THE DEVELOPMENT OF THE NOVEL

LITERARY SOURCES
&
DOCUMENTS

Portrait of Charles Dickens at his writing desk by Herbert Watkins, date unknown (c. 1850–1870).
By courtesy of the National Portrait Gallery, London.

The Development of the Novel

Literary Sources & Documents

Edited and with an Introduction by
Eleanor McNees

Volume II
The Nineteenth-Century Novel
The English Novel: Scott to James

HELM INFORMATION

Selection and editorial matter
© 2006 Helm Information Ltd
The Banks,
Mountfield,
near Robertsbridge,
East Sussex TN32 5JY,
U.K.

ISBN-10: 1-873403-62-3
ISBN-13: 978-1-873403-62-4

A CIP catalogue record for this book
is available from the British Library.

All rights reserved: No reproduction, copy
or transmission of this publication may be
made without written permission.

No paragraph of this publication may be
reproduced, copied or transmitted save
with written permission or in accordance
with the provisions of the Copyright Act
1956 (as amended), or under the terms of
any licence permitting limited copying
issued by the Copyright Licensing Agency,
7 Ridgmount Street, London WC1E 7AE.

Any person who does any unauthorised act
in relation to this publication may be liable
to criminal prosecution and civil claims for
damages.

Frontispiece: Portrait of Charles Dickens at his writing desk by
Herbert Watkins, date unknown (c. 1850–1870).
By courtesy of the National Portrait Gallery, London.

Printed on neutral-sized ('acid-free') paper through
Print Solutions Partnership, Wallington, Surrey, England.

Contents
VOLUME II
The Nineteenth-Century Novel

The English Novel: Scott to James
IV. Writers and Critics on the English Novel

42.	MARIA EDGEWORTH, "Author's Preface", *Castle Rackrent*, 1800	3
43.	[ANNA LETITIA] BARBAULD, "On the Origin and Progress of Novel Writing," *The British Novelists*, vol. 1, 1810	6
44.	SIR WALTER SCOTT, from *Waverley*, 1814	29
45.	SIR WALTER SCOTT, Review of *Emma*, *Quarterly Review*, 14, March 1816	33
46.	JANE AUSTEN, from *Northanger Abbey*, 1818	45
47.	WILLIAM HAZLITT, "On the English Novelists", 1818	47
48.	CHARLES DICKENS, "Preface", *The Posthumous Papers of the Pickwick Club*, 1837	70
49.	CHARLES DICKENS, "Preface", *The Adventures of Oliver Twist*, 1837–38	75
50.	SIR EDWARD BULWER-LYTTON, "Art in Fiction," 1838, *Critical and Miscellaneous Essays*, vol. 1, 1841	80
51.	WILLIAM THACKERAY, "Before the Curtain", *Vanity Fair*, 1847	104
52.	CHARLOTTE BRONTË, "Biographical Notice of Ellis and Acton Bell", *Wuthering Heights* by Emily Brontë, 1850	106
53.	CHARLOTTE BRONTË, "Editor's Preface to the New Edition of *Wuthering Heights*", 1850	112
54.	SIR JAMES FITZJAMES STEPHEN, "The Relation of Novels to Life", *Cambridge Essays*, 1855	116
55.	GEORGE ELIOT, "Silly Novels by Lady Novelists", *Westminster Review*, 66, October 1856	152
56.	GEORGE ELIOT, from *Adam Bede*, Book II, Chapter 17, 1859	169
57.	GEORGE ELIOT, from *Middlemarch*, Book II, Chapter 15, 1871–72	170
58.	GEORGE HENRY LEWES, "Criticism in Relation to Novels", *Fortnightly Review*, 3, 15 December 1865	171
59.	ANONYMOUS, "The Uses of Fiction", *The Saturday Review*, 22, 15 September 1866	181

60. WALTER BESANT, "The Value of Fiction", *Belgravia*, 16, November 1871 — 186
61. ANONYMOUS, "On the History of the Novel in England", *Argosy*, 14, 1872 — 190
62. ANONYMOUS, "The Art of Novel Writing", *Gentleman's Magazine*, 9, 1872 — 195
63. ANTHONY TROLLOPE, "Novel-Reading", *Nineteenth Century*, 5, January 1879 — 204
64. JOHN RUSKIN, "Fiction Fair and Foul", *Nineteenth Century*, 7, June 1880 — 222
65. ROBERT LOUIS STEVENSON, "A Gossip on Romance", *Longman's Magazine*, 1, 1882 — 242
66. ROBERT LOUIS STEVENSON, "A Humble Remonstrance", *Longman's Magazine*, 5.26, Winter 1883 — 251
67. WALTER BESANT, "The Art of Fiction", 1884 — 258
68. GEORGE MEREDITH, "Letter to G. P. Baker", 22 July 1887, *Letters of George Meredith*, vol. 2, 1882–1909, 1912 — 278
69. THOMAS HARDY, "The Profitable Reading of Fiction", 1888 — 281
70. OSCAR WILDE, "The Decay of Lying: A Dialogue", *The Nineteenth Century*, 25.143, January 1889 — 291
71. EDMUND GOSSE, "The Limits of Realism in Fiction", *The Forum*, June 1890 — 310
72. THOMAS HARDY, "The Science of Fiction", 1891 — 317
73. EDMUND GOSSE, "The Tyranny of the Novel", *National Review*, 19, 1892 — 321
74. GEORGE GISSING, et al., "The Place of Realism in Fiction: A Discussion", *The Humanitarian*, July 1895 — 332
75. VERNON LEE, "On Literary Construction", *Contemporary Review* 68, 1895 — 346
76. JOSEPH CONRAD, "Preface" to *The Nigger of the Narcissus*, 1897 — 360
77. FREDERICK KARL, "An Age of Fiction", *An Age of Fiction: The Nineteenth Century British Novel*, New York, 1964 — 364

The American Novel in the Nineteenth Century
V. Writers on the American Novel

78. JAMES FENIMORE COOPER, "Preface to the Leather-Stocking Tales", *The Deerslayer*, 1841 — 285
79. NATHANIEL HAWTHORNE, "Preface", *The House of the Seven Gables*, 1851 — 389
80. HARRIET BEECHER STOWE, "Preface", *Uncle Tom's Cabin; or, Life Among the Lowly*, 1853 — 393
81. WILLIAM DEAN HOWELLS, "Henry James", *The Century Illustrated*

	Monthly Magazine, 25, ns 3, November 1882	395
82.	HENRY JAMES, "The Art of Fiction", *Longman's Magazine*, Fall 1884	403
83.	HENRY JAMES, "The Future of the Novel", 1899	418
84.	WILLIAM DEAN HOWELLS, from *Criticism and Fiction*, 1892	426
85.	MARK TWAIN, "Fenimore Cooper's Literary Offences", *How to Tell a Story and Other Essays*, 1897	434
86.	HENRY JAMES, "Preface", *The Portrait of a Lady*, 1881	444

VI. Critics on the American Novel

87.	LILLIE DEMING LOSHE, "The Didactic and the Sentimental", *The Early American Novel*, 1907	457
88.	CARL VAN DOREN, "The Beginnings of Fiction", *The American Novel*, 1921	476
89.	LESLIE FIEDLER, "Come Back to the Raft Ag'in, Huck Honey!" *Partisan Review*, 15.6, June 1948	488
90.	JAMES BALDWIN, "Everybody's Protest Novel", *Partisan Review*, 16.6, June 1949	494
91.	PHILIP RAHV, "Paleface and Redskin", *Image and Idea: Twenty Essays on Literary Themes*, 1949; rev. ed. 1957	500
92.	ARTHUR MIZNER, "The Novel of Manners in America", *Kenyon Review*, 12.1, Winter 1950	504
93.	MALCOLM COWLEY, "Naturalism: No Teacup Tragedies", *The Literary Situation*, 1954	517
94.	PHILIP RAHV, "The Cult of Experience in American Writing", *Image and Idea: Twenty Essays on Literary Themes*. 1949; rev. ed. 1957	534
95.	RICHARD CHASE, "The Broken Circuit," *The American Novel and its Tradition*, 1957	546
96.	MARIUS BEWLEY, "The Question of Form", *The Eccentric Design: Form in the Classic American Novel*, 1957	563
97.	LESLIE A. FIEDLER, "The Novel and America", *Partisan Review*, 27.1, Winter 1960	570
98.	HAROLD BEAVER, "A Figure in the Carpet: Irony and the American Novel." *Essays and Studies*, 15, 1962	583
99.	JAMES W. TUTTLETON, "The Sociological Matrix of the Novel of Manners", *The Novel of Manners in America*, Chapel Hill, 1972	593

IV. The English Novel: Scott to James

The end of a novel, like the end of a children's dinner-party, must be made up of sweetmeats and sugar-plums.
        Anthony Trollope, *Barchester Towers*, Chapter 9, 1857.

Novels with a purpose are proverbially detestable, for a novel with a purpose means a book setting forth that a villain is hanged and a good man presented with a thousand pounds—that is silly and really immoral; for, in the first place, the imaginary event is no guarantee for the real event; secondly, a particular case does not proved a rule; thirdly, it is not ture that virtue is always rewarded and vice punished; and fourthly, virtue should not be inculcated with a simple view to money or the gallows. But even a novel should have a ruling thought, though it should not degenerate into a tract; and the thought should be one which will help to purify and sustain the mind by which it is assimilated, and therefore tend to make society so far healthier and happier.
    Stephen Leslie, "Art and Morality", *Cornhill Magazine*, 32, July 1875, p. 101.

Let me repeat that a novel is an impression, not an argument, and there the matter must rest, as one is reminded by a passage which occurs in the letters of Schiller to Goethe on judges of this class: "They are those who seek only their own ideas in a representation, and prize that which should be as higher than what is." The casue of the dispute, therefore, lies in the very first principles, and it would be utterly impossible to come to an understanding with them.
    Thomas Hardy, from "Preface" to the Fifth (English) Edition, *Tess of the D'Urbervilles*, 1892, rptd New York: The Modern Library, 1919, p. x.

Author's Preface to *Castle Rackrent*

MARIA EDGEWORTH

Irish novelist Maria Edgeworth (1767-1849) was admired both by Sir Walter Scott and Jane Austen. She wrote a number of novels and children's books in the early 1800s. In the following preface, she assumes the guise of an editor who transcribes the story of a family as told by Thady, "an illiterate old steward". Edgeworth distinguishes her work, a biography, from a history and thus departs from Defoe's and Richardson's claims to historicity. She argues that a history is often less accurate in delineating character than a biography because of the former's emphasis solely on the public aspects of a person. The biography's or memoir's attention to the private history of the domestic life via conversations, diaries and letters is therefore both more persuasive and more truthful. In addition, the retention of the native idiom and diction in a story lends credibility to the tale. Edgeworth avoids any mention of her work as a novel or a romance. The denomination of a novel as a biography is adopted later in the century by Fitzjames Stephen (see Chapter 46).

The prevailing taste of the public for anecdote has been censured and ridiculed by critics who aspire to the character of superior wisdom; but if we consider it in a proper point of view, this taste is an incontestable proof of the good sense and profoundly philosophic temper of the present times. Of the numbers who study, or at least who read history, how few derive any advantage from their labours! The heroes of history are so decked out by the fine fancy of the professed historian; they talk in such measured prose, and act from such sublime or such diabolical motives, that few have sufficient taste, wickedness, or heroism, to sympathise in their fate. Besides, there is much uncertainty even in the best authenticated ancient or modern histories; and that love of truth, which in some minds is innate and immutable, necessarily leads to a love of secret memoirs and private anecdotes. We cannot judge either of the feelings or of the characters of men with perfect accuracy,

Source: Maria Edgeworth, Author's Preface to *Castle Rackrent*, 1800, rptd London: Macmillan, 1895, pp. xlvii-xlx.

from their actions or their appearance in public; it is from their careless conversations, their half-finished sentences, that we may hope with the greatest possibility of success to discover their real characters. The life of a great or of a little man written by himself, the familiar letters, the diary of any individual published by his friends or by his enemies, after his decease, are esteemed important literary curiosities. We are surely justified, in this eager desire, to collect the most minute facts relative to the domestic lives, not only of the great and good, but even of the worthless and insignificant, since it is only by a comparison of their actual happiness or misery in the privacy of domestic life that we can form a just estimate of the real reward of virtue, or the real punishment of vice. That the great are not as happy as they seem, that the external circumstances of fortune and rank do not constitute felicity, is asserted by every moralist: the historian can seldom, consistently with his dignity, pause to illustrate this truth; it is therefore to the biographer we must have recourse. After we have beheld splendid characters playing their parts on the great theatre of the world, with all the advantages of stage effect and decoration, we anxiously beg to be admitted behind the scenes, that we may take a nearer view of the actors and actresses.

Some may perhaps imagine that the value of biography depends upon the judgment and taste of the biographer; but on the contrary it may be maintained, that the merits of a biographer are inversely as the extent of his intellectual powers and of his literary talents. A plain unvarnished tale is preferable to the most highly ornamented narrative. Where we see that a man has the power, we may naturally suspect that he has the will to deceive us; and those who are used to literary manufacture know how much is often sacrificed to the rounding of a period, or the pointing of an antithesis.

That the ignorant may have their prejudices as well as the learned cannot be disputed; but we see and despise vulgar errors: we never bow to the authority of him who has no great name to sanction his absurdities. The partiality which blinds a biographer to the defects of his hero, in proportion as it is gross, ceases to be dangerous; but if it be concealed by the appearance of candour, which men of great abilities best know how to assume, it endangers our judgment sometimes, and sometimes our morals. If her Grace the Duchess of Newcastle, instead of penning her lord's elaborate eulogium, had undertaken to write the life of Savage, we should not have been in any danger of mistaking an idle, ungrateful libertine for a man of genius and virtue. The talents of a biographer are often fatal to his reader. For these reasons the public often judiciously countenance those who, without sagacity to discriminate character, without elegance of style to relieve the tediousness of narrative, without enlargement of mind to draw any conclusions from the facts they relate, simply pour forth anecdotes, and retail conversations, with all the minute prolixity of a gossip in a country town.

The author of the following Memoirs has upon these grounds fair claims to the public favour and attention; he was an illiterate old steward, whose partiality to *the family*, in which he was bred and born, must be obvious to the reader. He tells the history of the Rackrent family in his vernacular idiom, and in the full confidence that Sir Patrick, Sir Murtagh, Sir Kit, and Sir Condy Rackrent's affairs will be as interesting to all the world as they were to himself. Those who were acquainted with the manners of a certain class of the gentry of Ireland some years ago, will want no evidence of the truth of honest Thady's narrative; to those who are totally unacquainted with Ireland, the following Memoirs will perhaps be scarcely intelligible, or probably they may appear perfectly incredible. For the information of the *ignorant* English reader, a few notes have been subjoined by the editor, and he had it once in contemplation to translate the language of Thady into plain English; but Thady's idiom is incapable of translation, and, besides, the authenticity of his story would have been more exposed to doubt if it were not told in his characteristic manner. Several years ago he related to the editor the history of the Rackrent family, and it was with some difficulty that he was persuaded to have it committed to writing; however, his feelings for "*the honour of the family,*" as he expressed himself, prevailed over his habitual laziness, and he at length completed the narrative which is now laid before the public.

The editor hopes his readers will observe that these are 'tales of other times;' that the manners depicted in the following pages are not those of the present age; the race of the Rackrents has long since been extinct in Ireland; and the drunken Sir Patrick, the litigious Sir Murtagh, the fighting Sir Kit, and the slovenly Sir Condy, are characters which could no more be met with at present in Ireland, than Squire Western or Parson Trulliber in England. There is a time when individuals can bear to be rallied for their past follies and absurdities, after they have acquired new habits and a new consciousness. Nations, as well as individuals, gradually lose attachment to their identity, and the present generation is amused, rather than offended, by the ridicule that is thrown upon its ancestors.

Probably we shall soon have it in our power, in a hundred instances, to verify the truth of these observations.

When Ireland loses her identity by an union with Great Britain, she will look back, with a smile of good-humoured complacency, on the Sir Kits and Sir Condys of her former existence.

43

On the Origin and Progress of Novel-writing

[ANNA LETITIA] BARBAULD

Anna Letitia Barbauld (1743-1825) was a minor English poet and essayist. She edited a collection of Samuel Richardson's letters and collected and printed in ten volumes a number of principal English novels, beginning with *Clarissa*. The following essay begins with a fairly lengthy survey of the origins of fictional tales in the early literature of ancient Greece and the Middle East. Barbauld's is one of the first essays on the origin of the novel to present a comparative view of the rise of the novel across cultures. While the focus is clearly eurocentric and ultimately anglocentric, Barbauld's assessments, especially of French precursors of the novel beginning with the troubadours of the tenth century and culminating in Mme de la Fayette's *Princesse de Cleves* and Le Sage's *Gil Blas*, prefigures much recent debate about multiple and simultaneous origins of the novel. Like many later critics, she acknowledges Cervantes's *Don Quixote* as spelling the death of the romance genre. In the last part of her essay, Barbauld considers the effects of novel reading on the British public. Like her later Victorian successors, she worries about the gap between the ideal world depicted by the novelist and the more mundane reality the female reader in particular is likely to experience. Though the "unpardonable sin in a novel is dullness" (48), Barbauld somewhat ambivalently appears to call for an increased realism among authors too prone to sensationalism. In this she appears to prepare the ground for Jane Austen's fiction.

A Collection of Novels has a better chance of giving pleasure than of commanding respect. Books of this description are condemned by the grave, and despised by the fastidious; but their leaves are seldom found unopened, and they occupy the parlour and the dressing-room while productions of higher name are often gathering dust on the shelf. It might not perhaps by difficult to show that

Source: Mrs [Anna Letitia] Barbauld, "On the Origin and Progress of Novel-Writing", *The British Novelists*, vol. 1, London, 1810, pp. 1-62.

this species of composition is entitled to a higher rank than has been generally assigned it. Fictitious adventures, in one form or other, have made a part of the polite literature of every age and nation. These have been grafted upon the actions of their heroes; they have been interwoven with their mythology; they have been moulded upon the manners of the age,—and, in return, have influenced the manners of the succeeding generation by the sentiments they have infused and the sensibilities they have excited.

Adorned with the embellishments of Poetry, they produce the epic; more concentrated in the story, and exchanging narrative for action, they become dramatic. When allied with some great moral end, as in the *Telemaque* of Fenelon, and Marmontel's *Belisaire*, they may be termed didactic. They are often made the vehicles of satire, as in Swift's *Gulliver's Travels*, and the *Candide* and *Babouc* of Voltaire. They take a tincture from the learning and politics of the times, and are made use of successfully to attack or recommend the prevailing systems of the day. When the range of this kind of writing is so extensive, and its effect so great, it seems evident that it ought to hold a respectable place among the productions of genius; nor is it easy to say, why the poet, who deals in one kind of fiction, should have so high a place allotted him in the temple of fame; and the romance-writer so low a one as in the general estimation he is confined to. To measure the dignity of a writer by the pleasure he affords his readers is not perhaps using an accurate criterion; but the invention of a story, the choice of proper incidents, the ordonnance of the plan, occasional beauties of description, and above all, the power exercised over the reader's heart by filling it with the successive emotions of love, pity, joy, anguish, transport, or indignation, together with the grave impressive moral resulting from the whole, imply talents of the highest order, and ought to be appretiated accordingly. A good novel is an epic in prose, with more of character and less (indeed in modern novels nothing) of the supernatural machinery.

If we look for the origin of fictitious tales and adventures, we shall be obliged to go to the earliest accounts of the literature of every age and country. The Eastern nations have always been fond of this species of mental gratification. The East is emphatically the country of invention. The Persians, Arabians, and other nations in that vicinity have been, and still are, in the habit of employing people whose business it is to compose and to relate entertaining stories (as Parnell's Hermit for instance) which have passed current in verse and prose through a variety of forms, may be traced up to this source. From Persia the taste passed into the soft and luxurious Ionia. The *Milesian Tales*, written by Aristides of Miletus, at what time is not exactly known, seem to have been a kind of novels. They were translated into Latin during the civil wars of Marius and Sylla. They consisted of loose love stories, but were very popular among the Romans; and the Parthian general who beat Crassus took occasion, from his finding a copy of them amongst the camp equipage, to reproach that nation with effeminacy, in not being able, even in time of danger, to dispense with such an amusement. From Ionia the taste of romances passed over to the Greeks about the time of Alexander the Great. The *Golden Ass* of Lucian, which is exactly in the manner of the Arabian Tales, is one of the few extant.

In the time of the Greek emperors these compositions were numerous, and had attained a form and a polish which assimilates them to the most regular and sentimental of modern productions. The most perfect of those which are come down to our time is *Theagenes and Chariclea*, a romance or novel, written by Heliodorus bishop of Tricca in Thessaly, who flourished under Arcadius and Honorius. Though his production was perfectly chaste and virtuous, he was called to account for it by a provincial synod, and ordered to burn his book or resign his bishopric; upon which, with the heroism of an author, he chose the latter. Of this work a new translation was given in 1789; and had this Selection admitted translations, it would have found a place here. It is not so much read as it ought to be; and it may not be amiss to inform the customers to circulating libraries, that they may have the pleasure of reading a genuine novel, and at the same time enjoy the satisfaction of knowing how people wrote in Greek about love, above a thousand years ago. The scene of this work is chiefly laid in Egypt. It opens in a striking and picturesque manner. A band of pirates, from a hill that overlooks the Heracleotic mouth of the Nile, see a ship lying at anchor, deserted by its crew; a feast spread on the shore; a number of dead bodies scattered round, indicating a recent skirmish or quarrel at an entertainment: the only living creatures, a most beautiful virgin seated on a rock, weeping over and supporting a young man of equally distinguished figure, who is wounded and apparently lifeless. These are the hero and heroine of the piece, and being thus let into the middle of the story, the preceding events are given in narration. The description of the manner of life of the pirates at the mouth of the Nile is curious, and no doubt historical. It shows that, as well then as in Homer's time, piracy was looked upon as a mode of honourable war, and that a captain who treated the women with respect, and took a regular ransom for his captives, and behaved well to his men, did not scruple to rank himself with other military heroes. Indeed it might be difficult to say why he should not. It is a circumstance worth observing, that Tasso has in all probability borrowed a striking circumstance from the Greek romance. *Chariclea* is the daughter of a queen of Æthiopia, exposed by her mother to save her reputation, as, in consequence of the queen, while pregnant, having gazed at a picture of Perseus and Andromeda, her infant was born with a fair complexion. This is the counterpart of the story of Clorinda, in the Gierusalemme Liberata, whose mother is surprised with the same phænomenon, occasioned by having had in her chamber a picture of St. George. The discovery is kept back to the end of the piece, and is managed in a striking manner. There is much beautiful description, of which the pomp of heathen sacrifices and processions makes a great part; and the love is at once passionate and chaste.

The pastoral romance of Longus is also extant in the Greek language. It is esteemed elegant, but it would be impossible to chastise it into decency. The Latins, who had less invention, had no writings of this kind, except the *Golden Ass* of Apuleius may be reckoned such. In it is found the beautiful episode of Cupid and Psyche, which has been elegantly modernized by Fontenelle. But romance writing was destined to revive with greater splendour under the Gothic powers, and it sprung out of the histories of the times, enlarged and exaggerated into fable. Indeed all fictions have probably grown out of real adventures. The actions of heroes would be the most natural subject for recital in a warlike age; a little flattery and a little love of the marvellous would overstep the modesty of truth in the narration. A champion of extraordinary size would easily be magnified into a giant. Tales of magic and enchantment probably took their rise from the awe and wonder with which the vulgar looked upon any instance of superior skill in mechanics or medicine, or acquaintance with any of the hidden properties of nature. The Arabian tales, so well known and so delightful, bear testimony to this. At a fair in Tartary a *magician* appears, who brings various curiosities, the idea of which was probably suggested by inventions they had heard of, which to people totally ignorant of the mechanical powers would appear the effect of enchantment. How easily might the exhibition at Merlin's, or the tricks of Jonas, be made to pass for magic in New Holland or Otaheite! Letters and figures were easily turned into talismans by illiterate men, who saw that a great deal was effected by them, and intelligence conveyed from place to place in a manner they could not account for. Medicine has always, in rude ages and countries, been accompanied with charms and superstitious practices, and the charming of serpents in the East is still performed in a way which the Europeans cannot discover. The total separation of scholastic characters from men of the world favoured the belief of magic; and when to these causes are added the religious superstitions of the times, we shall be able to account for much of the marvellous in the first instance. These stories, as well as the historical ones, would be continually embellished, as they passed from hand to hand, till the small mixture of truth in them was scarcely discoverable.

The first Gothic romances appeared under the venerable guise of history. Arthur and the knights of the round table, Charlemagne and his peers, were their favourite heroes. The extended empire of Charlemagne and his conquests naturally offered themselves as subjects for recital; but it seems extraordinary that Arthur, a British prince, the scene of whose exploits was in Wales, a country little known to the rest of Europe, and who was continually struggling against ill-fortune, should have been so great a favourite upon the continent. Perhaps, however, the comparative obscurity of his situation might favour the genius of the composition, and the intercourse between Wales and Brittany would contribute to diffuse and exaggerate the stories of his exploits. In fact, every song and record relating to this hero was kept with the greatest care in Brittany, and, together with a chronicle deducing Prince Arthur from Priam king of Troy, was brought to England about the year 1100, by Walter Mapes archdeacon of Oxford, when he returned from the continent through that province. This medley of historical songs, traditions, and invention, was put into Latin by Geoffry of Monmouth, with many additions of his own, and from Latin translated into French in the year 1115, under the title of *Brut d'Angleterre*. It is full of the grossest anachronisms. *Merlin*, the enchanter, is a principal character in it. He opposes his Christian magic to the Arabian sorcerers. About the same time appeared a similar story of *Charlemagne*. Two expeditions of his were particularly celebrated; his conversion of the Saxons by force of arms, and his expedition into

Spain against the Saracens; in returning from which he met with the defeat of Roncevaux, in which was slain the celebrated *Roland*. This was written in Latin by a monk, who published it under the name of Archbishop Turpin, a cotemporary of Charlemagne, in order to give it credit. These two works were translated into most of the languages of Europe, and became the groundwork of numberless others, each more wonderful than the former, and each containing a sufficient number of giants, castles and dragons, beautiful damsels and valiant princes, with a great deal of religious zeal, and very little morality. *Amadis de Gaul* was one of the most famous of this class. Its origin is disputed between France and Spain. There is a great deal of fighting in it, much of the marvellous, and very little of sentiment. It has been given lately to the public in an elegant English dress by Mr. Southey; but notwithstanding he has considerably abridged its tediousness, a sufficiency of that ingredient remains to make it rather a task to go through a work which was once so great a favourite. *Palmerin of England, Don Belianis of Greece*, and the others which make up the catalogue of Don Quixote's library, are of this stamp.

Richard Coeur de Lion and his exploits were greatly to the taste of the early romance writers. The Crusades kindled a taste for romantic adventure; the establishment of the Saracens in Spain had occasioned a large importation of genii and enchantments, and Moorish magnificence was grafted upon the tales of the Gothic chivalry. Of these heroic romances, the Troubadours were in France the chief composers: they began to flourish about the end of the tenth century. They by degrees mingled a taste for gallantry and romantic love with the adventures of heroes, and they gave to that passion an importance and a refinement which it had never possessed among the ancients. It was a compound of devotion, metaphysics, Platonism, and chivalry, making altogether such a mixture as the world had never seen before. There is something extremely mysterious in the manner in which ladies of rank allowed themselves to be addressed by these poetical lovers; sometimes no doubt a real passion was produced, and some instances there are of its having had tragical consequences: but in general it may be suspected that the addresses of the Troubadours and other poets were rather a tribute paid to rank than to beauty; and that it was customary for young men of parts, who had their fortune to make, to attach themselves to a patroness, of whom they made a kind of idol, sometimes in the hopes of rising by her means, sometimes merely as a subject for their wit. The manner in which Queen Elizabeth allowed herself to be addressed by her courtiers, the dedications which were in fashion in Dryden's time, the letters of Voiture, and the general strain of poetry of Waller and Cowley, may serve to prove that there may be a great deal of gallantry without any passion. it is evident that, while these romance writers worshipped their mistress as a distant star, they did not disdain to warm themselves by meaner and nearer fires; for the species of love or rather adoration they professed did not at all prevent them from forming connexions with more accessible fair ones. Of all the countries on the continent, France and Spain had the greatest number of these chivalrous romances. In Italy the genius of the nation and the facility of versification led them to make poetry the vehicle of this kind of entertainment. The Cantos of Boiardo and Ariosto are romances in verse.

In the mean time Europe settled into a state of comparative tranquillity: castles and knights and adventures of distressed damsels ceased to be the topics of the day, and romances founded upon them had begun to be insipid when the immortal satire of Cervantes drove them off the field, and they have never since been able to rally their forces. The first work of entertainment of a different kind which was published in France (for the *Pantagruel* of Rabelais is rather a piece of licentious satire than a romance) was the *Astrea* of M. d'Urfé. It is a pastoral romance, and became so exceedingly popular, that the belles and beaux of that country assumed the airs and language of shepherds and shepherdesses. A Celadon (the hero of the piece) became a familiar appellation for a languishing lover, and men of gallantry were seen with a crook in their hands, leading a tame lamb about the streets of Paris. The celebrity of this work was in great measure owing to its being strongly seasoned with allusions to the intrigues of the court of Henry the Fourth, in whose reign it was written. The volumes of *Astrea* are never opened in the present day but as a curiosity; to read them through would be a heavy task indeed. There is in the machinery a strange mixture of wood nymphs and druids. The work is full of anachronisms, but the time is supposed to be in the reign of Pharamond or his successors. That tale begins with the lover, who is under the displeasure of his mistress, throwing himself into the water, where he narrowly escapes drowning at the very outset of the piece. We find here the *fountain of love*, in which if a man looks, he sees, if he is beloved, the face of his mistress; but if not, he is presented with the countenance of his rival: long languishing speeches and little adventures of intrigue fill up the story. It is interspersed with little pieces of poetry, very tolerable for the time, but highly complimentary. One of them turns upon the incident of the poet's mistress having burnt her cheek with her curling-iron; on which he takes occasion to say, "*that the fire of her eyes caused the mischief.*" This work was however found so interesting by M. Huet, the grave bishop of Avranches, that when he read it along with his sisters, he was often obliged (as he tells us) to lay the book down, that he and they might give free vent to their tears.

Though Cervantes had laid to rest the giants and enchanters, a new style of fictitious writing was introduced, not less remote from nature, in the romances *de longue haleine*, which originated in France, and of which Calprenéde and Mad. Scudery were the most distinguished authors. The principle of these was high honour, impregnable chastity, a constancy unshaken by time or accident, and a species of love so exalted and refined, that it bore little resemblance to a natural passion. These, in the construction of the story, came nearer to real life than the former had done. The adventures were marvellous, but not impossible. The heroes and heroines were taken from ancient history, but without any resemblance to the personages whose names they bore. The manners therefore and passions referred to an ideal world, the creation of the writer; but the situations were often striking, and the sentiments always noble. It is a curious circumstance that Rousseau, who tells us that his childhood was conversant in these romances, (a course of reading which no doubt fed and inflamed his fine imagination) has borrowed from them an affecting incident in his *Nouvelle Heloise*. St. Preux, when his mistress lies ill of the small-pox, glides into the room, approaches the bed in order to imbibe the danger, and retires without speaking. *Julie*, when recovered, is impressed with a confused idea of having seen him, but whether in a dream, a vision, or a reality, she cannot determine. This striking circumstance is taken from the now almost forgotten *Cassandra* of Scudery. The complimentary language of these productions seems to have influenced the intercourse of common life, at least in the provinces, for Boileau introduces in his satires—

> Deux nobles campagnards, grands lecteurs de romans,
> Qui m'ont dit tout Cyrus dans leurs longs complimens.

The same author made a more direct attack upon these productions in a dialogue entitled *Les Héros de Roman*, a humorous little piece, in which he ridiculed these as Cervantes had done the others, and drove them off the stage.

Heroic sentiment and refined feeling, as expressed in romances and plays, were at their height about this time in France; and while the story and adventures were taken from the really chivalrous ages, it is amusing to observe how the rough manners of those times are softened and polished to meet the ideas of a more refined age. A curious instance of this occurs in Corneille's well-known play of the *Cid*. *Chimene*, having lost her father by the hand of her lover, not only breaks off the connexion, but throws herself at the feet of the king to entreat him to avenge her by putting *Rodrigues* to death: "*Sire, vengeance!*" But in the genuine chronicle of the *Cid*, with which curious and entertaining work Mr. Southey has lately obliged the public, the previous incidents of the combat are nearly the same, and Ximena in like manner throws herself at the feet of the king; but to beg what?—not vengeance upon the murderer of her father, but that the kind would be pleased to give her *Rodrigues* for a husband, to whom moreover she is not supposed to have had any previous attachment; her request seems to proceed from the simple idea that *Rodrigues*, by killing her father, having deprived her of one protector, it was but reasonable that he should give her another.

Rude times are fruitful of striking adventures; polished times must render them pleasing.—The ponderous volumes of the romance writers being laid upon the shelf, a closer imitation of nature began to be called for; not but that, from the earliest times, there had been stories taken from, or imitating, real life. The *Decameron* of Boccacio (a storehouse of tales, and a standard of the language in which it is written), the *Cent Nouvelles* of the Queen of Navarre, *Contes et Fabliaux* without number, may be considered as novels of a lighter texture; they abounded with adventure, generally of the humorous, often of the licentious kind, and indeed were mostly founded on intrigue, but the nobler passions were seldom touched. The *Roman Comique* of Scarron is a regular piece of its kind. Its subject is the adventures of a set of strolling players. Comic humour it certainly possesses, but the humour is very coarse and the incidents mostly low. Smollet seems to have formed himself very much upon this model.—But the *Zaide* and the *Princesse de Cleves* of Madame de la Fayette are esteemed to be the first which approach the modern novel of the serious kind, the latter especially. Voltaire says of them , that they were "*les premiers romans* où l'on vit les mœurs des honnêtes gens, et des avantures naturelles décrites avec grace. Avant elle on écrivoit d'un stile empoulé des choses peu vraisemblables." "They were the first novels which gave the manners of cultivated life and natural incidents related with elegance. Before the time of this lady, the style of these productions was affectedly turgid, and the adventures out of nature." The modesty of Mad. de la Fayette led her to shelter her productions, on their first publication, under the name of Segrais, her friend, under whose revision they had passed. Le Sage in his *Gil Blas*, a work of infinite entertainment though of dubious morality, has given us pictures of more familiar life, abounding in character and incident. The scene is laid in Spain, in which country he had travelled, and great part of it is imitated from the adventures of *Don Gusman d'Alvarache*; for Spain, though her energies have so long lain torpid, was earlier visited by polite literature than any country of Europe, Italy excepted. Her authors abounded in invention, so that the plots of plays and groundwork of novels were very frequently drawn from their productions. Cervantes himself, besides his Don Quixote, which has been translated and imitated in every country, wrote several little tales and novels, some of which he introduced into that work, for he only banished one species of fiction to introduce another. The French improved upon their masters. There is not perhaps a more amusing book than *Gil Blas*; it abounds in traits of exquisite humour and lessons of life, which, though not always pure, are many of them useful. In this work of Le Sage, like some of Smollet's, the hero of the piece excites little interest, and it rather exhibits a series of separate adventures, slightly linked together, than a chain of events concurring in one plan to the production of the catastrophe, like the *Tom Jones* of Fielding. The scenes of his *Diable Boiteux* are still more slightly linked together. That, and his *Bachelier de Salamanque*, are of the same stamp with *Gil Blas*, though inferior to it.

Marivaux excelled in a different style. His *Marianne* and *Paisan Parvenu* give a picture of French manners with all their refinement and delicacy of sentiment. He lays open the heart, particularly the female heart, in its inmost folds and recesses; its little vanities and affectations as well as its finer feelings. He abounds in wit, but it is of a refined kind, and requires thought in the reader to enter into it. He has also much humour, and describes comic scenes and characters amongst the lower and middle ranks with a great deal of the comic effect, but without the coarseness of Fielding. He eluded the difficulty of winding up a story by leaving both his pieces unfinished. Marivaux was contemporary with our Richardson: his style is found fault with by some French critics. From his time, novels of all kinds have made a large and attractive portion of French literature.

At the head of writers of this class stands the seductive, the passionate Rousseau,— the most eloquent writer in the most eloquent modern language: whether his glowing pencil paints the strong emotions of passion, or the enchanting scenery of nature in his own romantic country, or his peculiar cast of moral sentiment,—a charm is spread over every part of the work, which scarcely leaves the judgement free to condemn what in it is dangerous or reprehensible. His are truly the "Thoughts that breathe and words that burn." He has hardly any thing of story; he has but few figures upon his canvass; he wants them not; his characters are drawn more from a creative imagination than from real life, and we wonder that what has so little to do with nature should have so much to do with the heart. Our censure of the tendency of this work will be softened, if we reflect that Rousseau's aim, as far as he had a moral aim, seems to have been to give a striking example of fidelity in the *married* state, which, it is well known, is little thought of by the French; though they would judge with the greatest severity the more pardonable failure of an unmarried woman. But Rousseau has not reflected that *Julie* ought to have considered herself as indissolubly united to *St. Preux*; her marriage with another man was the infidelity. Rousseau's greatest rival in fame, Voltaire, has written many light pieces of fiction which can scarcely be called novels. They abound in wit and shrewdness, but they are all composed to subserve his particular views, and to attack systems which he assailed in every kind of way. His *Candide* has much strong painting of the miseries and vices which abound in this world, and is levelled against the only system which can console the mind under the view of them. In *L'Ingénu*, beside the wit, he has shown that he could also be pathetic. *Les Lettres Peruviennes*, by Mad. Grafigny, is a most ingenious and charming little piece. *Paul et Virginie*, by that friend of humanity St. Pierre, with the purest sentiment and most beautiful description, is pathetic to a degree that even distresses the feelings. *La Chaumiere Indienne*, also his, breathes the spirit of universal philanthropy. *Caroline de Lichtfeld* is justly a favourite; but it were impossible to enumerate all the elegant compositions of this class which later times have poured forth. For the expression of sentiment in all its various shades, for the most delicate tact, and a refinement and polish, the fruit of high cultivation, the French writers are superior to those of every other nation.

There is one species of this composition which may be called the *Didactic Romance*, which they have particularly made use of as a vehicle for moral sentiment, and philosophical or political systems and opinions.—Of this mature is the beautiful fiction of *Telémaque*, if it be not rather an Epic in prose; the high merit of which cannot be sufficiently appreciated, unless the reader bears in mind when and to whom it was written; that it dared to attack the fondness for war and the disposition to ostentatious profusion, under a monarch the most vain and ambitious of his age, and to draw, expressly as a pattern for his successor, the picture of a prince, the reverse of him in almost everything. *Les Voyages de Cyrus*, by Ramsay, and *Sethos*, by the Abbé Terrasson, are of the same kind; the former is rather dry and somewhat mystical: it enters pretty deeply into the mythology of the ancients, and aims at showing that the leading truths of religion,—an original state of happiness, a fall from that state, and the final recovery and happiness of all sentient beings,—are to be found in the mythological systems of all nations. Ramsay was a Scotchman by birth, but had lived long enough in France to write the language like a native; a rare acquisition! The latter, *Sethos*, contains, interwoven in its story, all that we know concerning the customs and manners of the ancient Egyptians; the trial of the dead before they are received to the honours of sepulture, and the various ordeals of the initiation, are very striking. A high and severe tone of morals reigns through the whole, and indeed both this and the last mentioned are much too grave for the readers of romance in general. That is not the case with the *Belisaire*, and *Les Incas*, of Marmontel, in which the incidents meant to strike the feelings and the fancy are executed with equal happiness with the preceptive part. Writings like these cooperated powerfully with the graver labours of the encyclopaedists in diffusing sentiments of toleration, a spirit of free enquiry, and a desire for equal laws and good government over Europe. Happy, if the mighty impulse had permitted them to stop within the bounds of justice and moderation! They French language is well calculated for eloquence. The harmony and elegance of French prose, the taste of their writers, and the grace and amenity which they know how to diffuse over every subject, give great effect to compositions of this kind. When *we* aim at eloquence in prose, we are apt to become turgid. Florian, though a feeble writer, is not void of merit. His *Galatée* is from Cervantes; his *Gonsalve de Cordoue* is built upon the history of that hero.

There is one objection to be made to these romances founded in history, which is, that if the personages are not judiciously selected, they are apt to impress false ideas on the mind. *Sethos* is well chosen for a hero in this respect. His name scarcely emerges from the obscurity of half fabulous times, and of a country whose records are wrapped in mystery; for all that is recorded of *Sethos* is, merely that there was such a prince, and that, for some reason or other, he entered into the priesthood. *Cyrus*, though so conspicuous a character, was probably thought a fair one for the purpose, as Xenophon has evidently made use of him in the same manner; but it may admit a doubt whether *Belisarius* is equally so; still less, many in more modern times that have been selected for writings of this kind. *Telemachus* is a character already within the precincts of poetry and fable, and may illustrate without any objection the graceful fictions of Fenelon. Our own Prince *Arthur* offers himself with equal advantage for poetry or romance. Where history says little, fiction may say much: events and men that are dimly seen through the obscurity of remote periods and countries, may be illuminated with these false lights; but where history throws her light steady and strong, no artificial colouring should be permitted. Impressions of historical characters very remote from the truth, often remain on the mind from dramatic compositions. If we examine into our ideas of the Henries and Richards of English history, we shall perhaps find that they are as much drawn from Shakespear as from Hume or Rapin. Some of our English romances are very faulty in this respect. A lady confessed that she could never get over a prejudice against the character of our Elizabeth, arising from her cruelty to two imaginary daughters of Mary Queen of Scots, who never existed but in the pages of a novel. The more art is shown, and much is often shown, in weaving the fictitious circumstances into the texture of the history, the worse is the tendency. A romance of which *Edward the Black Prince* is the hero, by Clara Reeves, has many curious particulars of the customs of that age; but the manners of his court are drawn with such a splendid colouring of heroic virtue, as certainly neither that court nor any other ever deserved.

Among the authors of perceptive novels, Mad. Genlis stands very high. Her *Adele et Théodore* is a system of education, the whole of which is given in action; there is infinite ingenuity in the various illustrative incidents: the whole has an air of the world and of good company; to an English reader it is also interesting as exhibiting traits of Parisian manners, and modern manners, from one who was admitted into the first societies. A number of characters are delineated and sustained with truth and spirit, and the stories of *Cecile* and the *Duchesse de C.* are uncommonly interesting and well told, while the sublime benevolence of M. and Mad. Lagaraye presents a cure for sorrow worthy of a Howard. From the system of Mad. Genlis many useful hints may be gathered, though the English reader will probably find much that differs from his own ideas. A good bishop, as Huet relates, conceiving of love as a most formidable enemy to virtue, entertained the singular project of writing, or procuring to be written, a number of novels framed in such a manner as to inspire an antipathy to this profane passion. Madame Genlis seems to have had the same idea, and in this manual of education, love is represented as a passion totally unfit to enter the breast of a young female; and in this, and in all her other works, she invariably represents as ending in misery, every connexion which is begun by mutual inclination. The parent, the mother rather, must dispose of her daughter; the daughter must be passive; and the great happiness of her life, is to be the having in her turn a daughter, in whose affections *she* is to be the prime object. Filial affection is no doubt much exaggerated by this writer. It is not natural that a young woman should make it an indispensable condition of marrying a young man that he will not separate her from her mother. We know in England what filial affection is, and we know it does not rise so high, and we know too that it ought not. There is another objection to Mad. Genlis' system of education, which applies also to Rousseau's *Emile*, which is, that it is too much founded upon deception. The pupil never sees the real appearance of life and manners: the whole of his education is a series of contrived artificial scenery, produced, as occasion demands, to serve a particular purpose. Few of these scenes would succeed at all; a number of them certainly never would. Indeed Mad. Genlis is not very strict in the point of veracity. A little fibbing is even enjoined to Adele occasionally on particular emergencies. *Les Veillées du Chateau*, by the same author, has great merit. A number of other productions which have flowed from her pen witness her fertility of invention and astonishing rapidity of execution: their merit is various; all have great elegance of style: but it is observable, that in some of her later novels, she has endeavoured to favour the old order of things, to make almost an object of worship of Louis the Fourteenth, and to revive the reverence for monastic seclusion, which, with so much pathos, she had attacked in her charming story of *Cecile*. The *Attala* of M. Chateau Briand is in like manner directed to prop the falling fabric of Romish faith.

    The celebrated daughter of Necker is one whose name cannot be passed over in this connexion. Her *Delphine* exhibits great powers: some of the situations are very striking; and the passion of love is expressed in such a variety of turns and changes, and with so many refined delicacies of sentiment, that it is surprising how any language could, and surely no language could but the French, find a sufficient variety of phrases in which to dress her ideas.—Yet this novel cannot be called a pleasing one. One monotonous colour of sadness prevails through the whole, varied indeed with deeper or lighter shades, but no where presenting the cheerful hues of contentment and pleasure. A heavier accusation lies against this work from its tendency, on which account it has been said that the author was desired by the present sovereign of France to leave Paris; but we may well suspect that a scrupulous regard to morality had less share than political motives in such a prohibition. *Corinne*, by the same author, is less exceptionable, and has less force. It has some charming descriptions, and a picture of English country manners which may interest our curiosity, though it will not greatly flatter our vanity. Elegant literature has sustained a loss in the recent death of Mad. Cotin. Her *Elizabeth* and *Matilde* have given her a deserved celebrity. The latter is however very enthusiastic and gloomy.

A number of other French writers of this class might have been mentioned, as Mad. Ricoboni, Mad. Elie de Beaumont, the Abbé Prévost, whose *Chevalier de Grieux* though otherwise not commendable, has some very pathetic parts. To these may be added Crebillon, and a number of writers of his class; for it must not be disguised, that besides the more respectable French novels, there are a number of others, which having passed no license of press, were said to be sold *sous le manteau*, and were not therefore the less read. These are not merely exceptionable, they are totally unfit to enter a house where the morals of young people are esteemed an object. They are generally not coarse in language, less so perhaps than many English ones which aim at humour; but gross sensual pleasure is the very soul of them. The awful frown with which the better part of the English public seem disposed to receive any approaches, either in verse or prose, to the French voluptuousness, does honour to the national character.

The Germans, formerly remarkable for the laborious heaviness and patient research of their literary labours, have, within this last century, cultivated with great success the field of polite literature. Plays, tales, and novels of all kinds, many of them by their most celebrated authors, were at first received with avidity in this country, and even made the study of their language popular. The tide has turned, and they are now as much depreciated. The *Sorrows of Werter*, by Goethe, was the first of these with which we were familiarized in this country: we received it through the medium of a French translation. It is highly pathetic, but its tendency has been severely, perhaps justly, censured; yet the author might plead that he has given warning of the probable consequences of illicit and uncontrolled passions by the awful catastrophe. It is certain, however, that the impression made is of more importance than the moral deduced; and if Schiller's fine play of *The Robbers* has had, as we are assured it has, the effect of leading some well-educated young gentlemen to commit depredations on the public, allured by the splendour of the principal character, we may well suppose that Werter's delirium of passion will not be less seducing. Goethe has written another novel, much esteemed, it is said, by the Germans, which contains, amongst other things, criticisms on the drama. The celebrated Wieland has composed a great number of works of fiction; the scene of most of them is laid in ancient Greece. His powers are great, his invention fertile, but his designs insidious. He and some others of the German writers of philosophical romances have used them as a frame to attack received opinions, both in religion and in morals. Two at least of his performances have been translated, *Agathon* and *Peregrine Proteus*. The former is beautifully written, but its tendency is seductive. The latter has taken for its basis a historical character; its tendency is also obvious. Klinger is an author who deals in the horrid. He subsists on murders and atrocities of all sorts, and introduces devils and evil spirits among his personages; he is said to have powers, but to labour under a total want of taste. In contrast to this writer and those of his class, may be mentioned *The Ghost Seer*, by Schiller, and *The Sorcerer* by another hand. These were written to expose the artifices of the Italian adepts of the school of Cagiostro. It is well known that these were spreading superstition and enthusiasm on the German part of the continent to an alarming degree, and had so worked upon the mind of the late king of Prussia, that he was made to believe he possessed the power of rendering himself invisible, and was wonderfully pleased when one of his courtiers (who, by the way, understood his trade) ran against and jostled him, pretending not to see his Majesty. These have been translated; as also a pleasant and lively satire on Lavater's system of physiognomy, written by Museus, author of *Popular Tales of the Germans*. The Germans abound in materials for works of the imagination; for they are rich in tales and legends of an impressive kind, which have perhaps amused generation after generation as nursery stories, and lain like or in the mine, ready for the hand of taste to separate the dross and polish the material: for it is infinitely easier, when a nation has gained cultivation, to polish and methodize than to invent. A very pleasing writer of novels, in the more common acceptance of the term, is Augustus La Fontaine; at least he has written some for which he merits that character, though perhaps more that are but indifferent. His *Tableaux de Famille* contains many sweet domestic pictures and touches of nature. It is imitated from *The Vicar of Wakefield.*— The Germans are a very book-making people. It is calculated that twenty thousand authors of that nation live by the exercise of the pen; and in the article of novels it is computed that seven thousand, either original or translated, have been printed by them within the last five-and-twenty years.

One Chinese novel has been translated. It is called *The Pleasing History, or the Adventures of Hau Kiou Choan*. It is said to be much esteemed, but can only be interesting to an European, as exhibiting something of the manners of that remote and singular country. It chiefly turns upon the stratagems used by the heroine to elude the ardour of her lover, and retard his approaches, till every circumstance of form and ceremony had been complied with. In their most tender assignations the lady is hid behind a curtain, as he is not permitted to see her face; and a female attendant conveys the tender speeches from one to the other; by which, according to our ideas, they would lose much of their pathos. The chief quality the heroine exhibits is cunning, and the adventures are a kind of hide-and-seek between the lovers. In short, *Shuy Ping Sin* to a Chinese may possibly be as great an object of admiration as *Clarissa*, but her accomplishments are not calculated for the meridian of this country.

In England, most of the earlier romances, from the days of Chaucer to James the First, were translations from the Spanish or French. One of the most celebrated of our own growth is Sir Philip Sidney's *Arcadia*, dedicated to his sister the Countess of Pembroke. It is a kind of pastoral romance, mingled with adventures of the heroic and chivalrous kind. It has great beauties, particularly in poetic imagery. It is a book which all have heard of, which some few possess, but which nobody reads. The taste of the times seems to have been for ponderous performances. The Duchess of Newcastle was an indefatigable writer in this way. Roger Boyle, earl of Orrery, published, in 1664, a romance called *Parthenissa*. It was in three volumes folio, and unfinished, to which circumstance alone his biographer, Mr. Walpole, attributes its being but little read. He must have had a capacious idea of the appetite of the readers of those days. There is a romance of later date, in one small volume, by the Hon. Robert Boyle—*The Martyrdom of Didymus and Theodora*, a Christian heroic tale. We had pretty early some celebrated political romances. Sir Thomas More's *Utopia*, Barclay's *Argenis*, and Harrington's *Oceana*, are of this kind: the two former are written in Latin. The *Utopia*, which is meant as a model of a perfect form of civil polity, is chiefly preserved in remembrance at present by having had the same singular fortune with the *Quixote* of Cervantes, of furnishing a new word, which has been adopted into the language as a permanent part of it; for we speak familiarly of an Utopian interesting without applying to the common resource of love. At length, in the reign of George the Second, Richardson, Fielding, and Smollet, appeared in quick succession; and their success raised such a demand for this kind of entertainment, that it has ever since been furnished from the press, rather as a regular and necessary supply, than as an occasional gratification. Novels have indeed been numerous "as leaves in Vallombrosa." The indiscriminate passion for them, and their bad effects on the female mind, became the object of the satire of Garrick, in a sprightly piece entitled *Polly Honeycomb*. A few deserve to be mentioned, either for their excellence or the singularity of their plan.

The history of *Gaudentio di Lucca*, published in 1725, is the effusion of a fine fancy and a refined understanding; it is attributed to Bishop Berkeley. It gives an account of an imaginary people in the heart of Africa, their manners and customs. They are supposed to be descended from the ancient Egyptians, and to be concealed from all the world by impenetrable deserts. The description of crossing the sands is very striking, and shows much information as well as fancy. It is not written to favour any particular system; the whole is the play of a fine imagination delighting itself with images of perfection and happiness, which it cannot find in any existing form of things. The frame is very well managed; the whole is supposed to be read in manuscript to the fathers of the Inquisition, and the remarks of the holy office are very much in character. A highly romantic air runs through the whole, but the language is far from elegant.

Another singular publication which appeared in 1756, was *The Memoirs of several Ladies*, by John Buncle, followed the next year by the *Life of Buncle*. These volumes are very whimsical, but contain entertainment. The ladies, whose memoirs he professes to give, are all highly beautiful and deeply learned; good Hebrew scholars; and, above all, zealous Unitarians. The author generally finds them in some sequestered dell, among the fells and mountains of Westmoreland, where, after a narrow escape of breaking his neck amongst rocks and precipices, he meets, like a true knight-errant, with one of these adventures. He marries in succession four or five of these prodigies, and the intervals between description and adventure are filled up with learned conversations on abstruse points of divinity. Many of the descriptions are taken from nature; and, as the book was much read, have possibly contributed to spread that taste for lake and mountain scenery which has since been so prevalent. The author was a clergyman.

A novel universally read at the time was *Chrysal, or the Adventures of a Guinea*. It described real characters and transactions, mostly in high life, under fictitious names; and certainly if a knowledge of the vicious part of the world be a desirable acquisition, *Chrysal* will amply supply it; but many of the scenes are too coarse not to offend a delicate mind, and the generation it describes is past away. *Pompey the Little*, with a similar frame, has less of personality, and is a lively pleasant satire. Its author is unknown.

About fifty years ago a very singular work appeared, somewhat in the guise of a novel, which gave a new impulse to writings of this stamp; namely, *The Life and Opinions of Tristram Shandy*, followed by *The Sentimental Journey*, by the rev. Mr. Sterne, a clergyman of York. They exhibit much originality, wit, and beautiful strokes of pathos, but a total want of plan or adventure, being made up of conversations and detached incidents. It is the peculiar characteristic of this writer, that he affects the heart, not by long drawn tales of distress, but by light electric touches which thrill the nerves of the reader who possesses a correspondent sensibility of frame. His characters, in like manner, are struck out by a few masterly touches. He resembles those painters who can give expression to a figure by two or three strokes of bold outline, leaving the imagination to fill up the sketch; the feelings are awakened as really by the story of *Le Fevre*, as by the narrative of *Clarissa*. The indelicacies of these volumes are very reprehensible, and indeed in a clergyman scandalous, particularly in the first publication, which however has the richest vein of humour. The two *Shandys*, Trim, Dr. Slop, are all drawn with a masterly hand. It is one of the merits of Sterne that he has awakened the attention of his readers to the wrongs of the poor negroes, and certainly a great spirit of tenderness and humanity breathes throughout the work. It is rather mortifying to reflect how little the power of expressing these feelings is connected with moral worth; for Sterne was a man by no means attentive to the happiness of those connected with him; and we are forced to confess that an author may conceive the idea of "brushing away flies without killing them," and yet behave ill in every relation of life.

It has lately been said that Sterne has been indebted for much of his wit to *Burton's Anatomy of Melancholy*. He certainly exhibits a good deal of reading in that and many other books out of the common way, but the wit is in the application, and that is his own. This work gave rise to the vapid effusions of a crowd of sentimentalists, may of whom thought they had seized the spirit of Sterne, because they could copy him in his breaks and asterisks. The taste spread, and for a while, from the pulpit to the playhouse, the reign of sentiment was established. Among the more respectable imitators of Sterne may be reckoned Mr. Mackenzie in his

Man of Feeling and his *Julia de Roubigné*, and Mr. Pratt in his *Emma Corbett*.

An interesting and singular novel, *The Fool of Quality*, was written by Henry Brooke, a man of genius, the author of *Gustavus Vasa* and many other productions. Many beautiful and pathetic episodical stories might be selected from it, but the story runs out into a strain romantic and improbable beyond the common allowed measure of this kind of writing; so that as a whole it cannot be greatly recommended: but it ought not to be forgotten that the very popular work of *Sandford and Merton* is taken from it. It has not merely given the hint for that publication; but the plan, the contrasted character of the two boys, and many particular incidents are so closely copied, that it will hardly be thought by one who peruses them both together, that Mr. Day has made *quite* sufficient acknowledgement in his preface. Rousseau had about this time awakened the public attention to the preference of natural manners in children, in opposition to the artificial usages of fashionable life; and much of the spirit of *Emile* is seen in this part of the work. The present generation have been much obliged to Mr. Day for separating this portion of the novel from the mass of improbable adventure in which it is involved, clothing it in more elegant language, and giving those additions which have made it so deservedly a favourite in the juvenile library. The religious feelings are often awakened in *The Fool of Quality*, not indeed without a strong tincture of enthusiasm, to which the author was inclined. Indeed, his imagination had at times prevailed over his reason before he wrote it.

A number of novels might be mentioned, which are, or have been, popular, though not of high celebrity. Sarah Fielding, sister to the author of *Tom Jones*, composed several; among which *David Simple* is the most esteemed: she was a woman of good sense and cultivation; and if she did not equal her brother in talent, she did not, like him, lay herself open to moral censure. She translated Xenophon's *Socrates*, and wrote a very pretty book for children, *The Governess, or Female Academy*.

Many tears have been shed by the young and tender-hearted over *Sidney Biddulph*, the production of Mrs. Sheridan, the wife of Thomas Sheridan the lecturer, an ingenious and amiable woman: the sentiments of this work are pure and virtuous, but the author seems to have taken pleasure in heaping distress upon virtue and innocence, merely to prove, what no one will deny, that the best dispositions are not always sufficient to ward off the evils of life. Why is it that women when they write are apt to give a melancholy tinge to their compositions? Is it that they suffer more, and have fewer resources against melancholy? Is it that men, mixing at large in society, have a brisker flow of ideas, and, seeing a greater variety of characters, introduce more of the business and pleasures of life into their productions? Is it that humour is a scarcer product of the mind than sentiment, and more congenial to the stronger powers of man? Is it that women nurse those feelings in secrecy and silence and diversify the expression of them with endless shades of sentiment, which are more transiently felt, and with fewer modifications of delicacy, by the other sex? The remark, if true, has no doubt many exceptions; but the productions of several ladies, both French and English, seem to countenance it.

Callistus, or The Man of Fashion, by Mr. Mulso, is a pathetic story; but it is written entirely for moral effect, and affords little of entertainment. Mr. Graves, an author of a very different cast, is known in this walk by *Columella* and his *Spiritual Quixote*. The latter is a popular work, and possesses some humour; but the humour is coarse, and the satire much too indiscriminately levelled against a society whose doctrines, operating with strong effect upon a large body of the most ignorant and vicious class, must necessarily include in their sweeping net much vice and folly, as well as much of sincere piety and corresponding morals. The design of his *Columella* is less exceptionable. It presents a man educated in polite learning and manners, who, from a fastidious rejection of the common active pursuits in life, rusticates in a country solitude, grows morose and peevish, and concludes with marrying his maid; no unusual consequence of a whimsical and morose singularity; the secret springs of which are, more commonly, a tincture of indolence and pride than superiority of genius. Mr. Graves was brought up originally for physic, but took orders and became rector of Claverton near Bath. He was the author of several publications, both translations and original; he was fond of writing, and published what he entitled his *Senilities* when at the age of near ninety. He died in 1804.—But it is time to retire from the enumeration of these works of fancy, or the reader might be as much startled with the number of heroes and heroines called up around him, as Ulysses was with the troops of shades that came flocking about him in the infernal regions.

If the end and object of this species of writing be asked, many no doubt will be ready to tell us that its object is,—to call in fancy to the aid of reason, to deceive the mind into embracing truth under the guise of fiction:

> Cosi a l'egro fanciul porgiamo aspersi
> Di soave licor gli orli del vaso,
> Succhi amari, ingannato in tanto ei beve,
> E da l'inganno suo vita riceve:

with such-like reasons equally grave and dignified. For my own part, I scruple not to confess that, when I take up a novel, my end and object is entertainment; and as I suspect that to be the case with most readers, I hesitate not to say that entertainment is their legitimate end and object. To read the productions of wit and genius is a very high pleasure to all persons of taste, and the avidity with which they are read by all such shows sufficiently that they are calculated to answer this end. Reading is the cheapest of pleasures: it is a domestic pleasure. Dramatic exhibitions give a more poignant delight, but they are seldom enjoyed in perfection, and never without expense and trouble. Poetry requires in the reader a certain elevation of mind and a practised ear. It is seldom relished unless a taste be formed for it pretty early. But the humble novel is always ready to enliven the gloom of solitude, to soothe the languor of debility and disease, to win the attention from pain or vexations occurrences, to take man from himself, (at many seasons the worst company he can be in,) and, while the moving picture of life passes before him, to make him forget the subject of his own complaints. It is pleasant to the mind to sport in the boundless regions of possibility; to find relief from the sameness of every-day occurrences by expatiating amidst brighter skies and fairer fields; to exhibit love that is always happy, valour that is always successful; to feed the appetite for wonder by a quick succession of marvellous events; and to distribute, like a ruling providence, rewards and punishments which fall just where they ought to fall.

It is sufficient therefore as an end, that these writings add to the innocent pleasures of life; and if they do no harm, the entertainment they give is a sufficient good. We cut down the tree that bears no fruit, but we ask nothing of a flower beyond its scent and colour. The unpardonable sin in a novel is dullness: however grave or wise it may be, if its author possesses no powers of amusing, he has no business to write novels; he should employ his pen in some more serious part of literature.

But it is not necessary to rest the credit of these works on amusement alone, since it is certain they have had a very strong effect in infusing principles and moral feelings. It is impossible to deny that the most glowing and impressive sentiments of virtue are to be found in many of these compositions, and have been deeply imbibed by their useful readers. They awaken a sense of finer feelings than the commerce of ordinary life inspires. Many a young woman has caught from such works as *Clarissa* or *Cecilia*, ideas of delicacy and refinement which were not, perhaps, to be gained in any society she could have access to. Many a maxim of prudence is laid up in the memory from these stores, ready to operate when occasion offers.

The passion of love, the most seductive of all the passions, they certainly paint too high, and represent its influence beyond what it will be found to be in real life; but if they soften the heart they also refine it. They mix with the natural passions of our nature all that is tender in virtuous affection; all that is estimable in high principle and unshaken constancy; all that grace, delicacy, and sentiment can bestow of touching and attractive. Benevolence and sensibility to distress are almost always insisted on in modern works of this kind; and perhaps it is not too much to say, that much of the softness of our present manners, much of that tincture of humanity so conspicuous amidst all our vices, is owing to the bias given by our dramatic writings and fictitious stories. A high regard to female honour, generosity, and a spirit of self-sacrifice, are strongly inculcated. It costs nothing, it is true, to an author to make his hero generous, and very often he is extravagantly so; still, sentiments of this kind serve in some measure to counteract the spirit of the world, where selfish considerations have always more than their due weight. In what discourse from the pulpit are religious feelings more strongly raised than in the prison sermon of *The Vicar of Wakefield*, or some parts of *The Fool of Quality?*

But not only those splendid sentiments with which, when properly presented, our feelings readily take part, and kindle as we read; the more severe and homely virtues of prudence and œconomy have been enforced in the writings of a Burney and an Edgeworth. Writers of their good sense have observed, that while these compositions cherished even a romantic degree of sensibility, the duties that have less brilliancy to recommend them were neglected. Where can be found a more striking lesson against unfeeling dissipation than the story of the *Harrels?* Where have order, neatness, industry, sobriety, been recommended with more strength than in the agreeable tales of Miss Edgeworth? If a parent wished his child to avoid caprice, irregularities of temper, procrastination, coquetry, affectation,—all those faults and blemishes which undermine family happiness, and destroy the every-day comforts of common life,—whence can he derive more impressive morality than from the same source? When works of fancy are thus made subservient to the improvement of the rising generation, they certainly stand on a higher ground than mere entertainment, and we revere while we admire.

Some knowledge of the world is also gained by these writings, imperfect indeed, but attained with more ease, and attended with less danger, than by mixing in real life. If the stage is a mirror of life, so is the novel, and perhaps a more accurate one, as less is sacrificed to effect and representation. There are many descriptions of characters in the busy world, which a young woman in the retired scenes of life hardly meets with at all, and many whom it is safer to read of than to meet; and to either sex it must be desirable that the first impressions of fraud, selfishness, profligacy and perfidy should be connected, as in good novels they will always be, with infamy and ruin. At any rate, it is safer to meet with a bad character in the pages of a fictitious story, than in the polluted walks of life; but an author solicitous for the morals of his readers will be sparing in the introduction of such characters.— It is an aphorism of Pope,

> Vice is a monster of such frightful mien
> As to be hated, needs but to be seen.

But he adds,

> But seen too oft, familiar with her face,
> We first endure, then pity, then embrace.

Indeed the former assertion is not true without considerable modifications. If presented in its naked deformity, vice will indeed give disgust; but it may be so surrounded with splendid and engaging qualities, that the disgust is lost in admiration. Besides, though the selfish and mean propensities are radically unlovely, it is not the same with those passions which all have felt, and few are even desirous to resist. To present these to the young mind in the glowing colours of a Rousseau or a Madame de Stael is to awaken and increase sensibilities, which it is the office of wise restraint to calm and to moderate. Humour covers the disgust which the grosser vices would occasion; passion veils the danger of the more seducing ones.

After all, the effect of novel-reading must depend, as in every other kind of reading, on the choice which is made. If the looser compositions of this sort are excluded, and the sentimental ones chiefly perused, perhaps the danger lies more in fixing the standard of virtue and delicacy too high for ready use, than in debasing it. Generosity is carried to such excess as would soon dissipate even a princely fortune; a weak compassion often allows a vice to escape with impunity; an over-strained delicacy, or regard to a rash vow, is allowed to mar all the prospects of a long life: dangers are despised, and self is annihilated, to a degree that prudence does not warrant, and virtue is far from requiring. The most generous man living, the most affectionate friend, the most dutiful child, would find his character fall far short of the perfections exhibited in a highly-wrought novel.

Love is a passion particularly exaggerated in novels. It forms the chief interest of, by far, the greater part of them. In order to increase this interest, a false idea is given of the importance of the passion. it occupies the serious hours of life; events all hinge upon it; everything gives way to its influence, and no length of time wears it out. When a young lady, having imbibed these notions, comes into the world, she finds that this formidable passion acts a very subordinate part on the great theatre of the world; that is vivid sensations are mostly limited to a very early period; and that it is by no means, as the poet sings,

> All the colour of remaining life.

She will find but few minds susceptible of its more delicate influences. Where it is really felt, she will see it continually overcome by duty, by prudence, or merely by a regard for the show and splendour of life; and that in fact it has a very small share in the transactions of the busy world, and is often little consulted even in choosing a partner for life. In civilized life both men and women acquire so early a command over their passions, that the strongest of them are taught to give way to circumstances; and a moderate liking will appear apathy itself, to one accustomed to see the passion painted in its most glowing colours. Least of all will a course of novels prepare a young lady for the neglect and tedium of life which she is perhaps doomed to encounter. If the novels she reads are virtuous, she has learned how to arm herself with proper reserve against the ardour of her lover; she has been instructed how to behave with the utmost propriety when run away with, like *Miss Byron*, or locked up by a cruel parent, like *Clarissa*; but she is not prepared for indifference and neglect. Though young and beautiful, she may see her youth and beauty pass away without conquests, and the monotony of her life will be apt to appear more insipid when contrasted with scenes of perpetual courtship and passion.

It may be added with regard to the knowledge of the world, which, it is allowed, these writings are calculated in some degree to give, that, let them be as well written and with as much attention to real life and manners as they can possibly be, they will in some respects give false ideas, from the very nature of fictitious writing. Every such work is a *whole*, in which the fates and fortunes of the personages are brought to a conclusion, agreeably to the author's own preconceived idea. Every incident in a well written composition is introduced for a certain purpose, and made to forward a certain plan. A sagacious reader is never disappointed in his forebodings. If a prominent circumstance is presented to him, he lays hold on it, and may be very sure it will introduce some striking event; and if a character has strongly engaged his affections, he need not fear being obliged to withdraw them: the personages never turn out differently from what their first appearance gave him a right to expect; they gradually open, indeed; they may surprise, but they never disappoint him. Even from the elegance of a name he may give a guess at the amenity of the character. But real life is a kind of chance-medley, consisting of many unconnected scenes. The great author of the drama of life has not finished his piece; but the author must finish his; and vice must be punished and virtue rewarded in the compass of a few volumes; and it is a fault in *his* composition if every circumstance does not answer the reasonable expectations of the reader. But in real life our reasonable expectations are often disappointed; many incidents occur which are like "passages that lead to nothing," and characters occasionally turn out quite different from what our fond expectations have led us to expect.

In short, the reader of a novel forms his expectations from what he supposes passes in the mind of the author, and guesses rightly at his intentions, but would often guess wrong if he were considering the real course of nature. It was very probable, at some periods of his history, that *Gil Blas*, if a real character, would come to be hanged; but the practised novel-reader knows well that no such event can await the hero of the tale. Let us suppose a person speculating on the character of *Tom Jones* as the production of an author, whose business it is pleasingly to interest his readers. He has no doubt but that, in spite of his irregularities and distresses, his history will come to an agreeable termination. He has no doubt but that his parents will be discovered in due time; he has no doubt but that his love for *Sophia* will be rewarded sooner or later with her hand; he has no doubt of the constancy of that young lady, or of their entire happiness after marriage. And why does he foresee all this? Not from the real tendencies of things, but from what he has discovered of the author's intentions. But what would have been the probability in real life? Why, that the parents would either never have been found, or have proved to be persons of no consequence—that *Jones* would pass from one vicious indulgence to another, till his natural good disposition was quite smothered under his irregularities—that *Sophia* would either have married her lover clandestinely, and have been poor and unhappy, or she would have conquered her passion and married some country gentleman with whom she would have lived in moderate happiness, according to the usual routine of married life. But the author would have done very ill so to have constructed his story. If *Booth* had been a real character, it is probable his *Amelia* and her family would not only have been brought to poverty, but left in it; but to the reader it is much more probable that by some means or other they will be rescued from it, and left in possession of all the comforts of life. It is *probable* in *Zeluco* that the detestable husband will some way or other be got rid of; but woe to the young lady, who, when married, should be led, by contemplating the possibility of such an event, to cherish a passion which ought to be entirely relinquished!

Though a great deal of trash is every season poured out upon the public from the English presses, yet in general our novels are not vicious; the food has neither flavour nor nourishment, but at least it is not poisoned. Our national taste and habits are still turned towards domestic life and matrimonial happiness, and the chief harm done by a circulating library is occasioned by the frivolity of its furniture, and the loss of time incurred. Now and then a girl perhaps may be led by them to elope with a coxcomb; or, if she is handsome, to expect the homage of a *Sir Harry* or *My lord*, instead of the plain tradesmen suitable to her situation in life; but she will not have her mind contaminated with such scenes and ideas as Crebillon, Louvet, and others of that class have published in France.

And indeed, notwithstanding the many paltry books of this kind published in the course of every year, it may safely be affirmed that we have more good writers in this walk living at the present time, than at any period since the days of Richardson and Fielding. A very great proportion of these are ladies: and surely it will not be said that either taste or morals have been losers by their taking the pen in hand. The names of D'Arblay, Edgeworth, Inchbald, Radcliffe, and a number more, will vindicate this assertion.

No small proportion of modern novels have been devoted to recommend, or to mark with reprobation, those systems of philosophy or politics which have raised so much ferment of late years. Mr. Holcroft's *Anna St. Ives* is of this number: its beauties, and beauties it certainly has, do not make amends for its absurdities. What can be more absurd than to represent a young lady gravely considering, in the disposal of her hand, how she shall promote the greatest possible good of the system? Mr. Holcroft was a man of strong powers, and his novels are by no means without merit, but his satire is often partial, and his representations of life unfair. On the other side may be reckoned *The modern Philosophers*, and the novels of Mrs. West. In the war of systems these light skirmishing troops have been often employed with great effect; and, so long as they are content with fair, general warfare, without taking aim at individuals, are perfectly allowable. We have lately seen the gravest theological discussions presented to the world under the attractive form of a novel, and with a success which seems to show that the interest, even of the generality of readers, is most strongly excited when some serious end is kept in view.

It is not the intention in these slight remarks to enumerate those of the present day who have successfully entertained the public; otherwise Mr. Cumberland might be mentioned, that veteran in every field of literature; otherwise a tribute ought to be paid to the peculiarly pathetic powers of Mrs. Opie; nor would it be possible to forget the very striking and original novel of *Caleb Williams*, in which the author, without the assistance of any of the common events or feelings on which these stories generally turn, has kept up the curiosity and interest of the reader in the most lively manner; nor his *St. Leon*, the ingenious speculation of a philosophical mind, which is also much out of the common track. It will bear an advantageous comparison with Swift's picture of the *Strulbrugs* in his *Voyage to Laputa*, the tendency of which seems to be to repress the wish of never-ending life in this world: but in fact it does not bear at all upon the question, for no one ever did wish for immortal life without immortal youth to accompany it, the one wish being as easily formed as the other; but *St. Leon* shows, from a variety of striking circumstances, that both together would pall, and that an immortal *human* creature would grow an insulated unhappy being.

With regard to this particular selection, it presents a series of some of the most approved novels, from the first regular productions of the kind to the present time: they are of very different degrees of merit; but none, it is hoped, so destitute of it as not to afford entertainment. Variety in manner has been attended to. As to the rest, no two people probably would make the same choice, nor indeed the same person at any distance of time. A few of superior merit were chosen without difficulty, but the list was not completed without frequent hesitation. Some regard it has been thought proper to pay to the taste and preference of the public, as was but reasonable in an undertaking in which their preference was to indemnify those who are at the expense and risk of the publication. Copyright also was not to be intruded on, and the number of volumes was determined by the booksellers. Some perhaps may think that too much importance has been already given to a subject so frivolous, but a discriminating taste is no where more called for than with regard to a species of books which every body reads. It was said by Fletcher of Saltoun, "Let me make the ballads of a nation, and I care not who makes the laws." Might it not be said with as much propriety, Let me make the novels of a country, and let who will make the systems?

44

From *Waverley;*
Or, 'Tis Sixty Years Since

SIR WALTER SCOTT

Scottish novelist Sir Walter Scott (1771-1832) is frequently credited with inventing the historical novel. Originally a poet, Scott turned to novel-writing with the publication of the first in a series of what are now termed his *Waverley Novels*. Variously and loosely chronicling the history of Scotland and England, the novels are often considered to be romances as opposed to realistic ficiton, though in the following introductory chapter to *Waverley*, Scott emphasizes his attempt to draw his characters and events "from the great book of Nature". His most famous novels include *Rob Roy* (1817), *The Heart of Midlothian* (1818), and *Ivanhoe* (1819). In the following chapter he engages the reader in a discussion of possible subtitles for his work, ones that would confine it alternately to the genres of Gothic romance or sentimental novel. He eschews both of these categories by focusing on the recent past—subtitling the novel *Or, 'Tis Sixty Years Since*. He notes that in doing so his emphasis will be on men rather than matters and on the recreation of historical fidelity to the period depicted.

Chapter First.
Introductory.

The title of this work has not been chosen without the grave and solid deliberation which matters of importance demand from the prudent. Even its first, or general denomination, was the result of no common research or selection, although, according to the example of my predecessors, I had only to seize upon the most sounding and euphonic surname that English history or topography affords, and elect it at once as the title of my work, and the name of my hero. But, alas! what could my readers have expected from the chivalrous epithets of Howard, Mordaunt, Mortimer, or Stanley, or from the softer and more sentimental sounds of Belmour,

Source: Sir Walter Scott, from *Waverley; Or, 'Tis Sixty Years Since*, 1814, rptd Boston: DeWolfe, Fiske and Co., 1880, pp. 21-4.

> # WAVERLEY
>
> ## OR 'TIS SIXTY YEARS SINCE
>
> ### By SIR WALTER SCOTT, Bart.
>
> Under which King, Bezonian? speak, or die!
> *Henry IV. Part II.*
>
> WAVERLEY HONOUR.
>
> BOSTON
> DeWOLFE, FISKE, & CO., PUBLISHERS
> 365 WASHINGTON STREET

Title page of *Waverley*

Belville, Belfield, and Belgrave, but pages of inanity, similar to those which have been so christened for half a century past? I must modestly admit I am too diffident of my own merit to place it in unnecessary opposition to preconceived associations: I have therefore, like a maiden knight with his white shield, assumed for my hero, Waverley, an uncontaminated name, bearing with its sound little of good or evil, excepting what the reader shall hereafter be pleased to affix to it. But my second or supplemental title was a matter of much more difficult election, since that, short as it is, may be held as pledging the author to some special mode of laying his scene, drawing his characters, and managing his adventures. Had I, for example, announced in my frontispiece, "Waverley, a Tale of other Days," must not every novel-reader have anticipated a castle scarce less than that of Udolpho, of which the eastern wing had long been uninhabited, and the keys either lost or consigned to the care of some aged butler or housekeeper, whose trembling steps, about the middle of the second volume, were doomed to guide the hero or heroine to the ruinous precipice? Would not the owl have shrieked and the cricket cried in my very title-page? and could it have been possible for me, with a moderate attention to decorum, to introduce any scene more lively than might be produced by the jocularity of a clownish but faithful valet, or the garrulous narrative of the heroine's fille-de-chamber, when rehearsing the stories of blood and horror which she had heard in the servants' hall? Again, had my title borne, "Waverley, a Romance from the German," what head so obtuse as not to image forth a profligate abbot, an oppressive duke, a secret and mysterious association of Rosicrucians and illuminati, with all their properties of black cowls, caverns, daggers, electrical machines, trap-doors, and dark-lanterns? Or if I had rather chosen to call my work a "Sentimental Tale," would it not have been a sufficient presage of a heroine with a profusion of auburn hair, and a harp, the soft solace of her solitary hours, which she fortunately finds always the means of transporting from castle to cottage, although she herself be sometimes obliged to jump out of a two-pair-of-stairs window, and is more than once bewildered on her journey, alone and on foot, without any guide but a blowsy peasant girl, whose jargon she hardly can understand? Or again, if my Waverley had been entitled "A Tale of the Times," wouldst thou not, gentle reader, have demanded from me a dashing sketch of the fashionable world, a few anecdotes of private scandal thinly veiled, and if lusciously painted, so much the better? a heroine from Grosvenor Square, and a hero from the Barouche Club, or the Four-in-Hand, with a set of subordinate characters from the elegantes of Queen Anne Street East, or the dashing heroes of the Bow Street Office? I could proceed in proving the importance of a title-page, and displaying at the same time my own intimate knowledge of the particular ingredients necessary to the composition of romances and novels of various descriptions: But it is enough, and I scorn to tyrannize longer over the impatience of my reader, who is doubtless already anxious to know the choice made by an author so profoundly versed in the different branches of his art.

By fixing, then, the date of my story Sixty Years before this present 1st November, 1805, I would have my readers understand that they will meet in the following pages neither a romance of chivalry, nor a tale of modern manners; that my hero will neither have iron on his shoulders, as of yore, nor on the heels of his boots, as is the present fashion of Bond Street; and that my damsels will neither be clothed "in purple and in pall," like the Lady Alice of an old ballad, nor reduced to the primitive nakedness of a modern fashionable at a rout. From this my choice of an æra the understanding critic may farther presage, that the object of my tale is more a description of men than manners. A tale of manners, to be interesting, must either refer to antiquity so great as to have become venerable, or it must bear a vivid reflection of those scenes which are passing daily before our eyes, and are interesting from their novelty. Thus the coat-of-mail of our ancestors, and the triple-furred pelisse of our modern beaux, may, though for very different reasons, be equally fit for the array of a fictitious character; but who, meaning the costume of his hero to be impressive, would willingly attire him in the court dress of George the Second's reign, with its no collar, large sleeves, and low pocket-holes? The same may be urged, with equal truth, of the Gothic hall, which, with its darkened and tinted windows, its elevated and gloomy roof, and massive oaken table garnished with boar's-head and rosemary, pheasants and peacocks, cranes and cygnets, has an excellent effect in fictitious description. Much may also be gained by a lively display of a modern fête, such as we have daily recorded in that part of a newspaper entitled the Mirror of Fashion, if we contrast these, or either of them, with the splendid formality of an entertainment given Sixty Years Since; and thus it will be readily seen how much the painter of antique or of fashionable manners gains over him who delineates those of the last generation.

Considering the disadvantages inseparable from this part of my subject, I must be understood to have resolved to avoid them as much as possible, by throwing the force of my narrative upon the characters and passions of the actors;—those passions common to men in all stages of society, and which have alike agitated the human heart, whether it throbbed under the steel corslet of the fifteenth century, the brocaded coat of the eighteenth, or the blue frock and white dimity waistcoat of the present day. Upon these passions it is no doubt true that the state of manners and laws casts a necessary coloring; but the bearings, to use the language of heraldry, remain the same, though the tincture may be not only different, but opposed in strong contradistinction. The wrath of our ancestors, for example, was colored *gules*; it broke forth in acts of open and sanguinary violence against the objects of its fury. Our malignant feelings, which must seek gratification through more indirect channels, and undermine the obstacles which they cannot openly bear down, may be rather said to be tinctured *sable*. But the deep-ruling impulse is the same in both cases; and the proud peer, who can now only ruin his neighbor according to law, by protracted suits, is the genuine descendant of the baron who wrapped the castle of his competitor in flames, and knocked him on the head as he endeavored to escape from the conflagration. It is from the great book of Nature, the same through a thousand editions, whether of black-letter, or wire-wove and hot-pressed, that I have venturously essayed to read a chapter to the public. Some favorable opportunities of contrast have been afforded me, by the state of society in the northern part of the island at the period of my history, and may serve at once to vary and to illustrate the moral lessons which I would willingly consider as the most important part of my plan, although I am sensible how short these will fall of their aim, if I shall be found unable to mix them with amusement,—a task not quite so easy in this critical generation as it was "Sixty Years Since."

45

Unsigned Review of *Emma*

SIR WALTER SCOTT

In the following review of Austen's novel, *Emma*, Sir Walter Scott acknowledges the distinction between his romantic tendencies and Austen's new brand of realism. Considering himself a romance novelist, Scott contrasts his portrayals of heightened adventures and heroic characters with the more mimetic and sbudued actions and characters of Austen's novels. Austen's work responds to the new taste for more realistic fiction, one that requests "characters and incidents [be] introduced more immediately from the current of ordinary life than was permitted by the former rules of the novel". The realistic author, Scott notes, is subject to more intense criticism than was the author of romance because the critic tends to measure novelistic success by the author's exactness of representation. In addition, characters must evince more depth to compensate for the dearth of adventure. After a synopsis of *Emma*, Scott compares Austen's novels to Flemish paintings in their stylistic finish and precision. Since she pursues the middle road, her novles are less likely than are romances to discompose young minds. However, Scott cautions the realists not to ignore the passions in their calculated attempts to represent people in ordinary cirumstances. This essay signals a split in the novels of the nineteenth century in both England and America. While particularly in the Americans—Cooper, Hawthorne, and Melville—and the British Brontë sisters, the tendency toward romance remains strong, the counter realistic thrust, represented by Austen, Thackeray, Trollope and Eliot, prevails.

There are some vices in civilized society so common that they are hardly acknowledged as stains upon the moral character, the propensity to which is nevertheless carefully concealed, even by those who most frequently give way to them; since no man of pleasure would willingly assume the gross epithet of a debauchee or a drunkard. One would almost think that novel-reading fell under this class of

Source: Sir Walter Scott, Unsigned Review of *Emma*, (October 1815), *Quarterly Review*, 14, March 1816, pp. 188-201

frailties, since among the crowds who read little else, it is not common to find an individual of hardihood sufficient to avow his taste for these frivolous studies. A novel, therefore, is frequently 'bread eaten in secret;' and it is not upon Lydia Languish's toilet alone that Tom Jones and Peregrine Pickle are to be found ambushed behind works of a more grave and instructive character. And hence it has happened, that in no branch of composition, not even in poetry itself, have so many writers, and of such varied talents, exerted their powers. It may perhaps be added, that although the composition of these works admits of being exalted and decorated by the higher exertions of genius; yet such is the universal charm of narrative, that the worst novel ever written will find some gentle reader content to yawn over it, rather than to open the page of the historian, moralist, or poet. We have heard, indeed, of one work of fiction so unutterable stupid, that the proprietor, diverted by the rarity of the incident, offered the book, which consisted of two volumes in duodecimo, handsomely bound, to any person who would declare, upon his honour, that he had read the whole from beginning to end. But although this offer was made to the passengers on board an Indiaman, during a tedious outward-bound voyage, the *Memoirs of Clegg the Clergyman*, (such was the title of this unhappy composition,) completely baffled the most dull and determined student on board, and bid fair for an exception to the general rule above-mentioned,—when the love of glory prevailed with the boatswain, a man of strong and solid parts, to hazard the attempt, and he actually conquered and carried off the prize!

The judicious reader will see at once that we have been pleading our own cause while stating the universal practice, and preparing him for a display of more general acquaintance with this fascinating department of literature, than at first sight may seem consistent with the graver studies to which we are compelled by duty: but in truth, when we consider how many hours of languor and anxiety, of deserted age and solitary celibacy, of pain even and poverty, are beguiled by the perusal of these light volumes, we cannot austerely condemn the source from which is drawn the alleviation of such a portion of human misery, or consider the regulation of this department as beneath the sober consideration of the critic.

If such apologies may be admitted in judging the labours of ordinary novelists, it becomes doubly the duty of the critic to treat with kindness as well as candour works which, like this before us, proclaim a knowledge of the human heart, with the power and resolution to bring that knowledge to the service of honour and virtue. The author is already known to the public by the two novels announced in her title-page, and both, the last especially, attracted, with justice, an attention from the public far superior to what is granted to the ephemeral productions which supply the regular demand of watering-places and circulating libraries. They belong to a class of fictions which has arisen almost in our own times, and which draws the characters and incidents introduced more immediately from the current of ordinary life than was permitted by the former rules of the novel.

In its first appearance, the novel was the legitimate child of the romance; and though the manners and general turn of the composition were altered so as to suit modern times, the author remained fettered by many peculiarities derived from the original style of romantic fiction. These may be chiefly traced in the conduct of the narrative, and the tone of sentiment attributed to the fictitious personages. On the first point, although

> The talisman and magic wand were broke
> Knights, dwarfs, and genii vanish'd into smoke,

still the reader expected to peruse a course of adventures of a nature more interesting and extraordinary than those which occur in his own life, or that of his next-door neighbours. The hero no longer defeated armies by his single sword, clove giants to the chine, or gained kingdoms. But he was expected to go through perils by sea and land, to be steeped in poverty, to be tried by temptation, to be exposed to the alternate vicissitudes of adversity and prosperity, and his life was a troubled scene of suffering and achievement. Few novelists, indeed, adventured to deny the hero his final hour of tranquillity and happiness, though it was the prevailing fashion never to relieve him out of his last and most dreadful distress until the finishing chapters of his history; so that although his prosperity in the record of his life was short, we were bound to believe it was long and uninterrupted when the author had done with him. The heroine was usually condemned to equal hardships and hazards. She was regularly exposed to being forcibly carried off like a Sabine virgin by some frantic admirer. And even if she escaped the terrors of masked ruffians, an insidious ravisher, a cloak wrapped forcibly around her head, and a coach with the blinds up driving she could not conjecture whither, she had still her share of wandering, of poverty, of obloquy, of seclusion, and of imprisonment, and was frequently extended upon a bed of sickness, and reduced to her last shilling before the author condescended to shield her from persecution. In all these dread contingencies the mind of the reader was expected to sympathize, since by incidents so much beyond the bounds of his ordinary experience, his wonder and interest ought at once to be excited. But gradually he became familiar with the land of fiction, and adventures of which he assimilated not with those of real life, but with each other. Let the distress of the hero or heroine be ever so great, the reader reposed an imperturbable confidence in the talents of the author, who, as he had plunged them into distress, would in his own good time, and when things, as Tony Lumpkin says, were in a concatenation accordingly, bring his favourites out of all their troubles. Mr. Crabbe has expressed his own and our feelings excellently on this subject.

> For should we grant these beauties all endure
> Severest pangs, they've still the speediest cure;
> Before one charm be wither'd from the face,
> Except the bloom which shall again have place,
> In wedlock ends each wish, in triumph all disgrace.
> And life to come, we fairly may suppose,
> One light bright contrast to these wild dark woes.

In short, the author of novels was, in former times, expected to tread pretty much in the limits between the concentric circles of probability and possibility; and as he was not permitted to transgress the latter, his narrative, to make amends, almost always went beyond the bounds of the former. Now, although it may be urged that the vicissitudes of human life have occasionally led an individual through as many scenes of singular fortune as are represented in the most extravagant of these fictions, still the causes and personages acting on these changes have varied with the progress of the adventurer's fortune, and do not present that combined plot, (the object of every skilful novelist,) in which all the more interesting individuals of the dramatis personae have their appropriate share in the action and in bringing about the catastrophe. Here, even more that in its various and violent changes of fortune, rests the improbability of the novel. The life of man rolls forth like a stream from the fountain, or it spreads out in to tranquillity like a placid or stagnant lake. In the latter case, the individual grows old among the characters with whom he was born, and is contemporary,—shares precisely the sort of weal and woe to which his birth destined him,—moves in the same circle,—and, allowing for the change of seasons, is influenced by, and influences the same class of persons by which he was originally surrounded. The man of mark and adventure, on the contrary, resembles, in the course of his life, the river whose mid-current and discharge in to the ocean are widely removed from each other, as well as from the rocks and wild flowers which its fountains first reflected; violent changes of time, of place, and of circumstances, hurry him forward from one scene to another, and his adventures will usually be found only connected to each other because they have happened to the same individual. Such a history resembles an ingenious, fictitious narrative, exactly in the degree in which an old dramatic chronicle of the life and death of some distinguished character, where all the various agents appear and disappear as in the page of history, approaches a regular drama, in which every person introduce plays an appropriate part, and every point of the action tends to one common catastrophe.

We return to the second broad line of distinction between the novel, as formerly composed, and real life,—the difference, namely, of the sentiments. The novelist professed to give an imitation of nature, but it was, as the French say, *la belle nature*. Human beings, indeed, were presented, but in the most sentimental mood, and with minds purified by a sensibility which often verged on extravagance. In the serious class of novels, the hero was usually

A knight of love, who never broke a vow.

And although, in those of a more humorous cast, he was permitted a license, borrowed either from real life or from the libertinism of the drama, still a distinction was demanded even from Peregrine Pickle, or Tom Jones; and the hero, in every folly of which he might be guilty, was studiously vindicated from the charge of infidelity of the heart. The heroine was, of course, still more immaculate; and to have conferred her affections upon any other than the lover to whom the reader had destined her from their first meeting, would have been a crime against sentiment which no author, of moderate prudence, would have hazarded, under the old *régime*.

Here, therefore, we have two essential and important circumstances, in which the earlier novels differed from those now in fashion, and were more nearly assimilated to the old romances. And there can be no doubt that, by the studied involution and extrication of the story, by the combination of incidents new, striking and wonderful beyond the course of ordinary life, the former authors opened that obvious and strong sense of interest which arises from curiosity; as by the pure, elevated, and romantic cast of the sentiment, they conciliated those better propensities of our nature which loves to contemplate the picture of virtue, even when confessedly unable to imitate its excellences.

But strong and powerful as these sources of emotion and interest may be, they are, like all others, capable of being exhausted by habit. The imitators who rushed in crowds upon each path in which the great masters of the art had successively led the way, produced upon the public mind the usual effect of satiety. The first writer of a new class is, as it were, placed on a pinnacle of excellence, to which, at the earliest glance of a surprised admirer, his ascent seems little less than miraculous. Time and imitation speedily diminish the wonder, and each successive attempt establishes a kind of progressive scale of ascent between the lately deified author, and the reader, who had deemed his excellence inaccessible. The stupidity, the mediocrity, the merit of his imitators, are alike fatal to the first inventor, by shewing how possible it is to exaggerate his faults and to come within a certain point of his beauties.

Materials also (and the man of genius as well as his wretched imitator must work with the same) become stale and familiar. Social life, in our civilized days, affords few instances capable of being painted in the strong dark colours which excite surprize and horror; and robbers, smugglers, bailiffs, caverns, dungeons, and madhouses, have been all introduced until they ceased to interest. And thus in the novel, as in every style of composition which appeals to the public taste, the more rich and easily worked mines being exhausted, the adventurous author must, if he is desirous of success, have recourse to those which were disdained by his predecessors as unproductive, or avoided as only capable of being turned to profit by great skill and labour.

Accordingly a style of novel has arisen, within the last fifteen or twenty years, differing from the former in the points upon which the interest hinges; neither alarming our credulity nor amusing our imagination by wild variety of incident, or by those pictures of romantic affection and sensibility, which were formerly as certain attributes of fictitious characters as they are of rare occurrence among those who actually live and die. The substitute for these excitements, which had lost much of their poignancy by the repeated and injudicious use of them, was the art of copying from nature as she really exists in the common walks of life, and presenting to the reader, instead of the splendid scenes of an imaginary world, a correct and striking representation of that which is daily taking place around him.

In adventuring upon this task, the author makes obvious sacrifices, and encounters peculiar difficulty. He who paints from *le beau idéal*, if his scenes and sentiments are striking and interesting, is in a great measure exempted from the difficult task of reconciling them with the ordinary probabilities of life: but he who paints a scene of common occurrence, places his composition within that extensive range of criticism which general experience offers to every reader. The resemblance of a statue of Hercules we must take on the artist's judgment; but every one can criticize that which is presented as the portrait of a friend, or neighbour. Something more than a mere sign-post likeness is also demanded. The portrait must have spirit and character, as well as resemblance; and being deprived of all that, according to Bayes, goes 'to elevate and surprize,' it must make amends by displaying depth of knowledge and dexterity of execution. We, therefore, bestow no mean compliment upon the author of *Emma*, when we say that, keeping close to common incidents, and to such characters as occupy the ordinary walks of life, she has produced sketches of such spirit and originality, that we never miss the excitation which depends upon a narrative of uncommon events, arising from the consideration of minds, manners, and sentiments, greatly above our own. In this class she stands almost alone; for the scenes of Miss Edgeworth are laid in higher life, varied by more romantic incident, and by her remarkable power of embodying and illustrating national character. But the author of *Emma* confines herself chiefly to the middling classes of society; her most distinguished characters do not rise greatly above well-bred country gentlemen and ladies; and those which are sketched with most originality and precision, belong to a class rather below that standard. The narrative of all her novels is composed of such common occurrences as may have fallen under the observation of most folks; and her dramatis personæ conduct themselves upon the motives and principles which the readers may recognize as ruling their own and that of most of their acquaintances. The kind of moral, also, which these novels inculcate, applies equally to the paths of common life, as will best appear from a short notice of the author's former works, with a more full abstract of that which we at present have under consideration.

Sense and Sensibility, the first of these compositions, contains the history of two sisters. The elder, a young lady of prudence and regulated feelings, becomes gradually attached to a man of excellent heart and limited talents, who happens unfortunately to be fettered by a rash and ill-assorted engagement. In the younger sister, the influence of sensibility and imagination predominates; and she, as was to be expected, also falls in love, but with a more unbridled and wilful passion. Her lover, gifted with all the qualities of exterior polish and vivacity, proves faithless, and marries a woman of large fortune. The interest and merit of the piece depend altogether upon the behaviour of the elder sister, while obliged at once to sustain her own disappointment with fortitude, and to support her sister, who abandons herself, with unsuppressed feelings, to the indulgence of grief. The marriage of the unworthy rival at length relieves her own lover from his imprudent engagement, while her sister, turned wise by precept, example, and experience, transfers her affection to a very respectable and somewhat too serious admirer, who had nourished an unsuccessful passion through the three volumes.

In *Pride and Prejudice* the author presents us with a family of young women, bred up under a foolish and vulgar mother, and a father whose good abilities lay hid under such a load of indolence and insensibility, that he had become contented to make the foibles and follies of his wife and daughters the subject of dry and humorous sarcasm, rather than of admonition, or restraint. This is one of the portraits from ordinary life which shews our author's talents in a very strong point of view. A friend of ours, whom the author never saw or heard of, was at once recognized by his own family as the original of Mr. Bennet, and we do not know if he has yet got rid of the nickname. A Mr. Collins, too, a formal, conceited, yet servile young sprig of divinity, is drawn with the same force and precision. The story of the piece consists chiefly in the fates of the second sister, to whom a man of high birth, large fortune, but haughty and reserved manners, becomes attached, in spite of the discredit thrown upon the object of his affection by the vulgarity and ill-conduct of her relations. The lady, on the contrary, hurt at the contempt of her connections, which the lover does not even attempt to suppress, and prejudiced against him on other accounts, refuses the hand which he ungraciously offers, and does not perceive that she has done a foolish thing until she accidentally visits a very handsome seat and grounds belonging to her admirer. They chance to meet exactly as her prudence had begun to subdue her prejudice; and after some essential services rendered to her family, the lover becomes encouraged to renew his addresses, and the novel ends happily.

Emma has even less story than either of the preceding novels. Miss Emma Woodhouse, from whom the book takes its name, is the daughter of a gentleman of wealth and consequence residing at his seat in the immediate vicinage of a country village called Highbury. The father, a good-natured, silly valetudinary, abandons the management of his household to Emma, he himself being only occupied by his summer and winter walk, his apothecary, his gruel, and his whist table. The latter is supplied from the neighbouring village of Highbury with precisely the sort of persons who occupy the vacant corners of a regular whilst table, when a village is in the neighbourhood, and better cannot be found within the family. We have the smiling and courteous vicar, who nourishes the ambitious hope of obtaining Miss Woodhouse's had. We have Mrs. Bates, the wife of a former rector, past every thing but tea and whist; her daughter, Miss Bates, a good-natured, vulgar, and foolish old maid; Mr. Weston, a gentleman of frank disposition and moderate fortune, in the vicinity, and his wife an amiable and accomplished person, who had been Emma's governess, and is devotedly attached to her. Amongst all these personages, Miss Woodhouse walks forth, the princess paramount, superior to all her companions in wit, beauty, fortune, and accomplishments, doated upon by her father and the Westons, admired, and almost worshipped by the more humble companions of the whist table. The object of most young ladies is, or at least is usually supposed to be, a desirable connection in marriage. But Emma Woodhouse, either anticipating the taste of a later period of life, or, like a good sovereign, preferring the weal of her subjects of Highbury to her own private interest, sets generously about making matches for her friends without thinking of matrimony on her own account. We are informed that she had been eminently successful in the case of Mr. and Miss Weston; and when the novel commences she is exerting her influence in favour of Miss Harriet Smith, a boarding-school girl without family or fortune, very good humoured, very pretty, very silly, and, what suited Miss Woodhouse's purpose best of all, very much disposed to be married.

In these conjugal machinations Emma is frequently interrupted, not only by the cautions of her father, who had a particular objection to any body committing the rash act of matrimony, but also by the sturdy reproof and remonstrances of Mr. Knightley, the elder brother of her sister's husband, a sensible country gentleman of thirty-five, who had known Emma from her cradle, and was the only person who ventured to find fault with her. In spite, however, of his censure and warning, Emma lays a plan of marrying Harriet Smith to the vicar; and though she succeeds perfectly in diverting her simple friend's thoughts from an honest farmer who had made her a very suitable offer, and in flattering her into a passion for Mr. Elton, yet, on the other hand, that conceited divine totally mistakes the nature of the encouragement held out to him, and attributes the favour which he found in Miss Woodhouse's eyes to a lurking affection on her own part. This at length encourages him into a presumptuous declaration of his sentiments; upon receiving a repulse, he looks abroad elsewhere, and enriches the Highbury society by uniting himself to a dashing young woman with as many thousands as are usually called ten, and a corresponding quantity of presumption and ill breeding.

While Emma is thus vainly engaged in forging wedlock-fetters for others, her friends have views of the same kind upon her, in favour of a son of Mr. Weston by a former marriage, who bears the name, lives under the patronage, and is to inherit the fortune of a rich uncle. Unfortunately Mr. Frank Churchill had already settled his affections on Miss Jane Fairfax, a young lady of reduced fortune; but as this was a concealed affair, Emma, when Mr. Churchill first appears on the stage, has some thoughts of being in love with him herself; speedily, however, recovering from that dangerous propensity, she is disposed to confer him upon her deserted friend Harriet Smith. Harriet has, in the interim, fallen desperately in love with Mr. Knightley, the sturdy, advice-giving bachelor; and, as all the village supposes Frank Churchill and Emma to be attached to each other, there are cross purposes enough (were the novel of a more romantic cast) for cutting half the men's throats and breaking all the women's hearts. But at Highbury Cupid walks decorously, and with good discretion, bearing his torch under a lanthorn, instead of flourishing it around to set the house on fire. All these entanglements bring on only a train of mistakes and embarrassing situations, and dialogues at balls and parties of pleasure, in which the author displays her peculiar powers of humour and knowledge of human life. The plot is extricated with great simplicity. The aunt of Frank Churchill dies; his uncle, no longer under her baneful influence, consents to his marriage with Jane Fairfax. Mr. Knightley and Emma are led, by this unexpected incident, to discover that they had been in love with each other all along. Mr. Woodhouse's objections to the marriage of his daughter are overpowered by the fears of housebreakers, and the comfort which he hopes to derive from having a stout son-in-law resident in the family; and the facile affections of Harriet Smith are transferred, like a bank bill by indorsation, to her former suitor, the honest farmer, who had obtained a favourable opportunity of renewing his addresses. Such is the simple plan of a story which we peruse with pleasure, if not with deep interest, and which perhaps we might more willingly resume than one of those narratives where the attention is strongly riveted, during the first perusal, by the powerful excitement of curiosity.

The author's knowledge of the world, and the peculiar tact with which she presents characters that the reader cannot fail to recognize, reminds us something of the merits of the Flemish school of painting. The subjects are not often elegant, and certainly never grand; but they are finished up to a nature, and with a precision which delights the reader. This is a merit which it is very difficult to illustrate by extracts, because it pervades the whole work, and is not to be comprehended from a single passage. The following is a dialogue between Mr. Woodhouse, and his elder daughter Isabella, who shares his anxiety about health, and has, like her father, a favourite apothecary. The reader must be informed that this lady, with her husband, a sensible, peremptory sort of person, has come to spend a week with her father.

> While they were thus comfortably occupied, Mr Woodhouse was enjoying a full flow of happy regrets and fearful affection with his daughter.
>
> "My poor dear Isabella," said he, fondly taking her hand, and interrupting, for a few moments, her busy labours for some one of her five children—"How long it is, how terribly long since you were here! And how tired you must be after your journey! You must go to bed early, my dear-and I recommend a little gruel to you before you go. You and I will have a nice basin of gruel together. My dear Emma, suppose we all have a little gruel."
>
> Emma could not suppose any such thing, knowing, as she did, that both the Mr Knightleys were as unpersuadable on that article as herself; and two basins only were ordered. After a little more discourse in praise of gruel, with some wondering at its not being taken every evening by every body, he proceeded to say, with an air of grave reflection,
>
> "It was an awkward business, my dear, your spending the autumn at South End instead of coming here. I never had much opinion of the sea air."
>
> "Mr Wingfield most strenuously recommended it, sir-or we should not have gone. He recommended it for all the children, but particularly for the weakness in little Bella's throat, both sea air and bathing."
>
> "Ah! my dear, but Perry had many doubts about the sea doing her any good; and as to myself, I have been long perfectly convinced, though perhaps I never told you so before, that the sea is very rarely of use to any body. I am sure it almost killed me once."
>
> "Come, come," cried Emma, feeling this to be an unsafe subject, "I must beg you not to talk of the sea. It makes me envious and miserable; I who have never seen it! South End is prohibited, if you please. My dear Isabella, I have not heard you make one inquiry after Mr Perry yet; and he never forgets you."
>
> "Oh! good Mr Perry-how is he, sir?"
>
> "Why, pretty well; but not quite well. Poor Perry is bilious, and he has not time to take care of himself-he tells me he has not time to take care of himself-which is very sad-but he is always wanted all round the country. I suppose there is not a man in such practice any where. But then, there is not so clever a man any where."
>
> "And Mrs Perry and the children, how are they? do the children grow? I have a great regard for Mr Perry. I hope he will be calling soon. He will be so pleased to see my little ones."

"I hope he will be here to-morrow, for I have a question or two to ask him about myself of some consequence. And, my dear, whenever he comes, you had better let him look at little Bella's throat."

"Oh! my dear sir, her throat is so much better that I have hardly any uneasiness about it. Either bathing has been of the greatest service to her, or else it is to be attributed to an excellent embrocation of Mr Wingfield's, which we have been applying at times ever since August."

"It is not very likely, my dear, that bathing should have been of use to her-and if I had known you were wanting an embrocation, I would have spoken to—"

"You seem to me to have forgotten Mrs and Miss Bates," said Emma, "I have not heard one inquiry after them."

"Oh! the good Bateses-I am quite ashamed of myself-but you mention them in most of your letters. I hope they are quite well. Good old Mrs Bates—I will call upon her to-morrow, and take my children. They are always so pleased to see my children. And that excellent Miss Bates! such thorough worthy people! How are they, sir?"

"Why, pretty well, my dear, upon the whole. But poor Mrs Bates had a bad cold about a month ago."

"How sorry I am! But colds were never so prevalent as they have been this autumn. Mr Wingfield told me that he had never known them more general or heavy-except when it has been quite an influenza."

"That has been a good deal the case, my dear; but not to the degree you mention. Perry says that colds have been very general, but not so heavy as he has very often known them in November. Perry does not call it altogether a sickly season."

"No, I do not know that Mr Wingfield considers it very sickly except-"

"Ah! my poor dear child, the truth is, that in London it is always a sickly season. Nobody is healthy in London, nobody can be. It is a dreadful thing to have you forced to live there! so far off! and the air so bad!"

"No, indeed— we are not at all in a bad air. Our part of London is so very superior to most others! You must not confound us with London in general, my dear sir. The neighbourhood of Brunswick Square is very different from almost all the rest. We are so very airy! I should be unwilling, I own, to live in any other part of the town; there is hardly any other that I could be satisfied to have my children in: but we are so remarkably airy! Mr Wingfield thinks the vicinity of Brunswick Square decidedly the most favourable as to air."

"Ah 1 my dear, it is not like Hartfield. You make the best of it-but after you have been a week at Hartfield, you are all of you different creatures; you do not look like the same. Now I cannot say, that I think you are any of you looking well at present."

"I am sorry to hear you say so, sir; but I assure you, excepting those little nervous head-aches and palpitations which I am never entirely free from any where, I am quite well myself; and if the children were rather pale before they went to bed, it was only because they were a little more tired than usual, from their journey and the happiness of coming. I hope you will think better of their looks to-morrow; for I assure you Mr Wingfield told me, that he did not believe he had ever sent us off altogether, in such good case. I trust, at least, that you do not think Mr Knightley looking ill," turning her eyes with affectionate anxiety towards her husband.

"Middling, my dear; I cannot compliment you. I think Mr John Knightley very far from looking well.

"What is the matter, sir? Did you speak to me?" cried Mr John Knightley, hearing his own name.

"I am sorry to find, my love, that my father does not think you looking well-but

I hope it is only from being a little fatigued. I would have wished, however, as you know, that you had seen Mr Wingfield before you left home."

"My dear Isabella," exclaimed he hastily, "pray do not concern yourself about my looks. Be satisfied with doctoring and coddling yourself and the children, and let me look as I chuse."

"I did not thoroughly understand what you were telling your brother," cried Emma, "about your friend Mr Graham's intending to have a bailiff from Scotland, to look after his new estate. But will it answer? Will not the old prejudice be too strong?"

And she talked in this way so long and successfully that, when forced to give her attention again to her father and sister, she had nothing worse to hear than Isabella's kind inquiry after Jane Fairfax; and Jane Fairfax, though no great favourite with her in general, she was at that moment very happy to assist in praising.

Perhaps the reader may collect from the preceding specimen both the merits and faults of the author. The former consists much in the force of a narrative conducted with much neatness and point, and a quiet yet comic dialogue, in which the characters of the speakers evolve themselves with dramatic effect. The faults, on the contrary, arise from the minute detail which the author's plan comprehends. Characters of folly or simplicity, such as those of old Woodhouse and Miss Bates, are ridiculous when first presented, but if too often brought forward or too long dwelt upon, their prosing is apt to become as tiresome in fiction as in real society. Upon the whole, the turn of this author's novels bears the same relation to that of the sentimental and romantic cast, that cornfields and cottages and meadows bear to the highly adorned grounds of a show mansion, or the rugged sublimities of a mountain landscape. It is neither so captivating as the one, nor so grand as the other, but it affords to those who frequent it a pleasure nearly allied with the experience of their own social habits; and what is of some importance, the youthful wanderer may return from his promenade to the ordinary business of life, without any chance of having his head turned by the recollection of the scene through which he has been wandering.

One word, however, we must say in behalf of that once powerful divinity, Cupid, king of gods and men, who in these times of revolution, has been assailed, even in his own kingdom of romance, by the authors who were formerly his devoted priests. We are quite aware that there are few instances of first attachment being brought to a happy conclusion, and that is seldom can be so in a state of society so highly advanced as to render early marriages among the better class, acts, generally speaking, of imprudence. But the youth of this realm need not at present be taught the doctrine of selfishness. It is by no means their error to give the world or the good things of the world all for love; and before the authors of moral fiction couple Cupid indivisibly with calculating prudence, we would have them reflect, that they may sometimes lend their aid to substitute more mean, more sordid, and more selfish motives of conduct, for the romantic feelings which their predecessors perhaps fanned into too powerful a flame. Who is it, that in his youth has felt a virtuous attachment, however romantic or however unfortunate, but can trace back its influence much that his character may possess of what is honourable, dignified, and disinterested? If he recollects hours wasted in unavailing hope, or saddened by doubt and disappointment; he may also dwell on many which have been snatched from folly or libertinism, and dedicated to studies which might render him worthy of the object of his affection, or pave the way perhaps to that distinction necessary to raise him to an equality with her. Even the habitual indulgence of feelings totally unconnected with ourself and our own immediate interest, softens, graces, and amends the human mind; and after the pain of disappointment is past, those who survive (and by good fortune those are the greater number) are neither less wise nor less worthy members of society for having felt, for a time, the influence of a passion which has been well qualified as the 'tenderest, noblest and best.'

From *Northanger Abbey*

JANE AUSTEN

Jane Austen (1775-1817) one of England's first and most famous realistic novelists, was the author of six novels, including *Pride and Prejudice* (1813) and *Emma* (1815). Though *Northanger Abbey* was begun in 1798 and thus appears to be Austen's first novel, it was not published until after her death. It satirises the genre of the Gothic novel in its characterisation of the gullible heroine Catherine Morland who is reading Radcliffe's *The Mysteries of Udolpho* during the course of the story. In the following excerpt from Chapter 5, Austen interrupts her description of Catherine's and Isabella's friendship to defend novels and novel-reading. At the conclusion of her defence, she criticises the male-dominated essays in the *Spectator*, the bulk of which she notes would "disgust a young person of taste" but are nevertheless elevated over the novel by reviewers and critics.

Yes, novels; for I will not adopt that ungenerous and impolitic custom, so common with novel writers, of degrading, by their contemptuous censure, the very performances to the number of which they are themselves adding: joining with their greatest enemies in bestowing the harshest epithets on such works, and scarcely ever permitting them to be read by their own heroine, who, if she accidentally takes up a novel, is sure to turn over its insipid pages with disgust. Alas! if the heroine of one novel be not patronised by the heroine of another, from whom can she expect protection and regard? I cannot approve of it. Let us leave it to the Reviewers to abuse such effusions of fancy at their leisure, and over every new novel to talk in threadbare strains of the trash with which the press now groans. Let us not desert one another; we are an injured body. Although our productions have afforded much more extensive and unaffected pleasure than those of any other literary corporation in the world, no species of composition has been so much decried. From pride, ignorance, or fashion, our foes are almost as many as our readers; and while the abilities of the nine-hundredth abridger of the *History of England*, or of

Source: Jane Austen, from *Northanger Abbey*, 1818, rptd *The Novels of Jane Austen*, London: Grant Richards, 1898, pp. 34-6.

the man who collects and publishes in a volume some dozen lines of Milton, Pope, and Prior, with a paper from the *Spectator*, and a chapter from Sterne, are eulogised by a thousand pens, there seems almost a general wish of decrying the capacity and undervaluing the labour of the novelist, and of slighting the performances which have only genius, wit, and taste to recommend them. 'I am no novel reader; I seldom look into novels; do not imagine that *I* often read novels; it is really very well for a novel.' Such is the common cant. 'And what are you reading, Miss —?' 'Oh! it is only a novel!' replies the young lady; while she lays down her book with affected indifference, or momentary shame. 'It is only *Cecilia*, or *Camilla*, or *Belinda*'; or, in short, only some work in which the greatest powers of the mind are displayed, in which the most thorough knowledge of human nature, the happiest delineation of its varieties, the liveliest effusions of wit and humour, are conveyed to the world in the best chosen language. Now, had the same young lady been engaged with a volume of the *Spectator*, instead of such a work, how proudly would she have produced the book, and told its name! though the chances must be against her being occupied by any part of that voluminous publication, of which either the matter or manner would not disgust a young person of taste; the substance of its papers so often consisting in the statement of improbable circumstances, unnatural characters, and topics of conversation, which no longer concern any one living; and their language, too, frequently so coarse as to give no very favourable idea of the age that could endure it.

On the English Novelists

WILLIAM HAZLITT

William Hazlitt (1778-1830), an acquaintance of Wordsworth, Coleridge and lamb, is best known as a prolific essayist on drama, literature and travel. He published pieces in The *Edinburgh Review* and in other major journals of the period. His *Lectures on the English Poets* (1818-19) and *Characters of Shakespeare's Plays* (1817-18) reveal his easy movement among the dominant literary genres of the period. In the following essay, he traces the history of eighteenth- and nineteenth-century British novelists backwards to *Don Quixote* and *Gil Blas*, noting their influence especially on Fielding and Smollett. Hazlitt attributes the eighteenth-century novelist's focus on character to the relative stability of George II's reign during which society began to acknowledge the importance of the individual. During George III's reign, novels conversely reflected the instability of the war-torn times with their emphasis on Gothic horrors. Hazlitt concludes with a comparison of Scott and Godwin, praising the latter for his psychological insight and the former for external observation.

Lecture VI.

On the English Novelists.

There is an exclamation in one of Gray's letters—"Be mine to read eternal romances of Marivaux and Crebillon!" If I did not utter a similar aspiration at the conclusion of the last new novel which I read (I would not give offence by being more particular as to the name) it was not from any want of affection for the class of writing to which it belongs; for without going so far as the celebrated French philosopher, who thought that more was to be learnt from good novels and romances than from the gravest treatises on history and morality, yet there are few works to which I am oftener tempted to turn for profit or delight, than to the standard productions in this species of composition. We find there a close imitation

Source: William Hazlitt, "On the English Novelists", 1818, rptd *Lectures on the English Comic Writers*. Ed. By his son. New York and London: John Wiley, 1849, pp. 124-56.

of men and manners; we see the very web and texture of society as it really exists, and as we meet with it when we come into the world. If poetry has "something more divine in it," this savours more of humanity. We are brought acquainted with the motives and characters of mankind, imbibe our notions of virtue and vice from practical examples, and are taught a knowledge of the world through the airy medium of romance. As a record of past manners and opinions, too, such writings afford the best and fullest information. For example, I should be at a loss where to find any authentic documents of the same period so satisfactory an account of the general state of society, and of moral, political, and religious feeling in the reign of George II as we meet with in the *Adventures of Joseph Andrews* and his friend Mr Abraham Adams. This work, indeed, I take to be a perfect piece of statistics in its kind. In looking into any regular history of that period, into a learned and eloquent charge to a grand jury or the clergy of a diocese or into a tract on controversial divinity, we should hear only of the ascendancy of the Protestant succession, the horrors of Popery, the triumph of civil and religious liberty, the wisdom and moderation of the sovereign, the happiness of the subject, and the flourishing state of manufactures and commerce. But if we really wish to know what all these fine-sounding names come to, we cannot do better than turn to the works of those who, having no other object than to imitate nature, could only hope for success from the fidelity of their pictures; and were bound (in self-defence) to reduce the boasts of vague theorists and the exaggerations of angry disputants to the mortifying standard of reality. Extremes are said to meet; and the works of imagination, as they are called, sometimes come the nearest to truth and nature. Fielding, in speaking on this subject, and vindicating the use and dignity of the style of writing in which he excelled against the loftier pretensions of professed historians, says, "that in their productions nothing is true but the names and dates, whereas in his everything is true but the names and dates." If so, he has the advantage on his side.

I will here confess, however, that I am a little prejudiced on the point in question; and that the effect of many fine speculations has been lost upon me, from an early familiarity with the most striking passages in the work to which I have just alluded. Thus nothing can be more captivating than the description somewhere given by Mr Burke of the indissoluble connexion between learning and nobility, and of the respect universally paid by wealth to piety and morals. But the effect of this ideal representation has always been spoiled by my recollection of Parson Adams sitting over his cup of ale in Sir Thomas Booby's kitchen. Echard *On the Contempt of the Clergy* is, in like manner, a very good book, and "worthy of all acceptation;" but somehow an unlucky impression of the reality of Parson Trulliber involuntarily checks the emotions of respect to which it might otherwise give rise; while, on the other hand, the lecture which Lady Booby reads to Lawyer Scout on the immediate expulsion of Joseph and Fanny from the parish, casts no very favourable light on the flattering accounts of our practical jurisprudence which are to be found in Blackstone or De Lolme. The most moral writers, after all, are those who do not pretend to inculcate any moral. The professed moralist almost unavoidably degenerates into the partisan of a system; and the philosopher is too apt to warp the evidence to his own purpose. But the painter of manners gives the facts of human nature, and leaves us to draw the inference; if we are not able to do this, or do it ill, at least it is our own fault.

The first-rate writers in this class, of course, are few; but those few we may reckon among the greatest ornaments and best benefactors of our kind. There is a certain set of them who, as it were, take their rank by the side of reality, and are appealed to as evidence on all questions concerning human nature. The principal of these are Cervantes and Le Sage, who may be considered as having been naturalised among ourselves; and, of native English growth, Fielding, Smollett, Richardson, and Sterne.[1] As this is a department of criticism which deserves more attention than has been usually bestowed upon it, I shall here venture to recur (not from choice but from necessity) to what I have said upon it in a well-known periodical publication;[2] and endeavour to contribute my mite towards settling the standard of excellence, both as to degree and kind, in these several writers.

I shall begin with the history of the renowned 'Don Quixote de la Mancha,' who presents something more stately, more romantic, and at the same time more real to the imagination, than any other hero upon record. His lineaments, his accoutrements, his pasteboard vizor, are familiar to us; and Mambrino's helmet still glitters in the sun! We not only feel the greatest love and veneration for the knight himself, but a certain respect for all those connected with him, the curate and Master Nicolas the barber, Sancho and Dapple, and even for Rosinante's leanness and his errors.—Perhaps there is no work which combines so much whimsical invention with such an air of truth. Its popularity is almost unequalled; and yet its merits have not been sufficiently understood. The story is the least part of them; though the blunders of Sancho, and the unlucky adventures of his master, are what naturally catch the attention of the majority of readers. The pathos and dignity of the sentiments are often disguised under the ludicrousness of the subject, and provoke laughter when they might well draw tears. The character of Don Quixote himself is one of the most perfect disinterestedness. He is an enthusiast of the most amiable kind; of a nature equally open, gentle, and generous; a lover of truth and justice; and one who had brooded over the fine dreams of chivalry and romance, till they had robbed him of himself, and cheated his brain into a belief of their reality. There cannot be a greater mistake than to consider *Don Quixote* as a merely satirical work, or as a vulgar attempt to explode "the long-forgotten order of chivalry." There could be no need to explode what no longer existed. Besides, Cervantes himself was a man of the most sanguine and enthusiastic temperament; and even through the crazed and battered figure of the knight, the spirit of chivalry shines out with undiminished lustre; as if the author had half-designed to revive the examples of past ages, and once more "witch the world with noble horsemanship." Oh! if ever the mouldering flame of Spanish liberty is destined to break forth, wrapping the tyrant and the tyranny in one consuming blaze, that the spark of generous sentiment and romantic enterprise, from which it must be kindled, has not been quite extinguished, will perhaps be owing to thee, Cervantes, and to thy *Don Quixote*!

The character of Sancho is not more admirable in itself, than as a relief to that of the knight. The contrast is as picturesque and striking as that between the figures of Rosinante and Dapple. Never was there a more complete *partie quarrée*,—they answer to one another at all points. Nothing need surpass the truth of physiognomy in the description of the master and man, both as to body and mind; the one lean and tall, the other round and short; the one heroical and courteous, the other selfish and servile; the one full of high-flown fancies, the other a bag of proverbs; the one always starting some romantic scheme, the other trying to keep to the safe side of custom and tradition. The gradual ascendancy, however, obtained by Don Quixote over Sancho, is as finely managed as it is characteristic. Credulity and a love of the marvellous are as natural to ignorance as selfishness and cunning. Sancho by degrees becomes a kind of lay-brother of the order; acquires a taste for adventures in his own way, and is made all but an entire convert by the discovery of the hundred crowns in one of his most comfortless journeys. Towards the end, his regret at being forced to give up the pursuit of knight-errantry, almost equals his master's; and he seizes the proposal of Don Quixote for them to turn shepherds with the greatest avidity—still applying it in his own fashion; for while the Don is ingeniously torturing the names of his humble acquaintance into classical terminations, and contriving scenes of gallantry and song, Sancho exclaims, "Oh, what delicate wooden spoons shall I carve! what crumbs and cream shall I devour!"—forgetting, in his milk and fruits, the pullets and geese at Camacho's wedding.

This intuitive perception of the hidden analogies of things, or, as it may be called, this *instinct of the imagination*, is, perhaps, what stamps the character of genius on the productions of art more than any other circumstance: for it works unconsciously, like nature, and receives its impressions from a kind of inspiration. There is as much of this indistinct keeping and involuntary unity of purpose in Cervantes as in any author whatever. Something of the same unsettled, rambling humour extends itself to all the subordinate parts and characters of the work. Thus we find the curate confidentially informing Don Quixote, that if he could get the ear of the government he has something of considerable importance to propose for the good of the state; and our adventurer afterwards (in the course of his peregrinations) meets with a young gentleman who is a candidate for poetical honours, with a mad lover, a forsaken damsel, a Mahometan lady converted to the Christian faith, &c.—all delineated with the same truth, wildness, and delicacy of fancy. The whole work breathes that air of romance, that aspiration after imaginary good, that indescribable longing after something more than we possess, that in all places and in all conditions of life,

> —*still prompts the eternal sigh,*
> *For which we wish to live, or dare to die!*

The leading characters in *Don Quixote* are strictly individuals; that is, they do not so much belong to, as form a class by themselves. In other words, the actions and manners of the chief *dramatis personæ* do not arise out of the actions and manners of those around them, or the situation of life in which they are placed, but out of the peculiar dispositions of the persons themselves, operated upon by certain impulses of caprice and accident. Yet these impulses are so true to nature, and their operation so exactly described, that we not only recognise the fidelity of the representation, but recognise it with all the advantage of novelty superadded. They are in the best sense *originals*, namely, in the sense in which nature has her originals. They are unlike anything we have seen before—may be said to be purely ideal; and yet identify themselves more readily with our imagination, and are retained more strongly in memory, than perhaps any others: they are never lost in the crowd. One test of the truth of this ideal painting is the number of allusions which *Don Quixote* has furnished to the whole of civilised Europe; that is to say, of appropriate cases and striking illustrations of the universal principles of our nature. The detached incidents and occasional descriptions of human life are more familiar and obvious; so that we have nearly the same insight here given us into the characters of innkeepers, bar-maids, ostlers, and puppet-show men, that we have in Fielding. There is a much greater mixture, however, of the pathetic and sentimental with the quaint and humorous, than there ever is in Fielding. I might instance the story of the countryman whom Don Quixote and Sancho met in their doubtful search after Dulcinea, driving his mules to plough at break of day, and "singing the ancient ballad of Roncesvalles!" The episodes, which are frequently introduced, are excellent, but have, upon the whole, been overrated. They derive their interest from their connexion with the main story. We are so pleased with that, that we are disposed to receive pleasure from everything else. Compared, for instance, with the serious tales in Boccacio, they are slight and somewhat superficial. That Marcella, the fair shepherdess, is, I think, the best. I shall only add, that *Don Quixote* was, at the time it was published, an entirely original work in its kind, and that the author claims the highest honour which can belong to one, that of being the inventor of a new style of writing. I have never read his *Galatea*, nor his *Loves of Persiles and Sigismunda*, though I have often meant to do it, and I hope to do so yet. Perhaps there is a reason lurking at the bottom of this dilatoriness: I am quite sure the reading of these works could not make me think higher of the author of *Don Quixote*, and it might, for a moment or two, make me think less.

There is another Spanish novel, *Guzman d'Alfarache*, nearly of the same age as *Don Quixote*, and of great genius, though it can hardly be ranked as a novel or a work of imagination. It is a series of strange, unconnected adventures, rather drily told, but accompanied by the most severe and sarcastic commentary. The satire, the wit, the eloquence, and reasoning, are of the most potent kind: but they are didactic rather than dramatic. They would suit a homily or a pasquinade as well or better than a romance. Still there are in this extraordinary book occasional sketches of character and humorous descriptions, to which it would be difficult to produce anything superior. This work, which is hardly known in this country except by name, has the credit, without any reason, of being the original of *Gil Blas*. There is one incident the same, that of the unsavoury ragout, which is served up for supper at the inn. In all other respects these two works are the very reverse of each other, both in their excellences and defects.—*Lazarillo de Tormes* has been more read than the *Spanish Rogue*, and is a work more readable, on this account among others, that it is contained in a duodecimo instead of a folio volume. This, however, is long enough, considering that it treats of only one subject, that of eating, or rather the possibility of living without eating. Famine is here framed into an art, and feasting is banished far hence. The hero's time and thoughts are taken up in a thousand shifts to procure a dinner; and that failing, in tampering with his stomach till supper time, when being forced to go supperless to bed, he comforts himself with the hopes of a breakfast the next morning, of which being again disappointed, he reserves his appetite for a luncheon, and then has to stave it off again by some meagre excuse or other till dinner; and so on, by a perpetual adjournment of this necessary process, through the four-and-twenty hours round. The quantity of food proper to keep body and soul together is reduced to a *minimum*; and the most uninviting morsels with which Lazarillo meets once a week as a God's-send, are pampered into the most sumptuous fare by a long course of inanition. The scene of this novel could be laid nowhere so properly as in Spain, that land of priestcraft and poverty, where hunger seems to be the ruling passion, and starving the order of the day.

Gil Blas has, next to *Don Quixote*, been more generally read and admired than any other novel; and in one sense deservedly so: for it is at the head of its class, though that class is very different from, and I should say inferior, to the other. There is little individual character in *Gil Blas*. The author is a describer of manners, and not of character. He does not take the elements of human nature, and work them up into new combinations (which is the excellence of *Don Quixote*;) nor trace the peculiar shifting shades of folly and knavery as they are to be found in real life (like Fielding;) but he takes off, as it were, the general, habitual impression which circumstances make on certain conditions of life, and moulds all his characters accordingly. All the persons whom he introduces carry about with them the badge of their profession, and you see little more of them than their costume. He describes men as belonging to distinct classes in society; not as they are in themselves, or with the individual differences which are always to be discovered in nature. His hero, in particular, has no character but that of the successive circumstances in which he is placed. His priests are only described as priests: his valets, his players, his women, his courtiers and his sharpers, are all alike. Nothing can well exceed the monotony of the work in this respect:—at the same time that nothing can exceed the truth and precision with which the general manners of these different characters are preserved, nor the felicity of the particular traits by which their common foibles are brought out. Thus the Archbishop of Grenada will remain an everlasting memento of the weakness of human vanity; and the account of Gil Blas' legacy, of the uncertainty of human expectations. This novel is also deficient in the fable as well as in the characters. It is not a regularly constructed story; but a series of amusing adventures told with equal gaiety and good sense, and in the most graceful style imaginable.

It has been usual to class our own great novelists as imitators of one or other of these two writers. Fielding, no doubt, is more like *Don Quixote* than *Gil Blas*; Smollett is more like *Gil Blas* than *Don Quixote*; but there is not much resemblance in either case. Sterne's *Tristram Shandy* is a more direct instance of imitation.

Richardson can scarcely be called an imitator of any one; or if he is, it is of the sentimental refinement of Marivaux, or of the verbose gallantry of the writers of the seventeenth century.

There is very little to warrant the common idea that Fielding was an imitator of Cervantes, except his own declaration of such an intention in the title-page of *Joseph Andrews*, the romantic turn of the character of Parson Adams (the only romantic character in his works,) and the proverbial humour of Partridge, which is kept up for only a few pages. Fielding's novels are, in general, thoroughly his own; and they are thoroughly English. What they are most remarkable for, is neither sentiment, nor imagination, nor wit, nor even humour, though there is an immense deal of this last quality; but profound knowledge of human nature, at least of English nature, and masterly pictures of the characters of men as he saw them existing. This quality distinguishes all his works, and is shown almost equally in all of them. As a painter of real life, he was equal to Hogarth; as a mere observer of human nature, he was little inferior to Shakespeare, though without any of the genius and poetical qualities of his mind. His humour is less rich and laughable than Smollett's; his wit as often misses as hits; he has none of the fine pathos of Richardson or Sterne; but he has brought together a greater variety of characters in common life, marked with more distinct peculiarities, and without an atom of caricature, than any other novel writer whatever. The extreme subtlety of observation on the springs of human conduct in ordinary characters, is only equalled by the ingenuity of contrivance in bringing those springs into play, in such a manner as to lay open their smallest irregularity. The detection is always complete, and made with the certainty and skill of a philosophical experiment, and the obviousness and familiarity of a casual observation. The truth of the imitation is indeed so great, that it has been argued that Fielding must have had his materials ready-made to his hands, and was merely a transcriber of local manners and individual habits. For this conjecture, however, there seems to be no foundation. His representations, it is true, are local and individual; but they are not the less profound and conclusive. The feeling of the general principles of human nature operating in particular circumstances, is always intense, and uppermost in his mind; and he makes use of incident and situation only to bring out character.

It is scarcely necessary to give any illustrations. *Tom Jones* is full of them. There is the account, for example, of the gratitude of the elder Blifil to his brother, for assisting him to obtain the fortune of Miss Bridget Alworthy by marriage; and of the gratitude of the poor in his neighbourhood to Alworthy himself, who had done so much good in the country that he had made every one in it his enemy. There is the account of the Latin dialogues between Partridge and his maid, of the assault made on him during one of these by Mrs Partridge, and the severe bruises he patiently received on that occasion, after which the parish of Little Baddington rung with the story, that the schoolmaster had killed his wife. There is the exquisite keeping in the character of Blifil, and the want of it in that of Jones. There is gradation in the lovers of Molly Seagrim, the philosopher Square succeeding to Tom Jones, who again finds that he himself had succeeded to the accomplished Will

Barnes who had the first possession of her person, and had still possession of her heart, Jones being only the instrument of her vanity, as Square was of her interest. Then there is the discreet honesty of Black George, the learning of Thwackum and Square, and the profundity of Squire Western, who considered it as a physical impossibility that his daughter should fall in love with Tom Jones. We have also that gentleman's disputes with his sister, and the inimitable appeal of that lady to her niece: "I was never so handsome as you, Sophy; yet I had something of you formerly. I was called the cruel Parthenissa. Kingdoms and states, as Tully Cicero says, undergo alteration, and so must the human form!" The adventure of the same lady with the highwayman, who robbed her of her jewels while he complimented her beauty, ought not to be passed over; nor that of Sophia and her muff, nor the reserved coquetry of her cousin Fitzpatrick, nor the description of Lady Bellaston, nor the modest overtures of the pretty widow Hunt, nor the indiscreet babblings of Mrs Honour. The moral of this book has been objected to without much reason; but a more serious objection has been made to the want of refinement and elegance in two principal characters. We never feel this objection, indeed, while we are reading the book; but at other times we have something like a lurking suspicion that Jones was but an awkward fellow, and Sophia a pretty simpleton. I do not know how to account for this effect, unless it is that Fielding's constantly assuring us of the beauty of his hero, and the good sense of his heroine, at last produces a distrust of both. The story of *Tom Jones* is allowed to be unrivalled; and it is this circumstance, together with the vast variety of characters, that has given the *History of a Foundling* so decided a preference over Fielding's other novels. The characters themselves, both in *Amelia* and *Joseph Andrews*, are quite equal to any of those in *Tom Jones*. The account of Miss Matthews and Ensign Hibbert in the former of these,—the way in which that lady reconciles herself to the death of her father,—the inflexible Colonel Bath, the insipid Mrs James, the complaisant Colonel Trent, the demure, sly, intriguing, equivocal Mrs Bennet, the lord who is her seducer, and who attempts afterwards to seduce Amelia by the same mechanical process of a concert-ticket, a book, and the disguise of a great coat,—his little, fat, short-nosed, red-faced, good-humoured accomplice, the keeper of the lodging-house, who, having no pretensions to gallantry herself, has a disinterested delight in forwarding the intrigues and pleasures of others (to say nothing of the honest Atkinson, the story of the miniature-picture of Amelia, and the hashed mutton, which are in a different style,) are master pieces of description. The whole scene at the lodging-house, the masquerade, &c., in *Amelia*, are equal in interest to the parallel scenes in *Tom Jones*, and even more refined in the knowledge of character. For instance, Mrs Bennet is superior to Mrs Fitzpatrick in her own way. The uncertainty in which the event of her interview with her former seducer is left, is admirable. Fielding was a master of what may be called the *double entendre* of character, and surprises you no less by what he leaves in the dark (hardly known to the persons themselves) than by the unexpected discoveries he makes of the real traits and circumstances in a character with which, till then, you find you were unacquainted. There is nothing at all heroic, however, in the usual style of his delineations. He does not draw lofty characters or strong passions; all his persons are of the ordinary stature as to intellect, and possess little elevation of fancy, or energy of purpose. Perhaps, after all, Parson Adams is his finest character. It is equally true to nature and more ideal than any of the others. Its unsuspecting simplicity makes it not only more amiable, but doubly amusing, by gratifying the sense of superior sagacity in the reader. Our laughing at him does not once lessen our respect for him. His declaring that he would willingly walk ten miles to fetch his sermon on vanity, merely to convince Wilson of his thorough contempt of this vice, and his consoling himself for the loss of Æschylus by suddenly recollecting that he could not read it if he had it, because it is dark, are among the finest touches of *naïveté*. The night adventures at Lady Booby's with Beau Didnapper and the amiable Slipslop are the most ludicrous; and that with the huntsman, who draws off the hounds from the poor parson because they would be spoiled by following *vermin*, the most profound. Fielding did not often repeat himself, but Dr Harrison, in *Amelia*, may be considered as a variation of the character of Adams; so also is Goldsmith's *Vicar of Wakefield*; and the latter part of that work, which sets out so delightfully, an almost entire plagiarism from Wilson's account of himself, and Adams's domestic history.

Smollett's first novel, *Roderick Random*, which is also his best, appeared about the same time as Fielding's *Tom Jones*, and yet it has a much more modern air with it; but this may be accounted for from the circumstances that Smollett was quite a young man at the time, whereas Fielding's manner must have been formed long before. The style of *Roderick Random* is more easy and flowing than that of *Tom Jones*; the incidents follow one another more rapidly (though, it must be confessed, they never come in such a throng, or are brought out with the same dramatic effect;) the humour is broader, and as effectual; and there is very nearly, if not quite, an equal interest excited by the story. What, then, is it that gives the superiority to Fielding? It is the superior insight into the springs of human character, and the constant development of that character through every change of circumstance. Smollett's humour often arises from the situation of the persons, or the peculiarity of their external appearance; as, from Roderick Random's carroty locks, which hung down over his shoulders like a pound of candles, or Strap's ignorance of London, and the blunders that follow from it. There is a tone of vulgarity about all his productions. The incidents frequently resemble detached anecdotes taken from a newspaper or magazine; and, like those in *Gil Blas*, might happen to a hundred other characters. He exhibits the ridiculous accidents and reverses to which human life is liable, not "the stuff" of which it is composed. He seldom probes to the quick, or penetrates beyond the surface; and, therefore, he leaves no stings in the minds of his readers, and in this respect is far less interesting than Fielding. His novels always enliven, and never tire us; we take them up with pleasure, and lay them down without any strong feeling of regret. We look on and laugh, as spectators of a highly amusing scene, without closing in with the combatants, or being made parties in the event. We read *Roderick Random* as an entertaining story, for the particular accidents and modes of life which it describes have ceased to exist; but we regard *Tom Jones* as a real history, because the author never stops short of those essential principles which lie at the bottom of all our actions, and in which we feel an immediate interest—*intus et in cute*. Smollett excels most as the lively caricaturist: Fielding as the exact painter and profound metaphysician. I am far from maintaining that this account applies uniformly to the productions of these two writers; but I think that, as far as they essentially differ, what I have stated is the general distinction between them. *Roderick Random* is the purest of Smollett's novels: I mean in point of style and description. Most of the incidents and characters are supposed to have been taken from the events in his own life; and are, therefore, truer to nature. There is a rude conception of generosity in some of his characters, of which Fielding seems to have been incapable, his amiable persons being merely good-natured. It is owing to this that Strap is superior to Partridge; as there is a heartiness and warmth of feeling in some of the scenes between Lieutenant Bowling and his nephew, which is beyond Fielding's power of impassioned writing. The whole of the scene on ship-board is a most admirable and striking picture, and, I imagine, very little if at all exaggerated, though the interest it excites is of a very unpleasant kind, because the irritation and resistance to petty oppression can be of no avail. The picture of the little profligate French friar, who was Roderick's travelling companion, and of whom he always kept to the windward, is one of Smollett's most masterly sketches.—*Peregrine Pickle* is no great favourite of mine, and *Launcelot Greaves* was not worthy of the genius of the author.

Humphry Clinker and *Count Fathom* are both equally admirable in their way. Perhaps the former is the most pleasant gossiping novel that was ever written; that which gives the most pleasure with the least effort to the reader. It is quite as amusing as going the journey could have been; and we have just as good an idea of what happened on the road as if we had been of the party. Humphry Clinker himself is exquisite; and his sweetheart, Winifred Jenkins, not much behind him. Matthew Bramble, though not altogether original, is excellently supported, and seems to have been the prototype of Sir Anthony Absolute in *The Rivals*. But Lismahago is the flower of the flock. His tenaciousness in argument is not so delightful as the relaxation of his logical severity, when he finds his fortune mellowing in the wintry smiles of Mrs Tabitha Bramble. This is the best preserved, and most severe of all Smollett's characters. The resemblance to *Don Quixote* is only just enough to make it interesting to the critical reader, without giving offence to anybody else. The indecency and filth in this novel are what must be allowed to all Smollett's writings.—The subject and characters in *Count Fathom* are, in general, exceedingly disgusting: the story is also spun out to a degree of tediousness in the serious and sentimental parts; but there is more power of writing occasionally shown in it than in any of his works. I need only refer to the fine and bitter irony of the Count's address to the country of his ancestors on his landing in England; to the robber scene in the forest, which has never been surpassed; to the Parisian swindler who personates a raw English country squire (Western is tame in the comparison;) and to the story of the seduction in the west of England. It would be difficult to point out, in any author, passages written with more force and mastery than these.

It is not a very difficult undertaking to class Fielding or Smollett;—the one as an observer of the characters of human life, the other as a describer of its various eccentricities. But it is by no means so easy to dispose of Richardson, who was neither an observer of the one nor a describer of the other, but who seemed to spin his materials entirely out of his own brain, as if there had been nothing existing in the world beyond the little room in which he sat writing. There is an artificial reality about his works which is nowhere else to be met with. They have the romantic air of a pure fiction, with the literal minuteness of a common diary. The author had the strongest matter-of-fact imagination that ever existed, and wrote the oddest mixture of poetry and prose. He does not appear to have taken advantage of anything in actual nature from one end of his works to the other; and yet, throughout all his works, voluminous as they are (and this, to be sure, is one reason why they are so,)—he sets about describing every object and transaction, as if the whole had been given in on evidence by an eye-witness. This kind of high finishing from imagination is an anomaly in the history of human genius; and certainly nothing so fine was ever produced by the same accumulation of minute parts. There is not the least distraction, the least forgetfulness of the end—every circumstance is made to tell. I cannot agree that this exactness of detail produces heaviness; on the contrary, it gives an appearance of truth, and a positive interest to the story; and we listen with the same attention as we should to the particulars of a confidential communication. I at one time used to think some parts of Sir Charles Grandison rather trifling and tedious, especially the long description of Miss Harriet Byron's wedding-clothes, till I was told of two young ladies who had severally copied out the whole of that very description for their own private gratification. After that I could not blame the author.

The effect of reading this work is like an increase of kindred. You find yourself all of a sudden introduced into the midst of a large family, with aunts and cousins to the third and fourth generation, and grandmothers both by the father's and mother's side; and a very odd set of people they are, but people whose real existence and personal identity you can no more dispute than your own senses, for you see and hear all that they do or say. What is still more extraordinary, all this extreme elaborateness in working out the story seems to have cost the author nothing; for, it is said, that the published works are mere abridgments. I have heard (though this I suspect must be a pleasant exaggeration) that Sir Charles Grandison was originally written in eight-and-twenty volumes.

Pamela is the first of Richardson's productions, and the very child of his brain. Taking the general idea of the character of a modest and beautiful country girl, and of the ordinary situation in which she is placed, he makes out all the rest, even to the smallest circumstance, by the mere force of a reassuring imagination. It would seem as if a step lost, would be as fatal here as in a mathematical demonstration. The development of the character is the most simple, and comes the nearest to nature that it can do, without being the same thing. The interest of the story increases with the dawn of understanding and reflection in the heroine: her sentiments gradually expand themselves, like opening flowers. She writes better every time, and acquires a confidence in herself, just as a girl would do, in writing such letters in such circumstances; and yet it is certain that no girl would write such letters in such circumstances. What I mean is this:—Richardson's nature is always the nature of sentiment and reflection, not of impulse or situation. He furnishes his characters, on every occasion, with the presence of mind of the author. He makes them act, not as they would from the impulse of the moment, but as they might upon reflection, and upon a careful review of every motive and circumstance in their situation. They regularly sit down to write letters: and if the business of life consisted in letter-writing, and was carried on by the post (like a Spanish game at chess,) human nature would be what Richardson represents it. All actual objects and feelings are blunted and deadened by being presented through a medium which may be true to reason, but is false in nature. He confounds his own point of view with that of the immediate actors in the scene; and hence presents you with a conventional and factitious nature, instead of that which is real. Dr Johnson seems to have preferred this truth of reflection to the truth of nature, when he said that there was more knowledge of the human heart in a page of Richardson than in all Fielding. Fielding, however, saw more of the practical results, and understood the principles as well; but he had not the same power of speculating upon their possible results, and combining them in certain ideal forms of passion and imagination, which was Richardson's real excellence.

It must be observed, however, that it is this mutual good understanding and comparing of notes between the author and the persons he describes, his infinite circumspection, his exact process of ratiocination and calculation, which gives such an appearance of coldness and formality to most of his characters,—which makes prudes of his women and coxcombs of his men. Everything is too conscious in his works. Everything is distinctly brought home to the mind of the actors in the scene, which is a fault undoubtedly: but then, it must be confessed, everything is brought home in its full force to the mind of the reader also; and we feel the same interest in the story as if it were our own. Can anything be more beautiful or more affecting than Pamela's reproaches to her "lumpish heart," when she is sent away from her master's at her own request; its lightness when she is sent for back; the joy which the conviction of the sincerity of his love diffuses in her heart, like the coming on of spring; the artifice of the stuff gown; the meeting with Lady Davers after her marriage; and the trial-scene with her husband? Who ever remained insensible to the passion of Lady Clementina, except Sir Charles Grandison himself, who was the object of it? *Clarissa* is, however, his masterpiece, if we except Lovelace. If she is fine in herself, she is still finer in his account of her. With that foil, her purity is dazzling indeed: and she who could triumph by her virtue, and the force of her love, over the regality of Lovelace's mind, his wit, his person, his accomplishments, and his spirit, conquers all hearts. I should suppose that never sympathy more deep or sincere was excited by the calamities of real life. The links in this wonderful chain of interest are not more finely wrought, than their whole weight is overwhelming and irresistible. Who can forget the exquisite gradations of her long dying-scene, or the closing of the coffin-lid, when Miss Howe comes to take her last leave of her friend; or the heart-breaking reflection that Clarissa makes on what was to have been her wedding day? Well does a certain writer exclaim—

> Books are a real world, both pure and good,
> Round which, with tendrils strong as flesh and blood,
> Our pastime and our happiness may grow!

Richardson's wit was unlike that of any other writer—his humour was so too. Both were the effect of intense activity of mind—laboured, and yet completely effectual. I might refer to Lovelace's reception and description of Hickman, when he calls out Death in his ear, as the name of the person with whom Clarissa had fallen in love; and to the scene at the glove-shop. What can be more magnificent than his enumeration of his companions—"Belton, so pert and so pimply—Tourville, so fair and so foppish!" &c. In casuistry this author is quite at home; and, with a boldness greater even than his puritanical severity, has exhausted every topic on virtue and vice. There is another peculiarity in Richardson, not perhaps so uncommon, which is, his systematically preferring his most insipid characters to his finest, though both were equally his own invention, and he must be supposed to have understood something of their qualities. Thus he preferred the little, selfish, affected, insignificant Miss Byron, to the divine Clementina; and again, Sir Charles Grandison to the nobler Lovelace. I have nothing to say in favour of Lovelace's morality; but Sir Charles is the prince of coxcombs,—whose eye was never once taken from his own person and his own virtues; and there is nothing which excites so little sympathy as this excessive egotism.

It remains to speak of Sterne; and I shall do it in few words. There is more of mannerism and affectation in him, and a more immediate reference to preceding authors; but his excellences, where he is excellent, are of the first order. His characters are intellectual and inventive, like Richardson's, but totally opposite in the execution. The one are made out by continuity, and patient repetition of touches; the others, by glancing transitions and graceful apposition. His style is equally different from Richardson's: it is at times the most rapid, the most happy, the most idiomatic of any that is to be found. It is the pure essence of English conversational style. His works consist only of *morceaux*—of brilliant passages. I wonder that Goldsmith, who ought to have known better, should call him "a dull fellow." His wit is poignant, though artificial; and his characters (though the groundwork of some of them had been laid before) have yet invaluable original differences; and the spirit of the execution the master-strokes constantly thrown into them, are not to be surpassed. It is sufficient to name them:—Yorick, Dr Slop, Mr Shandy, My Uncle Toby, Trim, Susanna, and the Widow Wadman. In these he has contrived to oppose, with equal felicity and originality, two characters, one of pure intellect, and the other of pure good nature, in My Father and My Uncle Toby. There appears to have been in Sterne a vein of dry, sarcastic humour, and of extreme tenderness of feeling; the latter sometimes carried to affectation, as in the tale of Maria, and the apostrophe to the recording angel; but at other times pure, and without blemish. The story of Le Fevre is perhaps the finest in the English language. My Father's restlessness, both of body and mind, is inimitable. It is the model from which all those despicable performances against modern philosophy ought to have been copied, if their authors had known anything of the subject they were writing about. My Uncle Toby is one of the finest compliments ever paid to human nature. He is the most unoffending of God's creatures; or, as the French express it, *un tel petit homme*! Of his bowling green, his sieges, and his amours, who would say or think anything amiss!

It is remarkable that our four best novel-writers belong nearly to the same age. We also owe to the same period (the reign of George II. the inimitable Hogarth, and some of our best writers of the middle style of comedy. If I were called upon to account for this coincidence, I should waive the consideration of more general causes, and ascribe it at once to the establishment of the Protestant ascendancy, and the succession of the House of Hanover. These great events appear to have given a more popular turn to our literature and genius, as well as to our government. It was found high time that the people should be represented in books as well as in Parliament. They wished to see some account of themselves in what they read; and not to be confined always to the vices, the miseries, and frivolities of the great. Our domestic tragedy, and our earliest periodical works, appeared a little before the same period. In despotic countries, human nature is not of sufficient importance to be studied or described. The *canaille* are objects rather of disgust than curiosity; and there are no middle classes. The works of Racine and Molière are either imitations of the verbiage of the court, before which they were represented, or fanciful caricatures of the manners of the lowest of the people. But in the period of our history in question, a security of person and property, and a freedom of opinion had been established, which made every man feel of some consequence to himself, and appear an object of some curiosity to his neighbours: our manners become more domesticated; there was a general spirit of sturdiness and independence, which made the English character more truly English than perhaps at any other period—that is, more tenacious of its own opinions and purposes. The whole surface of society appeared cut out into square enclosures and sharp angles, which extended to the dresses of the time, their gravel-walks and clipped hedges. Each individual had a certain ground-plot of his own to cultivate his particular humours in, and let them shoot out at pleasure; and a most plentiful crop they have produced accordingly. The reign of George II was, in a word, the age of *hobby-horses*: but, since that period, things have taken a different turn.

His present Majesty (God save the mark!) during almost the whole of his reign, has been constantly mounted on a great war-horse; and has fairly driven all the competitors out of the field. Instead of minding our own affairs, or laughing at each other, the eyes of his faithful subjects have been fixed on the career of the sovereign, and all hearts anxious for the safety of his person and government. Our pens and our swords have been alike drawn in their defence; and the returns of killed and wounded, the manufacture of newspapers and parliamentary speeches, have exceeded all former example. If we have had a little of the blessings of peace, we have had enough of the glories and calamities of war. His Majesty has indeed contrived to keep alive the greatest public interest ever known, by his determined manner of riding his hobby for half a century together, with the aristocracy, the democracy, the clergy, the landed and monied interest, and the rabble, in full cry after him;—and at the end of his career, most happily and unexpectedly succeeded, amidst empires lost and won, kingdoms overturned and created, and the destruction of an incredible number of lives, in restoring *the divine right of kings*, and thus preventing any future abuse of the example which seated his family on the throne!

It is not to be wondered at, if amidst the tumult of events crowded into this period, our literature has partaken of the disorder of the time; if our prose has run mad, and our poetry grown childish. Among those persons who "have kept the even tenor of their way," the author of *Evelina, Cecilia*, and *Camilla*, must be allowed to hold a distinguished place.[3] Mrs Radcliffe's "enchantments drear," and mouldering castles, derived part of their interest, no doubt, from the supposed tottering state of all old structure of the time; and Mrs Inchbald's *Nature and Art* would scarcely have had the same popularity, but that it fell in (as to its two main characters) with the prevailing prejudice of the moment, that judges and bishops were not invariably pure abstractions of justice and piety. Mrs Edgeworth's *Tales*, again, (with the exception of *Castle Rack-rent*, which is a genuine, unsophisticated, national portrait) are a kind of pedantic, pragmatical, common sense, tinctured with the pertness and pretensions of the paradoxes to which they are so self-complacently opposed. Madame D'Arblay is, on the contrary, quite of the old school, a mere common observer of manners, and also a very woman. It is this last circumstance which forms the peculiarity of her writings, and distinguishes them from those masterpieces which I have before mentioned. She is a quick, lively, and accurate observer of persons and things; but she always looks at them with a consciousness of her sex, and in that point of view in which it is the particular business and interest of women to observe them. There is little in her works of passion or character, or even manners, in the most extended sense of the word, as implying the sum-total of our habits and pursuits; her *forte* is in describing the absurdities and affectations of external behaviour, or the manners of people in company. Her characters, which are ingenious caricatures, are, no doubt, distinctly marked, and well kept up; but they are slightly shaded, and exceedingly uniform. Her heroes and heroines, almost all of them, depend on the stock of a single phrase or sentiment, and have certain mottoes or devices by which they may always be known. They form such characters as people might be supposed to assume for a night at a masquerade. She presents not the whole-length figure, nor even the face, but some prominent feature. In one of her novels, for example, a lady appears regularly every ten pages, to get a lesson in music for nothing. She never appears for any other purpose; this is all you know of her: and in this the whole wit and humour of the character consists. Meadows is the same, who has always the cue of being tired, without any other idea. It has been said of Shakespeare, that you may always assign his speeches to the proper characters; and you may infallibly do the same thing with Madame D'Arblay's, for they always say the same thing. The Braughton's are the best. Mr Smith is an exquisite city portrait. 'Evelina' is also her best novel, because it is the shortest; that is, it has all the liveliness in the sketches of character, and smartness of comic dialogue and repartee, without the tediousness of the story, and endless affectation of sentiment which disfigures the others.

Women, in general, have a quicker perception of any oddity or singularity of character than men, and are more alive to every absurdity which arises from a violation of the rules of society, or a deviation from established custom. This partly arises from the restraints on their own behaviour, which turn their attention constantly on the subject, and partly from other causes. The surface of their minds, like that of their bodies, seems of a finer texture than ours; more soft, and susceptible of immediate impulses. They have less muscular strength, less power of continued voluntary attention, of reason, passion, and imagination; but they are more easily impressed with whatever appeals to their senses or habitual prejudices. The intuitive perception of their minds is less disturbed by any abstruse reasonings on causes or consequences. They learn the idiom of character and manners, as they acquire that of language, by rote, without troubling themselves about the principles. Their observation is not the less accurate on that account, as far as it goes, for it has been well said that "there is nothing so true as habit."

There is little other power in Madame D'Arblay's novels than that of immediate observation; her characters, whether of refinement or vulgarity, are equally superficial and confined. The whole is a question of form, whether that form is adhered to or infringed upon. It is this circumstance which takes away dignity and interest from her story and sentiments, and makes the one so teazing and tedious, and the other so insipid. The difficulties in which she involves her heroines are too much 'Female Difficulties;' they are difficulties created out of nothing. The author appears to have no other idea of refinement than it is the reverse of vulgarity; but the reverse of vulgarity is fastidiousness and affectation. There is a true and a false delicacy. Because a vulgar country Miss would answer "yes" to a proposal of marriage in the first page, Madame D'Arblay makes it a proof of an excess of refinement, and an indispensable point of etiquette in her young ladies to postpone the answer to the end of five volumes, without the smallest reason for their doing so, and with every reason to the contrary. The reader is led every moment to expect a *denouement*, and is as often disappointed on some trifling pretext. The whole artifice of her fable consists in coming to no conclusion. Her ladies "stand so upon the order of their going," that they do not go at all. They will not abate an ace of their punctilio in any circumstances or on any emergency. They would consider it as quite indecorous to run down stairs though the house were in flames, or to move an inch off the pavement though a scaffolding was falling. She has formed to herself an abstract idea of perfection in common behaviour, which is quite as romantic and impracticable as any other idea of the sort; and the consequence has naturally been that she makes her heroines commit the greatest improprieties and absurdities in order to avoid the smallest. In opposition to a maxim in philosophy, they constantly act from the weakest motive, or rather from pure contradiction. The whole tissue of the fable is, in general, more wild and chimerical than anything in *Don Quixote*, without the poetical truth or elevation. Madame D'Arblay has woven a web of difficulties for her heroines, something like the green silken threads in which the shepherdesses entangled the steed of Cervantes' hero, who swore, in his fine enthusiastic way, that he would sooner cut his passage to another world than disturb the least of those beautiful meshes. To mention the most painful instance—the 'Wanderer,' in her last novel, raises obstacles lighter than "the gossamer that idles in the wanton summer air," into insurmountable barriers; and trifles with those that arise out of common sense, reason, and necessity. Her conduct is not to be accounted for directly out of the circumstances in which she is placed, but out of some factitious and misplaced refinement on them. it is a perpetual game at cross-purposes. There being a plain and strong motive why she should pursue any course of action, is a sufficient reason for her to avoid it, and the perversity of her conduct is in proportion to its levity—as the lightness of the feather baffles the force of the impulse that is given to it, and the slightest breath of air turns it back on the hand from which it is thrown. We can hardly consider this as the perfection of the female character!

I must say I like Mrs Radcliffe's romances better, and think of them oftener; and even when I do not, part of the impression with which I survey the full-orbed moon shining in the blue expanse of heaven, or hear the wind sighing through the autumnal leaves, or walk under the echoing archways of a Gothic ruin, is owing to a repeated perusal of the *Romance of the Forest*, and *The Mysteries of Udolpho*. Her descriptions of scenery, indeed, are vague and wordy to the last degree; they are neither like Salvator nor Claude, nor nature and she dwells on the effects of moonlight till we are sometimes weary of them; her characters are insipid, the of a shade, continued on, under different names, through all her novels; her story comes to nothing. But in harrowing up the soul with imaginary horrors, and making the flesh creep, and the nerves thrill with fond hopes and fears, she is unrivalled among her fair country-women. Her great power lies in describing the indefinable, and embodying a phantom. She makes her readers twice children; and from the dim and shadowy veil which she draws over the objects of her fancy, forces us to believe all that is strange, and next to impossible, of their mysterious agency; whether it is the sound of the lover's lute borne o'er the distant waters along the winding shores of Provence, recalling with its magic breath, some long-lost friendship or some hopeless love; or the full choir of the cloistered monks, chanting their midnight orgies; or the lonely voice of an unhappy sister in her pensive cell, like angels' whispered music; or the deep sigh that steals from a dungeon on the startled ear; or the dim apparition of ghastly features; or the face of an assassin hid beneath a monk's cowl; or the robber gliding through the twilight gloom of the forest. All the fascination that links the world of passion to the world unknown is hers, and she plays with it at her pleasure; she has all the poetry of romance, all that is obscure, visionary, and objectless in the imagination. It seems that the simple notes of Clara's lute, which so delighted her youthful heart, still echo among the rocks and mountains of the Valois; the mellow tones of the minstrel's songs still mingle with the noise of the dashing oar, and the rippling of the silver waves of the Mediterranean; the voice of Agnes is heard from the haunted tower, and Schedoni's form still stalks through the frowning ruins of Palinzi. The greatest treat, however, which Mrs Radcliffe's pen has provided for the lovers of the marvellous and terrible is the Provençal tale which Ludovico reads in the Castle of Udolpho as the lights are beginning to turn blue, and just before the faces appear from behind the tapestry that carry him off, and we hear no more of him. This tale is of a knight, who being engaged in a dance at some high festival of old romance, was summoned out by another knight clad in complete steel; and being solemnly adjured to follow him into the mazes of the neighbouring wood, his conductor brought him at length to a hollow glade in the thickest part, where he pointed to the murdered corse of another knight, and lifting up his beaver showed him by the gleam of moonlight which fell on it, that it had the face of his spectre-guide! The dramatic power in the character of Schedoni, the Italian monk, has been much admired and praised; but the effect does not depend upon the character, but the situations; not upon the figure, but upon the background. *The Castle of Otranto* (which is supposed to have led the way to this style of writing) is, to my notion, dry, meagre, and without effect. It is done upon false principles of taste. The great hand and arm which are thrust into the court-yard, and remain there all day long, are the pasteboard machinery of a pantomime; they shock the senses, and have no purchase upon the imagination. They are a matter-of-fact impossibility; a fixture, and no longer a phantom. *Quod sic mihi ostendis, incredulus odi.* By realising the chimeras of ignorance and fear, begot upon shadows and dim likenesses, we take away the very grounds of credulity and superstition; and, as in other cases, by facing out the imposture betray the secret to the contempt and laughter of the spectators. *The Recess*, and the *Old English Baron*, are also "dismal treatises," but with little in them "at which our fell of hair is like to rouse and stir as life were in it." They are dull and prosing, without the spirit of fiction or the air of tradition to make them interesting. After Mrs Radcliffe, Monk Lewis was the greatest master of the art of freezing the blood. The robber-scene in *The Monk* is only inferior to that in *Count Fathom*, and perfectly new in the circumstances and cast of the characters. Some of his descriptions are chargeable with unpardonable grossness, but the pieces of poetry interspersed in this far-famed novel, such as the fight of Roncesvalles and the Exile, in particular, have a romantic and delightful harmony, such as might be chanted by the moon-light pilgrim, or might lull the dreaming mariner on summer seas.

If Mrs Radcliffe touched the trembling chords of the imagination, making wild music there, Mrs Inchbald has no less power over the springs of the heart. She not only moves the affections but melts us into "all the luxury of woe." Her *Nature and Art* is one of the most pathetic and interesting stories in the world. It is, indeed, too much so; or the distress is too naked, and the situations hardly to be borne with patience. I think nothing, however, can exceed in delicacy and beauty the account of the love-letter which the poor girl, who is the subject of the story, receives from her lover, and which she is a fortnight in spelling out, sooner than show it to any one else; nor the dreadful catastrophe of the last fatal scene, in which the same poor creature, as her former seducer, now become her judge, is about to pronounce sentence of death upon her, cries out in agony—"Oh, not from you!" The effect of this novel upon the feelings, is not only of the most distressing, but withering kind.

It blights the sentiments, and haunts the memory. *The Simple Story* is not much better in this respect: the gloom, however, which hangs over it is of a more fixed and tender kind: we are not now lifted to ecstasy, only to be plunged into madness; and besides the sweetness and dignity of some of the characters, there are redeeming traits, retrospective glances on the course of human life, which brighten the backward stream, and smile in hope or patience to that last. Such is the account of Sandford, her stern and inflexible adviser, sitting by the bedside of Miss Milner, and comforting her in her dying moments; thus softening the worst pang of human nature, and reconciling us to the best, but not the most shining virtues in human character. The conclusion of *Nature and Art*, on the contrary, is a scene of heartless desolation, which must effectually deter any one from ever reading the book twice. Mrs Inchbald is an instance to confute the assertion of Rousseau, that women fail whenever they attempt to describe the passion of love.

I shall conclude this Lecture, by saying a few words of the author of *Caleb Williams*, and the author of *Waverley*. I shall speak of the last first. In knowledge, in variety, in facility, in truth of painting, in costume and scenery, in freshness of subject, and in untired interest, in glancing lights and the graces of a style passing at will "from grave to gay, from lively to severe," at once romantic and familiar, having the utmost force of imitation and apparent freedom of invention; these novels have the highest claims to admiration. What lack they yet? The author has all power given him from without—he has not, perhaps, an equal power from within. The intensity of the feeling is not equal to the distinctness of the imagery. He sits like a magician in his cell, and conjures up all shapes and sights to the view; and with a little variation we might apply to him what Spenser says of Fancy:—

> *His chamber was dispainted all within*
> *With sundry colours, in the which were writ*
> *Infinite shapes of things dispersed thin;*
> *Some such as in the world were never yet;*
> *Some daily scene and knowen by their names,*
> *Such as in idle fantasies do flit;*
> *Infernal hags, centaurs, fiends, hippodames,*
> *Apes, lions, eagles, owls, fools, lovers, children, dames.*

In the midst of all this phantasmagoria, the author himself never appears to take part with his characters, to prompt our affection to the good, or sharpen our antipathy to the bad. It is the perfection of art to conceal art; and this is here done so completely, that while it adds to our pleasure in the work, it seems to take away from the merit of the author. As he does not thrust himself forward in the foreground, he loses the credit of the performance. The copies are so true to nature, that they appear like tapestry figures taken off by the pattern; the obvious patchwork of tradition and history. His characters are transplanted at once from their native soil to the page which we are reading, without any traces of their having passed through the hot-bed of the author's genius or vanity. He leaves them as he found them; but this is doing wonders. The Laird and the Baillie of Bradwardine, the idiot rhymer, David Gallatly, Miss Rose Bradwardine, and Miss Flora Mac Ivor, her brother the Highland Jacobite chieftain, Vic Ian Vhor, the Highland rover, Donald Bean Lean, and the worthy page Callum Beg, Bothwell and Balfour of Burley, Claverhouse and Macbriar, Elsbie the Black Dwarf, and the Red Reever of Westburn Flat, Hobbie and Grace Armstrong, Ellengowan and Dominie Sampson, Dirk Hatteraick and Meg Merrilies, are at present "familiar in our mouths as household names," and whether they are actual persons or creations of the poet's pen, is an impertinent inquiry. The picturesque and local scenery is as fresh as the lichen on the rock: the characters are a part of the scenery. If they are put in action, it is a moving picture: if they speak, we hear their dialect and the tones of their voice. If the humour is made out by dialect, the character by the dress, the interest by the facts and documents in the author's possession, we have no right to complain, if it is made out; but sometimes it hardly is, and then we have a right to say so. For instance, in the *Tales of my Landlord*, Canny Elshie is not in himself so formidable or petrific a person as the real Black Dwarf, called David Ritchie, nor are his acts or sayings so staggering to the imagination. Again, the first introduction of this extraordinary personage, groping about among the hoary twilight ruins of the witch of Micklestane Moor and her Grey Geese, is as full of perternatural power and bewildering effect (according to the tradition of the country) as can be; while the last decisive scene, where the Dwarf, in his resumed character of Sir Edward Manley, comes from the tomb in the Chapel, to prevent the forced marriage of the daughter of his former betrothed mistress with the man she abhors, is altogether powerless and tame. No situation could be imagined more finely calculated to call forth an author's powers of imagination and passion; but nothing is done. The assembly is dispersed under circumstances of the strongest natural feeling, and the most appalling preternatural appearances, just as if the effect had been produced by a peace-officer entering for the same purpose. These instances of a falling-off are, however, rare; and if this author should not be supposed by fastidious critics to have original genius in the highest degree, he has other qualities which supply its place so well, his materials are so rich and varied, and he uses them so lavishly, that the reader is no loser by the exchange. We are not in fear that he should publish another novel; we are under no apprehension of his exhausting himself, for he has shown that he is inexhaustible.

Whoever else is, it is pretty clear that the author of *Caleb Williams* and *St Leon* is not the author of *Waverley*. Nothing can be more distinct or excellent in their several ways than these two writers. If the one owes almost everything to external observation and traditional character, the other owes everything to internal conception and contemplation of the possible workings of the human mind. There is little knowledge of the world, little variety, neither an eye for the picturesque, nor a talent for the humorous in *Caleb Williams* for instance, but you cannot doubt for a moment of the originality of the work and the force in the conception. The impression made upon the reader is the exact measure of the strength of the author's genius. For the effect, both in *Caleb Williams* and *St Leon*, is entirely made out, neither by facts, nor dates, by black-letter or magazine learning, by transcript or record, but by intense and patient study of the human heart, and by an imagination projecting itself into certain situations, and capable of working up its imaginary feelings to the height of reality. The author launches into the ideal world, and must sustain himself and the reader there by the mere force of imagination. The sense of power in the writer thus adds to the interest of the subject.—The character of Falkland is a sort of apotheosis of the love of fame. The gay, the gallant Falkland lives only in the good opinion of good men; for this he adorns his soul with virtue, and tarnishes it with crime; he lives only with this, and dies as he loses it. He is a lover of virtue but a worshipper of fame. Stung to madness by a brutal insult, he avenges himself by a crime of the deepest die, and the remorse of his conscience and the stain upon his honour prey upon his peace and reason ever after. It was into the mouth of such a character that a modern poet has put the words,

> —— Action is momentary,
> The motion of a muscle, this way or that;
> Suffering is long, obscure, and infinite.

In the conflict of his feelings he is worn to a skeleton, wasted to a shadow. But he endures this living death to watch over his undying reputation, and to preserve his name unsullied and free from suspicion. But he is at last disappointed in this his darling object, by the very means he takes to secure it, and by harassing and goading Caleb Williams (whose insatiable, incessant curiosity had wormed itself into his confidence) to a state of desperation, by employing every sort of persecution, and by trying to hunt him from society like an infection, makes him turn upon him, and betray the inmost secret of his soul. The last moments of Falkland are indeed sublime: the spark of life and the hope of imperishable renown are extinguished in him together; and bending his last look of forgiveness on his victim and destroyer, he dies a martyr to fame, but a confessor at the shrine of virtue! The re-action and play of these two characters into each other's hands (like Othello and Iago) is inimitably well managed, and on a par with anything in the dramatic art; but Falkland is the hero of the story, Caleb Williams is only the instrument of it. This novel is utterly unlike anything else that ever was written, and is one of the most original as well as powerful productions in the English language. *St Leon* is not equal to it in the plot and ground-work, though perhaps superior in the execution. In the one Mr Godwin has hit upon the extreme point of the perfectly natural and perfectly new; in the other he enters into the preternatural world, and comes nearer to the world of common place. Still the character is of the same exalted intellectual kind. As the ruling passion of the one was the love of fame, so in the other the sole business of life is thought. Raised by the fatal discovery of the philosopher's stone above mortality, he is cut off from all participation with its pleasures. He is a limb torn from society. In possession of eternal youth and beauty, he can feel no love; surrounded, tantalized, tormented with riches, he can do no good. The races of men pass before him as in a *speculum*: but he is attached to them by no common tie of sympathy or suffering. He is thrown back into himself and his own thoughts. He lives in the solitude of his own breast,—without wife or child, or friend, or enemy in the world. His is the solitude of the soul,—not of woods, or seas, or mountains,—

but the desert of society, the waste and desolation of the heart. His is himself alone. His existence is purely contemplative, and is therefore intolerable to one who has felt the rapture of affection or the anguish of woe. The contrast between the enthusiastic eagerness of human pursuits and their blank disappointment, was never, perhaps, more finely pourtrayed than in this novel. Marguerite, the wife of St Leon, is an instance of pure and disinterested affection in one of the noblest of her sex. It is not improbable that the author found the model of this character in nature.—Of *Mandeville*, I shall say only one word. It appears to me to be a falling off in the subject, not in the ability. The style and declamation are even more powerful than ever. But unless an author surpasses himself, and surprises the public as much the fourth or fifth time as he did the first, he is said to fall off, because there is not the same stimulus of novelty. A great deal is here made out of nothing, or out of a very disagreeable subject. I cannot agree that the story is out of nature. The feeling is very common indeed; though carried to an unusual and improbable excess, or to one with which from the individuality and minuteness of the circumstances, we cannot readily sympathise.

It is rare that a philosopher is a writer of romances. The union of the two characters in this author is a sort of phenomenon in the history of letters; for I cannot but consider the author of *Political Justice* as a philosophical reasoner of no ordinary stamp or pretensions. That work, whatever its defects may be, is distinguished by the most acute and severe logic, and by the utmost boldness of thinking, founded on a love and conviction of truth. It is a system of ethics, and one that, though I think it erroneous myself, is built on following up into its fair consequences, a very common and acknowledged principle, that abstract reason and general utility are the only test and standard of moral rectitude. If this principle is true, then the system is true: but I think that Mr Godwin's book has done more than anything to overturn the sufficiency of this principle by abstracting, in a strict metaphysical process, the influence of reason or the understanding in moral questions and relations from that of habit, sense, association, local and personal attachment, natural affection, &c.; and by thus making it appear how necessary the latter are to our limited, imperfect, and mixed being, how impossible the former as an exclusive guide of action, unless man were, or were capable of becoming, a purely intellectual being. Reason is no doubt one faculty of the human mind, and the chief gift of Providence to man; but it must itself be subject to and modified by other instincts and principles, because it is not the only one. This work then, even supposing it to be false, is invaluable in demonstrating an important truth by the *reductio ad absurdum*; or it is an *experimentum crucis* in one of the grand and trying questions of moral philosophy.—In delineating the character and feelings of the hermetic philosopher St Leon, perhaps the author had not far to go from those of a speculative philosophical Recluse. He who deals in the secrets of magic, or in the secrets of the human mind, is too often looked upon with jealous eyes by the world, which is no great conjurer; he who pours out his intellectual wealth into the lap of the public, is hated by those who cannot understand how he came by it; he who thinks beyond his age, cannot expect the feelings of his contemporaries to go along with him; he whose mind is of no age or country, is seldom properly recognized during his lifetime, and must wait, in order to have justice done him, for the late but lasting award of posterity:—"Where his treasure is, there his heart is also."

Notes

1. It is not to be forgotten that the author of *Robinson Crusoe* was also an Englishman. His other works, such as the *Life of Colonel Jack*, &c., are of the same cast, and leave an impression on the mind more like that of things than words.
2. The *Edinburgh Review*.
3. *The Fool of Quality*, *David Simple*, and *Sydney Biddulph*, written about the middle of the last century, belong to the ancient *régime* of novel-writing. Of the *Vicar of Wakefield* I have attempted a character elsewhere.

THE
POSTHUMOUS PAPERS
OF THE
PICKWICK CLUB

By CHARLES DICKENS

GADSHILL

WITH ILLUSTRATIONS BY SEYMOUR AND "PHIZ"

LONDON
THE CAXTON PUBLISHING CO.

Title page of the London Edition of *The Pickwick Papers*

48

Preface to *The Pickwick Papers*

CHARLES DICKENS

One of the most famous and prolific novelists of the Victorian period, Charles Dickens (1812–1870) was first a reporter of House of Commons debates for the *Morning Chronicle* and subsequently the author of the "Sketches by Boz" that appeared in several journals in the mid 1830s. He began publication of "The Posthumous Papers of the Pickwick Club" in April 1836, a series that ran thought twenty monthly numbers and was finally published in volume form in 1837 to considerable acclaim. In the following Preface, Dickens defends the episodic nature of the work, blaming the lack of plot on serial publication. He explains his use of satire to criticise "the cant of religion", not religion itself and hints that his humour serves a moral end. The end of the Preface contains Dickens's ruminations on the social reforms that have occurred since the commencement of the series of papers. Implicit in these retrospective paragraphs is the hope that his own writing may help to alleviate dire social and economic conditions.

An author who has much to communicate under this head, and expects to have it attended to, may be compared to a man who takes his friend by the button at a Theatre Door, and seeks to entertain him with a personal gossip before he goes in to the play.

Nevertheless, as Prefaces, though seldom read, are continually written, no doubt for the behoof of that so richly and so disinterestedly endowed personage, Posterity (who will come into an immense fortune), I add my legacy to the general remembrance.

It was observed, in the Preface to the original Edition, that the Pickwick Papers were designed for the introduction of diverting characters and incidents; that no ingenuity of plot was attempted, or even at that time considered very feasible by the author in connection with the desultory mode of publication adopted; and that

Source: Charles Dickens, Preface, *The Pickwick Papers*, 1837, rptd New York: Harper and Brothers, 1902, pp. iii–vii.

the machinery of the Club, proving cumbrous in the management, was gradually abandoned as the work progressed. Although, on one of these points, experience and study have since taught me something, and I could perhaps wish now, that these chapters were strung together on a stronger thread of general interest, still, what they are, they were designed to be.

I have seen various accounts in print, of the origin of these Pickwick Papers; which have, at all events, possessed—for me—the charm of perfect novelty. As I may infer, from the occasional appearance of such histories, that my readers have an interest in the matter, I will relate how they came into existence.

I was a young man of three-and-twenty, when the present publishers, attracted by some pieces I was at that time writing in the Morning Chronicle newspaper (of which one series had lately been collected and published in two volumes, illustrated by my esteemed friend Mr. George Cruikshank), waited upon me to propose a something that should be published in shilling numbers—then only known to me, or, I believe, to anybody else, by a dim recollection of certain interminable novels in that form, which used to be carried about the country by pedlers, and over some of which I remember to have shed innumerable tears, before I had served my apprenticeship to Life.

When I opened my door at Furnival's Inn to the managing partner who represented the firm, I recognized in him the person from whose hands I had bought, two or three years previously, and whom I had never seen before or since, my first copy of the Magazine in which my first effusion—dropped stealthily one evening at twilight, with fear and trembling, into a dark letter-box, in a dark office, up a dark court in Fleet Street—appeared in all the glory of print; on which memorable occasion—how well I recollect it!—I walked down to Westminster Hall, and turned into it for half an hour, because my eyes were so dimmed with joy and pride, that they could not bear the street, and were not fit to be seen there. I told my visitor of the coincidence, which we both hailed as a good omen; and so feel to business.

The idea propounded to me was, that the monthly something should be a vehicle for certain plates to be executed by Mr. Seymour; and there was a notion, either on the part of that admirable humorous artist, or of my visitor (I forget which), that a "Nimrod Club," the members of which were to go out shooting, fishing, and so forth, and getting themselves into difficulties through their want of dexterity, would be the best means of introducing these. I objected, on consideration, that although born and partly bred in the country, I was no great sportsman, except in regard of all kinds of locomotion; that the idea was not novel, and had been already much used; that it would be infinitely better for the plates to arise naturally out of the text; and that I should like to take my own way, with a freer range of English scenes and people, and was afraid I should ultimately do so in any case, whatever course I might prescribe to myself at starting. My views being deferred to, I thought of Mr. Pickwick, and wrote the first number; from the proof-sheets of which, Mr. Seymour made his drawing of the Club, and that happy portrait of its founder, by which he is always recognized, and which may be said to have made him a reality. I connected

Mr. Pickwick with a club, because of the original suggestion, and I put in Mr. Winkle expressly for the use of Mr. Seymour. We started with a number of twenty-four pages instead of thirty-two, and four illustrations in lieu of a couple. Mr. Seymour's sudden and lamented death before the second number was published, brought about a quick decision upon a point already in agitation; the number became one of thirty-two pages with two illustrations, and remained so to the end. My friends told me it was a low, cheap form of publication,[1] by which I should ruin all my rising hopes; and how right my friends turned out to be, everybody now knows.

"Boz," my signature in the Morning Chronicle, appended to the monthly cover of this book, and retained long afterwards, was the nickname of a pet child, a younger brother, whom I had dubbed Moses, in honor of the Vicar of Wakefield; which being facetiously pronounced through the nose, became Boses, and being shortened, became Boz. "Boz" was a very familiar household word to me, long before I was an author, and so I came to adopt it.

It has been observed of Mr. Pickwick, that there is a decided change in his character, as these pages proceed, and that he becomes more good and more sensible. I do not think this change will appear forced or unnatural to my readers, if they will reflect that in real life the peculiarities and oddities of a man who has anything whimsical about him, generally impress us first, and that it is not until we are better acquainted with him that we usually begin to look below these superficial traits, and to know the better part of him.

Lest there should be any well-intentioned persons who do not perceive the difference (as some such could not, when Old Mortality was newly published) between religion and the cant of religion, piety and the pretence of piety, a humble reverence for the great truths of Scripture, and an audacious and offensive obtrusion of its letter and not its spirit in the commonest dissensions and meanest affairs of life, to the extraordinary confusion of ignorant minds, let them understand that it is always the latter, and never the former, which is satirized here. Further, that the latter is here satirized, as being, according to all experience, inconsistent with the former, impossible of union with it, and one of the most evil and mischievous falsehoods existent in society—whether it establish its headquarters, for the time being, in Exeter Hall, or Ebenezer Chapel, or both. It may appear unnecessary to offer a word of observation on so plain a head. But, it is never out of season to protest against that coarse familiarity with sacred things, which is busy on the lip, and idle in the heart; or against the confounding of Christianity with any class of persons who, in the words of Swift, have just enough religion to make them hate, and not enough to make them love, one another.

I have found it curious and interesting, looking over the sheets of this reprint, to mark what important social improvements have taken place about us, almost imperceptibly, even since they were originally written. The license of Counsel, and the degree to which Juries are ingeniously bewildered, are yet susceptible of moderation; while an improvement in the mode of conducting Parliamentary Elections (especially for counties) is still within the bounds of possibility. But legal reforms have pared the claws of Messrs. Dodson and Fogg; a spirit of self-respect, mutual forbearance, education, and co-operation, for such good ends, has diffused itself among their clerks; places far apart are brought together, to the present convenience and advantage of the Public, and to the certain destruction, in time, of a host of petty jealousies, blindnesses, and prejudices, by which the Public alone have always been the sufferers; the laws relating to imprisonment for debt are altered; and the Fleet Prison is pulled down!

With such a retrospect comprised within so short a period, who knows, but it may be discovered, within this Century, that there are even magistrates in town and country, who should be taught to shake hands every day with Commonsense and Justice; that even Poor Laws may have mercy on the weak, the aged, and unfortunate; that Schools, on the broad principles of Christianity, are the best adornment for the length and breadth of this civilized land; that Prison-doors should be barred on the outside, no less heavily and carefully than they are barred within; that the universal diffusion of common means of decency and health is as much the right of the poorest of the poor, as it is indispensable to the safety of the rich, and of the State; that a few petty boards and bodies—less than drops in the great ocean of humanity, which roars around them—are not to let loose Fever and Consumption on God's creatures at their will, or always to keep their little fiddles going, for a Dance of Death!

Note

1. This book would have cost, at the then established price of novels, about four guineas and a half.

49

Preface to *The Adventures of Oliver Twist*

CHARLES DICKENS

One of the most famous British novelists of the nineteenth century, Charles Dickens published his first novel as a series of sketches in twenty monthly parts, *The Posthumous Papers of the Pickwick Club* (1836-37). He followed this with a serialised version of *Oliver Twist* in *Bentley's Miscellany*, one of the several journals he edited. Other works include *David Copperfield* (1849-50), *Bleak House* (1852-53), *Hard Times* (1854), *Great Expectations* (1860-61) and *Our Mutual Friend* (1864-65). In an early defence of his realistic subject matter in *Oliver Twist*, Dickens takes issue with moralistic critics who disdain portrayals of vice. He argues that accurate depictions of vicious characters serve to warn readers against such behaviour even more effectively than portrayals of virtuous characters act as models of behaviour. He ridicules readers who would prefer to have vice disguised and romanticised. A number of Dickens's works fall into the novelistic subgenre of the Social Problem Novel prominent in England in the 1840s.

"Some of the author's friends cried, 'Lookee, gentlemen, the man is a villain; but it is Nature for all that;' and the young critics of the age, the clerks, apprentices, &c., called it low, and fell a groaning."—Fielding.

The greater part of this Tale was originally published in a magazine. When I completed it, and put it forth in its present form, it was objected to on some high moral grounds in some high moral quarters.

It was, it seemed, a coarse and shocking circumstance, that some of the characters in these pages are chosen from the most criminal and degraded of London's population; that Sikes is a thief, and Fagin a receiver of stolen goods; that the boys are pickpockets, and the girl is a prostitute.

Source: Charles Dickens, Preface to *The Adventures of Oliver Twist*, 1837-38, rptd London: Chapman and Hall, 1866, pp. v-x.

OLIVER TWIST ASKS FOR MORE.

One of George Cruikshank's original illustrations for *Oliver Twist*

I have yet to learn that a lesson of the purest good may not be drawn from the vilest evil. I have always believed this to be a recognised and established truth, laid down by the greatest men the world has ever seen, constantly acted upon by the best and wisest natures, and confirmed by the reason and experience of every thinking mind. I saw no reason, when I wrote this book, why the dregs of life, so long as their speech did not offend the ear, should not serve the purpose of a moral, at least as well as its froth and cream. Nor did I doubt that there lay festering in Saint Giles's, as good materials towards the truth as any to be found in St. James's.

In this spirit, when I wished to show, in little Oliver, the principle of Good surviving through every adverse circumstance, and triumphing at last; and when I considered among what companions I could try him best, having regard to that kind of men into whose hands he would most naturally fall; I bethought myself of those who figure in these volumes. When I came to discuss the subject more maturely with myself, I saw many strong reasons for pursuing the course to which I was inclined. I had read of thieves by scores—seductive fellows (amiable for the most part), faultless in dress, plump in pocket, choice in horseflesh, bold in bearing, fortunate in gallantry, great at a song, a bottle, pack of cards or dice-box, and fit companions for the bravest. But I had never met (except in Hogarth) with the miserable reality. It appeared to me that to draw a knot of such associates in crime as really do exist; to paint them in all their deformity, in all their wretchedness, in all the squalid poverty of their lives; to show them as they really are, for ever skulking uneasily through the dirtiest paths of life, with the great, black, ghastly gallows closing up their prospect, turn them where they may; it appeared to me that to do this, would be to attempt a something which was greatly needed, and which would be a service to society. And therefore I did it as I best could.

In every book I know, where such characters are treated of at all, certain allurements and fascinations are thrown around them. Even in the Beggar's Opera, the thieves are represented as leading a life which is rather to be envied than otherwise; while Macheath, with all the captivations of command, and the devotion of the most beautiful girl and only pure character in the piece, is as much to be admired and emulated by weak beholders, as any fine gentleman in a red coat who has purchased, as Voltaire says, the right to command a couple of thousand men, or so, and to affront death at their head. Johnson's question, whether any man will turn thief because Macheath is reprieved, seems to me beside the matter. I ask myself, whether any man will be deterred from turning thief because of his being sentenced to death, and because of the existence of Peachum and Lockit; and remembering the captain's roaring life, great appearance, vast success, and strong advantages, I feel assured that nobody having a bent that way will take any warning from him, or will see anything in the play but a very flowery and pleasant road, conducting an honourable ambition, in course of time, to Tyburn Tree.

In fact, Gay's witty satire on society had a general object, which made him careless of example in this respect, and gave him other aims. The same may be said of Sir Edward Bulwer's admirable and powerful novel of Sir Paul Clifford, which cannot be fairly considered as having, or being intended to have, any bearing on this part of the subject, one way or other.

What manner of life is that which is described in these pages, as the everyday existence of a Thief? What charms has it for the young and ill-disposed, what allurements for the most jolter-headed of juveniles? Here are no canterings on moonlit heaths, no merry-makings in the suggest of all possible caverns, none of the attractions of dress, no embroidery, no lace, no jack-boots, no crimson coats and ruffles, none of the dash and freedom with which "the road" has been, time out of mind, invested. The cold, wet, shelterless midnight streets of London; the foul and frowsy dens, where vice is closely packed and lacks the room to turn; the haunts of hunger and disease, the shabby rags that scarcely hold together; where are the attractions of these things? Have they no lesson, and do they not whisper something beyond the little-regarded warning of an abstract moral precept?

But, there are people of so refined and delicate a nature, that they cannot bear the contemplation of these horrors. Not that they turn instinctively from crime; but that criminal characters, to suit them, must be, like their meat, in delicate disguise. A Massaroni in green velvet is an enchanting creature; but a Sikes in fustian is insupportable. A Mrs. Massaroni, being a lady in short petticoats and a fancy dress, is a thing to imitate in tableaux and have in lithograph on pretty songs; but a Nancy, being a creature in a cotton gown and cheap shawl, is not to be thought of. It is wonderful how Virtue turns from dirty stockings; and how Vice, married to ribbons and a little gay attire, changes her name, as wedded ladies do, and becomes Romance.

Now, as the stern and plain truth, even in the dress of this (in novels) much exalted race, was a part of the purpose of this book, I will not, for these readers, abate one hole in the Dodger's coat, or one scrap of curl-paper in the girl's dishevelled hair. I have no faith in the delicacy which cannot bear to look upon them. I have no desire to make proselytes among such people. I have no respect for their opinion, good or bad; do not covet their approval; and do not write for their amusement. I venture to say this without reserve; for I am not aware of any writer in our language having a respect for himself, or held in any respect by his posterity, who ever has descended to the taste of this fastidious class.

On the other hand, if I look for examples, and for precedents, I find them in the noblest range of English literature. Fielding, De Foe, Goldsmith, Smollett, Richardson, Mackenzie—all these for wise purposes, and especially the two first, brought upon the scene the very scum and refuse of the land. Hogarth, the moralist, and censor of his age—in whose great works the times in which he lived, and the characters of every time, will never cease to be reflected—did the like, without the compromise of a hair's breadth. Where does this giant stand now, in the estimation of his countrymen? And yet, if I turn back to the days in which he or any of these men flourished, I find the same reproach levelled against them every one, each in his turn, by the insects of the hour, who raised their little hum, and died and were forgotten.

Cervantes laughed Spain's chivalry away, by showing Spain its impossible and wild absurdity. It was my attempt, in my humble and far-distant sphere, to dim the false glitter surrounding something which really did exist, by showing it in its unattractive and repulsive truth. No less consulting my own taste, than the manners of the age, I endeavoured, while I painted it in all its fallen and degraded aspect, to banish from the lips of the lowest character I introduced, any expression that could by possibility offend; and rather to lead to the unavoidable inference that its existence was of the most debased and vicious kind, than to prove it elaborately by words and deeds. In the case of the girl, in particular, I kept this intention constantly in view. Whether it is apparent in the narrative, and how it is executed, I leave my readers to determine.

It has been observed of this girl, that her devotion to the brutal housebreaker does not seem natural, and it has been objected to Sikes in the same breath—with some inconsistency, as I venture to think—that he is surely overdrawn, because in him there would appear none of those redeeming traits which are objected to as unnatural in his mistress. Of the latter objection I will merely say, that I fear there are in the world some insensible and callous natures, that do become, at last, utterly and irredeemably bad. But whether this be so or not, of one thing I am certain: that there are such men as Sikes, who, being closely followed through the same space of time, and through the same current of circumstances, would not give, by one look or action of a moment, the faintest indication of a better nature. Whether every gentler human feeling is dead within such bosoms, or the proper chord to strike has rusted and is hard to find, I do not know; but that the fact is so, I am sure.

It is useless to discuss whether the conduct and character of the girl seems natural or unnatural, probable or improbable, right or wrong. It is true. Every man who has watched these melancholy shades of life knows it to be so. Suggested to my mind long ago, by what I often saw and read of, in actual life around me, I have tracked it through many profligate and noisome ways, and found it still the same. From the first introduction of that poor wretch, to her laying her bloody head upon the robber's breast, there is not one word exaggerated or over-wrought. It is emphatically God's truth, for it is the truth He leaves in such depraved and miserable breasts; the hope yet lingering behind; the last fair drop of water at the bottom of the dried-up, weed-choked, well. It involves the best and worst shades of our common nature; much of its ugliest hues, and something of its most beautiful; it is a contradiction, an anomaly, an apparent impossibility, but it is a truth. I am glad to have had it doubted, for in that circumstance I find a sufficient assurance that it needed to be told.

⁂·50·⁂

Art in Fiction

SIR EDWARD BULWER LYTTON

Edward George Earle Lytton Bulwer (1803–73) was a prolific minor novelist, dramatist, translator and essayist. Among his better known novels are *Paul Clifford* (1830), belonging to the sub genre of the criminal novel, and *The Last Days of Pompeii* (1834), an example of the historical novel. In the following essay, he lays out his criteria for good novels, emphasizing in particular delineation of manners, passions and character. In keeping with the Victorian emphasis on the necessity for moral rectitude, Lytton argues that the good novel should depict the ideal as opposed to copious realistic details. Yet, unlike Samuel Johnson, he notes the need for characters to be mixtures of good and bad in order to be psychologically interesting. In an extended (and unfair) comparison of Shakespeare and Scott, Lytton advises that conception should be superior to execution. Of Scott, he says, "He had no grandeur of conception, for he had no strong desire to render palpable and immortal some definite and abstract truth" (70). Comparing drama to fiction, he concedes that the latter permits more accidents and focuses less on a single catastrophe. Because it is under less pressure from a collective and confined audience, the novel can afford to be freer of restrictions than a play. The essay is a relatively early example of the novelist/critic's attempt to erect a specific taxonomy for the prospective novelist and thus to defend the genre's respectability.

Art is that process by which we give to natural materials the highest excellence they are capable of receiving.

We estimate the artist, not only in proportion to the success of his labours, but in proportion to the intellectual faculties which are necessary to that success. Thus, a watch by Breguét is a beautiful work of art, and so is a tragedy by Sophocles:— The first is even more perfect of its kind than the last, but the tragedy requires higher intellectual faculties than the watch; and we esteem the tragedian above the watchmaker.

Source: Sir Edward Bulwer Lytton, "Art in Fiction", *Monthly Chronicle*, 1838, rptd *Critical and Miscellaneous Essays*, vol. 1, Philadelphia: Lea and Blanchard, 1841, pp. 52–88.

The excellence of art consists in the fitness of the object proposed with the means adopted. Art carried to its perfection would be the union of the most admirable object with the most admirable means; in other words, it would require a greatness in the conception correspondent to the genius in the execution. But as mechanical art is subjected to more definite and rigorous laws than intellectual art, so, in the latter, a comprehensive critic regards the symmetry of the whole with large indulgence towards blemishes in detail. We contemplate mechanical art with reference to its utility—intellectual art with reference to its beauty. A single defect in a watch may suffice to destroy all the value of its construction—a single blemish in a tragedy may scarcely detract from its effect.

In regarding any work of art, we must first thoroughly acquaint ourselves with the object that the artist had in view. Were an antiquarian to set before us a drawing, illustrative of the costume of the Jews in the time of Tiberius, we should do right to blame him if he presented to our eye goblets in the fashion of the fifteenth century; but when Leonardo da Vinci undertook the sublime and moving representation of the Last Supper, we feel that his object is not that of an antiquary; and we do not regard it as a blemish that the apostles are seated upright instead of being recumbent, and that the loaves of bread are those of an Italian baker. Perhaps, indeed, the picture affected the spectators the more sensibly from their familiarity with the details; and the effect of art on the whole was only heightened by a departure from correctness in minutiae. So, in an anatomical drawing that professed to give the exact proportions of man, we might censure the designer if the length of the limbs were disproportioned to the size of the trunk; but, when the sculptor of the Apollo Belvidere desired to convey to the human eye the ideal of the God of Youth, the length of the limbs contributed to give an additional and super-human lightness and elasticity to the form; and the excellence of the art was evinced and promoted by the sacrifice of mechanical accuracy in detail. It follows, therefore, that intellectual art and technical correctness are far from identical—that one is sometimes proved by the disdain of the other. And, as this makes the distinction between mechanical and intellectual art, so is the distinction remarkable in proportion as that intellectual art is exercised in the highest degree—in proportion as it realizes the ideal. For the ideal consists not in the imitation, but the exaltation, of nature; and we must accordingly inquire, not how far it resembles what we have seen so much as how far it embodies what we can imagine.

It is not till we have had great pictures, that we can lay down the rules of painting—it is not till we have had great writers in a particular department of intellect, that we can sketch forth a code of laws for those who succeed them: for the theory of art resembles that of science; we must have data to proceed upon, and our inductions must be drawn from a vast store of experiments.

Prose fictions have been cultivated by modern writers of such eminence, and now form so wide and essential a part of the popular literature of Europe, that it may not be an uninteresting or a useless task to examine the laws by which the past may be tested, and the labours of future students simplified and abridged.

Prose fictions.

The novelist has three departments for his art: MANNERS, PASSIONS, CHARACTER.

Manners.

The delineation of manners embraces both past and present; the Modern and the Historical Romance.

The Historical.

We have a right to demand from the writer who professes to illustrate a former age, a perfect acquaintance with its characteristics and spirit. At the same time, as he intends rather to interest than instruct us, his art will be evinced in the illustrations he selects, and the skill with which they are managed. He will avoid all antiquarian dissertations not essentially necessary to the conduct of his tale. If, for instance, his story should have no connexion with the mysteries of the middle ages, he will take care how he weary us with an episodical description that changes his character from that of a narrator into that of a lecturer. In the tale of Notre Dame de Paris, by Victor Hugo, the description of the cathedral of Notre Dame is not only apposite, but of the deepest interest; for the cathedral is, by a high effort of art, made an absolute portion of the machinery of the tale. But the long superfluous description of the spectacle with which the story opens is merely a parade of antiquarian learning, because the scholars and the mysteries have no proportionate bearing whatever in the future development of the tale.

The usual fault of the historical novelist is over-minuteness in descriptions of dress and feasts, of pageants and processions. Minuteness is not accuracy. On the contrary, the more the novelist is minute, the more likely he is to mar the accurate effect of the whole, either by wearisome tameness, or some individual terror.

An over-antiquated phraseology is a common and a most inartistical defect: whatever diction the delineator of a distant age employs, can never be faithful to the language of the time, for if so, it would be unintelligible. So, in the German novels that attempt a classical subject, there is the prevalent vice of a cold imitation of a classic epistolary style. It is the very attempt at resemblance that destroys the illusion, as it is by the servility of a copy that we are most powerfully reminded of the difference between the copy and the original. The language of a former time should be presented to us in the freest and most familiar paraphrase we can invent. Thus the mind is relieved at once from the task of forming perpetual comparisons, and surrenders itself to the delusion the more easily, from the very candour with which the author will consider well what is the principal obstacle in the mind of his audience to the reception of his story. For instance, if he select a story of ancient Greece, the public will be predisposed to anticipate a frigid pedantry of style, and delineations of manners utterly different from those which are familiar to us now. The author will, therefore, agreeably surprise the reader, if he adopt a style as familiar and easy as that which a Greek would have used in common conversation; and show the classical spirit that pervades his diction, by the grace of the poetry, or the lightness of the wit, with which he can adorn his allusions and his dialogue. Thus, the very learning he must evince will only be but incidental and easy ornament. On the other hand, instead of selecting such specimens and modifications of human nature as are most different from, and unfamiliar to, the sympathies of modern times, he will rather prefer to appeal to the eternal sentiments of the heart, by showing how closely the men of one age resemble those of another. His hero, his lover, his epicure, his buffoon, his miser, his boaster, will be as close to the life as if they were drawn from the streets of London. The reader will be interested to see society different, yet men the same; and the manners will be relieved from the disadvantage of unfamiliarity by an entire sympathy with the humours they mask, or the passions on which they play.

Again, if the author propose to carry his reader to the times of Richard the First or of Elizabeth, he will have to encounter a universal repugnance from the thought of imitation of Ivanhoe or Kenilworth. An author who was, nevertheless, resolved to select such a period for his narrative would, accordingly, if an artist of sufficient excellence, avoid with care touching upon any of the points which may suggest the recollection of Scott. He would deeply consider all the features of the time, and select those neglected by his predecessor;—would carefully note all the deficiencies of the author of Kenilworth, and seize at once upon the ground which that versatile genius omitted to consecrate himself.

To take the same epoch, the same characters, even the same narrative, as a distinguished predecessor, is perfectly allowable; and, if successful, a proof at once of originality and skill. But if you find the shadow of the previous work flinging itself over your own—if you have not thoroughly escaped the influence of the first occupant of the soil—you will only invest your genius to unnecessary disadvantage, and build edifices, however graceful and laboured, upon the freehold of another.

In novels devoted to the delineation of existing manners, the young author will be surprised to find, that exact and unexaggerated fidelity has never been the characteristic of the greatest novelists of their own time. There would be, indeed, something inane and trifling, or mean and vulgar, in Dutch copies of the modern still life. We do not observe any frivolity in Walter Scott, when he describes with elaborate care the set of the ruffle, the fashion of the cloak of Sir Walter Raleigh, nor when he catches all the minutiae of the chamber of Rowena. But to introduce your hero of May Fair with an exact portraiture of the colour of his coat, and the length of his pantaloons, to item all the commodes and fauteuils of the boudoir of a lady Caroline or Frances, revolts our taste as an effeminate attention to trifles.

In humbler life, the same rule applies with equal strength. We are willing to know how Gurth was dressed, or Esmeralda lodged; but we do not require the same minuteness in describing the smock-frock of a labourer, or the garret of the girl who is now walking upon stilts for a penny. The greatest masters of the novel of modern life have usually availed themselves of humour as the illustration of manners; and have, with a deep and true, but, perhaps, unconscious, knowledge of art, pushed the humour almost to the verge of caricature. For as the serious ideal requires a certain exaggeration in the proportions of the natural, so also does the ludicrous. Thus, Aristophanes, in painting the humours of his time, resorts to the most poetical extravagance of machinery, and calls the clouds in aid of his ridicule of philosophy, or summons frogs and gods to unite in his satire on Euripides. The Don Quixote of Cervantes never lived, nor, despite the vulgar belief, ever could have lived, in Spain; but the art of the portrait is in the admirable exaltation of the humorous by means of the exaggerated. With more qualification, the same may be said of Parson Adams, of Sir Roger de Coverley, and even of the Vicar of Wakefield.

Where the author has not adopted the humorous as the best vehicle for the delineation of manners, he has sometimes artfully removed the scene from the country that he seeks to delineate, so that he might place his portraitures at a certain, and the most advantageous, distance from the eye. Thus, Le Sage obtains his object, of a consummate and masterly picture of the manners of his own land, though he has taken Spain for the theatre of the adventures of Gil Blas; and Swift has transferred all that his experience or his malice could narrate of the intrigues of courts, the chimeras of philosophy, the follies and vices of his nation and his time, to the regions of Lilliput and Laputa.

It may be observed that the delineation of manners is usually the secondary object of a novelist of high power. To a penetrating mind, manners are subservient to the illustration of views of life, or the consummation of original character. In a few years the mere portraiture of manners is obsolete. It is the knowledge of what is durable in human nature that alone preserves the work from decay. Lilly and Shakespeare alike painted the prevailing and courtly mannerism of their age. The Euphues rests upon our shelves—Don Armado will delight us as long as pedantry exists.

Character.

An author once said, "Give me a character, and I will find the play;" and, if we look to the most popular novels, we shall usually find, that where one reader speaks of the conduct of the story, a hundred readers will speak of the excellence of some particular character.

An author, before resolving on the characters he designs to portray, will do well to consider maturely, first, what part they are destined to play in his performance; and, secondly, what is the precise degree of interest which he desires them to create. Having thus considered, and duly determined, he will take care that no other character in the work shall interfere with the effect each is intended to produce. Thus, if his heroine is to be drawn gentle and mild, no second heroine, with the same attributes, should distract the attention of the reader, a rule that may seem obvious, but which is usually overlooked. When the author feels that he has thoroughly succeeded in a principal and predominant character, he will even sacrifice others, nominally more important, to increase the interest of the figure in the foreground. Thus, in the tale of Ivanhoe, Rowena, professedly the heroine, is very properly sacrificed to Rebecca. The more interesting the character of Rowena, the more pathetic the position she had assumed, the more we should have lost our compassion and admiration of the Jewess; and the highest merit of the tale, its pathos, would have been diminished. The same remark will apply to the Clementina and Harriet Byron of Richardson.

The author will take care not to crowd his canvass. He will select as few characters as are compatible with the full agency of his design. Too many plants in a narrow compass destroy each other. He will be careful to individualize each; but, if aspiring to the highest order of art, he will yet tone down their colours by an infinite variety of shades. The most original characters are those most delicately drawn, where the individual peculiarity does not obtrude itself naked and unrelieved. It was a very cheap purchase of laughter in Sir Walter Scott, and a mere trick of farce, which Shakespeare and Cervantes would have disdained, to invest a favourite humourist with some cant phrase, which he cannot open his mouth without disgorging. This was so special a device (because so easy and popular a mode of producing a ludicrous effect) with Sir Walter Scott, that it was almost his invariable source. The "Prodigious" of Dominie Sampson—the "My father, the baillie" of Nichol Jarvie—the "Provant" of Major Dalgettie—the "*Déjeuner* at Tillietudlem" of Lady Margaret Bellenden, &c., all belong to one source of humour, and that the shallowest and most hacknied. If your tale spread over a considerable space of time, you will take care that your readers may note the change of character which time has necessarily produced. You will quietly show the difference between the boy of eighteen and the man of forty; you will connect the change in the character with the influence of the events you have narrated. In the novel of Anastasius, this art of composition is skilfully and delicately mastered; more so than in *Gil Blas*.

If you bend all your faculties to the development of some single character, and you make us sensible that such is your object, the conduct of your story becomes but a minor consideration. Shakespeare, probably, cared but little whether the fencing scene in *Hamlet* was the best catastrophe he could invent; he took the incidents of the story as he found them, and lavished his genius on the workings of the mind, to which all external incidents on this side the grave had become trivial and uninfluential—weary, unprofitable, stale.

It must rely entirely on the nature of the interest you desire it to effect, whether you seek clearly to place before us, or dimly to shadow out, each particular character. If you connect your hero with supernatural agency, if you introduce incidents not accounted for by purely human means, if you resort to the legendary and mysterious, for the interest that you identify with any individual character, it may be most artistical to leave such a character vague, shadowy, and half incompleted. Thus, very skilfully is the Master of Ravenswood, over whose head hang ominous and weird predictions, left a less distinct and palpable creation than the broad-shouldered and much-eating heroes, whom Scott usually conducts through a labyrinth of adventures to marriage with a wealthy Ariadne.

The formation of characters improbable and grotesque, is not very compatible with a high conception of art, unless the work be one that so avowedly deals with beings different from those we mix with, that our imagination is prepared as to the extent of the demand upon its faith. Thus, when Shakespeare introduces us at once to the enchanted island, and we see the wand of the magician, and hear the song of Ariel, we are fully prepared to consider Caliban a proper inhabitant of such a soil; or when the Faust opens with the chorus of the angels, and the black dog appears in the chamber of the solitary student, the imagination finds little difficulty in yielding assent to the vagaries of the witches, and the grotesque diablerie of the Hartz Mountains; but we are wholly unprepared to find a human Caliban in the bellringer of a Parisian cathedral; and we see no reason why Quasimodo should not have been as well shaped as other people. The use of the grotesque in *The Abbot*, where Sir Percy Shafto is killed and revived, is an absurdity as gross and gratuitous as can well be conceived.

In the portraiture of evil and criminal characters lies the widest scope for an author profoundly versed in the philosophy of the human heart. In all countries, in all times, the delineation of crime has been consecrated in the highest order of poetry. For as the emotions of terror and of pity are those which it falls to the province of the sublimest genius to arouse, so it is chiefly, though not solely, in the machinations of guilt that may be found the source of the one, and in the misfortunes, sometimes of the victim of guilt, nay, sometimes of the guilty agent himself, that we arrive at the fountain of the softer passion. Thus, the murder of Duncan rouses our compassion, through our admission to all the guilty doubts and aspirations of Macbeth; and our terror is of a far higher and more enthralling order, because it is reflected back upon us from the bared and struggling heart of the murderer, than it would have been if we had seen the physical death of the victim. It may be observed, in deed, that, in a fine tragedy, it is the preparation to the death that is to constitute the catastrophe that usually most sensibly excites the interest of terror, and that the blow of the murderer, and the fall of the victim, is but a release to the suspense of fear, and changes the whole current of our emotions. But the grandest combination is when the artist unites in one person the opposite passions of terror and pity—when we feel at once horror of the crime, yet compassion for the criminal. Thus, in the most stirring of all the ancient dramas, the moment that we discover that Œdipus has committed the crimes from which we most revolt, homicide and incest, is the very moment in which, to the deepest terror of the crimes is united the most intense compassion for the criminal. So, again, before the final catastrophe of the mystic fate of Macbeth, when evil predictions are working to their close, and we feel that his hour is come, Shakespeare has paused, to draw from the dark bosom of the fated murderer those moving reflections, "My way of life," &c., which steal from us insensibly our hatred of his guilt, and awaken a new and softer interest in the approaching consummation of the usurper's doom. Again, in the modern play of Virginius, when the scene opens, and discovers the avenging father upon the body of the murdered Appius, it is in Virginius, at once criminal and childless, that are concentrated our pity and our terror.

In the portraiture of crime, however dark, the artist will take care to throw some redeeming light. The veriest criminal has some touch and remnant of human goodness; and it is according as this sympathy between the outcast and ourselves is indicated or insinuated, that the author profanes or masters the noblest mysteries of his art. Where the criminal be one, so resolute and hardened, so inexorable and preter-human, in his guilt, that he passes the bounds of flesh-and-blood inconsistencies and sympathies, a great artist will bring forth intellectual qualities to balance our disgust at the moral. Thus, in *Richard III*, it is with a masterly skill that Shakespeare relieves us of from the revolting contemplation of unmingled crime, by enlisting our involuntary and unconscious admiration on the side of the address, the subtle penetration into character, the affluent wit, the daring energy, the royal will, with which the ruthless usurper moves through the bloody scenes of his treachery. And, at the last, it is, if not by a relic of human virtue, at least by a relic of human weakness, by the working conscience, and the haunted pillow, that we are taught to remember that it is a man who sins and suffers, not a beast that ravages and is slain. Still, despite all the subtle shadings in the character of Richard, we feel that the guilt is overdrawn—that the dark spirit wants a moral as well as intellectual relief. To penetrating critics, it has always, therefore, been the most coarse of all the creations of Shakespeare; and will never bear a comparison, as a dissection of human nature, with the goaded and writhing wickedness of Macbeth.

In the delineation of a criminal, the author will take care to show us the motives of the crimes—the influences beneath which the character has been formed. He will suit the nature of the criminal to the state of society in which he is cast. Thus, he will have occasions for the noblest morality. By concentrating in one focus the vicious influences of any peculiar error in the social system, he will hold up a mirror to nations themselves.

As the bad man will not be painted as thoroughly and unredeemedly bad, so he, whom you represent as good, will have his foibles or infirmities. You will show where even the mainspring of his virtues sometimes calls into play a counter vice. Your just man will be sometimes severe—your generous man will be sometimes careless of the consequences of generosity. It is true that, in both these applications of art, you will be censured by shallow critics and pernicious moralists. It will be said of you in the one case, "He seeks to interest us in a murderer or a robber, an adulterer or a parricide;"—it will be said of you in the other, "And this man whom he holds up to us as an example, whom he calls wise and good, is a rascal, who indulges such an error, or commits such an excess." But no man can be an artist who does not prefer experience and human nature to all criticism; and, for the rest, he must be contented to stand on the same ground, or to have filled his urn from the same fountains, as Shakespeare and Boccaccio, as Goethe and Schiller, Fielding and Le Sage. If it be, however, necessary to your design to paint some character as almost faultless, as exempt from the common infirmities and errors, you will act skilfully if you invest it with the attributes of old age. When all the experience of error has been dearly bought, when the passions are laid at rest, and the mind burns clear as the night deepens, virtue does, in fact, become less and less wavering and imperfect. But youth without a fault, would be youth without a passion; and such a portrait would make us despair of emulation, and arm against reverence and esteem all the jealousies of self-love.

The Passions.

Delineation of passions is inseparable from the delineation of character. A novel, admirable in character, may, indeed, be drawn, in which the passions are but coldly and feebly shadowed forth: *Gil Blas* is an example. But either such novels are intended as representations of external life, not of the metaphysical operations of the inner man, or they deal with the humours and follies, not the grave and deep emotions, of our kind, and belong to the *comedy* of romance.

But if a novel of character can be excellent without passion, it would be impossible to create a novel of passion without character. The elementary passions themselves, like the elements, are few: it is the modifications they take in passing through different bodies that give us so inexhaustible a variety of lights and shadows, of loveliness and glory.

The passion of love is not represented by a series of eloquent rhapsodies, or even of graceful sentiments. It is represented, in fiction, by its effects on some particular character: the same with jealousy, avarice, revenge, &c. Therefore, in a certain sense of the word, all representations of passion in fiction may be considered *typical*. In Juliet, it is not the picture of love solely and abstractedly—it is the picture of love in its fullest effect on *youth*. In Anthony, it is love as wild, and as frantic, and as self-sacrificing; but it is love, not emanating from the enthusiasm of youth, but already touched with something of the blindness and infirmity of dotage.

In Macbeth, it is not the mere passion of ambition that is portrayed,—it is ambition operating on a man physically daring, and morally irresolute: a man whom the darkest agencies alone can compel, and whom the fullest triumphs of success cannot reconcile, to crime. So, if we review all the passionate characters of Shakespeare, we shall find that the passion is individualized and made original by the mould in which the fiery liquid is cast. Nor is the language of that passion declamation upon the passion itself, but the revelation of the effect it produces on a single subject. It is, accordingly, in the perfect harmony that exists between the character and the passion that the abstract and bodiless idea finds human force and corporeal interest. If you would place the passion before us in a new light, the character that represents it must be original. An artistical author, taking advantage of the multiform inconsistencies of human nature, will often give to the most hacknied passion a thoroughly new form, by placing it in a character where it could least be looked for. For instance, should you desire to portray avarice, you will go but on worn-out ground, if you resort to Plautus and to Molière for your model. But if you find in history the record of a brilliant courtier, a successful general, marked and signalized by the vice of Harpagon, the vice itself takes a new hue, and your portraiture will be a new addition to our knowledge of the mysteries of our kind. Such a representation, startling, untouched, and truthful, might be taken from the character of the Duke of Marlborough, the hero of Blenheim. In portraying the effect of a passion, the rarest art of the novelist is to give it its due weight and no more. Thus, in love novels, we usually find nothing but love; as if, in the busy and complicated life of man, there were no other spring to desire and action but

> Love, love;–eternal love.

Again, if an author portrays a miser, he never draws him otherwise than as a miser. He makes him, not the avaricious miser, but abstract avarice itself. Not so Shakespeare, when he created Shylock. Other things, other motives, occupy the spirit of the Jew besides his gold and his argosies: he is a grasping and relentless miser, yet he can give up avarice to revenge. He has sublime passions that elevate his mean ones.

If your novel be devoted to love and its effects, you will act more consistently with the truths of life, if you throw the main interest of the passion in the heroine. In the hero, you will increase our sense of the power of the passion, if you show us all the conflicting passions with which in men it usually contends—ambition, or honour, or duty: the more the effect of the love is shown by the obstacles it silently subdues, the more triumphant will be your success. You will recollect that in the novel, as in the drama, it is in the *struggle* of emotions that the science of the heart is best displayed; and, in the delineation of such struggles, there is ground little occupied hitherto by the great masters of English fiction. It was not in the province of Fielding or Smollett; and Scott but rarely indulges, and still more rarely succeeds in the metaphysical operations of stormy and conflicting feelings. He rather seems to have made it a point of art to imitate the ancient painter, and throw a veil over passions he felt inadequate to express. Thus, after the death and burial of Lucy, it is only by the heavy and unequal tread of Ravenswood, in his solitary chamber, that his agonies are to be conjectured. But this avoidance of the internal man, if constant and systematic, is but a clever trick to hide the want of power.

The Sentiment.

The sentiment that pervades a book is often its most effective moral, and its most universal charm. It is a pervading and indescribable harmony, in which the heart of the author himself seems silently to address our own. Through creations of crime and vice, there may be one pervading sentiment of virtue; through the humblest scenes, a sentiment of power and glory. It is the sentiment of Wordsworth of which his disciples speak, when they enlarge upon the attributes of holiness and beauty, which detached passages, however exquisite, do not suffice to justify; for the sentiment of a work is felt, not in its parts, but as a whole: it is undefinable and indefinite—it escapes while you seek to analyze it. Of all the qualities of fiction, the sentiment is that which we can least subject to the inquiries or codes of criticism. It emanates from the moral and predominant quality of the author—the perfume from his genius; and by it he unconsciously reveals himself. The sentiment of Shakespeare is in the strong sympathies with all that is human. In the sentiment of Swift, we see the reflection of a spirit discontented and malignant. Mackenzie, Goldsmith, Voltaire, Rousseau, betray their several characters as much in the prevalent sentiment of their writings, as if they had made themselves the heroes. Of all writers of great genius, Shakespeare has the most sentiment, and, perhaps, Smollett and Defoe the least. The student will distinguish between a work of sentiment and a sentimental work. As the charm of sentiment in a fiction is that it is latent and indefinite, so the charm vanishes the instant it becomes obtruding and importunate. The mistake of Kotebue and many of the Germans, of Metastasio, and a feeble and ephemeral school of the Italians, was in the confounding sentiment with passion.

Sentiment is capable of many classifications and subdivisions. The first and finest is that touched upon—the sentiment of the whole work: a sentiment of beauty or of grandeur—of patriotism or of benevolence—of veneration, of justice, or of piety. This may be perfectly distinct from the characters or scenes portrayed: it evinces itself insensibly and invisibly; and we do not find its effect till we sum up all the effects that the work has bequeathed. The sentiment is, therefore, often incorporated and identified with the moral tendency of the fiction.

There is also a sentiment that belongs to style, and gives depth and colouring to peculiar passages. For instance, in painting a pastoral life in the heart of a lonely forests, of by the side of unpolluted streams, the language and thoughts of the author glide into harmony with the images he creates; and we feel that he has, we scarcely know by what art, penetrated himself and us with the sentiment of repose.

A sentiment of this nature will be felt at once by the lovers of Spenser, and of Ariosto and Tasso. In the entrance to the Domains of Death, Milton breathes over the whole description the sentiment of awe.

The sentiments are distinct from the passions: sometimes they are most eloquent in the utter absence of passion itself; as the sentiment that pervades the poem of *The Castle of Indolence*;—at other times they are the neighbours, the intervening shades, between one passion and another; as the sentiment of a pleasing melancholy. Regret and awe are sentiments; grief and terror, passions.

As there is a sentiment that belongs to description, so there are characters in which sentiment supplies the place of passion. the character of Jacques, in *As You Like It*, is purely one of sentiment. Usually, sentiment is, in character, most effective when united with humour, as in Uncle Toby and Don Quixote, and, to quote a living writer, some of the masterly creations of Paul de Kock. For the very delicacy of the sentiment will be most apparent by the contrast of what seems to us at first the opposite quality; as the violet we neglect in a flower-bed enchants us in the hollow of a rock.

In a succeeding paper it is proposed to enter upon the construction of the fiction itself—the distinctions between the drama and the novel—and the mechanism, conduct, and catastrophe, of the different species of invented narrative.

The Conception.

A story may well be constructed, yet devoid of interest; on the other hand, the construction may be faulty and the interest vivid. This is the case even with the drama. Hamlet is not so well constructed a story as the Don Carlos of Alfieri; but there is no comparison in the degree of interest excited in either tragedy. Still, though we ought not to consider that excellence in the technical arrangement of incidents as a certain proof of the highest order of art, it is a merit capable of the most brilliant effects, when possessed by a master. An exquisite mechanism, in the construction of a mere story, not only gives pleasure in itself, but it displays other and loftier beauties to the best advantage. It is the setting of the jewels.

It is common to many novelists to commence a work without any distinct chart of the country which they intend to traverse—to suffer one chapter to grow out of another, and invention to warm as the creation grows. Scott has confessed to this mode of novel-writing[1] but Scott, with all his genius, was rather a great mechanist than a great artist. His execution was infinitely superior to his conception. It may be observed, indeed, that his conceptions are often singularly poor and barren, compared with the vigour with which they are worked out. He conceives a story with the design of telling it as well as he can, but is wholly insensible to the high and true aim of art, which is rather to consider for what objects the story should be told. Scott never appears to say to himself, "Such a tale will throw a new light upon human passions, or add fresh stores to human wisdom: for that reason I select it." He seems rather to consider what picturesque effects it will produce, what striking scenes, what illustrations of mere manners. He regards the story with the eye of the *property man*, though he tells it with the fervour of the poet. It is not thus that the greatest authorities in fiction have composed. It is clear to us that Shakespeare, when he selected the tale which he proposed to render χτῆμά ἰς ἀεί,—the everlasting possession of mankind, made it his first and paramount object to work out certain passions, or affections of the mind, in the most complete and profound form. He did not so much consider how the incidents might be made most striking, as how the truths of the human heart might be most clear. And it is a remarkable proof of his consummate art, that though in his best plays we may find instances, in which the mere incidents might be made more probable, and the theatrical effects more vivid, we can never see one instance in such plays where the passions he desired to represent, could have been placed in a broader light, or the character he designed to investigate, could have been submitted to a minuter analysis. We are quite sure that *Othello* and *Macbeth* were not written without the clear and deep and premeditated conception of the story to be told us. For with Shakespeare, the conception itself is visible and gigantic from the first line to the last. So in the greatest works of Fielding, a very obtuse critic may perceive that the author sat down to write in order to embody a design previously formed. The perception of moral truths urged him to the composition of his fictions. In Jonathan Wild, the finest prose satire in the English language, Fielding, before he set pen to paper, had resolved to tear the mask from false greatness. In his conception of the characters and histories of Blifil and Jones, he was bent on dethroning that popular idol—false virtue. The scorn of hipocrisy in all grades, all places, was the intellectual passion of Fielding; and his masterpieces are the results of intense convictions. That many incidents never contemplated would suggest them as he proceeded—that the technical plan of events might deviate and vary, according as he saw new modes of enforcing his aims, is unquestionable. But still Fielding always commenced *with* a plan—with a conception—with a moral end, to be achieved by definite agencies, and through the medium of certain characters pre-formed in his mind. If Scott had no preconcerted story when he commenced chapter the first of one of his delightful tales, it was because he was deficient in the highest attributes of art, viz., its philosophy and ethics. He never seemed to have imagined that the loftiest merit of a tale rests upon the effect it produces, not on the fancy, but on the intellect and the passions. He had no grandeur of conception, for he had no strong desire to render palpable and immortal some definite and abstract truth.

It is a sign of the low state of criticism in this country that Scott has been compared to Shakespeare. No two writers can be more entirely opposed to each other in the qualities of their genius, or the sources to which they applied. Shakespeare ever aiming at the development of the secret man, and half disdaining the mechanism of external incidents; Scott painting the ruffles and the dress, and the features and the gestures—avoiding the movements of the heart, elaborate in the progress of the incident. Scott never caught the mantle of Shakespeare, but he improved in the dresses of his wardrobe, and threw artificial effects into the scenes of his theatres.

Let us take an example: we will select one of the finest passages in Sir Walter Scott: a passage unsurpassed for its mastery over the PICTURESQUE. It is that chapter in *Kenilworth*, where Elizabeth has discovered Amy, and formed her first suspicions of Leicester.

> Leicester was at this moment the centre of a splendid group of lords and ladies, assembled together under an arcade or portico, which closed the alley. The company had drawn together in that place to attend the commands of her majesty when the hunting party should go forward, and their astonishment may be imagined, when, instead of seeing Elizabeth advance towards them, with her usual measured dignity of motion, they beheld her walking so rapidly, that she was in the midst of them ere they were aware; and then observed with fear and surprise, that her features were flushed betwixt anger and agitation, that her hair was loosened by her haste of motion, and that her eyes sparkled as they were wont when the spirit of Henry VIII. mounted highest in his daughter. Nor were they less astonished at the appearance of the pale, extenuated, half-dead, yet still lovely female, whom the queen upheld by main strength with one hand, while with the other she waved aside the ladies and nobles, who pressed towards her, under the idea that she was taken suddenly ill. "Where is my lord of Leicester?" she said, in a tone that thrilled with astonishment, all the courtiers who stood around—"Stand forth, my lord of Leicester!"
>
> If, in the midst of the most serene day of summer, when all is light and laughing around, a thunderbolt were to fall from the clear blue vault of heaven, and rend the earth at the very feet of some careless traveller, he could not gaze upon the

smouldering chasm which so unexpectedly yawned before him, with half the astonishment and fear which Leicester felt at the sight that so suddenly presented itself. He had that instant been receiving, with a political affectation of disavowing and misunderstanding their meaning, the half-uttered, half-intimated congratulations of the courtiers upon the favour of the queen, carried apparently to its highest pitch during the interview of that morning; from which most of them seemed to augur, that he might soon arise from their equal in rank to become their master. And now, while the subdued, yet proud smile with which he disclaimed those inferences was yet curling his cheek, the queen shot into the circle, her passions excited to the uttermost; and, supporting with one hand, and apparently without an effort, the pale and sinking form of his almost expiring wife, and pointing with the finger of the other, to her half-dead features, demanded in a voice that sounded to the ears of the astounded statesman like the last dread trumpet-call, that is to summon body and spirit to the judgment seat, "Knowest thou this woman?"

The reader will observe that the whole of this splendid passage is devoted to external effects: the loosened hair and sparkling eyes of Elizabeth—the grouping of the courtiers—the proud smile yet on the cheek of Leicester—the pale and sinking form of the wife. Only by external effects do we guess at the emotions of the agents. Scott is thinking of the costume and postures of the actors, not the passions they represent. Let us take a parallel passage in Shakespeare; parallel, for, in each, a mind disturbed with jealousy, is the real object placed before the reader. It is thus that Iago describes Othello, after the latter has conceived *his* first suspicions:

> [*Iago*]: Look where he comes! Not poppy, nor mandragora,
> Nor all the drowsy syrups of the world,
> Shall ever medicine thee to that sweet sleep
> Which thou ow'dst yesterday.
> *Othello*: Ha! ha! false to me?"

Here the reader will observe that there is no attempt at the picturesque—no sketch at the outward man. It is only by a reference to the wo that kills sleep that we can form any notion of the haggard aspect of the moor. So, if we compare the ensuing dialogue in the romance with that in the tragedy, we shall remark that Elizabeth utters only bursts of shallow passion, which convey none of the deep effects of the philosophy of jealousy; none of the sentiments that "inform us what we are." But every sentence uttered by Othello penetrates to the very root of the passion described: the farewell to fame and pomp, which comes from a heart that, finding falsehood in the prop it leaned on, sees the world itself, and all its quality and circumstance, crumbled away; the burst of vehement incredulity; the sudden return to doubt; the intense revenge proportioned to the intense love; the human weakness that must seek faith somewhere, and, with the loss of Desdemona, cast itself upon her denouncer; the mighty knowledge of the heart exhibited in those simple words of Iago, "I greet *thy* love;"—compare all this with the mere words of Elizabeth, which have no force in themselves, but are made effective by the picturesque grouping of the scene, and you will detect at once the astonishing distinction between Shakespeare and Scott. Shakespeare could have composed the most wonderful plays from the stories in Scott; Scott could have written the most excellent stage directions to the plays of Shakespeare.

If the novelist be contented with the secondary order of art in fiction, and satisfied if his incidents be varied, animating, and striking, he may write from chapter to chapter, and grope his way to a catastrophe in the dark; but if he aim at loftier and more permanent effects, he will remember that to execute grandly we must conceive nobly. He will suffer the subject he selects to lie long in his mind, to be revolved, meditated, brooded over, until, from the chaos breaks the light, and he sees distinctly the highest end for which his materials can be used, and the best process by which they can be reduced to harmony and order.

If, for instance, he found his tale upon some legend, the author, inspired with a great ambition, will consider what will be, not the most vivid interest, but the loftiest and most durable *order* of interest, he can extract from the incidents. Sometimes it will be in a great truth elicited by the catastrophe; sometimes by the delineation of one or more characters; sometimes by the mastery over, and development of, some complicated passion. Having decided what it is that he designs to work out, he will mould his story accordingly; but before he begin to execute, he will have clearly informed his mind of the conception that induces the work itself.

Interest.

No fiction can be first-rate if it fail to create interest. But the merit of the fiction is not, by any means, proportioned to the *degree* of excitement it produces, but to the *quality* of the excitement. It is certainly some merit to make us weep; but the great artist will consider from what sources our tears are to be drawn. We may weep as much at the sufferings of a beggar as at the agonies of Lear; but from what sublime sympathies arise our tears for the last? what commonplace pity will produce the first? We may have our interest much more acutely excited by the *Castle of Udolpho* than by *Anastasius*; but in the one, it is a melo-dramatic arrangement of hair-breadth escapes, and a technical skill in the arrangement of vulgar mysteries—in the other, it is the consummate knowledge of actual life, that fascinates the eye to the page. It is necessary, then, that every novel should excite interest, but one novel may produce a much more gradual, gentle, and subdued interest than another, and yet have infinitely more merit in the *quality* of the interest it excites.

Terror and Horror.

True art never disgusts. If, in descriptions intended to harrow us, we feel sickened and revolted by the very power with which the description is drawn, the author has passed the boundary of his province; he does not appal—he shocks. Thus, nothing is more easy than to produce a feeling of intense pain by a portrait of great bodily suffering, the vulgarest mind can do this, and the mistaken populace of readers will cry, "See the power of this author!" But all sympathy with bodily torture is drawn from our basest infirmities; all sympathy with mental torture from our deepest passions and our most spiritual nature. HORROR is generally produced by the one, TERROR by the other. If you describe a man hanging by a breaking bough over a precipice—if you paint his starting eyeballs, his erect hair, the death-sweat of his brow, the cracking of the bough, the depth of the abyss, the sharpness of the rock, the roar of the cataract below, you may make us dizzy and sick with sympathy; but you operate on the physical nerves, and our sensation is that of coarse and revolting pain. But take a *moral* abyss; Œdipus, for instance, on the brink of learning the awful secret which proclaims him an incestuous parricide. Show the splendour of his power, the depth of his wisdom, the loftiness of his pride, and then gradually, step by step, reveal the precipice on which he stands—and you work not on the body but the mind; you produce the true tragic emotion, *terror*. Even in this, you must stop short all that could make terror revolt while it thrills us. This, Sophocles has done by one of those fine perceptions of nature, which open the sublimest mysteries of art; we are not allowed time to suffer our thought to dwell upon the incest and self-assault of Œdipus, or upon the suicide of Jocasta, before, by the introduction of the children, terror melts into pity, and the parricide son assumes the new aspect of the broken-hearted father. A modern French writer, if he had taken this subject, would have disgusted us by details of the incest itself, or forced us from the riven heart to gaze on the bloody and eyeless sockets of the blind king; and the more he disgusted us, the more he would have thought that he excelled the tragedian of Colonos. Such of the Germans, on the contrary, as follow the school of Schiller, will often stop as far short of the true boundaries of terror, as the French romanticists would go beyond it. Schiller held it a principle of art never to leave the complete and entire effects of a work of art one of pain. According to him, the pleasure of the art should exceed the sympathy with the suffering. He sought to vindicate this principle by a reference to the Greek drama, but in this he confounded the sentiments with which we, moderns, read the works of Æschylus and Sophocles, with the sentiments with which *a Greek* would have read them. No doubt, to a Greek, religiously impressed with the truth and reality of the woes or the terror depicted, the *Agamemnon* of Æschylus, the *Œdipus Tyrannus* of Sophocles, and the *Medea* of Euripides, would have left a far more unqualified and overpowering sentiment of awe and painful sympathy than we now can entertain for victims, whom we believe to be shadows, to deities and destinies that we know to be chimeras. Were Schiller's rule universally adopted, we should condemn Othello and Lear.

Terror may then be carried up to its full extent, provided that it work upon us through the mind, not the body, and stop short of the reaction of recoil and disgust.

Description.

One of the greatest and most peculiar arts of the novelist is decription. It is in this that he has a manifest advantage over the dramatic poet. The latter will rarely describe scenery, costume, *personals*, for they ought to be placed before the eyes of the audience by the theatre and the actors. When he does so, it is generally understood by an intelligent critic, to be an episode introduced for the sake of some poetical beauty, which, without absolutely carrying on the plot, increases the agreeable and artistical effect of the whole performance. This is the case with the description of Dover cliff, in *Lear*, or with that of the chasm which adorns, by so splendid a passage, the monstrous tragedy of the "Cenci." In the classical French theatre, as in the Greek, description, it is true, becomes an essential part of the play itself, since the catastrophe is thrown into description. Hence, the celebrated picture of the death of Hippolyte, in the *Phèdre* of Racine—of the suicide of Hæmon in the *Antigone* of Sophocles. But it may be doubted whether both Sophocles and his French imitator did not, in this transfer of action to words, strike at the very core of dramatic art, whether ancient or modern; for it may be remarked—and we are surprised that it has not been remarked before, that Æschylus preferred placing the catastrophe before the eyes of the reader; and he who remembers the sublime close of the *Prometheus*, the storm, the lightning, the bolt, the shivered rock, and the mingled groans and threats of the Titan himself, must acknowledge that the effect is infinitely more purely tragical than it would have been if we had been told how it all happened by the Angelos or Messenger. So in the *Agamemnon* of the same sublime poet, though we do not see the blow given, the scene itself, opening, places before us the murderess and the corpse. No messenger intervenes—no description is required for the action. "I stand where I struck him," says Clytæmnestra. "The deed is done!"[2]

But without recurring farther to the drama of other nations, we may admit at once that in our own it is the received and approved rule that action, as much as possible, should dispense with description. With narrative fiction it is otherwise: the novel writer is his own scene painter; description is as essential to him as canvass is to the actor—description of the most various character.

In this art, none ever equalled Scott. In the comparison we made between him and Shakespeare, we meant not to censure the former for indulging in what the latter shunned; each did that which his art required. We only lament that Scott did not combine with external description an equal, or, at least, not very inferior, skill in metaphysical analysis. Had he done so, he would have achieved all of which the novelist is capable.

In the description of natural scenery, the author will devote the greatest care to such landscapes as are meant for the localities of his principal events. There is nothing, for instance, very attractive in the general features of a common; but if the author lead us through a common, on which, in a later portion of his work, a deed of murder is to be done, he will strive to fix deeply in our remembrance, the character of the landscape, the stunted tree, or the mantling pool, which he means to associate in our minds with an act of terror.

If the duration of time in a fiction be limited to a year, the author may be enabled artfully to show us the progress of time by minute descriptions of the gradual change in the seasons. This is attempted to be done in the tale of *Eugene Aram*: instead of telling us when it is July, and when it is October, the author of that fiction describes the signs and characteristics of the month, and seeks to identify our interest in the natural phenomena, with the approaching fate of the hero, himself an observer and an artist of the "clouds that pass to and fro," and the "herbs that wither and are renewed." Again, in description, if there be any natural objects that will bear upon the catastrophe, if, for instance, the earthquake or the inundation be intended as an agent in the fate of those whose history the narrative relates, incidental descriptions of the state of the soil, frequent references to the river or the sea, will serve to make the elements themselves minister to the interest of the plot; and the final catastrophe will be made at once more familiar, yet more sublime, if we have been prepared and led to believe that you have from the first designed to invoke to your aid the awful agencies of nature herself. Thus, in the Œdipus, at Colonos, the poet, at the very opening of the tragedy, indulges in the celebrated description of the seats of the dread goddesses, because the place, and the deities themselves, though invisible, belong yet more essentially to the crowning doom of the wanderer, than any of the characters introduced.

The description of *feelings* is also the property of the novelist. The dramatist throws the feelings into dialogue,—the novelist goes at once to the human heart, and calmly scrutinizes, assorts, and dissects them. Few, indeed, are the writers who have hitherto attempted this—the master mystery of the hierophant! Godwin has done so the most elaborately; Goethe the most skilfully. The first writer is, indeed, so minute, that he is often frivolous—so lengthened, that he is generally tedious; but the cultivator of the art, and not the art itself, is to be blamed for such defects. A few words will often paint the precise state of emotion as faithfully as the most voluminous essay; and in this department condensation and brevity are to be carefully studied. Conduct us to the cavern, light the torch, and startle and awe us by what you reveal; but if you keep us all day in the cavern, the effect is lost, and our only feeling is that of impatience and desire to get away.

Arrangement of Incidents.

Distinctions between the Novel and the Drama.

In the arrangement of incidents, the reader will carefully study the distinctions between the novel and the drama—distinctions the more important, because they are not, at the first glance, very perceptible.

In the first place, the incidents of a play must grow, progressively, out of each other. Each scene should appear the necessary consequence of the one that precedes it. This is far from being the case with the novel; in the last, it is often desirable to go back instead of forward—to wind, to vary, to shift the interest from person to person—to keep even your principal hero, your principal actor, in the background. In the novel, you see more of Frank Osbaldistone than you do of Rob Roy; but bring Rob Roy on the stage, and Frank Osbaldistone must recede at once into a fifth-rate personage.

In our closets, we should be fatigued with the incessant rush of events that we desire, when we make one of a multitude. Oratory and the drama in this, resemble each other—that the things best to hear are not always the best to read. In the novel, we address ourselves to the one person—on the stage, we address ourselves to a crowd: more rapid effects, broader and more popular sentiments, more condensed grasp of the universal passions are required for the last. The calm advice which persuades our friend, would only tire out the patience of the crowd. The man who writes a play for Covent Garden, ought to remember that the theatre is but a few paces distant from the Hustings: success at either place, the Hustings or the theatre, will depend upon a mastery over feelings, not perhaps the most commonplace, but the most commonly felt. If, with his strong effects on the stage, the dramatic poet can, like Shakespeare, unite the most delicate and subtle refinement, like Shakespeare, he will be a consummate artist. But the refinement will not do without the effects. In the novel it is different: the most enchanting and permanent kind of interest, in the latter, is often gentle, tranquillizing and subdued. The novelist can appeal to those delicate and subtle emotions, which are easily awakened when we are alone, which are torpid and unfelt in the electric contagion of popular sympathies. The most refining amongst us, will cease to refine when placed in the midst of a multitude.

There is a great distinction between the plot of a novel and that of a play; a distinction which has been indicated by Goethe in the "Wilhelm Meister." The novel allows *accident*, the drama never. In the former, your principal character may be thrown from his horse, and break his neck; in the latter, this would be a great burlesque on the first laws of the drama; for in the drama, the incidents must bring about the catastrophe; in the novel, there is no such necessity. Don Quixote at the last, falls ill, and dies in his bed; but in order that he should fall ill and die in his bed, there was no necessity that he should fight windmills, or mistake an inn for a castle. If a novelist had taken for his theme the conspiracy of Fiesco, after realizing his ambitious projects, is about to step into the ship, he slips from the plank, and the weight of his armour drowns him. This is accident, and this catastrophe would not only have been admissible in the novel, but would have conveyed, perhaps, a sublimer moral than any that fiction could invent. But when Schiller adapted Fiesco for the stage, he felt that accident was not admissible,[3] and his Fiesco falls by the hand of the patriot Verrina. The whole dialogue preceding the fatal blow is one of the most masterly adaptations of moral truth to the necessity of historical infidelity, in European literature.

In the "Bride of Lammermoor," Ravenswood is swallowed up by quicksand. This catastrophe is singularly grand in romance; it could not be allowable on the stage; for this again is *accident*, and not *result*.

The distinctions, then, between the novel and the drama, so far as the management of incidents is concerned, are principally these: that in the one, the interest must always progress—that in the other, it must often go back and often halt; that dealing with human nature in a much larger scale in the novel, you will often introduce events and incidents, not necessarily growing one out of the other, though all conducing to the completeness of the whole; that in the drama you have more impatience to guard against—you are addressing men in numbers, not the individual man; your effects must be more rapid and more startling; that in the novel you may artistically have more recourse to accident for the working out of your design—in the drama, never.

The ordinary faults of a play by the novelist,[4] and of a novel by the play-writer, will serve as an illustration of the principles which have insensibly regulated each. The novelist will be too diffuse, too narrative, and too refined in his effects for the stage; the play-writer will be too condensed, abrupt, and, above all, too exaggerated, for our notions of the natural when we are in the closet. Stage effect is a vice in the novel; but, how can we expect a man trained to write for the stage, to avoid what on the stage is a merit? A certain exaggeration of sentiment is natural, and necessary, for sublime and truthful effects when we address numbers; it would be ludicrous uttered to a friend in his easy chair. If Demosthenes, urging a young Athenian to conduct himself properly, had thundered out[5] that sublime appeal to the shades of Marathon, Platea, and Salamis, which thrilled the popular assembly, the young Athenian would have laughed in his face. If the dialogue of *Macbeth* were the dialogue of a romance on the same subject, it would be equally good in itself, but it would seem detestable bombast. If the dialogue in *Ivanhoe*, which is matchless of its kind for spirit and fire, were shaped into blank verse, and cut up into a five-act play, it would be bald and pointless. As the difference between the effective oration and the eloquent essay—between Pitt so great to hear, and Burke so great to read, so is the difference between the writing for the eye of one man, and the writing for the ears of three thousand.

Mechanism and Conduct.

The mechanism and conduct of the story ought to depend upon the nature of the preconceived design. Do you desire to work out some definite end, through the passions or through the characters you employ? Do you desire to carry on the interest less through character and passion than through incident? Or, do you rather desire to entertain and instruct by a general and wider knowledge of living manners or human nature? Or, lastly, would you seek to incorporate all these objects? As you are faithful to your conception, will you be attentive to, and precise in, the machinery you use? In other words, your *progress* must depend upon the order of interest you mean to be predominant. It is by not considering this rule that critics have often called that episodical or extraneous, which is in fact a part of the design. Thus, in *Gil Blas*,"the object is to convey to the reader a complete picture of the surface of society; the manners, foibles, and peculiarities of the time; elevated by a general, though not very profound, knowledge of the more durable and universal elements of human nature in the abstract. Hence, the numerous tales and nouvellettes scattered throughout the work, though episodical to the adventures of Gil Blas, are not episodical to the design of Le Sage. They all serve to complete and furnish out the conception, and the whole would be less rich and consummate in its effect without them. They are not passages which lead to nothing, but conduce to many purposes we can never comprehend, unless we consider well for what end the building was planned. So if you wish to bring out all the peculiarities of a certain character, you will often seem to digress into adventures which have no palpable bearing on the external plot of incident and catastrophe. This is constantly the case with Cervantes and Fielding; and the critic who blames you for it, is committing the gross blunder of judging the novel by the laws of the drama.

But as an ordinary rule, it may be observed that, since, both in the novel and the play, human life is represented by an epitome, so in both, it is desirable that all your characters should more or less be brought to bear on the conclusions you have in view. It is not necessary in the novel that they should bear on the physical events; they may sometimes bear on the mental and interior changes in the minds and characters of the persons you introduce. For instance, if you design in the life of your hero to illustrate the passion of a jealousy upon a peculiar conformation of mind, you may introduce several characters and several incidents, which will serve to ripen his tendencies, but not have the least bearing on the actual catastrophe in which those tendencies are confirmed into deeds. This is but fidelity to real life, in which it seldom happens that they who foster the passion are the witnesses or sufferers of the effects. This distinction between interior and external agencies will be made apparent by a close study of the admirable novel of Zeluco.

In the mechanism of external incidents, Scott is the greatest model that fiction possesses; and if we select from his works that in which this mechanism is most artistical, we instance not one of his most brilliant and popular, but one in which he combined all the advantages of his multiform and matured experience in the craft: we mean the *Fair Maid of Perth*. By noting well the manner in which, in this tale, the scene is ever varied at the right moment, and the exact medium preserved between abruptness and *longueur*; how all the incidents are complicated, so as to appear inextricable, yet the solution obtained by the simplest and shortest process, the reader will learn more of the art of *mechanical* construction, than by all the rules that Aristotle himself, were he living, could lay down.

Divisions of the work.

In the drama, the divisions of the plot into *Acts* are of infinite service in condensing and simplifying the design of the author. The novelist will find it convenient to himself to establish analogous divisions in the conduct of his story. The division into volumes is but the affair of the printer, and affords little help to the intellectual purposes of the author. Hence, most of our greatest novelists have had recourse to the more definite sub-partition of the work into *Books*; and if the student use this mode of division, not from capricious or arbitrary pleasure, but with the same purposes of art, for which, in the drama, recourse is had to the division into acts, he will find it of the greatest service. Properly speaking, each book should be complete in itself, working out the exact and whole purpose that the author meditates in that portion of his work. It is clear, therefore, that the number of his books will vary according to the nature of his design. Where you have shaped your story after a dramatic fashion, you will often be surprised to find how greatly you serve to keep your construction faithful to your design, by the mere arrangement of the work into the same number of sub-divisions as are adopted in the drama, viz., five books instead of five acts. Where, on the other hand, you avoid the dramatic construction, and lead the reader through great varieties of life and action, meaning, in each portion of the history of your hero, to illustrate separate views of society or human nature, you will probably find a much greater number of sub-divisions requisite. This must depend upon your design. Another advantage in these divisions consists in the rules that your own common sense will suggest to you with respect to the introduction of characters. It is seldom advisable to admit any new character of importance, after the interest has arrived at a certain point of maturity. As you would not introduce a new character of consequence to the catastrophe, in the fifth act of a play, so, though with more qualification and reserve, it will be inartistical to make a similar introduction in the corresponding portion of a novel. The most illustrious exception to this general rule is in *Clarissa*, in which the avenger, the brother of the heroine and the executioner of Lovelace, only appears at the close of the story, and for the single purpose of revenge; and here the effect is heightened by the lateness and suddenness of the introduction of the very person to whom the catastrophe is confided.

The Catastrophe.

The distinction between the novel and the drama is usually very visible in the catastrophe. The stage effect of bringing all the characters together in the closing chapter, to be married or stabbed as the thing may require, is, to a fine taste, eminently displeasing in a novel. It introduces into the very place where we most desire verisimilitude, a clap-trap and theatrical effect. For it must be always remembered, that in prose fiction we require more of the real than we do in the drama (which belongs, of right, to the regions of pure poetry,) and if the very last effect bequeathed to us be that of palpable delusion and trick, the charm of the whole work is greatly impaired. Some of Scott's romances may be justly charged with this defect.

Usually, the author is so far aware of the inartist-like effect of a final grouping of all the characters before the fall of the curtain, that he brings but few of the agents he has employed to be *present* at the catastrophe, and follows what may be called the wind-up of the main interest, by one or more epilogical chapters, in which we are told how Sir Thomas married and settled at his country seat, how Miss Lucy died an old maid, and how the miser Grub was found dead on his money chest; disposing in a few sentences of the lives and deaths of all to whom we have been presented—a custom that we think might now give place to less hacknied inventions.

The drama will bear but one catastrophe; the novel will admit of more. Thus, in

Ivanhoe, the more vehement and apparent catastrophe is the death of Bois Guilbert; but the marriage of Ivanhoe, the visit of Rebecca to Rowena, and the solemn and touching farewell of the Jewess, constitute, properly speaking, a catastrophe no less capital in itself, and no less essential to the completion of the incidents. So also there is often a moral catastrophe, as well as a physical one, sometimes identified each with the other, sometimes distinct. If you have been desirous to work out some conception of a principle or a truth, the design may not be completed till after the more violent effects which form the physical catastrophe. In the recent novel of *Alice, or the Mysteries*, the external catastrophe is in the vengeance of Cæsarini and the death of Vargrave, but the complete *dénouement* and completion of the more typical meanings and ethical results of the fiction are reserved to the moment when Maltravers recognises the natural to be the true ideal, and is brought, by the faith and beauty of simple goodness, to affection and respect for mankind itself. In the drama, it would be necessary to incorporate in one scene all the crowning results of the preceding events. We could not bear a new interest after the death of Bois Guilbert; and a new act of mere dialogue between Alice and Maltravers, after the death of Vargrave, would be insufferably tame and frigid. The perfection of a catastrophe is not so much in the power with which it is told, as in the feeling of completeness which it should leave on the mind. On closing the work, we ought to feel that we have read a *whole*—that there is a harmonious unity in all its parts—that its close, whether it be pleasing or painful, is that which is essentially appropriate to all that has gone before; and not only the mere isolated thoughts in the work, but the unity of the work itself, ought to leave its single and deep impression on the mind. The book itself should be a thought.

There is another distinction between the catastrophe of a novel and that of a play. In the last, it ought to be the most permanent and striking events that lead to the catastrophe; in the former, it will often be highly artistical to revive, for the consummating effect, many slight details—incidents the author had but dimly shadowed out—mysteries, that you had judged, till then, he had forgotten to clear up; and to bring a thousand rivulets, that had seemed merely introduced to relieve or adorn the way, into the rapid gulf which closes over all. The effect of this has a charm not derived from mere trick, but from its fidelity to the natural and life-like order of events. What more common in the actual world than that the great crises of our fate are influenced and coloured, not so much by the incidents and persons we have deemed most important, but by many things of remote date, or of seeming insignificance. The feather the eagle carelessly sheds by the way-side plumes the shaft that transfixes him. In this management and combination of incidents towards the grand end, knowledge of human nature can alone lead the student to the knowledge of ideal art.

These remarks form the summary of the hints and suggestions that, after a careful study of books, we submit to the consideration of the student in a class of literature now so widely cultivated, and hitherto almost wholly unexamined by the critic. We presume not to say that they form an entire code of laws for the art. Even Aristotle's immortal treatise on poetry, were it bequeathed to us complete, would still be but a skeleton; and though no poet could read that treatise without advantage, the most glorious poetry might be, and has been, written in defiance of nearly all its laws. Genius will arrive at fame by the light of its own star: but criticism can often serve as a sign-post to save many an unnecessary winding, and indicate many a short way. He who aspires to excel in that fiction which is the glass of truth, may learn much from books and rules, from the lecturer and the critic; but he must be also the imaginer, the observer. He will be ever examining human life in its most catholic and comprehensive aspects. Nor is it enough to observe—it is necessary to feel. We must let the heart be a student as well as the head. No man who is a passionless and cold spectator, will ever be an accurate analyst, of all the motives and springs of action. Perhaps, if we were to search for the true secret of creative genius, we should find that secret in the intenseness of its sympathies.

Notes

1. See Mr. Lockhart's *Life of Scott*, vol. vi. p. 232. "In writing, I never could lay down a plan," &c. Scott, however, has the candour to add, "I would not have young writers imitate my carelessness."

2. Even Sophocles, in one of his finest tragedies, has not scrupled to suffer the audience to witness the last moments of Ajax.

3. "The nature of the Drama," observes Schiller, in his preface to *Fiesco*, and in excuse for his corruption of history, "does not admit the hand of chance."

4. "Why is it that a successful novelist never has been a successful play-writer?" This is a question that has been so often put, that we have been frightened out of considering whether the premises involved in the question are true or not. It is something like the schoolboy question, "Why is a pound of feathers heavier than a pound of lead?" It is long before Tom or Jack ask, "Is it heavier?" *Is* it true that a successful novelist never has been a successful playwriter? We will not insist on Goldsmith, whose comedy of *She Stoops to Conquer*, and whose novel of the *Vicar of Wakefield*, are alike among the greatest ornaments of our language. But was not Goethe a great play-writer and a great novelist? Who will decide whether the palm in genius should be given to the *Tasso*, or the *Wilhelm Meister*, of that all-sided genius? Is not the *Ghost-seer* a successful novel? Does it not afford the highest and most certain testimony of what Schiller could have done as a writer of narrative fiction, and are not *Wallenstein*, and *Fiesco*, and *Don Carlos*, great plays by the same author? Are not *Candide* and *Zadig* imperishable masterpieces in the art of the novelist? And are not *Zaire* and *Mahomet* equally immortal? The three greatest geniuses that, in modern times, the Continent has produced, were both novelists and dramatists—equally great in each department. In France, at this day, Victor Hugo, who, with all his faults, is immeasurably the first writer in the school he has sought to found, is both the best novelist and the most powerful dramatist. That it has not happened *oftener* that the same man has achieved equal honour in the novel and the play is another question. But we might just as well ask why it has not happened oftener that the same man has been equally successful in tragedy and epic—in the ode and the didactic—why he, who is sublime as a poet, is often tame as a prose writer, and *vice versa*—why the same artist who painted the *Transfiguration*, did not paint the *Last Day*. Nature, circumstance, and education, have not fitted many men to be great in two lines which, though seemingly close to each other, run in parallel directions. The more subtle the distinctions between the novel and the play, the more likely they are to be overlooked by him who attempts both. It is the same with all departments of art; the closer the approximation of the boundaries, the more difficult the blending.

5. Dem. de Cor.

⁂ 51 ⁂

Before the Curtain

WILLIAM MAKEPEACE THACKERAY

William Makepeace Thackerary (1811-1863) shares his place as one of the prominent novelists of the nineteenth century together with Dickens, George Eliot and Anthony Trollope. In addiiton to writing for such Victorian journals as *Fraser's Magazine*, *Punch* and *Cornhill*, Thackeray published in serial form, in addition to *Vanity Fair, Pendennis* (1848), *Esmond* (1852) and *The Newcomes* (1853-55). Charlotte Brontë dedicated her second edition of *Jane Eyre* to him. In the following preface to *Vanity Fair*, Thackeray assumes the rôle of puppeteer in order to discuss his novelistic method. His moral, he says, is simply to depict the social manoeuvrings and foibles of a spectrum of Victorian society. Unlike his eighteenth-century predecessors who were keen to defend their novels as true histories, Thackeray deliberately emphasizes the fictional quality of his characters as well as his aesthetic distance from them. They are "puppets", "dolls", and "figures", as opposed to real people.

As the Manager of the Performance sits before the curtain on the boards, and looks into the Fair, a feeling of profound melancholy comes over him in his survey of the bustling place. There is a great quantity of eating and drinking, making love and jilting, dancing, and fiddling: there are bullies pushing about, bucks ogling the women, knaves picking pockets, policemen on the look-out, quacks (*other* quacks, plague take them!) bawling in front of their booths, and yokels looking up at the tinselled dancers and poor old rouged tumblers, while the light-fingered folk are operating upon their pockets behind. Yes, this is Vanity Fair; not a moral place certainly; not a merry one, though very noisy. Look at the faces of the actors and buffoons when they come off from their business; and Tom Fool washing the paint off his cheeks before he sits down to dinner with his wife and the little Jack Puddings behind the canvas. The curtain will be up presently, and he will be turning over head and heels, and crying, "How are you?"

Source: William Makepeace Thackeray, "Before the Curtain", *Vanity Fair*, 1847, rptd New York and Boston: Thomas D. Crowell & Co., 1898, pp. v-vi.

A man with a reflective turn of mind, walking through an exhibition of this sort, will not be oppressed, I take it, by his own or other people's hilarity. An episode of humor or kindness touches and amuses him here and there;—a pretty child looking at a gingerbread stall; a pretty girl blushing whilst her lover talks to her and chooses her fairing; poor Tom Fool, yonder behind the wagon, mumbling his bone with the honest family which lives by his tumbling; but the general impression is one more melancholy than mirthful. When you come home, you sit down, in a sober, contemplative, not uncharitable frame of mind, and apply yourself to your books or your business.

I have no other moral than this to tag to the present story of "Vanity Fair." Some people consider Fairs immoral altogether, and eschew such, with their servants and families: very likely they are right. But persons who think otherwise, and are of a lazy, or a benevolent, or a sarcastic mood, may perhaps like to step in for half an hour, and look at the performances. There are scenes of all sorts; some dreadful combats, some grand and lofty horse-riding, some scenes of high life, and some of very middling indeed; some love-making for the sentimental, and some light comic business; the whole accompanied by appropriate scenery, and brilliantly illuminated with the Author's own candles.

What more has the Manager of the Performance to say?—To acknowledge the kindness with which it has been received in all the principal towns of England through which the Show has passed, and where it has been most favorably noticed by the respected conductors of the public Press, and by the Nobility and Gentry. He is proud to think that his Puppets have given satisfaction to the very best company in this empire. The famous little Becky Puppet has been pronounced to be uncommonly flexible in the joints, and lively on the wire: the Amelia Doll, though it has had a smaller circle of admirers, has yet been carved and dressed with the greatest care by the artist: the Dobbin Figure, though apparently clumsy, yet dances in a very amusing and natural manner: the Little Boys' Dance has been liked by some; and please to remark the richly dressed figure of the Wicked Nobleman, on which no expense has been spared, and which Old Nick will fetch away at the end of this singular performance.

And with this, and a profound bow to the patrons, the Manager retires, and the curtain rises.

London, June 28, 1848.

52

Biographical Notice of Ellis and Acton Bell

CHARLOTTE BRONTË

Eldest of the three Brontë sisters, Charlotte Brontë (1816-1855), author of *Jane Eyre* (1847), *Shirley* (1849) and *Villette* (1853), corrects the erroneous view that *Wuthering Heights* and *Jane Eyre* are by the same author. In the following notice to her edition of her sister's novel, she explains the genesis of her own and her sisters' novels and defends *Wuthering Heights* against ruthless critics. She calls *Wuthering Heights* the product of an immature, powerful but uninstructed mind. Of her sister Anne's *The Tenant of Wildfell Hall*, she has less praise, condemning its realism and its fidelity to minute and sordid details as critics of naturalism will do a half century later. In Charlotte's defence of her sisters' works, she indicates traits for which she herself is ridiculed by critics—reliance on intuition, impulse and limited observation of nature.

It has been thought that all the works published under the names of Currer, Ellis, and Acton Bell, were, in reality, the production of one person. This mistake I endeavoured to rectify by a few words of a disclaimer prefixed to the third edition of *Jane Eyre*. These, too, it appears, failed to gain general credence, and now, on the occasion of a reprint of *Wuthering Heights* I am advised distinctly to state how the case really stands.

Indeed, I feel myself that it is time the obscurity attending these two names—Ellis and Acton—was done away. The little mystery, which formerly yielded some harmless pleasure, has lost its interest; circumstances are changed. It becomes, then, my duty to explain briefly the origin of the authorship of the books written by Currer, Ellis, and Acton Bell.

About five years ago, my two sisters and myself, after a somewhat prolonged period of separation, found ourselves reunited, and at home. Resident in a remote district, where education had made little progress, and where, consequently, there

Source: Charlotte Brontë, "Biographical Notice of Ellis and Acton Bell", *Wuthering Heights* by Emily Brontë, 1850, rptd New York: The Modern Library, 1926, pp. xi-xix.

An example of a manuscript page by Charlotte Brontë

was no inducement to seek social intercourse beyond our own domestic circle, we were wholly dependent on ourselves and each other, on books and study, for the enjoyments and occupations of life. The highest stimulus, as well as the liveliest pleasure we had known from childhood upwards, lay in attempts at literary composition; formerly we used to show each other what we wrote, but of late years this habit of communication and consultation had been discontinued; hence it ensued, that we were mutually ignorant of the progress we might respectively have made.

One day, in the autumn of 1845, I accidentally lighted on a MS. volume of verse in my sister Emily's handwriting. Of course, I was not surprised, knowing that she could and did write verse: I looked it over, and something more than surprise seized me,—a deep conviction that these were not common effusions, nor at all like the poetry women generally write. I thought them condensed and terse, vigorous and genuine. To my ear, they had also a peculiar music—wild, melancholy, and elevating.

My sister Emily was not a person of demonstrative character, nor one on the recesses of whose mind and feelings, even those nearest and dearest to her could, with impunity, intrude unlicensed; it took hours to reconcile her to the discovery I had made, and days to persuade her that such poems merited publication. I knew, however, that a mind like hers could not be without some spark of honourable ambition, and refused to be discouraged in my attempts to fan that spark to flame.

Meantime, my younger sister quietly produced some of her own compositions, intimating that, since Emily's had given me pleasure, I might like to look at hers. I could not but be a partial judge, yet I thought that these verses, too, had a sweet sincere pathos of their own.

We had very early cherished the dream of one day becoming authors. This dream, never relinquished even when distance divided and absorbing tasks occupied us, now suddenly acquired strength and consistency: it took the character of a resolve. We agreed to arrange a small selection of our poems, and, if possible, get them printed. Averse to personal publicity, we veiled our own names under those of Currer, Ellis, and Acton Bell; the ambiguous choice being dictated by a sort of conscientious scruple at assuming Christian names positively masculine, while we did not like to declare ourselves women, because—without at that time suspecting that our mode of writing and thinking was not what is called "feminine"—we had a vague impression that authoresses are liable to be looked on with prejudice; we had noticed how critics sometimes use for their chastisement the weapon of personality, and for their reward, a flattery which is not true praise.

The bringing out of our little book was hard work. As was to be expected, neither we nor our poems were at all wanted; but for this we had been prepared at the outset; though inexperienced ourselves, we had read the experience of others. The great puzzle lay in the difficulty of getting answers of any kind from the publishers to whom we applied. Being greatly harrassed by this obstacle, I ventured to apply to the Messrs. Chambers, of Edinburgh, for a word of advice; *they* may have forgotten the circumstance, but *I* have not, for from them I received a brief and business-like, but civil and sensible reply, on which we acted, and at last made a way.

The book was printed: it is scarcely known, and all of it that merits to be known are the poems of Ellis Bell. The fixed conviction I held, and hold, of the worth of these poems has not indeed received the confirmation of much favourable criticism; but I must retain it notwithstanding.

Ill-success failed to crush us: the mere effort to succeed had given a wonderful zest to existence; it must be pursued. We each set to work on a prose tale: Ellis Bell produced *Wuthering Heights*, Acton Bell *Agnes Grey*, and Currer Bell also wrote a narrative in one volume. These MSS. were perseveringly obtruded upon various publishers for the space of a year and a half; usually, their fate was an ignominious and abrupt dismissal.

At last *Wuthering Heights* and *Agnes Grey* were accepted on terms somewhat impoverishing to the two authors; Currer Bell's book found acceptance nowhere, nor any acknowledgment of merit, so that something like the chill of despair began to invade his heart. As a forlorn hope, he tried one publishing house more—Messrs. Smith, Elder and Co. Ere long, in a much shorter space than that on which experience had taught him to calculate—there came a letter, which he opened in the dreary expectation of finding two hard hopeless lines, intimating that Messrs. Smith, Elder and Co. "were not disposed to publish the MS.," and instead took out of the envelope a letter of two pages. He read it trembling. It declined, indeed, to publish the tale, for business reasons, but it discussed its merits and demerits so courteously, so considerately, in a spirit so rational, with a discrimination so enlightened, that this very refusal cheered the author better than a vulgarly expressed acceptance would have done. It was added, that a work in three volumes would meet with careful attention.

I was just then completing *Jane Eyre*, at which I had been working while the one-volume tale was plodding its weary way round in London: in three weeks I sent it off; friendly and skilful hands took it in. This was in the commencement of September 1847; it came out before the close of October, following, while *Wuthering Heights* and *Agnes Grey*, my sisters' works, which had already been in the press for months, still lingered under a different management.

They appeared at last. Critics failed to do them justice. The immature but very real powers revealed in *Wuthering Heights* were scarcely recognised; its import and nature were misunderstood; the identity of its author was misrepresented; it was said that this was an earlier and ruder attempt of the same pen which had produced *Jane Eyre*. Unjust and grievous error! We laughed at it at first, but I deeply lament it now. Hence, I fear, arose a prejudice against the book. That writer who could attempt to palm off an inferior and immature production under cover of one successful effort, must indeed by unduly eager after the secondary and sordid result of authorship, and pitiably indifferent to its true and honourable meed. If reviewers and the public truly believed this, no wonder that they looked darkly on the cheat.

Yet I must not be understood to make these things subject for reproach or complaint; I dare not do so; respect for my sister's memory forbids me. By her any such querulous manifestation would have been regarded as an unworthy and offensive weakness.

It is my duty, as well as my pleasure, to acknowledge one exception to the general rule of criticism. One writer,[1] endowed with the keen vision and fine sympathies of genius, has discerned the real nature of *Wuthering Heights*, and has, with equal accuracy, noted its beauties and touched upon its faults. Too often do reviewers remind us of the mob of Astrologers, Chaldeans, and Soothsayers gathered before the "writing on the wall," and unable to read the characters or make known the interpretation. We have a right to rejoice when a true seer comes at last, some man in whom is an excellent spirit, to whom have been given light, wisdom, and understanding; who can accurately read the "Mene, Mene, Tekel, Upharsin" of an original mind (however unripe, however inefficiently cultured and partially expanded that mind may be); and who can say with confidence, "This is the interpretation thereof."

Yet even the writer to whom I allude shares the mistake about the authorship, and does me the injustice to suppose that there was equivoque in my former rejection of this honour (as an honour I regard it). May I assure him that I would scorn in this and in every other case to deal in equivoque; I believe language to have been given us to make our meaning clear, and not to wrap it in dishonest doubt.

The Tenant of Wildfell Hall, by Acton Bell, had likewise an unfavourable reception. At this I cannot wonder. The choice of subject was an entire mistake. Nothing less congruous with the writer's nature could be conceived. The motives which dictated this choice were pure, but, I think, slightly morbid. She had, in the course of her life, been called on to contemplate, near at hand, and for a long time, the terrible effects of talents misused and faculties abused; hers was naturally a sensitive, reserved, and dejected nature; what she saw sank very deeply into her mind; it did her harm. She brooded over it till she believed it to be a duty to reproduce every detail (of course with fictitious characters, incidents, and situations), as a warning to others. She hated her work, but would pursue it. When reasoned with on the subject, she regarded such reasonings as a temptation to self-indulgence. She must be honest: she must not varnish, soften, or conceal. This well-meant resolution brought on her misconstruction, and some abuse, which she bore, as it was her custom to bear whatever was unpleasant, with mild, steady patience. She was a very sincere and practical Christian, but the tinge of religious melancholy communicated a sad shape to her brief, blameless life.

Neither Ellis nor Acton allowed herself for one moment to sink under want of encouragement; energy nerved the one, and endurance upheld the other. They were both prepared to try again; I would fain think that hope and the sense of power was yet strong within them. But a great change approached: affliction came in that shape which to anticipate is dread: to look back on, grief. In the very heat and burden of the day, the labourers failed over their work.

My sister Emily first declined. The details of her illness are deep-branded in my memory, but to dwell on them, either in thought or in narrative, is not in my power. Never in all her life had she lingered over any task that lay before her, and she did not linger now. She sank rapidly. She made haste to leave us. Yet, while physically she perished, mentally she grew stronger than we had yet known her. Day by day, when I saw with what a front she met suffering, I looked on her with an anguish of wonder and love. I have seen nothing like it; but, indeed, I have never seen her parallel in anything. Stronger than a man, simpler than a child, her nature stood alone. The awful point was, that while full of ruth for others, on herself she had no pity; the spirit was inexorable to the flesh; from the trembling hand, the unnerved limbs, the faded eyes, the same service was exacted as they had rendered in health. To stand by and witness this, and not dare to remonstrate, was a pain no words can render.

Two cruel months of hope and fear passed painfully by, and the day came at last when the terrors and pains of death were to be undergone by this treasure, which had grown dearer and dearer to our hearts as it wasted before our eyes. Towards the decline of that day, we had nothing of Emily but her mortal remains as consumption left them. She died December 19, 1848.

We thought this enough: but we were utterly and presumptuously wrong. She was not buried ere Anne fell ill. She had not been committed to the grave a fortnight, before we received distinct intimation that it was necessary to prepare our minds to see the younger sister go after the elder. Accordingly, she followed in the same path with slower step, and with a patience that equalled the other's fortitude. I have said that she was religious, and it was by leaning on those Christian doctrines in which she firmly believed that she found support through her most painful journey. I witnessed their efficacy in her latest hour and greatest trial, and must bear my testimony to the calm triumph with which they brought her through. She died May 28, 1849.

What more shall I say about them? I cannot and need not say much more. In externals, they were two unobtrusive women; a perfectly secluded life gave them retiring manners and habits. In Emily's nature the extremes of vigour and simplicity seemed to meet. Under an unsophisticated culture, inartificial tastes, and an unpretending outside, lay a secret power and fire that might have informed the brain and kindled the veins of a hero; but she had no worldly wisdom; her powers were unadapted to the practical business of life: she would fail to defend her most manifest rights, to consult her most legitimate advantage. An interpreter ought always to have stood between her and the world. Her will was not very flexible, and it generally opposed her interest. Her temper was magnanimous, but warm and sudden; her spirit altogether unbending.

Anne's character was milder and more subdued; she wanted the power, the fire, the originality of her sister, but was well endowed with quiet virtues of her own. Long-suffering, self-denying, reflective, and intelligent, a constitutional reserve and taciturnity placed and kept her in the shade, and covered her mind, and especially her feelings, with a sort of nun-like veil, which was rarely lifted. Neither Emily nor Anne was learned; they had no thought of filling their pitchers at the well-spring of other minds; they always wrote from the impulse of nature, the dictates of intuition, and from such stores of observation as their limited experience had enabled them to amass. I may sum up all by saying, that for strangers they were nothing, for superficial observers less than nothing; but for those who had known them all their lives in the intimacy of close relationship, they were genuinely good and truly great.

This notice has been written, because I felt it a sacred duty to wipe the dust off their gravestones, and leave their dear names free from soil.

Currer Bell.
(Charlotte Brontë.)

September 19, 1850.

Note

1. See the *Palladium* for September, 1850.

❧ 53 ☙

Editor's Preface to the New Edition of *Wuthering Heights*

CHARLOTTE BRONTË

In an eloquent Preface to her own edition of Emily Brontë's *Wuthering Heights*, Charlotte Brontë offers an incisive ciriticism of her sister's novel and, by implication, of her own practice as a novelist. She defends the provincialism of *Wuthering Heights* against accusations of rudeness and unintelligibility, noting that it captures in many aspects the nature of the moors of northern England even if it darkens the inhabitants. She apologises for her sister's harsh portrayal and intimates that had Emily been raised in a more genteel environment and lived longer, she would have produced a softer and more palatable work. In Heathcliff, Charlotte Brontë finds only one remotely redeemable trait—his ambivalent care for Hareton Earnshaw and his esteem for Nelly Dean, *not* his love for Catherine. In her concluding paragraphs Charlotte Brontë offers her romanticised theory of composition, a theory often embodied in her characters' mental conflicts between imagination and reason. In a statement reminiscent of the Romantic poets' descriptions of inspiration, she claims that the impulse to create often overwhelms the writer's conscious intentions, violating novelistic rules and holding the rational mind subject to the imagination. She compares *Wuthering Heights* to a giant statue wrought with a "rude chisel, and from no model but the vision of his [the author's] meditations" (xxvi). Critics of the novel throughout both nineteenth and twentieth centuries, taking their cue from Charlotte Brontë's Preface, have difficulty categorising the novel. Though some insist on its mystical and mythical qualities and thus identify it as purely romantic, others view the work as a site of conflict between the opposed genres of romance and realism.

I have just read over *Wuthering Heights*, and, for the first time, have obtained a clear glimpse of what are termed (and, perhaps, really are) its faults; have gained

Source: Charlotte Brontë, "Editor's Preface to the New Edition of *Wuthering Heights*", 1850, rptd *Wuthering Heights*, by Emily Brontë, New York: The Modern Library, 1926, pp. xxi–xxvi.

a definite notion of how it appears to other people—to strangers who knew nothing of the author; who are unacquainted with the locality where the scenes of the story are laid; to whom the inhabitants, the customs, the natural characteristics of the outlying hills and hamlets in the West Riding of Yorkshire are things alien and unfamiliar.

To all such *Wuthering Heights* must appear a rude and strange production. The wild moors of the north of England can for them have no interest; the language, the manners, the very dwellings and household customs of the scattered inhabitants of those districts, must be to such readers in a great measure unintelligible, and—where intelligible—repulsive. Men and women who, perhaps naturally very calm, and with feelings moderate in degree, and little marked in kind, have been trained from their cradle to observe the utmost evenness of manner and guardedness of language, will hardly know what to make of the rough, strong utterance, the harshly manifested passions, the unbridled aversions, and headlong partialities of unlettered moorland hinds and rugged moorland squires, who have grown up untaught and unchecked, except by mentors as harsh as themselves. A large class of readers, likewise, will suffer greatly from the introduction into the pages of this work of words printed with all their letters, which it has become the custom to represent by the initial and final letter only—a blank line filling the interval. I may as well say at once that, for this circumstance, it is out of my power to apologise; deeming it, myself, a rational plan to write words at full length. The practice of hinting by single letters those expletives with which profane and violent persons are wont to garnish their discourse, strikes me a proceeding which, however well meant, is weak and futile. I cannot tell what good it does—what feelings it spares—what horror it conceals.

With regard to the rusticity of *Wuthering Heights*, I admit the charge, for I feel the quality. It is rustic all through. It is moorish, and wild, and knotty as a root of heath. Nor was it natural that it should be otherwise; the author being herself a native and nursling of the moors. Doubtless, had her lot been cast in a town, her writings, if she had written at all, would have possessed another character. Even had chance or taste led her to choose a similar subject, she would not have treated it otherwise. Had Ellis Bell been a lady or gentleman accustomed to what is called "the world," her view of a remote and unreclaimed region, as well as of the dwellers therein, would have differed greatly from that actually taken by the homebred country girl. Doubtless it would have been wider—more comprehensive: whether it would have been more original or more truthful is not so certain. As far as the scenery and locality are concerned, it could scarcely have been so sympathetic: Ellis Bell did not describe as one whose eye and taste alone found pleasure in the prospect; her native hills were far more to her than a spectacle; they were what she lived in, and by, as much as the wild birds, their tenants, or as the heather, their produce. Her descriptions, then, of natural scenery, are what they should be, and all they should be.

Where delineation of human character is concerned, the case is different. I am bound to avow that she had scarcely more practical knowledge of the peasantry amongst whom she lived, than a nun has of the country people who sometimes pass her convent gates. My sister's disposition was not naturally gregarious; circumstances favoured and fostered her tendency to seclusion; except to go to church or take a walk on the hills, she rarely crossed the threshold of home. Though her feelings for the people round was benevolent, intercourse with them she never sought; nor, with very few exceptions, ever experienced. And yet she knew them: knew their ways, their language, their family histories; she could hear of them with interest, and talk of them with detail, minute, graphic, and accurate; but *with* them, she rarely exchanged a word. Hence it ensued that what her mind had gathered of the real concerning them was too exclusively confined to those tragic and terrible traits of which, in listening to the secret annals of every rude vicinage, the memory is sometimes compelled to receive the impress. Her imagination, which was a spirit more sombre than sunny, more powerful than sportive, found in such traits material whence it wrought creations like Heathcliff, like Earnshaw, like Catherine. Having formed these beings she did not know what she had done. If the auditor of her work when read in manuscript, shuddered under the grinding influence of natures so relentless and implacable, of spirits so lost and fallen; if it was complained that the mere hearing of certain vivid and fearful scenes vanished sleep by night, and disturbed mental peace by day, Ellis Bell would wonder what was meant, and suspect the complainant of affectation. Had she but lived, her mind would of itself have grown like a strong tree, loftier, straighter, wider-spreading, and its matured fruits would have attained a mellowed ripeness and sunnier bloom; but on that mind time and experience alone could work: to the influence of other intellects, it was not amenable.

Having avowed that over much of *Wuthering Heights* there broods a "horror of great darkness"; that, in its storm-heated and electrical atmosphere, we seem at times to breathe lightning, let me point to those spots where clouded daylight and the eclipsed sun still attest their existence. For a specimen of true benevolence and fidelity, look at the character of Nelly Dean; for an example of constancy and tenderness, remark that of Edgar Linton. (Some people will think these qualities do not shine so well incarnate in a man as they would do in a woman, but Ellis Bell could never be brought to comprehend this notion; nothing moved her more than any insinuation that the faithfulness and clemency, the long-suffering and loving kindness which are esteemed virtues in the daughters of Eve, become foibles in the sons of Adam. She held that mercy and forgiveness are the divinest attributes of the Great Being who made both man and woman, and that what clothes the Godhead in glory, can disgrace no form of feeble humanity.) There is a dry saturnine humour in the delineation of old Joseph, and some glimpses of grace and gaiety animate the younger Catherine. Nor is even the first heroine of the name destitute of a certain strange beauty in her fierceness, or of honesty in the midst of perverted passion and passionate perversity.

Heathcliff, indeed, stands unredeemed; never once swerving in his arrow-straight course to perdition, from the time when "the little black-haired swarthy thing, as dark as if it came from the Devil," was first unrolled out of the bundle and set on its feet in the farmhouse kitchen, to the hour when Nelly Dean found the grim, stalwart corpse laid on its back in the panel-enclosed bed, with wide-gazing eyes that seemed "to sneer at her attempt to close them, and parted lips and sharp white teeth that sneered too."

Heathcliff betrays one solitary human feeling, and that is *not* his love for Catherine; which is a sentiment fierce and inhuman; a passion such as might boil and glow in the bad essence of some evil genius; a fire that might form the tormented centre—the ever-suffering soul of a magnate of the infernal world: and by its quenchless and ceaseless ravage effect the execution of the decree which dooms him to carry Hell with him wherever he wanders. No; the single link that connects Heathcliff with humanity is his rudely-confessed regard for Hareton Earnshaw—the young man whom he has ruined; and then his half-implied esteem for Nelly Dean. These solitary traits omitted, we should say he was child neither of Lascar nor gipsy, but a man's shape animated by demon life—a Ghoul—an Afreet.

Whether it is right or advisable to create beings like Heathcliff, I do not know: I scarcely think it is. But this I know: the writer who possesses the creative gift owns something of which he is not always master—something that, at times, strangely wills and works for itself. He may lay down rules and devise principles, and to rules and principles it will perhaps for years lie in subjection; and then, haply without any warning of revolt, there comes a time when it will no longer consent to "harrow the valleys, or be bound with a band in the furrow"—when it "laughs at the multitude of the city, and regards not the crying of the driver"—when, refusing absolutely to make ropes out of sea-sand any longer, it sets to work on statue-hewing, and you have a Pluto or a Jove, a Tisiphone or a Psyche, a Mermaid or a Madonna, as Fate or Inspiration direct. Be the work grim or glorious, dread or divine, you have little choice left but quiescent adoption. As for you—the nominated artist—your share in it has been to work passively under dictates you neither delivered nor could question—that would not be uttered at your prayer, nor suppressed nor changed at your caprice. If the result be attractive, the World will praise you, who little deserve praise; if it be repulsive, the same World will blame you, who almost as little deserve blame.

Wuthering Heights was hewn in a wild workshop with simple tools, out of homely materials. The statuary found a granite block on a solitary moor; gazing thereon, he saw how from the crag might be elicited a head, savage, swart, sinister; a form moulded with at least one element of grandeur—power. He wrought with a rude chisel, and from no model but the vision of his meditations. With time and labour, the crag took human shape; and there it stands colossal, dark, and frowning, half statue, half rock in the former sense, terrible and goblinlike; in the latter almost beautiful, for its colouring is of mellow grey, and moorland moss clothes it; and heath, with its blooming bells and balmy fragrance, grows faithfully close to the giant's foot.

CURRER BELL.
(Charlotte Brontë.)

54

The Relation of Novels to Life

SIR JAMES FITZJAMES STEPHEN

In one of the more discerning Victorian discussions of the nature of the novel, Sir James Fitzjames Stephen (brother of Leslie Stephen) defines the novel as a fictionalised biography in which the emphasis falls on the life of a character as opposed to dramatic incident. From this perspective Stephen judges the principal Victorian novelists to be deficient either in realistic portrayal (Dickens) or in depth of description (Thackeray). According to Stephen, only Defoe's *Robinson Crusoe* from the previous century fits his definition of the novel as realistic biography. Above all, Stephen admires Defoe's objective approach to his characters and his refusal to accumulate tedious details. Apart from his Victorian tendency to debate the moral efficacy of novels, Stephen's essay anticipates the modern focus on character over plot and the withdrawal of the meddling narrator.

We have discarded many of the amusements of our fore-fathers. Out-of-door games are almost inaccessible to the inhabitants of cities; and if they were not, people are too much tired, both in nerve and muscle, to care for them. Theatres and spectacles are less frequented than they used to be; whilst the habit of reading has become universal. These causes increase the popularity and the influence of novels, and, measured by these standards, their importance must be considered very great.

The majority of those who read for amusement, read novels. The number of young people who take from them nearly all their notions of life is very considerable. They are widely used for the diffusion of opinions. In one shape or another, they enter into the education of us all. They constitute very nearly the whole of the book-education of the unenergetic and listless.

Familiar as the word "novel" may be, it is almost the last word in the language to suggest any formal definition; but it is impossible to estimate the influence of this species of literature, or to understand how its character is determined, unless we

Source: Sir James Fitzjames Stephen, "The Relation of Novels to Life", *Cambridge Essays*, London: Parker, 1855, pp. 148-92.

have some clear notion as to what is, and what is not, included in the word.

The first requisite of a novel is, that it should be a biography,—an account of the life, or part of the life, of a person. When this principle is neglected or violated, the novel becomes tiresome; after a certain point it ceases to be a novel at all, and becomes a mere string of descriptions.

The *Arabian Nights*, perhaps, contain as slight a biographical substratum as is consistent with anything like romance. The extravagance of the incidents and scenery is their principal charm, and the different characters might be interchanged amongst the different stories, almost without notice. Who would relish the *Diamond Valley* and the *Roc's Egg* the less, if they were introduced in the *History of the three Calendars*, or in the *Adventures of Prince Caramalzaman*? and who would notice the change if either of those personages were to be substituted for *Sinbad the Sailor*? Who, on the other hand, could interchange the incidents, or the personages, of the *Memoirs of a Cavalier*, and *Robinson Crusoe*?

Perhaps the essentially biographical character of novels will be more fully displayed by comparing less extreme cases. In what does the superiority of Fielding over Mr Dickens consist? Is it not in the fact the *Tom Jones* and *Joseph Andrews* are *bona fide* histories of those persons; whilst *Nicholas Nickleby* and *Oliver Twist* are a series of sketches, of all sorts of things and people, united by various grotesque incidents, and interspersed with projects for setting the world to rights?

There is a class of books which wants only a biographical substratum to become novels. In so far as it is an account of Sir Roger de Coverley, and the Club, the *Spectator* is one of the best novels in the language; and if the original conception had been more fully carried out, that fact would have been universally recognised. It employs fictitious personages to describe manners and characters, and it sustains the interest which they excite by fictitious incidents. Yet no one would call those parts of the *Spectator* which are not biographical a novel.

Novels must also be expressly and intentionally fictitious. No amount of carelessness or dishonesty would convert into a novel what was meant for a real history. It would, for example, be an unjustifiable stretch of charity to consider the *Histoire des Girondins*, or the *Histoire de la Restauration*, as romances. On the other hand, a very small amount of intentional fiction, artistically introduced, will make a history into a novel. All the events related may be substantially true, and the fictitious characters may play a very subordinate part, and yet the result may be a novel, in the fullest sense of the word. In the *Memoirs of a Cavalier*, Gustavus Adolphus, Charles, and Fairfax occupy the most prominent places. The scenes in which they take part are generally represented with great historical fidelity. The cavalier himself, and his adventures, are only introduced as a medium for the display of the events through which he passes; but they are introduced so naturally as incidents in his life, and the gaps between them are filled with such probably and appropriate domestic occurrences, that the result is the most perfect of all historical novels.

We understand, then, by the word *novel*, a fictitious biography. Books written primarily for the purposes of instruction, or for the sake of illustrating a theory, do not fall within this definition, because they are not, properly speaking, biographies. If we suppose the hero to have been a real person, and then consider whether the object of the book was to deduce some moral, or to illustrate some theory, by his life, or to describe the man as he was, we shall be able to say whether the book is, or is not, a novel.

Thus, we should not call Plato's *Dialogues* novels, though they resemble them more nearly than any other ancient books.[1] Nor should we call the "Vision," in Tucker's *Light of Nature*, a novel, although it would fall expressly within the terms of our definitions, if it were not written merely to illustrate a theory. The miraculous separation of Search's body from his vehicle—the inconvenience which he sustained from the rays of light—his conversation with Locke—his interview with his wife—his absorption into the mundane soul—and his re-introduction into his body, form an imaginary posthumous biography, with a beginning, middle, and end; but it cannot be called a novel, inasmuch as Search and his adventures are introduced slowly in order to give life to a philosophical speculation, which is never for an instant lost sight of.

Pilgrim's Progress and the *Holy War* come nearer to the character of novels. The artistic bias of Bunyan's mind was so strong, that we should be inclined to think that he sacrificed the allegory to the story more frequently than the story to the allegory. The death of Faithful, for example, is an incident which, if the book is a novel, is as well conceived as executed; but it is consistent with the allegory, which would have required that Faithful should go to Heaven in the sense of travelling along the actual highroad till he got there. So, too, the Siege of Mansoul is much more like the Siege of Leicester than the temptations of the Devil.

There is another class of books which would be excluded from our definition by the word "fictitious." As fiction is sometimes used as a mere vehicle for opinions, so it is sometimes a mere embellishment of facts. There is a class of books in which the life of a real person is made to illustrate some particular time or country, and in which just so many fictitious circumstances are introduced as may be necessary to give a certain unity to the scenes described. The most perfect instance of his form of writing with which we are acquainted is M. Bungener's *Trois Sermons sous Louis XV.*, which is partly a history of French Protestants in the eighteenth century, partly a fictitious biography of the real man Rabaut. It has the inconvenience of constantly suggesting to the reader the impression than the author considers him incapable of taking an interest in the subject unless it is baited with a certain amount of fiction.

It is commonly said that novels supply the place of comedies; and it would perhaps be hard to put into words the distinction between them, otherwise than by the definition which we have suggested. A drama is the representation of an incident—a novel is the history of a life. Thus, the plays which composed an Æschylean trilogy consisted of the representation of separate incidents in the life of some person or the fortunes of some royal house; but if they had been permitted to run into each other, such an interference would have been a violation of the rules of dramatic art, and would have made them into a novel.

It is not always easy to say what is incident and what is biography. Shakespeare's historical plays do not fall very appropriately under either division. Some, for example, of Crabbe's tales, are miniature novels, others undramatized plays. It cannot, however, be doubted that in cases upon which no one hesitates our distinction holds good. Thus, *Waverley* is undeniably a novel, and *Romeo and Juliet* is undeniably a play. We should have been displeased if Shakespeare had introduced into his play anything not bearing upon the single subject of the love of the principal persons in it. It is, on the other hand, one of the beauties of *Waverley* that it incidentally illustrates a great number of subjects in which the hero of the novel had not personally much interest.

Novels, in the proper sense of the word, are used for a greater number of purposes than any other species of literature. Their influences on their readers may, however, be reduced within a very narrow compass. In early boyhood and in mature life they are read merely for amusement; and indulgence in them will be beneficial, or otherwise, according to the ordinary rules upon that subject. But at that time of life which intervenes between these two periods they exercise a far greater influence. They are then read as commentaries upon the life which is just opening before the reader, and as food for passions which are lately awakened but have not yet settled down to definite objects.

It may be questioned how far the habit of reading novels contributes to knowledge of the world. The undue prominence given to particular passions—such as love, the colouring used for artistic purposes, and a variety of other circumstances, are so much calculated to convey false impressions, that it may be plausibly doubted whether the impressions formed are, in fact, better than none at all.

Such a judgment appears to us too severe. If a young man were, according to Mr Carlyle's suggestion, to be shut up in a glass case from eighteen to twenty-five, and were, during that period, to be supplied with an unlimited number of novels, he would no doubt issue from his confinement with extremely false notions of the world to which he was returning; but if, during such an imprisonment, he had made it a point of conscience never to open a novel, he would, in the absence of extraordinary powers of observation and generalization, be strangely puzzled on re-entering life.

What we call knowledge of the world is acquired by the same means as other kinds of knowledge, and consists not in mere acquaintance with maxims about life, but in applying appropriate ideas to clear facts. This application can only be made by a proper arrangement and selection of the material parts of the facts observed; and this arrangement is effected, to a very great degree, by guesses and hypotheses. No one will be able to make any use of his experience of life, or to classify it in such a manner as to add to his real knowledge, unless he is provided in the first instance with some schemes or principles of classification, which he starts with, and which he enlarges, narrows, or otherwise modifies as he sees cause.

> Discoveries, it has been said,[2] are not improperly described as happy *guesses*, and guesses, in these, as in other instances, imply various suppositions made, of which some one turns out to be the right one. We may, in such cases, conceive the discoverer as inventing and trying many conjectures, till he finds one which answers

the purpose of combining the scattered facts into a single rule. The discovery of general truths from special facts is performed, commonly at least, and more commonly than at first appears, by the use of a series of suppositions, or *hypotheses*, which are looked at in quick succession, and of which the one which really leads to truth is rapidly detected, and when caught sight of, firmly held, verified, and followed to its consequences.

Nor does the indistinctness and incompleteness of their suggestions render them useless. The same author observes,—

> A maxim which it may be useful to recollect is this, that hypotheses may often be of service to science, when they involve a certain portion of incompleteness and even of errour. The object of such inventions is to bind together facts which, without them, are loose and detached; and if they do this, they may lead the way to a perception of the true rule by which the phenomena are associated together, even if they themselves misstate the matter. The imagined arrangement enables us to contemplate as a whole a collection of special cases, which perplex and overload our minds when they are considered in succession; and if our scheme has so much of truth in it as to conjoin what is really connected, we may afterwards duly connect, or limit the mechanism of this connexion.[3]

φθονερὸν ὁ δαίμων—φίλοι οὐ φίλος. "Friends follow fortune," and a thousand other proverbs, are instances of these hypothetical "guesses at truth," which are not intended to be exhaustive, but merely to set in a strong light one lesson gathered from human affairs. Novels, perhaps, offer a greater number of such hypotheses than are to be derived from any other source; and though they give them in a very confused, indefinite manner, they gain in liveliness and variety what they want in precision.

It is, however, by the materials which it affords for self-examination that novel reading enlarges our experience most efficiently. It was, if we are not mistaken, Lord Chesterfield's advice to his son, that if he wished to understand mankind he ought to be always saying to himself, "If I were to act towards that man as he acts towards me, he would feel towards me as I feel towards him." The thought that they often do act like characters represented in novels, and that people do in consequence feel towards them as they themselves regard such characters, must occur, we should think pretty frequently, to novel readers. It would be a great effort of self-denial to many of us to read *Murad the Unlucky*, or *To-morrow*; and we should think that few men could become acquainted with *George Osborne* or *Arthur Pendennis* without acquiring a consciousness of a multitude of small vanities and hypocrisies which would otherwise have escaped their attention. To produce or to stimulate self-consciousness by such means, may not be altogether a healthy process, but it is unquestionably one which has powerful effects.

In a large class of readers, novels operate most strongly by producing emotion. Strange as it seems, many people sympathize more intensely with fictitious then with historical characters. Persons who would read Carlyle's *History of the French Revolution* unmoved, would not be proof against such books as *Uncle Tom's Cabin*, or the *Heir of Redclyffe*; and we suspect that Mr Dickens has caused a great deal more emotion by some of his luscious death-bed scenes, than by what we have always considered one of the most fearful stories, both in matter and manner, which we ever read, the papers entitled *Transported for Life*,[4] in *Household Words*. Habitual emotion, whatever may be the exciting cause, produces some moral effects. A man who had really seen a negro flogged to death, or had attended a young man on his wedding tour, in a fatal illness, would probably be in some respects altered for a longer or shorter time afterwards. Whatever would be the effect of habitually witnessing such scenes, the same effect would follow in a much slighter degree from habitually reading descriptions of them; but in order to make the parallel complete we much suppose the witnessing of the scenes to be as much a matter of choice as the reading of the novels; a person who went to see a man die because he liked it would receive very different impressions from one who saw such a sight because he could not help it.

It is sometimes broadly stated that emotion produced by fiction is an evil, and tends to harden the heart. This statement goes further than its authors suppose. The parables are fictions, but we do not think any one was ever hurt by emotion produced by reading the parable of the Prodigal Son, or that of Dives and Lazarus. Emotion, also, is of many kinds. Laughter implies emotion. Is it wrong to laugh at Falstaff or Mrs Quickly? Admiration is an emotion. Even amusement, in so far as it involves interest, and is not a mere suspension of thought, implies emotion. So, too, wonder is an emotion. No one thinks it wrong to produce these emotions by fiction. In fact, the emotions of tenderness or terror are the only ones which are objected to; and since the objection will not lie against producing emotion by fiction, but only against producing these particular emotions, it must be contended that the emotions are bad in themselves, and ought only to be submitted to when unavoidably forced upon the mind. Few people would maintain this proposition when nakedly set before them.

It may, however, be remarked, that it is not easy to say what is and what is not fiction for these purposes. Is the story of *Lucretia* fiction, within the meaning of this objection? Or has it only become so since the publication of Niebuhr's *History*, and as to so many people who have read it? Or would it cease to be fiction if its substantial truth were to be established by new evidence?

Would *Mansfield Park* cease to be fiction for the purposes of the objection, if it were to appear that Miss Austen had drawn from the life, and that the grouping and connexion alone of the circumstances were invented by her? Or, if the intention of the author be considered as the test of fiction, it would be necessary to contend that a description of incidents which in all essential particulars occurred as described, ought not to produce emotion, merely because the person describing them was not aware of the degree in which his description coincided with the facts.

The moral effects of novel reading being the enlargement of the reader's knowledge of the world, and the excitement of his feelings, in what respects do such effects differ from those which similar objects might excite in real life? In other words, what adjustments and allowances must we make before the suggestions of novels can be accepted as additions to our experience?

If novels were perfectly-executed pictures of life, they would increase the reader's knowledge of life, just as paintings add to his knowledge of scenery and incident; but no information, or only very false information, is to be derived from the pictures either of novelists or of painters, unless proper allowance is made, not only for the limitations imposed upon them by the rules of their art, but also for the faults of conception and of execution most common amongst them.

One of the most obvious causes which makes novels unlike real life is the necessity under which they lie of being interesting, an object which can only be obtained by a great deal of *suppressio veri*, whence arises that *suggestio falsi* of which it is our object to point out the principal varieties.

Who would infer from one of the trial scenes which occur in almost every one of the *Waverley Novels*, what a real criminal trial was like? The mere *coup d'oeil* presented by the judges, the barristers, the prisoner, the witnesses, and the crowd of spectators, might be pretty accurately represented to any sufficiently imaginative reader by the account of the trial of Fergus McIvor and Evan Dhu Maccombich. The *State Trials* would give a juster notion of the interminable length of the indictments, the apparently irrelevant and unmeaning examinations and cross-examinations of witnesses, the skirmishing of the counsel on points of law, and the petitions of the prisoners, often painfully reasonable, for some relaxation of the rules of evidence, or procedure; but to any one who seeks mere amusement, such reading is intolerably tedious, and even when accomplished, it gives a very faint representation of the actual scene as it appeared to those who sat or stood, day after day, in all the heat, and dust, and foul air of the court-house at Carlisle or Southwark, half understanding, and—as the main points at issue got gradually drowned in their own details—half attending to the proceedings on which the lives and deaths of their friends depended. A man really present on such an occasion, and personally interested, would probably bring away impressions which a life-time would not destroy. In a novel, such a scene is at once more and less interesting than it is in fact. There are more points of interest, more dramatic situations; the circumstances are more clearly defined, and more sharply brought out than they ever would be in real life; but at the same time, that from which such circumstances derive their interest is wanting: the necessity of thought and attention, the consciousness that what is passing is most real and serious business, which it is not open to the spectators to hurry over, or to lay down and take up again at pleasure. In one word, the reality. It is in order to supply the absence of this source of interest that recourse is had to the other.

If we imagine a novel written for a reader seeking, not amusement, but information, it would be not only insupportably dull, but would be more laborious reading than any other kind of literature. Suppose that in addition to the present novel of *Waverley*, we had the muster-roll of Captain Waverley's troop, with extracts from the *Army List* of that time as to Gardiner's dragoons;—suppose we had full statements of the route of the Pretender's army, short-hand writers' notes of the proceedings of all his councils of war;—suppose the MSS. of the Jacobite divinity of Waverley's tutor, or at any rate, the plan of the work, with copious extracts, were actually printed, and all the proceedings against Fergus McIvor, and respecting the pardon of Waverley and the Baron incorporated in the book;—and suppose on the part of the reader sufficient interest and patience to go through all this mass of matter, no one can doubt that he would know much more about Waverley and his fortunes than ordinary readers do know. If, however, *Waverley* had been composed upon this principle, the conversations and descriptions, which give it all its charm, would have been greatly curtailed. A person who had toiled, notebook and atlas in hand, through all sorts of authorities, geographical, historical, antiquarian, and legal, about the Highland line, black-mail, and the heritable jurisdictions, would have little taste for the conversations between Waverley, Rose Bradwardine, Even Dhu, and the Baron, upon the same subjects. They contemplate a frame of mind altogether different.[5]

The *suppressio veri* which occurs in novels may therefore be considered as an essential feature of that kind of literature, but it involves a *suggestio falsi* which is not so obvious, and has more tendency to mislead readers.

It requires but very little experience of life to be aware that the circumstances stated in a novel form a very small part of what must have actually occurred to the persons represented; but it requires more experience to see in what respects the fact that all dull matter is suppressed, falsifies the representation of what is actually described.

The most remarkable of all the modifications with which novels represent real life consists in the way in which such suppressions distort their representations of character.

These representations differ from the thing represented much as a portrait differs from a real face. A child would probably prefer the portrait to the face, because its colours are more definite, smoother, and less altered by the various disturbing causes which act upon the living body. This difference is a consequence of yielding to the temptation, under which novelists continually labour, of taking an entirely different view of character from those who seek not to represent, but to understand it.

The easiest way of representing character is to represent it as a set of qualities which belong to different men, as colour, weight, and form belong to different substances; to represent brave actions as resulting from a quality of courage in one man, or wise actions from a quality of wisdom in another, just as knives cut because they are sharp, or lead sinks because it is heavy. No one who takes his views of character from life would accept this as a fair representation of it. Whatever ultimate differences not resolvable by any analysis there may be between one man and another, no one can seriously doubt that far the most important differences between men are differences of habit. What we call character is little else than a collection of habits, whether their formation is to be traced to original organic differences or to any other causes.

Almost everybody likes and dislikes the same things. Everybody likes praise, everybody likes knowledge, everybody likes distinction, everybody likes action; but everybody likes rest, and ease, and safety, and dislikes trouble, risk, and defeat. The difference between different people is that in some, for whatever reason, the passions which involve immediate self-denial conquer those which involve immediate self-indulgence, whilst in others the opposite happens, and thus some habits are acquired with great ease and completeness, others at the expense of a good deal of effort and self-restraint, and therefore much less completely. A man may be a very brave man, and yet do very cowardly things, as he may be very prudent, and yet do very foolish things.

Probably no one can look back upon his own history without recalling innumerable inconsistencies in his own conduct and in the conduct of those about him, with the principles which it has been their most earnest desire to recognise, and the habits which they have been forming for years. But though life is full of shortcomings and inconsistencies arising from this cause, novels are not. The difficulty of conceiving or representing differences which vary in every case would of course be very great, and the flow of the story would be interrupted by them. Character, in novels, therefore, is represented as far more homogeneous and consistent than it ever really is. Men are made cowards or brave, foolish or wise, affectionate or morose, just as they are represented as being tall or short, red-haired or black-haired, handsome or ugly.

It is to this origin that we are indebted for the mass of melodramatic or merely conventional characters, which form the staple of some novel writers, and which appear in greater or less numbers even in the most distinguished.

The heroes of the Waverley novels, one and all, belong to this class. They have certain characters assigned to them, and act accordingly throughout the whole story, never rising above or falling below a certain ill-defined, but well-understood, level of thought and conduct which is appropriated to such persons. There is no effort, no incompleteness, about these characters. Any one of them could be described by a certain number of adjectives. All of them possess certain muscular and amatory qualifications for their office of hero, all of them are brave, most of them generous, some determined, and some irresolute, but none of them display the variety, the incompleteness, the inconsistency, which almost all men show in real life.

If we look either at history, or at the very highest class of fiction, we shall find it impossible to exhaust a man's character by adjectives. Who could describe Cromwell, or William III., or Voltaire, or Falstaff, or Hamlet in this manner? It is only by reflection and comparison that we can tell what kind of persons Shakespeare's characters were intended to represent, just as it is only by studying and reflecting upon the different actions of their lives that we can become acquainted with any real personage whatever, historical or contemporary. The great mass of characters in novels may be weighed and measured, and their qualities may be enumerated, with as much ease and precision as we could count the squares in a chess-board, and describe their colours.

A novelist always has some kind of scheme in his mind, according to which he draws his picture; and this scheme becomes sufficiently obvious to the reader long before he has finished the novel. In real life, on the contrary, we are obliged to take people as they come, and to form our opinions of their characters as time and opportunity happen to display them to us.

Men whose opinion is worth anything upon such matters are very cautious indeed in describing characters by a few broad phrases; for no lesson is sooner learnt than that such general language requires to be modified in innumerable ways before it can, with any kind of correctness, be applied to any individual case. In life character is inferred from actions, in most novels actions are ascribed to particular people in order to illustrate the author's conceptions respecting their character. Language, therefore, is as inadequate, when applied to real persons, as it is adequate and exhaustive when applied to the common run of fictitious ones.

Even the most prominent figures in a novel are represented in a very imperfect manner. The object of a fictitious biography is to enlist the curiosity, which a real biography presupposes. It therefore seeks to lay before the reader rather a vivid picture than an historical account of a character. To exhibit a great man as he really is the novelist would have to be himself a greater man than the person represented, and the few cases in which this has really been done are universally recognised as the very highest efforts of genius. Hamlet, King Lear, and Henry V., Satan in *Paradise Lost*,[6] and to some extent perhaps Prometheus, not only act as people capable of great things might act, but they absolutely do the great things themselves before us. It is, however, only in the very highest class of fiction that this is possible. In ordinary novels the labour necessary to effect such an object would be improvidently invested. If any one of the numerous biographies of popular clergymen which are so common in the present day were from beginning to end an entire fiction, it would be no doubt the most extraordinary feat of imagination ever performed. But few people, and those members of a very limited class, would care to read it. Novelists, therefore, are generally in the habit of representing people rather by their behaviour in the less than in the more important affairs of life. They say, A. B., being otherwise a remarkable man, acted thus or thus in relation to his marriage. We assume, for the purposes of the novel, that he was a remarkable man *aliunde*, and we consider the representation successful or not according as it corresponds or otherwise with this assumption.

There is always, however, a certain amount of risk that the reader will suppose that the author means to describe a man as he is, instead of giving a mere sketch, more or less perfect, of certain features in his manners. Hence they might come to draw a wider inference from the book than it was calculated to support, and to suppose that, because in this or that particular case, certain qualities were displayed by particular symptoms, there is, therefore, a necessary and universal connexion between the characters and the symptoms. Thus Byron suggests to many persons an association between misery and gloom on the one hand, and genius on the other, though, if we look at the books themselves, we have only Lord Byron's own word for the power or capacity of any kind, of Lara, and the Giaour, and the rest. No doubt he only exercised in author's prerogative in making such statements respecting them as matter of fact; but all that he shows of their characters is not in any way inconsistent with their having been as weak as they were bad. Byron's is an extreme case, but almost every writer who has obtained any considerable popularity has, more or less, misled his readers in this manner. To be able to do so is a proof, which few people can give, of the power of interesting and enlisting sympathy.

The most remarkable instance of this is afforded by Mr Thackeray. As there is no writer who has shown greater genius in representing a particular view of life, so there is none whose books contain greater omissions, or whose omissions are more likely to mislead, on account of the wonderful impartiality and many-sidedness of his characters. The first impression received from reading almost any one of his books is, that it exhausts the subject to which it refers; but a very little experience will show that the perfection of the observation, so far as it goes, is only equalled by the narrowness of its range. In the whole of Mr Thackeray's books, there is hardly a hint of such a thing as the serious business in life. All his characters are represented either in their leisure moments, or as men whose whole life is leisure. Hardly any important transaction of any kind whatever (except the usual number of marriages) enters into any one of his books. Even when the course of his story brings him near an event in which the stronger passions and energies are displayed, he instinctively avoids it, often with consummate skill. The wonderful description of the scenes which passed at Brussels, during the battle of Waterloo is, perhaps, the most striking instance of this. *Scriberis Vario* is his constant motto; and we have the actors in one of the greatest scenes in history set before us, as they flirted, and danced, and lounged—not as they planned, and felt, and fought.

There is not in all Mr Thackeray's novels a character who is described by his great qualities; all are described by their small peculiarities. Yet a man of his genius cannot have failed to observe that men differ from each other far more radically in the great leading habits which they have acquired than in the small affectations or weaknesses by which he generally specifies them. In *Pendennis*, for example, the principal characters are literary barristers, but nothing turns upon their law or their literature, except that it is stated as a matter of fact, that they earned an income by the last. Warrington is represented as being a man of great originality—full of powerful thought, scholarship, and knowledge of various kinds; but we have none of the powerful thought, or scholarship, or knowledge, produced in the book; still less are any incidents introduced to give scope to them. We certainly get the impression that Warrington was a man of vigorous understanding; but we get it from learning that he behaved in the commonest affairs of life as such a man might be supposed to behave, not from any description of the remarkable things which he did. To prove that he really was what Mr Thackeray calls him, we ought to have had an account of his social, political, and legal opinions, and the reasons why he adopted them. We ought to have had specimens of his reviews and leading articles.

Suppose two writers had invented, out of their own heads, such a character as Lord Chatham, and that one of them had described him talking to his sons, rehearsing his orations, flannel and crutch all prepared, keeping five or six dinners cooking all at once, and so forth; and that the other had invented the whole scheme of his policy in relation to the Seven Years' War, and had composed and put into his mouth the speeches which he made about the American Revolution. The first would have shown how a great man might behave, and the second would have shown what a great man was. The mistake into which such novels as Mr Thackeray's might easily lead an inexperienced person, is the supposition that he had read a book of the second, and not of the first kind.

We do not venture to criticise Mr Thackeray's choice of characters. We only wish to point out that the very perfection with which parts of them are represented might lead some persons to suppose that the representation is more complete than Mr Thackeray meant it to be.

It would be difficult to find in Mr Thackeray's works an example of another fault, very common amongst novelists, and perhaps more fatal than any other to the correctness of their representations of life. In fact, his whole career may be considered as a protest against it. This is what Mr Macaulay has called the *lues Boswelliana*, applied to the creations of a man's own brain.

The hero-worship of authors is a love passing the love of women. The hero of a novel is the child of the author's experience, of his love, of his passions, of his vanity, of his philosophy; yet he is not a picture of himself in such a sense as to establish between them that unlimited liability for each others' shortcomings which is the essence of partnership. A hero is an embodied day-dream, with paper and ink for flesh and blood; and all of us know how large a part we ourselves play in our own day-dreams. The hero of a novel may not be like the author. He may be ludicrously unlike; but it is hardly possible that the furniture of his mind should not have been supplied by the author from his own mental stores, although its arrangement in the two men may differ. The reason is, that we know our own feelings, but we only know other men's actions, and infer from them that they feel as we should feel if we were to act in the same manner. Therefore, when we are to describe feelings as they present themselves to us upon introspection, and not as we view them in, or infer them from, other people's acts, we must necessarily draw from ourselves, as we have no other models. I know that when A. was angry he spoke harshly, that B. imputed ungenerous motives, that C. misrepresented, and so on; but I can only infer the feelings of A., B., and C., when they so acted, from my own experience of my own feelings when I acted in the same way. But though a writer cannot but invest his characters with many of his own feelings, he by no means necessarily identifies himself with all or any of them. Conscious that he is likely to be charged with drawing from himself, he probably avoids doing so explicitly and consciously, whilst he allows the favourite points of his own character to look out upon him, more or less, from his canvas. An author, under such circumstances, has some resemblance to an artist colouring a photograph. The main lines are drawn for him, and recall his own features, but he is at liberty to add what he pleases. Sometimes, probably, he paints his hero as he would wish to be, sometimes as he would not wish to be; but, unless such characters as he represents at full length, with all their feelings and mental peculiarities, have some relation to him, it is hard to say to what they are related.

Whatever may be the origin of the fact, we take the fact to be quite certain, that there is a large class of novels in which all the incidents are arranged so as to give prominence to one particular view of life, and to present it, as it might be supposed to present itself to the eyes of some one person, who, (with some modifications) acts as hero in a whole series of novels.

Perhaps there is no one thing which so entirely distorts facts as this habit. It is like looking at the world through coloured spectacles; and it engenders a wretched class of imitators, who, as we seriously believe, do harm in society.

The vexed question, as to the morality of representing bad characters in a novel, is possibly to be solved upon this principle. If it is universally true that the representation of wicked characters is objectionable, it would be hard to deny that all representation of human character is objectionable; inasmuch as there is no character which does not contain some admixture of wickedness. On the other hand, it is impossible to deny that there are some vices which can hardly be represented without mischief both to the writer and the reader. It would appear that the morality or immorality of such representations by no means depends upon the heinousness of the character described. It would be difficult to imagine a more wicked character than Iago, or a less immoral play than *Othello*. The Bible is full of descriptions of most atrocious crimes of all sorts, and it would be natural to suppose that the fact that they are related historically would make them more, and not less, injurious than they would be if related as fictions, because the interest is greater.

The moral effect of men upon each other depends upon their intimacy. No one is made wicked by knowing that bad people exist. Most people would become wicked if all their intimate friends were so. Characters in novels may be considered as being more or less intimate acquaintances, and as they are represented upon two different principles, they may be divided into two classes.

The characters of one class are represented from without—those of the other class from within. The classification is neither exact nor complete, because almost all characters are depicted partly from one point of view, partly from the other; but these are the limits towards which such representations approximate in a greater or less degree. We should say that the latter class exercise very little moral influence over any one. They are merely more or less honest and accurate representations of facts. The other class of characters exercises the same *kind* of influence over readers as actual acquaintances with the living persons. In order to ascertain the *degree* of influence, we must not only suppose the acquaintanceship to have been limited to the time consumed in reading or thinking over the novel, and to the circumstances mentioned in it, but as existing subject to those deductions which we have indicated above as implied in the existence of novels. How far such acquaintanceship is injurious or otherwise, is a question for individuals.

It is to be observed, however, that the immoral writing which gives the greatest and most reasonable offence, is immoral specifically, and consists of detailed descriptions of subjects on which the mind cannot be suffered to rest without injury. This class of offences is mostly of a sufficiently obvious kind. It is nearly allied to what, in our own time and country, is a far more probably evil—a conscious delicacy, which suggests improper thoughts by carefully avoiding all mention of vices which must be referred to if life is to be depicted at all, and which would excite no improper feelings if referred to without unnecessary detail.

The secondary characters in a novel are, perhaps, even more distorted than the heroes. The existence of a plot makes it necessary to represent men and women in their relation to the groups of which they form parts, and not substantively. Hence the different personages have apparently a much closer connexion, and more intimate sympathy with each other, than they would have under similar circumstances in real life.

If *The Antiquary*, for example, had been a real history, it would have been incorrect, amongst other things, in representing Lovel, the antiquary, Sir Arthur Wardour, and the rest of the characters, as taking a much deeper interest in each other than they did in fact. If Jonathan Oldbuck had been a real man, he would have had, after a very few years, to consider and recollect himself before he could say precisely in which year it was that Miss Wardour was married, and he would have been far more likely to have fixed the date of her marriage by its coincidence with some of his every-day business, than to have dated his dissertations from it. This is not the impression which the novel leaves on the reader's mind.

He considers all its characters as forming one group, and as taking that kind of intimate interest in each others' fortunes which they would take if they formed such a group by nature, instead of being compressed into it for artistic purposes. The connexion stated between the different characters of a novel, is generally such as in real life would attract but little attention; but the fact that nothing is known of such characters, except what is contained in the novel, makes the reader forget that in real life the secondary characters would have histories of their own, and suggests to him the conclusion, that they had nothing else to love or care for in life except the hero and heroine, and nothing to look forward to except their marriage. If a distant mountain range forms the background of a picture, it is represented by very few and very slight strokes of the brush; but if the rest of the picture were cut away, no one would know that these strokes were intended to represent mountains, nor would any one, on seeing real mountains, recognise them by their resemblance to those so represented.

In the same way the less prominent characters of a novel are only like one particular aspect of the real persons, and not only throw almost no light at all upon such characters in real life, but sometimes mislead people into the notion that, by reason of their acquaintance with some of their prominent peculiarities, they are better acquainted with them than is, in fact, the case.

For example, there is, in one of Sir E. Lytton's novels, an old soldier whose character it is, to boast of his selfishness and knowledge of the world. In another, the hero lodges with a man whose character it is to keep constantly making the same pun about rolls and swallows. In a third, there is a strolling vagabond, whose character it is to quote scraps of Shakespeare. All of these men would, in real life, have had a great deal more in them than this; they would have had schemes, objects in life, connexions, talents—in a word, characters,—and such caprices as these would go but a very little way towards displaying them.

It is a great beauty in a novel to give glimpses of the life which the secondary characters lived when they were not within the field of the novelist's camera obscura. In *Pendennis* we get a most ingeniously contrived glimpse of the career of the gentleman who lent his chambers to the hero. How he was presented at court, and entangled himself in a lady's train, who turned out to be the daughter of "that eminent Queen's Counsel, Mr Kewsy," who subsequently became his wife, and he a county-court judge. Many writers would have left on their readers no other impression about this person than that he had lent Mr Pendennis his chambers, and was in the habit of making some pet speech, or indulging some whimsical caprice.

The incompleteness, and consequent incorrectness of the information conveyed by novels, distorts facts even more than characters. The most familiar of all illustrations of the defect is to be found in novels of adventure. Captain Marryat, Cooper, and other writers of that class, not only suppress a great many facts for the sake of interest, but, by the very fact of such suppression, they entirely falsify the characters of those which are represented.

Thus, Captain Marryat leaves on the mind the impression that curious companions, strange adventures, and ever-changing excitement, in one shape or another, are the staple of a sailor's life, instead of being exceptional occurrences. Compare Southey's *Life of Nelson*, with its dreary tracts of blockading, cruising, delay, and disappointments of all kinds,—or a volume of James's *Naval History*, with its indecisive, unromantic actions and enterprises,—with *Peter Simple* or *Midshipman Easy*, which are one continued series of wonderful storms and battles, and the nature of the varnish applied by novelists to reality will become curiously evident. This is an extreme case, but the same principle must be applied more or less to all novels before their suggestions can be accepted as fair representations of life. Even Miss Austen, whose books convey an impression of reality altogether extraordinary, culls out and pieces together a succession of small incidents, so contrived as to develop, step by step, the characters of the persons represented. Each incident, taken by itself, is so exquisitely natural, and so carefully introduced, that it requires considerable attention to detect the improbability of the story. That improbability consists in the sequence of the incidents wanted. It is likely enough that incidents should sometimes happen which throw a light on character, but it is not probable that a series of incidents should occur, one after the other, all throwing light on different parts of the same character, as if they had been arranged for the express purpose of bringing out every feature of it in succession. Nor must it be forgotten that the importance and significance of an incident is much greater when it is one in a series, as in a novel, than where it stands by itself, as in real life.

The circumstances which, when combined and arranged, form a novel, would, in reality, lie widely scattered over the surface of life, the attention of the actors in them being diverted to other affairs, quite unfit for the purposes of a novelist. Thus, when any of these events occurred, it would not strike those who were concerned in it, or who were witnesses of it, as being in any degree a romantic incident. Its connexion with the other circumstances which impart to it its romantic character, would be so overlaid by the other affairs of life, that their relation to each other would escape observation.

Few novels have been written with a plot more elaborately contrived, or dexterously brought out, than *Caleb Williams*; but would the circumstances have impressed themselves upon the mind of a person who witnessed their real occurrence in the connected pictorial manner in which they appear to the readers of the novel?

Caleb Williams is taken into the service of a rich gentleman, Mr Falkland, whom he discovers to have murdered Mr Tyrrel, some years before. Incautiously informing his master of his discovery, he tempts him to take advantage of an opportunity of accusing him, with every appearance of truth, of committing an aggravated robbery. His master, satisfied with destroying his character, offers no evidence against him at the trial, and he is acquitted. Wherever he goes he is followed by Falkland's agents, who expose his character and deprive him of one situation after another, until, at last, he resolves to turn upon his master in self-defence, reiterates accusations (which he had formerly made and retracted) of the murder of Tyrrel, and choosing his time for the accusation[7] ingeniously, extorts from Mr Falkland a confession, not only of his murder of Tyrrel, but of the falsehood of his accusations against himself.

Nothing can be more remarkable than the skill with which this story is developed step by step, each leading to, and each bearing upon the next. But if we suppose the events really to have occurred, would any ordinary person have remarked their connexion? In the novel, Caleb Williams's introduction to Falkland's house, and the story he hears from the steward about his master's history, at once arrest the reader's attention, and introduce all that follows. In real life, the gossip of two servants about their master's affairs would attract no attention at all, or would only be noticed as one of the little vexations incidental to keeping a large establishment. When Falkland has been introduced in a manner calculated to awaken attention and curiosity, a variety of small characteristic conversations and allusions—immediately detected by the least experienced novel reader as being characteristic and important—are introduced in order to heighten the mystery and curiosity. In real life, such things would have passed unnoticed, or, if noticed, any one but a confirmed meddler and gossip would have set them down to the account of casual ill-temper or bad digestion, or to any other insignificant cause. The transaction about the robbery would have amounted to this—that there was strong reason to suppose a clerk had robbed his master; that there was a kind of possibility that the master wanted to get rid of the clerk; and so the matter would have stood for many months, and in the meantime Falkland, and his relations, and servants, and acquaintance would have hardly given a thought to Caleb Williams and his affairs. They would have had business, and formed habits and connexions far more interesting to themselves than any in which Williams had a part, and he and his trial would have subtended a very small angle indeed in their range of vision, instead of forming, as by the novelist's art they are made to do, the centre upon which all their fortunes depend.

Perhaps the necessity of modifying the representation made by novels of the different events which occur in them, may be more fully illustrated by supposing that the story of *Caleb Williams* is only his way of accounting for, and connecting, certain admitted facts: such as the fact that Mr Tyrrel was murdered; that Mr Falkland was tried for the murder, and acquitted; that he led a retired life; that Caleb Williams was taken into his service, and left it under an accusation, true or false, of robbery; that Williams was committed to gaol; that he escaped, was retaken, tried, and, by the kindness of his prosecutor, acquitted; that he wandered about the country, and lost situations from a report of his conduct; that he went to Mr Falkland's house during his last illness, accused him of murder, and caused him to make certain statements. Might it not be open to Mr Falkland's friends to contend, and would they not contend with the greatest force, that the story was all false from beginning to end, and that it bore upon it every mark of being so; that all the tales about Falkland's conversations with Williams were mere fictions, artfully constructed on information obtained from a gossiping old man, in order to supply a means of explaining conduct which was in fact a treacherous robbery of a master by a confidential servant; that Williams's escape from prison was a confession of guilt; that his subsequent acquittal was simply owing to his master's reluctance to have him hanged; that his loss of his situations was the natural and necessary consequence of his crime; that his report of Falkland's last conversation was a garbled account of the weak, confused language of a dying man about matters in which he had at any rate suffered most cruelly; and that to suppose Falkland guilty of murder merely because a discharged servant, who had formerly made and retracted the same accusation, a probable robber, and a man who, according to his own confession, associated with a gang of highwaymen, said that his master had chosen him of all mankind as his confessor, would be to consider the solemn verdict of a jury as less cogent than the unsupported evidence of a single interested and untrustworthy witness.

This, however, is not the impression which the mere perusal of the novel leaves upon the mind. It is of the essence of a novel to assume not only the infallibility of the narrator as to the matters of fact which he relates, but also as to the bearing of the facts related upon each other; and it would lead to constant mistakes to suppose that the circumstances which in a novel prove the guilt, or the love, or the wisdom, which the novelist attributes to his hero, would prove the same things in real life. A still more curious illustration of this is the alterations of facts which occur in historical novels. As novels cannot be taken to be histories without a good deal of management and allowance, so history cannot be readily woven into novels without corresponding distortions.

Two curious instances of this are to be found in Colonel Everard, the hero of *Woodstock*, and Henry Morton, the hero of *Old Mortality*. Characters of that stamp were not likely to be found amongst Puritans or Covenanters. Sir Walter Scott was not the man to enter into the feelings either of Cromwell or of Balfour of Burley, in such a manner as to make their passions real objects of interest. Inasmuch, however, as some hero with whom his readers could sympathize was necessary, he provides two young men who talk the language and think the thoughts of the end of the eighteenth century to the men of the seventeenth, with a sort of unconscious simplicity and *bonâ fide* belief in their own superiority over those amongst whom they live, which is not only curious in itself, but is especially curious as an illustration of the radical differences between romance and history.

There is something in the quiet, easy, plausible solution of all the difficulties, which seemed so vital to all the greatest men of their time, at which Everard and Morton have arrived, and in the calm superiority with which they estimate and patronize them, with more or less disapproval, which in real life would be contemptible, but which in a novel does not exactly shock us, because we understand, or at any rate feel, its congruity with the scope of such books. Far the most curious illustration of this predominance of the novel atmosphere over fact which we can remember, is to be found in Mr Lockhart's novel of *Valerius*. The curious Paleyan process by which Valerius, on reading a MS. of one of the Gospels lent him by a Christian under persecution, becomes convinced of "the candour and veracity of the author," would have astonished the contemporaries of Origen about as much as the acquisition of an estate worth something like a million and a half sterling as the providential reward of a pagan's conversion to Christianity.

Somewhat similar in its effects is the habit of supposing that the importance of events in real life is commensurate with their importance in novels. The well-known dogma of Aristotle, that the object of a tragedy is to excite terror and pity, might be paraphrased by saying that it is the object of a novel to describe love ending in marriage. Marriage in novels occupies almost always the position which death occupies in real life: it is the art of transition into a new state, with which novelists (with some very rare exceptions) have little or nothing to do. No doubt, a happy marriage is to a woman what success in any of the careers of life is to a man. It is almost the only profession which society, as at present constituted, opens to her. The mistake of novelists lies not so much in overrating the importance of marriage, as in the assumed universality of the passion of love, in their sense of the word. The notion which so many novels suggest—that if two people who have a violent passion for each other marry, they have necessarily acted wisely,—is as unfounded as the converse, that if two people marry without such a passion, they act unwisely.

It would be impossible for any one to dispute altogether the existence of some such passion as is the foundation of most novels; but it may safely be affirmed that it is very uncommon, that it is a very doubtful good when it exists, and that the love which the Prayer Book seems to consider as a condition subsequent to marriage, is something much more common and very different. In novels it is considered as the cause, in the Prayer Book as what ought to be the effect of marriage; and we suspect that the divines have been shrewder observers of human nature than the men of the world. In the morality of almost all novelists, the promise ought to be, not "I will love," but "I declare that I do love." The wisdom or otherwise of a step upon which so much of the happiness of life must turn, is made to depend, not on the mutual forbearance and kindly exertions of the two persons principally interested, but upon their feeling an exceptional and transitory passion at a particular moment.

To attempt to give an accurate definition, or even description of love, would be presumptuous, if not pedantic; but it may safely be affirmed that one of its most important constituent parts, if not its essence, is to be found in a willingness to discharge the duties implied in the relation of the persons loving, in order to please or benefit each other. Love between the sexes is not the only kind of love in the world. Its specific peculiarities arise, like the specific peculiarities of all other kinds of love, from the peculiar relations and duties implied in the relation of husband and wife, which, however, operate principally by giving colour to the common sentiments of friendship and confidence, and, above all, to those which spring from the habits of society. To use the language of a very great man (employed in maintaining a proposition which to some may seem questionable)—

> It must be carefully remembered, that the general happiness of married life is secured by its indissolubility. When people understand that they must live together, except for a very few reasons known to the law, they learn to soften, by mutual accommodation, that yoke which they know they cannot shake off, and become good husbands and good wives from the necessity of remaining husbands and wives. For necessity is a powerful master in teaching the duties. If it were once understood that, upon mutual disgust, married persons might be legally separated, many a couple who now pass through the world with mutual comfort, with attention to their common offspring, and to the moral order of civil society, might have been at this moment living in a state of mutual unkindness, in a state of estrangement from their common offspring, in a state of the most licentious morality.[8]

The habit of finishing a novel with the marriage of the hero and heroine, is quite in accordance with the view of love which we have been reprobating. It would seem ludicrous to conclude the history of a man's professional career with the act of his entering upon his profession; but it is an all but universal practice to conclude a representation of him, as a social and feeling being, with his marriage. Why? Because a person is supposed to enter on a profession in order to do something in it, and to marry only to gratify his passions.

The necessity of interesting the reader by what is represented, and the necessity of suppressing all that is dull, taken together, are the reasons why novelists fall into the habit of distorting facts in order to produce an unnatural excitement of feeling.

In real life, the announcement of a person's death, or marriage, produces a certain effect, varying with our attachment to the person concerned. The same announcement about a fictitious character would produce no effect at all by its own weight; therefore, in order to make it affecting, novelists are obliged to have recourse to what we now call sentimentality. "Affectation," if the word were used in a more restricted sense than it generally bears, would be a more correct, though perhaps less expressive, name for the habit of mind which we wish to describe.

Etymologically, "sentimental" ought to mean, capable of sentiment; and, inasmuch as sentiment is nothing else than feeling, every man, and indeed every animal, might be described as being in that sense "sentimental;" but the meaning which we popularly attach to the word has become considerably extended in some respects, and much narrowed in others. It denotes, not a capability of any sort of feeling, but the habitual indulgence of one particular class of feelings; that is to say, tenderness, and principally tenderness by way of association, and it is seldom used without implying disapprobation. There are certain secondary pleasures attendant upon almost all kinds of sorrow. Sorrow calls out many good qualities, the recollection of which is in itself pleasant. The sorrow of others furnishes an occasion for the feelings of pity and generosity, as well as for that less amiable gratification implied in the "*Suave mari magno.*" There is a certain interest and sympathy of which people in unfortunate circumstances are the object, both at their own hands and at the hands of others, such as Charles Lamb has very agreeably described in his essay on the *Pleasures of Sickness*. Now, when a man describes sorrow in writing, painting, or speaking, not substantively, but with an eye to these alleviations and associations, we call such a description sentimental. Thus, the description of Lefevre's death, in *Tristram Shandy*, is sentimental, because it is impossible to read it without feeling that it is introduced in order to set off Uncle Toby's generosity and Lefevre's affection for his son; but no one would call Burns' address to *Mary in Heaven* sentimental, because there the grief is the substantive part of the poem, and the description of scenery merely an accessory.

For our present purposes, therefore, "sentimentality" may be described as being that way of writing which makes use of emotions of tenderness or the like, as accessories for the purpose of heightening an artistic effect, whether that effect is to be produced by the description of other feelings, or merely by the skilful handling of details. The state of human affairs is probably such that no one could conceive a consistent story without being naturally and unavoidably led to describe many painful things, and no one can be blamed for describing such subjects in a spirited manner, if he describes them gravely, and because they lie straight in his path; but we do not know of a habit more likely to injure the interests, both of art and of morals, than that of describing death and kindred subjects as accessories to matters of inferior importance, or for the sake of displaying skill in handling details.

There is one writer in our own day who entirely exemplifies our meaning: this is Mr Dickens.

We will take only one instance of his sentimentality,—his treatment of the subject of death. There are some aspects of death of which we wish to say nothing; but if we consider it simply as it affects the survivors, it cannot be regarded as connected exclusively with painful associations. The feelings excited by the death of a friend are, first, a feeling of solemn awe, which is not deepened, but weakened, by anything which diverts the attention from the naked fact. "He is dead," is all that is to be said upon the subject; and any phrases whatever beyond that or its equivalents have a tendency to distract the mind, and so far to lessen the solemnity of the feelings excited. It would not be true to say that this sensation is entirely painful. To a sluggish imagination, the mere excitement is far from being altogether unpleasant. The dim view of a world of mysteries, in the midst of which we live and move, has something in it which relieves the tedium and ennobles the trivialities of common life; but when we weigh this against the utter separation, the end—for aught we know, the final end—of so many kindly sympathies and warm activities, there is something loathsome in the notion of a man's being willing to call up the one set of associations for the sake of playing with the other; and when we recollect the lighter associations which accompany death, the expressions of affection, the leave-takings, the little touching incidents to which the unconscious simplicity of the dying person may give rise, we cannot but feel that the mere recollection of such things involves an unutterable, an almost sacred sadness, and that there is an absence of feeling in displaying that which gives them all their sadness in order to set off their beauty, which reminds us of nothing so much as the mumbling satisfaction of the old Grandmother in the *Antiquary*, at the wine and cakes handed round at her grandson's funeral. Now, Mr

Dickens, not once or twice, but continually, brings death upon the stage, apparently for no one reason but that of showing his skill in arranging affecting details so as to give them this horrible pungency. Paul Dombey, Eleanor Trent, Dora Copperfield, Richard Carstone (who dies partly to spite the Court of Chancery, and partly to give Miss Summerson an opportunity of showing how conscious she is of her unconscious sweetness and piety), Oliver Twist's mother, and Smike,[9] are a few of the instances which occur to us of this toying with the disgrace of our nature. We do not wish to write lightly on such a subject; but let us compare Mr Dickens's treatment of death with some others.

Having to describe the death of a young woman who dies very unnecessarily, after rambling about the country with her grandfather, Mr Dickens first introduces a little boy dying quietly enough, then he brings in an old sexton of seventy-nine, whose peculiarity is that he does *not* die, and does not expect to do so. Appended to the sexton are a church and out-houses, with carved wainscots, and windows looking out on the graves. Having arranged the scene, we have the time—a winter night and a snow-storm—and the chorus, in the shape of all sorts of anxious admirers; then comes the scene over which so many foolish tears have been shed, and which reminds us of nothing so much as the hackneyed quotation about the difficulty of driving a dog from a greasy hide. He gloats over the girl's death as if it delighted him; he looks at it from four or five points of view; touches, tastes, smells, and handles it as if it was some savoury dainty which could not be too fully appreciated.

The description consists of six paragraphs (some in blank verse) of which three begin with the words, "She was dead." The first is introductory; the second describes her as being asleep; the third relates to the bed; the fourth to a certain bird; the fifth to the subject's beautiful appearance; and the sixth to its face. The whole concludes with a questionable statement as to what the angels will look like, which suggests that even upon artistic grounds it is as well not to intrude into things which we have not seen.

Perhaps the prophet Ezekiel thought of death as solemnly as Mr Dickens, and loved his wife as much as Mr Dickens cared for his little tragedy queen; but he tells us nothing of her bed, nor of what he put on it, nor about her face, nor her bird—

> *Ezekiel* xxiv. 15-18. "Son of man, behold I take from thee the desire of thine eyes with a stroke, yet neither shalt thou mourn nor weep, neither shall thy tears run down. Forbear to cry, make no mourning for the dead, bind the tire of thy head upon thee, and put on they shoes upon thy feet, and cover not thy lips, and eat not the bread of men. So I spake unto the people in the morning, and at even my wife died; and I did in the morning as I was commanded."

Though Ezekiel was commanded not to mourn, it does not appear that he was forbidden to linger on the details of his wife's death, to describe her face, her bed, her ornaments, and to put little bits of pretty simplicity into her mouth. But he was not only an inspired prophet, but a brave man, who wrote with modesty and self-respect.

This is but one illustration out of ten thousand, of the spirit which leads people to indulge their timidity or their love of luxury, by disregarding the essential points of observation for the sake of accessories, and instead of looking death, and grief, and pain in the face, to trifle with the dramatic incidents by which they may be attended.

Another consequence of the suppression of so large a proportion of the facts which in real life carry on the business of the world is to be found in the invention of masses of what the critics in the last century used to call "machinery," and what is perhaps better known in the present day under its theatrical slang name of "business." Almost every author has his *Di minorum* or *majorum gentium* in reserve for such knots as may occur in his story. Scott or Sir E. Lytton have generally some funny man—some Andrew Fairservice, or Corporal Bung—hanging about the story, ready to help matters on as a kind of prose comic chorus, or to disentangle any embarrassment which may arise, by throwing an air of absurdity over it.

If hardship, or poverty, or sickness is to be represented, almost all writers of novels bring in a Caleb Balderstone, to invent shifts for filling his hero's larder, or a Mrs Flanagan, to steal his spirits under pretence of giving him medicine, that the reader's mind may not be unduly shocked.

Mr Dickens seems to us the greatest master of this kind of artifice, but his method is most peculiar. It consists in giving an entirely factitious prominence to minute peculiarities. He constantly gives expression, almost personality, to inanimate objects. He invests the most ordinary affairs of life with a certain charm and poetry. It is abundantly clear that this is what none but a man of genius could do. Nor is it an illusion which would be likely to deceive any one. Nobody ever lived in the world without finding plenty of dullness in it, and no quantity of verbal artifice would make him forget it; but though artifices like these may not deceive, they are still deviations from reality, and are to be allowed for before a novel can be considered as a picture of life.

There are dwarfs in real life, and the circumstance of bodily deformity no doubt exercises a powerful influence over character, but a little imp, with some slight resemblance to a man and a vast preponderance of the devil, like Quilp, or a "recluse," like the Black Dwarf, are what Addison calls "machines" peculiar to novelists, and without representatives in real life.

Descriptions of scenery, especially in modern novels, often act as machines. We are tolerant of improbability and of gaps in a story, such as "Five years elapsed," &c. &c., when they are covered by pictures of still life, such as the charming descriptions of South America, which fill up about half a volume and three very uneventful years in the wanderings of Sir Amyas Leigh, knight. Such, too, are some of Mr Dickens's descriptions of nature, which contain extremely picturesque sentences, but generally offend our taste by their obvious effort and elaboration; such, for example, is the account of the great storm at Yarmouth or of the Swiss valley, in *David Copperfield*. They would furnish very good drop-scenes to a theatre; but in the history of a man's life we can dispense with drop-scenes.[10] The description of nature in *Gil Blas*, in Defoe, occasionally in Fielding, and continually in Smollett, are never obtrusive or over elaborate. They are the simple vivid impression left by striking scenery upon men who had no inclination to go about in the world in the spirit of landscape painters, but who could appreciate a fine view when it came their way. Gil Blas' journey through the Asturias, the Cavaliers' wanderings in Yorkshire, the hill on which Tom Jones and Partridge lost their way, and the infinite variety of pictures hinted at rather than drawn, in Roderick Random's journey to London, are instances of our meaning.

It is a great beauty in a novel, when the story, as it were, tells itself, without the introduction of machines to help it out.

Perhaps the most remarkable result of the arbitrary power which novel writers exercise in the selection of facts to be represented and facts to be suppressed, is to be found in the morality which they teach.

Nothing is more common than for novel writers to set out with the assumption of the truth of certain maxims of morality, and to arrange the facts of their story upon the hypothesis that every violation of those maxims entails all sorts of calamity; instead of looking at the world, and seeing for themselves whether, in point of fact, experience confirms them in the notions which they have formed as to the sanctions provided for the enforcement of such maxims. Those who act thus do not see that the honour which they intend to pay to morality is mere lip-service, and conceals a real doubt as to whether there is such a thing as a natural sanction of morality at all. If they believe that human nature and society are so constituted that the laws of morality are self-executing, they ought to recollect that the sanctions are adjusted by some fixed rule, and if so, the question, what those sanctions are, can be learnt only from experience.

Miss Edgeworth affords perhaps the most complete instance of this fault, and it is almost the only blemish which we can think of in her admirable works. Indeed, her morals are so good, so kindly, and so wise, that it seems unnatural to find fault with them. The number of capital punishments for small offences in her moral tales and tales of fashionable life is dreadful. No one, we suppose, would doubt the evils of procrastination, but it is not a fair representation of life to call as a witness to bad effects a man of great talents and many opportunities, who is five or six times on the point of making his fortune, and is as often baffled by putting something off which he might have done before. The character might, we apprehend, be objected to on artistic grounds. No one would be so inveterately and invariably procrastinating as the unhappy Mr Lowe; but independently of this, secondary punishments would, we think, have answered Miss Edgeworth's purpose quite as well, and have been much more true to nature. She might have made him miss one or two openings in life, and succeed less well in others than a more punctual man; but in her anxiety to preach up punctuality, she seems to forget that there is no good in being punctual if a man cannot do his business when he has kept his appointment.

A novel with a moral bears the same relation to other novels as a panegyric to a biography. Instead of illustrating the particular virtues of his subject simply and naturally, the novelist is always on the watch for opportunities of bringing them in at any cost, and, if we may trust our own experience, seldom fails to make the reader utterly rebel against the maxim, or hero, as the case may be.

There are, indeed, cases in which morals become absolute Juggernauts, and the more questionable they are the bloodier are the sacrifices which they obtain. We do not recollect a more salient example of this than the fate of all the low-churchmen, freethinkers, and Jesuits introduced into *Hawkstone*. The account stands thus:—

Bentley. For being an evangelical clergyman, and for having belonged to a debating club at Cambridge—Subjected to extortion of money by threats of false accusations, unlawfully detained in custody, twice nearly murdered, and thrown at last into a quasi convent, by way of restitution.

Webster. For Atheism—Falls into melted lead, falling on his hands in the first instance, and sinking slowly on his face.

Pearce. For being a Jesuit—Eaten by rats in a secret passage of his own contrivance. From the position of what was left of him, it appeared that the vital parts had been attacked last.

The old French penal code was merciful compared to this. Webster, perhaps, might have met with treatment not materially milder at the hands of the judges who sentenced Damien and La Barre, but the fate of Jesuits in the time of Louis XV., or of Jansenists in that of Louis XIV., was far more tolerable than that of heretics convicted by the inexorable and infallible author of *Hawkstone*.

A parallel instance is that of Eugene Sue, whom the author of *Hawkstone* so much resembles, and with whom, we suppose, he so fully sympathises. Jesuits, hypocrites, and immoral persons generally, get their poetical justice served out, like the boiling pitch which Robinson Crusoe's cook distributed amongst the Chinese. Dying of recondite diseases, having holes burnt in their flesh with blow-pipes, being blinded, and kicked in tender parts,—and in some of the less serious cases, drowning, hanging, guillotining, and other not very painful forms of death, are the punishments with which M. Sue visits the crimes which he takes so much pleasure in describing; and no doubt it is fair enough to hang all the characters, if the scene is always laid in Newgate.

Poetical justice is, however, not confined to such instances as these: it extends far higher, and is a taint from which few authors have escaped. Sir Edward Lytton generally puts on the black cap when his hero and heroine are, or are about to be, married. Surely the execution of Randal Leslie, in the last chapter of *My Novel*, is very unnecessary. The character is certainly abundantly mean and base; but his very selfishness and insensibility of conscience would have prevented him from throwing up the game of life, which he had played so unscrupulously, merely because he was discovered in discreditable tricks by a set of people who must have kept their discoveries to themselves, for fear of compromising the character of their connexions. Leslie must have known very well that the wish to protect the character of the lady whom he had injured from public discussion, would have been quite motive enough to prevent his exposure by his former friends; and that many paths of life were open to him in which he might gratify his ambition. Instead of doing so, he utterly ruins himself, taking some trouble to do it, and takes to drinking, merely from a sense of duty to Sir E. Lytton; and because he feels that if a wicked man in a novel were to become rich, all the foundations of morality would be out of course. George Sand's works abound in curious instances of an inverted poetical justice. We think it would be hard to prove that the arrangements of life, and the existing notions of morality, uniformly produce misery.

In this, as in almost every department of novel literature, Mr Thackeray appears to us to have conferred immense benefits on novel readers. He is the only writer that we know who does not shrink from allowing all kinds of villainy to go unpunished, except by its own badness, and who makes his readers feel without preaching or effort how complete a punishment that is. The reason of this may perhaps be, that few authors feel so strongly as Mr Thackeray that mere wealth and success in life are not all that we ought to live or to wish for; and that it is a beggarly reward, after all, for goodness, to make it heir to a large estate and a fine house. We think that Mr Morgan "living to be one of the most respectable men in the parish of St. James's," and Becky Sharpe keeping one of the most well-conducted stalls in Vanity Fair, are really far more edifying representations than any number of saints, pampered, very strangely to all readers of the New Testament, with all sorts of luxury, and any number of sinners consigned to a fate to which they certainly were not accustomed, when they were not plagued like other men, nor afflicted like other men,—when they had children at their desire, and left the rest of their substance to their babes.

We would recommend to all who think it necessary to warp facts in order to justify morality, the words of one of the greatest of English wits and poets:—

> *Think we, like some weak prince, th'Eternal Cause*
> *Prone for his favourites to reverse his laws?*
>
> . . . .
>
> *"If" sometimes virtue wants while vice is fed,*
> *What then? is the reward of virtue bread?*
> *That vice may merit, 'tis the price of toil,*
> *The knave deserves it when he tills the soil;*
> *The knave deserves it when he tempts the main,*
> *Where folly fights for kings, or dives for gain.*
>
> *What nothing earthly gives, or can destroy—*
> *The soul's calm sunshine, and the heart-felt joy,—*
> *Is virtue's prize: a better would you fix?*
> *Then give humility a coach-and-six,*
> *Justice a conqueror's sword, or Truth a gown,*
> *Or public spirit its great cure—a crown.*

In conclusion, we will indicate—it would require a book to do more—a few of the principal historical causes of the imperfect representations of life by novelists.

The most remarkable of these are traditional plots, the requisitions of which can hardly be complied with without a considerable warping of facts. The great majority of these plots are composed of two elements,—the adventurous, and the amatory.

The oldest European form of the adventurous element in novels, and its introduction into modern literature, has been curiously described by M. Guizot:—

> Independently (he says) of the satisfaction which they afforded to morality and to human sensibility, the condition of which in the external world was so bad, the legends corresponded to other faculties and other necessities. We hear much in the present day of the interest, the movement, which in the course of what is vaguely called the middle ages, gave animation to common life. It seems as if great adventures, spectacles, and histories constantly excited the imagination; as if society were a thousand times more varied, more amusing, than it is with us. This might be the case with a few men who belonged to the higher classes, or were thrown into singular situations; but, for the mass of the population, life was, on the contrary, prodigiously monotonous, insipid, tiresome. It was destined to pass in one place, amidst the constant repetition of the same scenes. With hardly any external movement, and still less from within, it had as little pleasure as happiness, and the condition of its intelligence was not more agreeable than its material existence. There was no nourishment for the active imagination and love of adventure which have so much empire over men, except in the lives of the saints. To the Christians of this time—I may be allowed a merely literary comparison,—the legends were what the long stories, the brilliant and varied histories of which the *Thousand and One Nights* are a specimen, were to the Orientals. It was there that the popular imagination wandered freely in an unknown and wonderful world, full of action and poetry. It is difficult for us, at the present day, to share all the pleasure which they afforded twelve hundred years ago. Habits have changed, amusements besiege us; but we can at least understand that this kind of literature derived hence a powerful interest.[11]

In the authors of the Legends of the Saints are probably to be found the literary ancestors of our modern novels of adventure; and possibly their miracles may have had some connexion with the habit of mind which leads so many novelists to suppose, or at least to suggest, that the divine government of the world is carried on entirely *ex machiná*, and not by the orderly operation of general laws. It would of course be fanciful to rate very highly the influence of the legends on the writers of the present day. We merely refer to them as being the earliest instances of the operation of causes which are still in full vigour, and as having exercised some influence over those who were the earliest professors of the art of novel writing.

The commonest form of the combination of the adventurous and amatory element is pleasantly described by Mr Thackeray:—

> I suppose, as long as novels last, and authors aim at interesting their public, there must be in a story a virtuous and gallant hero, a wicked monster his opposite, and a pretty girl who finds a champion. Bravery and virtue conquer beauty; and vice, after seeming to triumph through a certain number of pages, is sure to be discomfited in the last volume, when justice overtakes him, and honest folks come by their own. There never was, perhaps, a greatly popular story, but this simple plot was carried through it. Mere satiric wit is addressed to a class of readers and thinkers quite different to those simple souls who laugh and weep over a novel.

This description (although strangely inapplicable to the four most popular novels ever written—*Don Quixote*, *Pilgrim's Progress*, *Gil Blas*, and *Robinson Crusoe*), seems to us to characterise very happily a vast proportion of the plots of novels, which are constructed in neglect of the principles which distinguish them from plays. A play is addressed to an audience, a novel to readers; therefore many deviations from nature are necessary in plays which are clumsy in novels. In a play, situations which form *tableaux*, surprises, mistaken identity, coincidences, and so forth, are unavoidable, because without their help the audience would not be able to take in the whole bearing of the piece, during its representation; but their improbability makes them displeasing in a novel, which presumes a certain amount of attention and leisure on the part of the reader.

If, indeed, a novel is merely an unacted play, like *Monte Christo*, its plot is good in proportion to the exactness with which dramatic principles are employed in its construction; but where it is professedly a picture of life, an incident borrowed from the stage is out of place. Take from *Monte Christo* the plots of Dantés and the Abbé, the discovery of the treasure, the intrigues against Dantés' enemies, and all the list of catastrophes at the end, and the book is not worth reading.

If, on the other hand, we take from *David Copperfield* the surprising recognitions of old acquaintance, the poetical justice, and the Magdalene and death-bed "business" of Emily, Martha, and Dora, the reminiscences of the hero's youth and childhood, the sketch of the Yarmouth boatmen, and the gentleman who is always expecting "something to turn up," become sketches as exquisite in their playfulness and humour as anything in *Household Words*. It would be hard to give them higher praise.

It has always seemed to us that the confusion of the two classes of plots of which we have spoken, spoils all novels in which it exists. The wonderful superiority of Swift and Defoe over all succeeding novelists, is owing, to a great extent, to their almost absolute freedom from this fault. Grant Gulliver his postulates, and his book is as sober, dignified, and probable as Arthur Young's *Travels in France*. Smollett and Fielding have but very little of the dramatic element in their plots. *The Vicar of Wakefield* has a sort of sentimental, operatic atmosphere cast over it by Burcham's incognito, and Squire Thornhill's marriage. If Olivia's character had never been reinstated at all, the story would have been far more life-like.

Next to those of Swift and Defoe, we should most unquestionably place the plots of Fielding. They are marvellous in their simplicity and nature; and the various adventures by which they are illustrated form, as they would in real life, not the ground-work of the story told, but mere ornaments and episodes.

The whole story, for example, of *Joseph Andrews* may be told in a sentence: Joseph Andrews being dismissed from his place in London, goes into the country and marries Fanny Williams. The adventures related are merely incidental, and might all be struck out of the book without disarranging the continuity of the story. Most novels are, as it were, articulated by means of various more or less well-known dramatic contrivances.

Another curious case of an extrinsic disturbing force acting upon novels is to be found in the habit, which of late years has become so common, of using novels to ventilate opinions.

It is a common, but not, we think, a very fair objection to such books, to complain that the author does not give his critics a fair shot—that he shelters himself behind his hero, and expresses, not his own, but his puppets' opinions.

To those who consider authors as a sort of waste, over which they are entitled to common abuse, some comfort may be given by the reflection, that by abusing the hero instead of the author, and by abusing him for those qualities which he shares with the author, they may still inflict a reasonable amount of pain; but those who are willing to consider that the object of such novels is rather to display the manner in which opinions act upon those who hold them, than to inculcate the opinions on their own grounds, will probably be content with considering how far the representation is honest.

Opinions and states of mind may, no doubt, be legitimately made the subjects of representation as adventures, but the dangers of partiality, of dishonesty, of false morality on the part of authors, and of hasty misconception on the part of readers, is obviously at a maximum in this class of books. *Pendennis* is, perhaps, the most notable and trustworthy specimen of the class which could be mentioned. The irresolute, half-ashamed, sceptical hero, conscious of his own weakness, conscious of his own ignorance, conscious, too, of his capacity for both power and knowledge,—half envious of the vigorous delusions with which he sees one part of mankind possessed, half sympathizing with the vigorous pleasure-hunting of another class,—governed by tastes and circumstances instead of principles, but clinging, firm to old habits, to traditional lessons of truth and honour,—jotting down, sketch-book in hand, all the quaint irregularities or picturesque variations of the banks as he drifts, half-pleased, half-melancholy, down the river of life, not very bad, nor very good, nor very anything,—looking, half-respectfully, half-derisively, at what the world venerates,—despising, more or less, though on other grounds, what it hates,—is one of the saddest, as it is one of the most masterly memorials of the times in which he lived which any writer ever drew for posterity.

Our most remarkable writer of this kind, after Mr Thackeray, appears to us to be, beyond all comparison, Mr Kingsley. That he is a poet and a man of genius, that he has almost unrivalled power of description, and that he reproduces, with a fidelity almost marvellous, the feelings of that particular generation and class in which his lot is cast, no one, we think, who belongs to the same class and generation can doubt. The perplexities of Lancelot Smith, the certainties of Amyas Leigh—who is a Lancelot Smith without perplexities,—the opinions, or rather sentiments of Alton Locke and his friend—who may be like tailors, but are most unquestionably like gentlemen accidentally reduced to that occupation,—are most undeniable likenesses of the genus Englishman, species of Cantabrigian tempore 184–. Mr Kingsley knows much more about Alexandria in the days of Cyril, and about England in the days of Elizabeth, than we do; therefore we shall only say that it is very curious that their inhabitants should have so exactly, so curiously, and intimately resembled that particular class to which we have referred, as, from Mr Kingsley's novels, we find they did.

Novels are also made use of at the present day, as social or political *argumenta ad miericordium*,—when they fall within the remarks which we have made upon novels written with a moral. Such, for example, are Mrs Gaskell's novel of *Mary Barton*, written in order to bring forward certain observations of the author, and apparently to advocate a particular set of feelings respecting the condition of the poor in Manchester; and her novel of *Ruth*, written, apparently, to show that the regulations of society, with respect to female virtue, sometimes produce hardship. We have already expressed our opinion upon the general question of the introduction of morality into novels; historically considered, all these novels will have to be read with large allowances, on the score of their having been, to a great extent, party pamphlets. It is curious to observe how the artistic bias of the writer's mind gets the better of her theories. *Mary Barton* remains an excellent novel after its utter uselessness, politically speaking, is fully recognised. That poor people out of work in Manchester were very discontented and very miserable, and that being so, they behaved much as the authoress of *Mary Barton* describes their behaviour, will continue to be a fact worth representing, however notorious it may always have been, long after everybody has recognised the truth, that that fact has little or nothing to do with either the cause or the remedy of their wretchedness.

Ruth has much in it that is beautiful, even in the eyes of those who cannot see that if it were literally true it would prove anything at all. All that it shows is, that it is possible to put a case of a person who, for violating the letter, and not the spirit of the law, gets more severely punished than she would have been if the law had been made to provide for her individual case. This must be the case with all human laws. What has to be proved is that the punishments of the social law, on the subject to which *Ruth* refers, are too severe, when not only the letter, but the spirit also, of the law is violated. You do not prove that imprisonment is too severe a punishment for theft by putting the case of a child being so punished, though it had hardly realised the notion of property: you must show that it is unjust to imprison a commonplace London pickpocket.

A person who reads either *Ruth* or *Mary Barton* without notice of the various social and political discussions which suggested these novels, will hardly be able to derive much experience from them. It is like reading *Caleb Williams* without knowing that Godwin was the author of *Political Justice*.

The personal character of the authors is the last disturbing force which is to be taken into account.

Life puts on very special colours when it is looked at through the medium of the feelings of a man like Swift, who seems to have been, in sober earnest, very much the kind of person that Byron wished himself to be thought. The *sæva indignatio* which prompted him constantly to write what, if not inscribed with, is continually suggestive of lamentations, and mourning, and woe—showed him all things in a sort of glare, which, like the light of some distant conflagration, forms a background to all the playfulness and irony of *Gulliver's Travels*, and becomes, at last, their one great characteristic; so that after being amused at Lilliput, interested in Brobdignag, and astonished at Laputa, we feel the same kind of relief on finishing the account of the Houyhnhms as we experience on passing into the open air and cheerful streets from the ulcers and abortions of a medical museum.

Goldsmith, on the other hand, saw everything *couleur de rose*. If young Primrose has to travel through Europe, he makes rather a pleasant business of it. He enjoys himself more, as he tells us, with his crown piece over a bowl of punch, than the old crimp to whom he has just paid its last companion with his fifty thousand pounds. When he lands on the continent he finds ways and means to see the world, not unpleasantly; he gets his board and lodging from "those who are poor enough to be very merry," and disputes his way cheerfully through university towns as yet unknown to tourists.

Now if anyone were to draw from Swift's book the moral that life was utterly foul and monstrous, or from Goldsmith the conclusion that even to a penniless vagabond it was a pleasant amusement,—he would be transferring to the picture the colour of the glass through which he looks at it. It would be a curious thing to construct a scale of the allowances necessary to be made in the books of different authors on this ground, like the rates of going which are ascertained for chronometers at the Greenwich Observatory.

We do not know a better corrective for timidity and despondence than the tone of "unabashed" Defoe. Most men would have described Robinson Crusoe's career as something between life in a mad-house and life in gaol. So, too, Lockhart's *Life of Scott* is a not uninstructive commentary on the *Waverley Novels*. There is another side to that prosperous, easy-going enjoyment of life, and fine scenery, and middle-age costume, which is to be taken into account before we can let the stalwart heroes— who are constantly "accompanying their thanks with a kiss," and plausibly settling all the difficulties of the world,—walk out of the canvas into real life. All those volumes of correspondence about plate, linen, and furniture—all the adding house to house, and field to field—the final bankruptcy—the tragical and fruitless efforts which followed it—and the gradual breaking up of a great genius and an iron frame, are melancholy proofs that the world has more in it after all than is to be solved by the sort of boisterous, noisy, straightforward sense—sense in more ways than one— which the *Waverley Novels* seem to suggest as that sum of the whole matter which the Wise Man expressed somewhat differently.

In conclusion, we will take as an illustration of the manner in which the disturbing forces of which we have spoken may be minimized, an instance of a novel which appears to us to be, in these particulars, almost faultless; and which adds to the information and excites the feelings of its readers in a manner almost as natural and complete as if it were a real history of real facts. We allude to *Robinson Crusoe*.

Whichever of the tests we have been discussing is applied to this book, we shall find it equally sound. Consider it with reference to the variations from real life introduced into it for artistic purposes. It is almost impossible to point out a single such variation. There is no factitious completeness in the incidents or scenery; characters come and go, and are mentioned and criticised as they happen to affect Crusoe's career, but they are never brought in for any other purpose, nor are their separate adventures followed farther than the occasion requires. Sir Walter Scott remarked, very justly, that the elder brother, who was colonel of the regiment of German infantry, and the boy Xury, both vanish from the book just as they would have vanished from the history of a real man's life, and are not brought in at the end, as they would have been in any ordinary novel, to rejoice in the hero's fortunate catastrophe. One of Mr Dickens's critics praised *Bleak House* because it was so like life, in containing such an infinite variety of characters. Compare *Bleak House* with *Robinson Crusoe*. The old English gentleman—the eccentric bachelor, the surgeon, the heroine, Joe the sweeper, the law-writer, all the parties concerned in the Chancery suit, Mr Jarndyce, the philanthropic lady, the attorney's clerk—who wants to make an offer of marriage "without prejudice"—and fifty others, are all woven into one series of adventures, in which they are all interested, and from which, when they have performed their several tasks, they all depart in different dramatic positions, each with his appropriate piece of poetical justice. Can any one pretend that this is like life? Thousands of people affect us, and we affect thousands of others; but each of us works out the romance or history of our own life with but very occasional and fragmentary assistance from each other. Men are not, as Mr Dickens seems to think, like characters in a play; they far more resemble a complicated set of forces, each acting in its own direction, and each influenced by, though independent of the others. In *Robinson Crusoe* this truth is far more fully apprehended. After the skipper of the Hull trader has been wrecked in Yarmouth Roads, and has given Crusoe some good advice, he goes on his way, and we see him no more. The old sailor who takes him a Guinea voyage dies when he returns. The Sallee rovers remain in the Mediterranean; the Portuguese captain and the Brazilian planters all stay at home; and when Crusoe wants them for a specific purpose, he has to go and look for them as any common person would. A modern novelist would have rolled them all into one mass; would have made the Portuguese captain marry the English captain's widow, who would have turned out to be connected with Friday, and to have a secret sorrow pressing on her on account of the bad behaviour of the colonel of Lockhart's foot, and the book would have closed with eating and drinking, marrying and giving in marriage, according to the universal practice in that behalf.

If we examine Crusoe's character, we shall see that it is a simple ordinary character, in no respect distorted for the purposes of art. What a picture of a stern, swarthy youth, scowling or smiling in horrible sympathy at the winds and the waves, and displaying the most heroic courage when the oldest sailors quailed, would many modern authors have painted if they had had to draw Crusoe on his first voyage. Defoe simply represents him as "most inexpressibly sick both in mind and body"—as making all sorts of good resolutions only to break them,—as cheering up and "pumping as well as another," when there was something actually to be done.

Is there any modern novelist who, wishing to represent a very brave, adventurous, young man, would have sufficient confidence in himself to make him beat his breast, and sob and cry like a madman, trusting to his resources to prove that such conduct was a part of the bravest, hardiest, and most indomitable character that genius ever conceived? Defoe knew that courage is not a positive quality which some men have and others want; that it is that willingness to do disagreeable things which we have all acquired in some measure, but that there are acts of courage which the very bravest are only just able to do, and in which even they falter and tremble. How nobly is this brought out in Crusoe's behaviour on the island. At first he is in a passion of grief almost amounting to madness,—"but I thought that would do little good, so I began to make a raft," &c. Little by little he calms down, often fairly giving way to the horrors of his situation, but always, after a time, setting to work manfully on whatever comes next to hand, until at last his mind grows into a state of settled content and cheerfulness, to which none but a man ribbed with triple steel would have attained. There is a fearless humility about the whole conception of Crusoe, of which we have almost lost even the tradition.

There is perhaps no novel which affords so little excuse for hasty generalisation on the part of readers. The admirable fidelity to nature with which the book is executed would prevent anyone from supposing that it represented a larger section of society than it really does represent; and the plan of the work affords constant hints of states of society quite unconnected with each other or with the main purpose of the book.

No one passion is invested with an exaggerated importance. Even Crusoe's love for wandering is made to arise principally out of his unsettled circumstances. It is not a bad test of the propriety with which passions are represented in a novel, to look upon the novel as an autobiography of the hero, and to consider what would be the feelings with which we should look upon a man who so described the events of his own life. If we apply this test to *Robinson Crusoe*, we shall see with what self-respect and consistency the story is told. First in order comes the serious business of his life—his trade, his travels, his management of his affairs in his island. Then come the principles upon which he lived, his reflections upon Providence, and the Divine plans of which he conceived himself to be the subject. His purely personal matters, his marriage, his wife's death, and the like, are modestly kept in the background, as matter which he had no particular wish to publish to the world at large.

Contrast this with David Copperfield's memoirs, "which he never meant to have published on any account." If David Copperfield had been a real man, we think his intention would have been eminently judicious. What would be thought of a real autobiography disclosing all a man's most secret thoughts and most sacred affections. It would be considered a great breach of decency: and why is this less an offence in a novel than it would be in real life? It is seldom wholesome to dwell upon descriptions of those thoughts and feelings in others which we would instinctively veil if they were our own.

It is observable that Defoe never worships his hero. He does not in the least degree warp facts, or allow them to be coloured by his own peculiarities. It is impossible to read the book without feeling that it is, to use a much-abused word, eminently objective; that is, the circumstances are drawn from a real study of things as they are, and not in order to exemplify the workings of a particular habit of mind.

With respect to the manner in which Defoe's work acts upon the feelings, a few very simple instances will be sufficient to show his superiority over modern pathos. On gay subjects he is gay, on pathetic subjects pathetic, but he never goes out of his way to look for affecting incidents or details. When he returns to England, after nearly forty years' absence, he simply says, "I went down to Yorkshire to look for my relatives." We are not even told whether he went on horseback or by coach, whom he met on the road by a series of surprising coincidences, how many shops had been rebuilt, or young people grown old.

When he has occasion to speak of his wife's death he does it simply and quietly. We are not told whether there were any, and what, reflections of the sun upon the wall on the occasion, nor what his wife wore, nor who told him of her death, nor what the angels had to say upon the subject, nor, indeed, anything but the essential facts and the eternal feelings—

> But in the middle of all this felicity one blow from Divine Providence unhinged me at once. This blow was the loss of my wife. She was, in a few words, the stay of all my affairs, the centre of all my enterprises, the engine that, by her prudence, reduced me to that happy compass I was in, and from the most extravagant and ruinous project that fluttered in my head as above, and did more to guide my rambling genius than a mother's tears and a father's instructions, a friend's counsel, or all my own reasoning powers could do. I was happy in being moved by her tears and in listening to her entreaties, and to the last degree desolate and disconsolate in the world by the loss of her. When she was gone, the world looked awkwardly round me.

As for his descriptions of nature, we give but one instance in illustration of our remarks on that subject:—

> Accordingly, we set out from Pampeluna, with our guide, on the 15th of November; and, indeed, I was surprised, when, instead of going forward, he came directly back with us on the same road that we came from Madrid, about twenty miles, when, having passed two rivers, and come into the plain country, we found ourselves in a warm climate again, where the country was pleasant, and no snow to be seen; but on a sudden turning to his left, he approached the mountains another way; and though it is true the hills and precipices looked dreadful, yet he made so many turns, such meanders, and led us by such winding ways, that we insensibly passed the height of the mountains without being much incumbered with the show; and, all of a sudden, he showed us the pleasant fruitful provinces of Languedoc and Gascony, all green and flourishing, though, indeed, at a great distance, and we had some rough way to pass still.

Perhaps the most extraordinary part of Defoe's book is its morality. The continual speculations upon the subject of Providence may seem, at first sight, to fall within the limits of that eagerness to justify existing notions which we have criticised. We apprehend, however, that this is not the case. All the incidents described are to the last degree simple, natural, and regular. The story is told so well, that the author can make the hero comment upon his own life as simply and quietly as if he were a real man commenting upon real occurrences. To invent facts in order to justify a theory is one thing,—to apply facts fairly represented in a particular manner is quite another thing. That a sailor should be cast upon a desert island, escape from it, and travel over the world afterwards, is not in itself improbable. That he should have the piety and good sense to make such observations upon it as Crusoe makes, is much to be desired.

A somewhat similar justification may be offered for his constant introduction of omens and presentiments. It is well known, from other quarters, that Defoe had a strong belief in the existence of such warnings. Believing in them as matters of fact, it is natural that he should introduce them into a picture of life; but it is remarkable that the omens are not very specific. He arranges the details of the facts as is most suitable to the story; and introduces considerable variations between the facts and the presentiments. He dreams, for example, that a savage man will run into his wood, but he says, "I did not let my dream come true in this, for I took him another way," &c. A common writer would have made the details match exactly, in order to heighten the supernatural character of the warning, but Defoe gives the impression of not going beyond experience and reason, even where his opinions of what experience and reason teach are most peculiar to himself.

The historical and personal disturbing forces to be allowed for in reading *Robinson Crusoe* are few. There is hardly anything conventional in the structure of the story. The book is written to serve no turn—moral, political, or religious. It might probably be inferred, from the general character of the religious speculations contained in it, that it had been written by a man to whom the Act of Toleration was the announcement of a new era, and who thought and felt upon those subjects as a contemporary of Locke would naturally think and feel.

We have already remarked that the charm of Crusoe's adventures is owing to the circumstances that they are described by a man who had, as he says, "undergone as great risk as a grenadier on a counterscarp," though a great part of his life, and who was by nature pre-eminently qualified to run such risks; and that, described by a man more dependent on society—by Fielding, for example, they would have been a series of awful calamities and miseries.

Taken as a whole, there is probably no book in the range of novel literature which would form an addition to the experience of its readers so nearly equivalent to that which it would have formed if it had been literally true. In so far as a novel is a poem, or a satire, or a play, or a depository for beauties, *Robinson Crusoe* has been surpassed again and again; but if a novel is properly and primarily a fictitious biography, and if we have fairly stated its general objects and effects, it is not only unsurpassed, but we may almost say unsurpassable.

It may perhaps be regretted that novels should form so large a part of the reading of young men, though it is doubtful whether in any case they are an unmixed evil. Those who idle over novels would, in their absence, idle over something else; those who are unnaturally excited by them would find a vent for that habit of mind elsewhere. But be they good or bad, useless or necessary, they circulate over the land in every possible form, and enter more or less into the education of almost every one who can read. They hold in solution a great deal of experience. It would therefore surely be a most useful thing to provide rules by which the experience might be precipitated, and to ascertain the process by means of which the precipitate might be made fit for use. We are not so vain as to suppose that we have done much towards the accomplishment of such a task. We have done our best to point out the limits and directions of the instructions which are wanted.

F. S.

Notes

1. Apuleius' *Ass* is, no doubt, strictly a novel, and Lucian's *Dialogues* have much of the same character.
2. Whewell, *Philo. Ind. Sci.*, vol. ii., p. 41. The quotation is slightly modified.
3. *Ib.*, p. 60. This is followed by a characteristically beautiful illustration taken from the utility of the false maxim as to nature's *fuga vacui*, in the progress of science.
4. They are a simple relation of the experience (we believe) of Mr Barber, transported twelve or thirteen years since for forgery, and pardoned o the discovery of his innocence. See *Household Words*, vol. v., p. 455, &c.
5. It has indeed become a sort of commonplace, or what may perhaps be called a secondary commonplace (for which the authority of M. A. Thierry may be pleaded), to extol the representations of novelists and memoir writers over the more authorized mediums of obtaining historical and social knowledge. This surely is confounding facts and possibilities. It may be very true that more knowledge about the relations of the Saxons and Normans after the Conquest is gained from *Ivanhoe* than from Hume's *History*, but that is surely owing to the fact that, for one person who studies Hume and Hume's authorities with sufficient attention to place a clear picture of the twelfth and thirteenth centuries before his mind, thousands will read *Ivanhoe*. It is not because Mr Macaulay's prefaces to his ballads contain more information than Niebuhr's *History* that they have informed a far greater number of people of the nature of the sources from whence we derive our knowledge of early Rome.
6. Satan's rebellion is made the subject of a substantive description, which is not the case with the theft of Prometheus.
7. It is a curious instance of the almost universal inability of novelists to write about law without making mistakes, that Godwin, who had a considerable acquaintance with criminal law, forgets that Falkland could not be tried a second time for the murder of Tyrrel, although he seems quite aware that Williams could not be tried twice for the theft.

In Miss Bronte's remarkable novel, *Wuthering Heights*, the legal relations of the different characters towards the close of the book are most perplexed. They involve a perfect wilderness of questions about disseisin, forcible entries, mortgages, and the wills and marriages of minors. Even Mr Thackeray, generally so careful in such matters, falls, we conceive, into a legal mistake in *The Newcomes*. Mrs Newcome leaves behind her a letter to her attorney written on the day of her death (before 1838) saying in effect, "I desire to bequeath" 5000l. to Clive Newcome. "Prepare a codicil to my will to that effect, and bring it on Saturday." This is written on Tuesday, on which day she dies. Mr Pendennis, on the discovery of the letter, tells Miss Newcome that "it is not worth a penny," being only "a wish on the part of Mrs Newcome," and Mr Luce, the attorney, confirms this.

Now, in *Passmore v. Passmore*, I Phillim. 218, Sir J. Nicholl expressly says, "That the instrument as in the form of a letter is no conclusive objection to it,—nor has it been held necessary that they" (such instruments) "should be in direct and imperative terms, *wishes and requests have been deemed sufficient*."

In *Allen v. Manning*, 2 Add. 490, instructions to an attorney to prepare a will were admitted to probate on the ground that the testator died five days after giving them, and before he could execute the will. See, too, *Torre v. Castle*, I Curt. 303, and *Hattat v. Hattat*, 4 Hagg. 411. This would be somewhat minute criticism, if it were not for the fact, that Mr Pendennis gives his opinion expressly as a lawyer.

8. Judgment of Lord Stowell in *Evans v. Evans*. I Hagg. Cons. Rep. 36, 37.
9. A list of the killed, wounded, and missing amongst Mr Dickens's novels would read like an *Extraordinary Gazette*. An interesting child runs as much risk there as any of the troops who stormed the Redan.
10. It may be worth while to remark that Mr Dickens often writers unintentional verse, like the "*Urbem Romam a principio reges habuere*," or the iambics, which occur sometimes in *Thucydides*. For example:

> Yoho, beside the village green,
> Where cricket players linger yet,
> And every little indentation made

In the fresh grass
By bat or wicket, ball, or player's foot,
Sheds out its perfume on the night. Away,
With four fresh horses from the Bald-faced Stag.

The last line is wonderfully Tennysonian. The following description of the shadow of a mail-coach might have well been written by Wordsworth:—

Yoho, yoho, through ditch and brake,
Upon the ploughed land and the smooth,
Along the steep hill-side and steeper wall,
As if it were a Phantom Hunter.

11. *Civilisation en France*, Leçon 17me, p. 276, 277. Bruss. Edn. 1843.

Silly Novels by Lady Novelists

GEORGE ELIOT

George Eliot (Marian Evans 1818–1880) was the principal female British novelist of the latter half of the nineteenth century. Assistant editor of The *Westminster Review*, she published an anonymous translation of Strauss's *Life of Jesus* in 1846. During the 1850s, 60s, and 70s she wrote a number of novels, including *Adam Bede* (1859), *The Mill on the Floss* (1860), *Middlemarch* (1871–2) and *Daniel Deronda* (1874–76). In the following essay she satirizes the facile sentimental novels written by "lady novelists". She divides the novles into four categories—the "mind and millinery species", the "oracular species", the "white neck-cloth species" and the "modern-antique species". Her principal complaints about all the types are their artificial style and their lack of "genuine observation, humour and passion". Like a number of mid-to-late nineteenth-century writers and critics, Eliot deplores the burgeoning number of popular novels that cater to a mass audience.

Silly Novels by Lady Novelists are a species, determined by the particular quality of silliness that predominates in them—the frothy, the prosy, the pious, or the pedantic. But it is a mixture of all of these—a composite order of feminine fatuity, that produces the largest class of such novels, which we shall distinguish as the mind-and-millinery species. The heroine is usually an heiress, probably a peeress in her own right, with perhaps a vicious baronet, an amiable duke, and an irresistible younger son of a marquis as lovers in the foreground, a clergyman and a poet sighing for her in the middle distance, and a crowd of undefined adorers dimly indicated beyond. Her eyes and her wit are both dazzling; her nose and her morals are alike free from any tendency to irregularity; she has a superb *contralto* and a superb intellect; she is perfectly well dressed and perfectly religious; she dances like a sylph, and reads the Bible in the original tongues. Or it may be that the heroine is not

Source: George Eliot, "Silly Novels by Lady Novelists", *Westminster Review*, October 1856, pp. 243–54.

only an heiress—that rank and wealth are not the only things in which she is deficient; but she infallibly gets into high society, she has the triumph of refusing many matches and securing the best, and she wears some family jewels or other as a sort of crown of righteousness at the end. Rakish men either bite their lips in impotent confusion at her repartees, or are touched to penitence by her reproofs, which, on appropriate occasions, rise to a lofty strain of rhetoric; indeed, there is a general propensity in her to make speeches, and to rhapsodize at some length when she retires to her bedroom. In her recorded conversations she is amazingly eloquent, and in her unrecorded conversations, amazingly witty. She is understood to have a depth of insight that looks through and through the shallow theories of philosophers, and her superior instincts are a sort of dial by which men have only to set their clocks and watches, and all will go well. The men play a very subordinate part by her side. You are consoled now and then by a hint that they have affairs, which keeps you in mind that the working-day business of the world is somehow being carried on, but ostensibly the final cause of their existence is that they may accompany the heroine on her "starring" expedition through life. They see her at a ball, and are dazzled; at a flower-show, and they are fascinated; on a riding excursion, and they are witched by her noble horsemanship; at church, and they are awed by the sweet solemnity of her demeanour. She is the ideal woman in feelings, faculties, and flounces. For all this, she as often as not marries the wrong person to begin with, and she suffers terribly from the plots and intrigues of the vicious baronet; but even death has a soft place in his heart for such a paragon, and remedies all mistakes for her just at the right moment. The vicious baronet is sure to be killed in a duel, and the tedious husband dies in his bed requesting his wife, as a particular favour to him, to marry the man she loves best, and having already dispatched a note to the lover informing him of the comfortable arrangement. Before matters arrive at this desirable issue our feelings are tried by seeing the noble, lovely, and gifted heroine pass through many *mauvais moments*, but we have the satisfaction of knowing that her sorrows are wept into embroidered pocket-handkerchiefs, that her fainting form reclines on the very best upholstery, and that whatever vicissitudes she may undergo, from being dashed out of her carriage to having her head shaved in a fever, she comes out of them all with a complexion more blooming and locks more redundant than ever.

We may remark, by the way, that we have been relieved from a serious scruple by discovering that silly novels by lady novelists rarely introduce us to any other than very lofty and fashionable society. We had imagined that destitute women turned novelists, as they turned governesses, because they had no other "lady-like" means of getting their bread. On this supposition, vacillating syntax and improbable incident had a certain pathos for us; like the extremely supererogatory pin-cushions and ill-devised nightcaps that are offered for sale by a blind man. We felt the commodity to be a nuisance, but we were glad to think that the money went to relieve the necessitous, and we pictured to ourselves lonely women struggling for a maintenance, or wives and daughters devoting themselves to the production of "copy" out of pure heroism,—perhaps to pay their husband's debts or to purchase luxuries for a sick father. Under these impressions we shrank from criticising a lady's novel: her English might be faulty, but we said to ourselves her motives are irreproachable; her imagination may be uninventive, but her patience is untiring. Empty writing was excused by an empty stomach, and twaddle was consecrated by tears. But no! This theory of ours, like many other pretty theories, has had to give way before observation. Women's silly novels, we are now convinced are written under totally different circumstances. The fair writers have evidently never talked to a tradesman except from a carriage window; they have no notion of the working-classes except as "dependents;" they think five hundred a-year a miserable pittance; Belgravia and "baronial halls" are their primary truths; and they have no idea of feeling interest in any man who is not at least a great landed proprietor, if not a prime minister. It is clear that they write in elegant boudoirs, with violet-coloured ink and a ruby pen; that they must be entirely different to publishers' accounts, and inexperienced in every form of poverty except poverty of brains. It is true that we are constantly struck with the want of verisimilitude in their representations of society in which they seem to live; but then they betray no closer acquaintance with any other form of life. If their peers and peeresses are improbable, their literary men, tradespeople, and cottagers are impossible; and their intellect seems to have the peculiar impartiality of reproducing both what they *have* seen and heard, and what they have *not* seen and heard, with equal unfaithfulness.

There are few women, we suppose, who have not seen something of children under five years of age, yet in "Compensation," a recent novel of the mind-and-millinery species, which calls itself a "story of real life," we have a child of four and a half years old talking in this Ossianic fashion—

"Oh, I am so happy, dear gran'mamma;—I have seen,—I have seen such a delightful person; he is like everything beautiful,—like the smell of sweet flowers, and the view from Ben Lomond;—or no, *better than that*—he is like what I think of and see when I am very, very happy; and he is really like mamma, too, when she sings; and his forehead is like *that distant sea*," she continued, pointing to the blue Mediterranean; "there seems no end—no end; or like the clusters of stars I like best to look at on a warm fine night . . .Don't look so . . . your forehead is like Loch Lomond, when the wind is blowing and the sun gone in; I like the sunshine best when the lake is smooth . . . So now—I like it better than ever . . . it is more beautiful still from the dark cloud that has gone over it, *when the sun suddenly lights up all the colours of the forests and shining purple rocks, and it is all reflected in the waters below.*"

We are not surprised to learn that the mother of this infant phenomenon, who exhibits symptoms so alarmingly like those of adolescence repressed by gin, is herself a phœnix. We are assured, again and again, that she had a remarkably original mind, that she was a genius, and "conscious of her originality," and she was fortunate enough to have a lover who was also a genius and a man of "most original mind."

This lover, we read, though "wonderfully similar" to her "in powers and capacity," was "infinitely superior to her in faith and development," and she saw in him " 'Agape'—so rare to find—of which she had read and admired the meaning in her Greek Testament; having, *from her great facility in learning languages*, read the

Scriptures in their original *tongues*." Of course! Greek and Hebrew are mere play to a heroine; Sanscrit is no more than *a b c* to her; and she can talk with perfect correctness in any language, except English. She is a polking polyglott, a Creuzer in crinoline. Poor men! There are so few of you who know even Hebrew; you think it something to boast of if, like Bolingbroke, you only "understand that sort of learning and what is writ about it;" and you are perhaps adoring women who can think slightingly of you in all the Semitic languages successively. But, then, as we are almost invariably told, that a heroine has a "beautifully small head," and as her intellect has probably been early invigorated by an attention to costume and deportment, we may conclude that she can pick up the Oriental tongues, to say nothing of their dialects, with the same aerial facility that the butterfly sips nectar. Besides, there can be no difficulty in conceiving the depth of the heroine's erudition, when that of the authoress is so evident.

In "Laura Gay," another novel of the same school, the heroine seems less at home in Greek and Hebrew, but she makes up for the deficiency by a quite playful familiarity with the Latin classics—with the "dear old Virgil," "the graceful Horace, the humane Cicero, and the pleasant Livy;" indeed, it is such a matter of course with her to quote Latin, that she does it at a picnic in a very mixed company of ladies and gentlemen, having, we are told, "no conception that the nobler sex were capable of jealousy on this subject. And if, indeed," continues the biographer of Laura Gay, "the wisest and noblest portion of that sex were in the majority, no such sentiment would exist; but while Miss Wyndhams and Mr. Redfords abound, great sacrifices must be made to their existence." Such sacrifices, we presume, as abstaining from Latin quotations, of extremely moderate interest and applicability, which the wise and noble minority of the other sex would be quite as willing to dispense with as the foolish and ignoble majority. It is as little the custom of well-bred men as of well-bred women to quote Latin in mixed parties; they can contain their familiarity with "the humane Cicero" without allowing it to boil over in ordinary conversation, and even references to "the pleasant Livy" are not absolutely irrepressible. But Ciceronian Latin is the mildest form of Miss Gay's conversational power. Being on the Palatine with a party of sightseers, she falls into the following vein of well-rounded remark:— "Truth can only be pure objectively, for even in the creeds where it predominates, being subjective, and parcelled out into portions, each of these necessarily receives a hue of idiosyncrasy, that is, a taint of superstition more or less strong; while in such creeds as the Roman Catholic, ignorance, interest, the basis of ancient idolatries, and the force of authority, have gradually accumulated on the pure truth, and transformed it, at last, in to a mass superstition for the majority of its votaries; and how few there are, alas! whose zeal, courage, and intellectual energy are equal to the analysis of this accumulation, and to the discovery of the pearl of great price which lies hidden beneath this heap of rubbish." We have often met with women much more novel and profound in their observations than Laura Gay, but rarely with any so inopportunely long-winded. A clerical lord, who is half in love with her, is alarmed by the daring remarks just quoted, and begins to suspect that she is inclined to free-thinking. But he is mistaken; when in a moment of sorrow he delicately begs leave to "recal to her memory, a *depot* of strength and consolation under affliction, which, until we are hard pressed by the trials of life, we are too apt to forget," we learn that she really has "recurrence to that sacred depot," together with the tea-pot. There is a certain flavour of orthodoxy mitigated by study of "the humane Cicero," and by an "intellectual disposition to analyse."

"Compensation" is much more heavily dosed with doctrine, but then it has a treble amount of snobbish worldliness and absurd incident to tickle the palate of pious frivolity. Linda, the heroine, is still more speculative and spiritual than Laura Gay, but she has been "presented," and has more, and far grander, lovers; very wicked and fascinating women are introduced—even a French *lionne*, and no expense is spared to get up as exciting a story as you will find in the most immoral novels. In fact, it is a wonderful *pot pourri* of Almack's, Scotch second-sight, Mr. Rogers's breakfasts, Italian brigands, death-bed conversions, superior authoresses, Italian mistresses, and attempts at poisoning old ladies, the whole served up with a garnish of talk about "faith and development," and "most original minds." Even Miss Susan Barton, the superior authoress, whose pen moves in a "quick, decided manner when she is composing," declines the finest opportunities of marriage; and though old enough to be Linda's mother (since we are told that she refused Linda's father), has her hand sought by a young earl, the heroine's rejected lover. Of course, genius and morality must be backed by eligible offers, or they would seem rather a dull affair; and piety, like other things, in order to be *comme il faut*, must be in society, and have admittance to the best circles.

"Rank and Beauty" is a more frothy and less religious variety of the mind-and-millinery species. The heroine, we are told "if she inherited her father's pride of birth and her mother's beauty of person, had in herself a tone of enthusiastic feeling that, perhaps, belongs to her age, even in the lowly born, but which is refined into the high spirit of wild romance only in the far descended, who feel that it is their best inheritance." This enthusiastic young lady, by dint of reading the newspaper to her father, falls in love with the *prime minister*, who through the medium of leading articles and "the *resumé* of the debates," shines upon her imagination as a bright particular star, which has no parallax for her living in the country as simple Miss Wyndham. But she forthwith becomes Baroness Umfraville in her own right, astonishes the world with her beauty and accomplishments when she bursts upon it from her mansion in Spring Gardens, and, as you foresee, will presently come into contact with the unseen *objet aimé*. Perhaps the words "prime minister" suggest to you a wrinkled or obese sexagenarian; but pray dismiss the image. Lord Rupert Conway has been "called while still almost a youth to the first situation which a subject can hold in the "*universe*," and even leading articles and a *resumé* of the debates have not conjured up a dream that surpasses the fact.

> The door opened again, and Lord Rupert Conway entered. Evelyn gave one glance. It was enough; she was not disappointed. It seemed as if a picture on which she had once gazed was suddenly instinct with life, and had stepped from its frame before her. His tall figure, the distinguished simplicity of his air—it was a living Vandyke, a cavalier, one of his noble cavalier ancestors, or one to whom her fancy

had always likened him, who long of yore had with an Umfraville fought the Paynim, far beyond the sea. Was this reality?

Very little like it, certainly.

By-and-by it becomes evident that the ministerial heart is touched. Lady Umfraville is on a visit to the Queen at Windsor and,—

> The last evening of her stay, when they returned from riding, Mr. Wyndham took her and a large party to the top of the Keep, to see the view. She was leaning on the battlements, gazing from that 'stately height' at the prospect beneath her, when Lord Rupert was by her side. "What an unrivalled view!" exclaimed she.
> "Yes, it would have been wrong to go without having been up here. You are pleased with your visit?"
> "Enchanted! A Queen to live and die under, to live and die for!"
> "Ha!' cried he, with sudden emotion and with a *eureka* expression of countenance, as if he had *indeed found a heart in unison with his own.*"

The "*eureka* expression of countenance," you see at once to be prophetic of marriage at the end of the third volume; but before that desirable consummation, there are very complicated misunderstandings, arising chiefly from the vindictive plotting of Sir Luttrel Wycherley, who is a genius, a poet, and in every way a most remarkable character indeed. He is not only a romantic poet, but a hardened rake and a cynical wit; yet his deep passion for Lady Umfraville has so impoverished his epigrammatic talent, that he cuts an extremely poor figure in conversation. When she rejects him, he rushes into the shrubbery and rolls himself in the dirt; and on recovering, devotes himself to the most diabolical and laborious schemes of vengeance, in the course of which he disguises himself as a quack physician, and enters into general practice, foreseeing that Evelyn will fall ill, and that he shall be called in to attend her. At last, when all his schemes are frustrated, he takes leave of her in a long letter, written, as you will perceive from the following passage, entirely in the style of an eminent literary man:—

> Oh, lady, nursed in pomp and pleasure, will you ever cast one thought upon the miserable being who addresses you? Will you ever, as your gilded galley is floating down the unruffled stream of prosperity, will you ever, while lulled by the sweetest music—thine own praises,—hear the far-off sigh from that world to which I am going?

On the whole, however, frothy as it is, we rather prefer "Rank and Beauty" to the two other novels we have mentioned. The dialogue is more natural and spirited; there is some frank ignorance and no pedantry; and you are allowed to take the heroine's astounding intellect upon trust, without being called on to read her conversational refutations of sceptics and philosophers, or her rhetorical solutions of the mysteries of the universe.

Writers of the mind-and-millinery school are remarkably unanimous in their choice of diction. In their novels there is usually a lady or gentleman, who is more or less of a upas tree; the lover has a manly breast; minds are redolent of various things; hearts are hollow; events are utilized; friends are consigned to the tomb; infancy is an engaging period; the sun is a luminary that goes to his Western couch, or gathers the rain-drops into his refulgent bosom; life is a melancholy boon; Albion and Scotia are conversational epithets. There is a striking resemblance, too, in the character of their moral comments, such, for instance, as that "It is a fact, no less true than melancholy, that all people, more or less, richer or poorer, are swayed by bad example;" that "Books, however trivial, contain some subjects from which useful information may be drawn;" that "Vice can too often borrow the language of virtue;" that "Merit and nobility of nature must exist, to be accepted, for clamour and pretension cannot impose upon those too well read in human nature to be easily deceived;" and that, "In order to forgive, we must have been injured." There is doubtless a class of readers to whom these remarks appear peculiarly pointed and pungent; for we often find them doubly and trebly scored with the pencil, and delicate hands giving in their determined adhesion to these hardy novelties by a distinct *très vrai*, emphasized by many notes of exclamation. The colloquial style of these novels is often marked by much ingenious inversion, and a careful avoidance of such cheap phraseology as can be heard every day. Angry young gentlemen exclaim— "'Tis ever thus, methinks;" and in the half-hour before dinner a young lady informs her next neighbour that the first day she read Shakespeare she "stole away into the park, and beneath the shadow of the greenwood tree, devoured with rapture the inspired page of the great magician." But the most remarkable efforts of the mind-and-millinery writers lie in their philosophic reflections. The authoress of "Laura Gay," for example, having married her hero and heroine, improves the event by observing that "if those sceptics, whose eyes have so long gazed on matter that they can no longer see aught else in man, could once enter with heart and soul, into such bliss as this, they would come to say that the soul of man and the polypus are not of common origin, or of the same texture." Lady novelists, it appears, can see something else besides matter; they are not limited to phenomena, but can relieve their eyesight by occasional glimpses of the *noumenon*, and are, therefore, naturally better able than any one else to confound sceptics, even of that remarkable, but to us unknown school, which maintains that the soul of man is of the same texture as the polypus.

The most pitiable of all silly novels by lady novelists are what we may call the *oracular* species—novels intended to expound the writers' philosophical or moral theories. There seem to be a notion abroad among women, rather akin to the superstition that the speech and actions of idiots are inspired, and that the human being most entirely exhausted of common sense is the fittest vehicle of revelation. To judge from their writings, there are certain ladies who think that an amazing ignorance, both of science and of life, is the best possible qualification for forming an opinion on the knottiest moral and speculative questions. Apparently, their recipe for solving all such difficulties is something like this:—Take a woman's head, stuff it with a smattering of philosophy and literature chopped small, and with false notions of society baked hard, let it hang over a desk a few hours every day, and serve up hot in feeble English, when not required. You will rarely meet with a lady novelist of the oracular class who is diffident of her ability to decide on theological questions,—who has any suspicion that she is not capable of discriminating with the nicest accuracy between the good and evil in all church parties,—who does not see precisely how it is that men have gone wrong hitherto,—and pity philosophers in general that they have not had the opportunity of consulting her. Great writers, who have modestly contented themselves with putting their experience into fiction, and have thought it quite a sufficient task to exhibit men and things as they are, she sighs over as deplorably deficient in the application of their powers. "They have solved no great questions"— and she is ready to remedy their omission by setting before you a complete theory of life and manual of divinity, in a love story, where ladies and gentlemen of good family go through genteel vicissitudes, to the utter confusion of Deists, Puseyites, and ultra-Protestants, and to the perfect establishment of that peculiar view of Christianity which either condenses itself into a sentence of small caps, or explodes into a cluster of stars on the three hundred and thirtieth page. It is true, the ladies and gentlemen will probably seem to you remarkably little like any you have had the fortune or misfortune to meet with, for, as a general rule, the ability of a lady novelist to describe actual life and her fellow-men, is in inverse proportion to her confident eloquence about God and the other world, and the means by which she usually chooses to conduct you to true ideas of the invisible is a totally false picture of the visible.

As typical a novel of the oracular kind as we can hope to meet with is "The Enigma: a Leaf from the Chronicles of the Wolchorley House." The "enigma" which the novel is to solve, is certainly one that demands powers no less gigantic than those of a lady novelist, being neither more nor less than the existence of evil. The problem is stated, and the answer dimly foreshadowed on the very first page. The spirited young lady, with raven hair, says, "All life is an inextricable confusion;" and the meek young lady, with auburn hair, looks at the picture of the Madonna which she is copying, and— "*There* seemed the solution of that mighty enigma." The style of this novel is quite as lofty as its purpose; indeed, some passages on which we have spent much patient study are quite beyond our reach, in spite of the illustrative aid of italics and small caps; and we must await further "development" in order to understand them. Of Ernest the model young clergyman, who sets every one right on all occasions, we read that "he held not of marriage in the marketable kind, after a social desecration;" that, on one eventful night, "sleep had not visited his divided heart, where tumultuated, in varied type and combination, the aggregate feelings of grief and joy," and that, "for the *marketable* human article he had no toleration, be it of what sort, or set for what value it might, whether for worship or class, his upright soul abhorred it, whose ultimatum, the self-deceiver, was to him the *great spiritual lie*, 'living in a vain show, deceiving and being deceived;' since he did not suppose the phylactery and enlarged border on the garment to be *merely* a social trick." (The italics and small caps are the author's, and we hope they assist the reader's comprehension.) Of Sir Lionel, the model old gentleman, we are told that "the simple ideal of the middle age, apart from its anarchy and decadence, in him most truly seemed to live again, when the ties which knit men together were of heroic cast. The first-born colours of pristine faith and truth engraven on the common soul of man, and blent into the wide arch of brotherhood, where the primæval law of *order* grew and multiplied each perfect after his kind, and mutually inter-dependent." You see clearly, of course, how colours are first engraven on the soul, and then blent into a wide arch, on which arch of colours—apparently a rainbow—the law of order grew and multiplied, each—apparently the arch and the law—perfect after his kind? If, after this, you can possibly want any further aid towards knowing what Sir Lionel was, we can tell you, that in his soul "the scientific combinations of thought could educe no fuller harmonies of the good and the true, than lay in the primæval pulses which floated as an atmosphere around it!" and that, when he was sealing a letter, "Lo! the responsive throb in that good man's bosom echoed back in simple truth the honest witness of a heart that condemned him not, as his eye, bedewed with love, rested, too, with something of ancestral pride, on the undimmed motto of the family—'Loiaute.'"

The slightest matters have their vulgarity fumigated out of them by the same elevated style. Commonplace people would say that a copy of Shakespeare lay on a drawing-room table; but the authoress of "The Enigma," bent on edifying periphrasis, tells you that there lay on the table, "that fund of human thought and feeling, which teaches the heart through the little name, 'Shakespeare.'" A watchman sees a light burning in an upper window rather longer than usual, and thinks that people are foolish to sit up late when they have an opportunity of going to bed; but, lest this fact should seem too low and common, it is presented to us in the following striking and metaphysical manner: "He marvelled—as a man *will* think for others in a necessarily separate personality, consequently (though disallowing it) in false mental premise,—how differently *he* should act, how gladly *he* should prize the rest so lightly held of within." A footman—an ordinary Jeames, with large calves and aspirated vowels—answers the door-bell, and the opportunity is seized to tell you that he was a "type of the large class of pampered menials, who follow the curse of Cain— 'vagabonds' on the face of the earth, and whose estimate of the human class varies in the graduated scale of money and expenditure....These, and such as these, O England, be the false lights of they morbid civilization!" We have heard of various "false lights," from Dr. Cumming to Robert Owen, from Dr. Pusey to the Spirit-rappers, but we never before heard of the false light that emanates from plush and powder.

In the same way very ordinary events of civilized life are exalted into the most awful crises, and ladies in full skirts and *manches à la Chinoise*, conduct themselves not unlike the heroines of sanguinary melodramas. Mrs. Percy, a shallow woman of the world, wishes her son Horace to marry the auburn-haired Grace, she being an heiress; but he, after the manner of sons, falls in love with the raven-haired Kate, the heiress's portionless cousin; and moreover, Grace herself shows every symptom of perfect indifference to Horace. In such cases, sons are often sulky or fiery, mothers are alternately manœuvring and waspish, and the portionless young lady often lies awake at night and cries a good deal. We are getting used to these things now, just as we are used to eclipses of the moon, which no longer set us howling and beating tin kettles. We never heard of a lady in a fashionable "front" behaving like Mrs. Percy under these circumstances. Happening one day to see Horace talking to Grace at a window, without in the least knowing what they are talking about, or having the least reason to believe that Grace, who is mistress of the house and a person of dignity, would accept her son if he were to offer himself, she suddenly rushes up to them and clasps them both, saying, "with a flushed countenance and in an excited manner"—"This is indeed happiness; for, may I not call you so, Grace?—my Grace—my Horace's Grace!—my dear children!" Her son tells her she is mistaken, and that he is engaged to Kate, whereupon we have the following scene and tableau:—

> Gathering herself up to an unprecedented height, (!) her eyes lightening forth the fire of her anger:—
> "Wretched boy!" she said, hoarsely and scornfully, and clenching her hand,
> "Take then the doom of your own choice! Bow down your miserable head and let a mother's—'
> "Curse not!" spake a deep low voice from behind, and Mrs. Percy started, scared, as though she had seen a heavenly visitant appear, to break upon her in the midst of her sin.
> Meantime, Horace had fallen on his knees at her feet, and hid his face in his hands.
> Who, then, is she—who! Truly his "guardian spirit" hath stepped between him and the fearful words, which, however unmerited, must have hung as a pall over his future existence;—a spell which could not be unbound—which could not be unsaid.
> Of an earthly paleness, but calm with the still, iron bound calmness of death—the only calm one there,—Katherine stood; and her words smote on the ear in tones whose appallingly slow and separate intonation rung on the heart like the chill, isolated tolling of some fatal knell.
> "He would have plighted me his faith, but I did not accept it; you cannot, therefore—you *dare* not curse him. and here," she continued, raising her hand to heaven, whither her large dark eyes also rose with a chastened glow, which, for the first time, *suffering* had lighted in those passionate orbs,—"here I promise, come weal, come woe, that Horace Wolchorley and I do never interchange vows without his mother's sanction—without his mother's blessing!"

Here, and throughout the story, we see that confusion of purpose which is so characteristic of all silly novels written by women. It is a story of quite modern drawing room society—a society in which polkas are played and Puseyism discussed; yet we have characters, and incidents, and traits of manner introduced, which are mere shreds from the most heterogeneous romances. We have a blind Irish harper, "relic of the picturesque bards of yore," startling us at a Sunday-school festival of tea and cake in an English village; we have a crazy gipsy, in a scarlet cloak, singing snatches of romantic song, and revealing a secret on her deathbed which, with the testimony of a dwarfish miserly merchant, who salutes strangers with a curse and a devilish laugh, goes to prove that Ernest, the model young clergyman, is Kate's brother; and we have an ultra-virtuous Irish Barney, discovering that a document is forged, by comparing the date of the paper with the date of the alleged signature, although the same document has passed through a court of law, and occasioned a fatal decision. The "Hall" in which Sir Lionel lives is the venerable country seat of an old family, and this, we suppose, sets the imagination of the authoress flying to donjons and battlements, where "lo! the warder blows his horn; for, as the inhabitants are in their bed-rooms on a night certainly within the recollection of Pleaceman X., and a breeze springs up, which we are at first told was faint, and then that it made the old cedars bow their branches to the greensward, she falls into this mediæval vein of description (the italics are ours): "The banner *unfurled it* at the sound, and shook its guardian wing above, while the startled owl *flapped her* in the ivy; the firmament looking down through her 'argus eyes,'—

Ministers of heaven's mute melodies.

And lo! two strokes tolled from out the warder tower, and 'Two o'clock' re-echoed its interpreter below."

Such stories as this of "The Enigma" remind us of the pictures clever children sometimes draw "out of their own head," where you will see a modern villa on the right, two knights in helmets fighting in the foreground, and a tiger grinning in a jungle on the left, the several objects being brought together because the artist thinks each pretty, and perhaps still more because he remembers seeing them in other pictures.

But we like the authoress much better on her mediæval stilts than on her oracular ones,—when she talks of the *Ich* and of "subjective" and "objective," and lays down the exact line of Christian verity, between "right-hand excesses and left-hand declensions." Persons who deviate from this line are introduced with a patronizing air of charity. Of a certain Miss Inshquine she informs us, 'with all the lucidity of italics and small caps, that "*function*, not *form*, as *the inevitable outer expression of the spirit in this tabernacled age*, weakly engrossed her." And *a propos* of Miss Mayjar, an evangelical lady who is a little too apt to talk of her visits to sick women and the state of their souls, we are told that the model clergyman is "not one to disallow, through the *super* crust, the undercurrent towards good in the *subject*, or the positive benefits, nevertheless, to the *object*." We imagine the double-refined accent and protrusion of chin which are feebly represented by the italics in this lady's sentences! We abstain from quoting any of her oracular doctrinal passages, because they refer to matters too serious for our pages just now.

The epithet "silly" may seem impertinent, applied to a novel which indicates so much reading and intellectual activity as "The Enigma;" but we use this epithet advisedly. If, as the world has long agreed, a very great amount of instruction will not make a wise man, still less will a very mediocre amount of instruction make a wise woman. And the most mischievous form of feminine silliness is the literary form, because it tends to confirm the popular prejudice against the more solid education of women. When men see girls wasting their time in consultations about bonnets and ball dresses, and in giggling or sentimental love-confidences, or middle-aged women mismanaging their children, and solacing themselves with a little acrid gossip, they can hardly help saying, "For Heaven's sake, let girls be better educated; let them have some better objects of thought—some more solid occupations." But after a few hours' conversation with an oracular literary woman, or a few hours' reading of her books, they are likely enough to say, "After all, when a woman gets some knowledge, see what use she makes of it! Her knowledge remains acquisition, instead of passing into culture; instead of being subdued into modesty and simplicity by a larger acquaintance with thought and fact, she has a feverish consciousness of her attainments; she keeps a sort of mental pocket-mirror, and is continually looking in it at her own 'intellectuality;' she spoils the taste of one's muffin by questions of metaphysics; puts down men at a dinner table with her superior information; and seizes the opportunity of a *soirée* to catechise us on the vital question of the relation between mind and matter. And then, look at her writings! She mistakes vagueness for depth, bombast for eloquence, and affectation for originality; she struts on one page, rolls her eyes on another, grimaces in a third, and is hysterical in a fourth. She may have read many writings of great men, and a few writings of great women; but she is as unable to discern the difference between her own style and theirs as a Yorkshireman is to discern the difference between his own English and a Londoner's: rhodomontade is the native accent of her intellect. No—the average nature of women is too shallow and feeble a soil to bear much tillage; it is only fit for the very lightest crops."

It is true that the men who come to such a decision on such very superficial and imperfect observation may not be among the wisest in the world; but we have not now to contest their opinion—we are only pointing out how it is unconsciously encouraged by many women who have volunteered themselves as representatives of the feminine intellect. We do not believe that a man was ever strengthened in such an opinion by associating with a woman of true culture, whose mind had absorbed her knowledge instead of being absorbed by it. A really cultured woman, like a really cultured man, is all the simpler and less intrusive for her knowledge; it has made her see herself and her opinions in something like just proportions; she does not make it a pedestal from which she flatters herself that she commands a complete view of men and things, but makes it a point of observation from which to form a right estimate of herself. She neither spouts poetry nor quotes Cicero on slight provocation; not because she thinks that a sacrifice must be made to the prejudices of men, but because that mode of exhibiting her memory and Latinity does not present itself to her as edifying or graceful. She does not write books to confound philosophers, perhaps because she is able to write books that delight them. In conversation she is the least formidable of women, because she understands you, without wanting to make you aware that you *can't* understand her. She does not give you information, which is the raw material of culture—she gives you sympathy, which is its subtlest essence.

A more numerous class of silly novels than the oracular (which are generally inspired by some form of High Church, or transcendental Christianity), is what we may call the *white neck cloth* species, which represent the tone of thought and feeling in the Evangelical party. This species is a kind of genteel tract on a large scale, intended as a sort of medicinal sweetmeat for Low Church young ladies; an Evangelical substitute for the fashionable novel, as the May Meetings are a substitute for the Opera. Even Quaker children, one would think, can hardly have been denied the indulgence of a doll; but it must be a doll dressed in a drab gown and a coal-scuttle bonnet!—not a worldly doll, in gauze and spangles. And there are no young ladies, we imagine,—unless they belong to the Church of the United Brethren, in which people are married without any love-making—who can dispense with love stories. Thus, for Evangelical young ladies there are Evangelical love stories, in which the vicissitudes of the tender passion are sanctified by saving views of Regeneration and Atonement. These novels differ from the oracular ones, as a Low Churchwoman often differs from a High Churchwoman: they are a little less supercilious, and a great deal more ignorant, a little less correct in their syntax, and a great deal more vulgar.

The Orlando of Evangelical literature is the young curate, looked at from the point of view of the middle class, where cambric bands are understood to have as thrilling an effect on the hearts of young ladies as epaulettes have in the classes above and below it. In the ordinary type of these novels, the hero is almost sure to be a young curate, frowned upon, perhaps, by worldly mammas, but carrying captive the hearts of their daughters, who can "never forget *that* sermon;" tender glances are seized from the pulpit stairs instead of the opera-box; *tête-à-têtes* are seasoned with quotations from Scripture, instead of quotations from the poets; and questions as to the state of the heroine's affections are mingled with anxieties as to the state of her soul. The young curate always has a background of well-dressed and wealthy, if not fashionable society;—for Evangelical silliness is as snobbish as any other kind of silliness; and the Evangelical lady novelist, while she explains to you the type of the scapegoat on one page, is ambitious on another to represent the manners and conversation of aristocratic people. Her pictures of fashionable society are often curious studies, considered as efforts of the Evangelical imagination, but in one particular the novels of the White Neck-cloth School are meritoriously realistic,— their favourite hero, the Evangelical young curate, is always rather an insipid personage.

The most recent novel of this species that we happen to have before us, is "The Old Grey Church." It is utterly tame and feeble; there is no one set of objects on which the writer seems to have a stronger grasp than on any other; and we should be entirely at a loss to conjecture among what phases of life her experience has been gained, but for certain vulgarisms of style which sufficiently indicate that she has had the advantage, though she has been unable to use it, of mingling chiefly with men and women whose manners and characters have not had all their bosses and angles rubbed down by refined conventionalism. It is less excusable in an Evangelical novelist, than in any other, gratuitously to seek her subjects among titles and carriages. The real drama of Evangelicalism—and it has abundance of fine drama for any one who has genius enough to discern and reproduce it—lies among the middle and lower classes; and are not Evangelical opinions understood to give an especial interest in the weak things of the earth, rather than in the mighty? Why, then, cannot our Evangelical lady novelists show us the operation of their religious views among people (there really are many such in the world) who keep no carriage, "not so much as a brass-bound gig," who even manage to eat their dinner without a silver fork, and in whose mouths the authoress's questionable English would be strictly consistent? Why can we not have pictures of religious life among the industrial classes in England, as interesting as Mrs. Stowe's pictures of religious life among the negroes? Instead of this, pious ladies nauseate us with novels which remind us of what we sometimes see in a worldly woman recently "converted;"—she is as fond of a fine dinner table as before, but she invites clergy-men instead of beaux; she thinks as much of her dress as before, but she adopts a more sober choice of colours and patterns; her conversation is as trivial as before, but the triviality is flavoured with gospel instead of gossip. In "The Old Grey Church," we have the same sort of Evangelical travesty of the fashionable novel, and of course the vicious, intriguing baronet is not wanting. It is worth while to give a sample of the style of conversation attributed to this high-born rake—a style that, in its profuse italics and palpable innuendoes is worthy of Miss Squeers! In an evening visit to the ruins of the Colosseum, Eustace, the young clergyman, has been withdrawing the heroine, Miss Lushington, from the rest of the party, for the sake of a *tête-à-tête*. The baronet is jealous, and vents his pique in this way:—

> There they are, and Miss Lushington, no doubt, quite safe; for she is under the holy guidance of Pope Eustace the First, who has, of course, been delivering her an edifying homily on the wickedness of the heathens of yore, who, as tradition tells us, in this very place let loose the wild *beastises* on poor St. Paul!—Oh no!, by-the-bye, I believe, I am wrong, and betraying my want of clergy, and that it was not at all St. Paul, nor was it here. But no matter, it would equally serve as a text to preach from, and from which to diverge to the degenerate *heathen* Christians of the present day, and all their naughty practices, and so end with an exhortation to 'come out from among them, and be separate;'—and I am sure, Miss Lushington, you have most scrupulously conformed to that injunction this evening, for we have seen nothing of you since our arrival. But every one seems agreed it has been a *charming party of pleasure*, and I am sure we all feel *much indebted* to Mr. Grey for having *suggested* it; and as he seems so capital a cicerone, I hope he will think of something equally agreeable to *all*.

This drivelling kind of dialogue, and equally drivelling narrative, which, like a bad drawing, represents nothing, and barely indicates what is meant to be represented, runs through the book; and we have no doubt is considered by the amiable authoress to constitute an improving novel, which Christian mothers will do well to put into the hands of their daughters. But everything is relative; we have met with American vegetarians whose normal diet was dry meal, and who, when their appetite wanted stimulating, tickled it with *wet* meal; and so, we can imagine that there are Evangelical circles in which "The Old Grey Church" is devoured as a powerful and interesting fiction.

But, perhaps, the least readable of silly women's novels, are the *modern-antique* species, which unfold to us the domestic life of Jannes and Jambres, the private love affairs of Sennacherib, or the mental struggles and ultimate conversion of Demetrius the silversmith. From most silly novels we can at least extract a laugh; but those of the modern antique school have a ponderous, a leaden kind of fatuity, under which we groan. What can be more demonstrative of the inability of literary women to measure their own powers, than their frequent assumption of a task which can only be justified by the rarest occurrence of acquirement with genius? The finest effort to reanimate the past is of course only approximative—as always more or less an infusion of the modern spirit into the ancient form,—

> *Was ihr den Geist der Zeiten heisst,*
> *Das ist im Grund der Herren eigner Geist,*
> *In dem die Zeiten sich bespiegeln.*

Admitting that genius which has familiarized itself with all the relics of an ancient period can sometimes, by the force of its sympathetic divination, restore the missing notes in the "music of humanity," and reconstruct the fragments into a whole which will really bring the remote past nearer to us, and interpret it to our duller apprehension,—this form of imaginative power must always be among the very rarest, because it demands as much accurate and minute knowledge as creative vigour. Yet we find ladies constantly choosing to make their mental mediocrity more conspicuous, by clothing it in a masquerade of ancient names; by putting their feeble sentimentality into the mouths of Roman vestals or Egyptian princesses, and attributing their rhetorical arguments to Jewish high-priests and Greek philosophers. A recent example of this heavy imbecility is, "Adonijah, a Tale of the Jewish Dispersion," which forms part of a series, "uniting," we are told, "taste, humour, and sound principles." "Adonijah," we presume, exemplifies the tale of "sound principles;" the taste and humour are to be found in other members of the series. We are told on the cover, that the incidents of this tale are "fraught with unusual interest," and the preface winds up thus: "To those who feel interested in the dispersed of Israel and Judea, these pages may afford, perhaps, information on an important subject, as well as amusement." Since the "important subject" on which this book is to afford information is not specified, it may possibly lie in some esoteric meaning to which we have no key; but if it has relation to the dispersed of Israel and Judea at any period of their history, we believe a tolerably well-informed school-girl already knows much more of it than she will find in this "Tale of Jewish Dispersion." "Adonijah" is simply the feeblest kind of love story, supposed to be instructive, we presume, because the hero is a Jewish captive, and the heroine a Roman vestal, because they and their friends are converted to Christianity after the shortest and easiest method, approved by the "Society for Promoting the Conversion of the Jews," and because, instead of being written in plain language, it is adorned with that peculiar style of grandiloquence which is held by some lady novelists to give an antique colouring, and which we recognise at once in such phrases as these:— "the splendid regnal talent, undoubtedly possessed by the Emperor Nero"—"the expiring scion of a lofty stem"—"the virtuous partner of his couch"—"ah, by Vesta!"— and "I tell thee, Roman!" Among the quotations which serve at once for instruction and ornament on the cover of this volume, there is one from Miss Sinclair, which informs us that "Works of imagination are *avowedly* read by men of science, wisdom, and piety;" from which we suppose the reader is to gather the cheering inference that Dr. Daubeny, Mr. Mill, or Mr. Maurice, may openly indulge himself with the perusal of "Adonijah," without being obliged to secrete it among the sofa cushions, or read it by snatches under the dinner table.

"Be not a baker if your head be made of butter," says a homely proverb, which, being interpreted, may mean, let no woman rush into print who is not prepared for the consequences. We are aware that our remarks are in a very different tone from that of the reviewers who, with perennial recurrence of precisely similar emotions, only paralleled, we imagine, in the experience of monthly nurses, tell one lady novelist after another that they "hail" her productions "with delight." We are aware that the ladies at whom our criticism is pointed are accustomed to be told, in the choicest phraseology of puffery, that their pictures of life are brilliant, their characters well drawn, their style fascinating, and their sentiments lofty. But if they are inclined to resent our plainness of speech, we ask them to reflect for a moment on the chary praise, and often captious blame, which their panegyrists give to writers whose works are on the way to become classics. No sooner does a woman show that she has genius or effective talent, than she receives the tribute of being moderately praised and severely criticised. By a peculiar thermometric adjustment, when a woman's talent is at zero, it is already at no more than summer heat; and if ever she reaches excellence, critical enthusiasm drops to the freezing point. Harriet Martineau, Currer Bell, and Mrs. Gaskell have been treated as cavalierly as if they had been men. And every critic who forms a high estimate of the share women may ultimately take in literature, will, on principle, abstain from any exceptional indulgence towards the productions of literary women. For it must be plain to every one who looks impartially and extensively into feminine literature, that its greatest deficiencies are due hardly more to the want of intellectual power than to the want of those moral qualities that contribute to literary excellence—patient diligence, a sense of the responsibility involved in publication, and an appreciation of the sacredness of the writer's art. In the majority of women's books you see that kind of facility which springs from the absence of any high standard; that fertility in imbecile combination or feeble imitation which a little self-criticism would check and reduce to barrenness; just as with a total want of musical ear people will sing out of tune, while a degree more melodic sensibility would suffice to render them silent. The foolish vanity of wishing to appear in print, instead of being counterbalanced by any consciousness of the intellectual or moral derogation implied in futile authorship, seems to be encouraged by the extremely false impression that to write *at all* is a proof of superiority in a woman. On this ground, we believe that the average intellect of women is unfairly represented by the mass of feminine literature, and that while the few women who write well are very far above the ordinary intellectual level of their sex, the many women who write ill are far below it. So that, after all, the severer critics are fulfilling a chivalrous duty in depriving the mere fact of feminine authorship of any false prestige which may give it a delusive attraction, and in recommending women of mediocre faculties—as at least a negative service they can render their sex—to abstain from writing.

The standing apology for women who become writers without any special qualification is, that society shuts them out from other spheres of occupation. Society is a very culpable entity, and has to answer for the manufacture of many unwholesome commodities, from bad pickles to bad poetry. But society, like "matter," and Her Majesty's Government, and other lofty abstractions, has its share of excessive blame as well as excessive praise. Where there is one woman who writes from necessity, we believe there are three women who write from vanity; and, besides, there is something so antiseptic in the mere healthy fact of working for one's bread, that the most trashy and rotten kind of feminine literature is not likely to have been produced under such circumstances. "In all labour there is profit;" but ladies' silly novels, we imagine, are less the result of labour than of busy idleness.

Happily, we are not dependent on argument to prove that Fiction is a department of literature in which women can, after their kind, fully equal men. A cluster of great names, both living and dead, rush to our memories in evidence that women can produce novels not only fine, but among the very finest;—novels, too, that have a precious speciality, lying quite apart from masculine aptitudes and experience. No educational restrictions can shut women out from the materials of fiction, and there is no species of art which is so free from rigid requirements. Like crystalline masses, it may take any form, and yet be beautiful; we have only to pour in the right elements—genuine observation, humour, and passion. But it is precisely this absence of rigid requirement which constitutes the fatal seduction of novel-writing to incompetent women. Ladies are not wont to be very grossly deceived as to their power of playing on the piano; here certain positive difficulties of execution have to be conquered, and incompetence inevitably breaks down. Every art which has its absolute *technique* is, to a certain extent, guarded from the intrusions of mere left-handed imbecility. But in novel-writing there are no barriers for incapacity to stumble against, no external criteria to prevent a writer from mistaking foolish facility for mastery. And so we have again and again the old story of La Fontaine's ass, who puts his nose to the flute, and, finding that he elicits some sound, exclaims, "Moi, aussi, je joue de la flute;"—a fable which we commend, at parting, to the consideration of any female reader who is in danger of adding to the number of "silly novels by lady novelists."

56

From *Adam Bede*

GEORGE ELIOT

In her first published novel, Eliot defends her realistic technique, using the analogy of a defective mirror. She is anticipating and responding to readers' calls for romanticised or idealised portraits, ones she had condemned in her essay, "Silly Novels by Lady Novelists", in the *Westminster Review* (see previous chapter) several years before. The characterisation in *Adam Bede* sets the tone for all of Eliot's later novels.

From Book II.
Chapter XVII.

In which the story pauses a little.

"This Rector of Broxton is little better than a pagan!" I hear one of my readers exclaim. "How much more edifying it would have been if you had made him give Arthur some truly spiritual advice! You might have put into his mouth the most beautiful things—quite as good as reading a sermon."

Certainly I could, if I held it the highest vocation of the novelist to represent things as they never have been and never will be. Then, of course, I might refashion life and character entirely after my own liking; I might select the most unexceptionable type of clergyman, and put my own admirable opinions into his mouth on all occasions. But it happens, on the contrary, that my strongest effort is to avoid any such arbitrary picture, and to give a faithful account of men and things as they have mirrored themselves in my mind. The mirror is doubtless defective; the outlines will sometimes be disturbed, the reflection faint or confused; but I feel as much bound to tell you as precisely as I can what that reflection is, as if I were in the witness-box narrating my experience on oath. [. . .]

Source: George Eliot, from *Adam Bede*, Book II, Chapter 17, 1859, rptd New York: John W. Lovell Co., 1890, pp. 171-2.

57

From *Middlemarch*

GEORGE ELIOT

In the following passage from her best known novel, Eliot advances the analogy of the web to describe her attempts at realistic characterisation. She contrasts her own method with that of Fielding, noting that Fielding could afford to be expansive, to digress in the inter chapters throughout his novels. Viewing herself and her contemporaries as "belated historians", Eliot comments on the central purpose in her novel: to investigate the social interactions among a select group of characters living in a particular community.

From Book II, Chapter 15

A great historian, as he insisted on calling himself, who had the happiness to be dead a hundred and twenty years ago, and so to take his place among the colossi whose huge legs our living pettiness is observed to walk under, glories in his copious remarks and digressions as the least imitable part of his work, and especially in those initial chapters to the successive books of his history, where he seems to bring his arm-chair to the proscenium and chat with us in all the lusty ease of his fine English. But Fielding lived when the days were longer (for time, like money, is measured by our needs), when summer afternoons were spacious, and the clock ticked slowly in the winter evenings. We belated historians must not linger after his example; and if we did so, it is probable that our chat would be thin and eager, as if delivered from a camp-stool in a parrot-house. I at least have so much to do in unravelling certain human lots, and seeing how they were woven and interwoven, that all the light I can command must be concentrated on this particular web, and not dispersed over that tempting range of relevancies called the universe.

Source: George Eliot, from *Middlemarch*, Book II, Chapter 15, 1871–72, rptd Boston: Estes and Lauriat, 1894, pp. 191–2.

❦ 58 ❦

Criticism in Relation to Novels

GEORGE HENRY LEWES

One of the principal critics and reviewers of the Victorian period, G. H. Lewes insisted that in order to represent reality, a novelist needed sincerity and clarity of vision. In the following essay he condemns the low standard of the circulating libraries and the really low level of critical appraisal in the major periodicals. Like his predecessors and contemporaries, he distinguishes between romance and realism, noting that the latter, which presents a picture of life, is both preferable and more difficult to achieve. He follows Matthew Arnold in his call for a higher level of criticism, a criticism that might inspire the novelist to attend more closely to the fit between language and subject matter. This essay builds on Lewes's earlier distinction between realism and "falsism" in a review of German fiction in the *Westminster Review* of October 1858. As early as 1847 in his review of Brontë's *Jane Eyre*, Lewes had condemned the use of melodramatic incident as false and unconvincing. He recommended that Charlotte Brontë read Jane Austen for an example of realistic portraiture.

Criticism in relation to novels.[1]

Although the fame of a great novelist is only something less than the fame of a great poet, and the reputation of a clever novelist is far superior to that of a respectable poet, the general estimation of prose fiction as a branch of Literature has something contemptuous in it. This is shown not only in the condescending tone in which critics speak, and the carelessness with which they praise, but also in the half-apologetic phrases in which very shallow readers confess that they have employed their leisured ignorance on such light literature. It is shown, moreover, in the rashness with which writers, confessedly incapable of success in far inferior efforts, will confidently attempt fiction, as if it were the easiest of literary tasks; and in the insolent assumption that "anything will do for a novel."

Source: George Henry Lewes, "Criticism in Relation to Novels", *Fortnightly Review*, 3, 15 December 1865, pp. 352-61.

The reason of this fame, and the reason of this contempt, are not difficult to find. The fame is great because the influence of a fine novel is both extensive and subtle, and because the combination of high powers necessary for the production of a fine novel is excessively rare. The contempt is general, because the combination of powers necessary for the production of three volumes of Circulating Library reminiscences is very common; and because there is a large demand for the amusement which such reminiscences afford. The intellectual feebleness of readers in general prevents their forming a discriminating estimate of the worth of such works; and most of those who are capable of discrimination have had their standard of expectation so lowered by the profusion of mediocrity, that they languidly acquiesce in the implied assumption that novels are removed from the canons of common-sense criticism. Hence the activity of this commerce of trash. The sterile abundance casts a sort of opprobrium on the art itself. The lowered standard invites the incapable. Men and women who have shown no special aptitudes for this difficult art flatter themselves, and not unreasonably, that they may succeed as well as others whom openly they despise. And their friends are ready to urge them on this path. No one looking over the sketchbook of an amateur turns to him with the question—"Why not try your hand at a fresco?" But many men, on no better warrant, say to a writer—"Why not try you hand at a novel?" And there is a great alacrity in trying the hand.

There is thus action and reaction: acquiescence in mediocrity increases the production of mediocrity and lowers the standard, which thus in turn admits of inferior production. We critics are greatly to blame. Instead of compensating for the inevitable evils of periodical criticism by doing our utmost to keep up the standard of public taste, too many of us help to debase it by taking a standard from the Circulating Library, and by a half-contemptuous, half-languid patronage of what we do not seriously admire. The lavish eulogies which welcome very trivial works as if they were masterpieces, are sometimes the genuine expression of very ignorant writers (for easy as it is to write a poor novel, to review it is easier still; and the very language of the reviews often betrays the intellectual condition of the writers); but sometimes they are judgments formed solely in reference to the degraded standard which the multitude of poor works has introduced. Thus although the same terms of commendation are applied to the last new novel which are applied to "Vanity Fair," or "Pride and Prejudice," the standard is nevertheless insensibly changed, and the critic who uses the same language respecting both really thinks of placing both in the same class.

The general public knows nothing of this change of standards; and thus a foreigner, casting his eye over our advertisements, would suppose, from the "opinions of the press," that England boasted of two or three score writers of exquisite genius; but if, seduced by this supposition, he familiarised himself with the masterpieces thus extolled; he would perhaps conclude that England was suffering from a softened brain. One thing would certainly arouse his curiosity, and that would be to meet with a sample of what are everywhere called "the ordinary run of novels." He would hear that Mr. A's work was far superior to this ordinary run; that Mrs.

B's exquisite story was carefully separated from the ordinary run; that Miss C's tale displayed a delicacy of conception, a depth of insight into character and passion, and a purity of moral tone sought for in vain in the ordinary run of novels. But he would appeal to Mudie in vain for a novel which was acknowledged as one of the ordinary run.

Although I have a very high opinion of Fiction as a form of Literature, and read no kind of Literature with more delight and gratitude, I cannot pretend to an extensive acquaintance with recent novels; indeed there are writers of considerable reputation whose works I have never opened, either because they have not fallen in my way in hours of leisure, or because those whose judgment I respect have not by their praises induced me to make a trial. Nevertheless, living in a great literary centre, and naturally inclined to seek the immense gratification which a good novel always gives, I have become tolerably acquainted with the typical specimens, and come to the conclusion that if many of the novels of to-day are considerably better than those of twenty or thirty years ago, because they partake of the general advance in culture, and its wider diffusion; the vast increase of novels, mostly worthless, is a serious danger to public culture, a danger which tends to become more and more imminent, and can only be arrested by an energetic resolution on the part of the critics to do their duty with conscientious rigour. At present the duty is evaded, or performed fitfully. There is plenty of sarcasm and ill-nature; too much of it; there is little serious criticism which weighs considerately its praise and its blame. Even in the best journals poor novels are often praised in terms strictly applicable to works of genius alone. If a thoughtful reader opens one of these novels, he sees such violations of common sense and common knowledge, such style and such twaddle, as would never gain admission into the critical journals themselves, for these journals recommend to readers what they would refuse to print. The reason generally is that critics have ceased to regard novels as Literature, and do not think of applying to the style and sentiments of a fiction those ordinary canons which would be applied to a history, an article, or a pamphlet.

And there is sometimes a certain justification for this exception; only it should be always brought prominently forward. The distinctive element in Fiction is that of plot-interest. The rest is vehicle. If critics would carefully specify the qualities which distinguish the work they praise, and not confound plot-interest with other sources of interest, above all not confound together the various kinds of plot-interest, readers would be guided in their choice, and have their taste educated. For example, it is quite fair to praise Miss Braddon for the skill she undoubtedly displays in plot-interest of a certain kind—in selecting situations of crime and mystery which have a singular fascination for a large number of readers; and the success she has obtained is due to the skill with which she has prepared and presented these situations so as to excite the curiosity and sympathy of idle people. It is a special talent she possesses; and the critic is wrong who fails to recognise in it the source of her success. But he would be equally wrong, I think, if he confounded this merit with other merits, which her novels do not display. I have only read two of her works—"Lady Audley's Secret," and "Sir Jasper's Tenant"—but from those I have no hesitation in concluding that her grasp of character, her vision of realities, her regard for probabilities, and her theoretical views of human life, are very far from being on a level with her power over plot-interest. In praising stories there should be some discrimination of the kind of interest aimed at, and the means by which the aim is reached. A criminal trial will agitate all England, when another involving similar degrees of crime, but without certain adjuncts of interest, will be read only by the seekers of the very vulgarest stimulants. It is not the crime, but the attendant circumstances of horror and mystery, of pathetic interest, and of social suggestions, which give importance to a trial. In like manner the skill of the story-teller is displayed in selecting the attendant circumstances of horror, mystery, pathos, and social suggestion, bringing the events home to our experience and sympathy. And the critic should fix his attention on this mode of presentation, not demanding from the writer qualities incompatible with, or obviously disregarded by his method. In a story of wild and startling incidents, such as "Monte Christo," it is absurd to demand a minute attention to probabilities; provided the improbabilities are not glaringly obtrusive, that is, provided our imaginative sympathy is not checked by a sense of the incongruous, we grant the author a large licence. But in proportion as the story lies among scenes and characters of familiar experience, in proportion as the writer endeavours to engage our sympathy by pictures of concrete realities, and not by *abstractions* of passion and incident, the critic demands a closer adherence to truth and experience. Monte Christo may talk a language never heard off the stage, but Major Pendennis must speak as they speak in Pall Mall. It is obviously a much easier task to tell a story involving only the abstractions of life, than to tell one which moves amidst its realities. It is easier to disregard all those probabilities which would interfere with the symmetrical arrangement of incidents in a culminating progression, and all those truths of human character which in real life would complicate and thwart any scheme of pre-arranged events, than to tell a story which carries with it in every phase of its evolution a justification of what is felt, said, and done, so that the reader seems, as it were, to be the spectator of an actual drama. Nevertheless, both are legitimate forms of art; and although the latter is incomparably the more difficult, and the more valuable in its results, the former is and always will be popular with the mass of readers. A picture made up of improbable combinations and unreal elements may interest us once; but unless it be a pure play of fancy avowedly soaring away into regions beyond or beside this life of ours, it cannot sustain its interest, for it cannot withstand the inevitable scrutiny of deliberation. It will not bear re-reading. It cannot be thought of without misgiving. A picture made up of nature's sequences will interest for all time.

Plot-interest is, as I said, the distinctive element in Fiction; and the critic ought to mark plainly what the nature of the interest is no less than the skill with which it is presented. Having done this, if he speak of the historical, pictorial, moral, religious, or literary details, he should speak of them as amenable to the ordinary canons. Nonsense is not excusable because it forms part of the padding of a story. People ought to be ashamed of having written, or of having praised trash, wherever it may have appeared. And a little critical rigour exercised with respect to the descriptions, dialogues, and reflections which accompany a story, would act beneficially in two ways: first, in affording a test whereby the writer's pretensions might be estimated; secondly, by making writers more vigilant against avoidable mistakes.

As a test: You may have a very lively sense of the unreality with which a writer has conceived a character, or presented a situation, but it is by no means easy to make him see this, or to make his admirers see it. In vain would you refer to certain details as inaccurate; he cannot recognise their inaccuracy. In vain would you point to the general air of unreality, the conventional tone of the language, the absence of those subtle, individual traits which give verisimilitude to a conception; he cannot see it; to him the conception does seem lifelike; he may perhaps assure you that it is taken from the life. But failing on this ground, you may succeed by an indirect route. In cases so complex as those of human character and human affairs, the possibilities of misapprehension are numerous; and if we find a man liable to mistake sound for sense, to misapprehend the familiar relations of daily life, to describe vaguely or inaccurately the objects of common experience, or to write *insincerely* in the belief that he is writing eloquently, then we may *à fortiori* conclude that he will be still more liable to misapprehend the complexities of character, to misrepresent psychological subtleties, to put language into peoples mouths which is not the language of real feeling, and to modify the course of events according to some conventional prejudice. In a word, if he is feeble and inaccurate in ordinary matters, he may be believed to be feeble and inaccurate in higher matters. If he writes nonsense, or extravagant sentimentality, in uttering his own comments, we may suspect his sense and truthfulness when his personages speak and act.

Before proceeding to the second result of critical rigour it will be desirable to apply the test in a specific instance, and I select "Maxwell Drewitt" for this purpose, rather than "Sir Jasper's Tenant," because the author has been specially lauded for powers of portraiture which I have been unable to recognise. It is but right to add that I have read none of this author's previous works; and to add further that there is much even in this work which I shall presently have to praise. If any of my remarks seem severe, let them be understood as at least implying the compliment of serious criticism. It is because I wish to treat her novel as Literature, and because she has an earnestness of purpose and a literary ability which challenge respect, that I make choice of her work for illustration; though at first sight any selection must seem invidious where so many examples abound.

"Maxwell Drewitt" is not a novel of incident, but a picture of life and character. Its interest is not meant to lie in the skilful combination of the abstractions of passion and situation, irrespective of concrete probabilities, irrespective of real human motives in the common transactions of life; in other words, it is not a romance, it is not a sensation story, trusting solely to the power of ideal presentation of abstractions, or to the appeal to our sympathies with mystery and crime. The obvious aim of the writer is to paint a picture of Irish life, and to inculcate a moral lesson. The aim is high; and being high, it challenges criticism as to its means. The aim is one which tasks a writer's powers; and success can only be proportionate to the verisimilitude with which the picture is painted. I do not think the degree of verisimilitude attained is such as to justify the praises which have been awarded it. There are excellent intentions; but the execution is approximative, inaccurate, wanting in the sharp individuality which comes from clear vision and dramatic insight. The first hazy conception of the characters is not condensed into distinctness. The careless, good-natured, indolent Irish landlord—always in difficulties, always cheery and improvident—is described, but not depicted. His energetic, clever, scheming, hard-hearted nephew is drawn with more detail, but nevertheless falls very short of a recognisable portrait. The rascally Irish lawyer, and the virtuous English lawyer, are pale, lifeless conventionalities. The reckless Harold and the vindictive but virtuous Brian, are shadows. The coquettish Lady Emeline, the loving Jenny Bourke, and the patient Mrs. Drewitt, are lay figures. The language has never that nice dramatic propriety which seems as if it could only come from the persons. None of the characters have the impress of creative genius. The same haziness and conventionality may be noted of the attempts to represent the fluctuations of feeling, and the combinations of motive, in the actors. We are informed at great length of what the people felt, we listen to their conversation and soliloquies, but we never seem to hear a real human voice, we never see a soul laid bare.

Such briefly is the impression produced on my mind by this novel as a picture of life and character. I do not really *see* the election riot, I do not feel myself ideally present at those scenes; I do not seem to know Archibald Drewitt's improvidence; nor does Maxwell's patient prosecution of his plans for improving the estate and making his fortune, although told at some length, come home to me like an experience. Both are described, neither is vividly painted. The scenes in Dublin and London are weak and shadowy. In fact, the execution is wanting in the sharpness of distinct vision, where it is not absolutely inaccurate. At the best it is but approximative, never lifelike.

But having said thus much, I should leave a false impression if I did not add that I have been judging "Maxwell Drewitt" by a higher standard than that of the novels which are produced by the score. There is a certain gloomy earnestness in the writer, and a rhetorical power which carry you unwearied, though not unoffended, through the volumes. There is, moreover, a certain distinctiveness in the mode of treatment, and in the selection of the subjects. Without knowing anything of Ireland, I am quite sure that life at Connemara was not like what it appears in these pages; but then the fact that we are taken to unfamiliar scenes lightens our sense of the imperfect verisimilitude. The *suggestions* of the novel are interesting. The obvious effort of the writer to depict the improvidence and ignorance of the Irish and the ready means by which the land may be immensely improved, gives it a more serious aim than if it were a mere love story, or story of incident. What I consider its gravest defects, are the absence of sufficient clearness of Vision, and of sufficient attention to the principle of Sincerity (as these have formerly been explained in this Review); which defects might to a great extent be remedied by a resolute determination on her part not to writer until her vision became clear, and only to write what she had distinctly in her mind.

Let us see what the application of our Test will do towards justifying such an impression. We find the hero, a young man of our own day, talking thus to himself:—

> "Yes, yes," he cried at last, halting suddenly, and looking away towards the hills that rose to heaven—"yes, yes, Kincorth, you shall yet be mine—you and many a fair property beside; but you in especial, because I have sworn that neither man nor devil shall keep you from me. And shall a woman? No, before God!' And the veins came swelling up in his forehead as he stretched out one clenched hand towards Kincorth, and registered his oath.

It is difficult to suppose the author hearing her characters talk in this style, or believing it to be a representation of modern life, which could be accepted by a reflecting reader. Still worse is this rhapsody—

> "I love the wind," she thought; "it is fresh and pure, and it comes from travelling over the great sea, instead of bringing the taint of large cities on its breath;" and she turned, even while she was thinking this, round Eversbeg Head, and the wide Atlantic and the full force of the western breeze burst upon her at once.
>
> Thousands of miles! Millions upon millions of tossing billows! Oh! thou great God Almighty! who can look across the restless ocean and not think of Thee? Who can forget, while standing by the sea and watching the great waters come thundering upon the shore, that Thou hast set bounds to the waters and said, 'Here shall thy proud waves be stayed'—who, looking over the trackless expanse of ocean, but must feel that all unseen the feet of the Most High have traversed it?
>
> When we see this work of the Lord, His wonders in the deep; when we perceive how at His command the floods arise, and how at His word the storm ceases; when we remember that though the waves of the sea are mighty and rage horribly, still that the Lord God who dwelleth on high is mightier; when we think that He holds the waters in the hollow of His hand, do we not seem, for a moment, amid raging tempests and foaming billows, to catch a glimpse of the Infinite? Looking over the waste of waters, does not our weak mortality appear able to grasp for an instant the idea of immortality? Can we not imagine that no material horizon bounds our view—that we are gazing away and away across the ocean into eternity?
>
> Thousands of miles, friends! Which of us has not at one time or other let his heart go free over the waters? Who has not stood by the shore silent, while his inner self—his self that never talks save to his god and his own soul—has gone out from his body and tossed with the billows, and answered the sullen roar of the waters, and risen and sunk with the waters as they rose and fell, rose and fell, and felt the breaking of the foam, the sobbing plash of the great ocean, as it rolls up on the sands and over the rocks and stones and shells of earth, while depth calleth unto depth, and the giant floods clap their hands together?
>
> And oh! with what a terrible sadness does that second self come back to us! It has been out listening to strange voices, hearing strange sounds, learning solemn truths. It has been out on the billows, on the foam, among the spray and the clouds and the tempest—out and away to the very confines of the invisible world. It has been restless like the ocean, and it comes back to be set within the bounds of flesh; it has been free, and behold it must return to chains and fetters; it has been telling off its troubles to the ocean, and the ocean has lift up its mighty arms and mourned out its sorrowful reply.
>
> Mourning—mourning—never silent, never still—now lashing itself up into fury—now tossing hither and thither as it seems to us without plan or purpose; now wave following after wave, as man follows after man in the ranks of a vast army; now flinging its waters on the shore—now striving to climb the steep sides of some

ragged rock; fretting itself as we fret ourselves—moaning as we moan—toiling as we toil—restless as we are; now receding—now advancing—but never at peace; in its strong moods wild and tumultuous—in its calmest moments stirred by the ground swell, ruffled by the lightest breeze! Well may man love this deep, inexplicable, unfathomable ocean, for as it through the ages has gone on sobbing and mourning and struggling, so man through the years of his life goes mourning and struggling too.

Some thoughts like these passed through Mrs. Drewitt's mind as she stood at the base of Eversbeg Head, and looked out over the Atlantic.

This ambitious, but most injudicious passage is given as a representation of the thoughts which passed through the mind of a gentle, unhysterical, matter-of-fact woman! On reading it, every one will be able to form an estimate of the probability of a writer, who could present such a picture with a belief in its truthfulness being able to delineate truly the complexities of character under exceptional conditions. It is quite clear that she was led away by the temptation of "fine writing" to substitute what she considered an eloquent passage about the sea, for what Mrs. Drewitt is likely to have felt by the sea-shore. This is what I have named insincerity; and it is one of the common vices of literature.

There is an unpleasant redundance of "fine writing" and emphatic platitudes in these volumes. The desire to be eloquent, and the desire to sermonise, lead to pages upon pages which offend the taste, and which, if found out of a novel or a sermon, would provoke the critic's ridicule; but on the assumption that novels are not to be criticised as Literature, they pass without rebuke. Imagine any one of ordinary cleverness called upon to meditate on a truism thus ambitiously worded:—

Within a week Ryan took a house in Duranmore next door to his office, and moved his furniture and himself and his sister away from the pretty cottage by the shore. *But the waves came rolling up the bay for all that*: though there was no human ear to listen to their music, they still rippled over the stones and sand—the shutters of the cottage windows were closed and fastened, *but the fuchsias bloomed the same as ever*—no Jenny now stood by the stream, singing her love songs, dreaming her love fantasies, *but the stream* went dancing over the stones to the sea none the less joyously—there were none to look up at the evelasting hills, *but the summer's sun shone on them*, and the winter's snows lay on them, as the sun had shone and the show had lain since the beginning of time.

For whose instruction is this wisdom proffered? Was it a *possible* supposition that the removal of Jenny should cause the disappearance of the mountains and the cessation of the tides, or that fuchsias would cease to bloom because the window shutters were closed? Surely common sense ought not to be thus disregarded in the search for eloquence?

The truth seems to be that writing hastily, and unchecked by any sense of her responsibilities, never pausing to ask herself whether what she was setting down had truth or value, and would bear reflection, she indulged a propensity to vague moralising, feeling that anything was good enough for a novel. Thus, having killed her hero, she preaches a sermon on his career, in which we have remarks like this:—

Pitiful! most pitiful! In his prime this man was taken away from among his treasures—from the place he had longed to possess—from the country of his birth—from the scenes he had loved to gaze over. What did it matter, then, whether he had been rich or poor, wealthy or indigent, lofty or lowly, peer or peasant?—what did it matter? what even in life had the lands and the houses, had the silver and the gold, profited him?"

And this—

> Never more may he walk by the sea shore, or stand under the arching trees that shade the avenue, or ride by lake or river, past mountains and through the valleys—never more for ever . . . The great mountains rear their blue summits to heaven, the lakes ripple and ripple, the rivers flow onward to the sea, and the boulders and the blocks of granite lie scattered about on the hill sides—the great Atlantic beats against the iron-bound coast, and up the thousand bays the waves steal gently as ever—on that strange country through which Maxwell rode when he was still young, when he had life all before him, the moon looks down with as cold a light, playing as many fantastic tricks, creeping up the hills, and lying in the waters just as she did then.

There are several other passages I had marked for comment,[2] but those already given will suffice to confirm both my opinion of the quality of "Maxwell Drewitt," and my position respecting the advantage of testing a writer's quality by a consideration of the way in which he handles minor points. If we find him wanting in truthfulness, insight, and good sense in these minor points, we may be prepared to find him inaccurate, inadequate, and conventional in the more difficult representation of life and character. He may make foolish remarks, and yet tell a story well; but if his remarks are deviations from common sense, his story will be a deviation from human experience; and the critic who detects this may avoid the appearance of arbitrariness in his judgment on higher matters less easily brought within the scope of ordinary recognition, by showing that a writer who is not to be trusted in the one case cannot be trusted in the other.

This leads me to the second benefit which would accrue from a more stringent criticism, especially applied to minor points. It would soon greatly purge novels of their insincerities and nonsense. If critics were vigilant and rigorous, they would somewhat check the presumptuous facility and *facundia* of indolent novelists, by impressing on them a sense of danger in allowing the pen to wander at random. It would teach them that what they wrote would not only be read, but reflected on; and if their glittering diction proved on inspection to be tinsel, they would suffer from the exposure. This would lead to a more serious conception of the art, and a more earnest effort to make their works in all respects conformable to sense and artistic truth. The man who begins to be vigilant as to the meaning of his phrases is already halfway towards becoming a good writer. The man who before passing on to his next sentence has already assured himself that the one just written expresses the thought actually in his mind, as well as he can express it, and declines to believe that insincere expressions or careless approximative phrases are good enough for a novel, will soon learn to apply the same vigilance to his conception of character and incident, and will strive to attain clearness of vision and sincerity of expression. Let criticism only exact from novels the same respect for truth and common sense which it exacts from other literary works; let it stringently mark where the approbation of a novel is given to it as Literature, and where it is given to plot-interest of a more or less attractive nature, and some good may be effected both on writers and readers.

Editor.

Notes

1. *Maxwell Dewitt*. By F. G. Trafford, author of *George Geith*, &c. 3 vols. Tinsley Brothers. 1865.

Sir Jasper's Tenant. By the Author of *Lady Audley's Secret*, &c. 3 vols. Maxwell and Co. 1865.

2. Among the slight but significant indications of imperfect attention to accuracy, may be mentioned the inadvertency with which the French language is treated on the two occasions when French phrases are used: *bête noir* might be charitably accepted as a misprint, but *au discrétion* tasks even charity.

❦ 59 ❧

The Uses of Fiction.

ANONYMOUS

The author addresses the impact of fiction on the reading public, noting two specific effects of a good novel: (1) the expansion of the reader's imagination to incorporate, in Wordsworthian terms, the absent as if present; and (2) the elevation of the moral fibre of society. The first, the essayist argues, would be helpful for statesmen and others of a practical mindset who currently fail to see the value of imagination in expanding one's understanding of others. The second reinforces the prevalent notion in nineteenth-century England that he worth novel tends to elevate character by presenting ideals for which the reader can strive. Opposed to such "good" novels are those that pander to popular taste for economic gain.

Mr Mill has said, in one of his Dissertations, that the only two modes in which an individual mind could hope to exercise much direct influence upon the minds of contemporaries were as a member of Parliament or as the editor of a London newspaper. This limitation may have been correct enough when Mr Mill made it some thirty years ago, but we think there can be little doubt that in these days a third influence ought to be added to the list—namely, that of the popular novelist. It is perhaps scarcely necessary to say that we refer exclusively to novelists who, by profound reflection or a quick natural insight into character and life, have arrived at something like consistent and manageable theories of the social conditions which surround them; and not to novelists whose chief claim to popularity is the skill with which they can keep the reader, for so many hundred pages, in suspense as to whether the charming heroine has really murdered her first husband, or what may be her exact relationship to the mysterious orphan. Novels which depend for their success upon ingenuity of this kind may be classed with clever conjuring tricks, fearful ascents up spiral staircases, tremendous headers into unseen feather-beds, or any other feats whose sole object is to excite and amuse. They enable any one in

Source: Anonymous, "The Uses of Fiction", *Saturday Review*, 22, 15 September 1866, pp. 323-4.

want of occupation to get through so many hours without being bored; and hence the large demand which nowadays exists for them among the constantly increasing class, popularly typified by young ladies and guardsmen, who take to light literature, as rich men take to politics, or any other profession, merely as a means of killing time.

But a novelist who has clear and definite views upon the social or other problems of contemporary life may, it appears to us, exercise in these days a scarcely less direct, though obviously a less immediate, influence upon his age than either of the two classes formerly singled out by Mr Mill. Indeed, he owes his influence, in some measure, to the very cause which apparently induced Mr Mill to make this limitation—namely, to the fact that, from the countless multitude of books yearly issuing from the press, it is generally considered necessary to have a superficial acquaintance with so many authors that it becomes impossible thoroughly to master the doctrines of any one. Even the best books are, as a rule, "bolted"—rarely, after Bacon's advice, "chewed"; and there is, accordingly, no process of intellectual digestion sufficient to leave a permanent effect upon the mind. The effect is scarcely more durable than that made by one forcible article in a daily newspaper, or one telling speech in Parliament; and, inasmuch as articles and speeches innumerable may be given in succession to the public in the time that it takes to mature and produced one thoughtful book, the author has no chance whatever against the journalist or the politician. This complaint of Mr Mill's may be applicable to books written solely for instruction, especially if they rise beyond the level of the ordinary popular point of view. Books of this class may as well be left unread altogether as bolted, for any permanent salutary effect they can produce upon the mind. Indeed, they are better left unread, since a too hasty perusal will not merely leave the reader as ignorant as it found him, which would involve nothing worse than loss of time, but will expose him to what Plato pronounced the most dangerous of all forms of ignorance—the ignorance of one's ignorance. But Mr Mill's theory does not appear to us to be applicable to the novel, since, unlike a didactic work, it may be bolted, and yet leave upon the mind a perfectly clear and lasting impression of the doctrine it is intended to convey. The reasons of this are obvious. The doctrine is not clothed in abstract conceptions which, to be fully and clearly comprehended, require thoughtful reflection, but in concrete instances which come home at once to the feeblest comprehension. It may, moreover, be spread over a long and varied series of incidents, each more or less remotely illustrative of it, and this with a diffuseness and amplification which would be utterly inadmissible in a philosophical treatise. To borrow Archbishop Whately's simile, just as food must have bulk as well as nutriment, the stomach requiring a "certain degree of distention" to enable it to act properly, so do the generality of minds assimilate knowledge far more readily and perfectly if it is spread for them over a tolerably large surface, than if it is concentrated, no matter how clearly and forcibly, in small compass. And although, as we have already observed, the novelist must exercise a less immediate influence than the journalist or the politician, he has, on the other hand, this advantage over them, if he be a popular writer of the first class, that he addresses a far larger audience among that educated portion of the community who do most to create public opinion on important questions of the day. A really first-rate novel is read, sooner or later, by almost every one with any pretensions to education, while there are thousands of educated people who only occasionally interest themselves in a newspaper article or a political speech. The great majority of women, while they make it a point of honour to read the first, rarely trouble themselves about the two last, and the share which women contribute to the formation of public opinion on all really fundamental questions is far greater than it appears.

But it is indirectly—in subtle and permanent impressions upon the whole character, not in the direct formation of this or that special opinion—that the influence of a novelist of high order is most powerfully exercised upon his age. It is astonishing how little Englishmen, as a rule, appreciate the tendency of the novel to develop imagination, or rather, how little importance they attach to the cultivation of this faculty. Nine fathers out of ten, for instance, would far rather see their children absorbed in scientific experiments with the microscope, or puzzling their brains over tough botanical names, than poring over one of Scott's novels. In some families the last amusement is strictly interdicted, and in nearly all it is rather tolerated than encouraged, as an inevitable concession to the great truth that boys will be boys. Even this amiable concession is confined to the well-to-do classes; and works of fiction are regarded, like indigestible sweetmeats and heavy puddings, as unwholesome luxuries only to be adventured upon by the rich. Few teachers would have courage enough to countenance the startling heresy that the child of a poor man is not grievously wasting his time if he devotes to works of imagination hours that might be occupied in acquiring a knowledge of chemistry or mechanics. It may be sound enough, as an educational theory, that the development of the imaginative faculty should precede that of the faculties which natural science is best adapted to train. But then this theory assumes that imagination has uses which make its development worth aiming at; and the ordinary notion of the so-called practical mind, the commonest type of the English mind, is that imagination may be all very well for those who want to be poets or artists or novelists, but that it is a gift rather dangerous than otherwise to those who would qualify themselves for more lucrative or more substantial professions. It may be a question, it is said, how far even the son of the rich man, who has his way in the world smoothed before him, ought deliberately to be encouraged in the cultivation of a faculty so likely to give him a romantic and un-business-like turn of mind; but there can be no question that it is absurd to encourage the indulgence of such vagaries in the poor. The practical people who hold this view strangely enough overlook the strictly practical effects of imagination upon character and the conduct of life. We mean more especially that kind of imagination which it is the direct and immediate tendency of fiction to educe and strengthen, and which we may call the dramatic imagination—"the power by which one human being enters into the mind and circumstances of another," or which "enables us, by a voluntary effort, to conceive the absent as if it were present, the imaginary as if it were real, and to clothe it in the feelings which, if it were indeed real, it would being along with it." This is the power which fiction does most to foster, which can be cultivated to its proper perfection only when the mind still retains the plasticity and impressibility of youth, and the strictly practical consequences of which are altogether overlooked when it is treated as if it were of no marketable value to any one but the intellectual artist. Fanciful as to some may appear the connection between the want of this dramatic faculty and the prevalence of crime among the poorer classes, there can be no doubt that a large proportion of crimes are directly traceable to the criminal's inability to realize, with sufficient vividness to serve as a deterrent, the ultimate consequences of his act. At least this is the opinion of a really practical man like Lord Stanley, who has devoted much time and labour to statistics bearing upon the condition of the poorer population, and who rarely delivers an opinion which he has not matured. He holds that the sudden, and sometimes almost unintelligible, acts of brutal violence for which the very poor are comparatively notorious, are for the most part due to the fact that the criminal, like a mere animal, cannot "conceive the absent as if it were present"—cannot bring before his mind, with lifelike distinctness, the fatal results that must follow from his crime. The temptation is visibly present before him; his punishment lies in the unseen future. Upon this incapacity is based the only philosophical defence of public executions. They impress vividly upon the popular mind consequences which it has not imagination enough to picture for itself. We have instanced the poorer classes simply because their case exhibits most forcibly the practical value of imagination, and an extreme case does as well as any other for the purpose of illustration. But of course the same principle applies, in greater or less degree, to all classes and professions. Imagination is often most wanted in those pursuits from which the "practical mind" would be most anxious to exclude it. It is, for instance, about the last quality which would be considered desirable for a statesman by Englishmen of the class who despise novels as conveying unpractical, unmarketable knowledge, and who would think a taste for mechanics a more promising symptom in the youthful mind than a taste for *Ivanhoe*. Yet it is to Lord Dalhousie's want of imagination that an historian of Mr Kaye's ability attributes the fatal policy that led to the Indian mutiny. In his Life of Lord George Bentinck, Mr Disraeli declares this same defect to have been the weak point in the political genius of Sir Robert Peel; and Mr Mill finds the defect vitiating the whole philosophical system of so great a thinker as Bentham.

The use of fiction in developing what we have called dramatic imagination has a scarcely less important bearing upon the moral, than we have seen it to have upon the intellectual, side of character. Deficiency in the two great social virtues, justice and benevolence, is less often due to conscious dishonesty or heartlessness than to inability to "enter into the mind and circumstances" of the suffering or the injured— to look at the matter not exclusively from your own, but also from his, point of view. People cry over fictitious suffering in a novel who hear almost unmoved of the far worse miseries actually inflicted by our workhouse system upon the poor. A superficial observer may pronounce such people guilty of sham sentiment, and assert that they sympathize so readily with fictitious woe merely because it threatens no demand upon the pocket. But a more charitable, and certainly not less philosophical, explanation of their inconsistency is that the imagination of the novelist brings far more vividly before them the suffering which is fictitious than their own imagination can bring the suffering which has the advantage of being real. It is certainly odd that good and pious people should wage such strenuous war against a class of writings which contribute perhaps more than any other towards the foundation of all true goodness and piety, the power of enlarged and ready sympathy. How far such writings conduce to what should be their other great function, that of elevating the character by setting before the reader great aims and ennobling conceptions of life, must depend very much upon whether the author is prepared to make a certain sacrifice of popularity. It is perhaps impossible for a writer of fiction to work on a level much above the ordinary national character, the average aspirations and pursuits of the day, and yet remain generally popular. And, since popularity means money—and novels, like most other things, are, as a rule, made to sell—there is an almost insuperable temptation to endeavour to keep on a level with, and reflect, the national sentiment, rather than to endeavour to raise and refine it. The larger and more varied the number of readers, the greater becomes the necessity of consulting average tastes. This is, we think, the main cause why most of the popular fiction of the present day is so intensely commonplace in its general tone—why it so studiously avoids whatever borders on the heroic. The noblest novel that our generation has yet seen, *Romola*, is by no means popular; we might almost say that it is unpopular, considering its author's commanding reputation. And in *Felix Holt* the same great writer has no doubt sacrificed popularity in presenting a hero for whom the money-making, pushing "gigmanity" of this age has so little sympathy. But although contemporaneous fiction is so far obliged to abdicate its proper functions and refrain from working counter to national prejudice, it may still claim the credit of reflecting the healthiest and heartiest aspects of the national character; for the sensational trash which is just now all the rage seems only an excrescence which will pass away as suddenly as it appeared. And the present practical age scarcely does sufficient justice to the beneficial influence which fiction, even when it works only at the average level, may exercise upon the national mind.

⚜ 60 ⚜

The Value of Fiction

WALTER BESANT

Walter Besant (1836–1901), founder of the Society of Authors and minor British novelist, is today best known for provoking Henry James's response, "The Art of Fiction". In the following essay, he present a typically Victorian defence of the novel as an escape from both boredom and worry and as a guide to morality. By giving the reader a wide variety of characters, both good and evil, the novelist exposes the reader to situations that involve moral and ethical choices. In addition, such exposure induces tolerance for people unlike oneself. Besant's defence of the novel is another attempt to enforce the novel's legitimacy as a genre in light of Puritan criticism of the previous century.

It is interesting to mark the sudden rush with which the old Puritanical dislike for novels has collapsed, at last, in the present generation. It took a long time to destroy; but then it took a long time to grow. It sprang originally from a very pardonable protest against plays; this itself being due, not so much to the dramatists of the Restoration, as to those of the later years of James I., the decadence of the Elizabethan drama. The suspicious hatred with which all works of fiction alike were regarded was strengthened by the free-and-easy morals of Smollett and Fielding, and not even lessened by the virtuous Richardson, who was looked upon as the single exception which proved the rule. And it went on spreading, till, like a vast cloud, it shut out altogether the sunshine of fancy and imagination from the dull homes of thousands, whose deadened thoughts turned upon themselves, and ate out their hearts in the gloom of a hopeless Calvinism, and a red-brick-and-stucco civilisation. There has been hard work to blow this cloud away, but it is done at last; and now, when not a single voice is lifted up against developing the imaginative faculty in men and women, we may perhaps ask ourselves, what is likely to be the real gain to us from reading or writing works of fiction.

Unquestionably the chief gain is, that it is good at times to get our minds away from ourselves. Life is mostly made up of little cares; in nine cases out of ten, cares arising from want of means; in the tenth case, often enough, from the spectre of

Source: Walter Besant, "The Value of Fiction," *Belgravia*, 16, November 1871, pp. 48–51.

some remote probability, conjured up by too much dwelling on contingencies. Little things become great things by being steadily looked at; and when society, change of scene, and lively companionship do not create a diversion, the mind may be, and often is, tortured almost to madness by imaginary horrors, the spectres of a morbid fancy. Consider the lives of most young girls in country towns. They should be painted of a dull gray colour throughout, under a cloudy sky. Their recreations are principally lectures and croquet; they have an occasional dance; one or two of them marry; the rest settle down to a life which is one long repression of desires, till desires are killed outright. Desire of society; desire of change; desire of knowing the world; desire for that strange madness called love; desire of feeling, if only for once, the pulse quicken, and the blood course through the veins: all these have to be met in the face and sternly subdued, until, wearied with defeat, they rise no more. Into these lives comes the novel, like the dream of another world. Leaving the little narrow town, with its dreary street and woeful monotony of emptiness, the mind travels far away to share in sorrow and joys alien to its own experiences—to feel the burst of life in action, and to smooth out its withered cheek to meet the kiss of love. Surely, if the novel were invented for no other purpose than to cheer the dull and purposeless lives of our women, it has done good work.

Consider, again, the fagged merchant, the barrister after a long term; worse, the physician when he gets a brief holiday: what is it not worth to him to sit idly and toy with the leaves of a novel, while the shadows shift on the hill sides, and the clouds chase each other on the sea? He is taken out from himself; while he is in another world, Nature the restorer is busily putting him to rights; and Imagination the mesmeriser charms him to sleep, to let the healing process go on.

This is fiction considered as an alterative. But it may be considered as a great educational power.

As dealing with different aspects of life, it teaches the nature of the world we live in. Ladies who read *Belgravia* do not often penetrate into the slums of the East-end. Fagin and his tribe are as unknown to them as the Esquimaux. It is not, however, bad for ladies to know that such things exist. A knowledge of evil *quà* evil is not to be desired; but a knowledge of all those forms of evil which can be remedied by money or self-denial is surely a good thing; and this the novel gives us. Moreover, if it is a good thing to know the different *kinds* of men and women there are—kinds which have as little affinity with one another as the Gibraltar monkey with the great gorilla; men and women who, if brought together, would have no one common topic of talk—these the novel shows us. And if it is a good thing to warn young men of the perils in their way, no sermons ever preached can have half the effect of the novel. Moreover, preachers of sermons have very seldom—certainly never since leaving college—encountered these perils. The novel sets them forth, giving them full dramatic effect. It shows the pitfall; the unwary youth hastening to take the fatal step; the ruin he brings on himself; the sorrow he brings on those who love him.

The so-called sensational novels generally turn upon some such catastrophe. Most of them show the downward progress of a character only weak at first, reckless at last. We see the man whose desires are beyond his means or his hopes; the struggles he undergoes to place himself in a better position—the temptation which prompts him by unlawful means to rise above his cares—his fall, and the infinitely greater cares that accompany it. In this class of novel we have, it is true, plenty of incident; but we have more—we have, condensed in a short space, and therefore intensified, all the sorrow and suffering that surround the fall of a man from his high estate of self-respect. Is it nothing to show to the world, in the most effective manner possible, that sin brings with it its own punishment, and that the most carefully-protected secret of crime is liable to discovery by the simplest accident? The problem of suffering and sorrow is that which lies at the root of all novels: it forms the interest and pathos of every life; it is the *fous et origo lagrimarum*; without it there would be no romance, for there would be no doubt; and where the milk-and-water novelist takes infinitesimal pinches, creating imaginary sorrows out of fictitious sins—a heroine laughs in a church, or forgets to tell her mamma that Philip kissed her—the 'sensational writer' takes his materials from the annals of the world, and narrates stories which, without the dramatic touch, the stroke of genius which makes the actors alive, and not mere puppets, may be read any day in our newspapers. If a novel is but faithful to life, it cannot but be wholesome in its effects, because it will be based on the great moral laws which govern the issues of life. I contend that a good 'sensational' novel—honest and truthful, free from the false sensibility of the French school, the mawkish cant of the pietistic, the rubbish of the young-lady school—can produce, of itself, no harm. It is true that young ladies are more apt to laugh in church than to commit murders; but the novel is not written to warn ladies against murder. It is a record of men and women, the actual types of whom *do exist*, who belong to our own class of life, who elbow us in places of resort, and whose stories are sometimes narrated for the edification of the world in the newspapers, without the concomitant circumstances which explain or mitigate the guilt, and which may warn the reader. There never has been a time when the desire for that money will bring has been a more ready prompter to evil, or has called for more clear warning, than the present. Since the theatre has retired from the post of educator, for example, and the young men of the day decline to attend the gratuitous education by precept which is provided regularly every Sunday, it is surely a good thing that the novel should step in. Fiction has, farther, this advantage for the writer: suppose, by dint of contemplating a man's character, as shown in his letters, his writings, his talk, his daily bearing, an intending biographer arrives at the discovery of the kind of man his hero wished to be, or to be thought. This gives him a sort of key-note to his history. He can, by bringing out all those traits which belong to this side of his character, and suppressing all the rest, produced exactly the effect desired—at the expense of honesty. This is how all biographies, except Boswell's, seem to have been written. The writer describes his man as he thinks he wished to be considered. It does not at all follow that he *was* that kind of man; and presently the facts are stated and theories broached, which contradict the biographer from beginning to end. Not so the novelist. He sees in A. the rudimentary conception of a character which A.—like his fellows, generally a weak sort of creature, who drifts—has not the power or the will to carry on. The novelist takes the character, and puts it into the person of an imaginary man who has the will, and he then follows it up to its legitimate consequences. Thus we get John Halifax (a beautiful life, which no biography could give us), Augustine Caxton, Colonel Newcome, Frank Fairleigh, and a thousand creations which are as real to us as our brothers and sisters, whom we love twice as well, and who teach us ten times as much.

A great deal more might be said, but it suffices. Fiction lessens our anxieties, by preventing that perpetual brooding which magnifies them; it brightens our real world, by giving us an ideal one—more happy, more varied, more joyous, richer, and *fuller* than our own; it teaches us tolerance, by showing us the different ways in which our fellows live; and it perpetually, under a thousand new forms, impresses the good old maxim, that the 'only way to be happy is by the narrow road.'

·❦·61·❧·

On the History of the Novel in England

ANONYMOUS

The essay represents a fairly typical mid-nineteenth century view of the rise of the novel in England. The author regards Chaucer's few prose tales as well as the chivalric romances that extended into the fifteenth century as early examples of pre-novelistic prose. The only exception to the political and theological treatises of the seventeenth century was Bunyan's *The Pilgrim's Progress*, followed in the early eighteenth century by Defoe's *Robinson Crusoe*. However, the novel does not achieve legitimacy until Richardson and Fielding, "the founders of an entirely new school of literature" (275). The essayist nods briefly to the female authors of the period—Burney, Radcliffe and Inchbald—and considers Austen and Edgeworth worthy of recognition after Sir Walter Scott who "rescue the novel from the condemnation of the judicious" (277). The essay concludes with a Johnsonian recommendation of the novel as a relaxant for the overworked and a balm for the sick as long as it presents stories of virtue as opposed to vice.

What is a novel? Referring to the dictionary we find it described as "a small tale, generally of love." But is this definition satisfactory? By no means. Novels are most frequently anything but "small tales," and though the theme of love must be "generally" interwoven with the story, as it is universally in the many-coloured tissue of human life, it does not follow that the whole, or even the principal interest of the novel, should turn upon the involvements of the tender passion.

The word novel is derived from the Italian "novella" and originally no doubt, denoted a short prose story, such as was formerly so common in Italian literature. But the modern novel differs even more widely from this, than from the romance that succeeded the novella in the public taste. Perhaps the best definition given is a "prose epic," as an essential quality is a gradual development of the plot, leading up to a climax, where the principal characters may be left happy, or otherwise, as the

Source: Anonymous, "On the History of the Novel in England", *Argosy*, 14, 1872, pp. 273-7.

case may be. Something of the dramatic element is also required, it being desirable that the author himself should be lost sight of in the characters he pourtrays. And lastly, a certain realism, truth to human nature, and incidents that apparently evolve themselves as a sequence from given circumstances, acting upon various idiosyncrasies, all go to make up the received ideas of a novel.

As in youth, when thought and feeling, stirring brain and heart, first strive to mould themselves into form, their usual utterance is metrical, so in the early ages of the world, tales and romances in verse preceded the novella in prose. First the oratio vincta or bound speech; secondly the oratio soluta, or loosened speech. We find this hold good in all countries alike, England being no exception. But one prose romance has been discovered in Anglo-Saxon, founded on the well known story of Apollonius of Tyre, the same incident from which the *Pericles* of Shakspeare was taken.

For several centuries the art of the story-teller continued to be almost entirely exercised in verse, though a few prose legends of the San Greal date back as far as the time of Henry the Second. It was not until the close of the fourteenth century that prose had become a popular medium for such stories; at this period, however, many of the old metrical narratives were recast in this new shape.

Chaucer, though most of his stories are in verse, has left us some few tales in prose, as a relief to the never-ending romances of chivalry then in vogue,— productions the sameness and dulness of which give us a singular idea of our ancestors' monotonous mode of life, and the utter barrenness of the subjects of though and imagination that could leave room for pleasure in these constantly repeated fables.

That these romances still held their ground in popular favour in the fifteenth century we have plain proof, inasmuch as Caxton, after some demur, not only printed Sir Thomas Malory's wonderful collection of King Arthur legends, "for to passe the tyme," as he says, though he is careful to add, "to gyve fayth and byleve that al is trewe that is contayned herein, ye be at your lyberte," but other tales of chivalry also appeared from his press, notably *The History of the noble Right Valiant, and Right Worthy Knight Paris, and of the Fair Vienne*, and *The History of King Blachardine and Queen Eglantine his wife*.

In the first half of the sixteenth century the English language had become so far polished and enriched as to lend itself readily to "the loosened speech," and we now begin to find something approaching to that vigour and elegance of diction from this time so assiduously cultivated. Even the "Euphuism" of Lyly, at the end of this century, much as it has been held up to ridicule, may not have been without its use in refining and elevating the vulgar tongue.

This leads us to one of the brightest eras in English literary history, an era that may well be called "that sunny morning of a new day." This period had been ushered in by a time of turmoil and struggle, and by many striking and important events and discoveries, trying the spirits of men, stirring and expanding the intellect and imagination. Thus the national mind was prepared for great achievements, when a sense of security had restored ease and freedom of thought, commercial prosperity had brought wealth and leisure, and the increasing power and renown of England had inspired emulation with the literary fame of other countries.

Italy up to this period had made the greatest advances in civilization; consequently we find the influence of Italy greatly prevailing in the sixteenth and first half of the seventeenth centuries, when it was to be superseded by French taste. Translations of numerous Italian novelle were published, and even Shakspeare did not disdain to avail himself of the treasures thus opened out, his *Romeo and Juliet*, as one instance, being little more than a dramatised version of the old Italian story as it appears translated in Paynter's *Palace of Pleasure*, though transmuted by his genius from quaint prose into the loftiest poetry.

Still, we are led to imagine that reading could have been but little resorted to for pleasant entertainment amongst the generality of the English, however much books must have been sought by the learned few, for the literary genius of this era found its outlet almost exclusively in works, not for the closet, but for dramatic representation, as far as fiction is concerned; few pastoral and heroical romances being excepted, of which Sir Philip Sidney's *Arcadia*, and Boyle's *Parthenissa* may be cited as the best examples.

England was destined soon again to become the prey of internal dissension, and men had other matters to think of; the realities of life pressed too heavily upon them for fictitious narratives to attract attention. We cannot, therefore, be surprised to find the writings published in England during the middle portion of the seventeenth century almost exclusively political and theological. One imaginative work appeared, however, destined to survive most of this political and theological lore, Bunyan's *Pilgrim's Progress*, a work so eagerly read by those who would have been terrified by the very name of romance, as to prove the very inherent craving after stories.

After the Restoration, Puritanism still formed a strong element in the country; literature grew and flourished mainly in the sunshine of Court favour, there being as yet no public by whom the author could hope to live. Poets and wits, writers of odes and epigrams, pamphlets and satires abounded, but neither romancist nor novelist, these being too serious for the frivolous and licentious Court, and "snares of the evil one" to the mass of community. Baxter, speaking but the voice of his time, holds forth against the reading of romances and feigned histories," and in his "Christian Directory," says, "I presuppose that you keep the devil's books out of your hand and house, I mean cards and idle tales, and play-books, and romances or love-books, and false bewitching stories;" and this belief of the danger, if not sinfulness, of novel-reading long continued to prevail.

Defoe is the first writer of fiction after this epoch whose name arrests us; though he had previously become well known as a newspaper writer and pamphleteer, he had passed his fifty-eighth year before he gave to the world his *Robinson Crusoe*, which was only published in 1719. From this time he produced a succession of fictitious narratives, several of which had misled wise heads by the air of reality he knew so well how to cast over the creations of his fancy. *The History of the Plague* has been more than once quoted as an authentic narrative, and Lord Chatham is said to have been in the habit of recommending *The Memoirs of a Cavalier*, to his friends, as the best account of the civil wars.

But Defoe, vivid as were his delineations, and perfectly as he identified himself with the supposed narrator of the adventures that form the basis of his fictions, cannot, properly speaking, be termed a novelist. He fails in dramatic power, he is at best only a story-teller, a distinction that is plainly felt as we turn to his successors, Richardson and Fielding.

These two authors may be considered as the founders of an entirely new school of literature, and *Pamela* and *Joseph Andrews* as our two first English novels properly so called. During the lapse of years, wonderful strides had been made in language and style. English had become more polished, as well as more vigorous, under the reign of Queen Anne and the first two Georges, preparing for a new development under George the Third, when literature was sufficiently cultivated and appreciated to allow the novelist to make his bow before an audience extensive enough to permit of a hope of remuneration for his labours.

Richardson, a respectable tradesman, living a quiet, if not secluded existence, having passed middle age before taking pen in hand, has given us in his pages rather human nature than human life, universal sentiments and passions rather than individual character. He anatomizes for us the heart to its inmost recesses, while Fielding causes the personages of his novels to act and speak before us. We are perfectly acquainted with the appearance and manners of Fielding's creations; we follow them in their adventures, but if we wish to know any more of them than what is patent to all the world, we are baffled and left to guess-work, as far as the author is concerned, for he refuses to let us into the secret.

Richardson's style, though it is said he was unacquainted with a word of any language but his own, has something of the inflated French manner of that day. Fielding and his rival Smollett were more natural and animated, but they had no scruple in describing a coarse and vicious state of society just as they found it, a state which we can scarcely be too thankful was, and is no longer.

There is one novel amongst those of the last century, the mention of which must be omitted, Goldsmith's *Vicar of Wakefield*, a tale which, notwithstanding all its faults of construction, and all its improbabilities, takes a hold of the memory and affections through the power of the genius that inspires it, as much as any story in the language; possessing as it does, in spite of all critics may say of its ill-conceived plot and badly contrived incidents, that "touch of nature that makes the whole world kin."

Women now began to put in their claim to a niche in the temple of Fame, producing works that achieved success, more or less. Amongst the most eminent of these may be mentioned Miss Burney, afterwards Madame D'Arblay, Mrs Radcliffe, and Mrs Inchbald.

It must be confessed that at this period the prejudice against novels, especially as mental food for the young, was not without foundation. Inflated style, high-flown sentimentality, and romantic improbabilities were but too much calculated to vitiate the taste, give false views of life and character, and render the mind discontented with the wholesome food of everyday existence. These remarks, however, do not apply to such works as Miss Burney's *Evelina*, and *Cecilia*, and Mrs Inchbald's *Simple Story*; and though Mrs Radcliffe's and mysteries no longer interest, the merit must be conceded to her or powers of description of no common order.

Everything, physically and morally, seems to have its ebb and flow, and at the time when the stream of fiction was at its shallowest, up sprang a mighty fountain, pouring its fertilizing waters through the then barren land of imagination. In 1814 Waverley appeared, followed in quick succession by a series of manly and brilliant fictions, that took the world by storm, attained from the beginning an unexampled popularity, and at once rescued the novel from the condemnation of the judicious. To this end, Miss Austen and Miss Edgeworth also assisted; the one by her truthful pictures of life and the absence of false sentiment, the other by equally graphic delineation united to shrewd and often humorous common sense.

From this time the novel has not only become a necessity of the age, but has taken a high place in literature, adding to the old gift of story-telling a new purpose. Professor Masson classifies novels under thirteen heads, a few of which are, the Novel of English Manners, the Fashionable Novel, the Novel of Illustrious Villany, the Traveller's Novel, the Novel of Supernatural Phantasy, the Art and Culture Novel, and the Historical Novel.

He also informs us that on the shelves of the British Museum Library there were only twenty-six novels, a published in the year 1820, when the Waverley novels were at the height of their popularity; and that in 1850, the yield was ninety-eight new novels, thus showing that the number of novels produced had been quadrupled in the space of twenty years. Such was the impetus given to works of fiction.

As it is difficult to conceive of anything in the form of a book more offensive and mischievous than a novel devoted to the description of vice set forth in an alluring manner; so, on the contrary, when the novel holds up to detestation everything mean and base, enforcing the paramount claims of duty, and the beauty of high-souled purity of life, the good influence exercised can scarcely be over-estimated. Nor when a story is related merely as a means of ministering to amusement, is it therefore to be despised. For those also who offer us recreation and rest for over-worked brain and nerve, who afford an hour's solace to the sick, causing them to forget their pain, or who add cheerfulness to our firesides, are surely amongst the benefactors of mankind.

·❦·62·❧·

The Art of Novel Writing.

ANONYMOUS

The author of the following essay represents the mid-Victorian concern with the morality of the novel. He divides the novel into three types, giving priority to the first two and denigrating the third. The first type, the novel that aims at correcting social abuse (later termed the social problem novel), requires the author to identify and sympathise with the class about which he is writing in order to make the novel an effective mouthpiece for change. The second (and seemingly most elevated) type is the fictional biography that forces plot to the background and highlights one character, in order in the highest instances to provide a model of virtuous behaviour for the reader. The third type, "the ordinary novel", is a product of society's demand for adventure and sensation; it often lacks the portrayal of virtue requisite in a good novel and falls prey to the lowest common moral denominator. The author concludes with a eulogy for the recently deceased Charles Dickens whose novels will always uphold "a pure morality" and consequently, will be perennially popular.

Of all branches of literature, many and multiform as they are, none perhaps has gained so many votaries as the art of writing fiction: and this fact need be the cause of no surprise. The work of the novelist is essentially a pleasant and grateful work, and one of endless variety and interest. He appeals to a wider class of readers than any other writer. His sympathies must be more general, his experience larger, than that of other men. The subject of his pen is no abstract question of philosophy—no theory of metaphysics to be argued and proved with logical precision; but he has to deal with the world around him. His subjects are the men and women who cross his daily path. His study is the human heart, the fountain source of the actions that compose his story. If he is to attain any eminence in his profession he must be a man of quick perception and fearless language; he must have an intimate knowledge of men and manners, founded on a personal experience. The cynic will gain but few listeners. Satire, however pointed, if it proceed from simply misanthropy and point to no practical result will be a dead letter. The

Source: Anonymous, "The Art of Novel Writing", *Gentleman's Magazine*, 9, 1872, pp. 384-93.

province of the novelist is strictly social: he deals with human character not as being self-formed and self-existent, but as being dependent upon the bearing and intercourse of others for its natural growth and development. He does not confine himself to one class of society, but shows each in its relation to the other. He stands upon the vantage ground of a common humanity, and takes an impartial view of each, with respect to its opportunities and its capabilities. His success, therefore, will mainly depend upon his experience and his ability to trace the virtues and vices of social life to their producing causes. His triumph will be the upholding of the one and the suppression of the other.

It would indeed be difficult to overestimate the influence of fiction as a motive power for good or evil. The standard of a nation's morality is seen in its literature; and in proportion as the effect of fiction is more vivid, and, as we have already shown, the circle of its readers is more extended, so will its responsibility be greater; and since its manifest object is to present under the form of a narrative the truths and realities that affect social life, the novelist becomes at once the exponent and investigator of public morality. His work, moreover, is especially important in the power that he has of applying the rules and axioms of this morality to individuals, showing its bearing upon society both severally and collectively; and here it takes precedence of a mere methodical essay, which from the nature of its composition is harder to be understood. The latter deals with first principles in themselves, while the former, by identifying them with some particular character, shows them in their application and active exercise.

And since this is the case, it necessarily follows that the power of fiction will be greater, and its standard of morality more eminently productive of practical results. It pervades every class of society, sowing broadcast seeds which will infallibly expand and ripen. Sorrow and crime, indeed, have been too often engendered by it. Pure waters, poisoned by the deadly stream of perverted truth, have pointed to it as the fountain-head from whence the pollution came. Hearts drawn away by the insidious attractions of vice delicately handled and carefully glossed over have owed to it their first propensity. But this is only one side of the picture, and there is another, we trust paramount, at all events no less true. Studies of human life, with its infinite capabilities for good, and stories of noble and devoted lives, by suggesting the glorious possibilities that still lie within our reach, have formed the soil from whence have sprung generous aspirations and heroic deeds. Using this means earnest men have pleaded for the eternal laws of truth and justice; philanthropists have urged the claims of particular classes for education and advancement; practical philosophers have striven for the domestic improvement of the poor—have proved the impossibility of even social decency with crowded dwellings and vicious influences—calling upon the higher classes, with their superior advantages, to assist in promoting a speedy and urgently needed reform. Appealing to motives of self-interest, if all others fail, they have pointed out how the corrupt morals of an individual class affect society at large, making rotten the very foundation on which it stands. Others have directed their attack against the higher and better educated classes themselves, insisting upon their responsible position in respect to their fellow men, baring the hypocrisy of conventional forms, and striking sometimes a well-aimed blow at popular vices which lurk behind the scenes of social indulgence.

Now, these are tangible and well defined results, and they may be attempted and have been already attained by the novelist. Only he must first acquire his materials by his own personal experience, and then know how to mould them skilfully. For, as we have endeavoured to point out, fiction is a sketch; but if it is to avail anything it must be a sketch taken from life.

Having, therefore, thus briefly summed up its nature and scope, and having shown its importance as affecting public morality, we have now in the second place to consider fiction in its construction and treatment. And to this end we may perhaps be permitted to class novels roughly under three prominent heads. First we will take into consideration those which are written with some particular practical object in view—such, for example, as the furtherance of education, or the correction of any social abuse. Now, with regard to a work of this sort it may be briefly said that its influence and success will depend upon the spirit in which it is written. To render it effective, the author must be a man of strict impartiality and uniform justice. If his object be the advancement or the reformation of a certain class of people, he must regard their errors and delinquencies from their own stand-point. He must adapt himself to their circumstances, taking into account their opportunities and becoming, as it were, one of them. If he wish to improve them he must consult their temporal interest as well as their moral obligations, and must show how the two are essentially bound up together and depend upon one another for their very existence. And this is more especially important with respect to the lower or less educated classes. The satirist may and has with good effect launched his sarcasms against the pitiful anomalies and furtive vices that disfigure a higher and more artificial state of society. But in dealing with the great working class, whose daily labour is the source from whence they derive their sustenance, and whose life is in many cases an unremitting struggle to support their families and themselves, he who would do a public service must go upon a different tack. Satire falls blunted. Mere schemes of philanthropy do not even gain a hearing. The author must take the world as he finds it, and, making acknowledged facts the subject matter of his work, can first show their practical bearing and their tendency, and then how far they admit of alteration. One well drawn sketch framed on this model will at once commend itself to those for whose benefit it is intended. The exposure of a vicious custom in its origin and effect will probably lead to a desire for its eradication. The exemplification of true human virtues in the exercise of their powers will endue existence with a nobler and less selfish aim. Only let the author be true to his own experience, and true to the human nature which he professes to illustrate, and the beauty of a pure and consistent life will recommend itself to the world, no less by the dignity it confers upon the possessors, than by the light which it reflects upon all who come within the range of its influence.

But in all attempts after social reform the writer must be careful to distinguish between the accidental qualities of a class and their essential characteristics. If an evil be inherent in and inseparably connected with a system, he will strike at the root of the system itself. The corrupt fruit is the product of the corrupt tree, but the fruit that is allowed to degenerate or grow rotten, though coming from a good stock, owes its worthlessness, not to the parent tree, but to the want of proper care and culture. And this, although it really involved a truism, would seem to be an axiom constantly disregarded by modern philanthropists. How is it, on the one hand, that schemes charitably devised and perhaps well carried out for the social and moral improvement of the humanity that centres and crowds in the heart of our great cities, passing an existence at which the civilisation of the nineteenth century blushes for very shame, have been so often frustrated, or at least have failed to realise the expectations which they held out? The reason is plain. Simply because they have not penetrated to the origin of the disease which they professed to cure. Because they regarded the evil in itself only, and neglected the principle to which it owed its birth. They attempted a partial reformation where the whole thing was fundamentally and radically wrong. On the other hand, error in the opposite direction has promoted wild and impracticable propositions, such as the fusion of classes, the general distribution of lands, and other equally Quixotic devices for the well-being and contentment of mankind at large.

The author must steer clear between these two faults, and in proportion as he effects this, and in proportion as he is able to prove the influence of external circumstances in the formation of character, and to show the co-extension of moral responsibility with the training necessary for its complete realisation, so will the practical value of his work be great or small.

Without, then, entering further into this subject, which would perhaps lead us somewhat astray from our main purpose, we will now pass on to a second class of novels, entirely different to the last both in their nature and in their object. These are books whose theme is the delineation and development of one particular character. They are, in fact, biographies, although this designation is usually applied to narratives of facts, whereas we are still in the province of fiction. Now, this class is numerically small, and in no work have authors more generally failed; and this is chiefly owing to the fact that the main interest of the book does not depend upon any plot or combination of extraordinary circumstances, but is centred upon one prominent figure—circumstances are but the background; accessory characters are grouped around it only to throw it into greater relief. In the portrayal, therefore, of this centre figure the greatest care must be observed. The reader's interest in it must be cherished and increased as the story proceeds, and never be allowed to flag or drift away into any side channel. A work of this kind, well conceived and well written, possesses great literary value and demands a very high order of talent. It exacts, moreover, the very closest attention, not only from the author, but from the reader also. It is, in fact, an abstract study of human nature—an analysis of character in its formation, its gradual growth, and subsequent maturity, dependent to a greater or less extent upon the external circumstances by which it is surrounded.

What, then, we proceed to ask, is necessary to make a work of this kind effective?

In the first place, it is manifest that the subject must either be one taken from the everyday world with which we are cognizant, or be a picture of the personification of some perfection of which the author believes humanity to be capable. If it be the former, the task is comparatively easy, a successful construction depending more than anything else upon the writer's experience and power of description and the general analogy of his sketch to nature; but where the character is ideal the author must to a great extent fall back upon himself. Premising that he wishes to show the capacity of human nature for the attainment of a certain moral elevation, his invention will rest upon the groundwork of his own personal conception with respect to men. In other words, he lifts up a standard of morality which, be it high or low, worthy or unworthy, is blazoned through the world for good or evil. It is important, because intended to command respect and admiration. The character is not a mere speculation, nor is it simply imaginary. It has a potential existence, and may therefore be imitated. Hence the author is himself responsible for the example which he has set up and the impression that is left upon the reader.

Now, if a work of this kind is to exercise any influence at all over the minds of men it must be distinguished by certain general characteristics. If, for instance, the conception of the author be one altogether incompatible with human fallibility, or if it be inconsistent in itself, or if its position in the world be an extraordinary and entirely unusual one, much, if not all, of the effect will be lost; for it is evident that the wider a writer wishes the range of his influence to extend, the more universally recognised must be the virtues and affections the personification of which in their combination and perfection makes up his ideal character.

In the first place, then, it is necessary that these virtues should recommend themselves by their practical results. In other words, they must be such as manifest themselves in social life and intercourse. The lofty meditations of the recluse, inspired by solitude and retirement from the world, possess little interest and still less practical value to the busy man of the world, who has to battle his way against hard facts and stubborn realities. He is not in a position to understand them, nor has he time even to take them into consideration. The bright world of the enthusiast is an unknown land to him, and the sounds that come from it awaken no responsive echo in his heart. But take a picture that has its origin in the world that surrounds him—draw something that he may compare with his own experience of mankind—and he is immediately interested. Let him once recognise the outlines of a familiar face, and the first point is gained—his attention is aroused. Then let the details be carefully filled in and the attributes most held up for admiration be thrown into prominence, either by exhibiting them against the dark background of their opposite vices, or by showing their value in their social and personal application, and we have at once a practical result. Such a work, well performed, is a complete picture of what a man in his own position, and with the same opportunities, may attain to.

Secondly, these virtues must recommend themselves by their possibility of general appropriation. There are certain qualities often called virtues, though not perhaps rightly included under this classification, which are either the idiosyncrasies of a class or lie only within the reach of a superior mental cultivation. Without particularising further it is sufficient to say that these, though valuable in themselves, are practically useless to ordinary men. They presuppose a state of mind which is not naturally but artificially obtained. They omit to mention the steps by which it is gained, or if they do so it is only to show that they are not attainable by mankind at large: hence they are less important because no essential virtue can be the monopoly of a class, but must in justice lie open to the acceptance of all.

Thirdly, and lastly, they must recommend themselves by their intrinsic value. Important as we have shown it to be that they should manifest themselves in the various phases of social life, it is still more important that they should be subjectively good. In other words, they must have their origin in and take their stand upon the eternal laws of right and wrong—laws that are unaffected by position in the world, or by circumstance, or by time—but remain the same to all and for ever. If, indeed, the author frame his work with respect to these he has high privileges and a noble opportunity. But if, on the other hand, his conception have no intrinsic claim to merit, but rest its pretensions to respect and admiration upon the affectation of a spurious, time-serving code of expediency, falsely called morality, he will have incurred a responsibility that rests upon himself alone.

Thus far, therefore, we have endeavoured to show the range and importance of fictitious biography, and have roughly pointed out one or two general characteristics needed to make it useful to the world at large. We will now pass on to the third class into which we have ventured to divide our subject. It has to do with what we may perhaps call the ordinary novel, a kind of literature with which the press is overcharged. It is found everywhere, and lies within the reach of all who are able to read. None so ignorant as not to find a book of this sort to suit his capacity; none so poor as not to be able to afford himself this amusement. From the penny magazine, with its weekly or monthly quantum, to the three volumes at one-and-twenty shillings, there is a library to accommodate every taste and inclination. Here may be found the matter-of-fact narrative of daily life, with its joys and sorrows, or the romantic love tale, the serious or amusing story, horrible tragedies, strange complications of events, inexplicable mysteries, all mingled together in wild confusion, and offering a choice and variety such as assuredly no other branch of literature ever can.

Now in dealing with such a wide class as this it is obvious that the remarks which we have to make must be very general, and must be accepted as such. In the first place it differs from the two others of which we have spoken in this essential particular: the interest of the ordinary novel usually depends more upon the story or combination of events, followed by a suitable *dénouement*, than upon the successful delineation of character. It is not necessarily written with any philanthropic object, nor does it confine itself to the study of one life. But it deals with facts of common experience and draws a general sketch of what is passing in the world around us. The talent required for a work of this sort is less common because less intellectual. For it is easier to take a general and comprehensive view of life than to take one character from the throng and analyse its nature and develop its capabilities. If a painter give us a picture embracing different subjects, we are disposed to be contented if the effect of the whole is good; but if he give us a portrait of a single figure we are hyper-critical with regard to the least defect. And so in the case of the novelist. Provided that he take us from place to place, that he afford us rapid changes and constant excitement, we are interested for the time being, even though his work possess no intrinsic literary merit. In short, while the former depends upon the detail of its composition, the latter rests upon its general effect.

Here, however, we must draw a line and make a very important distinction; for it is not uncommon in works of this sort, and especially prevalent in the more careless compositions of the present day, to make the actors in a story evidently subservient to the plot. With a view to originality events are made to take an unusual if not an unnatural course, and the characters are fitted with it to bring about the desired result; hence there is no conception of character at all. Cause and effect change places. Human nature is distorted and twisted into fantastic shapes to make a startling *tableau*, and the product of all this is a tissue of absurdity and contradiction, involving such an obvious inconsistency as hardly to entitle it to a passing allusion. It is, however, owing to the elements of this illogical construction that novels as a rule possess a literary value comparatively low, and are, with some exceptions, not ranked among standard works.

From what has been said, then, we may draw this general conclusion: that in the formation of a story the conception must first be of human nature; that events which are the result of human action must harmonise with it, although upon these events, in their connection and effect, will still depend the chief interest of the book.

A second remark that we have to make is especially applicable to this class. In all novels there are one or more prominent figures to which the attention of the male reader is particularly drawn. Round these are grouped accessory or subordinate characters; and it is with regard to these that we wish to make one statement.

In the histrionic art it has always been the custom to give the least important *rôles* to inferior artists, who play a minor and therefore less influential part in the play. But it has always been found necessary, in order to ensure a real and legitimate success, that the actors thus chosen, though less gifted than those who represent the chief characters, should still render their parts, however small, as nearly perfect as possible. A really fine play has often been ruined by inattention to this point. Dramatic writers have seen their compositions fail, and good artists have been disheartened in their performance by the want of intelligent actors, to fill the subordinate parts. Now the rule that applies to the acted drama is relevant also to the written story. And precisely as we call a play generally good or bad, according as the different characters back up and support one another, so the skilful or careless delineation of the accidental or accessory characters that are needed to make up the novel will determine it to be the work of a genius or that of an ordinary writer. How far they are to be developed, and to what point their peculiar traits may be brought out, and yet not divert the natural current of the narrative, must be left to the good sense and the tact of the author.

To enter into further detail about works of this sort would involve too long a labour. The subject, indeed, admits of too many variations in its treatment, and rules which might be applicable in one place would not be admissible in another.

We may, however, here put in a caution against a fault unfortunately prevalent among authors at the present time—namely, that of writing with a view to gratify the tastes and inclinations of a particular class. Hence the publication of books that pander to a morbid delight in scenes of crime and guilt, which seem to have a special attraction to uneducated and debased minds. Hence, too, the appearance and the toleration of what is commonly called the sensational novel, written to gratify a craving after excitement; a story abounding in hair-breadth adventures and constant *tableaux*, the aggregate literary and practical value of which is insignificant to the last degree. In all such cases the author can never have a real or lasting reward for the trouble which he has taken. Instead of endeavouring to improve those for whom he writes, he accommodates himself to their lower inclinations. Instead of trying to elevate their tastes, he sinks himself to their level. He starts with an ignoble object, and gains an ignoble end. Nor will his pitiful work ever gain a permanent reputation, but having at the most outrun a transient popularity, will sink into the oblivion that it richly deserves.

Thus have we, in rough and imperfect outline, attempted to show the more prominent forms that fiction is able to assume. We are proud to think that our own country can boast a literature second to none in the whole world, and that in this branch she especially excels—that from her have sprung high-minded and impartial authors of fiction, the brilliancy of whose writing is no less conspicuous than the purity of their moral teaching—that by this instrumentality education has been advanced, social abuse rectified, and virtue generally encouraged. True it is that among us, as well as among others, there is a dark side to the picture. There is, we greatly fear, in the present day a tendency to shift the standard of truth in order to suit the position that we have taken up—to accommodate morality to society—and then to make the exigency of its demands an excuse for what is essentially wrong. There is a want of openness and candour in some of our modern novels—they are either brilliant and artificial, or they lack life and originality. Others, far worse, are invested with a false and pernicious charm; they refuse to speak plainly, but suggest the corrupt thought and by an insidious inuendo do incalculable mischief. We read them with a half apprehension of their drift and meaning. We are fascinated for a moment, but we nervously put them out of the reach of our children. The influence of these is fatally dangerous. They involve a great and vital error, and one which has already contaminated the popular literature of a clever and polished people. Let us beware of it, for it is a deadly social poison, the more to be dreaded because its flavour is for the moment pleasant, though it leaves an after-taste bitter as gall. Let us check the incipient growth of it in the composition of our works of fiction, or it will gradually pollute the source from whence we derive some of our best and most innocent pleasures. Let it be our care to preserve that high reputation which our imaginative literature has always had, not only for distinguished authorship and eminent ability, but also for impartial discrimination and pure and abiding principles.

And in bringing this subject to a close, we cannot do less than pay our tribute of grateful respect to the memory of one who perhaps more than any other has contributed to this end, and who not long since was still among us, holding us to the very last entranced by the fascination of his wonderful genius. The name of Charles Dickens recalls an irreparable loss. His works are enshrined no less among the most precious archives of English literature than among the household treasures of every English home. We look in vain for one to fill the vacant place. The deep insight into human nature, the keen penetration, the ready wit, the gentle pathos were pre-eminently his. The easy and familiar style of writing, the universal and kindly fellow-feeling that he had for humanity at large, are no less remarkable than the fearless way in which he exposed the vicious practices of the age in which he lived. He had a wide and varied experience of the world, and he wrote about things with which he was personally conversant. His works will never lose their value, for they are a true picture of life, and they uphold a pure morality, the principles of which can never change.

☙ 63 ☙

Novel-Reading

ANTHONY TROLLOPE

Himself a major Victorian novelist best known for his Barsetshire series of six novels beginning with *The Warden* (1855) and ending with *The Last Chronicle of Barset* (1867), Anthony Trollope (1815-1882) defends the novel as a viable genre whose central purposes are to please, to teach and to avoid dullness. Beginning with Defoe and concluding with Dickens and Thackeray, Trollope measures the success of the novel by its moral effectiveness. According to this Johnsonian criterion, Richardson is the first true British novelist; Fielding and Smollett fail to inculcate proper moral values, and Goldsmith's *Vicar of Wakefield* is the most enduring novel of the eighteenth century. In the second half of the essay, Trollope praises Scott, Dickens and Thackeray for their ability to present vice as abhorrent, virtue as a quality to emulate. Little concerned with form in this essay, Trollope argues that the best novels combine truth of character with truth of description. He sees no conflict between realistic and sensational modes if the successful author can offer readers convincing characters. In his *Autobiography* (1883) he further evaluates the work of his contemporaries, again judging their success by their portrayal of realistic characters caught in either tragic or exciting circumstances.

The Works of Charles Dickens.
The Works of William Makepeace Thackeray.[1]

In putting at the head of this paper the names of two distinguished English novelists whose tales have been collected and republished since their death,[1] it is my object to review rather the general nature of the work done by English novelists of latter times than the contributions specially made by these two to our literature. Criticism has dealt with them, and public opinion has awarded to each his own position in the world of letters. But it may be worth while to inquire what is and what will be

Source: Anthony Trollope, "Novel-Reading", *Nineteenth Century*, 5, January 1879, pp. 24-43

the result of a branch of reading which is at present more extended than any other, and to which they have contributed so much. We used to regard novels as ephemeral; and a quarter of a century since were accustomed to consider those by Scott, with a few others which, from *Robinson Crusoe* downwards, had made permanent names to themselves, as exceptions to this rule. Now we have collected editions of one modern master of fiction after another brought out with all circumstances of editorial luxury and editorial cheapness. The works of Dickens are to be bought in penny numbers; and those of Thackeray are being at the present moment reissued to the public with every glory of paper, print, and illustration, at a proposed cost to the purchaser of 33*l*. 12*s*., for the set. I do not in the least doubt that the enterprising publishers will find themselves justified in their different adventures. The popular British novel is now so popular that it can be neither too cheap nor too dear for the market.

> *Æquo pulsat pede pauperum tabernas*
> *Regumque turres.*

I believe it to be a fact that of no English author has the sale of the works been at the same time so large and so profitable for the first half-dozen years after his death as of Dickens; and I cannot at the moment remember any edition so costly as that which is now being brought out of Thackeray's novels, in proportion to the amount and nature of the work. I have seen it asserted that the three English authors whose works are most to be found in the far-off shores of our colonists—in Australia, Canada, and South Africa—are Shakespeare, Macaulay, and Dickens. Shakespeare no doubt is there, as he is in the houses of some of us not so far off, for the sake of national glory. Macaulay and Dickens, perhaps, share between them the thumbs of the family, but the marks of affection bestowed on the novelist will be found to be the darker.

With such evidence before us of the wide-spread and enduring popularity of popular novels, it would become us to make up our minds whether this coveted amusement is of its nature prone to do good or evil. There cannot be a doubt that the characters of those around us are formed very much on the lessons which are thus taught. Our girls become wives, and our wives mothers, and then old women, very much under these inspirations. Our boys grow into manhood, either nobly or ignobly partly as they may teach, and in accordance with such teaching will continue to bear their burdens gallantly or to repudiate them with cowardly sloth.

Sermons have been invented, coming down to us from the Greek Chorus, and probably from times much antecedent to the Greek dramatists, in order that the violence of the active may be controlled by the prudence of the inactive, and the thoughtlessness of the young by the thoughtfulness of the old. And sermons have been very efficacious for these purposes. There are now among us preachers influencing the conduct of many, and probably delighting the intellectual faculties of more. But it is, we think, felt that the sermon which is listened to with more or less of patience once or twice a week does not catch a hold of the imagination as it used to do, so as to enable us to say that those who are growing up among us are formed as to their character by the discourses which they hear from the pulpit. Teaching to be efficacious must be popular. The birch has, no doubt, saved many from the uttermost depth of darkness, but it never yet made a scholar. I am inclined to think that the lessons inculcated by the novelists at present go deeper than most others. To ascertain whether they be good or bad, we should look not only to the teaching but to that which has been taught,—not to the masters only but the scholars. To effect this thoroughly, an essay on the morals of the people would be necessary,—of such at least of the people as read sufficiently for the enjoyment of a novel. We should have to compare the conduct of the present day with that of past years, and our own conduct with that of other people. So much would be beyond our mark. But something may be done to show whether fathers and mothers may consider themselves safe in allowing to their children the latitude in reading which is now the order of the day, and also in giving similar freedom to themselves. It is not the daughter only who now reads her *Lord Aimworth* without thrusting him under the sofa when a strange visitor comes, or feels it necessary to have Fordyce's sermons open on the table. There it is, unconcealed, whether for good or bad, patent to all and established, the recognised amusement of our lighter hours, too often our mainstay in literature, the former of our morals, the code by which we rule ourselves, the mirror in which we dress ourselves, the *index expurgatorius* of things held to be allowable in the ordinary affairs of life. No man actually turns to a novel for a definition of honour, nor a woman for that of modesty; but it is from the pages of many novels that men and women obtain guidance both as to honour and modesty. As the writer of the leading article picks up his ideas of politics among those which he finds floating about the world, thinking out but little for himself and creating but little, so does the novelist find his ideas of conduct, and then create a picture of that excellence which he has appreciated. Nor does he do the reverse with reference to the ignoble or the immodest. He collects the floating ideas of the world around him as to what is right and wrong in conduct, and reproduces them with his own colouring. At different periods in our history, the preacher, the dramatist, the essayist, and the poet have been efficacious over others;—at one time the preacher, and at one the poet. Now it is the novelist. There are reasons why we would wish it were otherwise. The reading of novels can hardly strengthen the intelligence. But we have to deal with the fact as it exists, deprecating the evil as far as it is an evil, but acknowledging the good if there be good.

Fond as most of us are of novels, it has to be confessed that they have had a bad name among us. Sheridan, in the scene from which we have quoted, has put into Lydia's mouth a true picture of the time as it then existed. Young ladies, if they read novels, read them on the sly, and married ladies were not more free in acknowledging their acquaintance with those in English than they are now as to those in French. That freedom was growing then as is the other now. There were those who could read unblushingly; those who read and blushed; and those who sternly would not read at all. At a much later date than Sheridan's it was the ordinary practice in well-conducted families to limit the reading of novels. In many houses such books were not permitted at all. In others Scott was allowed, with those probably of Miss

Edgeworth and Miss Austen. And the amusement, though permitted, was not encouraged. It was considered to be idleness and a wasting of time. At the period of which we are speaking,—say forty years ago,—it was hardly recognised by any that much beyond amusement not only might be, but must be, the consequence of such reading. Novels were ephemeral, trivial,—of no great importance except in so far as they might perhaps be injurious. As a girl who is, as a rule, duly industrious, may be allowed now and then to sit idle over the fire, thinking as nearly as possible of nothing,—thus refreshing herself for her daily toils; as a man may, without reproach, devote a small portion of his day to loafing and lounging about his club; so in those perhaps healthier days did a small modicum of novel-reading begin to be permitted. Where now is the reading individual for whom a small modicum suffices?

And very evil things have been said of the writers of novels by their brethren in literature; as though these workers, whose work has gradually become so efficacious for good or evil, had done nothing but harm in the world. It would be useless, or even ungenerous now, to quote essayists, divines, and historians who have written of novelists as though the mere providing of a little fleeting amusement,—generally of pernicious amusement,—had been the only object in their view. But our readers will be aware that if such criticism does not now exist, it has not ceased so long but that they remember its tone. The ordinary old homily against the novel, inveighing against the frivolities, the falsehood, and perhaps the licentiousness, of a fictitious narrative, is still familiar to our ears. Though we may reckon among our dearest literary possessions the pathos of this story, the humour of another, the unerring truth to nature of a third; though we may be aware of the absolute national importance to us of a *Robinson Crusoe* or *Tom Jones*, of an *Ivanhoe* or an *Esmond*; though each of us in his own heart may know all that a good novel has done for him,—still there remains something of the bad character which for years has been attached to the art.

> *Quo semel est imbuta recens, servabit odorem*
> *Testa diu.*

Even though it be true that the novels of the present day have in great measure taken the place of sermons, and that they feed the imagination too often in lieu of poetry, still they are admitted to their high functions not without forebodings, not without remonstrances, not without a certain sense that we are giving up our young people into the hands of an Apollyon. Is this teacher an Apollyon; or is he better because stronger, and as moral—as an archbishop?

It is certainly the case that novels deal mainly with one subject—that, namely, of love; and equally certain that love is a matter in handling which for the instruction or delectation of the young there is much danger. This is what the novelist does daily, and, whatever may be the danger, he is accepted. We quite agree with the young lady in the *Hunchback* who declared that Ovid was a fool. 'To call that thing an art which art is none.'

> *No art but taketh time and pains to learn.*
> *Love comes with neither.*

So much the novelist knows as well as Sheridan Knowles's young lady, and therefore sets about his work with descriptive rather than didactic lessons. His pupils would not accept them were he to tell them that he came into the house as a tutor in such an art. But still as a tutor he is accepted. What can be of more importance to us than to know whether we who all of us encourage such tutors in our houses, are subjecting those we love to good teaching or to ill? We do not dare to say openly to those dear ones, but we confess it to ourselves, that the one thing of most importance to them is whether they shall love rightly or wrongly. The sweet, innocent, bashful girl, who never to her dearest bosom friend dares to talk upon the matter, knows that it must be so for herself. Will it be her happy future to be joined to some man who, together with the energy necessary for maintaining her and her children, shall also have a loving heart and a sweet temper?—or shall she, through dire mistake, in this great affair of her life fall into some unutterable abyss of negligence, poverty, and heartless indifference? All this is vague, though still certain, to the girl herself. But to the mother it is in no way vague. Night and morning it must be her dearest prayer that the man who shall take her girl from her shall be worthy of her girl. And the importance to the man, though not so strongly felt, is equal. As it is not his lot to rise and fall in the world as his partner may succeed or the reverse, the image of a wife does not force itself upon his thoughts so vividly as does that of a husband on the female mind: but, as she is dependent of him for all honour, so he is on her for all happiness. It suits us to speak of love as a soft, sweet, flowery pastime, with many roses and some thorns, in which youth is apt to disport itself; but there is no father, no mother, no daughter, and should be no son, blind to the fact that, of all matters concerning life, it is the most important. That Ovid's *Art of Love* was nothing, much worse than nothing, we admit. But nevertheless the art is taught. Before the moment comes in which heart is given to heart, the imagination has been instructed as to what should accompany the gift, and what should be expected in accompaniment; in what way the gift should be made, and after what assurance; for how long a period silence should be held, and then how far speech should be unguarded.

By those who do not habitually read at all, the work is done somewhat roughly,—we will not say thoughtlessly, but with little of those precautions which education demands. With those who do read, all that literature gives them helps somewhat in the operation of which we are speaking. History tells us much of love's efficacy, and much of the evil that comes from the want of it. Biography is of course full of it. Philosophy deals with it. Poetry is hardly poetry without it. The drama is built on it almost as exclusively as are the novels. But it is from novels that the crowd of expectant and ready pupils obtain that constant flow of easy teaching which fills the mind of all readers with continual thoughts of love. The importance of the teaching is mainly to the young, but the existence of the teaching is almost equally present to the old. Why is it that the judge when he escapes from the bench, the bishop even,—as we are told,—when he comes from his confirmation, the politician as he sits in the library of the House, the Cabinet Minister when he has a half-hour to himself, the old dowager in almost all the hours which she has to herself,—seek for distraction and reaction in the pages of a novel? It is because there is an ever-recurring delight in going back to the very rudiments of those lessons in love.

'My dear,' says the loving but only half-careful mother to her daughter, 'I wish you wouldn't devote so many of your hours to novel-reading. How far have you got with your Gibbon?' Whereupon the young lady reads a page or two of Gibbon, and then goes back to her novels. The mother knows that her girl is good, and does not make herself unhappy. Is she justified in her security by the goodness of the teaching? There is good and bad, no doubt. In speaking of good and bad we are not alluding to virtue and vice themselves, but to the representations made of them. If virtue be made ridiculous, no description of it will be serviceable. If vice be made alluring, the picture will certainly be injurious. Sydney Smith, as far as it went, did an injury to morality at large when he declared in one of his letters that the Prime Minister of the day was 'faithful to Mrs. Percival.' Desiring to make the Prime Minister ridiculous, he endeavoured to throw a stone at that domesticity which the Prime Minister was supposed to cherish, and doing so he taught evil. Gay did injury to morality when he persuaded all the town to sympathise with a thief. The good teaching of a novel may be evinced as much in displaying the base as the noble, if the base be made to look base as the noble is made to look noble.

If we look back to the earlier efforts of English novel writing, the lessons taught were too often bad. Though there was a wide world of British fiction before the time of Charles the Second, it generally took the shape of the drama, and of that, whether good or bad, in its results we have at present nothing to say. The prose romances were few in number, and entertained so limited an audience that they were not efficacious for good or evil. The people would flock to see plays, where plays could be produced for them, as in London—but did not as yet care to feed their imaginations by reading. Then came the novelists of Charles the Second, who, though they are less profligate and also more stupid than is generally supposed of them, could certainly do no good to the mind of any reader. Of our novelists the first really known is Defoe, who, though he was born almost within the Commonwealth, did not produce his *Robinson Crusoe* till the time of George the First. *Robinson Crusoe* did not deal with love. Defoe's other stories, which are happily forgotten, are bad in their very essence. *Roxana* is an accurate sample of what a bad book may be. It relates the adventures of a woman thoroughly depraved, and yet for the most part successful,—in intended to attract by its licentiousness, and puts off till the end the stale scrap of morality which is brought in as a salve to the conscience of the writer. Putting aside *Robinson Crusoe*, which has been truly described as an accident, Defoe's teaching as a novelist has been altogether bad. Then, mentioning only the names which are well known to us, we come first to Richardson, who has been called the inventor of the modern English novel. It certainly was his object to write of love, so that young women might be profited by what he wrote,—and we may say that he succeeded. It cannot be doubted that he had a strong conscience in his work,—that he did not write only to please, or only for money, or only for reputation, nor for those three causes combined; but that he might do good to those for whom he was writing. In this respect he certainly was the inventor of the modern English novel. That his works will ever become popular again we doubt. Macaulay expressed an exaggerated praise for *Clarissa*, which brought forth new editions,—even an abridgment of the novel; but the tone is too melancholy, and is played too exclusively on a single string for the taste of a less patient age. Nor would his teaching, though it was good a hundred and thirty years ago, be good now. Against the horrors to which his heroine was subjected, it is not necessary to warn our girls in this safer age,—or to speak of them.

Of Fielding and Smollett,—whom, however, it is unfair to bracket,—it can hardly be said that their conscience was as clear in the matter of what they wrote as was that of Richardson, though probably each of them felt that the aim he had in view was to satirise vice. Defoe might have said the same. But when the satirist lingers lovingly over the vice which he castigates so as to allure by his descriptions, it may be doubted whether he does much service to morality. Juvenal was perhaps the sternest moral censor whom the world of letters has produced; but he was, and even in his own age must have been felt to be, a most lascivious writer. Fielding, who in the construction of a story and the development of a character is supreme among novelists, is, we think, open to the same reproach. That Smollett was so the readers of *Roderick Random* and his other stories are well aware; and in him the fault was more conspicuous than in Fielding,—without the great redeeming gifts. Novelists followed, one after another, whose tales were good enough to remain in our memories, though we cannot say that their work was effective for any special purpose. Among those Goldsmith was the first and the greatest. His *Vicar of Wakefield* has taken a hold on our national literature equalled perhaps by no other novel.

It is not my purpose to give a history of English fiction. Its next conspicuous phase was that of the awe-striking mysterious romances, such as the *Mysteries of Udolpho* and the *Italian*, by which we may say no such lessons were taught as those of which we are speaking, either for good or bad. The perusal of them left little behind beyond a slightly morbid tone of the imagination. They excited no passions, and created no beliefs. There was Godwin, a man whose mind was prone to revel in the injuries which an unfortunate might be subjected to by the injustice of the world; and Mrs. Inchbald, who longed to be passionate, though in the *Simple Story*, by which we know her, she hardly rose to the height of passion; and Miss Burney, who was a Richardson in petticoats, but with a woman's closer appreciation of the little details of life. After them, or together with them, and together also with the names which will follow them, flourished the Rosa Matilda school of fiction, than which the desire to have something to read has produced nothing in literature more vapid or more mean. Up to this time there was probably no recognised attempt on the part of the novelist himself, except by Richardson, and perhaps by Miss Burney, to teach any lesson, to give out any code of morals, to preach as it were a sermon from his pulpit, as the parson preaches his sermon. The business was chance business,— the tendency being good if the tendency of the mind of the worker was good;—or bad if that was bad. Then came Miss Edgeworth and Miss Austen, who, the one in Ireland and the other in England, determined to write tales which should have a wholesome bearing. In this they were thoroughly successful, and were the first to convince the British matron that her darling girl might be amused by light literature without injury to her purity. For there had been about Miss Burney, in spite of her morality, a smell of the torchlights of iniquity which had been offensive to the nose of the ordinary British matron. Miss Edgeworth, indeed, did fall away a little towards the end of her long career; but, as we all know, a well-established character may bear a considerable strain. Miss Austen from first to last was the same,—with no touch of rampant fashion. Her young ladies indeed are very prone to look for husbands; but when this is done with proper reticence, with no flavour of gaslight, the British matron can excuse a little evil in that direction for the sake of the good.

Then Scott arose, who still towers among us as the first of novelists. He himself tells us that he was prompted to write Scotch novels by the success of Miss Edgeworth's Irish tales. 'Without being so presumptuous as to hope to emulate the rich humour, pathetic tenderness, and admirable tact of my accomplished friend, I felt that something might be done for my own country of the same kind with that which Miss Edgeworth achieved for Ireland.' It no doubt was the case that the success of Miss Edgeworth stimulated him to write prose fiction; but we cannot but feel that there must have been present to him from first to last, through his long career of unprecedented success, a conviction of his duty as a teacher. In all those pages, in the telling of those incidents between men and women, in all those narratives of love, there is not a passage which a mother would feel herself constrained to keep from the eye of her daughter. It has been said that Scott is passionless in his descriptions of love. He moves us to our heart's core by his Meg Merrilies, his Edie Ochiltree, his Balfour of Burley, and a hundred other such characters; but no one sheds a tear over the sorrows of Flora Mac Ivor, Edith Bellenden, or Julia Mannering. When we weep for Lucy Ashton, it is because she is to be married to one she does not love, not because of her love. But in admitting this we ought to acknowledge at the same time the strain which Scott put upon himself so that he should not be carried away into the seducing language of ill-regulated passion. When he came to tell the story of unfortunate love, to describe the lot in life of a girl who had fallen,—when he created Effie Deans,—then he could be passionate. But together with this he possessed the greater power of so telling even that story, that the lesson from beginning to end should be salutary.

From Scott downwards I will mention no names till we come to those which I have prefixed to this paper. There have been English novelists by the score,—by the hundred we may say. Some of them have been very weak; some utterly inefficacious for the good or evil; some undoubtedly mischievous in their tendencies. But there has accompanied their growth a general conviction that it behoves the English novelist to be pure. As on the English stage and with the English periodical press, both scurrility and lasciviousness may now and again snatch a temporary success; so it is with English fiction. We all know the writers who endeavour to be so nearly lascivious that they may find an audience among those whose taste lies in that direction. But such is not the taste of the nation at large; and these attempts at impropriety, these longings to be as bold and wicked as some of our neighbours, do not pay in the long run. While a true story of genuine love, well told, will win the heart of the nation and raise the author to a high position among the worthies of his country, the prurient dabbler in lust hardly becomes known beyond a special class. The number of those who read novels have become millions in England during the last twenty-five years. In our factories, with our artisans, behind our counters, in third-class railway carriages, in our kitchens and stables, novels are now read unceasingly. Much reaches those readers that is poor. Much that is false in sentiment and faulty in art no doubt finds its way with them. But indecency does not thrive with them, and when there comes to them a choice of good or bad, they choose the better. There has grown up a custom of late, especially among tea dealers, to give away a certain number of books among their poorer customers. When so much tea has been consumed, then shall be a book given. It came to my ears the other day that eighteen thousand volumes of Dickens's works had just been ordered for this purpose. The bookseller suggested that a little novelty might be expedient. Would the benevolent tea-dealer like to vary his presents? But no! The tradesman, knowing his business, and being anxious above all things to attract, declared that Dickens was what he wanted. He had found that the tea-consuming world preferred their Dickens.

In wide-spread popularity the novels of Charles Dickens have, I believe, exceeded those of any other British novelist, though they have not yet reached that open market of unrestricted competition which a book reaches only when its copyright has run out. Up to this present time over 800,000 copies of *Pickwick* have been sold in this country, and the book is still copyright property. In saying this I make no invidious comparison between Scott and Dickens. I may, indeed, be in error in supposing the circulation of *Waverley* to have been less. As it is open to any bookseller to issue Scott's novels, it would be difficult to arrive at a correct number. Our object is simply to show what has been the circulation of a popular novel in Great Britain. The circulation outside the home market has been probably as great,— perhaps greater, as American readers are more numerous than the English. Among the millions of those into whose hands these hundreds of thousands of volumes have fallen, there can hardly be one who has not received some lesson from what he has read. It may be that many dissent from the mode of telling which Dickens adopted in his stories, that they are indifferent to the stories themselves, that they question the taste, and fail to interest themselves in the melodramatic incidents and unnatural characters which it was his delight to portray. All that has no bearing on the issue which we now attempt to raise. The teaching of which we are speaking is not instruction as to taste, or art,—is not instruction as to style or literary excellence. By such lessons as Dickens taught will the young man learn to be honest or dishonest, noble or ignoble? Will the girl learn to be modest or brazen-faced? Will greed be engendered and self-indulgence? Will a taste for vicious pleasure be created? Will the young of either sex be taught to think it is a grand thing to throw off the conventional rules which the wisdom of the world has established for its guidance; or will they unconsciously learn from the author's pages to recognise the fact that happiness is to be obtained by obeying, and not by running counter to the principles of morality? Let memory run back for a few moments over those stories, and it will fail to find an immodest girl who has been made alluring to female readers, or an ill-conditioned youth whose career a lad would be tempted to envy. No ridicule is thrown on marriage constancy; no gilding is given to fictitious pleasure; no charm is added to idleness; no alluring colour is lent to debauchery. Pickwick may be softer, and Ralph Nickleby harder than the old men whom we know in the world; but the lessons which they teach are all in favour of a soft heart, all strongly opposed to hardness of heart. 'What an impossible dear old duffer that Pickwick is!' a lady said to me the other day, criticising the character as I though very correctly. Quite impossible, and certainly a duffer,—if I understand the latter phrase,—but so dear! That an old man, as he grows old, should go on loving everybody around him, loving the more the older he grows, running over with philanthropy, and happy through it all in spite of the susceptibility of Mrs. Bardell and the failings of Mr. Winkle! That has been the lesson taught by *Pickwick*; and though probably but few readers have so believed in Pickwick as to think that nature would produce such a man, still they have been unconsciously taught the sweetness of human love.

Such characters as those of Lord Frederick Veresopht and Sir Mulberry Hawk have often been drawn by dramatists and novelists,—too frequently with a dash of attractive fashion,—in a manner qualified to conceal in the mind of the unappreciating reader the vices of the men under the brightness of their trappings. Has any young man been made to wish that he should be such as Lord Frederick Veresopht, or should become as Sir Mulberry Hawk? Kate Nickleby is not to us an entirely natural young woman. She lacks human life. But the girls who have read her adventures have all learnt to acknowledge the beauty and the value of modesty. It is not your daughter, my reader, who has needed such a lesson;—but think of the eight hundred thousands!

Of all Dickens's novels *Oliver Twist* is perhaps artistically the best, as in it the author adheres most tenaciously to one story, and interests us most thoroughly by his plot. But the characters are less efficacious for the teaching of lessons than in his other tales. Neither can Bill Sikes nor Nancy, nor can even the great Bumble, be credited with having been of much service by deterring readers from vice;—but then neither have they allured readers, as has been done by so many writers of fiction who have ventured to deal with the world's reprobates.

In *Martin Chuzzlewit*, in *David Copperfield*, in *Bleak House*, and *Little Dorrit*, the tendency of which I speak will be found to be the same. It is indeed carried through every work that he wrote. To whom has not the kindness of heart been made beautiful by Tom Pinch, and hypocrisy odious by Pecksniff? The peculiar abominations of Pecksniff's daughters are made to be abominable to the least attentive reader. Unconsciously the girl-reader declares to herself that she will not at any rate be like that. This is the mode of teaching which is in truth serviceable. Let the mind be induced to sympathise warmly with that which is good and true, or be moved to hatred against that which is vile, and then an impression will have been made, certainly serviceable, and probably ineradicable. It may be admitted in regard to Dickens's young ladies that they lack nature. Dora, Nelly, Little Dorrit, Florence

Dombey, and a host of others crowd upon our memory, not as shadows of people we have really known,—as do Jeanie Deans, for instance, and Jane Eyre;—but they have affected us as personifications of tenderness and gentle feminine gifts. We have felt each character to contain, not a woman, but something which will help to make many women. The Boythorns, Tulkinghorns, Cheerybles and Pickwicks, may be as unlike nature as they will. They are unlike nature. But they nevertheless charm the reader, and leave behind on the palate of his mind a sweet savour of humanity. Our author's heroes, down to Smike, are often outrageous in their virtues. But their virtues are virtues. Truth, gratitude, courage, and manly self-respect are qualities which a young man will be made not only to admire, but to like, by his many hours spent over these novels. And so it will be with young women as to modesty, reticence, and unselfish devotion.

The popularity of Thackeray has been very much less extended than that of Dickens, and the lessons which he has taught have not, therefore, been scattered afield so widely. Dickens, to use a now common phrase, has tapped a stratum lower in education and wealth, and therefore much wider, than that reached by his rival. The genius of Thackeray was of a nature altogether different. Dickens delighted much in depicting with very broad lines very well-known vices under impossible characters, but was, perhaps, still more thoroughly at home in representing equally well-known virtues after the same fashion. His Pinches and Cheerybles were nearer to him than his Ralph Nicklebys and his Pecksniffs. It seems specially to have been the work of Thackeray to cover with scorn the vices which in his hands were displayed in personages who were only too realistic. With him there is no touch of melodrama. From first to last you are as much at home with Barry Lyndon, the most complete rascal, perhaps, that ever was drawn, as with your wife, or your private secretary, if you have one, or the servant who waits upon you daily. And when he turns from the strength of his rascals to the weaker idiosyncrasies of those whom you are to love for their virtues, he is equally efficacious. Barry Lyndon was a man of infinite intellectual capacity, which is more than we can say for Colonel Newcome. But was there ever a gentleman more sweet, more loveable, more thoroughly a gentleman in all points, than the Colonel? How many a young lad has been taught to know how a gentleman should act and speak, by the thoughts and words and doings of the Colonel! I will not say that Barry Lyndon's career has deterred many from rascaldom, as such a career can only be exceptional; but it has certainly enticed no lad to follow it.

Vanity Fair, though not in my opinion the best, is the best known of Thackeray's works. Readers, though they are delighted, are not satisfied with it, because Amelia Sedley is silly, because Osborne is selfish, because Dobbin is ridiculous, and because Becky Sharp alone is clever and successful,—while at the same time she is as abominable as the genius of a satirist can make her. But let him or her who has read the book think of the lessons which have been left behind by it. Amelia is a true loving woman, who can love her husband even though he be selfish—loving, as a woman should love, with enduring devotion. Whatever is charming in her attracts; what is silly repels. The character of Osborne is necessary to that of Dobbin, who is one of the finest heroes ever drawn. Unselfish, brave, modest, forgiving, affectionate, manly all over,—his is just the character to teach a lesson. Tell a young man that he ought to be modest, that he ought to think more of the heart of the girl he loves than of his own, that even in the pursuit of fame he should sacrifice himself to others, and he will ridicule your advice and you too. But if you can touch his sentiment, get at him in his closet,—or perhaps rather his smoking-room,—without his knowing it, bring a tear to his eye and perhaps a throb to his throat, and then he will have learned something of that which your less impressive lecture was incapable of teaching. As for Becky Sharp, it is not only that she was false, unfeminine and heartless. Such attributes no doubt are in themselves unattractive. But there is not a turn in the telling of the story which, in spite of her success, does not show the reader how little is gained, how much is lost, by the exercise of that depraved ingenuity.

Pendennis is an unsteady, ambitious, clever but idle young man, with excellent aspirations and purposes, but hardly trustworthy. He is by no means such a one as an anxious father would wish to put before his son as an example. But he is lifelike. Clever young men, ambitious but idle and vacillating, are met every day, whereas the gift of persistency in a young man is uncommon. The Pendennis phase of life is one into which clever young men are apt to run. The character if alluring would be dangerous. If reckless idle conceit had carried everything before it in the story,—if Pendennis had been made to be noble in the midst of his foibles,—the lesson taught would have been bad. But the picture which becomes gradually visible to the eyes of the reader is the reverse of this. Though Pendennis is, as it were, saved at last by the enduring affection of two women, the idleness and the conceit and the vanity, the littleness of the *soi-disant* great young man, are treated with so much disdain as to make the idlest and vainest of male readers altogether fort the time out of love with idleness and vanity. And as for Laura, the younger of the two women by whom he is saved, she who becomes his wife,—surely no female character ever drawn was better adapted than hers to teach that mixture of self-negation, modesty and affection which is needed for the composition of the ideal woman whom we love to contemplate.

Of Colonel Newcome we have already spoken. Of all the characters drawn by Thackeray it is the most attractive, and it is so because he is a man *sans peur* and *sans reproche*. He is not a clever old man,—not half so amusing as that worldly old gentleman, Major Pendennis, with whom the reader of the former novel will have become acquainted,—but he is one who cannot lie, who cannot do a mean thing, who can wear his gown as a bedesman in the Grey Friars Hospital,—for to that he comes,—with all the honour that can hang about a judge's ermine.

Esmond is undoubtedly Thackeray's greatest work,—not only because in it his story is told with the directest purpose, with less of vague wandering than in the others,—but by reason also of the force of the characters portrayed. The one to which we will specially call attention is that of Beatrix, the younger heroine of the story. Her mother, Lady Castlewood, is an elder heroine. The term as applied to the personages of a modern novel,—as may be said also of hero,—is not very appropriate;

but it is the word which will best convey the intended meaning to the reader. Nothing sadder than the story of Beatrix can be imagined,—nothing sadder though it falls so infinitely short of tragedy. But we speak specially of it here, because we believe its effect on the minds of girls who read it to be thoroughly salutary. Beatrix is a girl endowed with great gifts. She has birth, rank, fortune, intellect and beauty. She is blessed with that special combination of feminine loveliness and feminine wit which men delight to encounter. The novelist has not merely said that it is so, but has succeeded in bringing the girl before us with such vivid power of portraiture that we know her, what she is, down to her shoe-ties,—know her, first to the loving of her, and then to the hating of her. She becomes as she goes on the object of Esmond's love,—and could she permit her heart to act in this matter, she too would love him. She knows well that he is a man worthy to be loved. She is encouraged to love him by outward circumstances. Indeed, she does love him. But she has decided within her own bosom that the world is her oyster, which has to be opened by her, being a woman, not by her sword but by her beauty. Higher rank than her own, greater fortune, a bigger place in the world's eyes, grander jewels, have to be won. Harry Esmond, oh, how good he is; how fit to be the lord of any girl,—if only he were a duke, or such like! This is her feeling, and this is her resolve. Then she sets her cap at a duke, a real duke, and almost gets him,—would have got him only her duke is killed in a duel before she has been made a duchess. After that terrible blow she sinks lower still in her low ambition. A scion of banished royalty comes dangling after her, and she, thinking that the scion may be restored to his royal grandeur, would fain become the mistress of a king.

It is a foul career, the reader will say; and there may be some who would ask whether such is the picture which should be presented to the eyes of a young girl by those who are anxious, not only for the amusement of her leisure hours, but also for her purity and worth. It might be asked, also, whether the Commandments should be read in her ears, lest she be taught to steal and to murder. Beautiful as Beatrix is, attractive, clever, charming,—prone as the reader is to sympathise with Esmond in his love for this winning creature,—yet by degrees the vileness becomes so vile, the ulcered sores are so revolting, the whited sepulchre is seen to be so foul within, that the girl who reads the book is driven to say, 'Not like that; not like that! Whatever fate may have in store for me, let it not be like that.' And this conviction will not come from any outward suffering,—not from poverty, ill-usage, from loss of beauty or youth. No condign punishment of that easy kind is inflicted. But the vice is made to be so ugly, so heartbreaking to the wretched victim who has encouraged it, that it strikes the beholder with horror. Vice is heartbreaking to its victim. The difficulty is to teach the lesson,—to bring the truth home. Sermons too often fail to do it. the little story in which Tom the naughty boy breaks his leg, while Jack the good boy gets the apples, does not do it. The broken leg and the apples do not find credence. Beatrix in her misery is believed to be miserable.

I will not appeal to further instances of good teaching among later British novelists, having endeavoured to exemplify my meaning by the novels of two masters who have appeared among us in latter days, whose works are known to all of us, and who have both departed from among us; but I think that I am entitled to vindicate the character of the British novelist generally from aspersions often thrown upon it by quoting the works of those to whom I have referred. And I am anxious also to vindicate that public taste in literature which has created and nourished the novelist's work. There still exists the judgment,–prejudice, I think I may call it,–which condemns it. It is not operative against the reading of novels, as is proved by their general acceptance. But it exists strongly in reference to the appreciation in which they are professed to be held, and it robs them of much of that high character which they may claim to have earned by their grace, their honesty, and good teaching.

By the consent of all mankind who read, poetry takes the highest place in literature. That nobility of expression, and all but divine grace of words, which she is bound to attain before she can make her footing good, is not compatible with prose. Indeed, it is that which turns prose into poetry. When that has been in truth achieved, the reader knows that the writer has soared above the earth, and can teach his lessons somewhat as a god might teach. He who sits down to write his tale in prose makes no such attempt, nor does he dream that the poet's honour is within his reach. But his teaching is of the same nature, and his lessons tend to the same end. By either, false sentiment may be fostered, false notions of humanity may be engendered, false honour, false love, false worship may be created; by either, vice instead of virtue may be taught. But by each equally may true honour, true love, true worship, and true humanity be inculcated; and that will be the greatest teacher who will spread such truth the widest. At present, much as novels, as novels, are sought and read, there still exists an idea,–a feeling which is very prevalent,–that novels at their best are but innocent. Young men and women,–and old men and women too,–read more of them than they read of poetry because such reading is easier; but they read them as men eat pastry after dinner,–not without some inward conviction that the taste is vain if not vicious. We think that it is not vicious or vain,–unless indeed the employment be allowed to interfere with the graver duties of life.

A greater proportion of the teaching of the day than any of us have as yet acknowledged comes, no doubt, from the reading of these books. Whether the teaching be good or bad, that is the case. It is from them that girls learn what is expected from them, and what they are to expect when lovers come; and also from them that young men unconsciously learn what are, or should be, or may be, the charms of love. Other lessons also are taught. In these days, when the desire to be honest is pressed so hard on the heel by ambition to be great, in which riches are the easiest road to greatness; when the temptations to which men are subjected dull their eyes to the perfected iniquities of others; when it is so hard for a man to decide vigorously that the pitch which so many are handling will defile him if it be touched,–men's conduct will be actuated much by that which is from day to day depicted to them as leading to glorious or inglorious results. The woman who is described as having obtained all that the world holds to be precious by lavishing her charms and caresses unworthily and heartlessly, will induce other women to do the same with theirs; as will she who is made interesting by exhibition of bold passion teach others to be spuriously passionate. The young man who in a novel becomes a hero,—perhaps a member of Parliament or almost a Prime Minister,—by trickery, falsehood, and flash cleverness, will have as many followers in his line as Jack Sheppard or Macheath will have in theirs; and will do, if not as wide, a deeper mischief.

To the novelist, thinking of all this, it must surely become a matter of deep conscience how he shall handle those characters by whose words and doings he hopes to interest his readers. It may frequently be the case that he will be tempted to sacrifice something for effect; to say a word or two here, or to draw a picture there, for which he feels that he has the power, and which, when spoken or drawn, would be alluring. The regions of absolute vice are foul and odious. The savour of them, till custom has hardened the palate and the nose, is disgusting. In these he will hardly tread. But there are outskirts on these regions in which sweet-smelling flowers seem to grow and grass to be green. It is in these border-lands that the danger lies. The novelist may not be dull. If he commit that fault, he can do neither harm nor good. He must please; and the flowers and the soft grass in those neutral territories sometimes seem to give too easy an opportunity of pleasing!

The writer of stories must please, or he will be nothing. And he must teach, whether he wish to teach or not. How shall he teach lessons of virtue, and at the same time make himself a delight to his readers? Sermons in themselves are not thought to be agreeable; nor are disquisitions on moral philosophy supposed to be pleasant reading for our idle hours. But the novelist, if he have a conscience, must preach his sermons with the same purpose as the clergyman, and must have his own system of ethics. If he can do this efficiently, if he can make virtue alluring and vice ugly, while he charms his reader instead of wearying him, then we think that he should not be spoken of generally as being among those workers of iniquity who do evil in their generation. So many have done so, that the English novelist as a class may, we think, boast that such has been the result of their work. Can any one, by search through the works of the fine writers whose names we have specially mentioned,—Miss Edgeworth, Miss Austen, Scott, Dickens, and Thackeray,—find a scene, a passage, or a word that could teach a girl to be immodest or a man to be dishonest? When men in their pages have been described as dishonest, or women as immodest, has not the reader in every instance been deterred by the example and its results? It is not for the novelist to say simply and baldly: 'Because you lied here, or were heartless there; because you, Lydia Bennet, forgot the lessons of your honest home, or you, Earl Leicester, were false through your ambition, or you, Beatrix, loved too well the glitter of the world, therefore you shall be scourged with scourges either here or hereafter;' but it is for him to show, as he carries on his tale, that his Lydia, or his Leicester, or his Beatrix, will be dishonoured in the estimation of all by his or her vices. Let a woman be drawn clever, beautiful, attractive, so as to make men love her and women almost envy her; and let her be made also heartless, unfeminine, ambitious of evil grandeur, as was Beatrix,—what danger is there not in such a character! To the novelist who shall handle it, what peril of doing harm! But if at last it has been so handled that every girl who reads of Beatrix shall say: 'Oh, not like that! let me not be like that!' and that every youth shall say: 'Let me not have such a one as that to press to my bosom,—anything rather than that!' Then will not the novelist have preached his sermon as perhaps no other preacher can preach it?

Very much of a novelist's work, as we have said above, must appertain to the intercourse between young men and young women. It is admitted that a novel can hardly be made interesting or successful without love. Some few might be named in which the attempt has been made, but even in them it fails. *Pickwick* has been given as an exception to this rule, but even in *Pickwick* there are three or four sets of lovers whose amatory flutterings give a softness to the work. In this frequent allusion to the passion which most strongly stirs the imagination of the young, there must be danger, as the novelist is necessarily aware. Then the question has to be asked, whether the danger may not be so handled that good shall be the result, and to be answered. The subject is necessary to the novelist, because it is interesting to all; but as it is interesting to all, so will the lessons taught respecting it be widely received. Every one feels it, has felt it, or expects to feel it,—or else regrets it with an eagerness which still perpetuates the interest. If the novelist, therefore, can so treat his subject as to do good by his treatment of it, the good done will be very wide. If a writer can teach politicians and statesmen that they can do their work better by truth than by falsehood, he does a great service; but it is done in the first instance to a limited number of persons. But if he can make young men and women believe that truth in love will make them happy, then, if his writings be popular, he will have a very large class of pupils. No doubt that fear which did exist as to novels came from the idea that this whole matter of love would be treated in an inflammatory and unwholesome manner. 'Madam,' says Sir Anthony in the play, 'a circulating library in a town is an evergreen tree of diabolical knowledge. It blossoms through the year; and, depend upon it, Mrs. Malaprop, they who are so fond of handling the leaves, will long for the fruit at last.' Sir Anthony, no doubt, was right. But he takes it for granted that longing for the fruit is an evil. The novelist thinks differently, and believes that the honest love of an honest man is a treasure which a good girl may fairly hope to win, and that, if she can be taught to wish only for that, she will have been taught to entertain only wholesome wishes.

There used to be many who thought, and probably there are some who still think, that a girl should hear nothing of love till the time comes in which she is to be married. That was the opinion of Sir Anthony Absolute and of Mrs. Malaprop. But we doubt whether the old system was more favourable to purity of manners than that which we have adopted of late. Lydia Languish, though she was constrained by fear of her aunt to hide the book, yet had *Peregrine Pickle* in her collection. While human nature talks of love so forcibly, it can hardly serve out turn to be silent on the subject. 'Naturam expelles furca, tamen usque recurret.' There are countries in which it has been in accordance with the manners of the upper classes that the girl should be brought to marry the man almost out of the nursery,—or rather, perhaps, out of the convent,—without having enjoyed any of the freedom of thought which the reading of novels and poetry will certainly produce; but we do not know that the marriages so made have been thought to be happier than our own.

Among English novels of the present day, and among English novelists, a great division is made. There are sensational novels, and anti-sensational; sensational novelists, and anti-sensational; sensational readers, and anti-sensational. The novelists who are considered to be anti-sensational are generally called realistic. The readers who prefer the one are supposed to take delight in the elucidation of character. They who hold by the other are charmed by the construction and gradual development of a plot. All this we think to be a mistake,—which mistake arises from the inability of the inferior artist to be at the same time realistic and sensational. A good novel should be both,—and both in the highest degree. If a novel fail in either, there is a failure in art. Let those readers who fancy that they do not like sensational scenes, think of some of those passages from our great novelists which have charmed them most,—of Rebecca in the castle with Ivanhoe; of Burley in the cave with Morton; of the mad lady tearing the veil of the expectant bride in *Jane Eyre*; of Lady Castlewood as, in her indignation, she explains to the Duke of Hamilton Harry Esmond's right to be present at the marriage of his Grace with Beatrix. Will any one say that the authors of these passages have sinned in being over-sensational? No doubt a string of horrible incidents, bound together without truth in details, and told as affecting personages without character,—wooden blocks who cannot make themselves known to readers as men and women,—does not instruct, or amuse, or even fill the mind with awe. Horrors heaped upon horrors, which are horrors only in themselves, and not as touching as any recognised and known person, are not tragic, and soon cease even to horrify. Such would-be tragic elements of a story may be increased without end and without difficulty. The narrator may tell of a woman murdered, murdered in the same street with you, in the next house; may say that she was a wife murdered by her husband, a bride not yet a week a wife. He may add to it for ever. He may say that the murderer burnt her alive. There is no end to it. he may declare that a former wife was treated with equal barbarity, and that the murderer when led away to execution declared his sole regret to be that he could not live to treat at third after the same fashion. There is nothing so easy as the creation and cumulation of fearful incidents after this fashion. If such creation and cumulation be the beginning and the end of the novelist's work,—and novels have been written which seem to be without other attraction,—nothing can be more dull and nothing more useless. But not on that account are we averse to tragedy in prose fiction. As in poetry, so in prose, he who can deal adequately with tragic elements is a greater artist, and reaches a higher aim, than the writer whose efforts never carry him above the mild walks of everyday life. The *Bride of Lammermoor* is a tragedy throughout in spite of its comic elements. The life of Lady Castlewood is a tragedy. Rochester's wretched thraldom to his mad wife in *Jane Eyre* is a tragedy. But these stories charm us, not simply because they are tragic, but because we feel that men and women with flesh and blood, creatures with whom we can sympathise, are struggling amidst their woes. It all lies in that.

No novel is anything, for purposes either of comedy or tragedy, unless the reader can sympathise with the characters whose names he finds upon the page. Let the author so tell his tale as to touch his reader's heart and draw his reader's tears, and he has so far done his work well. Truth let there be,—truth of description, truth of character, human truth as to men and women. If there be such truth, I do not now that a novel can be too sensational.

Note

1. *The Collected Works of Charles Dickens.* In 20 volumes. Chapman & Hall; *The Collected Works of W. M. Thackeray.* In 22 volumes. Smith, Elder, & Co.

⚜·64·⚜

Fiction–Fair and Foul

JOHN RUSKIN

Artist, art historian and social critic, John Ruskin (1819–1900) is best known today for his five-volume work, *Modern Painters* (1843–1860) in which he champions the major painters of the age, Turner and the Pre-Raphaelites. His preference for Gothic over Renaissance architecture is the subject of his essay, "The Nature of the Gothic", included in his three-volume *The Stones of Venice* (1851–1853). Throughout his writings as evinced in the following essay as well, Ruskin's chief keynote was the connection between art and morality. In the following essay, the first of a five-part series published form 1880 to 1881 in *Nineteenth Century*, he deplores the dehumanisation of the industrialised urban classes, and sees this condition reinforced by such diverse novelists as Scott and Dickens. Both authors, but especially Dickens, Ruskin argues, are guilty of clogging their works with gratuitous and undeserved deaths. Dickens's and Hugo's descriptions of Londonian and Parisian squalor he believes merely pander to a debauched public taste for low life. Ruskin terms such works literature "of the prison house" in their refusal to strive towards an ideal morality. Interestingly, Ruskin exempts *Oliver Twist* from the "loathsome mass" of other novels of "prison house", noting that it "is an earnest and uncaricatured record of states of criminal life, written with didactic purpose . . . "

On the first mild—or, at least, the first bright—day of March, in this year, I walked through what was once a country lane, between the hostelry of the Half-moon at the bottom of Herne Hill, and the secluded College of Dulwich.

In my young days, Croxsted Lane was a green bye-road traversable for some distance by carts; but rarely so traversed, and, for the most part, little else than a narrow strip of untilled field, separated by blackberry hedges from the better cared-for meadows on each side of it: growing more weeds, therefore, than they, and perhaps in spring a primrose or two—white archangel—daisies plenty, and purple thistles in autumn. A slender rivulet, boasting little of its brightness, for there are

Source: John Ruskin, ""Fiction–Fair and Foul", *Nineteenth Century*, 7, June 1880, pp. 941–62.

no springs at Dulwich, yet fed purely enough by the rain and morning dew, here trickled—there loitered—through the long grass beneath the hedges, and expanded itself, where it might, into moderately clear and deep pools, in which, under their veils of duckweed, a fresh-water shell or two, sundry curious little skipping shrimps, any quantity of tadpoles in their time, and even sometimes a tittlebat, offered themselves to my boyhood's pleased, and not inaccurate, observation. There, my mother and I used to gather the first buds of the hawthorn; and there, in after years, I used to walk in the summer shadows, as in a place wilder and sweeter than our garden, to think over any passage I wanted to make better than usual in *Modern Painters*.

So, as aforesaid, on the first kindly day of this year, being thoughtful more than usual of those old times, I went to look again at the place.

Often, both in those days, and since, I have put myself hard to it, vainly, to find words wherewith to tell of beautiful things; but beauty has been in the world since the world was made, and human language can make a shift, somehow, to give account of it, whereas the peculiar forces of devastation induced by modern city life have only entered the world lately; and no existing terms of language known to me are enough to describe the forms of filth, and modes of ruin, that varied themselves along the course of Croxsted Lane. The fields on either side of it are now mostly dug up for building, or cut through into gaunt corners and nooks of blind ground by the wild crossings and concurrencies of three railroads. Half a dozen handfuls of new cottages, with Doric doors, are dropped about here and there among the gashed ground: the lane itself, now entirely grassless, is a deep-rutted, heavy-hillocked cart-road, diverging gatelessly into various brickfields or pieces of waste; and bordered on each side by heaps of—Hades only knows what!—mixed dust of every unclean thing that can crumble in drought, and mildew of every unclean thing that can rot or rust in damp: ashes and rags, beer-bottles and old shoes, battered pans, smashed crockery, shreds of nameless clothes, door-sweepings, floor-sweepings, kitchen garbage, back-garden sewage, old iron, rotten timber jagged with out-torn nails, cigar-ends, pipe-bowls, cinders, bones, and ordure, indescribable; and, variously kneaded into, sticking to, or fluttering foully here and there over all these,—remnants broadcast, of every manner of newspaper, advertisement or big-lettered bill, festering and flaunting out their last publicity in the pits of stinking dust and mortal slime.

The lane ends now where its prettiest windings once began; being cut off by a cross-road leading out of Dulwich to a minor railway station: and on the other side of this road, what was of old the daintiest intricacy of its solitude is changed into a straight, and evenly macadamised carriage drive, between new houses of extreme respectability, with good attached gardens and offices—most of these tenements being larger—all more pretentious, and many, I imagine, held at greatly higher rent than my father's, tenanted for twenty years at Herne Hill. And it became a matter of curious meditation to me what much here become of children resembling my poor little dreamy quondam self in temper, and thus brought up at the same distance from London, and in the same or better circumstances of worldly fortune; but with only Croxsted Lane in its present condition for their country walk. The trimly kept road before their doors, such as one used to see in the fashionable suburbs of Cheltenham or Leamington, presents nothing to their study but gravel, and gas-lamp posts; the modern addition of a vermilion letter-pillar contributing indeed to the splendour, but scarcely to the interest of the scene; and a child of any sense or fancy would hastily contrive escape from such a barren desert of politeness, and betake itself to investigation, such as might be feasible, of the natural history of Croxsted Lane.

But, for its sense of fancy, what food, or stimulus, can it find, in that foul causeway of its youthful pilgrimage? What would have happened to myself, so directed, I cannot clearly imagine. Possibly, I might have got interested in the old iron and wood-shavings; and become an engineer or a carpenter: but for the children of to-day, accustomed from the instant they are out of their cradles, to the sight of this infinite nastiness, prevailing as a fixed condition of the universe, over the face of nature, and accompanying all the operations of industrious man, what is to be the scholastic issue? unless, indeed, the thrill of scientific vanity in the primary analysis of some unheard-of process of corruption—or the reward of microscopic research in the sight of worms with more legs, and acari of more curious generation then ever vivified the more simply smelling plasma of antiquity.

One result of such elementary education is, however, already certain; namely, that the pleasure which we may conceive taken by the children of the coming time, in the analysis of physical corruption, guides, into fields more dangerous and desolate, the expatiation of imaginative literature: and that the reactions of moral disease upon itself, and the conditions of languidly monstrous character developed in an atmosphere of low vitality, have become the most valued material of modern fiction, and the most eagerly discussed texts of modern philosophy.

The many concurrent reasons for this mischief may, I believe, be massed under a few general heads.

I. There is first the hot fermentation and unwholesome secrecy of the populations crowded into large cities, each mote in the misery lighter, as an individual soul, than a dead leaf, but becoming oppressive and infectious each to his neighbour, in the smoking mass of decay. The resulting modes of mental ruin and distress are continually new; and in a certain sense, worth study in their monstrosity: they have accordingly developed a corresponding science of fiction, concerned mainly with the description of such forms of disease, like the botany of leaf-lichens.

In De Balzac's story of *Father Goriot*, a grocer makes a large fortune, of which he spends on himself as much as may keep him alive; and on his two daughters, all that can promote their pleasures or their pride. He marries them to men of rank, supplies their secret expenses, and provides for his favourite a separate and clandestine establishment with her lover. On his deathbed, he sends for this favourite daughter, who wishes to come, and hesitates for a quarter of an hour between doing so, and going to a ball at which it has been for the last month her chief ambition to be seen. She finally goes to the ball.

This story is, of course, one of which the violent contrasts and spectral catastrophe could only take place, or be conceived, in a large city. A village grocer cannot make a large fortune, cannot marry his daughters to titled squires, and cannot die without having his children brought to him, if in the neighbourhood, by fear of village gossip, if for no better cause.

II. But a much more profound feeling than this mere curiosity of science in morbid phenomena is concerned in the production of the carefullest forms of modern fiction. The disgrace and grief resulting from the mere trampling pressure and electric friction of town life, become to the sufferers peculiarly mysterious in their undeservedness, and frightful in their inevitableness. The power of all surroundings over them for evil; the incapacity of their own minds to refuse the pollution, and of their own wills to oppose the weight of the staggering mass that chokes and crushes them into perdition, brings every law of healthy existence into question with them, and every alleged method of help and hope into doubt. Indignation, without any calming faith in justice, and self-contempt, without any curative self-reproach, dull the intelligence, and degrade the conscience, into sullen incredulity of all sunshine outside the dunghill, or breeze beyond the wafting of its impurity; and at last a philosophy develops itself, partly satiric, partly consolatory, concerned only with the regenerative vigour of manure, and the necessary obscurities of fimetic Providence; showing how everybody's fault is somebody else's, how infection has no law, digestion no will, and profitable dirt no dishonour.

And thus an elaborate and ingenious scholasticism, in what may be called the Divinity of Decomposition, has established itself in connection with the more recent forms of romance, giving them at once a complacent tone of clerical dignity, and an agreeable dash of heretical impudence; while the inculcated doctrine has the double advantage of needing no laborious scholarship for its foundation, and no painful self-denial for its practice.

III. The monotony of life in the central streets of any great modern city, but especially in those of London, where every emotion intended to be derived by men from the sight of nature, or the sense of art, is forbidden for ever, leaves the craving of the heart for a sincere, yet changeful, interest, to be fed from one source only. Under natural conditions the degree of mental excitement necessary to bodily health is provided by the course of the seasons, and the various skill and fortune of agriculture. In the country every morning of the year brings with it a new aspect of springing or fading nature; a new duty to be fulfilled upon earth, and a new promise or warning in heaven. No day is without its innocent hope, its special prudence, its kindly gift, and its sublime danger; and in every process of wise husbandry, and every effort of contending or remedial courage, the wholesome passions, pride, and bodily power of the labourer are excited and exerted in happiest unison. The companionship of domestic, the care of serviceable, animals, soften and enlarge his life with lowly charities, and discipline him in familiar wisdoms and unboastful fortitudes; while the divine laws of seed-time which cannot be recalled, harvest which cannot be hastened, and winter in which no man can work, compel the impatiences and coveting of his heart into labour too submissive to be anxious, and rest too sweet to be wanton. What thought can enough comprehend the contrast between such life, and that in streets where summer and winter are only alternations of heat and cold; where snow never fell white, nor sunshine clear; where the ground is only a pavement, and the sky no more than the glass roof of an arcade; where the utmost power of a storm is to choke the gutters, and the finest magic of spring, to change mud into dust: where—chief and most fatal difference in state, there is no interest of occupation for any of the inhabitants but the routine of counter or desk within doors, and the effort to pass each other without collision outside; so that from morning to evening the only possible variation of the monotony of the hours, and lightening of the penalty of existence, must be some kind of mischief, limited, unless by more than ordinary godsend of fatality, to the fall of a horse, or the slitting of a pocket.

I said that under these laws of inanition, the craving of the human heart for some kind of excitement could be supplied from *one* source only. It might have been thought by any other than a sternly tentative philosopher, that the denial of their natural food to human feelings would have provoked a reactionary desire for it; and that the dreariness of the street would have been gilded by dreams of pastoral felicity. Experience has shown the fact to be otherwise; the thoroughly trained Londoner can enjoy no other excitement than that to which he has been accustomed, but asks for *that* in continually more ardent or more virulent concentration; and the ultimate power of fiction to entertain him is by varying to his fancy the modes, and defining for his dulness the horrors, of Death. In the single novel of *Bleak House* there are nine deaths (or left for death's, in the drop scene) carefully wrought out or led up to, either by way of pleasing surprise, as the baby's at the brickmaker's, or finished in their threatenings and sufferings, with as much enjoyment as can be contrived in the anticipation, and as much pathology as can be concentrated in the description. Under the following varieties of method:—

One by assassination	Mr Tulkinghorn.
One by starvation, with phthisis	Joe.
One by chagrin	Richard.
One by spontaneous combustion	Mr Krook.
One by sorrow	Lady Dedlock's lover.
One by remorse	Lady Dedlock.
One by insanity	Miss Flite.
One by paralysis	Sir Leicester.

Besides the baby, by fever, and a lively young Frenchwoman left to be hanged.

And all this, observe, not in a tragic, adventurous, or military story, but merely as the further enlivenment of a narrative intended to be amusing; and as a properly representative average of the statistics of civilian mortality in the centre of London.

Observe further, and chiefly. It is not the mere number of deaths (which, if we count the odd troopers in the last scene, is exceeded in *Old Mortality*, and reached, within one or two, both in *Waverley* and *Guy Mannering*) that marks the peculiar tone of the modern novel. It is the fact that all these deaths, but one, are of inoffensive, or at least in the world's estimate respectable persons; and that they are all grotesquely either violent or miserable, purporting thus to illustrate the modern theology that the appointed destiny of a large average of our population is to die like rats in a drain, either by trap or poison. Not, indeed, that a lawyer in full practice can be usually supposed as faultless in the eye of heaven as a dove or a woodcock; but it is not, in former divinities, thought the will of Providence that he should be dropped by a shot from a client behind his fire-screen, and retrieved in the morning by his housemaid under the chandelier. Neither is Lady Dedlock less reprehensible in her conduct than many women of fashion have been and will be: but it would not therefore have been thought poetically just, in old-fashioned morality, that she should be found by her daughter lying dead, with her face in the mud of a St. Giles's churchyard.

In the work of the great masters death is always either heroic, deserved, or quiet and natural (unless their purpose be totally and deeply tragic, when collateral meaner death is permitted, like that of Polonius or Roderigo). In *Old Mortality*, four of the deaths, Bothwell's, Ensign Grahame's, Macbriar's, and Evandale's, are magnificently heroic; Burley's and Oliphant's long deserved, and swift; the troopers', met in the discharge of their military duty, and the old miser's, as gentle as the passing of a cloud, and almost beautiful in its last words of—now unselfish—care.

> "Ailie" (he aye ca'd me Ailie, we were auld acquaintance,) "Ailie, take ye care and haud the gear weel thegither; for the name of Morton of Milnwood's gane out like the last sough of an auld sang." And sae he fell out o' ae dwam into another, and ne'er spak a word mair, unless it were something we cou'dna mak out, about a dipped candle being gude enough to see to dee wi'. He cou'd ne'er bide to see a moulded ane, and there was ane, by ill luck, on the table.

In *Guy Mannering*, the murder, though unpremeditated, of a single person, (himself not entirely innocent, but at least by heartlessness in a cruel function earning his fate,) is avenged to the uttermost on all the men conscious of the crime; Mr Bertram's death, like that of his wife, brief in pain, and each told in the space of half-a-dozen lines; and that of the heroine of the tale, self-devoted, heroic in the highest, and happy.

Nor is it ever to be forgotten, in the comparison of Scott's with inferior work, that his own splendid powers were, even in early life, tainted, and in his latter years destroyed, by modern conditions of commercial excitement, then first, but rapidly, developing themselves. There are parts even in his best novels coloured to meet tastes which he despised; and many pages written in his later ones to lengthen his article for the indiscriminate market.

But there was one weakness of which his healthy mind remained incapable to the last. In modern stories prepared for more refined or fastidious audiences than those of Dickens, the funereal excitement is obtained, for the most part, not by the infliction of violent or disgusting death; but in the suspense, the pathos, and the more or less by all felt, and recognised, mortal phenomena of the sick-room. The temptation, to weak writers, of this order of subject is especially great, because the study of it from the living—or dying—model is so easy, and to many has been the most impressive part of their own personal experience; while, if the description be given even with mediocre accuracy, a very large section of readers will admire its truth, and cherish its melancholy. Few authors of second or third rate genius can either record or invent a probable conversation in ordinary life; but few, on the other hand, are so destitute of observant faculty as to be unable to chronicle the broken syllables and languid movements of an invalid. The easily rendered, and too surely recognised, image of familiar suffering is felt at once to be real where all else had been false; and the historian of the gestures of fever and words of delirium can count on the applause of a gratified audience as surely as the dramatist who introduces on the stage of his flagging action a carriage that can be driven or a fountain that will flow. But the masters of strong imagination disdain such work, and those of deep sensibility shrink from it.[1] Only under conditions of personal weakness, presently to be noted, would Scott comply with the cravings of his lower audience in scenes of terror like the death of Front-de-Bœuf. But he never once withdrew the sacred curtain of the sick-chamber, nor permitted the disgrace of wanton tears round the humiliation of strength, or the wreck of beauty.

IV. No exception to this law of reverence will be found in the scenes in Cœur de Lion's illness introductory to the principal incident in the *Talisman*. An inferior writer would have made the king charge in imagination at the head of his chivalry, or wander in dreams by the brooks of Aquitaine; but Scott allows us to learn no more startling symptoms of the king's malady than that he was restless and impatient, and could not wear his armour. Nor is any bodily weakness, or crisis of danger, permitted to disturb for an instant the royalty of intelligence and heart in which he examines, trusts and obeys the physician whom his attendants fear.

Yet the choice of the main subject in this story and its companion—the trial, to a point of utter torture, of knightly faith, and several passages in the conduct of both, more especially the exaggerated scenes in the House of Baldringham, and hermitage of Engedi, are signs of the gradual decline in force of intellect and soul which those who love Scott best have done him the worst injustice in their endeavours to disguise or deny. The mean anxieties, moral humiliations, and mercilessly demanded brain-toil, which killed him, show their sepulchral grasp for many and many a year before their final victory; and the states of more or less dulled, distorted, and polluted imagination which culminate in *Castle Dangerous*, cast a Stygian hue over *St. Ronan's Well*, *The Fair Maid of Perth*, and *Anne of Geierstein*, which lowers them, the first altogether, the other two at frequent intervals, into fellowship with the normal disease which festers throughout the whole body of our lower fictitious literature.

Fictitious! I use the ambiguous word deliberately; for it is impossible to distinguish in these tales of the prison-house how far their vice and gloom are thrown into their manufacture only to meet a vile demand, and how far they are an integral condition of thought in the minds of men trained from their youth up in the knowledge of Londinian and Parisian misery. The speciality of the plague is a delight in the exposition of the relations between guilt and decrepitude; and I call the results of it literature "of the prison-house," because the thwarted habits of body and mind, which are the punishment of reckless crowding in cities, become, in the issue of that punishment, frightful subjects of exclusive interest to themselves; and the art of fiction in which they finally delight is only the more studied arrangement and illustration, by coloured firelights, of the daily bulletins of their own wretchedness, in the prison calendar, the police news, and the hospital report.

The reader will perhaps be surprised at my separating the greatest work of Dickens, *Oliver Twist*, with honour, from the loathsome mass to which it typically belongs. That book is an earnest and uncaricatured record of states of criminal life, written with didactic purpose, full of the gravest instruction, nor destitute of pathetic studies of noble passion. Even the *Mysteries of Paris* and Gaboriau's *Crime d'Augival* are raised, by their definiteness of historical intention and forewarning anxiety, far above the level of their order, and may be accepted as photographic evidence of an otherwise incredible civilisation, corrupted by the infernal fact of it, down to the genesis of such figures as the Vicomte d'Augival, the Stabber,[2] the Skeleton, and the She-wolf. But the effectual head of the whole cretinous school is the renowned novel in which the hunchbacked lover watches the execution of his mistress from the tower of Notre-Dame; and its strength passes gradually away into the anatomical preparations, for the general market, of novels like *Poor Miss Finch*, in which the heroine is blind, the hero epileptic, and the obnoxious brother is found dead with his hands dropped off, in the Arctic regions.[3]

This literature of the Prison-house, understanding by the word not only the cell of Newgate, but also and even more definitely the cell of the Hôtel-Dieu, the Hôpital des Fous, and the grated corridor with the dripping slabs of the Morgue, having its central root thus in the Ile de Paris—or historically and pre-eminently the "Cité de Paris"—is, when understood deeply, the precise counter-corruption of the religion of the Sainte Chapelle, just as the worst forms of bodily and mental ruin are the corruption of love. I have therefore called it "Fiction mécroyante," with literal accuracy and precision; according to the explanation of the word which the reader may find in any good French dictionary,[4] and round its Arctic pole in the Morgue, he may gather into one Caina of gelid putrescence the entire product of modern infidel imagination, amusing itself with the destruction of the body, and busying itself with aberration of the mind.

Aberration, palsy, or plague, observe, as distinguished from normal evil, just as the venom of rabies or cholera differs from that of a wasp or a viper. The life of the insect and serpent deserves, or at least permits, our thoughts; not so the stages of agony in the fury-driven hound. There is some excuse, indeed, for the pathologic labour of the modern novelist in the fact that he cannot easily, in a city population, find a healthy mind to vivisect: but the greater part of such amateur surgery is the struggle, in an epoch of wild literary competition, to obtain novelty of material. The varieties of aspect and colour in healthy fruit, be it sweet or sour, may be within certain limits described exhaustively. Not so the blotches of its conceivable blight: and while the symmetries of integral human character can only be traced by harmonious and tender skill, like the branches of a living tree, the faults and gaps of one gnawed away by corroding accident can be shuffled into senseless change like the wards of a Chubb lock.

V. It is needless to insist on the vast field for this dice-cast or card-dealt calamity which opens itself in the ignorance, money-interest, and mean passion, of city marriage. Peasants know each other as children—meet, as they grow up in testing labour; and if a stout farmer's son marries a handless girl, it is his own fault. Also in the patrician families of the field, the young people know what they are doing, and marry a neighbouring estate, or a covetable title, with some conception of the responsibilities they undertake. But even among these, their season in the confused metropolis creates licentious and fortuitous temptation before unknown; and in the lower middle orders, an entirely new kingdom of discomfort and disgrace has been preached to them in the doctrines of unbridled pleasure which are merely an apology for their peculiar forms of ill-breeding. It is quite curious how often the catastrophe, or the leading interest, of a modern novel, turns upon the want, both in maid and bachelor, of the common self-command which was taught to their grandmothers and grandfathers as the first element of ordinarily decent behaviour. Rashly inquiring the other day the plot of a modern story from a female friend, I elicited, after some hesitation, that it hinged mainly on the young people's "forgetting themselves in a boat;" and I perceive it to be accepted as nearly an axiom in the code of modern civic chivalry that the strength of amiable sentiment is proved by our incapacity on proper occasions to express, and on improper ones to control it. The pride of a gentleman of the old school used to be in his power of saying what he meant, and being silent when he ought, (not to speak of the higher nobleness which bestowed love where it was honourable, and reverence where it was due); but the automatic amours and involuntary proposals of recent romance acknowledge little further law of morality than the instinct of an insect, or the effervescence of a chemical mixture.

There is a pretty little story of Alfred de Musset's,—La Mouche, which, if the reader cares to glance at it, will save me further trouble in explaining the disciplinarian authority of mere old-fashioned politeness, as in some sort protective of higher things. It describes, with much grace and precision, a state of society by no means pre-eminently virtuous, or enthusiastically heroic; in which many people do extremely wrong, and none sublimely right. But as there are heights of which the achievement is unattempted, there are abysses to which fall is barred; neither accident nor temptation will make any of the principal personages swerve from an adopted resolution, or violate an accepted principle of honour; people are expected as a matter of course to speak with propriety on occasion, and to wait with patience when they are bid: those who do wrong, admit it; those who do right don't boast of it; everybody knows his own mind, and everybody has good manners.

Nor must it be forgotten that in the worst days of the self-indulgence which destroyed the aristocracies of Europe, their vices, however licentious, were never, in the fatal modern sense, "unprincipled." The vainest believed in virtue; the vilest respected it. "Chaque chose avait son nom,"[5] and the severest of English moralists recognises the accurate wit, the lofty intellect, and the unfretted benevolence, which redeemed from vitiated surroundings the circle of d'Alembert and Marmontel.[6]

I have said, with too slight praise, that the vainest, in those days, "believed" in virtue. Beautiful and heroic examples of it were always before them; nor was it without the secret significance attaching to what may seem the least accidents in the work of a master, that Scott gave to both his heroines of the age of revolution in

England the name of the queen of the highest order of English chivalry.[7]

It is to say little for the types of youth and maid which alone Scott felt it a joy to imagine, or thought it honourable to portray, that they act and feel in a sphere where they are never for an instant liable to any of the weaknesses which disturb the calm, or shake the resolution, of chastity and courage in a modern novel. Scott lived in a country and time, when, from highest to lowest, but chiefly in the dignified and nobly severe[8] middle class to which he himself belonged, a habit of serene and stainless thought was as natural to the people as their mountain air. Women like Rose Bradwardine and Ailie Dinmont were the grace and guard of almost every household (God be praised that the race of them is not yet extinct, for all that Mall or Boulevard can do), and it has perhaps escaped the notice of even attentive readers that the comparatively uninteresting character of Sir Walter's heroes had always been studied among a class of youths who were simply incapable of doing anything seriously wrong; and could only be embarrassed by the consequences of their levity or imprudence.

But there is another difference in the woof of a Waverley novel from the cobweb of a modern one, which depends on Scott's larger view of human life. Marriage is by no means, in his conception of man and women, the most important business of their existence;[9] nor love the only reward to be proposed to their virtue or exertion. It is not in his reading of the laws of Providence a necessity that virtue should, either by love or any other external blessing, be rewarded at all;[10] and marriage is in all cases thought of as a constituent of the happiness of life, but not as its only interest, still less its only aim. And upon analysing with some care the motives of his principal stories, we shall often find that the love in them is merely a light by which the sterner features of character are to be irradiated, and that the marriage of the hero is as subordinate to the main bent of the story as Henry the Fifth's courtship of Katherine is to the battle of Agincourt. Nay, the fortunes of the person who is nominally the subject of the tale are often little more than a background on which grander figures are to be drawn, and deeper fates forth-shadowed. The judgments between the faith and chivalry of Scotland at Drumclog and Bothwell bridge owe little of their interest in the mind of a sensible reader to the fact that the captain of the Popinjay is carried a prisoner to one battle, and returns a prisoner form the other: and Scott himself, while he watches the white sail that bears Queen Mary for the last time from her native land, very nearly forgets to finish his novel, or to tell us—and with small sense of any consolation to be had out of that minor circumstance,—that "Roland and Catherine were united, spite their differing faiths."

Neither let it be thought for an instant that the slight, and sometimes scornful, glance with which Scott passes over scenes which a novelist of our own day would have analysed with the airs of a philosopher, and painted with the curiosity of a gossip, indicate any absence in his heart of sympathy with the great and sacred elements of personal happiness. An era like ours, which has with diligence and ostentation swept its heart clear of all the passions once known as loyalty, patriotism, and piety, necessarily magnifies the apparent force of the one remaining sentiment which sighs through the barren chambers, or clings inextricably round the chasms of ruin; nor can it but regard with awe the unconquerable spirit which still tempts or betrays the sagacities of selfishness into error or frenzy which is believed to be love.

That Scott was never himself, in the sense of the phrase as employed by lovers of the Parisian school, "ivre d'amour," may be admitted without prejudice to his sensibility,[11] and that he never knew "l'amor che move 'l sol et l'altre stelle," was the chief, though unrecognised, calamity of his deeply chequered life. But the reader of honour and feeling will not therefore suppose that the love which Miss Vernon sacrifices, stooping for an instant from her horse, is of less noble stamp, or less enduring faith, than that which troubles and degrades the whole existence of Consuelo; or that the affection of Jeanie Deans for the companion of her childhood, drawn like a field of soft blue heaven beyond the cloudy wrack of her sorrow, is less fully in possession of her soul than the hesitating and self-reproachful impulses under which a modern heroine forgets herself in a boat, or compromises herself in the cool of the evening.

I do not wish to return over the waste ground we have traversed, comparing, point by point, Scott's manner with those of Bermondsey and the Faubourgs; but it may be, perhaps, interesting at this moment to examine, with illustration from those Waverley novels which have so lately retracted the attention of a fair and gentle public, the universal conditions of "style," rightly so called, which are in all ages and above all local currents or wavering tides of temporary manners, pillars of what is for every strong, and models of what is for ever fair.

But I must first define, and that within strict horizon, the works of Scott, in which his perfect mind may be known, and his chosen ways understood.

His great works of prose fiction, excepting only the first half-volume of *Waverley*, were all written in twelve years, 1814-26 (of his own age forty-three to fifty-five), the actual time employed in their composition being not more than a couple of months out of each year; and during that time only the morning hours and spare minutes during the professional day. "Though the first volume of *Waverley* was begun long ago, and actually lost for a time, yet the other two were begun and finished between the 4th of June and the 1st of July, during all which I attended my duty in court, and proceeded without loss of time or hindrance of business."[12]

Few of the maxims for the enforcement of which, in *Modern Painters*, long ago, I got the general character of a lover of paradox, are more singular, or more sure, than the statement, apparently so encouraging to the idle, that if a great thing can be done at all, it can be done easily. But it is in that kind of ease with which a tree blossoms after long years of gathered strength, and all Scott's great writings were the recreations of a mind confirmed in dutiful labour, and rich with organic gathering of boundless resource.

Omitting from our count the two minor and ill-finished sketches of the *Black Dwarf* and *Legend of Montrose*, and, for a reason presently to be noticed, the unhappy *St. Ronan's*, the memorable romances of Scott are eighteen, falling into three distinct groups, containing six each.

The first group is distinguished from the other two by characters of strength and felicity which never more appeared after Scott was struck down by his terrific illness in 1819. It includes *Waverley, Guy Mannering,* The Antiquary, *Rob Roy, Old Mortality,* and *The Heart of Midlothian.*

The composition of these occupied the mornings of his happiest days, between the ages of 43 and 48. On the 8th of April, 1819 (he was 48 on the preceding 15th of August) he began for the first time to dictate—being unable for the exertion of writing—*The Bride of Lammermuir*, "the affectionate Laidlaw beseeching him to stop dictating, when his audible suffering filled every pause. 'Nay, Willie' he answered, 'only see that the doors are fast. I would fain keep all the cry as well as all the wool to ourselves; but as for giving over work, that can only be when I am in woollen.'"[13] From this time forward the brightness of joy and sincerity of inevitable humour, which perfected the imagery of the earlier novels, are wholly absent, except in the two short intervals of health unaccountably restored, in which he wrote *Redgauntlet* and *Nigel.*

It is strange, but only a part of the general simplicity of Scott's genius, that these revivals of earlier power were unconscious, and that the time of extreme weakness in which he wrote *St.Ronan's Well*, was that in which he first asserted his own restoration.

It is also a deeply interesting characteristic of his noble nature that he never gains anything by sickness; the whole man breathes or faints as one creature: the ache that stiffens a limb chills his heart, and every pang of the stomach paralyses the brain. It is not so with inferior minds, in the workings of which it is often impossible to distinguish native from narcotic fancy, and the throbs of conscience from those of indigestion. Whether in exaltation or languor, the colours of mind are always morbid, which gleam on the sea for the "Ancient Mariner," and through the casements on "St. Agnes' Eve;" but Scott is at once blinded and stultified by sickness; never has a fit of the cramp without spoiling a chapter, and is perhaps the only author of vivid imagination who never wrote a foolish word but when he was ill.

It remains only to be noticed on this point that any strong natural excitement, affecting the deeper springs of his heart, would at once restore his intellectual powers in all their fulness, and that, far towards their sunset: but that the strong will on which he prided himself, though it could trample upon pain, silence grief, and compel industry, never could warm his imagination, or clear the judgment in his darker hours.

I believe that this power of the heart over the intellect is common to all great men: but what the special character of emotion was that alone could lift Scott above the power of death, I am about to ask the reader, in a little while, to observe with joyful care.

The first series of romances, then, above named, are all that exhibit the emphasis of his unharmed faculties. The second group, composed in the three years subsequent to illness all but mortal, bear every one of them more or less the seal of it.

They consist of the *Bride of Lammermuir, Ivanhoe,* the *Monastery,* the *Abbot,*

Kenilworth, and the *Pirate*.[14] The marks of broken health on all these are essentially twofold—prevailing melancholy, and fantastic improbability. Three of the tales are agonisingly tragic, the *Abbot* scarcely less so in its main event, and *Ivanhoe* deeply wounded through all its bright panoply; while even in that most powerful of the series, the impossible archeries and axestrokes, the incredibly opportune appearances of Locksley, the death of Ulrica, and the resuscitation of Athelastane, are partly boyish, partly feverish. Caleb in the *Bride*, Triptolemus and Halcro in the *Pirate*, are all laborious, and the first incongruous; half a volume of the *Abbot* is spent in extremely dull detail of Roland's relations with his fellow-servants and his mistress, which have nothing whatever to do with the future story; and the lady of Avenel herself disappears after the first volume, "like a snaw-wreath when it's thaw, Jeanie." The public has for itself pronounced on the *Monastery*, though as much too harshly as it has foolishly praised the horrors of *Ravenswood* and the nonsense of *Ivanhoe*; because the modern public finds in the torture and adventure of these, the kind of excitement which it seeks at an opera, while it has no sympathy whatever with the pastoral happiness of Glandearg, or with the lingering simplicities of superstition which give historical likelihood to the legend of the White Lady.

But both this despised tale and its sequel have Scott's heart in them. The first was begun to refresh himself in the intervals of artificial labour on *Ivanhoe*. "It was a relief," he said, "to interlay the scenery most familiar to me[15] with the strange world for which I had to draw so much on imagination."[16] Through all the closing scenes of the second he is raised to his own true level by his love for the queen. And within the code of Scott's work to which I am about to appeal for illustration of his essential powers, I accept the *Monastery* and *Abbot*, and reject from it the remaining four of this group.

The last series contains two quite noble ones, *Redgauntlet* and *Nigel*; two of very high value, *Durward* and *Woodstock*; the slovenly and diffuse *Peveril*, written for the trade; the sickly *Tales of the Crusaders*, and the entirely broken and diseased *St. Ronan's Well*. This last I throw out of count altogether, and of the rest accept only the four first named as sound work; so that the list of the novels in which I propose to examine his methods and ideal standards, reduces itself to the following twelve (named in order of production): *Waverley*, *Guy Mannering*, the *Antiquary*, *Rob Roy*, *Old Mortality*, the *Heart of Midlothian*, the *Monastery*, the *Abbot*, the *Fortunes of Nigel*, *Quentin Durward*, and *Woodstock*.[17]

It is, however, too late to enter on my subject in this article, which I may fitly close by pointing out some of the merely verbal characteristics of his style, illustrative in little ways of the questions we have been examining, and chiefly of the one which may be most embarrassing to many readers, the difference, namely, between character and disease.

One quite distinctive charm in the Waverleys is their modified use of the Scottish dialect; but it has not generally been observed, either by their imitators, or the authors of different taste who have written for a later public, that there is a difference between the dialect of a language, and its corruption.

A dialect is formed in any district where there are persons of intelligence enough to use the language itself in all its fineness and force, but under the particular conditions of life, climate, and temper, which introduce words peculiar to the scenery, forms of word and idioms of sentence peculiar to the race, and pronunciations indicative of their character and disposition.

Thus "burn" (of a streamlet) is a word possible only in a country where there are brightly running waters, "lassie" a word possible only where girls are as free as the rivulets, and "auld," a form of the southern "old," adopted by a race of finer musical ear than the English.

On the contrary, mere deteriorations, or coarse, stridulent, and, in the ordinary sense of the phrase, "broad" forms of utterance, are not dialects at all, having nothing dialectic in them, and all phrases developed in states of rude employment, and restricted intercourse, are injurious to the tone and narrowing to the power of the language they affect. Mere breadth of accent does not spoil a dialect as long as the speakers are men of varied idea and good intelligence; but the moment the life is contracted by mining, millwork, or any oppressive and monotonous labour, the accents and phrases become debased. It is part of the popular folly of the day to find pleasure in trying to write and spell these abortive, crippled, and more or less brutal forms of human speech.

Abortive, crippled, or brutal, are however, not necessarily "corrupted" dialects. Corrupt language is that gathered by ignorance, invented by vice, misused by insensibility, or minced and mouthed by affectation, especially in the attempt to deal with words of which only half the meaning is understood, or half the sound heard. Mrs Gamp's "aperiently so"—and the "underminded" with primal sense of undermine, of—I forget which gossip, in the *Mill on the Floss*, are master- and mistress-pieces in this latter kind. Mrs Malaprop's "allegories on the banks of the Nile" are in a somewhat higher order of mistake: Mrs Tabitha Bramble's ignorance is vulgarised by her selfishness, and Winifred Jenkins' by her conceit. The "wot" of Noah Claypole, and the other degradations of cockneyism (Sam Weller and his father are in nothing more admirable than in the power of heart and sense that can purify even these); the "trewth" of Mr Chadband, and "natur" of Mr Squeers, are examples of the corruption of words by insensibility: the use of the word "bloody" in modern low English is a deeper corruption, not altering the form of the word, but defiling the thought in it.

Thus much being understood, I shall proceed to examine thoroughly a fragment of Scott's Lowland Scottish dialect; not choosing it of the most beautiful kind; on the contrary, it shall be a piece reaching as low down as he ever allows Scotch to go—it is perhaps the only unfair patriotism in him, that if he ever wants a word or two of really villanous slang, he gives it in English or Dutch—not Scotch.

I had intended in the close of this paper to analyse and compare the characters of Andrew Fairservice and Richie Moniplies, for examples, the former of innate evil, unaffected by external influences, and undiseased, but distinct from natural goodness as a nettle is distinct from balm or lavender; and the latter of innate goodness, contracted and pinched by circumstance, but still undiseased, as an oak-leaf crisped by frost, not by the worm. This, with much else in mind, I must put off;

but the careful study of one sentence of Andrew's will give us a good deal to think of.

I take his account of the rescue of Glasgow Cathedral at the time of the Reformation.

> Ah! it's a brave kirk—nane o' yere whigmaleeries and curliewurlies and opensteek hems about it—a' solid, weel-jointed mason-wark, that will stand as lang as the warld, keep hands and gunpowther aff it. It had amaist a douncome lang syne at the Reformation, when the pu'd doun the kirks of St. Andrews and Perth, and thereawa', to cleanse them o' Papery, and idolatry, and image-worship, and surplices, and sic-like rags o' the muckle hure that sitteth on seven hills, [. . .] they behoved to come into Glasgow ae fair morning, to try their hand on purging the High Kirk o' Popish nicknackets. But the townsmen o' Glasgow, they were feared their auld edifice might slip the girths in gaun through siccan rough physic, sae they rang the common bell, and assembled the train-bands wi' took o' drum. By good luck, the worthy James Rabat was Dean o' Guild that year—(and a gude mason he was himsell, made him the keener to keep up the auld bigging), and the trades assembled, and offered downright battle to the commons, rather than their kirk should coup the crans, as others had done elsewhere. It wasna for luve o' Paperie—na, na!—nane could ever say that o' the trades o' Glasgow—Sae they sune came to an agreement to take a' the idolatrous statues of sants (sorrow be on them!) out o' their neuks— And sae the bits o' stane idols were broken in pieces by Scripture warrant, and flung into the Molendinar burn, and the auld kirk stood as crouse as a cat when the flaes are kaimed aff her, and a'body was alike pleased. And I hae heard wise folk say, that if the same had been done in ilka kirk in Scotland, the Reform wad just hae been as pure as it is e'en now, and we had hae mair Christian-like kirks; for I hae been sae lang in England, that naething will drived out o' my head, that the dog-kennel at Osbaldistone-Hall is better than mony a house o' God in Scotland.

MISSING Words

Now this sentence is in the first place a piece of Scottish history of quite inestimable and concentrated value. Andrew's temperament is the type of a vast class of Scottish—shall we call it "*sow*-thistlian"—mind, which necessarily takes the view of either Pope or saint that the thistle in Lebanon took of the cedar or lilies in Lebanon; and the entire force of the passions which, in the Scottish revolution, foretold and forearmed the French one, is told in this one paragraph; the coarseness of it, observe, being admitted, not for the sake of the laugh, any more than an onion in broth merely for its flavour, but for the meat of it; the inherent constancy of that coarseness being a fact in this order of mind, and an essential part of the history to be told.

Secondly, observe that this speech, in the religious passion of it, such as there may be, is entirely sincere. Andrew is a thief, a liar, a coward, and, in the Fair service from which he takes his name, a hypocrite; but in the form of prejudice, which is all that his mind is capable of in the place of religion, he is entirely sincere. He does not in the least pretend detestation of image worship to please his master, or any one else; he honestly scorns the "carnal morality as dowd and fusionless as rue-leaves at Yule" of the sermon in the upper cathedral; and when wrapt in critical attention to the "real savour o' doctrine" in the crypt, so completely forgets the hypocrisy of his fair service as to return his master's attempt to disturb him with hard punches of the elbow.

Thirdly. He is a man of no mean sagacity, quite up to the average standard of Scottish common sense, not a low one; and, though incapable of understanding any manner of lofty thought or passion, is a shrewd measurer of weaknesses, and not without a spark or two of kindly feeling. See first his sketch of his master's character to Mr Hammorgaw, beginning: "He's no a'thegither sae void o' sense, neither;" and then the close of the dialogue: "But the lad's no a bad lad after a', and he needs some carefu' body to look after him."

Fourthly. He is a good workman; knows his own business well, and can judge of other craft, if sound, or otherwise.

All these four qualities of him must be known before we can understand this single speech. Keeping them in mind, I take it up, word by word.

You observe, in the outset, Scott makes no attempt whatever to indicate accents or modes of pronunciation by changed spelling, unless the word becomes a quite definitely new, and scarcely writeable one. The Scottish way of pronouncing "James," for instance, is entirely peculiar, and extremely pleasant to the ear. But it is so, just because it does *not* change the word into Jeems, nor into Jims, nor into Jawms. A modern writer of dialects would think it amusing to use one or other of these ugly spellings. But Scott writes the name in pure English, knowing that a Scots reader will speak it rightly, and an English one be wise in letting it alone. On the other hand he writes "weel" for "well," because that word is complete in its change, and may be very closely expressed by the double *e*. The ambiguous "*u*"s in "gude" and "sune" are admitted, because far liker the sound than the double *o* would be, and that in "hure," for grace' sake, to soften the word;—so also "flaes" for "fleas." "Mony" for "many" is again positively right in sound, and "neuk" differs from our "nook" in sense, and is not the same word at all, as we shall presently see.

Secondly, observe, not a word is corrupted in any decent haste, slowness, slovenliness, or incapacity of pronunciation. There is no lisping, drawling, slobbering, or snuffling: the speech is as clear as a bell and as keen as an arrow: and its elisions and contractions are either melodious, ("na," for "not,"—"pu'd," for "pulled,") or as normal as in a Latin verse. The long words are delivered without the slightest bungling: and "bigging" finished to its last *g*.

I take the important words now in their places.

Brave. The old English sense of the word in "to go brave" retained, expressing Andrew's sincere and respectful admiration. Had he meant to insinuate a hint of the church's being too fine, he would have said "braw."

Kirk. This is of course just as pure and unprovincial a word as "Kirche," or "église."

Whigmaleerie. I cannot get at the root of this word, but it is one showing that the speaker is not bound by classic rules, but will use any syllables that enrich his meaning. "Nipperty-tipperty" (of his master's "poetry-nonsense") is another word of the same class. "Curlieurlie" is of course just as pure as Shakespeare's "Hurly-burly." But see first suggestion of the idea to Scott at Blair-Adam (L. vi. 264).

Opensteek hems. More description, or better, of the later Gothic cannot be put into four syllables. "Steek," melodious for stitch, has a combined sense of closing or fastening. And note that the later Gothic, being precisely what Scott knew best (in Melrose) and liked best, it is, here as elsewhere, quite as much himself[18] as Frank, that he is laughing at, when he laughs *with* Andrew, whose "opensteek hems" are only a ruder metaphor for his own "willow-wreaths changed to stone."

Gunpowther. "-Ther" is a lingering vestige of the French "-dre."

Syne. One of the melodious and mysterious Scottish words which have partly the sound of wind and stream in them, and partly the range of softened idea which is like a distance of blue hills over border land ("far in the distant Cheviot's blue"). Perhaps even the least sympathetic "Englisher" might recognise this, if he heard "Old Long Since" vocally substituted for the Scottish words to the air. I do not know the root; but the word's proper meaning is not "since," but before or after an interval of some duration, "as weel sune as syne." "But first on Sawnie gies a ca', Syne, bauldly in she enters."

Behoved (*to come*). A rich word, with peculiar idiom, always used more or less ironically of anything done under a partly mistaken and partly pretended notion of duty.

Siccan. Far prettier, and fuller in meaning than "such." It contains an added sense of wonder; and means properly "so great" or "so unusual."

Took (*o' drum*). Classical "tuck" from Italian "toccata," the precluding "touch" or flourish, on any instrument (but see Johnson under word "tucket," quoting *Othello*). The deeper Scottish vowels are used here to mark the deeper sound of the bass drum, as in more solemn warning.

Bigging. The only word in all the sentence of which the Scottish form is less melodious than the English, "and what for no," seeing that Scottish architecture is mostly little beyond Bessie Bell's and Mary Gray's? "They biggit a bow're by yon burnside, and theekit it ow're wi rashes." But it is pure Anglo-Saxon in roots; see glossary to Fairbairn's edition of the Douglas *Virgil*, 1710.

Coup. Another of the much-embracing words; short for "upset," but with a sense of awkwardness as the inherent cause of fall; compare Richie Moniplies (also for sense of "behoved"): "Ae auld hirplin deevil of a potter behoved just to step in my way, and offer me a pig (earthen pot—etym. dub.), as he said "just to put my Scotch ointment in;" and I gave him a push, as but natural, and the tottering deevil coupit owre amang his own pigs, and damaged a score of them." So also Dandie Dinmont in the postchaise: "'Od! I hope they'll no coup us."

The Crans. Idiomatic; root unknown to me, but it means in this use, full, total, and without recovery.

Molendinar. From "molendium," the grinding-place. I do not know if actually the local name,[19] or Scott's invention. Compare Sir Piercies's "Molinaras." But at all events used here with bye-sense of degradation of the formerly idle saints to grind at the mill.

Crouse. Courageous, softened with a sense of comfort.

Ilka. Again a word with azure distance, including the whole sense of "each" and "every." The reader must carefully and reverently distinguish these comprehensive words, which gather two or more perfectly understood meanings into one *chord* of meaning, and are harmonies more than words, from the above-noted blunders between two half-hit meanings, struck as a bad piano-player strikes the edge of another note. In English we have fewer of these combined thoughts; so that Shakespeare rather plays with the distinct light of his words, than melts them into one. So again Bishop Douglas spells, and doubtless spoke, the word "rose," differently, according to his purpose; if as the chief or governing ruler of flowers, "rois," but if only in her own beauty, rose.

Christian-like. The sense of decency and order proper to Christianity is stronger in Scotland than in any other country, and the word "Christian" more distinctly opposed to "beast." Hence the back-handed cut at the English for their over-pious care of dogs.

I am a little surprised myself at the length to which this examination of one small piece of Sir Walter's first-rate work has carried us, but here I must end for this time, trusting, if the Editor of the *Nineteenth Century* permit me, yet to trespass, perhaps more than once, on his readers' patience; but, at all events, to examine in a following paper the technical characteristics of Scott's own style, both in prose and verse, together with Byron's, as opposed to our fashionably recent dialects and rhythms; the essential virtues of language, in both the masters of the old school, hinging ultimately, little as it might be thought, on certain unalterable views of theirs concerning the code called "of the Ten Commandments," wholly at variance with the dogmas of automatic morality which, summed again by the witches' line, "Fair is foul, and foul is fair," hover through the fog and filthy air of our prosperous England.

Notes

1. Nell, in the *Old Curiosity Shop*, was simply killed for the market, as a butcher kills a lamb (see Forster's *Life*), and Paul was written under the same conditions of illness which affected Scott—a part of the ominous palsies, grasping alike author and subject, both in *Dombey* and *Little Dorrit*.

2. "Chourineur" not striking with dagger-point, but ripping with knife-edge. Yet I do him, and La Louve, injustice in classing them with the two others; they are put together only as parts in the same phantasm. Compare with La Louve, the strength of wild virtue in the "Louvécienne" (Lucienne) of Gaboriau—she, province-born and bred; and opposed to Parisian civilisation in the character of her sempstress friend.

> De ce Paris où elle était née, elle savait tout—elle connaissait tout. Rien ne l'étonnait, nul ne l'intimidait. Sa science des détails matériels de l'existence était inconcevable. Impossible de la duper!—Eh bien! cette fille si laborieuse et si économe n'avait même pas la plus vague notion des sentiments qui sont l'honneur de la femme. Je n'avais pas idée d'une si complète absence de sens moral; d'une si inconsciente dépravation, d'une impudence si effrontément naïve.—*L'Argent des autres*, vol. i. p. 358.

3. The reader who cares to seek it may easily find medical evidence of the physical effects of certain states of brain disease in producing especially images of truncated and Hermes-like deformity, complicated with grossness. Horace, in the *Epodes*, scoffs at it, but not without horror. Luca Signorelli and Raphael in their arabesques are deeply struck by it: Durer, defying and playing with it alternately, is almost beaten down again and again in the distorted faces, hewing halberts, and suspended satyrs of his arabesques round the polyglot Lord's Prayer; it

takes entire possession of Balzac in the *Contes Drolatiques*; it struck Scott in the earliest days of his childish "visions" intensified by the axe-stroke murder of his grand aunt; L. i. 142, and see close of this note. It chose for him the subject of the *Heart of Midlothian*, and produced afterwards all the recurrent ideas of executions, tainting Nigel, almost spoiling Quentin Durward—utterly the Fair Maid of Perth: and culminating in Bizarro, L. x. 149. It suggested all the deaths by falling, or sinking, as in delirious sleep—Kennedy, Eveline Neville (nearly repeated in Clara Mowbray), Amy Robsart, the Master of Ravenswood in the quicksand, Morris, and Corporal Grace-be-here—compare the dream of Gride, in *Nicholas Nickleby*, and Dickens's own last words, *on the ground*, (so also, in my own inflammation of the brain, two years ago, I dreamed that I fell through the earth and came out on the other side). In its grotesque and distorting power, it produced all the figures of the Lay Goblin, Pacolet, Flibbertigibbet, Cockledemoy, Geoffrey Hudson, Fenella, and Nectabanus; in Dickens it in like manner gives Quilp, Krook, Smike, Smallweed, Miss Mowcher, and the dwarfs and waxwork of Nell's caravan; and runs entirely wild in *Barnaby Rudge*, where, with a *corps de drame* composed of one idiot, two madmen, a gentleman fool who is also a villain, a shop-boy fool who is also a blackguard, a hangman, a shrivelled virago, and a doll in ribands—carrying this company through riot and fire, till he hangs the hangman, one of the madmen, his mother, and the idiot, runs the gentleman-fool through in a bloody duel, and burns and crushes the shop-boy fool into shapelessness, he cannot yet be content without shooting the spare lover's leg off, and marrying him to the doll in a wooden one; the shapeless shop-boy being finally also married off in *two* wooden ones. It is this mutilation, observe, which is the very sign manual of the plague; joined, in the artistic forms of it, with a love of thorniness—(in their mystic root, the truncation of the limbless serpent and the spines of the dragon's wing. Compare *Modern Painters*, vol. iv., "Chapter on the Mountain Gloom," s. 19); and in *all* forms of it, with petrifaction or loss of power by cold in the blood, whence the last Darwinian process of the witches' charm—"cool it with a baboon's *blood, then* the charm is firm and good." The two frescoes in the colossal handbills which have lately decorated the streets of London (the baboon with the mirror, and the Maskelyne and Cooke decapitation) are the final English forms of Raphael's arabesque under this influence; and it is well worth while to get the number for the week ending April 3, 1880, of *Young Folks*—"a magazine of instructive and entertaining literature for boys and girls of all ages," containing "A Sequel to Desdichado" (the modern development of Ivanhoe), in which a quite monumental example of the kind of art in question will be found as a leading illustration of this characteristic sentence, "'See, good Cerberus,' said Sir Rupert, '*my hand has been struck off. You must make me a hand of iron, one with springs in it, so that I can make it grasp a dagger.*'" The text is also, as it professes to be, instructive; being the ultimate degeneration of what I have above called the "folly" of *Ivanhoe*; for folly begets folly down, and down; and whatever Scott and Turner did wrong has thousands of imitators—their wisdom none will so much as hear, how much less follow!

In both of the Masters, it is always to be remembered that the evil and good are alike conditions of literal *vision*: and therefore also, inseparably connected with the state of the health. I believe the first elements of all Scott's errors were in the milk of his consumptive nurse, which all but killed him as an infant, L. i. 19—and was without doubt the cause of the teething fever that ended in his lameness (L. i. 20). Then came (if the reader cares to know what I mean by *Fors*, let him read the page carefully) the fearful accidents L. i. 17; then the madness of his nurse, who planned his own murder (21), then the stories continually told him of the executions at Carlisle (24), his aunt's husband having seen them; issuing, he himself scarcely knows how, in the unaccountable terror that came upon him at the sight of statuary, 31—especially Jacob's ladder; then the murder of Mrs Swinton, and finally the nearly fatal bursting of the bloodvessel at Kelso, with the succeeding nervous illness, 65-7—solaced, while he was being "bled and blistered till he had scarcely a pulse left," by that history of the Knights of Malta—fondly dwelt on and realised by actual modelling of their fortress, which returned to his mind for the theme of its last effort in passing away.

4. "Se dit par dénigrement, d'un chrétien qui ne croit pas les dogmes de sa religion."—Fleming, vol. ii. p. 659.

5. "A son nom," properly. The sentence is one of Victor Cherbuliez's, in *Prosper Randoce*, which is full of other valuable ones. See the old nurse's "ici bas les chose vont de travers, comme un chien qui va à vépres," p. 93; and compare Prosper's treasures, "la petite Vénus, et le petit Christ d'ivoire," p. 121; also Madame Brehanne's request for the divertissement

of "quelque belle batterie à coups de couteau" with Didier's answer. "Hélas! madame, vous jouez de malheur, ici dans la Drôme, l'on se massacre aussi peu que possible," p. 33.

6. Edgeworth's *Tales* (Hunter, 1827), "Harrington and Ormond," vol. iii. p. 260.

7. Alice of Salisbury, Alice Lee, Alice Bridgnorth.

8. Scott's father was habitually ascetic. "I have heard his son tell that it was common with him, if any one observed that the soup was good, to taste it again, and say, 'Yes—it is too good, bairns,' and dash a tumbler of cold water into his plate."—Lockhart's *Life* (Black, Edinburgh, 1869), vol. i. p. 312. In other places I refer to this book in the simple form of "L."

9. A young lady sand to me, just before I copied out this page for press, a Miss Somebody's "great song," "Live, and Love, and Die." Had it been written for nothing better than silkworms, it should at least have added—Spin.

10. See passage of introduction to *Ivanhoe*, wisely quoted in L. vi. 106.

11. See below, note 17, p. 957, on the conclusion of *Woodstock*.

12. L. iv. 177.

13. L. iv. 67.

14. "One other such novel, and there's an end; but who can last for ever? who ever lasted so long?"—Sydney Smith (of the *Pirate*) to Jeffrey, December 30, 1821. (*Letters*, vol. ii. p. 223.)

15. L. vi. p. 188. Compare the description of Fairy Dean, vii. 192.

16. All, alas! were now in a great measure so written. *Ivanhoe*, *The Monastery*, *The Abbot*, and *Kenilworth* were all published between December 1819 and January 1821, Constable & Co. giving five thousand guineas for the remaining copyright of them, Scott clearing ten thousand before the bargain was completed; and before the *Fortunes of Nigel* issued from the press Scott had exchanged instruments and received his bookseller's bills for not less than four "works of fiction," not one of them otherwise described in the deeds of agreement, to be produced in unbroken succession, *each of them to fill up at least three volumes, but with proper saving clauses as to increase of copy money in case any of them should run to four*; and within two years all this anticipation had been wiped off by *Peveril of the Peak*, *Quentin Durward*, *St. Ronan's Well*, and *Red Gauntlet*.

17. *Woodstock* was finished 26th March 1826. He knew then of his ruin; and wrote in bitterness, but not in weakness. The closing pages are the most beautiful of the book. But a month afterwards Lady Scott died; and he never wrote glad word more.

18. There are three definite and international portraits of himself, in the novels, each giving a separate part of himself: Mr Oldbuck, Frank Osbaldistone, and Alan Fairford.

19. Andrew knows Latin, and might have coined the word in his conceit; but, writing to a friend in Glasgow, I find brook was called "Molyndona" even before the building of the Sub-dean Mill in 1446. See also account of the locality in Mr George's admirable volume, *Old Glasgow*, pp. 129, 149, &c. The Protestantism of Glasgow, since throwing that powder of saints into her brook Kidron, has presented it with other pious offerings; and my friend goes on to say that the brook, once famed for the purity of its waters (much used for bleaching), "has for nearly a hundred years been a crawling stream of loathsomeness. It is now bricked over, and a carriage-way made on the top of it; underneath the foul mess still passes through the heat of the city, till it falls into the Clyde close to the harbour."

⛯·65·⛯

A Gossip on Romance

ROBERT LOUIS STEVENSON

Scottish poet, novelist and essayist, Robert Louis Stevenson (1850-94) is best known for his collection of poems, *A Child's Garden of Verses*, and for the novels, *Treasure Island* (1883) and *Kidnapped* (1886), though he wrote a host of essays and short stories as well. In the following piece, he defends the romance against the late nineteenth-century thrust towards realism evident in the vogue for detailed descriptions of characters. Approaching his defence from the perspective of the reader, he avers that the reader prefers incident to character. For Stevenson, only the "epoch-making scenes" (72) are those we remember long after we have read a novel. Such scenes require the reader to enter into the story as a child would a game. Stevenson concludes the essay with a discussion of Sir Walter Scott as "the king of the romantics" (77), a writer who, though often inartistic, grants priority to incidents that capture the reader's desire to participate in the story.

In anything fit to be called by the name of reading, the process itself should be absorbing and voluptuous; we should gloat over a book, be rapt clean out of ourselves, and rise from the perusal, our mind filled with the busiest, kaleidoscopic dance of images, incapable of sleep or of continuous thought. The words, if the book be eloquent, should run thenceforward in our ears like the noise of breakers, or the story, if it be a story, repeat itself in a thousand coloured pictures to the eye. It was for this last pleasure that we read so closely, and loved our books so dearly, in the bright, troubled period of boyhood. Eloquence and thought, character and conversation, were but obstacles to brush aside as we dug blithely after a certain sort of incident, like a pig for truffles. For my part, I liked a story to begin with an old wayside inn where, "towards the close of the year 17–," several gentlemen in three-cocked hats were playing bowls. A friend of mine preferred the Malabar coast in a storm, with a ship beating to windward, and a scowling fellow of Herculean proportions striding along the beach: he, to be sure, was a pirate. This was further

Source: Robert Louis Stevenson, "A Gossip on Romance", *Longman's Magazine*, 1, November 1882 to April 1883, London: Longmans, Green, and Co., 1883, pp. 69-79.

afield than my home-keeping fancy loved to travel, and designed altogether for a larger canvas than the tales that I affected. Give me a highwayman and I was full to the brim; a Jacobite would do, but the highwayman was my favourite dish. I can still hear that merry clatter of the hoofs along the moonlit land; night and the coming of day are still related in my mind with the doings of John Rann or Jerry Abershaw; and the words "postchaise," the "great North road," "ostler," and "nag" still sound in my ears like poetry. One and all, at least, and each with his particular fancy, we read story-books in childhood, not for eloquence or character or thought, but for some quality of the brute incident. That quality was not mere bloodshed or wonder. Although each of these was welcome in its place, the charm for the sake of which we read depended on something different from either. My elders used to read novels aloud; and I can still remember four different passages which I heard, before I was ten, with the same keen and lasting pleasure. One I discovered long afterwards to be the admirable opening of *What will he Do with It*: it was no wonder I was pleased with that. The other three still remain unidentified. One is a little vague: it was about a dark, tall house at night, and people groping on the stairs by the light that escaped from the open door of a sick-room. In another, a lover left a ball, and went walking in a cool, dewy park, whence he could watch the lighted windows and the figures of the dancers as they moved. This was the most sentimental impression I think I had yet received, for a child is somewhat deaf to the sentimental. In the last, a poet, who had been tragically wrangling with his wife, walked forth on the sea-beech on a tempestuous might and witnessed the horrors of a wreck. Different as they are, all these early favourites have a common note—they have all a touch of the romantic.

Drama is the poetry of conduct, romance the poetry of circumstance. The pleasure that we take in life is of two sorts—the active and the passive. Now we are conscious of a great command over our destiny; anon we are lifted up by circumstance, as by a breaking wave, and dashed we know not how into the future. Now we are pleased by our conduct, anon merely pleased by our surroundings. It would be hard to say which of these modes of satisfaction is the more effective, but the latter is surely the more constant. Conduct is three parts of life, but it is not all the four. There is a vast deal in life and letters both which is not immoral, but simply a-moral; which either does not regard the human will at all, or deals with it in obvious and healthy relations; where the interest turns, not upon what a man shall choose to do, but on how he manages to do it; not on the passionate slips and hesitations of the conscience, but on the problems of the body and of the practical intelligence, in clean, open-air adventure, the shock of arms, or the diplomacy of life. With such material as this it is impossible to build a play, for the serious theatre exists solely on moral grounds, and is a standing proof of the dissemination of the human conscience. But it is possible to build, upon this ground, the most joyous of verses, and the most lively, beautiful, and buoyant tales.

One thing in life calls for another; there is a fitness in events and places. The sight of a pleasant arbour puts it in our mind to sit there. One place suggests work, another idleness, a third early rising and long rambles in the dew. The effect of night, of any flowing water, of lighted cities, of the peep of day, of ships, of the open ocean, calls up in the mind an army of anonymous desires and pleasures. Something, we feel, should happen; we know not what, yet we proceed in quest of it. And many of the happiest hours of life fleet by us in this vain attendance on the genius of the place and moment. It is thus that tracts of young fir, and low rocks that reach into deep surroundings, particularly torture and delight me. Something must have happened in such places, and perhaps ages back, to members of my race; and when I was a child I tried in vain to invent appropriate games for them, as I still try, just as vainly, to fit them with the proper story. Some places speak distinctly. Certain dank gardens cry aloud for a murder; certain old houses demand to be haunted; certain coasts are set apart for a shipwreck. Other spots again seem to abide their destiny, suggestive and impenetrable, "miching mallecho." The inn at Burford Bridge, with its arbours and green garden and silent, eddying river—though it is known already as the place where Keats finished his "Endymion" and Nelson parted from his Emma—still seems to wait the coming of the appropriate legend. Within these ivied walls, behind these old green shutters, some further business smoulders, waiting for its hour. The old Hawes Inn at the Queen's Ferry is another. There it stands, apart from the town, beside the pier, in a climate of its own, half inland, half marine—in front, the ferry bubbling with the tide and the guardship swinging to her anchor; behind, the old garden with the trees. Americans seek it already for the sake of Lovel and Oldbuck, who dined there at the beginning of *The Antiquary*. But you need not tell me—that is not all; there is some story, unrecorded or not yet complete, which must express the meaning of that inn more fully. So it is with names and faces; so it is with incidents that are idle and inconclusive in themselves, and yet seem like the beginning of some quaint romance, which the all-careless author leaves untold. How many of these romances have we not seen determine at their birth; how many people have met us with a look of meaning in their eye, and sunk at once into idle acquaintances; to how many places have we not drawn near, with express intimations—"here my destiny awaits me"—and we have but dined there and passed by! I have lived both at the Hawes and Burford in a perpetual flutter, on the heels, as it seemed, of some adventure that should justify the place; but though the feeling had me to bed at night and called me again at morning in one unbroken round of pleasure and suspense, nothing befell me in either worth remark. The man or the hour had not yet come; but some day, I think, a boat shall put off from the Queen's Ferry, fraught with a dear cargo, and some frosty night a horseman, on a tragic errand, rattle with his whip upon the green shutters of the inn at Burford.

Now, this is one of the natural appetites with which any lively literature has to count. The desire for knowledge, I had almost added the desire for meat, is not more deeply seated than this demand for fit and striking incident. The dullest of clowns tells, or tries to tell, himself a story, as the feeblest of children uses invention in his play; and even as the imaginative grown person, joining in the game, at once enriches it with many delightful circumstances, the great creative writer shows us the realisation and the apotheosis of the daydreams of common men. His stories may be nourished with the realities of life, but their true mark is to satisfy the nameless longings of the reader and to obey the ideal laws of the daydream. The right kind of thing should fall out in the right kind of place; the right kind of thing should follow; and not only the characters talk aptly and think naturally, but all the circumstances in a tale answer one to another like notes in music. The threads of a story come from time to time together and make a picture in the web; the characters fall from time to time into some attitude to each other or to nature, which stamps the story home like an illustration. Crusoe recoiling from the footprint, Achilles shouting over against the Trojans, Ulysses bending the great bow, Christian running with his fingers in his ears, there are each culminating moments in the legend, and each has been printed on the mind's eye for ever. Other things we may forget; we may forget the words, although they are beautiful; we may forget the author's comment, although perhaps it was ingenious and true; but these epoch-making scenes, which put the last mark of truth upon a story and fill up, at one blow, our capacity for sympathetic pleasure, we so adopt into the very bosom of our mind that neither time nor tide can efface or weaken the impression. This, then, is the plastic part of literature: to embody character, thought, or emotion in some act or attitude that shall be remarkably striking to the mind's eye. This is the highest and hardest thing to do in words; the thing which, once accomplished, equally delights the schoolboy and the sage, and makes, in its own right, the quality of epics. Compared with this, all other purposes in literature, except the purely lyrical or the purely philosophic, are bastard in nature, facile of execution, and feeble in result. It is one thing to write about the inn at Burford, or to describe scenery with the word-painters; it is quite another to seize on the heart of the suggestion and make a country famous with a legend. It is one thing to remark and to dissect, with the most cutting logic, the complications of life, and of the human spirit; it is quite another to give them body and blood in the story of Ajax or of Hamlet. The first is literature, but the second is something besides, for it is likewise art.

English people of the present day are apt, I know not why, to look somewhat down on incident, and reserve their admiration for the clink of tea-spoons and the accents of the curate. It is thought clever to write a novel with no story at all, or at least with a very dull one. Reduced even to the lowest terms, a certain interest can be communicated by the art of narrative; a sense of human kinship stirred; and a kind of monotonous fitness, comparable to the words and air of *Sandy's Mull*, preserved among the infinitesimal occurrences recorded. Some people work, in this manner, with even a strong touch. Mr Trollope's inimitable clergymen naturally arise to the mind in this connection. But even Mr Trollope does not confine himself to chronicling small beer. Mr Crawley's collision with the Bishop's wife, Mr Melnotte dallying in the deserted banquet-room, are typical incidents, epically conceived, fitly embodying a crisis. If Rawdon Crawley's blow were not delivered, *Vanity Fair* would cease to be a work of art. That scene is the chief ganglion of the tale; and the discharge of energy from Rawdon's fist is the reward and consolation of the reader. The end of *Esmond* is a yet wider excursion from the author's customary fields; the scene at Castlewood is pure Dumas; the great and wily English borrower has here borrowed from the great, unblushing French thief; as usual, he has borrowed admirably well, and the breaking of the sword rounds off the best of all his books with a manly, martial note. But perhaps nothing can more strongly illustrate the necessity for marking incident than to compare the living fame of *Robinson Crusoe* with the discredit of *Clarissa Harlowe*. *Clarissa* is a book of a far more startling import, worked out, on a great canvas, with inimitable courage and unflagging art; it contains wit, character, passion, plot, conversations full of spirit and insight, letters sparkling with unstrained humanity; and if the death of the heroine be somewhat frigid and artificial, the last days of the hero strike the only note of what we now call Byronism, between the Elizabethan and Byron himself. And yet a little story of a shipwrecked sailor, with not a tenth part of the style nor a thousandth part of the wisdom, exploring none of the arcana of humanity and deprived of the perennial interest of love, goes on from edition to edition, ever young, while *Clarissa* lies upon the shelves unread. A friend of mine, a Welsh blacksmith, was twenty-five years old, and could neither read nor write, when he heard a chapter of *Robinson* read aloud in a farm kitchen. Up to that moment he had sat contented, huddled in his ignorance; but he left that farm another man. There were daydreams, it appeared, divine daydreams, written and printed and bound, and to be bought for money and enjoyed at pleasure. Down he sat that day, painfully learned to read Welsh, and returned to borrow the book. It had been lost, nor could he find another copy but one that was in English. Down he sat once more, learned English, and at length, and with entire delight, read *Robinson*. It is like the story of a love-chase. If he had heard a letter from Clarissa, would he have been fired with the same chivalrous ardour? I wonder. Yet *Clarissa* has every quality that can be shown in prose, one alone excepted: pictorial, or picture-making romance. While *Robinson* depends, for the most part and with the overwhelming majority of its readers, on the charm of circumstance.

In the highest achievements of the art of words, the dramatic and the pictorial, the moral and romantic interest rise and fall together by a common and organic law. Situation is animated with passion, passion clothed upon with situation. Neither exists for itself, but each inheres indissolubly with the other. This is high art; and not only the highest art possible in words, but the highest art of all, since it combines with greatest mass and diversity of the elements of truth and pleasure. Such are epics, and the few prose tales that have the epic weight. But as from a school of works, aping the creative, incident and romance are ruthlessly discarded, so may character and drama be omitted or subordinated to romance. There is one book, for example, more generally loved than Shakespeare, that captivates in childhood, and still delights in age—I mean the *Arabian Nights*—where you shall look in vain for moral or for intellectual interest. No human face or voice greets us among that wooden crowd of kings and genies, sorcerers and beggarmen. Adventure, on the most naked terms furnishes forth the entertainment and is found enough. Dumas approaches perhaps the nearest of any modern to these Arabian authors in the purely material charm of his romances. The early part of *Monte Christo*, down to the finding of the treasure, is a piece of perfect story-telling; the man never breathed who shared these moving incidents without a tremor; and yet Faria is a thing of packthread and Dantè is little more than a name. The sequel is one long-drawn error, gloomy, bloody, unnatural and dull; but as for these early chapters, I do not believe there is another volume extant where you can breathe the same unmingled atmosphere of romance. It is very thin and light, to be sure, as on a high mountain; but it is brisk and clear and sunny in proportion. I saw the other day, with envy, and old and very clever lady setting forth on a second or third voyage into *Monte Christo*. Here are stories, which powerfully affect the reader, which can be reperused at any age, and where the characters are no more than puppets. The bony fist of the showman visibly propels them; their springs are an open secret; their faces are of wood, their bellies filled with bran; and yet we thrillingly partake of their adventures. And the point may be illustrated still further. The last interview between Lucy and Richard Feverell is pure drama; more than that, it is the strongest scene, since Shakespeare, in the English tongue. Their first meeting by the river, on the other hand, is pure romance; it has nothing to do with character; it might happen to any other boy and maiden, and be none the less delightful for the change. And yet I think he would be a bold man who should choose between these passages. Thus, in the same book, we may have two scenes, each capital in its order: in the one, human passion, deep calling unto deep, shall utter its genuine voice; in the second, according circumstances, like instruments in tune, shall build up a trivial but desirable incident, such as we love to prefigure for ourselves; and in the end, in spite of the critics, we may hesitate to give the preference to either. The one may ask more genius—I do not say it does; but at least the other dwells as clearly in the memory.

True romantic art, again, makes a romance of all things. It reaches into the highest abstraction of the ideal; it does not refuse the most pedestrian realism. *Robinson Crusoe* is as realistic as it is romantic; both qualities are pushed to an extreme, and neither suffers. Nor does romance depend upon the material importance of the incidents. To deal with strong and deadly elements, banditti, pirates, war, and murder, is to conjure with great names, and, in the event of failure, to double the disgrace. The arrival of Haydn and Consuelo at the Canon's villa is a very trifling incident; yet we may read a dozen boisterous stories from beginning to end, and not receive so fresh and stirring an impression of adventure. It was the scene of Crusoe at the wreck, if I remember rightly, that so bewitched my blacksmith. Nor is the fact surprising. Every single article the castaway recovers from the hulk is "a joy for ever" to the man who reads of them. They are the things he ought to find, and the bare enumeration stirs the blood. I found a glimmer of the same interest the other day in a new book, *The Sailor's Sweetheart*, by Mr Clark Russell. The whole business of the brig *Morning Star* is very rightly felt and spiritedly written; but the clothes, the books, and the money satisfy the reader's mind like things to eat. We are dealing here with the old cut-and-dry, legitimate interest of treasure trove. But even treasure trove can be made dull. There are few people who have not groaned under the plethora of goods that fell to the lot of the Swiss Family Robinson, that dreary family. They found article after article, creature after creature, from milk kine to pieces of ordnance, a whole consignment; but no informing taste had presided over the selection, there was no smack or relish in the invoice; and all these riches left the fancy cold. The box of goods in Verne's "Mysterious Island" is another case in point: there was no gusto and no glamour about that; it might have come from a shop. But the two hundred and seventy-eight Australian sovereigns on board the *Morning Star* fell upon me like a surprise that I had expected; whole vistas of secondary stories, besides the one in hand, radiated forth from that discovery, as they radiate from a striking particular in life; and I was made for the moment as happy as a reader has the right to be.

To come at all at the nature of this quality of romance, we must bear in mind the peculiarity of our attitude to any art. No art produces illusion; in the theatre, we never forget that we are in the theatre; and while we read a story, we sit wavering between two minds, now merely clapping our hands at the merit of the performance, now condescending to take an active part in fancy with the characters. This last is the triumph of story-telling: when the reader consciously plays at being the hero, the scene is a good scene. Now in character-studies the pleasure that we take is critical; we watch, we approve, we smile at incongruities, we are moved to sudden heats of sympathy with courage, suffering, or virtue, but the characters are still themselves; they are not us; the more clearly they are depicted, the more widely do they stand away from us, the more imperiously do they thrust us back into our place as spectator. I cannot identify myself with Rawdon Crawley or with Eugene de Rastignac, for I have scarce a hope or fear in common with them. It is not character, but incident, that wooes us out of our reserve. Something happens, as we desire to have it happen to ourselves; some situation, that we have long dallied with in fancy, is realised in the story with enticing and appropriate details. Then we forget the characters; then we push the hero aside; then we plunge into the tale in our own person and bathe in fresh experience; and then, and then only, do we say we have been reading a romance. It is not only pleasurable things that we imagine in our daydreams; there are lights in which we are willing to contemplate even the idea of our own death; ways in which it seems as if it would amuse us to be cheated, wounded, or calumniated. It is thus possible to construct a story, even of tragic import, in which every incident, detail, and trick of circumstance shall be welcome to the reader's thoughts. Fiction is to the grown man what play is to the child. It is there that he changes the atmosphere and tenor of his life. And when the game so chimes with his fancy that he can join in it with all his heart, when it pleases him with every turn, when he loves to recall it and dwells upon its recollection with entire delight, fiction is called romance.

Walter Scott is out and away the king of the romantics. *The Lady of the Lake* has no indisputable claim to be a poem beyond the inherent fitness and desirability of the tale. It is just such a story as a man would make up for himself, walking, in the best health and temper, through just such scenes as it is laid in. Hence it is that a charm dwells undefinable among these slovenly verses, as the unseen cuckoo fills the mountains with his note; hence, even after we have flung the book aside, the scenery and adventures remain present to the mind, a new and green possession, not unworthy of that beautiful name, *The Lady of the Lake,* or that direct, romantic opening—one of the most spirited and poetical in literature—"The stag at eve had drunk his fill." The same strength and the same weaknesses adorn and disfigure the novels. In that ill-written, ragged book, *The Pirate,* the figure of Cleveland—cast up by the sea on the resounding foreland of Dunrossness—moving, with the blood on his hands and the Spanish words on his tongue, among the simple islanders—singing a serenade under the window of his Shetland mistress—is conceived in the very highest manner of romantic invention. The words of his song, "Through the groves of palm," sung in such a scene and by such a lover, clench, as in a nutshell, the emphatic contrast upon which the tale is built. In *Guy Mannering,* again, every incident is delightful to the imagination; and the scene when Harry Bertram lands at Ellengowan is a model instance of romantic method.

> "I remember the tune well," he says, "though I cannot guess what should at present so strongly recall it to my memory." He took his flageolet from his pocket and played a simple melody. Apparently the tune awoke the corresponding associations of a damsel. . . .She immediately took up the song:—
>
> *Are these the links of Forth, she said;*
> *Or are they the crooks of Dee,*
> *Or the bonny woods of Warroch Head*
> *That I would fain so see?*
>
> "By heaven!" said Bertram, "it is the very ballad."

On this quotation two remarks fall to be made. First, as an instance of modern feeling for romance, this famous touch of the flageolet and the old song is selected by Miss Braddon for omission. Miss Braddon's idea of a story, like Mrs Todger's idea of a wooden leg, were something strange to have expounded. As a matter of personal experience, Meg's appearance to old Mr Bertram on the road, the ruins of Derncleugh, the scene of the flageolet, and the Dominie's recognition of Harry, are the four strong notes that continue to ring in the mind after the book is laid aside. The second point is still more curious. The reader will observe a mark of excision in the passage as quoted by me. Well, here is how it runs in the original: "A damsel, who, close behind a find spring about half-way down the descent, and which had once supplied the castle with water, was engaged in bleaching linen." A man who gave in such a copy would be discharged from the staff of a daily paper. Scott has forgotten to prepare the reader for the presence of the "damsel"; he has forgotten to mention the spring and its relation to the ruin; and now, face to face with his omission, instead of trying back and starting fair, crams all this matter, tail foremost, into a single shambling sentence. It is not merely bad English, or bad style; it is abominably bad narrative besides.

Certainly the contrast is remarkable; and it is one that throws a strong light upon the subject of this paper. For here we have a man, of the finest creative instinct, touching with perfect certainty and charm the romantic junctures of his story; and we find him utterly careless, almost, it would seem, incapable, in the technical matter of style; and not only frequently weak, but frequently wrong, in points of drama. In character parts, indeed, and particularly in the Scotch, he was delicate, strong, and truthful; but the trite, obliterated features of too many of his heroes have already wearied two generations of readers. At times, his characters will speak with something far beyond propriety, with a true heroic note; but on the next page they will be wading wearily forward with an ungrammatical and undramatic rigmarole of words. The man who could conceive and write the character of Elspeth of the Craigburnfoot, as Scott has conceived and written it, had not only splendid romantic, but splendid tragic, gifts. How comes it, then, that he could so often fob us off with languid, inarticulate twaddle?

It seems to me that the explanation is to be found in the very quality of his surprising merits. As his books are play to the reader, so were they play to him. He conjured up the beautiful with delight, but he had hardly patience to describe it. He was a great daydreamer, a seeër of fit and beautiful and humorous visions; but hardly a great artist; hardly, in the manful sense, an artist at all. He pleased himself, and so he pleases us. Of the pleasures of his art he tasted fully; but of its toils and vigils and distresses never man knew less. A great romantic—an idle child.

66

A Humble Remonstrance

ROBERT LOUIS STEVENSON

In response to Walter Besant's and Henry James's essays on the art of fiction, Stevenson takes issue with James's emphasis on the truth of the novelist's vision. Interpreting truth as fidelity to external reality, Stevenson argues that the novelist should not try to compete with reality; rather he or she should choose from the welter of reality the typical incident or character around which to frame the story. When guided by a central motif, the author must work to make incident, character and style cohere in a unified artistic pattern. Stevenson also disagrees with James's refusal to categorise novels into those of character and incident. In this essay he divides novels into three types—those of adventure, character and drama. The dramatic novel, he argues, constitutes the highest and most engaging of these categories in its presentation of passion. Though he does not focus specifically on the romance in this essay, Stevenson positions himself clearly on the side of the romantic writer who, unlike Henry James, focuses on" the brushes, the palette, and the north light" as opposed to "the finished picture" (146).

We have recently enjoyed a quite peculiar pleasure: hearing, in some detail, the opinions about the art they practise of Walter Besant and Mr Henry James; two men certainly of very different calibre: Mr James so precise of outline, so cunning of fence, so scrupulous of finish, and Mr Besant so genial, so friendly, with so persuasive and humorous a vein of whim: Mr James the very type of the deliberate artist, Mr Besant the impersonation of good nature. That such doctors should differ will excite no great surprise; but one point in which they seem to agree fills me, I confess, with wonder. For they are both content to talk about the "art of fiction;" and Mr Besant, waxing exceedingly bold, goes on to oppose this so-called "art of fiction" to the "art of poetry." By art of poetry he can mean nothing but the art of verse, an art of handicraft, and only comparable with the art of prose. For that heat and height of sane emotion which we agree to call by the name of poetry,

Source: Robert Louis Stevenson, "A Humble Remonstrance", *Longman's Magazine*, 5.26, Winter 1883, pp. 139–47.

is but a libertine and vagrant quality; present, at times, in any art, more often absent from them all; too seldom present in the prose novel, too frequently absent from the ode and epic. Fiction is in the same case; it is no substantive art, but an element which enters largely into all the arts but architecture. Homer, Wordsworth, Phidias, Hogarth, and Salvini, all deal in fiction; and yet I do not suppose that either Hogarth or Salvini, to mention but these two, entered in any degree into the scope of Mr Besant's interesting lecture or Mr James's charming essay. The art of fiction, then, regarded as a definition, is both too ample and too scanty. Let me suggest another; let me suggest that what both Mr James and Mr Besant had in view was neither more nor less than the art of narrative.

But Mr Besant is anxious to speak solely of "the modern English novel," the stay and bread-winner of Mr Mudie; and in the author of the most pleasing novel on that roll, "All Sorts and Conditions of Men," the desire is natural enough. I can conceive then, that he would hasten to propose two additions, and read thus: the art of *fictitious* narrative *in prose*.

Now the fact of the existence of the modern English novel is not to be denied; materially, with its three volumes, leaded type, and gilded lettering, it is easily distinguishable form other forms of literature; but to talk at all fruitfully of any branch of art, it is needful to build our definitions on some more fundamental ground than binding. Why, then, are we to add "in prose"? The *Odyssey* appears to me among the best of romances; *The Lady of the Lake* to stand high in the second order; and Chaucer's tales and prologues to contain more of the matter and art of the modern English novel than the whole treasury of Mr Mudie. Whether a narrative be written in blank verse or the Spenserian stanza, in the long period of Gibbon or the chipped phrase of Charles Reade, the principles of the art of narrative must be equally observed. The choice of a noble and swelling style in prose affects the problem of narration in the same way, if not to the same degree, as the choice of measured verse; for both imply a closer synthesis of events, a higher key of dialogue, and a more picked and stately strain of words. If you are to refuse *Don Juan*, it is hard to see why you should include *Zanoni* or (to bracket works of very different value) *The Scarlet Letter*; and by what discrimination are you to open your doors to *The Pilgrim's Progress* and close them on the *Faery Queen*? To bring things closer home, I will here propound to Mr Besant a conundrum. A narrative called *Paradise Lost* was written in English verse by one John Milton; what was it then? It was next translated by Chateaubriand into French prose; and what was it then? Lastly, the French translation was, by some inspired compatriot of George Gilfillan (and of mine), turned bodily into an English novel; and, in the name of clearness, what was it then?

But, once more, why should we add "fictitious"? The reason why is obvious. The reason why not, if something more recondite, does not want for weight. The art of narrative, in fact, is the same, whether it is applied to the selection and illustration of a real series of events or of an imaginary series. Boswell's *Life of Johnson* (a work of cunning and inimitable art) owes its success to the same technical manœuvres as (let us say) *Tom Jones*: the clear conception of certain characters of man, the choice and presentation of certain incidents out of a great number that offered, and the invention (yes, invention) and preservation of a certain key in dialogue. In which these things are done with the more art—in which with the greater air of nature—readers will differently judge. Boswell's is, indeed, a very special case, and almost a generic; but it is not only Boswell, it is in every biography with any salt of life, it is in every history where events and men, rather than ideas, are presented—in Tacitus, in Carlyle, in Michelet, in Macaulay—that the novelist will find many of his own methods most conspicuously and adroitly handled. He will find besides that he, who is free—who has the right to invent or steal a missing incident, who has the right, more precious still, of wholesale omission—is frequently defeated, and, with all his advantages, leaves a less strong impression of reality and passion. Mr James utters his mind with a becoming fervour on the sanctity of truth to the novelist; on a more careful examination truth will seem a word of very debateable propriety, not only for the labours of the novelist, but for those of the historian. No art—to use the daring phrase of Mr James—can successfully "compete with life"; and the art that does so is condemned to perish *montibus aviis*. Life goes before us, infinite in complication; attended by the most various and surprising meteors; appealing at once to the eye, to the ear, to the mind—the seat of wonder, to the touch—so thrillingly delicate, and to the belly—so imperious when starved. It combines and employs in its manifestation the method and material, not of one art only, but of all the arts. Music is but an arbitrary trifling with a few of life's majestic chords; painting is but a shadow of its gorgeous pageantry of light and colour; literature does but drily indicate that wealth of incident, of moral obligation, of virtue, vice, action, rapture, and agony, with which it teems. To "compete with life," whose sun we cannot look upon, whose passions and diseases waste and slay us—to compete with the flavour of wine, the beauty of the dawn, the scorching of fire, the bitterness of death and separation—here is, indeed, a projected escalade of heaven; here are, indeed, labours for a Hercules in a dress coat, armed with a pen and a dictionary to depict the passions, armed with a tube of superior flake-white to paint the portrait of the insufferable sun. No art is true in this sense: none can 'compete with life': not even history, built indeed of indisputable facts, but these facts robbed of their vivacity and sting; so that even when we read of the sack of a city or the fall of an empire, we are surprised, and justly commend the author's talent, if our pulse be quickened. And mark, for a last differentia, that this quickening of the pulse is, in almost every case, purely agreeable; that these phantom reproductions of experience, even at their most acute, convey decided pleasure; while experience itself, in the cockpit of life, can torture and slay.

What, then, is the object, what the method, of an art, and what the source of its power? The whole secret is that no art does "compete with life." Man's one method, whether he reasons or creates, is to half-shut his eyes against the dazzle and confusion of reality. The arts, like arithmetic and geometry, turn away their eyes from the gross, coloured, and mobile nature at our feet, and regard instead a certain figmentary abstraction. Geometry will tell us of a circle, a thing never seen in nature; asked about a green circle or an iron circle, it lays its hand upon its mouth. So with the arts. Painting, ruefully comparing sunshine and flake-white, gives up truth of colour, as it had already given up relief and movement; and instead of vying with nature, arranges a scheme of harmonious tints. Literature, above all in its most typical mood, the mood of narrative, similarly flees the direct challenge and pursues instead an independent and creative aim. So far as it imitates at all, it imitates not life but speech: not the facts of human destiny, but the emphasis and the suppressions with which the human actor tells of them. The real art that dealt with life directly was that of the first men who told their stories round the savage camp-fire. Our art is occupied, and bound to be occupied, not so much in making stories true as in making them typical; not so much in capturing the lineaments of each fact, as in marshalling all of them towards a common end. For the welter of impressions, all forcible but all discrete, which life presents, it substitutes a certain artificial series of impressions, all indeed most feebly represented, but all aiming at the same effect, all eloquent of the same idea, all chiming together like consonant notes in music or like the graduated tints in a good picture. From all its chapters, from all its pages, from all its sentences, the well-written novel echoes and re-echoes its one creative and controlling thought; to this must every incident and character contribute; the style must have been pitched in unison with this; and if there is anywhere a word that looks another way, the book would be stronger, clearer, and (I had almost said) fuller without it. Life is monstrous, infinite, illogical, abrupt, and poignant; a work of art, in comparison, is neat, finite, self-contained, rational, flowing, and emasculate. Life imposes by brute energy, like inarticulate thunder; art catches the ear, among the far louder noises of experience, like an air artificially made by a discrete musician. A proposition of geometry does not compete with life; and a proposition of geometry is a fair and luminous parallel for a work of art. Both are reasonable, both untrue to the crude fact; both inhere in nature, neither represents it. The novel which is a work of art exists, not by its resemblances to life, which are forced and material, as a shoe must still consist of leather, but by its immeasurable difference from life, which is designed and significant, and is both the method and the meaning of the work.

The life of man is not subject of novels, but the inexhaustible magazine from which subjects are to be selected; the name of these is legion; and with each new subject—for here again I must differ by the whole width of heaven from Mr James—the true artist will vary his method and change the point of attack. That which was in one case an excellence, will become a defect in another; what was the making of one book, will in the next be impertinent or dull. First each novel, and then each class of novels, exists by and for itself. I will take, for instance, three main classes, which are fairly distinct: first, the novel of adventure, which appeals to certain almost sensual and quite illogical tendencies in man; second, the novel of character, which appeals to our intellectual appreciation of man's foibles and mingled and inconstant motives; and third, the dramatic novel, which deals with the same stuff as the serious theatre, and appeals to our emotional nature and moral judgment.

Now first for the novel of adventure. Mr James refers, with generosity of praise, to a little book about a quest for hidden treasure; but he lets fall, by the way, some rather startling words. In this book he misses what he calls the "immense luxury" of being able to quarrel with his author. The luxury, to most of us, is to lay by our judgment, to be submerged by the tale as by a billow, and only to awake, and begin to distinguish and find fault, when the piece is over and the volume laid aside. Still more remarkable is Mr James's reason. He cannot criticise the author, as he goes, "because," says he, comparing it with another work, "*I have been a child, but I have never been on a quest for buried treasure.*" Here is, indeed, a wilful paradox; for if he has never been on a quest for buried treasure, it can be demonstrated that he has never been a child. There never was a child (unless Master James) but has hunted for gold, and been a pirate, and a military commander, and a bandit of the mountains; but has fought, and suffered shipwreck and prison, and imbrued its little hands in gore, and gallantly retrieved the lost battle, and triumphantly protected innocence and beauty. Elsewhere in his essay Mr James has protested with excellent reason against too narrow a conception of experience; for the born artist, he contends, the "faintest hints of life" are converted into revelations; and it will be found true, I believe, in a majority of cases, that the artist writes with more gusto and effect of those things which he has only wished to do, than of those which he has done. Desire is a wonderful telescope, and Pisgah the best observatory. Now, while it is true that neither Mr James nor the author of the work in question has ever, in the fleshly sense, gone questing after gold, it is probable that both have ardently desired and fondly imagined the details of such a life in youthful daydreams; and the author, counting upon that, and well aware (cunning and lowminded man!) that this class of interest, having been frequently treated, finds a readily accessible and beaten road to the sympathies of the reader, addressed himself throughout to the building up and circumstantiation of this boyish dream. Character go the boy is a sealed book; for him, a pirate is a beard in wide trousers and literally bristling with pistols. The author, for the sake of circumstantiation and because he was himself more or less grown up, admitted character, within certain limits, into his design; but only within certain limits. Had the same puppets figured in a scheme of another sort, they had been drawn to very different purpose; for in this elementary novel of adventure, the characters need to be presented with but one class of qualities—the warlike and formidable. So as they appear insidious in deceit and fatal in the combat, they have served their end. Danger is the matter with which this class of novel deals; fear, the passion with which it idly trifles; and the characters are portrayed only so for as they realise the sense of danger and provoke the sympathy of fear. To add more traits, to be too clever, to start the hare of moral or intellectual interest while we are running the fox of material interest, is not to enrich but to stultify your tale. The stupid reader will only be offended, and the clever reader lose the scent.

The novel of character has this difference from all others: that it requires no coherency of plot, and for this reason, as in the case of *Gil Blas*, it is sometimes called the novel of adventure. It turns on the humours of the persons represented; these are, to be sure, embodied in incidents, but the incidents themselves, being tributary, need not march in a progression; and the characters may be statically shown. As they enter, so they may go out; they must be consistent, but they need not grow. Here Mr James will recognise the note of much of his own work: he treats, for the most part, the statics of character, studying it at rest or only gently moved; and, with his usual delicate and just artistic instinct, he avoids those stronger passions which would deform the attitudes he loves to study, and change his sitters from the humourists of ordinary life to the brute forces and bare types of more emotional moments. In his recent *The Author of "Beltraffio,"* so just in conception, so nimble and neat in workmanship, strong passion is indeed employed; but observe that it is not displayed. Even in the heroine the working of the passion is suppressed; and the great struggle, the true tragedy, the *scène-à-faire*, passes unseen behind the panels of a locked door. The delectable invention of the young visitor is introduced, consciously or not, to this end: that Mr James, true to his method, might avoid the scene of passion. I trust no reader will suppose me guilty of undervaluing this little masterpiece. I mean merely that it belongs to one marked class of novel, and that it would have been very differently conceived and treated had it belonged to that other marked class, of which I now proceed to speak.

I take pleasure in calling the dramatic novel by that name, because it enables me to point out by the way a strange and peculiarly English misconception. It is sometimes supposed that the drama consists of incident. It consists of passion, which gives the actor his opportunity; and that passion must progressively increase, or the actor, as the piece proceeded, would be unable to carry the audience from a lower to a higher pitch of interest and emotion. A good serious play must therefore be founded on one of the passionate *cruces* of life, where duty and inclination come nobly to the grapple; and the same is true of what I call, for that reason, the dramatic novel. I will instance a few worthy specimens, all of our own day and language: Meredith's *Rhoda Fleming*, that wonderful and painful book, long out of print and hunted for at bookstalls like an Aldine; Hardy's *Pair of Blue Eyes*; and two of Charles Reade's, *Griffith Gaunt* and *The Double Marriage*, originally called "White Lies" and founded (by an accident quaintly favourable to my nomenclature) on a play by Maquet, the partner of the great Dumas. In this kind of novel the closed door of *The Author of "Beltraffio"* must be broken open; passion must appear upon the scene and utter its last word; passion is the be-all and the end-all, the plot and the solution, the protagonist and the *deus ex machinâ* in one. The characters may come anyhow upon the stage: we do not care; the point is, that, before they leave it, they shall become transfigured and raised out of themselves by passion. It may be part of the design to draw them with detail; to depict a full-length character, and then behold it melt and change in the furnace of emotion. But there is no obligation of the sort; nice portraiture is not required; and we are content to accept mere abstract types, so they be strongly and sincerely moved. A novel of this class may be even great, because it displays the workings of the perturbed heart and the impersonal utterance of passion; and with an artist of the second class it is, indeed, even more likely to be great, when the issue has thus been narrowed and the whole force of the writer's mind directed to passion alone. Cleverness again, which has its fair field in the novel of character, is debarred all entry upon this more solemn theatre. A far-fetched motive, an ingenious evasion of the issue, a witty instead of a passionate turn, offend us like an insincerity. All should be plain, all straightforward to the end. Hence it is that, in *Rhoda Fleming*, Mrs Lovel raises such resentment in the reader; her motives are too flimsy, her ways are too equivocal, for the weight and strength of her surroundings. Hence the hot indignation of the reader when Balzac, after having begun the *Duchesse de Langeais* in terms of strong if somewhat swollen passion, cuts the knot by the derangement of the hero's clock. Such personages and incidents belong to the novel of character; they are out of place in the high society of the passions; when the passions are introduced in art at their full height, we look to see them, not baffled and impotently striving, as in life, but towering above circumstance and acting substitutes for fate.

And here I can imagine Mr James, with his lucid sense, to intervene. To much of what I have said he would apparently demur; in much he would, somewhat impatiently, acquiesce. It may be true; but it is not what he desired to say or to hear said. He spoke of the finished picture and its worth when done; I, of the brushes, the palette, and the north light. He uttered his views in the tone and for the ear of good society; I, with the emphasis and technicalities of the obtrusive student. But the point, I may reply, is not merely to amuse the public, but to offer helpful advice to the young writer. And the young writer will not so much be helped by genial pictures of what an art may aspire to at its highest, as by a true idea of what it must be on the lowest terms. The best that we can say to him is this: Let him choose a motive, whether of character or passion; carefully construct his plot so that every incident is an illustration of the motive and every property employed shall bear to it a near relation of congruity or contrast; avoid a sub-plot, unless, as sometimes in Shakespeare, the sub-plot be a reversion or complement of the main intrigue; suffer not his style to flag below the level of the argument; pitch the key of conversation, not with any thought of how men talk in parlours, but with a single eye to the degree of passion he may be called on to express; and allow neither himself in the narrative nor any character in the course of the dialogue, to utter one sentence that is not part and parcel of the business of the story or the discussion of the problem involved. Let him not regret if this shortens his book; it will be better so; for to add irrelevant matter is not to lengthen but to bury. Let him not mind if he miss a thousand qualities, so that he keeps unflaggingly in pursuit of the one he has chosen. Let him not care particularly if he miss the tone of conversation, the pungent material detail of all the day's manners, the reproduction of the atmosphere and the environment. These elements are not essential: a novel may be excellent, and yet have none of them; a passion or a character is so much the better depicted as it rises clearer from material circumstance. In this age of the particular, let him remember the ages of the abstract, the great books of the past, the brave men that lived before Shakespeare and before Balzac. And as the root of the whole matter, let him bear in mind that his novel is not a transcript of life, to be judged by its exactitude; but a simplification of some side or point of life, to stand or fall by its significant simplicity. For although, in great men, working upon great motives, what we observe and admire is often their complexity, yet underneath appearances the truth remains unchanged: that simplification was their method, and that simplicity is their excellence.

❦ 67 ❧

The Art of Fiction

WALTER BESANT

Originally a lecture delivered to the Royal Institution on 25 April 1884, the essay presents a conventional defence of the novel's right to equal status among the legitimate arts of painting, music and poetry. Though the essay's significance today rests almost exclusively in the fact that it provoked Henry James's famous response, "The Art of Fiction", it serves as a late Victorian compendium of the rules of fiction. Besant insists on the centrality of character, sympathy, selection, truth, close observation and dramatic presentation. The novel must, he insists, tell a story, and it must have a "conscious moral purpose" (29). Furthermore, a writer should write from personal experience and observation to keep his characters convincing. Finally, Besant gives a nod to style which he terms workmanship. James will argue against such prescriptive rules, averring that the novelist should be free to employ whatever technique and subject he chooses.

The Art of Fiction:
A Lecture Delivered at the Royal Institution, 25 April 1884.

I desire, this evening, to consider Fiction as one of the Fine Arts. In order to do this, and before doing it, I have first to advance certain propositions. They are not new, they are not likely to be disputed, and yet they have never been so generally received as to form part, so to speak, of the national mind. These propositions are three, though the last two directly spring from the first. They are:—

1. That Fiction is an Art in every way worthy to be called the sister and the equal of the Arts of Painting, Sculpture, Music, and Poetry; that is to say, her field is as boundless, her possibilities as vast, her excellences as worthy of admiration, as may be claimed for any of her sister Arts.

2. That it is an Art which, like them, is governed and directed by general laws; and that these laws may be laid down and taught with as much precision and exactness as the laws of harmony, perspective, and proportion.

Source: Walter Besant, *The Art of Fiction*, a lecture given on 25 April 1884, Boston: De Wolfe, 1884.

3. That, like the other Fine Arts, Fiction is so far removed from the mere mechanical arts, that no laws or rules whatever can teach it to those who have not already been endowed with the natural and necessary gifts.

These are the three propositions which I have to discuss. It follows as a corollary and evident deduction that, these propositions once admitted, those who follow and profess the Art of Fiction must be recognized as artists, in the strictest sense of the word, just as much as those who have delighted and elevated mankind by music and painting; and that the great Masters of Fiction must be placed on the same level as the great Masters in the other Arts. In other words, I mean that where the highest point, or what seems the highest point, possible in this Art is touched, the man who has reached it is one of the world's greatest men.

I cannot suppose that there are any in this room who would refuse to admit these propositions; on the contrary, they will seem to most here self-evident; yet the application of theory to practice, of principle to persons, may be more difficult. For instance, so boundless is the admiration for great Masters such as Raphael or Mozart, that if one were to propose that Thackeray should be placed beside them, on the same level, and as an equal, there would be felt by most a certain shock. I am not suggesting that the art of Thackeray is to be compared with that of Raphael, or that there is any similarity in the work of two men; I only say that, Fiction being one Art, and Painting another and a sister Art, those who attain the highest possible distinction in either are equal.

Let us, however, go outside this room, among the multitudes by whom a novelist has never been considered an artist at all. To them the claim that a great novelist should be considered to occupy the same level as a great musician, a great painter, or a great poet, would appear at first a thing ludicrous and even painful. Consider for a moment how the world at large regards the novelist. He is, in their eyes, a person who tells stories, just as they used to regard the actor as a man who tumbled on the stage to make the audience laugh, and a musician as a man who fiddled to make the people dance. This is the old way of thinking, and most people think first as they have been taught to think; and next as they see others think. It is therefore quite easy to understand why the art of novel-writing has always been, by the general mass, undervalued. First, while the leaders in every other branch of Art, in every department of Science, and in every kind of profession, receive their share of the ordinary national distinctions, no one ever hears of honor being bestowed upon novelists. Neither Thackeray nor Dickens was ever, so far as I know, offered a Peerage; neither King, Queen, nor Prince in any country throughout the whole world takes the least notice of them. I do not say they would be any the better for this kind of recognition, but its absence clearly proves, to those who take their opinions from others, that they are not a class at all worthy of special honor. Then again, in the modern craze which exists for every kind of art—so that we meet everywhere, in every household, amateur actors, painters, etchers, sculptors, modellers, musicians, and singers, all of them serious and earnest in their aims—amateur novelists alone regard their Art as one which is learned by intuition. Thirdly, novelists are not associated as are painters; they hold no annual exhibitions, dinners, or conversazioni; they put no letters after their name; they have no President or Academy; and they do not themselves seem desirous of being treated as followers of a special Art. I do not say that they are wrong, or that much would be gained for Art if all the novelists of England were invited to Court and created into a Royal Academy. But I do say that for these three reasons it is easy to understand how the world at large does not even suspect that the writing of novels is one of the Fine Arts, and why they regard the story-teller with a sort of contempt. It is, I acknowledge, a kindly contempt—even an affectionate contempt; it is the contempt which the practical man feels for the dreamer, the strong man for the weak, the man who can do for the man who can only look on and talk.

The general—the Philistine—view of the Profession is, first of all, that it is not one which a scholar and a man of serious views should take up: the telling of stories is inconsistent with a well-balanced mind; to be a teller of stories disqualifies one from a hearing on important subjects. At this very day there are thousands of living people who will never understand how the author of *Coningsby* and *Vivian Grey* can possibly be regarded as a serious statesman—all the Disraeli literature, even to the comic cartoons, expresses the popular sentiment that a novelist must not presume to call himself a statesman: the intellect of a novelist, it is felt, if he have any intellect at all, which is doubtful, must be one of the most frivolous and lightest kind; how can a man whose mind is always full of the loves of Corydon and Amaryllis by trusted to form an opinion on practical matters? When Thackeray ventured to contest the city of Oxford, we know what happened. He thought his failure was because the people of Oxford had never even heard of him; I think otherwise. I think it was because it was whispered from house to house and was carried from shop to shop, and was mentioned in the vestry, that this fellow from London, who asked for their votes, was nothing but a common novelist.

With these people must not be confounded another class, not so large, who are prepared to admit that Fiction is in some qualified sense an Art; but they do this as a concession to the vanity of its followers, and are by no means prepared to allow that it is an Art of the first rank. How can that be an Art, they might ask, which has no lecturers or teachers, no school or college or Academy, no recognized rules, no text-books, and is not taught in any University? Even the German Universities, which teach everything else, do not have Professors of Fiction, and not one single novelist, so far as I know, has ever pretended to teach his mystery, or spoken of it as a thing which may be taught. Clearly, therefore, they would go on to argue, such art as is required for the making and telling of a story can and must be mastered without study, because no materials exist for the student's use. It may even, perhaps, be acquired unconsciously or by imitation. This view, I am sorry to say, largely prevails among the majority of those who try their chance in the field of fiction. Anyone, they think, can write a novel; therefore, why not sit down and write one? I would not willingly say one word which might discourage those who are attracted to this branch of literature; on the contrary, I would encourage them in every possible way. One desires, however, that they should approach their work at the outset with the same serious and earnest appreciation of its importance and its difficulties with which they undertake the study of music and painting. I would wish, in short, that from the very beginning their minds should be fully possessed with the knowledge that Fiction is an Art, and, like all other Arts, that it is governed by certain laws, methods, and rules, which it is their first business to learn.

It is then, first and before all, a real Art. It is the oldest, because it was known and practised long before Painting and her sisters were in existence or even thought of; it is older than any of the Muses from whose company she who tells stories has hitherto been excluded; it is the most widely spread, because in no race of men under the sun is it unknown, even though the stories may be always the same, and handed down from generation to generation in the same form; it is the most religious of all the Arts, because in every age until the present the lives, exploits, and sufferings of the gods, goddesses, saints, and heroes have been the favorite theme; it has always been the most popular, because it requires neither culture, education, nor natural genius to understand and listen to a story; it is the most moral, because the world has always been taught whatever little morality it possesses by way of story, fable, apologue, parable, and allegory. It commands the widest influence, because it can be carried easily and everywhere, into regions where pictures are never seen and music is never heard; it is the greatest teaching power, because its lessons are most readily apprehended and understood. All this, which might have been said thousands of years ago, may be said to-day with even greater force and truth. That world which exists not, but is an invention or an imitation—that world in which the shadows and shapes of men move about before our eyes as real as if they were actually living and speaking among us, is like a great theatre accessible to all of every sort, on whose stage are enacted, at our own sweet will, whenever we please to command them, the most beautiful plays: it is, as every theatre should be, the school in which manners are learned: here the majority of reading mankind learn nearly all that they know of life and manners, of philosophy and art; even of science and religion. The modern novel converts abstract ideas into living models; it gives ideas, it strengthens faith, it preaches a higher morality than is seen in the actual world; it commands the emotions of pity, admiration, and terror; it creates and keeps alive the sense of sympathy; it is the universal teacher; it is the only book which the great mass of reading mankind ever do read; it is the only way in which people can learn what other men and women are like; it redeems their lives from dulness, puts thoughts, desires, knowledge, and even ambitions into their hearts: it teaches them to talk, and enriches their speech with epigrams, anecdotes and illustrations. It is an unfailing source of delight to millions, happily not too critical. Why, out of all the books taken down from the shelves of the public libraries, four-fifths are novels, and of all those that are bought nine-tenths are novels. Compared with this tremendous engine of popular influence, what are all the other Arts put together? Can we not alter the old maxim, and say with truth, Let him who pleases make the laws if I may write the novels?

As for the field with which this Art of Fiction occupies itself, it is, if you please, nothing less than the whole of Humanity. The novelist studies men and women; he is concerned with their actions and their thoughts, their errors and their follies, their greatness and their meanness; the countless forms of beauty and constantly varying moods to be seen among them; the forces which act upon them; the passions, prejudices, hopes and fears which pull them this way and that. He has to do, above all, and before all, with men and women. No one, for instance, among novelists, can be called a landscape painter, or a painter of sea-pieces, or a painter of fruit and flowers, save only in strict subordination to the group of characters with whom he is dealing. Landscape, sea, sky, and air, are merely accessories introduced in order to set off and bring into greater prominence the figures on the stage. The very first rule in Fiction is that the human interest must absolutely absorb everything else. Some writers never permit anything at all in their pages which shall divert our thoughts one moment from the actors. When, for instance, Charles Reade—Alas! that we must say the late Charles Reade, for he is dead—when this great Master of Fiction, in his incomparable tale of the "Cloister and the Hearth," sends Gerard and Denis the Burgundian on that journey through France, it is with the fewest possible of words that he suggests the sights and persons met with on the way; yet, so great is the art of the writer, that, almost without being told, we see the road, a mere rough track, winding beside the river and along the valleys; we see the silent forests where lurk the *routiers* and the robbers, the cut-throat inn, the merchants, peasants, beggars, soldiers who go riding by; the writer does not pause in his story to tell us of all this, but yet we feel it—by the mere action of the piece and the dialogue we are compelled to see the scenery: the life of the fifteenth century passes before us, with hardly a word to picture it, because it is always kept in the background, so as not to interfere with the central figure of the young clerk journeying to Rome.

The human interest in Fiction, then, must come before aught else. It is of this world, wholly of this world. It might seem at first as if the limitation of this Art to things human placed it on a lower level than the Arts of Painting and Music. That, however, is not so. The stupendous subjects which were undertaken by the old Italian painters are, it is true, beyond the power of Fiction to attempt. It may be questioned whether they are not also, according to modern ideas, beyond the legitimate scope of painting. Certainly, just as there is nothing in the whole of creation more worthy of representation than men and women in action and in passion. The ancient poet placed the gods themselves upon the stage with the Furies and the Fates. Then we had the saints, confessors, and martyrs. We next descended to kings and great lords; in our times painter, poet, and novelist alike are contented with plain humanity, whether crowned or in rags. What picture, let us ask, what picture ever painted of angels and blessed souls, even if they are mounting the hill on which stands the Four Square City of the jasper wall, is able to command our interest and sympathy more profoundly than the simple and faithful story, truly and faithfully told, of a lover and his mistress?

It is, therefore, the especial characteristic of this Art, that, since it deals exclusively with men and women, it not only requires of its followers, but also creates in readers, that sentiment which is destined to be a most mighty engine in deepening and widening the civilization of the world. We call it Sympathy, but it means a great deal more than was formerly understood by the word. It means, in fact, what Professor Seeley once called the Enthusiasm of Humanity, and it first appeared, I think, about a hundred and fifty years ago, when the modern novel came into existence. You will find it, for instance, conspicuous for its absence in Defoe. The modern Sympathy includes not only the power to pity the sufferings of others, but also that of understanding their very souls; it is the reverence for man, the respect for his personality, the recognition of his individuality, and the enormous value of the one man, the perception of one man's relation to another, his duties and responsibilities. Through the strength of his newly-born faculty, and aided by the guidance of a great artist, we are enabled to discern the real indestructible man beneath the rags and filth of a common castaway, and the possibilities of the meanest gutter-child that steals in the streets for its daily bread. Surely that is a wonderful Art which endows the people—all the people—with this power of vision and of feeling. Painting has not done it, and could never do it; Painting has done more for nature than for humanity. Sculpture could not do it, because it deals with situation and form rather than action. Music cannot do it, because Music (if I understand rightly) appeals especially to the individual concerning himself and his own aspirations. Poetry alone is the rival of Fiction, and in this respect it takes a lower place, not because Poetry fails to teach and interpret, but because Fiction is, and must always be, more popular.

Again, this Art teaches, like the others, by suppression and reticence. Out of the great procession of Humanity, the *Comédie Humaine* which the novelist sees passing ever before his eyes, single figures detach themselves one after the other, to be questioned, examined, and received or rejected. This process goes on perpetually. Humanity is so vast a field that to one who goes about watching men and women, and does not sit at home and evolve figures out of inner consciousness, there is not, and can never be, any end or limit to the freshness and interest of these figures. It is the work of the artist to select the figures, to suppress, to copy, to group, and to work up the incidents which each one offers. The daily life of the world is not dramatic—it is monotonous; the novelist makes it dramatic by his silences, his suppressions, and his exaggerations. No one, for example, in fiction behaves quite in the same way as in real life; as on the stage, if an actor unfolds and reads a letter, the simple action is done with an exaggeration of gesture which calls attention to the thing and to its importance; so in romance, while nothing should be allowed which does not carry on the story, so everything as it occurs must be accentuated and yet deprived of needless accessory details. The gestures of the characters at an important juncture, their looks, their voices, may all be noted if they help to impress the situation. Even the weather, the wind and the rain, with some writers, have been made to emphasize a mood or a passion of a heroine. To know how to use these aids artistically is to the novelist exactly what to the actor is the right presentation of a letter, the handing of a chair, even the removal of a glove.

A third characteristic of Fiction, which should alone be sufficient to give it a place among the noblest forms of Art, is that, like Poetry, Painting, and Music, it becomes a vehicle, not only for the best thoughts of the writer, but also for those of the reader, so that a novelist may write truthfully and faithfully, but simply, and yet be understood in a far fuller and nobler sense than was present to his own mind. This power is the very highest gift of the poet. He has a vision and sees a thing clearly, yet perhaps afar off; another who reads him is enabled to get the same vision, to see the same thing, yet closer and more distinctly. For a lower intellect thus to lead and instruct a higher is surely a very great gift, and granted only to the highest forms of Art. And this it is which Fiction of the best kind does for its readers. It is, however, only another way of saying that Truth in Fiction produces effects similar to those produced by Truth in every other Art.

So far, then, I have showed that this Art of Fiction is the most ancient of all Arts and the most popular; that its field is the whole of humanity; that it creates and develops that sympathy which is a kind of second sight; that, like all other Arts, its function is to select, to suppress, and to arrange; that it suggests as well as narrates. More might be said— a great deal more—but enough has been said to show that in these, the leading characteristics of any Art, Fiction is on exactly the same level as her sisters. Let me only add that in this Art, as in the others, there is, and will be always, whatever has been done already, something new to discover, something new to express, something new to describe. Surgeons dissect the body, and account for every bone and every nerve, so that the body of one man, considered as a collection of bones and nerves, is so far exactly like the body of another man. But the mind of man cannot be so exhausted: it yields discoveries to every patient student; it is absolutely inexhaustible; it is to every one a fresh and virgin field: and the most successful investigator leaves regions and tracts for his successor as vast as those he has himself gone over. Perhaps, after all, the greatest Psychologist is not the metaphysician, but the novelist.

We come next to speak of the Laws which govern this Art. I mean those general rules and principles which must necessarily be acquired by every writer of Fiction before he can even hope for success. Rules will not make a man a novelist, any more than a knowledge of grammar makes a man know a language, or a knowledge of musical science makes a man able to play an instrument. Yet the Rules must be learned. And, in speaking of them, one is compelled, so close is the connection between the sister Arts, to use not only the same terms, but also to adopt the same rules, as those laid down by painters for their students. If these Laws appear self-evident, it is a proof that the general principles of the Art are well understood. Considering, however, the vast quantity of bad, inartistic work which is every week laid before the public, one is inclined to think that a statement of these principles may not be without usefulness.

First, and before everything else, there is the Rule that everything in Fiction which is invented and is not the result of personal experience and observation is worthless. In some other Arts, the design may follow any lines which the designer pleases: it may be fanciful, unreal, or grotesque; but in modern Fiction, whose sole end, aim, and purpose is to portray humanity and human character, the design must be in accordance with the customs and general practice of living men and women under any proposed set of circumstances and conditions. That is to say, the characters must be real, and such as might be met with in actual life, or, at least, the natural developments of such people as any of us might meet; their actions must be natural and consistent; the conditions of place, of manners, and of thought must be drawn from personal observation. To take an extreme case: a young lady brought up in a quiet country village should avoid descriptions of garrison life; a writer whose friends and personal experiences belong to what we call the lower middle class should carefully avoid introducing his characters into Society; a South-countryman would hesitate before attempting to reproduce the North-country accent. This is a very simple Rule, but one to which there should be no exception—never to go beyond your own experience.[1] Remember that most of the people who read novels, and know nothing about the art of writing them, recognize before any other quality that of fidelity: the greatness of a novelist they measure chiefly by the knowledge of the world displayed in his pages; the highest praise they can bestow upon him is that he has drawn the story to the life. It is exactly the same with a picture. If you go to the Academy any day, and listen to the comments of the crowd, which is a very instructive thing to do, and one recommended to young novelists, you will presently become aware that the only thing they look for in a picture is the story which it tells, and therefore the fidelity with which it is presented on the canvas. Most of the other qualities of the picture, and of the novel as well, all that has to do with the technique, escape the general observer.

This being so, the first thing which has to be acquired is the art of description. It seems easy to describe; any one, it seems, can set down what he sees. But consider. How much does he see? There is everywhere, even in a room, such a quantity of things to be seen: far, far more in field and hedge, in mountain and forest and beside the stream, are there countless things to be seen; the unpractised eye sees nothing, or next to nothing. Here is a tree, here is a flower, there is sunshine lying on the hill. But to the observant and trained eye, the intelligent eye, there lies before him everywhere an inexhaustible and bewildering mass of things to see. Remember how Mr Jefferies sits down in a coppice with his eyes wide open to see what the rest of us never dreamed of looking for. Long before he has half finished telling us what he has seen—behold! a volume, and one of the most delightful volumes conceivable. But, then, Mr Jefferies is a profound naturalist. We cannot all describe after his manner; nor should we try, for the simple reason that descriptions of still life in a novel must be strictly subordinated to the human interest. But while Mr Jefferies has his hedge and ditch and brook, we have our towns, our villages, and our assemblies of men and women. Among them we must not only observe, but we must select. Here, then, are two distinct faculties which the intending novelist must acquire; viz., observation and selection. As for the power of observation, it may be taught to any one by the simple method adopted by Robert Houdin, the French conjuror. This method consists of noting down continually and remembering all kinds of things remarked in the course of a journey, a walk, or the day's business. The learner must carry his note-book always with him, into the fields, to the theatre, into the streets—wherever he can watch man and his ways, or Nature and her ways. On his return home he should enter his notes in his commonplace-book. There are places where the production of a note-book would be embarrassing—say, at a dinner-party, or a street fight; yet the man who begins to observe will speedily be able to remember everything that he sees and hears until he can find an opportunity to note it down, so that nothing is lost.[2] The materials for the novelist, in short, are not in the books upon the shelves, but in the men and women he meets with everywhere; he will find them, where Dickens found them, in the crowded streets, in trains, tramcars and omnibuses, at the shop-windows, in churches and chapels: his materials are everywhere—there is nothing too low, nothing too high, nothing too base, nothing too noble, for the novelist. Humanity is like a kaleidoscope, which you may turn about and look into, but you will never get the same picture twice—it cannot be exhausted. But it may be objected, that the broad distinctive types have been long since all used. They *have* been used, but the comfort is that they can never be used up, and that they may be constantly used again and again. Can we ever be tired of them when a master hand takes one of them again and gives him new life? Are there to be no more hypocrites because we have already had Tartufe and Pecksniff? Do we suppose that the old miser, the young spendthrift, the gambler, the adventurer, the coquette, the drunkard, the soldier of fortune, are never to reappear, because they have been handled already? As long, on the contrary, as man shall continue story-telling, so long will these characters occur again and again, and look as fresh each time that they are treated by a master's hand as if they were newly discovered types.

Fidelity, therefore, can be only assured by acquiring the art of observation, which further assists in filling the mind with stored experience. I am quite sure that most men never see anything at all. I have known men who have even gone all round the world and seen nothing—no, nothing at all. Emerson says, very truly, that a traveller takes away nothing from a place except what he brought into it. Now, the observation of things around us is no part of the ordinary professional and commercial life; it has nothing at all to do with success and the making of money; so that we do not learn to observe. Yet it is very easy to shake people and make them open their eyes. Some of us remember, for instance, the time when Kingsley astonished everybody with his descriptions of the wonders to be seen on the seashore and to be fished out of every pond in the field. Then all the world began to poke about the seaweed and to catch tritons and keep water-grubs in little tanks. It was only a fashion, and it presently died out; but it did people good, because it made them understand, perhaps for the first time, that there really is a good deal more to see than meets the casual eye. At present the lesson which we need is not that the world is full of the most strange and wonderful creatures, all eating each other perpetually, but that the world is full of the most wonderful men and women, not one of whom is mean or common, but to each his own personality is a great and awful thing, worthy of the most serious study.

There are, then, abundant materials waiting to be picked up by any who has the wit to see them lying at his feet and all around him. What is next required is the power of Selection. Can this be taught? I think not, at least I do not know how, unless it is by reading. In every Art, selection requires that kind of special fitness for the Art which is included in the much abused word Genius. In Fiction the power of selection requires a large share of the dramatic sense. Those who already possess this faculty will not go wrong if they bear in mind the simple rule that nothing should be admitted which does not advance the story, illustrate the characters, bring into stronger relief the hidden forces which act upon them, their emotions, their passions, and their intentions. All descriptions which hinder instead of helping the action, all episodes of whatever kind, all conversation which does not either advance the story or illustrate the characters, ought to be rigidly suppressed.

Closely connected with selection is dramatic presentation. Given a situation, it should be the first care of the writer to present it as dramatically, that is to say as forcibly, as possible. The grouping and setting of the picture, the due subordination of description to dialogue, the rapidity of the action, those things which naturally suggest themselves to the practised eye, deserve to be very carefully considered by the beginner. In fact, a novel is like a play: it may be divided into scenes and acts, tableaus and situations, separated by the end of the chapter instead of the drop-scene: the writer is the dramatist, stage-manager, scene-painter, actor, and carpenter, all in one; it is his single business to see that none of the scenes flag or fall flat: he must never for one moment forget to consider how the piece is looking from the front.

The next simple Rule is that the drawing of each figure must be clear in outline, and, even if only sketched, must be sketched without hesitation. This can only be done when the writer himself sees his figures clearly. Characters in fiction do not, it must be understood, spring Minerva-like from the brain. They grow: they grow sometimes slowly, sometimes quickly. From the first moment of conception, that is to say, from the first moment of their being seen and caught, they grow continuously and almost without mental effort. If they do not grow and become every day clearer, they had better be put aside at once, forgotten as soon as may be, because that is a proof that the author does not understand the character he has himself endeavored to create. To have on one's hands a half-created being without the power of finishing him must be a truly dreadful thing. The only way out of it is to kill and bury him at once. I have always thought, for instance, that the figure of Daniel Deronda, whose portrait, blurred and uncertain as it is, has been drawn with the most amazing care and with endless touches and retouches, must have become at last to George Eliot a kind of awful veiled spectre, always in her brain, always seeming about to reveal his true features and his mind, but never doing it, so that to the end she never clearly perceived what manner of man he was, nor what was his real character. Of course, what the author cannot set down, the reader cannot understand. On the other hand, how possible, how capable of development, how real becomes a true figure, truly understood by the creator, and truly depicted! Do we not know what they would say and think under all conceivable conditions? We can dress them as we will; we can place them in any circumstances of life: we can always trust them because they will never fail us, never disappoint us, never change, because we understand them so thoroughly. So well do we know them that they become our advisers, our guides, and our best friends, on whom we model ourselves, our thoughts, and our actions. The writer who has succeeded in drawing to the life, true, clear, distinct, so that all may understand, a single figure of a true man or woman, has added another exemplar or warning to humanity. Nothing, then, it must be insisted upon as of the greatest importance, should be begun in writing until the characters are so clear and distinct in the brain, so well known, that they will act their parts, bend their dialogue, and suit their action to whatever situations they may find themselves in, if only they are becoming to them. Of course, clear outline drawing is best when it is accomplished in the fewest strokes, and the greater part of the figures in Fiction, wherein it differs from Painting, in which everything should be finished, require no more work upon them, in order to make them clear, than half-a-dozen bold, intelligible lines.

As for the methods of conveying a clear understanding of a character, they are many. The first and the easiest is to make it clear by reason of some mannerism or personal peculiarity, some trick of speech or carriage. This is the worst, as may generally be said of the easiest way. Another easy method is to describe your character at length. This also is bad, because a tedious, method. If, however, you read a page or two of any good writer, you will discover that he first makes a character intelligible by a few words, and then allows him to reveal himself in action and dialogue. On the other hand, nothing is more inartistic than to be constantly calling attention in a dialogue to a gesture or a look, to laughter or to tears. The situation generally requires no such explanation: in some well-known scenes which I could quote, there is not a single word to emphasize or explain the attitude, manner, and look of the speakers, yet they are as intelligible as if they were written down and described. That is the highest art which carries the reader along and makes him see, without being told, the changing expressions, the gestures of the speakers, and hear the varying tones of their voices. It is as if one should close one's eyes at the theatre, and yet continue to see the actors on the stage as well as hear their voices. The only writer who can do this is he who makes his characters intelligible from the very outset, causes them first to stand before the reader in clear outline, and then with every additional line brings out the figure, fills up the face, and makes his creatures grow from the simple outline more and more to the perfect and rounded figure.

Clearness of drawing, which includes clearness of vision, also assists in producing directness of purpose. As soon as the actors in the story become more real in the mind of the narrator, and not before, the story itself becomes real to him. More than this, he becomes straightway vehemently impelled to tell it, and he is moved to tell it in the best and most direct way, the most dramatic way, the most truthful way possible to him. It is, in fact, only when the writer believes his own story, and knows it to be every word true, and feels that he has somehow learned from everyone concerned the secret history of his own part in it, that he can really begin to write it.[3] We know how sometimes, even from a practised hand, there comes a work marred with the fatal defect that the writer does not believe in his own story. When this is the case, one may generally find on investigation that one cause at least of the failure is that the characters, or some of them, are blurred and uncertain.

Again, the modern English novel, whatever form it takes, almost always starts with a conscious moral purpose. When it does not, so much are we accustomed to expect it, that one feels as if there has been a debasement of the Art. It is, fortunately, not possible in this country for any man to defile and defame humanity and still be called an artist; the development of modern sympathy, the growing reverence for the individual, the ever-widening love of things beautiful and the appreciation of lives made beautiful by devotion and self-denial, the sense of personal responsibility among the English-speaking races, the deep-seated religion of our people, even in a time of doubt, are all forces which act strongly upon the artist as well as upon his readers, and lend to his work, whether he will or not, a moral purpose so clearly marked that it has become practically a law of English Fiction. We must acknowledge that this is a truly admirable thing, and a great cause for congratulation. At the same time, one may be permitted to think that the preaching novel is the least desirable of any, and to be unfeignedly rejoiced that the old religious novel, written in the interests of High Church or Low Church or any other Church, has gone out of fashion.

Next, just as in Painting and Sculpture, not only are fidelity, truth, and harmony to be observed in Fiction, but also beauty of workmanship. It is almost impossible to estimate too highly the value of careful workmanship, that is, of style. Everyone, without exception, of the great Masters in Fiction, has recognized this truth. You will hardly find a single page in any of them which is not carefully and even elaborately worked up. I think there is no point on which critics of novels should place greater importance than this, because it is one which young novelists are so very liable to ignore. There ought not to be in a novel, any more than in a poem, a single sentence carelessly worded, a single phrase which has not been considered. Consider, if you please, any one of the great scenes in Fiction—how much of the effort is due to the style, the balanced sentences, the very words used by the narrator! This, however, is only one more point of similarity between Fiction and the sister Arts. There is, I know, the danger of attaching too much attention to style at the expense of situation, and so falling a prey to priggishness, fashions, and mannerisms of the day. It is certainly a danger; at the same time, it sometimes seems, when one reads the slipshod, careless English which is often thought good enough for story-telling, that it is almost impossible to overrate the value of style. There is comfort in the thought that no reputation worth having can be made without attending to style, and that there is no style, however rugged, which cannot be made beautiful by attention and pains. "How many times," a writer once asked a girl who brought him her first effort for advice and criticism; "how many times have you re-written this page?" She confessed that she had written it once and for all, had never read it afterwards, and had not the least idea that there was such a thing as style. Is it not presumptuous in the highest degree to believe that what one has produced without pains, thought, or trouble will give any pleasure to the reader?

In fact every scene, however unimportant, should be completely and carefully finished. There should be no unfinished places, no sign anywhere of weariness or haste—in fact, no scamping. The writer must so love his work as to dwell tenderly on every age and be literally unable to send forth a single page of it without the finishing touches. We all of us remember that kind of novel in which every scene has the appearance of being hurried and scamped.

To sum up these few preliminary and general laws. The Art of Fiction requires first of all the power of description, truth, and fidelity, observation, selection, clearness of conception and of outline, dramatic grouping, directness of purpose, a profound belief on the part of the story-teller in the reality of his story, and beauty of workmanship. It is, moreover, an Art which requires of those who follow it seriously that they must be unceasingly occupied in studying the ways of mankind, the social laws, the religions, philosophies, tendencies, thoughts, prejudices, superstitions of men and women. They must consider as many of the forces which act upon classes and upon individuals as they can discover; they should be always trying to put themselves into the place of another; they must be as inquisitive and as watchful as a detective, as suspicious as a criminal lawyer, as eager for knowledge as a physicist, and withal fully possessed of that spirit to which nothing appears mean, nothing contemptible, nothing unworthy of study, which belongs to human nature.

I repeat that I submit some of these laws as perhaps self-evident. If that is so, many novels which are daily submitted to the reviewer are written in wilful neglect and disobedience of them. But they are not really self-evident; those who aspire to be artists in Fiction almost invariably begin without any understanding at all of these laws. Hence the lamentable early failures, the waste of good material, and the low level of Art with which both the novel-writer and the novel-reader are too often contented. I am certain that if these laws were better known and more generally studied, a very large proportion of the bad works of which our critics complain would not be produced at all. And I am in great hopes that one effect of the establishment of the newly founded Society of Authors will be to keep young writers of fiction from rushing too hastily into print, to help them to the right understanding of their Art and its principles, and to guide them into true practice of their principles while they are still young, their imaginations strong, and their personal experiences as yet not wasted in foolish failures.

After all these preliminary studies there comes the most important point of all—the story. There is a school which pretends that there is no need for a story: all the stories, they say, have been told already; there is no more room for invention: nobody wants any longer to listen to a story. One hears this kind of talk with the same wonder which one feels when a new monstrous fashion changes the beautiful figure of woman into something grotesque and unnatural. Men say these things gravely to each other, especially men who have no story to tell: other men listen gravely; in the same way women put on the newest and most preposterous fashions gravely, and look upon each other without either laughing or hiding their faces for shame. It is, indeed, if we think of it, a most strange and wonderful theory, that we should continue to care for Fiction and cease to care for the story. We have all along been training ourselves how to tell the story, and here is this new school which steps in, like the needy knife-grinder, to explain that there is no story left at all to tell. Why, the story is everything. I cannot conceive of a world going on at all without stories, and those strong ones, with incident in them, and merriment and pathos, laughter and tears, and the excitement of wondering what will happen next. Fortunately, these new theorists contradict themselves, because they find it impossible to write a novel which shall not contain a story, although it may but a puny bantling. Fiction without adventure—a drama without a plot—a novel without surprises—the thing is as impossible as life without uncertainty.[4]

As for the story, then. And here theory and teaching can go no farther. For every Art there is the corresponding science which may be taught. We have been speaking of the corresponding science. But the Art itself can neither be taught nor communicated. If the thing is in a man he will bring it out somehow, well or badly, quickly or slowly. If it is not, he can never learn it. Here, then, let us suppose that we have to do with the man to whom the invention of stories is part of his nature. We will also suppose that he has mastered the laws of his Art, and is now anxious to apply them. To such a man one can only recommend that he should with the greatest care and attention analyze and examine the construction of certain works, which are acknowledged to be of the first rank in fiction. Among them, not to speak of Scott, he might pay especial attention, from the constructive point of view, to the truly admirable shorter stories of Charles Reade, to George Eliot's "Silas Marner," the most *perfect* of English novels, Hawthorne's "Scarlet Letter," Holmes's "Elsie Venner," Blackmore's "Lorna Doone," or Black's "Daughter of Heth." He must not sit down to read them "for the story," as uncritical people say: he must read them slowly and carefully, perhaps backwards, so as to discover for himself how the author built up the novel, and from what original germ or conception it sprang. Let me take another novel by another writer to illustrate my meaning. It is James Payn's "Confidential Agent," a work showing, if I may be permitted to say so, constructive power of the very highest order. You have all, without doubt, read that story. As you know, it turns upon a diamond robbery. To the unpractised hand it would seem as if stories of theft had already been told *ad nauseam*. The man of experience knows better: he knows that in his hands every story becomes new, because he can place it upon the stage with new incidents, new conditions, and new actors. Accordingly, Payn connects his diamonds with three or four quite ordinary families: he does not search for strange and eccentric characters, but uses the folk he sees around him, plain middle-class people, to whom most of us belong. He does not try to show these people cleverer, better cultured, or in any respect at all other than they really are, except that some of them talk a little better than in real life they would be likely to do. That is to say, in dialogue he exercises the art of selection. Presently, in this quiet household of age and youth, love and happiness, there happens a dreadful thing: the young husband vanishes amid circumstances which give rise to the most horrible suspicions. How this event acts upon the minds of the household and their friends: how the faith, sorely tried, of one breaks down, and that of another remains steadfast: how the truth is gradually disclosed, and the innocence of the suspected man is made clear—all this should be carefully examined by the student as a lesson in construction and machinery. He will not, one hopes, neglect the other lesson taught him by this novel, which is the art of telling the story, selecting the actors, and skilfully using the plain and simply materials which lie around us everywhere ready to our hands. I am quite sure that the chief lesson to be learned form the study of nearly all our own modern novelists is that adventures, pathos, amusement, and interest, are far better sought among lives which seem dull, and among people who seem at first beyond the reach of romance, than from eccentricity and peculiarity of manner, or from violent and extreme reverses and accidents of fortune. This is, indeed, only another aspect of the increased value which we have learned to attach to individual life.

One thing more the Art student has to learn. Let him not only believe his own story before he begins to tell it, but let him remember that in story-telling, as in almsgiving, a cheerful countenance works wonders, and a hearty manner greatly helps the teller and pleases the listener. One would not have the novelist make continual efforts at being comic; but let him not tell his story with eyes full of sadness, a face of woe and a shaking voice. His story may be tragic, but continued gloom is a mistake in Art, even for a tragedy. If his story is a comedy, all the more reason to tell it cheerfully and brightly. Lastly, let him tell it without apparent effort: without trying to show his cleverness, his wit, his powers of epigram, and his learning. Yet let him pour without stint or measure into his work all that he knows, all that he has seen, all that he has observed, and all that he has remembered: all that there is of nobility, sympathy, and enthusiasm in himself. Let him spare nothing, but lavish all that he has, in the full confidence that the wells will not be dried up, and that the springs of fancy and imagination will flow again, even though he seem to have exhausted himself in this one effort.

Here, therefore, we may leave the student of this Art.[5] It remains for him to show whether he does wisely in following it farther. Of one thing for his encouragement he may rest assured; in the Art of Fiction more than in any other it is easy to gain recognition, far easier than in any of the sister Arts. In the English school of painting, for example, there are already so many good men in the field that it is most difficult to win an acknowledged position; in the drama it is next to impossible to get a play produced, in spite of our thirty London theatres; in poetry it seems almost hopeless to get a hearing, even if one has reached the second rank; but in Fiction the whole of the English-speaking race are always eager to welcome a newcomer; good work is instantly recognized, and the only danger is that the universal cry for more may lead to hasty and immature production. I do not mean that ready recognition will immediately bring with it a great pecuniary success. Unfortunately, there has grown up of late a bad fashion of measuring success too much by the money it seems to command. It is not always, remember, the voice of the people which elects the best man, and though in most cases it follows that a successful novelist commands a large sale of his works, it may happen that the Art of a great writer is of such a kind that it may never become widely popular. There have been among us two or three such writers. One case will immediately occur to most of us here. It is that of a man whose books are filled with wisdom, experience, and epigram: whose characters are most admirably studied from the life, whose plots are ingenious, situations fresh, and dialogues extraordinarily clever. Yet he has never been widely popular, and, I am sure, never will be. One may be pretty certain that this writer's money-value in the market is considerably less than that of many another whose genius is not half so great, but his popularity twice as large. So that a failure to hit the popular taste does not always imply a failure in Art. How, then, is one to know, when people do not ask for his work, if he has really failed or not? I think he must know without being told if he has failed to please. If a man sings a song he can tell in a moment, even before he has finished, if he has pleased his audience. So, if a man writes a novel, he can tell by the criticisms in the journals, by reading between the lines of what his friends tell him, by the expression of their eyes, by his own inner consciousness, if he has succeeded or failed. And if the latter, let him find out as quickly as may be through what causes. The unlucky dramatist can complain that his piece was badly mounted and badly acted. The novelist cannot, because he is sure not to be badly read. Therefore, if a novelist fail at first, let him be well assured that it is his own fault; and if, on his second attempt, he cannot amend, let him for the future be silent. One is more and more astonished at seeing the repeated efforts of writers whose friends should make them understand that they have not the least chance of success unless they unlearn all that they have learned and begin again upon entirely different methods and some knowledge of the science. It must be a cruel blow, after all the work that goes to make even a bad novel, after all the trouble of getting it published, to see it drop unnoticed, stillborn, thought hardly worthy to receive words of contempt. If the disappointment leads to examination and self-amendment, it may prove the greatest blessing. But he who fails twice probably deserves to fail, because he has learned nothing, and is incapable of learning anything, from the lessons of his first failure.

Let me say one word upon the present condition of this most delightful Art in England. Remember that the great Masters in every Art are rare. Perhaps one or two appear in a century: we ought not to expect more. It may even happen that those modern writers of our own whom we have agreed to call Masters will have to take lower rank among posterity, who will have great Masters of their own. I am inclined, however, to think that a few of the nineteenth-century novelists will never be suffered to die, though they may be remembered principally for one book—that Thackeray will be remembered for his "Vanity Fair," Dickens for "David Copperfield," George Meredith for the "Ordeal of Richard Feverel," George Eliot for "Silas Marner," Charles Reade for the "Cloister and the Hearth," and Blackmore for his "Lorna Doone." On the other hand, without thinking or troubling ourselves at all about the verdict of posterity, which matters nothing to us compared with the verdict of our contemporaries, let us acknowledge that it is a bad year indeed when we have not produced some good work, work of a very high kind, if not immortal work. An exhibition of the year's novels would generally show two or three, at least, of which the country may be, say, reasonably proud. Does the Royal Academy of Arts show every year more than two or three pictures—not immortal pictures, but pictures of which we may be reasonably proud? One would like, it is true, to see fewer bad novels published, as well as fewer bad pictures exhibited; the standard of the work which is on the borderland between success and failure should be higher. At the same time I am very sure and certain that there never has been a time when better works of Fiction have been produced, both by men and women. That Art is not declining, but is advancing, which is cultivated on true and not on false or conventional principles. Ought we not to be full of hope for the future, when such women as Mrs Oliphant and Mrs Thackeray Ritchie wrote for us—when such men as Meredith, Blackmore, Black, Payn, Wilkie Collins, and Hardy are still at their best, and such men as Louis Stevenson, Christie Murray, Clark Russell, and Herman Merivale have just begun? I think the fiction, and, indeed, all the imaginary work of the future will be far fuller in human interest than in the past; the old stories—no doubt they will still be the old stories—will be fitted to actors who up till recently were only used for the purposes of contrast; the drama of life which formerly was assigned to kings and princes will be played by figures taken as much from the great struggling, unknown masses. Kings and great lords are chiefly picturesque and interesting on account of their beautiful costumes, and a traditional belief in their power. Costume is certainly not a strong point in the lower ranks, but I think we shall not miss that, and wherever we go for our material, whether to the higher or the lower ranks, we may be sure of finding everywhere love, sacrifice, and devotion for virtues, with selfishness, cunning, and treachery for vices. Out of these, with their endless combinations and changes, that novelist must be poor indeed who cannot make a story.

Lastly, I said at the outset that I would ask you to accord to novelists the recognition of their place as artists. But after what has been said, I feel that to urge this further would be only a repetition of what has gone before. Therefore, though not all who write novels can reach the first, or even the second, rank, wherever you find good and faithful work, with truth, sympathy, and clearness of purpose, I pray you to give the author of that work the praise as to an Artist—an Artist like the rest—the praise that you so readily accord to the earnest student of any other Art. As for the great Masters of the Art—Fielding, Scott, Dickens, Thackeray, Victor Hugo—I, for one, feel irritated when the critics begin to appraise, compare, and to estimate them: there is nothing, I think, that we can give them but admiration that is unspeakable, and gratitude that is silent. This silence proves more eloquently than words how great, how beautiful an Art is that of Fiction.

Appendix.

I have been asked not to leave the young novelist at this point. Let me, therefore, venture upon a few words of advice. I do this without apology, because, like most men who write, I receive, every week, letters from young beginners asking for counsel and guidance. To all these I recommend the consideration of the rules I have laid down, and, above all, attention to truth, reality, and style.

I was once asked to read a MS. novel written by a young lady. The work was hurried, scamped, unreal—in fact, it had every fault. Yet there was something in it which made me think that there was hope for her. I therefore wrote to her, pointing out the faults, without sparing her. I added that, if she was not discouraged, but would begin again, and would prepare carefully the *scenario* of a novel, fitted with characters duly thought out, I would give her such further advice as was in my power. The *very next day* she sent me five *scenarios*. I have not heard from her since, and I hope she has renounced the Art whose very elements she could not understand.

Let me suppose, then, that the writer has got his novel completed. Here begins the "trouble," as the Americans say. And at this point my advice may be of use.

Remember that all publishers are eager to get good work: they are prepared to consider MSS. carefully—most of them pay men, on whose judgment they rely, men of literary standing, to read and "taste" for them; therefore it is a simple and obvious piece of advice that the writer should send his work to some good publisher, and it is perfectly certain that if the work is good it will be accepted and published. There is, as I have said in the lecture, little or no risk, even with an unknown author, over a really good novel. But, then, the first work almost always contains immaturities and errors which prevent it from being really good. More often than not, it is on the border line, not so good as to make publication desirable by a firm which will only issue good work, or by any means safe to pay its expenses. What then? I would advise the author never, from any considerations of vanity or self-confidence, to pay money to a publisher for bringing out his book. There are certain publishing houses, not the best, which bring out yearly quantities of novels, nearly every one of which is paid for by the author, because they are not good enough to pay their own expenses. Do not, I would say, swell the ranks of those who give the enemy reason to blaspheme this Art. Refuse absolutely to publish on such ignominious terms. Remember that to be asked for money to pay for the expense of publication is to be told that your work is not good enough to be published. If you have tried the half-dozen best publishers, and been refused by all, realize that the work *will not do*. Then, if you can, get the advice of some experienced man of letters upon it, and ponder over his judgment.

If you cannot, reconsider the whole story from the beginning, with special reference to the rules which are here laid down. If necessary, rewrite the whole. Or, if necessary, put the whole into the fire, and, without being disheartened, begin again with another and a better story. Do not aim at producing an absolutely new plot. You cannot do it. But persevere, if you feel that the root of the matter is in you, till your work is accepted; and *never*, never, never pay for publishing a novel.

Let me end with a little piece of personal history.

A good many years ago, there was a young man of four or five and twenty, who ardently desired before all things to become a novelist. He spent a couple of years, giving to the work all his unemployed hours, over a novel of modern life. He took immense pains with it, rewrote some of the scenes half a dozen times, and spared neither labor nor thought to make it as good as he could make it. When he really felt that he could do nothing more with it, he rolled it up and sent it to a friend with the request that he would place it anonymously in Mr Macmillan's hands. Mr Macmillan had it carefully read, and sent the author, still through the friend, his reader's opinion. The reader did not sign his opinion, but he was a Cambridge man, a critic of judgment, a man of taste, a kindly man, and he had once been, if he was not still, a mathematician. These things were clearly evident from his handwriting, as well as from the wording of his verdict. This was to the effect that the novel should not be published, for certain reasons which he proceeded to give. But he laid down his objections with very great consideration for the writer, indicating for his encouragement what he considered points of promise, suggesting certain practical rules of construction which had been violated, and showing where ignorance of the Art and inexperience of life had caused faults such as to make it most undesirable for the author, as well as impossible for a publisher of standing, to produce the work. The writer, after the first pangs of disappointment, plucked up heart and began to ponder over the lessons contained in that opinion. The young man has since become a novelist, "of a sort," and he takes this opportunity of returning his most sincere thanks to Mr Macmillan for his kindness in considering and refusing to publish an immature novel, and to his anonymous critic for his invaluable letter. Would that all publishers' readers were like unto that reader, as conscientious and as kindly, and as anxious to save beginners from putting forth bad work!

Notes

1. It has been objected to this Rule that, if followed, it would entirely shut out the historical novel. Not at all. The interest of the historical novel, as of any other novel, depends upon the experience and knowledge which the writer has of humanity, men and women being pretty much alike in all ages. It is not the setting that we regard, so much as the acting of the characters. The setting in an historical novel is very often absurd, incorrect, and incongruous; but the human interest, the skill and knowledge of character shown by the writer, may make us forget the errors of the setting. For instance, *Romola* is undoubtedly a great novel, not because it contains a true, and therefore valuable, reproduction of Florentine life in the time of the early Renaissance, for it does not; nor because it gives us the ideas of the age, for it does not; the characters, especially that of the heroine, being fully of nineteenth century ideas: but it is great as a study of character. On the other hand, in *The Cloister and the Hearth*, we do really have a description of the time and its ideas, taken bodily, sometimes almost literally, from the pages of the man who most truly represents them—Erasmus. So that here is a rule for the historical novelist—when he must describe, he must borrow. If it be objected, again, that he may do the same thing with contemporary life, I reply that he may, if he please, but he will *most assuredly be found out* through some blunder, omission, or confusion caused by ignorance. No doubt the same blunders are perpetrated by the historical novelist; but these are not so readily found out except by an archæologist. Of course, one who desires to reproduce a time gone by would not go to the poets, the divines, the historians, so much as to the familiar literature, the letters, comedies, tales, essayists, and newspapers.

2. I earnestly recommend those who desire to study this Art to begin by daily practice in the description of things, even common things, that they have observed, by reporting conversations, and by word portraits of their friends. They will find that the practice gives them firmness of outline, quickness of observation, power of catching important details, and, as regards dialogue, readiness to see what is unimportant. Preliminary practice and study of this kind will also lead to the saving of a vast quantity of valuable material, which is only wasted by being prematurely worked up into a novel written before the elements of the Art have been acquired.

3. Hardly anything is more important than this—to believe in your own story. Wherefore let the student remember that unless the characters exist and move about in his brain, all

separate, distinct, living, and perpetually engaged in the action of the story, sometimes at one part of it, sometimes at another, and that in scenes and places which must be omitted in the writing, he has got no story to tell and had better give it up. I do not think it is generally understood that there are thousands of scenes which belong to the story and never get outside the writer's brain at all. Some of these may be very beautiful and touching; but there is not room for all, and the writer has to select.

4. A correspondent asks me if I do not like the work of Mr Howells. Of course one cannot choose but like his writing. But one cannot also avoid comparing his work with that of his countryman, Nathaniel Hawthorne, who added to the charm of style the interest of a romantic and exciting story.

5. See Appendix.

68

Letter to G. P. Baker

GEORGE MEREDITH

Poet, journalist and novelist George Meredith (1828-1909) was a friend of Pre-Raphaelite painters and writers Rossetti and Swinburne. Throughout his long writing career he published such novels as *The Ordeal of Richard Feverel* (1859), *The Egoist* (1879) and *Diana of the Crossways* (1885). In the following letter he responds to a reviewer of his works by outlining his goals as a novelist. He notes that though he does not commence his novels with a set moral or theory, he aims to explore and expose characters "under stress of a fiery situation". While his comedies often employ an inflated rhetorical style, he allows the reality of human nature to dominate many of his portrayals of character.

To G. P. Baker.
Box Hill, Dorking,
England, July 22, 1887.

My dear Sir,—When at the conclusion of your article on my works, you say that a certain change in public taste, should it come about, will be to some extent due to me, you hand me the flowering wreath I covet. For I think that all right use of life, and the one secret of life, is to pave ways for the firmer footing of those who succeed us; as to my works, I know them faulty, think them of worth only when they point and aid to that end. Close knowledge of our fellows, discernment of the laws of existence, these lead to great civilization. I have supposed that the novel, exposing and illustrating the natural history of man, may help us to such sustaining roadside gifts. But I have never started on a novel to pursue the theory it developed. The dominant idea in my mind took up the characters and the story midway.

You say that there are few scenes. Is it so throughout? My method has been to prepare my readers for a crucial exhibition of the personae, and then to give the scene in the fullest of their blood and brain under stress of a fiery situation.

Source: George Meredith, Letter to G. P. Baker, 22 July 1887, in *Letters of George Meredith*, vol. 2, 1882-1909, London: Constable & Co. Ltd., 1912, pp. 398-99.

Concerning style, thought is tough, and dealing with thought produces toughness. Or when strong emotion is in tide against the active mind, there is perforce confusion. Have you found that scenes of simple emotion or plain narrative were hard to view? When their author revised for the new edition, his critical judgment approved these passages. Yet you are not to imagine that he holds his opinion combatively against his critics. The verdict is with the observer.

In the Comedies, and here and there where a concentrated presentment is in design, you will find a 'pitch' considerably above our common human; and purposely, for only in such a manner could so much be shown. Those high notes and condensings are abandoned when the strong human call is heard—I beg you to understand merely that such was my intention.

Again, when you tell me that Harvard has the works, and that Young Harvard reads them, the news if of a kind to prompt me to fresh productiveness and higher. In England I am encouraged but by a few enthusiasts. I read in a critical review of some verses of mine the other day that I was a 'harlequin and a performer of antics.' I am accustomed to that kind of writing, as our hustings orator is to the dead cat and the brickbat flung in his face—at which he smiles politely; and I too; but after many years of it my mind looks elsewhere. Adieu to you.—Most faithfully yours,

George Meredith.

Thomas Hardy by Olive Edis, 1914.
By courtesty of the National Portrait Gallery, London.

The Profitable Reading of Fiction

THOMAS HARDY

As his title indicates, in this essay Hardy is concerned with the impact of ficiton on the reader and the nature of the reader's response. He praises narratives that offer "a lesson life, mental enlargement from elements essential to the narratives themselves and from the reflections they engender" (60), as opposed to novels with purely didactic intentions. As in "The Science of Fiction" (see Chapter 64), Hardy distinguishes truth of character and action from scientifically observed reality, noting that art is often truer than history. Like Virginia Woolf's later criticism in "Modern Fiction" of the materialist authors, Hardy accuses the naturalists of substituting minute details for essence. In the second half of the essay he focuses on the necessity of organic form in an author's construction of the story. Finally, Hardy appeals to the reader's sense of discrimination to judge internal truth form outward pretense. His faith in his readers' judgements was to be irrevocably shattered with the charges of immorality his last novel, *Jude the Obscure*, elicited.

When the editor of this review courteously offered me space in his pages to formulate a few general notions upon the subject of novel reading, considered with a view to mental profit, I could not help being struck with the timelessness of the theme; for in these days the demand for novels has risen so high, in proportion to that for other kinds of literature, as to attract the attention of all persons interested in education. But I was by no means persuaded that one whose own writings have largely consisted in books of this class was in a position to say anything on the matter, even if he might be supposed to have anything to say. The field, however, is so wide and varied that there is plenty of room for impersonal points of regard; and I may as well premise that the remarks which follow, where not exclusively suggested by a consideration of the works of dead authors, are mere generalizations from a cursory survey, and no detailed analysis, of those of to-day.

Source: Thomas Hardy, "The Profitable Reading of Fiction", *The Forum*, New York, March 1888, rptd Greenberg Publisher, 1925, pp. 56-74.

If we speak of deriving good from a story, we usually mean something more than the gain of pleasure during the hours of its perusal. Nevertheless, to get pleasure out of a book is a beneficial and profitable thing, if the pleasure be a kind which, while doing no moral injury, affords relaxation and relief when the mind is overstrained or sick of itself. The prime remedy in such cases is change of scene, by which change of the material scene is not necessarily implied. A sudden shifting of the mental perspective into a fictitious world, combined with rest, is well known to be often as efficacious for renovation as a corporeal journey afar.

In such a case the shifting of scene should manifestly be as complete as if the reader had taken the hind seat on a witch's broomstick. The town man finds what he seeks in novels of the country, the countryman in novels of society, the indoor class generally in outdoor novels, the villager in novels of the mansion, the aristocrat in novels of the cottage.

The narrative must be of a somewhat absorbing kind, if not absolutely fascinating. To discover a book or books which shall possess, in addition to the special scenery, the special action required, may be a matter of some difficulty, though not always of such difficulty as to be insuperable; and it may be asserted that after every variety of spiritual fatigue there is to be found refreshment, if not restoration, in some antithetic realm of ideas which lies waiting in the pages of romance.

In reading for such hygienic purposes it is, of course, of the first consequence that the reader be not too critical. In other words, his author should be swallowed whole, like any other alterative pill. He should be believed in slavishly, implicitly. However profusely he may pour out his coincidences, his marvelous juxtapositions, his catastrophes, his conversions of bad people into good people at a stroke, and *vice versa*, let him never be doubted for a moment. When he exhibits people going out of their way and spending their money on purpose to act consistently, or taking a great deal of trouble to move in a curious and roundabout manner when a plain, straight course lies open to them; when he shows that heroes are never faithless in love, and that the unheroic always are so, there should arise a conviction that this is precisely according to personal experience. Let the invalid reverse the attitude of a certain class of critics—now happily becoming less numerous—who only allow themselves to be interested in a novel by the defeat of every attempt to the contrary. The aim should be the exercise of a generous imaginativeness, which shall find in a tale not only all that was put there by the author, put he it never so awkwardly, but which shall find there what was never inserted by him, never foreseen, never contemplated. Sometimes these additions which are woven around a work of fiction by the intensive power of the reader's own imagination are the finest parts of the scenery.

It is not altogether necessary to this tonic purpose that the stories chosen should be "of most disastrous chances, of moving accidents by flood and field." As stated above, the aim should be contrast. Directly the circumstances begin to resemble those of the reader, a personal connection, an interest other than an imaginative one, is set up, which results in an intellectual stir that is not in the present case to be desired.

It sets his serious thoughts at work, and he does not want them stimulated just now; he wants to dream.

So much may be said initially upon alleviating the effects of over-work and carking care by a course of imaginative reading. But I will assume that benefit of this sort is not that which is primarily contemplated when we speak of getting good out of novels, but intellectual or moral profit to active and undulled spirits.

It is obvious that choice in this case, though more limited than in the former, is by no means limited to compositions which touch the highest level in the essential constituents of a novel—those without which it would be no novel at all—the plot and the characters. Not only may the book be read for these main features—the presentation, as they may collectively be called—but for the accidents and appendages of narrative; and such are of more kinds than one. Excursions into various philosophies, which vary or delay narrative proper, may have more attraction than the regular course of the enactment; the judicious inquirer may be on the look-out for didactic reflection, such as is found in large lumps in 'Rasselas'; he may be a picker-up of trifles of useful knowledge, statistics, queer historic fact, such as sometimes occur in the pages of Hugo; he may search for specimens of the manners of good or bad society, such as are to be obtained from the fashionable writers; or he may even wish to brush up his knowledge of quotations from ancient and other authors by studying some chapters of *Pelham* and the disquisitions of Parson Adams in *Joseph Andrews*.

Many of the works which abound in appurtenances of this or a kindred sort are excellent as narrative, excellent as portraiture, even if in spite rather than in consequence of their presence. But they are the exception. Directly we descend from the highest levels we find that the majority are not effectual in their ostensible undertaking, that of giving us a picture of life in action; they exhibit a machinery which often works awkwardly, and at the instigation of unlikely beings. Yet, being packed with thoughts of some solidity, or more probably sprinkled with smart observations on men and society, they may be read with advantage even by the critical, who, for what they bring, can forgive the audible working of the wheels and wires and carpentry, heard behind the performance, as the wires and trackers of a badly constructed organ are heard under its tones.

Novels of the latter class—formerly more numerous than now—are the product of cleverness rather than of intuition; and in taking them up—bearing in mind that profit, and not amusement, is the student's aim—his manifest course is to escape from the personages and their deeds, gathering the author's wit or wisdom nearly as it would have presented itself if he had cast his thoughts in the shape of an essay.

But though we are bound to consider by-motives like these for reading fiction as praiseworthy enough where practicable, they are by their nature of an illegitimate character, more or less, and apart from the ruling interest of the genuine investigator of this department of literature. Such ingredients can be had elsewhere in more convenient parcels. Our true object is a lesson in life, mental enlargement form elements essential to the narratives themselves and from the reflections they engender.

Among the qualities which appertain to representations of life, construed, though not distorted, by the light of imagination—qualities which are seldom shared by views *about* life, however profound—is that of self-proof or obviousness. A representation is less susceptible of error than a disquisition; the teaching, depending as it does upon intuitive conviction, and not upon logical reasoning, is not likely to lend itself to sophistry. If endowed with ordinary intelligence, the reader can discern, in delineative art professing to be natural, any stroke greatly at variance with nature, which, in the form of moral essay, *pensée*, or epigram, may be so wrapped up as to escape him.

Good fiction may be defined here as that kind of imaginative writing which lies nearest to the epic, dramatic, or narrative masterpieces of the past. One fact is certain: in fiction there can be no intrinsically new thing at this stage of the world's history. New methods and plans may arise and come into fashion, as we see them do; but the general theme can neither be changed, nor (what is less obvious) can the relative importance of its various particulars be greatly interfered with. The higher passions must ever rank above the inferior—intellectual tendencies above animal, and moral above intellectual—whatever the treatment, realistic or ideal. Any system of inversion which should attach more importance to the delineation of man's appetites than to the delineation of his aspirations, affections, or humors, would condemn the old masters of imaginative creation from Æschylus to Shakespeare. Whether we hold the arts which depict mankind to be, in the words of Mr. Matthew Arnold, a criticism of life, or, in those of Mr. Addington Symonds, a revelation of life, the material remains the same, with its sublimities, its beauties, its uglinesses, as the case may be. The finer manifestations must precede in importance the meaner, without such a radical change in human nature as we can hardly conceive as pertaining to an even remote future of decline, and certainly do not recognize now.

In pursuance of his quest for a true exhibition of man, the reader will naturally consider whether he feels himself under the guidance of a mind who sees further into life than he himself has seen; or, at least, who can throw a stronger irradiation over subjects already within his ken that he has been able to do unaided. The new light needs not to be set off by a finish of phraseology or incisive sentences of subtle definition. The treatment may be baldly incidental, without inference or commentary. Many elaborate reflections, for example, have been composed by moralizing chroniclers on the effect of prosperity in blunting men's recollection of those to whom they have sworn friendship when they shared a hard lot in common. But the writer in Genesis who tells his legend of certain friends in such adverse circumstances, one of whom, a chief butler, afterward came to good fortune, and ends the account of this good fortune with the simple words, "Now the chief butler did not remember Joseph, but forgat him," brings out a dramatic sequence on ground prepared for an assent, shows us the general principle in the particular case, and hence writes with a force beyond that of aphorism or argument. It is the force of an appeal to the emotional reason rather than to the logical reason; for by their emotions men are acted upon, and act upon others.

If it be true, as is frequently asserted, that young people nowadays go to novels for their sentiments, their religion, and their morals, the question as to the wisdom or folly of those young people hangs upon their methods of acquisition in each case. A deduction from what these works exemplify by action that bears evidence of being a counterpart of life, has a distinct educational value; but an imitation of what may be called the philosophy of the personages—the doctrines of the actors, as shown in their conversation—may lead to surprising results. They should be informed that a writer whose story is not a tract in disguise has as his main object that of characterizing the people of his little world. A philosophy which appears between the inverted commas of a dialogue may, with propriety, be as full of holes as a sieve if the person or persons who advance it gain any reality of humanity thereby.

These considerations only bring us back again to the vital question how to discriminate the best in fiction. Unfortunately the two hundred years or so of the modern novel's development have not left the world so full of fine examples as to make it particularly easy to light upon them when the first obvious list has been run through. The, at first-sight, high-piled granary sifts down to a very small measure of genuine corn. The conclusion cannot be resisted, notwithstanding what has been stated to the contrary in so many places, that the scarcity of perfect novels in any language is because the art of writing them is as yet in its youth, if not in its infancy. Narrative art is neither mature in its artistic aspect, nor in its ethical or philosophical aspect; neither in form nor in substance. To me, at least, the difficulties of perfect presentation in both these kinds appear of such magnitude that the utmost which each generation can be expected to do is to add one or two strokes toward the selection and shaping of a possible ultimate perfection.

In this scarcity of excellence in novels as wholes the reader must content himself with excellence in parts; and his estimate of the degree to which any given modern instance approximates to greatness will, of course, depend not only upon the proportion that the finer characteristics bear to the mass, but upon the figure cut by those finer characteristics beside those of the admitted masterpieces as yet. In this process he will go with the professed critic so far as to inquire whether the story forms a regular structure of incident, accompanied by an equally regular development of character—a composition based on faithful imagination, less the transcript than the similitude of material fact. But the appreciative, perspicacious reader will do more than this. He will see what his author is aiming at, and by affording full scope to his own insight, catch the vision which the writer has in his eye, and is endeavoring to project upon the paper, even while it half eludes him.

He will almost invariably discover that, however numerous the writer's excellencies, he is what is called unequal; he has a specialty. This especial gift being discovered, he fixes his regard more particularly thereupon. It is frequently not that feature in an author's work which common repute has given him credit for; more often it is, while co-existent with his popular attribute, overshadowed by it lurking like a violet in the shade of the more obvious, possibly more vulgar, talent, but for which it might have received high attention. Behind the broad humor of one popular pen he discerns startling touches of weirdness; amid the colossal fancies of an other he sees strokes of the most exquisite tenderness; and the unobtrusive quality may grow to have more charm for him than the palpable one.

It must always be borne in mind, despite the claims of realism, that the best fiction, like the highest artistic expression in other modes, is more true, so to put it, than history or nature can be. In history occur from time to time monstrosities of human action and character explicable by no known law which appertains to sane beings; hitches in the machinery of existence, wherein we have not yet discovered a principle, which the artist is therefore bound to regard as accidents, hinderances to clearness of presentation, and hence, weakeners of the effect. To take an example from sculpture: no real gladiator ever died in such perfect harmony with normal nature as is represented in the well-known Capitoline marble. There was always a jar somewhere , a jot or tittle of something foreign in the real death-scene, which did not essentially appertain to the situation, and tended toward neutralizing its pathos; but this the sculptor omitted, and so consecrated his theme. In drama likewise. Observe the characters of any sterling play. No dozen persons who were capable of being animated by the profound reasons and truths thrown broadcast over *Hamlet* or *Othello*, of feeling the pulse of life so accurately, ever met together in one place in this world to shape an end. And, to come to fiction, nobody ever met an Uncle Toby who was Uncle Toby all round; no historian's Queen Elizabeth was ever so perfectly a woman as the fictitious Elizabeth of *Kenilworth*. What is called the idealization of characters is, in truth, the making of them too real to be possible.

It may seem something of a paradox to assert that the novels which most conduce to moral profit are likely to be among those written without a moral purpose. But the truth of the statement may be realized if we consider that the didactic novel is so generally devoid of *vraisemblance* as to teach nothing but the impossibility of tampering with natural truth to advance dogmatic opinions. Those, on the other hand, which impress the reader with the inevitableness of character and environment in working out destiny, whether that destiny be just or unjust, enviable or cruel, must have a sound effect, if not what is called a good effect, upon a healthy mind.

Of the effects of such sincere presentation on weak minds, when the courses of the characters are not exemplary, and the rewards and punishments ill adjusted to deserts, it is not our duty to consider too closely. A novel which does moral injury to a dozen imbeciles, and has bracing results upon a thousand intellects of normal vigor, can justify its existence; and probably a novel was never written by the purest-minded author for which there could not be found some invalid or other whom it was capable of harming.

To distinguish truths which are temporary from truths which are eternal, the accidental from the essential, accuracies as to custom and ceremony from accuracies as to the perennial procedure of humanity, is of vital importance in our attempts to read for something more than amusement. There are certain novels, both among the works of living and the works of deceased writers, which give convincing proof of much exceptional fidelity, and yet they do not rank as great productions; for what they are faithful in is life garniture and not life. You are fully persuaded that the personages are clothed precisely as you see them clothed in the street, in the drawing-room, at the assembly. Even the trifling accidents of their costume are rendered by the honest narrator. They use the phrases of the season, present or past, with absolute accuracy as to idiom, expletive, slang. They lift their tea-cups or fan themselves to date. But what of it, after our first sense of its photographic curiousness is past? In aiming at the trivial and the ephemeral they have almost surely missed better things. A living French critic goes even further concerning the novelists of social minutiae. "They are far removed," says he, "from the great imaginations which create and transform. They renounce free invention; they narrow themselves to scrupulous exactness; they paint clothes and places with endless detail."

But we must not, as inquiring readers, fail to understand that attention to accessories has its virtues when the nature of its regard does not involve blindness to higher things; still more when it conduces to the elucidation of higher things. The writer who describes his type of a jeweled leader of society by saying baldly how much her diamonds cost at So-and-So's, what the largest of them weighed and measured, how it was cut and set, the particular style in which she wore her hair, cannot convey much profit to any class of readers save two—those bent on making a purchase of the like ornaments or of adorning themselves in the same fashion; and, a century hence, those who are studying the costumes and expenditure of the period. But, supposing the subject to be the same, let the writer be one who takes less of a broker's view of his heroine and her adornments; he may be worth listening to, though his simplicity be quite child-like. It is immaterial that our example is in verse:

> Be you not proud of that rich hair
> Which wantons with the love-sick air;
> Whenas that ruby which you wear,
> Sunk from the tip of your soft ear,
> Will last to be a precious stone
> When all your world of beauty's gone.–Herrick.

And thus we are led to the conclusion that, in respect of our present object, our concern is less with the subject treated than with its treatment. There have been writers of fiction, as of poetry, who can gather grapes of thorns and figs of thistles.

Closely connected with the humanizing education found in fictitious narrative which reaches to the level of an illuminant of life, is the æsthetic training insensibly given by familiarity with story which, presenting nothing exceptional in other respects, has the merit of being well and artistically constructed. To profit of this kind, from this especial source, very little attention has hitherto been paid, though volumes have been written upon the development of the æsthetic sense by the study of painting and sculpture, and thus adding to the means of enjoyment. Probably few of the general body denominated the reading public consider, in their hurried perusal of novel after novel, that, to a masterpiece in story there appertains a beauty of shape, no less than to a masterpiece in pictorial or plastic art, capable of giving to the trained mind an equal pleasure. To recognize this quality clearly when present, the construction of the plot, or fable, as it used to be called, is to be more particularly observed than either in a reading for sentiments and opinions, or in a reading merely to discover the fates of the chief characters. For however real the persons, however profound, witty, or humorous the observations, as soon as the book comes to be regarded as an exemplification of the art of story-telling, the story naturally takes the first place, and the example is not noteworthy as such unless the telling be artistically carried on.

The distinguishing feature of a well rounded tale has been defined in various ways, but the general reader need not be burdened with many definitions. Briefly, a story should be an organism. To use the words applied to the epic by Addison, whose artistic feeling in this kind was of the subtlest, "nothing should go before it, be intermixed with it, or follow after it, that is not related to it." Tested by such consideration as these there are obviously many volumes of fiction remarkable, and even great, in their character-drawing, their feeling, their philosophy, which are quite second-rate in their structural quality as narratives. Instances will occur to every one's mind; but instead of dwelling upon these it is more interesting to name some which most nearly fulfill the conditions. Their fewness is remarkable, and bears out the opinion expressed earlier in this essay, that the art of novel-writing is as yet in its tentative stage only. Among them *Tom Jones* is usually pointed out as a near approach to perfection in this as in some other characteristics; though, speaking for myself, I do not perceive its great superiority in artistic form over some other novels of lower reputation. *The Bride of Lammermoor* is an almost perfect specimen of form, which is the more remarkable in that Scott, as a rule, depends more upon episode, dialogue, and description, for exciting interest, than upon the well-knit interdependence of parts. And the first thirty chapters of *Vanity Fair* may be instanced as well-nigh complete in artistic presentation, along with their other magnificent qualities.

Herein lies Richardson's real if only claim to be placed on a level with Fielding: the artist spirit that he everywhere displays in the structural parts of his work and in the interaction of the personages, notably those of *Clarissa Harlowe*. However cold, even artificial, we may, at times, deem the heroine and her companions in the pages of that excellent tale, however numerous the twitches of unreality in their movements across the scene beside those in the figures animated by Fielding, we feel, nevertheless, that we are under the guidance of a hand which has consummate skill in evolving a graceful, well-balanced set of conjectures, forming altogether one of those circumstantial wholes which, when approached by events in real life, cause the observer to pause and reflect, and say, "What a striking history!" We should look generously upon his deficiency in the robuster touches of nature, for it is the deficiency of an author whose artistic sense of form was developed at the expense of his accuracy of observation as regards substance. No person who has a due perception of the constructive art shown in Greek tragic drama can be blind to the constructive art of Richardson.

I have dwelt the more particularly upon this species of excellence, not because I consider it to rank in quality beside truth of feeling and action, but because it is one which so few nonprofessional readers enjoy and appreciate without some kind of preliminary direction. It is usually the latest to be discerned by the novel consumer, and it is often never discerned by him or her at all. Every intelligent reader with a little experience of life can perceive truth to nature in some degree; but a great reduction must be made for those who can trace in narrative the quality which makes Apollo and the Aphrodite a charm in marble. Thoughtful readers are continually met with who have no intuition that such an attribute can be claimed by fiction, except in so far as it is included in style.

The indefinite word style may be made to express almost any characteristic of story-telling other than subject and plot, and it is too commonly viewed as being some independent, extraneous virtue or varnish with which the substance of a narrative is artificially overlaid. Style, as far as the word is meant to express something more than literary finish, can only be treatment, and treatment depends upon the mental attitude of the novelist; thus entering into the very substance of a narrative, as into that of any other kind of literature. A writer who is not a mere imitator looks upon the world with his personal eyes, and in his peculiar moods; thence grows up his style, in the full sense of the term.

> Cui lecta potenter erit res,
> Nec facundia deseret hunc, nec lucidus ordo.[1]

Those who would profit from the study of style should formulate an opinion of what it consists in by the aid of their own educated understanding, their perception of natural fitness, true and high feeling, sincerity, unhampered by considerations of nice collocation and balance of sentences, still less by conventionally accepted examples. They will make the discovery that certain names have, by some accident or other, grown to be regarded as of high, if not of supreme merit in the catalogue of exemplars, which have no essential claims, in this respect, to be rated higher than hundreds of the rank and file of literature who are never mentioned by critic or considered by reader in that connection. An author who has once acquired a reputation for style may write English down to the depths of slovenliness if he choose, without losing his character as a master; and this probably because, as before observed, the quality of style is so vague and inapprehensible as a distinct ingredient that it may always be supposed to be something else than what the reader perceives to be indifferent.

Considerations as to the rank or station in life from which characters are drawn can have but little value in regulating the choice of novels for literary reasons, and the reader may thus leave much to the mood of the moment. I remember reading a lecture on novels by a young and ingenious, though not very profound, critic, some years ago, in which the theory was propounded that novels which depict life in the upper walks of society must, in the nature of things, be better reading than those which exhibit the life of any lower class, for the reason that the subjects of the former represent a higher stage of development than their less fortunate brethren. At the first blush this was a plausible theory; but when practically tested it is found to be based on such a totally erroneous conception of what a novel is, and where it comes from, as not to be worth a moment's consideration. It proceeds from the assumption that a novel is the thing, and not a view of the thing. It forgets that the characters, however they may differ, express mainly the author, his largeness of heart or otherwise, his culture, his insight, and very little of any other living person, except in such an inferior kind of procedure as might occasionally be applied to dialogue, and would take the narrative out of the category of fiction: *i.e.*, verbatim reporting without selective judgment.

But there is another reason, disconnected entirely from methods of construction, why the physical condition of the characters rules nothing of itself one way or the other. All persons who have thoughtfully compared class with class—and the wider their experience the more pronounced their opinion—are convinced that education has as yet but little broken or modified the waves of human impulse on which deeds and words depend. So that in the portraiture of scenes in any way emotional or dramatic—the highest province of fiction—the peer and the peasant stand on much the same level; the woman who makes the satin train and the woman who wears it. In the lapse of countless ages, no doubt, improved systems of moral education will considerably and appreciably elevate even the involuntary instincts of human nature; but at present culture has only affected the surface of those lives with which it has come in contact, binding down the passions of those predisposed to turmoil as by a silken thread only, which the first ebullition suffices to break. With regard to what may be termed the minor key of action and speech—the unemotional, every-day doings of men—social refinement operates upon character in a way which is oftener than not prejudicial to vigorous portraiture, by making the exteriors of men their screen rather than their index, as with untutored mankind. Contrasts are disguised by the crust of conventionality, picturesqueness obliterated, and a subjective system of description necessitated for the differentiation of character. In the one case the author's word has to be taken as to the nerves and muscles of his figures; in the other they can be seen as in an *écorché*.

The foregoing are a few imperfect indications how, to the best of my judgment, to discriminate fiction which will be the most desirable reading for the average man or woman of leisure, who does not wish the occupation to be wholly barren of results except in so far as it may administer to the pleasure of the hour. But, as with the horse and the stream in the proverb, no outside power can compel or even help a reader to gain good from such reading unless he has some natural eye for the finer qualities in the best productions of this class. It is unfortunately quite possible to read the most elevating works of imagination in our own or any language, and, by fixing the regard on the wrong sides of the subject, to gather not a grain of wisdom from them, nay, sometimes positive harm. What author has not had his experience of such readers?—the mentally and morally warped ones of both sexes, who will, where practicable, so twist plain and obvious meanings as to see in an honest picture of human nature an attack on religion, morals, or institutions. Truly has it been observed that 'the eye sees that which it brings with it the means of seeing.'

Note

1. Horace, "De Arte Poetica," 40.

The Decay of Lying: a Dialogue

OSCAR WILDE

Irish-born writer Oscar Wilde (1854-1900), though perhaps best known for his notorious behaviour, wrote one short novel, *The Picture of Dorian Gray* (1891), a series of essays and a number of plays, the most famous of which is *The Importance of Being Earnest* (1895). In the following polemical essay, disguised as a Socratic dialogue, Wilde's persona Vivian denigrates realism in art and laments its effects on an increasingly Philistine late nineteenth-century English culture. After a scathing criticism of British and French realism, especially the novels of Zola, Wilde praises Balzac for his ability to create, not copy, life. In his conclusion, Wilde offers three doctrines of his new aesthetics: 1)Art must express only itself without reference to life; 2) bad art results from attempting first to copy and then elevate nature; 3) life imitates art, not the reverse. In these three principles, Wilde effectively dismantles the nineteenth-century realist agenda that urged the novelist to represent a faithful picture of life. His novel, *The Picture of Dorian Gray*, reveals in the initial portrait of the eternally youthful Dorian the lie that Wilde claims art should embody: "the telling of beautiful untrue things".

SCENE.—*The Library of a Country House in England.*
PERSONS.—CYRIL *and* VIVIAN.

Cyril (*coming in through the open window from the terrace*). My dear Vivian, don't coop yourself up all day in the library. It is a perfectly lovely afternoon. Let us go and lie on the grass and smoke cigarettes and enjoy nature.

Vivian. Enjoy nature! I am glad to say that I have entirely lost that faculty. People tell us that art makes us love nature more than we loved her before; that it reveals her secrets to us; and that after a careful study of Corot and Constable we see things in her that had escaped us. My own experience is that the more we study art, the less we care for nature. What art really reveals to us is nature's lack of design, her curious crudities, her extraordinary monotony, her absolutely unfinished

Source: Oscar Wilde, "The Decay of Lying: a Dialogue", *Nineteenth Century*, 25, 143, January 1889, pp. 35-56.

condition. When I look at a landscape I cannot help seeing all its defects. It is fortunate for us, however, that nature is so imperfect, as otherwise we should have had no art at all. Art is our spirited protest, our gallant attempt to teach Nature her proper place. As for the infinite variety of Nature, that is a pure myth. It is not to be found in Nature herself, but in the imagination, or fancy, or cultivated blindness, of the man who looks at her.

C. Well, you need not look at the landscape. You can lie on the grass and smoke and talk.

V. But nature is so uncomfortable. Grass is hard and lumpy and damp, and full of horrid little black insects. Why, even Maple can make you a more comfortable seat than nature can. Nature pales before the Tottenham Court Road. I don't complain. If nature had been comfortable, mankind would never have invented architecture, and I prefer houses to the open air. In a house we all feel of the proper proportions. Everything is subordinated to us, fashioned for our use and our pleasure. Egotism itself, which is so necessary to a proper sense of human dignity, is absolutely the result of indoor life. Out of doors one becomes abstract and impersonal. One's individuality absolutely leaves one. And then nature is so indifferent, so unappreciative. Whenever I am walking in the park here, I always feel that I am not more to nature than the cattle that browse on the slope, or the burdock that blooms in the ditch. Nothing is clearer than that Nature hates Mind. Thinking is the most unhealthy thing in the world, and people die of it just as of any other disease. Fortunately, in England at least, it is not catching. Our splendid physique as a people is entirely due to our national stupidity. I only hope we shall be able to keep this great historic bulwark of our happiness for many years to come; but I am afraid that we are beginning to be over-educated; at least everybody who is incapable of learning has taken to teaching—that is really what our enthusiasm for education has come to. In the meantime you had better go back to your wearisome uncomfortable Nature, and leave me to correct my proofs.

C. Writing an article! That is not very consistent after what you have just said.

V. Who wants to be consistent? The dullard and the doctrinaire, the tedious people who carry out their principles to the bitter end of action, to the *reductio ad absurdum* of practice? Not I. Like Emerson, I write over the door of my library the word "Whim." Besides, my article is really a most salutary and valuable warning. If it is attended to, there may be a new Renaissance of Art.

C. What is the subject?

V. I intend to call it "The Decay of Lying: A Protest."

C. Lying! I should have thought our politicians kept up that habit.

V. I assure you they do not. They never rise beyond the level of misrepresentation, and actually condescend to prove, to discuss, to argue. How different from the temper of the true liar, with his frank, fearless statements, his superb irresponsibility, his healthy, natural disdain of proof of any kind! After all, what is a fine lie? Simply that which is its own evidence. If a man is sufficiently unimaginative to produce evidence in support of a lie, he might just as well speak the truth at once. No, the politicians won't do, and besides, what I am pleading for is lying in art. Shall I read you what I have written? It might do you a great deal of good.

C. Certainly, if you give me a cigarette. Thanks. By the way, what magazine do you intend it for?

V. For the *Retrospective Review*. I think I told you that we had revived it.

C. Whom do you mean by "we"?

V. Oh, the Tired Hedonists of course. It is a club to which I belong. We are supposed to wear faded roses in our button-holes when we meet, and to have a sort of cult for Domitian. I am afraid you are not eligible. You are too fond of simple pleasures.

C. I should be black-balled on the ground of animal spirits, I suppose?

V. Probably. Besides, you are a little too old. We don't admit anyone who is of the usual age.

C. Well, I should fancy you are all a good deal bored with each other.

V. We are. That is one of the objects of the club. Now, if you promise not to interrupt too often, I will read you my article.

C. (*flinging himself down on the sofa*). All right.

V. (*reading in a very clear, musical voice*). 'The Decay of Lying: a Protest.—One of the chief causes of the curiously commonplace character of most of the literature of our age is undoubtedly the decay of lying as an art, a science, and a social pleasure. The ancient historians gave us delightful fiction in the form of fact; the modern novelist presents us with dull facts under the guise of fiction. The blue-book is rapidly becoming his ideal both for method and manner. He has his tedious "*document humain*," his miserable little "*coin de la création*," into which he peers with his microscope. He is to be found at the Librairie Nationale, or at the British Museum, shamelessly reading up his subject. He has not even the courage of other people's ideas, but insists on going directly to life for everything, and ultimately, between encyclopædias and personal experience, he comes to the ground, having drawn his types from the family circle or from the weekly washerwoman, and having acquired an amount of useful information from which he never, even in his most thoughtful moments, can thoroughly free himself.

The loss that results to literature in general from this false ideal of our time can hardly be overestimated. People have a careless way of talking about a "born liar," just as they talk about a "born poet." But in both cases they are wrong. Lying and poetry are arts—arts, as Plato saw, not unconnected with each other—and they require the most careful study, the most disinterested devotion. Indeed, they have their technique, just as the more material arts of painting and sculpture have, their subtle secrets of form and colour, their craft-mysteries, their deliberate artistic methods. As one knows the poet by his fine music, so one can recognise the liar by his rich utterance, and in neither case will the casual inspiration of the moment suffice. Here, as elsewhere, practice must precede perfection. But in modern days while the fashion of writing poetry has become far too common, and should, if possible, be discouraged, the fashion of lying has almost fallen into disrepute. Many a young man starts in life with a natural gift for exaggeration which, if nurtured in congenial and sympathetic surroundings, or by the imitation of the best models, might grow into something really great and wonderful. But, as a rule, he comes to nothing. He either falls into careless habits of accuracy—

C. My dear Vivian!

V. Please don't interrupt in the middle of a sentence. 'He either falls into careless habits of accuracy, or takes to frequenting the society of the aged and the well-informed. Both things are equally fatal to his imagination, as indeed they would be fatal to the imagination of anybody, and in a short time he develops a morbid and unhealthy faculty of truth-telling, begins to verify all statements made in his presence, has no hesitation in contradicting people who are younger than himself, and often ends by writing novels which are so like life that no one can possibly believe them. This is no isolated instance that we are giving. It is simply one example out of many; and if something cannot be done to check, or at least to modify, our monstrous worship of facts, art will become sterile, and beauty will pass away from the land.

'Even Mr Robert Louis Stevenson, that delightful master of delicate and fanciful prose, is tainted with this modern vice, for we positively know no other name for it. There is such a thing as robbing a story of its reality by trying to make it too true, and *The Black Arrow* is so inartistic that it does not contain a single anachronism to boast of, while the transformation of Dr Jekyll reads dangerously like an experiment out of the *Lancet*. As for Mr Rider Haggard, who really has, or once had, the makings of a perfectly magnificent liar, he is now so afraid of being suspected of genius that when he does tell us anything marvellous, he feels bound to invent a personal reminiscence, and to put it into a footnote as a kind of cowardly corroboration. Nor are our other novelists much better. Mr Henry James writes fiction as if it was a painful duty, and wasted upon mean motives and imperceptible "points of view" his neat literary style, his felicitous phrases, his swift and caustic satire. Mrs Oliphant prattles pleasantly about curates, lawn-tennis parties, domesticity, and other wearisome things. Mr Marion Crawford has immolated himself upon the altar of local colour. He is like the lady in the French comedy who is always talking about "le beau ciel d'Italie." Besides, he has fallen into a bad habit of uttering moral platitudes. At times he is almost edifying. *Robert Elsmere* is of course a masterpiece—a masterpiece of the "genre ennuyeux", the one form of literature that the English people seem to thoroughly enjoy. Indeed it is only in England that such a novel could be possible. As for that great and daily increasing school of novelists for whom the sun always rises in the East-End, the only thing that can be said about them is that they find life crude, and leave it raw.

'In France, though nothing so deliberately tedious as *Robert Elsmere* has been produced, things are not much better. M. Guy de Maupassant, with his keen mordant irony and his hard vivid style, strips life of the few poor rags that still cover her, and shows us foul sore and festering wound. He writes lurid little tragedies in which everybody is ridiculous; bitter comedies at which one cannot laugh for very tears. M. Zola, true to the lofty principle that he lays down in one of his pronunciamientos on literature, "L'homme de génie n'a jamais de l'esprit," is determined to show that, if he has not got genius, he can at least be dull. And how well he succeeds! He is not without power. Indeed at times, as in *Germinal*, there is something almost epic in his work. But his work is entirely wrong from beginning to end, and wrong not on the ground of morals but on the ground of art. From any ethical standpoint his work is just what it should be. He is perfectly truthful, and describes things exactly as they happen. What more can any moralist desire? I have no sympathy at all with the moral indignation of our time against M. Zola. It is simply the rage of Caliban on seeing his own face in a glass. But from the standpoint of art, what can be said in favour of the author of *L'Assommoir, Nana,* and *Pot-Bouille*? Nothing. M. Ruskin once described the characters in George Eliot's novels as being like the sweepings of a Pentonville omnibus, but M. Zola's characters are much worse. They have their dreary vices, and their drearier virtues. The record of their lives is absolutely without interest. Who cares what happens to them? In literature we require distinction, charm, beauty, and imaginative power. We don't want to be harrowed and disgusted with an account of the doings of the lower orders. M. Daudet is better. He has *esprit*, a light touch, and an amusing style. But he has lately committed literary suicide. Nobody can possibly care for Delobelle with his "Il faut lutter pour l'art," or for Valmajour with his eternal refrain about the nightingale, or for the poet in *Jack* with his "mots cruels," now that we have learned from *Vingt Ans de ma Vie littéraire* that these characters were taken directly from life. To me they seem to have suddenly lost all their vitality, all the few qualities they ever possessed. The only real people are the people who never existed, and if a novelist is base enough to go to life for his personages he should at least pretend that they are creations and not boast of them as copies. As for M. Paul Bourget, the master of the *roman psychologique*, he commits the error of imagining that the men and women of modern life are capable of being infinitely analysed for an innumerable series of chapters. In point of fact what is interesting about people in good society—and M. Bourget never moves out of the Faubourg—is the mask that each one of them wears, not the reality that lies behind the mask. It is a humiliating confession, but we are all of us made out of the same stuff. In Falstaff there is something of Hamlet, in Hamlet there is not a little of Falstaff. The fat knight has his moods of melancholy, and the young prince his moments of coarse humour. Where we differ from each other is purely in accidentals: in dress, in manner, tone of voice, personal appearance, tricks of habit, and the like. The more one analyses people, the more all reasons for analysis disappear. Sooner or later one comes to that dreadful universal thing called human nature. Indeed, as anyone who has ever worked among the poor knows only too well, the brotherhood of man is no mere poet's dream, it is a terrible reality; and if a writer insists upon analysing the upper classes he might just as well write of match-girls and costermongers at once.' However, my dear Cyril, I will not detain you any further on this point. I quite admit that modern novels have many good points. All is say is that, as a class, they are quite unreadable.

C. That is certainly a very grave qualification, but I must say that I think you are rather unfair in some of your strictures. I like *Robert Elsmere* for instance. Not that I look upon it as a serious work. As a statement of the problems that confront the earnest Christian it is ridiculous and antiquated. It is simply Arnold's *Literature and*

Dogma with the literature left out. it is as much behind the age as Paley's *Evidences*, or Colenso's method of Biblical exegesis. Nor could anything be less impressive than the unfortunate hero gravely heralding a dawn that rose long ago, and so completely missing its true significance that he proposes to carry on the business of the old firm under the new name. On the other hand, it contains several clever caricatures, and a heap of delightful quotations, and Green's philosophy very pleasantly sugars the somewhat bitter pill of the author's fiction. I also cannot help expressing my surprise that you have said nothing about the two novelists whom you are always reading, Balzac and George Meredith. Surely they are realists, both of them?

V. Ah! Meredith! Who can define him? His style is chaos illumined by flashes of lightning. As a writer he has mastered everything, except language: as a novelist he can do everything, except tell a story: as an artist he is everything, except articulate. Somebody in Shakespeare—Touchstone, I think—talks about a man who is always breaking his shins over his own wit, and it seems to me that this might serve as the basis of a criticism of Meredith's style. But whatever he is, he is not a realist. Or rather I would say that he is a child of realism who is not on speaking terms with his father. By deliberate choice he has made himself a romanticist. He has refused to bow the knee to Baal, and after all, even if the man's fine spirit did not revolt against the noisy assertions of realism, his style would be quite sufficient of itself to keep life at a respectful distance. By its means he has planted round his garden a hedge full of thorns, and with some wonderful roses. As for Balzac, he was a most remarkable combination of the artistic temperament with the scientific spirit. The latter he bequeathed to his disciples: the former was entirely his own. The difference between such a book as M. Zola's *L'Assommoir* and Balzac's *Illusions Perdues* is the difference between unimaginative realism and imaginative reality. "All Balzac's characters," said Baudelaire, "are gifted with the same ardour of life that animated himself. All his fictions are as deeply coloured as dreams. Each mind is a weapon loaded to the muzzle with will. The very scullions have genius." A steady course of Balzac reduces our living friends to shadows, and our acquaintances to the shadows of shades. His characters have a kind of fervent fiery-coloured existence. They dominate us and defy scepticism. One of the greatest tragedies of my life is the death of Lucien de Rubempré. It is a grief from which I have never been able to completely rid myself. But Balzac is no more a realist than Holbein was. He created life, he did not copy it. I admit, however, that he set far too high a value on modernity of form, and that, consequently, there is no book of his that, as an artistic masterpiece, can rank with *Salammbô*, or *Esmond*, or *The Cloister and the Hearth*, or the *Vicomte de Bragelonne*.

C. Do you object to modernity of form then?

V. Yes. It is a huge price to pay for a very poor result. Pure modernity of form is always somewhat vulgarising. It cannot help being so. The public imagine that, because they are interested in their immediate surroundings, art should be interested in them also, and should take them as her subject-matter. But the mere fact that they are interested in these things makes them unsuitable subjects for art. The only beautiful things, as somebody once said, are the things that do not concern us. As long as a thing is useful necessary to us, or affects us in any way, either for pain or for pleasure, or appeals strongly to our sympathies, or is a vital part of the environment in which we live, it is outside the proper sphere of art. To art's subject-matter we should be more or less indifferent. We should, at any rate, have no preferences, no prejudices, no partisan feeling of any kind. It is exactly because Hecuba is nothing to us that her sorrows are such an admirable motive for a tragedy. I do not know anything in the whole history of literature sadder than the artistic career of Charles Reade. He wrote one beautiful book, *The Cloister and the Hearth*, a book as much above *Romola* as *Romola* is above *Daniel Deronda*, and wasted the rest of his life in a foolish attempt to be modern, to draw public attention to the state of our convict prisons and the management of private lunatic asylums. Charles Dickens was depressing enough in all conscience when he tried to arouse our sympathy for the victims of the poor-law administration; but Charles Reade, an artist, a scholar, a man with a true sense of beauty, raging and roaring over the abuses of modern life like a common pamphleteer or a sensational journalist, is really a sight for the angels to weep over. Believe me, my dear Cyril, modernity of form and modernity of subject-matter are entirely and absolutely wrong. We have mistaken the common livery of the age for the vesture of the Muses, and spend our days in the sordid streets and hideous suburbs of our vile cities when we should be out on the hillside with Apollo. Certainly we are a degraded race, and have sold our birthright for a mess of facts.

C. There is something in what you say, and there is no doubt that whatever amusement we may find in reading an absolutely modern novel, we have rarely any artistic pleasure in re-reading it. And this is perhaps the best rough test of what is literature and what is not. If one cannot enjoy a book over and over again, there is no good reading it at all. But what do you say about the return to Life and Nature? This is the panacea that is always being recommended to us.

V. (*taking up his proofs*). I will read you what I say on that subject. The passage comes later on in the article, but I may as well read it now:—

'The popular cry of our time is "Let us return to Life and Nature; they will recreate Art for us, and send the red blood coursing through her veins; they will give her feet swiftness and make her hand strong." But alas! we are mistaken in our amiable and well-meaning efforts. Nature is always behind the age; and as for Life, she is the solvent that breaks up Art, the enemy that lays waste her house.'

C. What do you mean by saying that nature is always behind the age?

V. Well, perhaps that is rather obscure. What I mean is this. If we take nature to mean natural simple instinct as opposed to self-conscious culture, the work produced under this influence is always old-fashioned, antiquated, and out of date. If, on the other hand, we regard nature as the collection of phenomena external to man, people only discover in her what they bring to her. She has no suggestions of her own. Wordsworth went to the lakes, but he was never a lake poet. He found in stones the sermons he had already hidden there. He went moralising about the district, but his good work was produced when he returned, not to nature but to poetry. Poetry gave him "Laodamia," and the fine sonnets, and the "Ode to

Immortality," and nature gave him "Martha Ray" and "Peter Bell."

C. I think that view might be questioned. I am rather inclined to believe in the "impulse from a vernal wood," though of course the artistic value of such an impulse depends entirely on the kind of temperament that receives it. However, proceed with your article.

V. (*reading*). 'Art begins with abstract decoration, with purely imaginative and pleasurable work dealing with what is unreal and non-existent. This is the first stage. Then Life becomes fascinated with this new wonder, and asks to be admitted into the charmed circle. Art takes Life as part of her rough material, recreates it, and refashions it in fresh forms, is absolutely indifferent to fact, invents, imagines, dreams, and keeps between herself and reality the impenetrable barrier of beautiful style, of decorative or ideal treatment. The third stage is when Life gets the upper hand, and drives Art out into the wilderness. This is the decadence, and it is from this that we are now suffering.

'Take the case of the English drama. At first in the hands of the monks dramatic art was abstract, decorative, and mythological. Then she enlisted life in her service, and using some of life's external forms, she created an entirely new race of beings, whose sorrows were more terrible than any sorrow man has ever felt, whose joys were keener than lover's joys, who had the rage of the Titans and the calm of the gods, who had monstrous and marvellous sins, monstrous and marvellous virtues. To them she gave a language different from that of actual life, a language full of resonant music and sweet rhythm, made stately by solemn cadence, or made delicate by fanciful rhyme, jewelled with wonderful words, and enriched with lofty diction. She clothed her children in strange raiment and gave them masks, and at her bidding the antique world rose from its marble tomb. A new Cæsar stalked through the streets of risen Rome, and with purple sail and flute-led oars another Cleopatra passed up the river to Antioch. Old myth and legend and dream took form and substance. History was entirely rewritten, and there was hardly one of the dramatists who did not recognise that *the object of art is not simple truth but complex beauty*. In this they were perfectly right. Art herself is simply a form of exaggeration; and selection, which is the very spirit of art, is nothing more than an intensified mode of over-emphasis.

'But life soon shattered the perfection of the form. Even in Shakespeare we can see the beginning of the end. It shows itself by the gradual breaking up of blank verse in the later plays, by the predominance given to prose, and by the over-importance assigned to characterisation. The passages in Shakespeare—and they are many—where the language is uncouth, vulgar, exaggerated, fantastic, obscene even, are due entirely to life calling for an echo of its own voice, and rejecting the intervention of beautiful style, through which alone it should be allowed to find expression. Shakespeare is not by any means a flawless artist. He is too fond of going directly to life, and borrowing life's natural utterance. He forgets that when *art surrenders her imaginative medium she surrenders everything*. Goethe says somewhere—

In der Beschränkung zeigt sich erst der Meister,

"It is in working within limits that the master reveals himself," and the limitation, the very condition, of any art is style. However, we will not linger any longer over Shakespeare's realism. 'The *Tempest* is the best of palinodes. All that we desired to point out was, that the magnificent work of the Elizabethan and Jacobean artists contained within itself the seeds of its own dissolution, and that if it drew some of its strength from using life as rough material, it drew all its weakness from using life as an artistic method. As the inevitable result of this substitution of an imitative for a creative medium, this surrender of an imaginative form, we have the modern English melodrama. The characters in these plays talk on the stage exactly as they would talk off it; they are taken directly from life and reproduce its vulgarity down to the smallest detail; they have the gait, manner, costume, and accent of real people; they would pass unnoticed in a third-class railway carriage. And yet how wearisome the plays are! They do not succeed in producing even that impression of reality at which they aim, and which is their only reason for existing. As a method realism is a complete failure.

'What is true about the drama and the novel is no less true about those arts that we call the decorative arts. The whole history of decorative art in Europe is the record of the struggle between Orientalism, with its frank rejection of imitation, its love of artistic convention, its dislike to the actual representation of any object in nature, and our own imitative spirit. Wherever the former has been paramount, as in Byzantium, Sicily, and Spain, by actual contact, or in the rest of Europe by the influence of the Crusades, we have had beautiful and imaginative work in which the visible things of life are transmuted into artistic conventions, and the things that life has not are invented and fashioned for her. But wherever we have returned to life and nature, our work has always become vulgar, common and uninteresting. Modern tapestry, with its aerial effects, its elaborate perspective, its broad expanses of waste sky, its faithful and laborious realism, has no beauty whatsoever. The pictorial glass of Germany is absolutely detestable. We are beginning to weave possible carpets in England, but only because we have returned to the method and spirit of the East. Our rugs and carpets of twenty years ago, with their healthy national feeling, their inane worship of nature, their sordid reproductions of visible objects, have become, even to the Philistine, a source of laughter. A cultured Mahomedan once remarked to me, 'You Christians are so occupied in misinterpreting the fourth commandment that you have never thought of making an artistic application of the second.' He was perfectly right, and the whole truth of the matter is this: *the proper school to learn art in is not Life but Art.*'

And now let me read you a passage which deals with the commonplace character of our literature:—

'It was not always thus. We need not say anything about the poets, for they, with the unfortunate exception of Mr Wordsworth, have always been faithful to their high mission, and are universally recognised as being absolutely unreliable. But in the works of Herodotus, who, in spite of the shallow and ungenerous attempts of modern sciolists to verify his history, may be justly called the "Father of Lies;" in the published speeches of Cicero and the biographies of Suetonius; in Tacitus at his best; in Pliny's *Natural History*; in Hanno's *Periplus*; in all the early chronicles; in the Lives of the Saints; in Froissart and Sir Thomas Mallory; in the travels of Marco Polo; in Olaus Magnus, and Aldrovandus, and Conrad Lycosthenes, with his magnificent *Prodigiorum et Ostentorum Chronicon*; in the autobiography of Benvenuto Cellini; in the memoirs of Casanuova; in Defoe's *History of the Plague*; in Boswell's *Life of Johnson*; in Napoleon's despatches, and in the works of our own Carlyle, whose *French Revolution* is one of the most fascinating historical romances ever written, facts are either kept in their subordinate position, or else entirely excluded on the general ground of dulness. Now everything is changed. Facts are not merely finding a footing in history, but they are usurping the domain of Fancy, and have invaded the kingdom of Romance. Their chilling touch is over everything. They are vulgarising mankind. The crude commercialism of America, its materialising spirit, its indifference to the poetical side of things, and its lack of imagination and of high, unattainable ideals, are entirely due to that country having adopted for its national hero, a man, who according to his own confession, was incapable of telling a lie, and it is not too much to say that the story of George Washington and the cherry-tree has done more harm, and in a shorter space of time, than any other moral tale in the whole of literature.'

C. My dear boy!

V. I assure you it is quite true, and the amusing part of the whole thing is that the story of the cherry-tree is an absolute myth. However, you must not think that I am too despondent about the artistic future of America or of our own country. Listen to this:—

'That some change will take place before this century has drawn to its close, we have no doubt whatsoever. Bored by the tedious and improving conversation of those who have neither the wit to exaggerate nor the genius to romance, tired of the intelligent person whose reminiscences are always based upon memory, whose statements are invariably limited by probability, and who is at any time liable to be corroborated by the merest Philistine who happens to be present, society sooner or later must return to its lost leader, the cultured and fascinating liar. Who he was who first, without ever having gone out to the rude chase, told the wondering cavemen at sunset how he had dragged the Megatherium from the purple darkness of its jasper cave, or slain the Mammoth in single combat and brought back its gilded tusks, we cannot tell, and not one of our modern anthropologists, with all their much-debated science, has had the ordinary courage to tell us. Whatever was his name or race, he was certainly the founder of social intercourse. For the aim of the liar is simply to charm, to delight, to give pleasure. He is the very basis of civilised society, and without him a dinner party, even at the mansions of the great, is as dull as a lecture at the Royal Society or a debate at the Incorporated Authors.

'Nor will he be welcomed merely by society. Art, breaking from the prison-house of realism, will run to greet him and will kiss his false, beautiful lips, knowing that he alone is in possession of the great secret of all her manifestations, the secret that truth is entirely and absolutely a matter of style. While Life—poor, probable, uninteresting human life—tired of repeating herself for the benefit of Mr Herbert Spencer, scientific historians, and the compilers of statistics in general, will follow meekly after him, and try to reproduce, in her own simple and untutored way, some of the marvels of which he talks.

'No doubt there will always be critics who, like a recent writer in the *Saturday Review*, will gravely censure the teller of fairy tales for his defective lack of knowledge of natural history, who will measure imaginative work by their own lack of any imaginative faculty, and who will hold up their inkstained hands in horror if some honest gentleman, who has never been farther than the yew trees of his own garden, pens a fascinating book of travels like Sir John Mandeville, or, like great Raleigh, writes a whole history of the world, in prison, and without knowing anything about the past. To excuse themselves they will try and shelter under the shield of him who made Prospero the magician, and gave him Caliban and Ariel as his servants, who heard the Tritons blowing their horns round the coral-reefs of the Enchanted Isle and the fairies singing to each other in a wood near Athens, who led the phantom kings in dim procession across the misty Scottish heath, and hid Hecate in a cave with the weird sisters. They will call upon Shakespeare—they always do—and will quote that hackneyed passage about Art holding up the mirror to Nature, forgetting that this unfortunate aphorism is deliberately said by Hamlet in order to convince the bystanders of his absolute insanity in art-matters.'

C. Ahem! Ahem! Another cigarette, please.

V. My dear fellow, whatever you may say, it is merely a dramatic utterance, and no more represents Shakespeare's real views upon art then the speeches of Iago represent his real views upon morals. But let me get to the end of the passage:—

'Art finds her own perfection within, and not outside, herself. She is not judged by any external standard of resemblance. She is a veil, rather than a mirror. She has flowers that no botanist knows of, birds that no museum possesses. She makes and unmakes many worlds, and can draw the moon from heaven with a scarlet thread. Hers are the "forms more real than living man," and hers the great archetypes of which things that have existence are but unfinished copies. Nature has, in her eyes, no laws, no uniformity. She can work miracles at her will, and when she calls monsters from the deep they come. She can bid the almond tree blossom in winter, and send the snow upon the ripe cornfield. At her word the frost lays its silver finger on the burning month of June, and the winged lions creep out from the hollows of the Lydian hills. The dryads peer from the thicket as she passes by, and the brown fauns smile strangely at her when she comes near them. She has hawk-faced gods that worship her, and the centaurs gallop at her side.'

C. Is that the end of the dangerous article?

V. No. There is one more passage, but it is purely practical. It simply suggests some methods by which we could revive this lost art of lying.

C. Well, before you read me that, I should like to ask you a question. What do you mean by saying that life, "poor, probable, uninteresting human life," will try to reproduce the marvels of art? I can quite understand your objection to art being treated as a mirror. You think it would reduce genius to the position of a cracked looking-glass. But you don't mean to say that you seriously believe that life imitates art, that life in fact is the mirror, and art the reality?

V. Certainly I do. Paradox though it may seem—and paradoxes are always dangerous things—it is none the less true that *life imitates art far more than art imitates life*. We have all seen in our own day in England how a certain curious and fascinating type of beauty, invented and emphasised by two imaginative painters, has so influenced life that whenever one goes to a private view or to an artistic salon one sees here the mystic eyes of Rossetti's dream, the long ivory throat, the strange square-cut jaw, the loosened shadowy hair that he so ardently loved, there the sweet maidenhood of "The Golden Stair," the blossom-like mouth and weary loveliness of the "Laus Amoris," the passion-pale face of Andromeda, the thin hands and lithe beauty of the Vivien in "Merlin's Dream." And it has always been so. A great artist invents a type, and Life tries to copy it, to reproduce it in a popular form, like an enterprising publisher. Neither Holbein nor Vandyck found in England what they have given us. They brought their types with them, and Life with her keen imitative faculty set herself to supply the master with the models. The Greeks, with their quick artistic instinct, understood this, and set in the bride's chamber the statue of Hermes or Apollo, that she might bear children like the works of art that she looked at. They knew that life gains from art not merely spiritually, depth of thought and passion, soul-turmoil or soul-peace, but that she can form herself on the very lines and colours of art, and can reproduce the dignity of Pheidias as well as the grace of Praxiteles. Hence came their objection to realism. They disliked it on purely social grounds. They felt that it inevitably makes people ugly, and they were perfectly right. We try to improve the conditions of the race by means of good air, sunlight, wholesome water, and hideous bare buildings for the better housing of the people. But these things merely produce health, they do not produce beauty. For this art is required, and the true disciples of the great artist are not his studio-imitators, but those who become like his works of art, be they plastic as in Greek days, or pictorial as in modern times: in fact, Life is Art's best, Art's only pupil.

As it is with the visible arts, so it is with literature. The most obvious and the vulgarest form in which this is shown is in the case of the silly boys who, after reading the adventures of Jack Sheppard or Dick Turpin, pillage the stalls of unfortunate apple-women, break into sweet-shops at night, and alarm old gentlemen who are returning from the city by leaping out on them, with black masks and loaded revolvers. This interesting phenomenon, which always occurs after the appearance of a new edition of either of the books I have named, is usually attributed to the influence of literature on the imagination. But this is a mistake. The imagination is essentially creative and always seeks for a new form. The boy-burglar is simply the inevitable result of life's imitative instinct. He is Fact, occupied, as Fact usually is, with trying to reproduce Fiction, and what we see in him is repeated on an extended scale through the whole of life. Schopenhauer has analysed the pessimism that characterises modern thought, but Hamlet invented it. The world has become sad because a puppet was once melancholy. The Nihilist, that strange martyr who has no faith, who goes to the stake without enthusiasm, and dies for what he does not believe in, is a purely literary product. He was invented by Tourgénieff, and completed by Dostoieffski. Robespierre came out of the pages of Rousseau, as surely as the People's Palace rose out of the *débris* of a novel. Literature always anticipates life. It does not copy it, but moulds it to its purpose. The nineteenth century, as we know it, is largely an invention of Balzac. Our Luciens de Rubempré, our Rastignacs, and De Marsays made their first appearance in the *Comédie Humaine*. We are merely carrying out, with footnotes and unnecessary additions, the whim or fancy of a great novelist. I once asked a lady, who knew Thackeray intimately, whether he had had any model for Becky Sharp. She told me that Becky was an invention, but that the idea of the character had been partly suggested by a governess who lived in the neighbourhood of Kensington Square, and was the companion of a very selfish and rich old woman. I inquired what became of the governess, and she replied that, oddly enough, some years after the appearance of *Vanity Fair*, the governess ran away with the nephew of the lady with whom she was living, and for a short time made a great splash in society, quite in Mrs Rawdon Crawley's style, and entirely by Mrs Rawdon Crawley's methods. Ultimately she came to grief, disappeared to the Continent, and used to be occasionally seen at Monte Carlo and other gambling places. The noble gentleman from whom the same great sentimentalist drew Colonel Newcome died a few months after *The Newcomes* had reached a fourth edition, with the word 'Adsum' on his lips. Shortly after Mr Stevenson published his curious psychological story of transformation, a friend of mine, called Mr Hyde, was in the north of London, and being anxious to get to a railway station, he took what he thought was a short cut, lost his way, and found himself in a network of mean, evil-looking streets. Feeling rather nervous he was walking extremely fast, when suddenly out of an archway ran a child right between his legs. The child fell on the pavement, he tripped over it, and trampled upon it. Being of course very much frightened and not a little hurt, it began to scream, and in a few seconds the whole street was full of rough people who kept pouring out of the houses like ants. They surrounded him, and asked him his name. He was just about to give it when he suddenly remembered the opening incident in Mr Stevenson's story. He was so filled with horror at having realised in his own person that terrible scene, and at having done accidentally what the Mr Hyde of fiction had done with deliberate intent, that he ran away as hard as he could go. He was, however, very closely followed, and he finally took refuge in a surgery, the door of which happened to be open, where he explained to a young man, apparently an assistant, who happened to be there, exactly what had occurred. The crown was induced to go away on his giving them a small sum of money, and as soon as the coast was clear he left. As he passed out, the name of the surgery caught his eye. It was 'Jekyll.'

Here the imitation was of course accidental. In the following case the imitation was self-conscious. In the year 1879, just after I had left Oxford, I met at a reception at the house of one of the Foreign Ministers a lady who interested me very much, not merely in appearance, but in nature. What interested me most in her was her strange vagueness of character. She seemed to have no personality at all, but simply the possibility of many types. Sometimes she would give herself up entirely to art, turn her drawing-room into a studio, and spend two or three days a week at picture-galleries or museums. Then she would take to attending race-meetings, would wear the most horsey clothes, and talk about nothing but betting. She was a kind of Proteus, and as much a failure in all her transformations as the sea-god was when Odysseus got hold of him. One day a serial began in one of the French magazines. At that time I used to read serial stories, and I well remember the shock of surprise I felt when I came to the description of the heroine. She was so like my friend that I brought her the magazine, and she recognised herself in it immediately, and seemed fascinated by the resemblance. I should tell you, by the way, that the story was translated from the Russian, so the author had not taken his type from my friend. Well, to put the matter briefly, some months afterwards I was in Venice, and finding the magazine in the reading-room of the hotel, I took it up to see what had become of the heroine. It was a most piteous tale, as the heroine had ended by running away with a man inferior to her, not merely in social station, but in nature and intellect also. I wrote to my friend that evening, and added a postscript to the effect that her double had behaved in a very silly manner. I don't know why I wrote, but I remember I had a sort of dread over me that she might do the same thing. Before my letter had reached her, she had run away with a man who deserted her in six months. I saw her in 1884 in Paris, where she was living with her mother, and I asked her whether the story had anything to do with her action. She told me that she had felt an absolutely irresistible impulse to follow the heroine step by step in her strange and fatal progress, and that it was with a feeling of real terror that she had looked forward to the last few chapters of the story. When they appeared it seemed to her that she was compelled to reproduce them in life, and she did so. It was a most clear example of this imitative instinct of which I was speaking, and an extremely tragic one.

However, I do not wish to dwell any further upon individual instances. Personal experience is a most vicious and limited circle. All that I desire to point out is the general principle that life imitates art far more than art imitates life, and I feel sure that if you think seriously about it you will find that it is true. Life holds the mirror up to art, and either reproduces some strange type imagined by painter or sculptor, or realises in fact what has been dreamed in fiction. Scientifically speaking, the basis of life—the energy of life, as Aristotle would call it—is simply the desire for expression, and art is always presenting various forms through which this expression can be attained. Life seizes on them and uses them, even if they be to her own hurt. Young men have committed suicide because Rolla did so, have died by their own hand because by his own hand Werther died. Think of what we owe to the imitation of Christ, of what we owe to the imitation of Cæsar.

C. The theory is certainly a very curious one. But even admitting this strange imitative instinct in life, surely you would acknowledge that art expresses the temper of its age, the spirit of its time, the moral and social conditions that surround it, and under whose influence it is produced.

V. Certainly not! *Art never expresses anything but itself.* This is the principle of my new æsthetics; and it is this, and not any vital connection between form and substance, as Mr Pater fancies, that makes music the true type of all the arts. Of course, nations and individuals, with that healthy natural vanity which is the secret of life, are always under the impression that it is of them that the Muses are talking, always trying to find in the calm dignity of imaginative art some mirror of their own turbid passions, always forgetting that the singer of life is not Apollo, but Marsyas. Remote from reality, and with her eyes turned away from the shadows of the cave, Art reveals her own perfection, and the wondering crowd that watches the opening of the marvellous, many-petalled rose fancies that it is its own history that is being told to do it, its own spirit that is finding expression in a new form. But it is not so. The highest art rejects the burden of the human spirit, and gains more from a new medium or a fresh material than she does from any enthusiasm for art, or from any lofty passion, or from any great awakening of the human consciousness. She develops purely on her own lines. She is not symbolic of any age. It is the ages that are her symbols, her reflections, her echoes.

Even those who hold that Art is representative of time and place and people, cannot help admitting that the more imitative an art is, the less it represents to us the spirit of its age. The evil faces of the Roman emperors look out at us from the foul porphyry and spotted jasper in which the realistic artists of the day delighted to work, and we fancy that in those cruel lips and heavy sensual jaws we can find the secret of the ruin of the Empire. But it was not so. The vices of Tiberius could not destroy that great civilisation, any more than the virtues of Antonines could save it. It fell for other, for greater reasons. The sybyls and prophets of the Sistine may indeed serve to interpret for some that new birth of the emancipated spirit that we call the Renaissance; but what do the drunken boors and brawling peasants of Dutch art tell us about the great soul of Holland? The more abstract, the more ideal an art is, the more it reveals to us the temper of its age. If we wish to understand a nation by means of its art, let us look at its architecture or its music.

C. I do not quite agree with you there. The spirit of an age may be best expressed in the abstract ideal arts, for the spirit itself is abstract and ideal; but for the spiritual aspect of an age, for its look, as the phrase goes, we must surely go to the arts of imitation.

V. I don't think so. After all, what the imitative arts really give us are merely the various styles of particular artists, or of particular schools of artists. Surely you don't imagine that people of the Middle Ages bore any resemblance at all to the figures on mediæval stained glass, or in mediæval stone and wood carving, or on mediæval metal-work, or tapestries, or illuminated MSS. They were probably very ordinary-looking people, with nothing grotesque, or remarkable, or fantastic about them. The Middle Ages, as we know them in art, are simply a form of style, and there is no reason at all why an artist with this style should not be produced in the nineteenth century. No great artist ever sees things as they really are. If he did, he would cease to be an artist. Take an example from our own day. I know that you are fond of Japanese art. Now, do you really imagine that the Japanese people, as they are presented to us in art, have any existence? If you do, you have never understood Japanese art at all. The Japanese people are the deliberate creation of certain artists.

If you set a picture by Hokusai, or Hokkei, or any of the great native painters, beside a real Japanese lady gentleman or lady, you will see that there is not the slightest resemblance between them. The actual people who live in Japan are not unlike the general run of English people; that is to say, they are extremely commonplace, and have nothing curious or extraordinary about them. In fact the whole of Japan is a pure invention. There is no such country, there are no such people. One of our most charming painters, whose tiny full-length portraits of children are so beautiful and so powerful that he should be named the Velasquez to the Court of Lilliput, went recently to Japan in the foolish hope of seeing the Japanese. All he saw, all he had the chance of painting, were a few lanterns and some fans. He was unable to discover the inhabitants, as the delightful exhibition at Messrs. Dowdeswell's Gallery showed only too well. He did not know that the Japanese people are, as I have said, simply a mode of style, a whimsical fancy of art. Take the Greeks. Do you think that Greek art ever tells us what the Greek people were like? Do you believe that the Athenian women were like the stately dignified figures of the Parthenon frieze, or like those marvellous goddesses who sat in the triangular pediments of the same building? If you judge from the art, they certainly were so. But read an authority, like Aristophanes for instance. You will find that the Athenian ladies laced tightly, wore high-heeled shoes, dyed their hair yellow, painted and rouged their faces, and were exactly like any silly fashionable or fallen creature of our own day. We look back on the ages entirely through the medium of Art, and Art very fortunately has never once told us the truth.

C. But modern portraits by English painters, what of them? Surely they are like the people they pretend to represent?

V. Quite so. They are so like them that a hundred years from now no one will believe in them. The only portraits that one believes in are portraits where there is very little of the sitter and a great deal of the artist. Holbein's portraits of the men and women of his time impress us with a sense of their absolute reality. But this is simply because Holbein compelled life to accept his conditions, to restrain itself within his limitations, to reproduce his type, and to appear as he wished it to appear. It is style that makes us believe in a thing—nothing but style. Most of our modern portrait painters never paint what they see. *They paint what the public sees, and the public never sees anything.*

C. Well, after that I think I should hear the end of your article.

V. With pleasure. Whether it will do any good I really cannot say. Ours is certainly the dullest and most prosaic century possible. Why, even Sleep has played us false, and has closed up the gates of ivory, and opened the gates of horn. The dreams of the great middle classes of this country, as recorded in Mr Myers's two bulky volumes on the subject and in the Transactions of the Psychical Society, are the most depressing things I have ever read. There is not even a fine nightmare among them. They are commonplace, sordid, and probable. As for the Church I cannot conceive anything better for the culture of a country than the presence in it of a body of men whose duty it is to believe in the supernatural, to perform daily miracles, and to keep alive that mythopœic faculty which is so essential for the imagination.

But in the English Church a man succeeds, not through his capacity for belief, but through his capacity for disbelief. Ours is the only Church where the sceptic stands at the altar, and where St. Thomas is regarded as the ideal apostle. Many a worthy clergyman, who passes his life in good works of kindly charity, lives and dies unnoticed and unknown; but it is sufficient for some shallow uneducated passman out of either University to get up in his pulpit and express his doubts about Noah's ark or Balaam's ass or Jonah and the whale, for half of London to flock to his church and to sit open-mouthed in rapt admiration at his superb intellect. The growth of common sense in the English Church is a thing very much to be regretted. It is really a degrading concession to a low form of realism. However, I must read the end of my article:—

'What we have to do, what at any rate it is our duty to do, is to revive this old art of lying. Much of course may be done, in the way of educating the public, by amateurs in the domestic circle, at literary lunches, and at afternoon teas. But this is merely the light and graceful side of lying, such as was probably heard at Cretan dinner parties. There are many other forms. Lying for the sake of gaining some immediate personal advantage, for instance—lying for a moral purpose, as it is usually called—though of late it has been rather looked down upon, was extremely popular with the antique world. Athena laughs when Odysseus tells her what a Cambridge professor once elegantly termed as a 'whopper,' and the glory of mendacity illumes the pale brow of the stainless hero of Euripidean tragedy, and sets amongst the noble women of the world the young bride of one of Horace's most exquisite odes. Later on what at first had been merely a natural instinct was elevated into a self-conscious science. Elaborate rules were laid down for the guidance of mankind, and an important school of literature grew up round the subject. Indeed, when one remembers the excellent philosophical treatise of Sanchez on the whole question, one cannot help regretting that no one has ever thought of publishing a cheap and condensed edition of that great casuist. A short primer, "When to Lie and how," if brought out in an attractive and not too expensive form, would no doubt command a large sale, and would prove of real practical service to many earnest and deep-thinking people. Lying for the sake of the improvement of the young, which is the basis of home education, still lingers amongst us, and its advantages are so admirably set forth in the early books of the *Republic* that it is unnecessary to dwell upon them here. It is a form of lying for which all good mothers have peculiar capabilities, but it is capable of still further development, and has been sadly overlooked by the School Board. Lying for the sake of a monthly salary is of course well known in Fleet Street, and the profession of a political leader-writer is not without its advantages. But it is said to be a somewhat dull occupation, and it certainly does not lead to much beyond a kind of ostentatious obscurity. The only form of lying that is absolutely beyond reproach is lying for its own sake, and the highest development of this is, as we have already pointed out, lying in Art. Just as those who do not love Plato more than truth cannot pass beyond the threshold of the Academe, so those who do not love beauty more than truth never know the inmost shrine of Art. The solid stolid British intellect lies in the desert sands like the

Sphinx in Flaubert's marvellous tale, and fantasy, *La Chimère*, dances round it, and calls to it with her false, flute-toned voice. It may not hear her now, but surely some day, when we are all bored to death with the commonplace character of modern fiction, it will hearken to her and try to borrow her wings.

'And when that day dawns, or sunset reddens, how joyous we shall all be! Facts will be regarded as discreditable, Truth will be found mourning over her fetters, and Romance, with her temper of wonder, will return to the land. The very aspect of the world will change to our startled eyes. Out of the sea will rise Behemoth and Leviathan, and sail round the high-pooped galleys, as they do on the delightful maps of those ages when books on geography were actually readable. Dragons will wander about the waste places, and the phœnix will soar from her nest of fire into the air. We shall lay our hands upon the basilisk, and see the jewel in the toad's head. The hippogriff will stand in our stalls, champing his gilded oats, and over our heads will float the Blue Bird singing of beautiful and impossible things, of things that are lovely and that never happen, of things that are not and that should be. But before this comes to pass we must cultivate the lost art of lying.'

C. Then we must certainly cultivate it at once. But in order to avoid making any error I want you to briefly tell me the doctrines of the new æsthetics.

V. Briefly, then, they are these. Art never expresses anything but itself. It has an independent life, just as Thought has, and develops purely on its own lines. It is not necessarily realistic in an age of realism, nor spiritual in an age of faith. So far from being the creation of its time, it is usually in direct opposition to it, and the only history that it preserves for us is the history of its own progress. Sometimes it returns on its own footsteps, and revives some old form, as happened in the archaistic movement of late Greek art, and in the pre-Raphaelite movement of our own day. At other times it entirely anticipates its age, and produces in one century work that it takes another century to understand, to appreciate, and to enjoy. In no case does it reproduce its age. To pass from the art of a time to the time itself is the great fallacy of all historians.

The second doctrine is this. All bad art comes from returning to life and nature, and elevating them into ideals. Life and nature may sometimes be used as part of art's rough material, but before they are of any real service to art they must be translated into artistic conventions. The moment art surrenders its imaginative medium it surrenders everything. As a method Realism is a complete failure, and the two things that every artist should avoid are modernity of form and modernity of subject-matter. To us, who live in the nineteenth century, any century is a suitable subject for art except our own. The only beautiful things are things that do not concern us. It is, to have the pleasure of quoting myself, exactly because Hecuba is nothing to us that her sorrows are so suitable a motive for a tragedy.

The third doctrine is that Life imitates Art far more than Art imitates Life. This results not merely from Life's imitative instinct, but from the fact that the desire of Life is simply to find expression, and that Art offers it certain beautiful forms through which it may realise that energy. It is a theory that has never been formularised before, but it is extremely fruitful, and throws an entirely new light on the history of Art.

The last doctrine is that Lying, the telling of beautiful untrue things, is the proper aim of Art. But of this I think I have spoken at sufficient length. And now let us go out on the terrace, where 'the milk-white peacock glimmers like a ghost,' while the evening star 'washes the dusk with silver.' At twilight nature becomes a wonderfully suggestive effect and is not without loveliness, though perhaps its chief use is to illustrate quotations from the poets. Come! We have talked long enough.

71

The Limits of Realism in Fiction

EDMUND GOSSE

Sir Edmund William Gosse (1849–1928), best known for his novel, *Father and Son* (1907), here beings by lamenting the British reaction to Zola's experimental novel and the naturalist tradition Zola's writings spawned. Though he proceeds to criticise the experimental novelists' "anatomist" attention to surface detail as opposed to psychological insight, he credits Zola with concentrating "the threads of Flaubert and Daudet, Dostoiefsky and Tolstoi, Howells and Henry James... into anything like a single system". Gosse sees the English focus on realism, beginning with Austen ("the perfection of the realistic ideal"), as a harbinger of Zola's later preoccupation with extreme realism. He concludes by predicting a reaction against the experimental novel toward "the mystical and the introspective", a reaction perhaps best evinced in England by Virgina Woolf in both her novels and her critical essays, especially "Modern Fiction" (1919) and "Mr Bennett and Mrs Brown" (1924).

In the last new Parisian farce, by M. Sarcey's clever young son-in-law, there is a conscientious painter of the realistic school who is preparing for the Salon a very serious and abstruse production. The young lady of his heart says, at length: "It's rather a melancholy subject; I wonder you don't paint a sportsman, crossing a rustic bridge, and meeting a pretty girl." This is the climax, and the artist breaks off his relations with Young Lady No. 1. Toward the end of the play, while he is still at work on his picture, Young Lady No. 2 says: "If I were you, I should take another subject. Now, for instance, why don't you paint a pretty girl, crossing a rustic bridge, and met by a sportsman?" This is really an allegory, whether M. Gandillot intends it or not. Thus have those charming, fresh, ingenuous, ignorant, and rather stupid young ladies, the English and American publics, received the attempts which novelists have made to introduce among them what is called, outside the Anglo-Saxon world, the experimental novel. The present writer is no defender of that class of fiction; least of all is he an exclusive defender of it; but he is tired to death of the criticism

Source: Edmund Gosse, "The Limits of Realism in Fiction", *The Forum*, June 1890, pp. 391–400.

on both sides of the Atlantic, which refuses to see what the realists are, whither they are tending, and what position they are beginning to hold in the general evolution of imaginative literature. He is no great lover of what they produce, and most certainly does not delight in their excesses; but when they are advised to give up their studies and paint pretty girls on rustic bridges, he is almost stung into partisanship. The present article will have no action nearer home than Zambeziland; but to those who have perceived that in almost every country in the world the novel of manners has been passing through a curious phase, it may possibly not be uninteresting to be called upon to inquire what the nature of that phase has been, and still more what is to be the outcome of it.

So far as the Anglo-Saxon world is concerned, the experimental or realistic novel is mainly to be studied in America, Russia, and France. It exists now in all the countries of the European Continent, but we know less about its manifestations there. It has had no direct development in England, except in the clever but imperfect stories of Mr George Moore. Ten years ago the realistic novel, or at all events the naturalist school, out of which it proceeded, was just beginning to be talked about, and there was still a good deal of perplexity, outside Paris, as to its scope and as to the meaning of its name. Russia, still unexplored by the Vicomte de Vogüé and his disciples, was represented to Western readers solely by Turgeneff, who was a great deal too romantic to be a pure naturalist. In America, where now almost every new writer of merit seems to be a realist, there was but one, Mr Henry James, who, in 1877, had inaugurated the experimental novel in the English language, with his "American." Mr Howells, tending more and more in that direction, was to write on for several years before he should produce a thoroughly realistic novel.

Ten years ago, then, the very few people who take an interest in literary questions were looking with hope or apprehension, as the case might be, to Paris, and chiefly to the study of M. Zola. It was from the little villa at Médan that revelation on the subject of the coming novel was to be expected; and in the autumn of 1880 the long-expected message came, in the shape of the grotesque, violent, and narrow, but extremely able volume of destructive and constructive criticism called "*Le Roman Expérimental*." People had complained that they did not know what M. Zola was driving at; that they could not recognize a "naturalistic" or "realistic" book when they saw it; that the "scientific method" in fiction, the "return to nature," "experimental observation" as the basis of a story, were mere phrases to them, vague and incomprehensible. The Sage of Médan determined to remove the objection and explain everything. He put his speaking-trumpet to his lips, and, disdaining to address the crassness of his countrymen, he shouted his system of rules and formulas to the Russian public, that all the world might hear.

In 1880 he had himself proceeded far. He had published the Rougon-Macquart series of his novels, as far as *Une Page d'Amour*. He has added to the bulk of his works since then, with six or seven novels, and he has published many forcible and fascinating and many repulsive pages. But since 1880 he has not altered his method or pushed on to any further development. He had already displayed his main qualities—his extraordinary mixture of versatility and monotony, his enduring force, his plentiful lack of taste, his cynical disdain for the weaknesses of men, his admirable constructive power, his inability to select the salient points in a vast mass of observations. He had already shown himself what I must take the liberty of saying that he appears to me to be, one of the leading men of genius in the second half of the nineteenth century, one of the strongest novelists in the world: and that in spite of faults so serious and so eradicable that they would have hopelessly wrecked a writer a little less overwhelming in strength and resource. Zola seems to me to be the Vulcan among our later gods, afflicted with moral lameness from his birth, and coming to us sooty and brutal from the forge, yet as indisputably great as any Mercury-Hawthorne or Apollo-Thackeray of the best of them. It is to Zola, and to Zola only, that the concentration of the scattered tendencies of naturalism is due. It is owing to him that the threads of Flaubert and Daudet, Dostoiefsky and Tolstoi, Howells and Henry James can be drawn into anything like a single system. It is Zola who discovered a common measure for all these talents, and a formula wide enough and yet close enough to distinguish them from the outside world and bind them to one another. It is his doing that for ten years the experimental novel has flowed in a definite channel, and has not spread itself abroad in a thousand whimsical directions.

To a serious critic, then, who is not a partisan, but who sees how a large body of carefully-composed fiction the naturalistic school has produced, it is of great importance to know what is the formula of M. Zola. He has defined it, one would think, clearly enough, but to see it intelligently repeated is rare indeed. It starts from the negation of fancy—not of imagination, as that word is used by the best Anglo-Saxon critics, but of fancy—the romantic and rhetorical elements that novelists have so largely used to embroider the home-spun fabric of experience with. It starts with the exclusion of all that is called "ideal," all that is not firmly based on the actual life of human beings, all, in short, that is grotesque, unreal, nebulous, or didactic. I do not understand Zola to condemn the romantic writers of the past; I do not think he has spoken of Dumas *père* or of George Sand as Mr Howells has spoken of Dickens. He has a phrase of contempt—richly deserved, it appears to me—for the childish evolution of Victor Hugo's plots, and in particular of that of *Notre Dame de Paris*; but, on the whole, his aim is rather to determine the outlines of a new school than to attack the recognized masters of the past. If it be not so, it should be so; there is room in the Temple of Fame for all good writers, and it does not blast the laurels of Walter Scott that we are deeply moved by Dostoiefsky.

With Zola's theory of what the naturalistic novel should be, it seems impossible at first sight to quarrel. It is to be contemporary; it is to be founded on and limited by actual experience; it is to reject all empirical modes of awakening sympathy and interest; its aim is to place before its readers living beings, acting the comedy of life as naturally as possible. It is to trust to principles of action and to reject formulas of character; to cultivate the personal expression; to be analytical rather than lyrical; to paint men as they are, not as you think they should be. There is no harm in all this. There is not a word here that does not apply to the chiefs of one of the two great parallel schools of English fiction. It is hard to conceive of a novelist whose work is more experimental than Richardson. Fielding is personal and analytical above all things. If France points to George Sand among its romanticists, we can point to a realist who is greater than she, in Jane Austen. There is not a word to be found in M. Zola's definitions of the experimental novel that is not fulfilled in the pages of *Emma*; which is equivalent to saying that the most advanced realism may be practiced by the most innocent as well as the most captivating of novelists. Miss Austen did not observe over a wide area, but within the circle of her experience she disguised nothing, neglected nothing, glossed over nothing. She is the perfection of the realistic ideal, and there ought to be a statue of her in the vestibule of the forthcoming *Académie des Goncourts*. Unfortunately, the lives of her later brethren have not been so sequestered as hers, and they, too, have thought it their duty to neglect nothing and to disguise nothing. It is not necessary to repeat here the rougher charges which have been brought against the naturalist school in France—charges which in mitigated form have assailed their brethren in Russia and America. On a carefully-reasoned page in the copy of M. Zola's essay "Du Roman" which lies before me, one of those idiots who write in public books has scribbled the remark, "They see nothing in life but filth and crime." This ignoble wielder of the pencil but repeats what more ambitious critics have been saying in solemn terms for the last fifteen years. Even as regards Zola himself, as the author of the delicate comedy of *La Conquête de Plassans*, and the moving tragedy of *Une Page d'Amour*, this charge is utterly false, and in respect of the other leaders it is simply preposterous. None the less, there are sides upon which the naturalistic novelists are open to serious criticism in practice. It is with no intention of underrating their eminent qualities that I suggest certain points at which, as it appears to me, their armor is conspicuously weak. There are limits to realism, and they seem to have been readily discovered by the realists themselves. These weak points are to be seen in the jointed harness of the strongest book that the school has yet produced in any country, *Crime et Châtiment*.

When the ideas of Zola were first warmly taken up, about ten years ago, by the most earnest and sympathetic writers who then were young, the theory of the experimental novel seemed unassailable, and the range within which it could be worked to advantage practically boundless. But the fallacies of practice remained to be experienced, and looking back upon what has been written by the leaders themselves, the places where the theory has broken down are patent. It may not be uninteresting to take up the leading dogmas of the naturalistic school, and to see what elements of failure, or, rather, what limitations to success, they contained. The outlook is very different in 1890 from what it was in 1880; and a vast number of exceedingly clever writers have labored to no avail, if we are not able at the latter date to gain a wider perspective than could be obtained at the earlier one. Ten years ago, most ardent and generous young authors, outside the frontiers of indifferent Albion, were fired with enthusiasm at the results to be achieved by naturalism in fiction. It was to be the Revealer and the Avenger. It was to display society as it is, and to wipe out all the hypocrisies of convention. It was to proceed from strength to strength. It was to place all imagination upon a scientific basis, and to open boundless vistas to sincere and courageous young novelists. We have seen with what ardent hope and confidence its principles were accepted by Mr Howells. We have seen all the Latin races, in their coarser way, embrace and magnify the system. We have seen M. Zola, like a heavy father in high comedy, bless a budding generation of novel-writers, and prophesy that they will all proceed further than he along the road of truth and experiment. Yet the naturalistic school is really less advanced, less thorough, than it was ten years ago. Why is this?

It is doubtless because the strain and stress of production have brought to light those weak places in the formula which were not dreamed of. The first principle of the school was the exact reproduction of life. But life is wide and it is elusive. All that the finest observer can do is to make a portrait of one corner of it. By the confession of the master spirit himself, this portrait is not be a photograph. It must be inspired by imagination, but sustained and confined by the experience of reality. It does not appear at first sight as though is should be difficult to attain this, but in point of fact it is found almost impossible to approach this species of perfection. The result of building up a long work on this principle is, I hardly know why, to produce the effect of a reflexion in a convex mirror. The more accurately experimental some parts of the picture are, the more will the want of balance and proportion in other parts be felt. I will take at random two examples. No better work in the naturalistic direction has been done than is to be found in the beginning of M. Zola's *La Joie de Vivre*, or in the early part of the middle of Mr James's *Bostonians*. The life in the melancholy Norman house upon the cliff, the life among the uncouth fanatic philanthropists in the American city, these are given with a reality, a brightness, a personal note which have an electrical effect upon the reader. But the remainder of each of these remarkable books, built up as they are with infinite toil by two of the most accomplished architects of fiction now living, leaves on the mind a sense of strained reflection, of images blurred or malformed by a convexity of the mirror. As I have said, it is difficult to account for this, which is a feature of blight on almost every specimen of the experimental novel; but perhaps it can in a measure be accounted for by the inherent disproportion which exists between the small flat surface of a book and the vast arch of life which it undertakes to mirror, those studies being least liable to distortion which reflect the smallest section of life, and those in which ambitious masters endeavor to make us feel the mighty movements of populous cities and vast bodies of men being the most inevitably misshapen.

Another leading principle of the naturalists is the disinterested attitude of the narrator. He who tells the story must not act the part of Chorus, must not praise or blame, must have no favorites; in short, must not be a moralist but an anatomist. This excellent and theoretical law has been a snare in practice. The nations of continental Europe are not bound down by conventional laws to the same extent as we English are. The Anglo-Saxon race is now the only one that has not been touched by that pessimism of which the writings of Schopenhauer are the most prominent and popular exponent. This fact is too often overlooked when we scornfully ask why the foreign nations allow themselves so great a latitude in the discussion of moral subjects. It is partly, no doubt, because of our beautiful

Protestant institutions; because we go to Sunday schools and take a lively interest in the souls of other people; because, in short, we are all so virtuous and godly, that our novels are so prim and decent. But it is also partly because our hereditary dullness in perceiving delicate ethical distinctions has given the Anglo-Saxon race a tendency to slur over the dissonances between man and nature. This tendency does not exist among the Latin races, who run to the opposite extreme and exaggerate these discords. The consequence has been that they have, almost without exception, been betrayed by the disinterested attitude into a contemplation of crime and frailty (notoriously more interesting than innocence and virtue) which has given by-standers excuse for saying that these novelists are lovers of that which is evil. In the same way they have been tempted by the Rembrandtesque shadows of pain, dirt, and obloquy to overdash their canvases with the subfuse hues of sentiment. In a word, in trying to draw life evenly and draw it whole, they have introduced such a brutal want of tone as to render the portrait a caricature. The American realists, who were guarded by fashion from the Scylla of brutality, have not wholly escaped, on their side, and for the same reason, the Charybdis of insipidity.

It would take us too far, and would require a constant reference to individual books, to trace the weaknesses of the realistic school of our own day. Human sentiment has revenged itself upon them for their rigid regulations and scientific formulas, by betraying them into faults the possibility of which they had not anticipated. But above all other causes of their limited and temporary influence, the most powerful has been the material character which their rules forced upon them, and their excess of positivism and precision. In eliminating the grotesque and the rhetorical they drove out more than they wished to lose; they pushed away with their scientific pitchfork the fantastic and intellectual elements. How utterly fatal this was may be seen, not in the leaders, who have preserved something of the reflected color of the old romance, but in those earnest disciples who have pushed the theory to its extremity. In their somber, grimy, and dreary studies in pathology, clinical bulletins of a soul dying of atrophy, we may see what the limits are of realism, and how impossible it is that human readers should much longer go on enjoying this sort of literary aliment.

If I have dwelt upon these limitations, however, it has not been to cast a stone at the naturalistic school. It has been rather with the object of clearing away some critical misconceptions about the future development of it. Anglo-Saxon criticism of the perambulating species might, perhaps, be persuaded to consider the realists with calmer judgment, if it looked upon them, not as a monstrous canker that was slowly spreading its mortal influence over the whole of literature, which it would presently overwhelm and destroy, but as a natural and timely growth, taking its due place in the succession of products, and bound, like other growths, to bud and blossom and decline. I venture to put forth the view that the novel of experiment has had its day; that it has been made the vehicle of some of the loftiest minds of our age; that is has produced a huge body of fiction, none of it perfect, perhaps, much of it bad, but much of it, also, exceedingly intelligent, vivid, sincere, and durable; and that it is now declining, to leave behind it a great memory, the prestige of persecution, and a library of books which every highly-educated man in the future will be obliged to be familiar with.

It would be difficult, I think, for any one but a realistic novelist to overrate the good that realism in fiction has done. It has cleared the air of a thousand follies, has pricked a whole fleet of oratorical bubbles. Whatever comes next, we cannot return, in serious novels, to the inanities and impossibilities of the old "well-made" plot, to the children changed at nurse, to the madonna heroine and the god-like hero, to the impossible virtues and melodramatic vices. In future, even those who sneer at realism and misrepresent it most wilfully, will be obliged to put in their effects in ways more in accord with veritable experience. The public has eaten of the apple of knowledge, and will not be satisfied with mere marionettes. There will still be novel-writers who address the gallery, and who will keep up the gaudy old convention, and the clumsy "Family Herald" evolution, but they will no longer be distinguished people of genius. They will no longer sign themselves George Sand and Charles Dickens.

In the meantime, wherever I look I see the novel ripe for another reaction. The old leaders will not change. It is not to be expected that they will write otherwise than in the mode which has grown mature with them. But in France, among the younger men, every one is escaping from the realistic formula. The two young athletes for whom M. Zola predicted ten years ago an "experimental" career more profoundly scientific than his own, are realists no longer. M. Guy de Maupassant has become a psychologist, and M. Huysmans a mystic. M. Bourget, who set all the ladies dancing after his ingenious, musky books, never has been a realist; nor has Pierre Loti, in whom, with a fascinating freshness, the old exiled romanticism comes back with a laugh and a song. All points to a reaction in France; and in Russia, too, if what we hear is true, the next step will be one toward the mystical and the introspective. Tolstoi's *Sonata*, still unpublished as I write these lines, is understood to be wholly distinct from his earlier novels—to be psychological and imaginative. In America it would be rash for a foreigner to say what signs of change are evident. The time has hardly come when we look to America for the symptoms of literary initiative. But it is my conviction that the limits of realism have been reached; that no great writer who has not already adapted the experimental system will do so; and that we ought now to be on the outlook to welcome (and, of course, to persecute) a school of novelists with a totally new aim, part of whose formula must unquestionably be a concession to the human instinct for mystery and beauty.

72

The Science of Fiction

THOMAS HARDY

One of the principal British poets and novelists of the latter part of the nineteenth century, Thomas Hardy (1840-1928) classified his novels into three categories: those of Character and Environment, those of Romance and Fantasy and those of Ingenuity. The most famous of these—the Wessex novels from *Far From the Madding Crowd* (1874) to *Jude the Obscure* (1896)—belong to the first category. In the following essay on the art of fiction, Hardy continues the debate among authors of the 1890s on the merits of realistic, romantic and naturalistic fiction. Here and in his essay, "The Profitable Reading of Fiction" (see Chapter 61), he criticizes the scientific realism propounded by Zola, noting that the true naturalist would be merely a copyist, "an automatic reproducer of all impressions." Zola's theories are not embodied in his novels, argues Hardy. Though he acknowledges the validity of the naturalist's rebellion against false or exaggerated subjects and characters, Hardy calls for a power of observation that exceeds perception of surface details. This power derives more from mental intuition than from an exacting eye; it entails sympathy and feeling.

Since Art is science with an addition, since some science underlies all Art, there is seemingly no paradox in the use of such a phrase as "the Science of Fiction." One concludes it to mean that comprehensive and accurate knowledge of realities which must be sought for, or intuitively possessed, to some extent, before anything deserving the name of an artistic performance in narrative can be produced.

The particulars of this science are the generals of almost all others. The materials of Fiction being human nature and circumstances, the science thereof may be dignified by calling it the codified law of all things as they really are. No single pen can treat exhaustively of this. The Science of Fiction is contained in that large work, the cyclopædia of life.

In no proper sense can the term "science" be applied to other than this fundamental matter. It can have no part or share in the construction of a story,

Source: Thomas Hardy, "The Science of Fiction", *The New Review*, April, 1891, rptd *Life and Art*, New York: Greenberg Publisher, 1925, pp. 85-90.

however recent speculations may have favoured such an application. We may assume with certainty that directly the constructive stage is entered upon, Art—high or low—begins to exist.

The most devoted apostle of realism, the sheerest naturalist, cannot escape, any more than the withered old gossip over her fire, the exercise of Art in his labour or pleasure of telling a tale. Not until he becomes an automatic reproducer of all impressions whatsoever can he be called purely scientific, or even a manufacturer on scientific principles. If in the exercise of his reason he select or omit, with an eye to being more truthful than truth (the just aim of Art), he transforms himself into a technicist at a move.

As this theory of the need for the exercise of the Dædalian faculty for selection and cunning manipulation has been disputed, it may be worth while to examine the contrary proposition. That it should ever have been maintained by such a romancer as M. Zola, in his work on the *Roman Expérimental*, seems to reveal an obtuseness to the disproof conveyed in his own novels which, in a French writer, is singular indeed. To be sure that author—whose powers in story-telling, rightfully and wrongfully exercised, may be partly owing to the fact that he is not a critic—does in a measure concede something in the qualified counsel that the novel should keep as close to reality *as it can*; a remark which may be interpreted with infinite latitude, and would no doubt have been cheerfully accepted by Dumas *père* or Mrs Radcliffe. It implies discriminative choice; and if we grant that we grant all. But to maintain in theory what he abandons in practice, to subscribe to rules and to work by instinct, is a proceeding not confined to the author of *Germinal* and *La Faute de l'Abbé Mouret*.

The reasons that make against such conformation of story-writing to scientific processes have been set forth so many times in examining the theories of the realist, that it is not necessary to recapitulate them here. Admitting the desirability, the impossibility of reproducing in its entirety the phantasmagoria of experience with infinite and atomic truth, without shadow, relevancy, or subordination, is not the least of them. The fallacy appears to owe its origin to the just perception that with our widened knowledge of the universe and its forces, and man's position therein, narrative, to be artistically convincing, must adjust itself to the new alignment, as would also artistic works in form and colour, if further spectacles in their sphere could be presented. Nothing but the illusion of truth can permanently please, and when the old illusions begin to be penetrated, a more natural magic has to be supplied.

Creativeness in its full and ancient sense—the making a thing or situation out of nothing that ever was before—is apparently ceasing to satisfy a world which no longer believes in the abnormal—ceasing at least to satisfy the van-couriers of taste; and creative fancy has accordingly to give more and more place to realism, that is, to an artificially distilled from the fruits of closest observation.

This is the meaning deducible from the work of the realists, however stringently they themselves may define realism in terms. Realism is an unfortunate, an ambiguous word, which has been taken up by literary society like a view-halloo, and has been assumed in some places to mean copyism, and in others pruriency, and has led to two classes of delineators being included in one condemnation.

Just as bad a word is one used to express a consequence of this development, namely "brutality," a term which, first applied by French critics, has since spread over the English school like the other. It aptly hits off the immediate impression of the thing meant; but it has the disadvantage of defining impartiality as a passion, and a plan as a caprice. It certainly is very far from truly expressing the aims and methods of conscientious and well-intentioned authors who, notwithstanding their excesses, errors, and rickety theories, attempt to narrate the *vérité vraie*.

To return for a moment to the theories of the scientific realists. Every friend to the novel should and must be in sympathy with their error, even while distinctly perceiving it. Though not true, it is well found. To advance realism as complete copyism, to call the idle trade of story-telling a science, is the hyperbolic flight of an admirable enthusiasm, the exaggerated cry of an honest reaction from the false, in which the truth has been impetuously approached and overleapt in fault of lighted on.

Possibly, if we only wait, the third something, akin to perfection, will exhibit itself on its due pedestal. How that third something may be induced to hasten its presence, who shall say? Hardly the English critic.

But this appertains to the Art of novel-writing, and is outside the immediate subject. To return to the "science." . . . Yet what is the use? Its very comprehensiveness renders the attempt to dwell upon it a futility. Being an observative responsiveness to everything within the cycle of the suns that has to do with actual life, it is easier to say what it is not than to categorise its *summa genera*. It is not, for example, the paying of a great regard to adventitious externals to the neglect of vital qualities, not a precision about the outside of the platter and an obtuseness to the contents. An accomplished lady once confessed to the writer that she could never be in a room two minutes without knowing every article of furniture it contained and every detail in the attire of the inmates, and, when she left, remembering every remark. Here was a person, one might feel for the moment, who could prime herself to an unlimited extent and at the briefest notice in the scientific data of fiction; one who, assuming her to have some slight artistic power, was a born novelist. To explain why such a keen eye to the superficial does not imply a sensitiveness to the intrinsic is a psychological matter beyond the scope of these notes; but that a blindness to material particulars often accompanies a quick perception of the more ethereal characteristics of humanity, experience continually shows.

A sight for the finer qualities of existence, an ear for the "still sad music of humanity," are not to be acquired by the outer senses alone, close as their powers in photography may be. What cannot be discerned by eye and ear, what may be apprehended only by the mental tactility that comes from a sympathetic appreciativeness of life in all its manifestations, this is the gift which renders its possessor a more accurate delineator of human nature than many another with twice his powers and means of external observation, but without that sympathy. To see in half and quarter views the whole picture, to catch from a few bars the whole tune, is the intuitive power that supplies the would-be story-writer with the scientific bases for his pursuit. He may not count the dishes at a feast, or accurately estimate the value of the jewels in a lady's diadem; but through the smoke of those dishes, and the rays from these jewels, he sees written on the wall:—

> We are such stuff
> As dreams are made of, and our little life
> Is rounded with a sleep.

Thus, as aforesaid, an attempt to set forth the Science of Fiction in calculable pages is futility; it is to write a whole library of human philosophy, with instructions how to feel.

Once in a crowd a listener heard a needy and illiterate woman saying of another poor and haggard woman who had lost her little son years before: "You can see the ghost of that child in her face even now."

That speaker was one who, though she could probably neither read nor write, had the true means towards the "Science" of Fiction innate within her; a power of observation informed by a living heart. Had she been trained in the technicalities, she might have fashioned her view of mortality with good effect; a reflection which leads to a conjecture that, perhaps, true novelists, like poets, are born, not made.

73

The Tyranny of the Novel

EDMUND GOSSE

As in his earlier essay, Gosse bemoans the mediocrity of the current race of British fiction writers. Advising that they are about to exhaust their sources, he calls (not unlike Virginia Woolf will do in 'Modern Fiction' in 1919) for a broader view of life, a grasp of subject matter outside the conventional love story. He connects the periodic failures of the novel since the 1740s with the novelist's refusal to look beyond conventional plots. Again citing Zola as the best example of the drive toward realistic detail, he requests a photographic rendering of the character 'with his every-day expression on his face, and the localities in which he spends his days accurately visible around him' (175). This essay may effectively be contrasted with that of Robert Louis Stevenson a decade earlier.

A Parisian Hebraist has been attracting a moment's attention to his paradoxical and learned self by announcing that strong-hearted and strong-brained nations do not produce novels. This gentleman's soul goes back, no doubt, in longing and despair to the heart of Babylon and the brain of Gath. But if he looks for a modern nation that does not cultivate the novel, he must, I am afraid, go far afield. Finland and Roumania are certainly tainted; Bohemia lies in the bond of naturalism, Probably Montenegro is the one European nation which this criterion would leave strong in heart and brain. The amusing absurdity of this whim of a pedant may serve to remind us how universal is now the reign of prose fiction. In Scandinavia the drama may claim an equal prominence, but no more. In all other countries the novel takes the largest place, claims and obtains the widest popular attention, is the admitted tyrant of the whole family of literature.

This is so universally acknowledged now-a-days that we scarcely stop to ask ourselves whether it is a heaven-appointed condition of things, existing from the earliest times, or whether it is an innovation. As a matter of fact, the predominance of the novel is a very recent event. Most other classes of literature are as old as the art of verbal expression: lyrical and narrative poetry, drama, history, philosophy,—

Source: Edmund Gosse, "The Tyranny of the Novel", *National Review*, 19, 1892, pp. 166–75.

all these have flourished since the sunrise of the world's intelligence. But the novel is a creation of the late afternoon of civilization. In the true sense, though not the pedantic one, the novel began in France with *La Princesse de Clèves*, and in England with *Pamela*—that is to say, in 1677 and in 1740 respectively. Compared with the dates of the beginning of philosophy and of poetry, these are as yesterday and the day before yesterday. Once started, however, the sapling of prose fiction grew and spread mightily. It took but a few generations to overshadow all the ancient oaks and cedars around it, and with its monstrous foliage to dominate the forest.

It would not be uninteresting, if we had space to do so here, to mark in detail the progress of this astonishing growth. It would be found that, in England at least, it has not been by any means regularly sustained. The original magnificent outburst of the English novel lasted for exactly a quarter of a century, and closed with the publication of *Humphrey Clinker*. During this period of excessive fertility in a hitherto unworked field, the novel produced one masterpiece after another, positively pushing itself to the front and securing the best attention of the public at a moment when such men as Gray, Butler, Hume, and Warburton were putting forth contributions to the old and long-established sections of literature. Nay: such was the force of the new kind of writing that the gravity of Johnson and the grace of Goldsmith were seduced into participating in its facile triumphs.

But, at the very moment when the novel seemed about to sweep everything before it, the wave subsided and almost disappeared. For nearly forty years, only one novel of the very highest Class was produced in England; and it might well seem as though prose fiction, after its brief victory, had exhausted its resources, and had sunken for ever into obscurity. During the close of the eighteenth century and the first decade of the nineteenth, no novel, except *Evelina*, could pretend to disturb the laurels of Burke, of Gibbon, of Cowper, of Crabbe. The publication of *Caleb Williams* is a poor event to set against that of the *Lyical Ballads*; even *Thalaba the Destroyer* seemed a more impressive phenomenon than the *Monk*. But the second great burgeoning of the novel was at hand. Like the tender ash, it delayed to clothe itself when all the woods of romanticism were green. But in 1811 came *Sense and Sensibility*, in 1814 *Waverley*; and the novel was once more at the head of the literary movement of the time.

It cannot be said to have stayed there very long. Miss Austen's brief and brilliant career closed in 1817. Sir Walter Scott continued to be not far below his best until about ten years later. But a period of two decades included not only the work of these two great novelists, but the best books also of Galt, of Mary Ferrier, of Maturin, of Lockhart, of Banim. It saw the publication of *Hajji Baba*, of *Frankenstein*, of *Anastatius*. Then, for the second time, prose fiction ceased for a while to hold a position of high predominance. But Bulwer Lytton was already at hand; and five or six years of comparative obscurity prepared the way for Dickens, Lever, and Lover. Since the memorable year 1837 the novel has reigned in English literature; and its tyranny was never more irresistible than it is to-day. The Victorian has been peculiarly the age of the triumph of fiction.

In the history of France something of the same fluctuation might be perceived, although the production of novels of a certain literary pretension has been a feature of French much longer and more steadily than of English life. As Mr Saintsbury has pointed out, 'it is particularly noteworthy that every one of the eight names which have been set at the head' of the nineteenth-century literature of France 'is the name of a novelist.' Since the days or Flaubert—for the last thirty years, that is to say—the novel has assumed a still higher literary function than it held even in the hands of George Sand and Balzac. It has cast aside the pretence of merely amusing, and has affected the airs of guide, philosopher, and friend. M. Zola, justified to some extent by the amazing vogue of his own writings, and the vast area covered by their prestige, has said that the various classes of literary production are being merged in the novel, and are ultimately to disappear within it:

> Apollo, ran, and Love,
> And even Olympia Jove
> Grow faint, for killing Truth hath glared on them;
> Our hills, and seas, and streams,
> Dispeopled of their dreams,

become the more primary material for an endless series of naturalistic stories. And even to-day, when the young David of symbolism rises to smite the Goliath Zola, the smooth stones he takes out of his scrip are works of fiction by Maurice Barrès and Elouard Rod. Schools pass and nicknames alter; but the novel rules in France as it does elsewhere.

We have but to look around us at this very moment to see how complete the tyranny of the novel is. If one hundred educated and grown men—not, of course, themselves the authors of other books—were to be asked which are the three most notable works published in London during the present season, would not ninety-and-nine be constrained to answer, with a parrot uniformity, *Tess of the D'Urbervilles*, *David Grieve*, *The Little Minister*? These are the books which have been most widely discussed, most largely bought, most vehemently praised, most venomously attacked. These are the books in which the 'trade' has taken most interest, the vitality of which is most obvious and indubitable. It may be said that the conditions of the winter of 1892 were exceptional—that no books of the first class in other branches were produced. This may be true; and yet Mr Jebb has issued a volume of his Sophocles, Mr William Morris a collection of the lyric poems of years, Mr Froude his *Divorce of Catherine of Aragon*, and Mr Tyndall his *New Fragments*. If the poets in chorus had blown their silver trumpets and the philosophers their bold bassoons, the result would have been the same: they would have won some respect and a little notice for their performances; but the novelists would have carried away the money and the real human curiosity. Who shall say that Mr Freeman was not a better historian than Robertson was? yet did he make £4,500 by his *History of Sicily*? I wish I could believe it. To-day Mr Swinburne may publish a new epic, Mr Gardiner discover to us the head of Charles I. on the scaffold, Mr Herbert Spencer explore a fresh province of sociology, or Mr Pater analyze devils in the accents of an angel,—none of these important occurrences will successfully compete, for more than a few moments, among educated people, with the publication of what is called, in publishers' advertisements, 'the new popular and original novel of the hour.' We are accustomed to this state of things, and we bow to it. But we may, perhaps, remind ourselves that it is a comparatively recent condition. It was not so in 1730, nor in 1800, nor even in 1835.

Momentary aberrations of fashion must not deceive us as to the general tendency of taste. Mr Hall Caine would have us believe that the public has suddenly gone crazy for stage-plays. 'Novels of great strength and originality,' says the author of *The Scapegoat*, 'occasionally appear without creating more than a flutter of interest,' and, meanwhile, plays of one-tenth their power and novelty are making something like a profound impression.' What plays are these? Not the Ollendorfian attitudinizings of M. Maeterlinck surely! The fact is that two years ago it would have been impossible for anyone to pen that sentence of Mr Caine's, and it is now possible merely because a passion for the literary drama has been flogged into existence by certain able critics. With a limited class, the same class which appreciates poetry, the literary drama may find a welcome; but to suppose that it competes, or can, in this country, even pretend to compete, with the novel is a delusion, and Mr Caine may safely abandon his locusts and wild honey.

That we see around us a great interest in the drama is, of course, a commonplace. But how much of that is literary? When the delights of the eye are removed from the sum of pleasure, what is left? Our public is interested in the actors and their art, in the scenery and the furniture, in the notion of large sums of money expended, lost or won. When all these incidental interests are extracted from the curiosity excited by a play, not very much is left for the purely literary portion of it,—not nearly so much, at all events, as is awakened by a great novel. After all that has been said about the publication of plays, I suspect that the sale of dramatic contemporary literature remains small and uncertain. Mr Pinero is read; but one swallow does not make a summer. Where are the dramatic works of Mr Sydney Grundy, which ought—if Mr Caine be correct—to be seen on every book-shelf beside the stories of Mr Hawley Smart?

If, however, I venture to emphasize the fact of the tyranny of the novel in our current literature, it is without a murmur that I do so. Like the harmless bard in *Lady Geraldine's Courtship*, I 'write no satire,' and, what is more, I mean none. It appears to me natural and rational that this particular form of writing should attract more readers than any other. It is so broad and flexible, includes so vast a variety of appeals to the emotions, makes so few painful demands upon an overstrained attention, that it obviously lays itself out to please the greatest number. For the appreciation of a fine poem, of a learned critical treatise, of a contribution to exact knowledge, peculiar aptitudes are required: the novel appeals to all. Experience, moreover, proves that the gentle stimulus of reading about the cares, passions, and adventures of imaginary personages, and their relations to one another, a mild and irresponsible mirroring of real life on a surface undisturbed by responsibility, or memory, or personal feeling of any kind, is the most restful, the must refreshing, of all excitements which literature produces.

It is commonly said, in all countries, that women are the chief readers of novels.

It may well be that they are the most numerous, and that they read more exhaustively than men, and with less selection. They have, as a rule, more time. The general notion seems to be that girls of from sixteen to twenty form the main audience of the novelist. But I am inclined to think that the real audience consists of young married women, sitting at home in the first year of their marriage. They find themselves without any constraint upon their reading: they choose what they will, and they read incessantly. The advent of the first-born baby is awaited in silent drawing-rooms, where through long hours the novelists supply the sole distraction. These young matrons form a much better audience than those timorous circles of flaxen-haired girls, watched by an Argus-eyed mamma, which the English novelist seems to consider himself doomed to cater for. I cannot believe that it is anything but a fallacy that young girls do read. They are far too busy with parties and shopping, chatting and walking, the eternal music and the eternal tennis. Middle-aged people in the country, who are cut off from much society, and elderly ladies, whose activities are past, and who like to resume the illusions of youth, are far more assiduous novel-readers than girls. But, if we take these and all other married and unmarried women into consideration, there is still apparently an exaggeration in saying that it is they who make the novelist's reputation. Men read novels a great deal more than is supposed, and it is probably from men that the first-class novel receives its *imprimatur*. Men have made Mr Thomas Hardy, who owes nothing to the fair sex; if women read him now, it is because the men have told them that they must. Occasionally we see a very original writer who decidedly owes his fame to the plaudits of the ladies. M. Paul Bourget is the most eminent example that occurs to the memory. But such instances are rare, and it is probably to the approval of male readers that most eminent novelists owe that prestige which ultimately makes them the favourites of the women. Not all men are pressed by the excessive agitations of business life which are habitually attributed to their sex. Even those who are most busy find time to read, and we have been lately informed that among the most constant and assiduous students of new novels are Lord Tennyson and Mr Gladstone. Every storyteller, I think, ought to write as though he believed himself addressing these illustrious veterans.

As I say, I do not revolt against the supremacy of the novel. I acknowledge too heavy a debt of gratitude to my great contemporaries to assume any but a thankful attitude towards them. In my dull and weary hours each has come like the angel Israfel, and let me listen to the beating of his heart, be it lyre or guitar, a solemn instrument or a gay one. I should be bankrupt instantly if I sought to repay to Mr Meredith or Mr Besant, Mr Hardy or Mr Norris, Mr Stevenson or Mr Kipling—to name no others—one-tenth part of the pleasure which, in varied quantity and quality, the stories of each have given me. I admit (for which I shall be torn in pieces) that the ladies please me less, with some exceptions; but that is because, since the days of the divine Mrs Gaskell, they have been so apt to be either too serious or not serious enough. I suppose that the composition of *The Wages Sin* and of *Donovan* serves some excellent purpose. Doubtless these books are useful to great growing girls. But it is not to such stories as these that I owe any gratitude, and it is not to their authors that I address the presumptuous remarks which follow.

A question which constantly recurs to my mind is this: Having secured the practical monopoly of literature, having concentrated public attention on their wares, what are the novelists going to do next? To what use will they put the unprecedented opportunity thrown in their way? It is quite plain that to a certain extent the material out of which the English novel has been constructed is in danger of becoming exhausted. Why do the American novelists inveigh against plots? Not, we may be sure, through any inherent tenderness of conscience, as they would have us believe; but because their eminently sane and somewhat timid natures revolt against the effort of inventing what is extravagant. But all the obvious plots, all the stories which are not in some degree extravagant, seem to have been told already, and for a writer with the temperament of Mr Howells there is nothing left but the careful portraiture of a small portion of the limitless field of ordinary humdrum existence. So long as this is fresh, this also may amuse and please; to the practitioners of this kind of work it seems as though the infinite prairie of life might be surveyed thus for centuries, acre by acre. But that is not possible. A very little while suffices to show that in this direction also the material is promptly exhausted. Novelty, freshness, and excitement are to be sought for at all hazards, and where can they be found?

The novelists hope many things from the happy system of nature, that supplies them, year by year, with fresh generations of the ingenuous young. The procession of adolescence moves on and on, and the front rank of it, for a month or a year, is duped by the novelist's report of that astonishing phenomenon, the passion of love. In a certain sense, we might expect to be tired of love-stories as soon as, and not before, we grow tired of the ever-recurring March mystery of primroses and daffodils. Each generation takes its tale of love under the hawthorn-tree as something quite new, peculiar to itself, not to be comprehended by its elders; and the novelist pipes as he will to this idyllic audience, sure of pleasing, if he adapt himself never so little to their habits and the idiosyncracies of their time. That theory would work well enough if the novelist held the chair of Erotics at the University of life, and might blamelessly repeat the same (or very slightly modified) lectures to none but the students of each successive year. But, unfortunately, we who long ago took our degree, who took it, perhaps, when the Professor was himself in pinafores, also continue to attend his classes. We are hardly to be put off with the old, old commonplaces about hearts and darts. Yet our adult acquiescence is necessary for the support of the Professor. How is he to freshen up his oft-repeated course of lectures to suit our jaded appetites?

It would be curious to calculate how many tales of love must have been told since the vogue of the modem story began. Three hundred novels a year is, I believe, the average product of the English press. In each of these there has been at least one pair of lovers, and generally there have been several pairs. It would be a good question to set in a mathematical examination: What is the probable number of young persons who have conducted one another to the altar in English fiction during the last hundred years? It is almost terrible to think of this multitude of fictitious love-makings,—

> For the lovers of years meet and gather;
> The sound of them all grows like thunder:
> O into what bosom, I wonder,
> Is poured the whole passion of years?

One would be very sorry to have the three hundred of one year poured into one's own mature bosom. But how curious is the absolute unanimity of it all! Thousands and thousands of books, every one of them, without exception, turning upon the attraction of Edwin to Angelina, exactly as though no other subject on earth interested a single human being! The novels in which love has not formed a central feature are so few that I suspect that they could be counted on the fingers of one hand. At this moment, I can but recall a single famous novel in which love has no place. This is, of course, *L'Abbé Tigrane*, that delightful story in which all the interest revolves around the intrigues of two priestly factions in a provincial cathedral. But, although M. Ferdinand Fabre achieved so great a success in this book, and produced an acknowledged masterpiece, he never ventured to repeat the experiment. Eros revels in the pages of all his other stories.

This would be the opportunity to fight the battle of the novelists against Mrs Grundy. But I am not inclined to waste ink on that conceded cause. After the reception of books like *Tess of the D'Urbervilles* and even *David Grieve*, it is plain that the English novelist, who cares and dares, may say almost anything he or she likes without calling flame out of heaven upon his head. There has been a great reform in this respect, since the days when our family friend Mr Punch hazarded his very existence by referring, in grimmest irony, to the sufferings of 'the gay.' We do not want to claim the right which the French have so recklessly abused of describing at will, and secure against all censure, the brutal, the abnormal and the horrible. No doubt a silly prudishness yet exists. Where are still clergymen's wives who write up indignantly from The Vicarage, Little Pedlington. I have just received an epistle from such an one, telling me that certain poor productions I am editing 'make young hearts acquainted with vice, and put hell-fire in their hearts.' 'Woe unto you in your evil work,' says this lady, doubtless a most sincere and conscientious creature, but a little behind the times. Of her and her race individually I wish to say nothing but what is kind; but I confess I am glad to know that the unreflecting spirit they represent is passing away. It is passing away so rapidly that there is really no need to hearten the novelists against it. If they are so poor-spirited as to be afraid to say what they feel they ought to say because of this kind of criticism, their exposition of the verities is not likely to be of very high value.

But I should like to ask our friends the leading novelists whether they do not see their way to enlarging a little the sphere of their labours. What is the use of this tyranny which they wield, if it does not enable them to treat life broadly and to treat it whole? The varieties of amatory intrigue form a fascinating subject, which is not even yet exhausted. But, surely, all life is not love-making. Even the youngest have to deal with other interests, although this may be the dominant one; while, as we advance in years, Venus ceases to be even the ruling divinity. Why should there not be novels written for middle-aged persons? Has the struggle for existence a charm only in its reproductive aspects? If every one of us regards his or her life seriously, with an absolute and unflinching frankness, it will be admitted that love, extended so as to include all its forms—its sympathetic, its imaginative, its repressed, as well as its fulfilled and acknowledged, forms—takes a place far more restricted than the formulæ of the novelist would load the inhabitant of some other planet to conjecture.

Unless the novelists do contrive to enlarge their borders, and take in more of life, that misfortune awaits them which befell their ancestors just before the death of Scott. About the year 1830 there was a sudden crash of the novel. The public found itself abandoned to Lady Blessington and Mr Plumer Ward, and it abruptly closed its account with the novelists. The large prices which had been, for twenty years past, paid for novels were no longer offered. The book-clubs, throughout the Kingdom, collapsed, or else excluded novels. When fiction reappeared, after this singular epoch of eclipse, it had learned its lesson, and the new writers were men who put into their work their best observation and ripest experience. It does not appear in the thirties that any one understood what was happening. The stuff produced by the novelists was so ridiculous and ignoble that 'the nonsense of that divil of a Bullwig' seemed positively unrivalled in its comparative sublimity, although these were the days of *Ernest Maltravers*. It never occurred to the authors when the public suddenly declined to read their books (it read 'Bullwig's' in the lack of anything else) that the fault was theirs. The excuses were made that are made now,— 'necessary to write down to a wide audience;' 'obliged to supply the kind of article demanded;' 'women the only readers to be catered for;' 'mammas so solicitous for the purity of what is laid before their daughters.' And the crash came.

The crash will come again, if the novelists do not take care. The same silly piping of the loves of the drawing-room, the same obsequious attitude towards a supposititious public clamouring for the commonplace, inspire the majority of the novel writers of to-day. Happily, we have, what our fathers in 1835 had not, half a dozen careful and vigorous men of letters who write, not what the foolish publishers ask for, but what they themselves choose to give. The future rests with these few recognized masters of fiction, and with their successors, the vigorous younger men who are preparing to take their place. What are these novelists going to do? They were set down to farm the one hundred acres of an estate called Life, and because one corner of it—the two or three acres hedged about, and called the kitchen-garden of Love—offered peculiar attractions, and was very easy to cultivate, they have neglected the other ninety-seven acres. The result is that by over-pressing their garden, and forcing crop after crop out of it, it is well-nigh exhausted, and will soon refuse to respond to the incessant hoe and spade; while, all the time, the rest of the estate, rich and almost virgin soil, is left to cover itself with the weeds of newspaper police-reports.

It is supposed that to describe one of the positive employments of life,—a business or a profession, for example,—would alienate the tender reader, and check that circulation about which novelists talk as nervously as if they were delicate invalids.

But what evidence is there to show that an attention to real things does frighten away the novel reader? The experiments which have been made in this country to widen the field of fiction in one direction, that of religious and moral speculation, have not proved unfortunate. What was the source of the great popular success of *John Inglesant* and then of *Robert Elsmere*, if not the intense delight of readers in being admitted, in a story, to a wider analysis of the interior workings of the mind than is compatible with the mere record of the billing and cooing of the callow young? We are afraid of words and titles. We are afraid of the word 'psychology,' and, indeed, we have seen follies committed in its name. But the success of the books I have just mentioned was due to their psychology, to their analysis of the effect of associations and sentiments on a growing mind. To make such studies of the soul even partially interesting, a great deal of knowledge, intuition, and workmanlike care must be expended. The novelist must himself be acquainted with something of the general life of man.

But the interior life of the soul is, after all, a very much less interesting study to an ordinarily healthy person than the exterior. It is surprising how little our recent novelists have taken this into consideration. One reason, I cannot doubt, is that they write too early and they write too fast. Fielding began with *Joseph Andrews*, when he was thirty-five; seven years later he published *Tom Jones*; during the remainder of his life, which closed when he was forty-seven, he composed one more novel. The consequence is that into these three books he was able to pour the ripe knowledge of an all-accomplished student of human nature. But our successful novelist of to-day begins when he is two- or three-and-twenty. He 'catches on,' as they say, and he becomes a laborious professional writer. He toils at his novels as if he were the manager of a bank or the captain of an ocean steamer. In one narrow groove he slides up and down, up and down, growing infinitely skilful at his task of making bricks out of straw. He finishes the last page of 'The Writhing Victim' in the morning, lunches at his club, has a nap; and, after dinner, writes the first page of 'The Swart Sombrero.' He cannot describe a trade or a profession, for he knows none but his own. He has no time to look at life, and he goes on weaving fancies out of the ever-dwindling stores of his childish and boyish memories. As these grow exhausted, his works get more and more shadowy, till at last even the long-suffering public that once loved his merits, and then grew tolerant of his tricks, can endure him no longer.

The one living novelist who has striven to give a large, competent, and profound view of the movement of life, is M. Zola. When we have said the worst of the *Rougon-Macquart* series, when we have admitted the obvious faults of these books,—their romantic fallacies on the one hand, their cold brutalities on the other,—it must be admitted that they present the results of a most laudable attempt to cultivate the estate outside the kitchen-garden. Hardly one of the main interests of the modern man has been neglected by M. Zola, and there is no doubt at all that to the future student of nineteenth-century manners his books will have an interest outweighing that of all other contemporary novels. An astonishing series of panoramas he has unrolled before us. Here is *Le Ventre de Paris*, describing the whole system by which a vast modern city is daily supplied with food; here is *Au Bonheur des Dames*, the romance of a shop, which is pushed upwards and outwards by the energy of a single ambitious tradesman, until it swamps all its neighbours, and governs the trade of a district; here is *L'Argent*, in which, with infinite pains and on a colossal scale, the passions which move in *la haute finance* are analyzed, and a great battle of the money-world chronicled; here, above all, is *Germinal*, that unapproachable picture of the agony and stress of life in a great mining community, with a description of the processes so minute and so technical that this novel is accepted by experts as the best existing record of conditions which are already obsolete.

In these books of M. Zola's, as every one knows, successive members of a certain family stand out against a background of human masses in incessant movement. The peculiar characteristic of this novelist is that he enables us to see why these masses are moved, and in what direction. Other writers vaguely tell us that the hero 'proceeded to his daily occupation,' if, indeed, they deign to allow that he had an occupation. M. Zola tells us what that occupation was, and describes the character of it carefully and minutely. More than this: he shows us how it affected the hero's character, how it brought him into contact with others, in what way it represented his share of the universal struggle for existence. So far from the employment being a thing to be slurred over or dimly alluded to, M. Zola loves to make that the very hero of his piece, a blind and vast commercial monster, a huge all-embracing machine, in whose progress the human persons are hurried helplessly along, in whose iron wheels their passions and their hopes are crushed. He is enabled to do this by the exceptional character of his genius, which is realistic in its power of retaining and repeating details, and romantic, also to an extreme, in its power of massing these details on a huge scale, in vast and harmoniously-balanced compositions.

I would not be misunderstood, even by the most hasty reader, to recommend an imitation of M. Zola. What suits his peculiarly-constituted genius might ill accord with the characteristics of another; Nor do I mean to say that we are entirely without something analogous in the writings of the more intelligent of our later novelists. The study of the Dorsetshire dairy-farms in Mr Hardy's superb *Tess of the D'Urbervilles* is of the highest value, and more thorough and intelligible than what we enjoyed in *The Woodlanders*, the details of the apple-culture in the same county. To turn to a totally different school: Mr Hall Caine's *Scapegoat* is a very interesting experiment in fresh fields of thought and experience, more happily conceived, if I may be permitted to say so, than fortunately executed, though even in execution far above the ruck of popular novels. A new Cornish story, called *Inconsequent Lives*, by that very promising young story-teller, Mr Pearce, seemed, when it opened, to be about to give us just the vivid information we want about the Newlyn pilchard-fishery; but the novelist grew timid, and forebore to fill in his sketch. These are instances in which, occasionally, or fantastically, or imperfectly, the real facts of life have been dwelt upon in recent fiction. But when we have mentioned or thought of a few exceptions, to what inanities do we not presently descend!

If we could suddenly arrive from another planet, and read a cluster of novels from Mudie's, without any previous knowledge of the class, we should be astonished at the conventionality, the narrowness, the monotony. All I ask for is a larger study of life. Have the stress and turmoil of a successful political career no charm? Why, if novels of the shop and the counting-house be considered sordid, can our novelists not describe the life of a sailor, of a game-keeper, of a railway-porter, of a civil engineer? What capital central figures for a story would be the whip of a leading hunt, the foreman of a colliery, the master of a fishing smack, or a speculator on the Stock Exchange! It will be suggested that persons engaging in one or other of these professions are commonly introduced into current fiction, and that I am proposing as a novelty what is amply done already. My reply is that our novelists may indeed present to us a personage who is called a stoker or a groom, a secretary of state or a pin-maker, but that, practically, they merely write these denominations clearly on the breasts of lay-figures. For all the enlightenment we get into the habits of action and the habits of thought entailed by the occupation of each, the fisherman might be the groom and the pin-maker the stockbroker. It is more than this that I ask for. I want to see the man in his life. I am tired of the novelist's portrait of a gentleman, with gloves and hat, leaning against a pillar, upon a vague landscape background. I want the gentleman as he appears in a snap-shot photograph, with his every-day expression on his face, and the localities in which he spends his days accurately visible around him. I cannot think that the commercial and professional aspects of life are unworthy of the careful attention of the novelist, or that he would fail to be rewarded by a larger and more interested audience for his courage in dealing closely with them. At all events, if it is too late to ask our accepted tyrants of the novel to enlarge their borders, may we not, at all events, entreat their heirs-apparent to do so?

74

The Place of Realism in Fiction: A Discussion

GEORGE GISSING et AL.

George Gissing (1857-1903), British author of numerous novels, especially *New Grub Street* (1891), *The Odd Women* (1893) and *The Private Papers of Henry Ryecroft* (1903), as well as a critical study of Charles Dickens, joins nine other authors in the following discussion of realism in fiction. All ten writers lament the degeneration of the term realism to connote vulgarity, harshness and ugliness. In general they all call upon a realistic author to strive for balance and truth to his or her own vision instead of photographic detail. Most agree that Balzac is the founder of the realistic school, followed by Flaubert and Zola. Gissing notes that the terms naturalism and realism arose as authors began to reject the insincerity of their predecessors. Refusing, however, to see objectivity as an alternative to insincerity, he argues that any pretence to objectivity in the realistic author is false, since the author's personality invariably shapes the work. Gissing favours abandoning the tainted labels of naturalism and realism and concentrating instead on sincerity and craftsmanship in fiction.

The Place of Realism in Fiction:
A Discussion By

DR WILLIAM BARRY
ALPHONSE DAUDET
ELLA HEPWORTH DIXON
SIR GEORGE DOUGLAS
GEORGE GISSING

W. H. MALLOCK
RICHARD PRYCE
ADELINE SERGEANT
FREDERICK WEDMORE
W. H. WILKINS

Source: George Gissing, et al., "The Place of Realism in Fiction: A Discussion", *The Humanitarian*, July 1895, pp. 7-23.

I.—Dr William Barry
(Author of *A New Antigone*)

Fiction, as I should maintain, is, whether exalted or humble, in prose or in verse, a branch of poetry; and Mr Arnold has told us that poetry should be "a criticism of life." Again, criticism, the same writer lays down, is the effort which we make to "see things as they really are." On these principles, one can easily imagine that a Realist who knew what he proposed to himself in story-telling, would take his stand. For he is always passionately in love with the truth of things, if we may believe M. Zola; he desires to see them as they are, and so to paint them; his voice is lifted up against shams, conventions, hypocrisies; and he would fain tear asunder the veil which hides reality from our deluded vision, and show us the picture itself.

Science, life, and poetry will thus be reconciled; a fresh era will dawn upon European literature; and the great democratic movement make an end of idealists and dreamers, who fashioned their worlds out of smoke, or saw them reflected in soap-bubbles, and thought the result very fine. Now, in an age of unfaith, when experience alone will persuade men to believe, "things as they are,"—and not as we fancy them,—must amuse, distract, awaken, intoxicate us. Facts are facts; the True is the Beautiful—nay, suppose it to be the ugly, the grotesque, the bestial, what then? Had we not better know it? Your Raphaels and Michel Angelos did not show the human figure half so well as a photograph, carefully taken, will show it. In like manner, the novelist who dips into life, anywhere and at what depth soever, will bring to light strange, curious, exciting specimens of reality, far beyond Molière and Shakspere. Let him only not go fishing for his own dreams!

Thus, it seems to me, will the Realist perorate, confident that science (in the person of Claude Bernard) is with him; and life, also, as photographed in police reports; and the democratic movement which means progress. What shall we who come from our classics, Greek or Roman, from our Elizabethan drama, from Goethe and Lessing,—nay, from Victor Hugo and George Sand—reply to his somewhat truculent demand for our money *and* our life? This bold person is nothing if not scientific, on his own showing. May we, then, appeal to the induction of instances, and whisper in the subdued tones which become mere antiques, that fiction, beginning with Homer, culminating in Shakspere and Cervantes, appears to have flourished mightily, yet never on the methods of realism? All these handle details with the most careless freedom. The vision wherein they see things is not of the flesh; it pierces beyond phenomena; it is "a light that never *was* on land or sea." Could a legion of photographers working their machines for ten years in all the available sunshine have given us, at last, an Iliad? Or take M. de Goncourt's *Diary*—it is the Kodak unsleeping and pitiless turned upon private life,—well, may we suppose that in its pages Hamlet would have quite eclipsed that other Prince of Denmark, founded, as we all must allow, not upon photography? My chief objection to the new method is, that, when loyally carried through it eliminates the photographer, and I humbly conceive that there may be some inconvenience in so doing. I would even affirm,—M. Flaubert not swallowing me down his capacious throat,—I would go so far even as to think no less than affirm, that in the absence of the Greek tragedians we should have had no Greek tragedy; that I never heard of anyone but Dante who was capable of writing the   ; that Balzac himself, the father of Realists, hitherto has been found inimitable; and that we shall probably wait in vain for a second George Meredith. Such are my fancies, absurd perhaps, but in any case requiring to be dealt with by "the masters of those that know." Great and splendid fiction the world certainly has, but we owe it to genius, not to machinery. And Realism, if it means an impersonal method, is machinery in literature.

"Tell me what you see, and I will tell you what you are." That is the touchstone I should apply in this question. Whose eyes are opened, and to what kind of vision? I read   ; I perceive that the writer has turned his gaze on the trivialities, the baseness, the horrors, the meanness of human things, on this alone, and on nothing else. Then, I say, the vision is false; it leaves out the sky and the stars. "But these phenomena exist, or they would not be seen; why not paint them?" Why not? Because they fail to render the proportion which is in life truly considered, and they distort its meaning. M. Flaubert, M. Zola, would have endeavoured to give a certain scene upon Calvary long ago, had either been standing by, with infinite precision of grouping and colour, to make it audible, visible to eye and sense. The Realist would have failed even in this attempt; for the endless aspects or any one incident, the multitude of particulars reflecting themselves on all sides, cannot be given, can only be suggested by the writer's shorthand. But, unless he had another insight than that which comes by looking and peeping,—if he were destitute of faith,—he would go away blind and deaf to the real story which had been there enacted, full of the execution with its shame and horror, simply ignorant that in those heartrending, nay, those ignoble details of a day of rebuke and blasphemy, a great "divine event" was passing before his eyes, to which the whole creation has ever since moved.

So it is in the heights and so in the deeps of existence. Romantic fiction is a device, or an economy, by means of which wisest masters teach us their thoughts concerning life, death, duty, self-sacrifice, the scope of suffering, the laws of righteousness. They exhibit ideals in visible forms; but their genius, personal, incommunicable, unique in the measure of their endowments, is like a plate sensitive only to certain sounds or colours; their thought is a vital energy peculiar to themselves. Others, indeed, may learn what has once been revealed. But here is the truth against which photographic Realism will always be dashed in pieces: supreme art is Revelation, and the mind wherein it is shadowed forth by no means an indifferent plane mirror, but a living spirit which reacts upon its materials and gives them its own stamp. Thus, the method of the Realist,—which, however, no one practices consistently, and Flaubert in his frantic efforts to carry it out, was struck down paralysed,—that method, were it possible, would be inhuman, and would sacrifice genius to the "not divine" average, which its disciples term the democratic,—to mediocrity as vulgar as uninteresting. The science which it affects to rest its claims upon is nothing but materialism; the experience it loves to depict that of the shambles, the hospital, and the house of infamy; the end it has in view is sensation, "thrill," and mental pasturings upon the forbidden. Once let it be understood that the human is more than the brutish, and reason above instinct and impulse, from that moment Realism will be found out.

II.—Alphonse Daudet.

I do not believe in *enregimentations*, I have never once in my life written the word "naturalism" or "realism," and I confess that I hardly know what one or the other may mean. Is it the research, as intense as possible, of truth by each one of us, and its expression, when found, according to the temperament of each? For my part, when in one of my books—it was in *Le Nabab*—I wished to depict a very beautiful, very significant, and yet a very repulsive scene, where the love-letters of that Don Juan statesman were being torn up and flung into the *necessarium* by one of his friends, because there was no fire in any of the fireplaces in which to burn them, I spent several hours over my description, seeking to avoid vulgar and realistic expressions, which would have dirtied my page without in any way adding to its power. When, in speaking or these letters, I had found the phrase: "They go down to oblivion by a road of shame" (*Elles vont à l'oubli par un chemin honteux*), I was filled with a true artistic joy. It is my opinion that the writer may say everything, but that a certain cleanliness is indispensable in true art. There are laws of decency and of salubrity which, in literature also, must be observed.

III.—Ella Hepworth Dixon.

"What is Truth?" said Pontius Pilate, unconsciously choosing a time and a place for his question which has sent it resounding, with its eternal note of interrogation, through the slowly evolving centuries. "What is Realism?" the bewildered student of literature is not unnaturally tempted to enquire when confronted with so formidable a problem as the place of realism in fiction. Nor are the two questions unconnected; for realism, we may take it, is truth, *la verité vraie*, as the French quaintly phrase it; that impalpable something which raises a book into a work of art, and not, as many honest folk seem to think (Anglo-Saxon these, and with a fine Puritanical out-look on life and literature) as another and more euphemistic name for the Nasty. It would puzzle some of these worthies to be told that English literature, in its higher manifestations, has always been largely realistic, from the first of the school, Chaucer, who, with marvellous fidelity, depicted life as be saw it; through Shakespeare, to whom no phase, no emotion, no secret of human nature was unknown; through Defoe, with his astonishing genius for the *vraisemblable*; through Fielding, who "saw life steadily and saw it whole"; through Jane Austen, who invented the modern novel; through Thackeray, with his untiring observation, his intimate knowledge of the upper middle-class, down to Mr George Meredith, in whom we have to-day the most brilliant and profound exponent of realism in

English fiction.

Indeed, to raise the question of realism in fiction at the end of a century which, from a literary point of view, may fairly be described as the century of the Realistic Novel seems, at the first blush, a vain wasting of ink. Have any of the masters of the novel disdained to ally themselves with actuality? Did Balzac—the real founder of the French Realistic School? Or his literary children, Flaubert, the Goncourts, Zola, Maupassant? And, further afield, did Turgenieff, though essentially a prose poet, ignore the part which realism must play in fiction to touch a generation which has cast down its old gods and worships the real in the guise of science? Did Tolstoï with his prose epic of *Peace and War*, and his powerful tragedy of the modern woman, *Anna Karenina*? Does Björnsen, in his lurid pictures of Scandinavian manners, or the great symbolist Ibsen, whose more poignant dramas are so many pages torn from suffering human lives? Strip Dickens of his inimitable Gamps and Pecksniffs—startling *silhouettes* of the early Victorian era—and you have little that would endure. It is for the realism of his Squeers and his Mrs Nickleby that we forgive Dickens his cheap pathos, his lumbering plots, and his insupportable heroes and heroines. These things were demanded by his period, but we may be sure (indeed we know) that it was in his extraordinary realisations of contemporary types that the artist chiefly delighted. Strange is it indeed to remember that the same year in which Dickens was writing *A Tale of Two Cities*, a young author was offering to a shocked and bewildered British public the famous Richmond-dinner scene, together with the Shakespearian nurse, the end of the century Adrian (with his selfishness, his epigrams and his cold viciousness), and the audacious and winning courtesan of *The Ordeal of Richard Feveril*. Like Stendhal with his curiously prophetic phrase, "I write for 1890!" Mr Meredith went on his way, regardless of the foolish gibes, the puerile accusations of his critics, convinced, one may reasonably hope, that one day his generation would find him out and elect to do him honour. And Thackeray, girding as he did at the hypocrisy, the false modesty of the 'fifties, and who frankly invites us to read between the lines in *Pendennis*, even the author of *Vanity Fair* and *Esmond* did not shrink from the apotheosis of the Minx in his Becky and his Beatrix, admirable and realistic creations by whom it is not improbable that Thackeray will live when his idealistic Lauras and Amelias are forgotten.

That there are realists and realists is of course obvious. Most people would imagine that in the stories of Guy de Maupassant we have art and reality united in a felicitous marriage, yet, in a recent volume of the *Journal*, we find Edmond de Goncourt speaking of "*Fort comme la Mort*" as one would speak in England of a novel by Miss Rhoda Broughton or Sir Walter Besant. "*Oui*" writes the septuagenarian author of *Germinie Lacerteux*, "*c'est positif: le roman, et un roman tel que 'Fort comme la Mort,' à l'heure actuelle n'a plus d'intérêt pour moi. Je n'aime plus que ls livres qui contiennent des morceaux de vie vraiment vraie, et sans preoccupation de dénouement, et non arrange à l'usage de lecteur bête que demandent les grandes ventes. Non, je ne suis plus intéressé que par les dévoilements d'âme d'un être reel et non l'être chimérique qu'est toujours un héros de roman, par son amalgame avec la convention et le mensonage.*"

And here, tersely put, we have the credo of the advanced realistic school. "*Des morceaux de vie vraiment vraie*,"—that is to say, bits of life selected by an artist, and therefore truer than life itself; this is the pre-occupation of the masters of realistic fiction, no less than that profound sympathy with the poor, the suffering and the down-trodden, which is the most characteristic note of our century—a century which, in casting off the creeds and dogmas which have formed a parasitical growth round the truest and most beautiful of all religions, has emerged triumphantly and essentially Christian. Yes, profoundly, if unconsciously Christian, did M. Zola reveal himself when he wrote *Germinal* and *La Guerre*; nothing could be more un-pagan than Mr Thomas Hardy's poetical and tragic story of a wronged woman in *Tess of the d'Urberville's*; nowhere has the eternal woman's tragedy been touched with a more sympathetic hand than by Maupassant in *Une Vie*, or by the Goncourts in *Soeur Philomène, Germinie Lacerteux, Chérie* and *Renée Manpérin*. Again Ibsen, though chiefly concerned in showing us woman in revolt, is yet Christian in his demand for justice for women—a demand which is the one dominant note in all the great living writers of fiction, and which may fairly be described as the ethical attitude or the end or the nineteenth century. And so it may be that Realism, allied as it is to our religious, our ethical, and our artistic ideals, will probably unite itself in the future more closely still with fiction, an alliance which will afford the appropriate spectacle of a sober bridegroom married to a beguiling bride.

IV.—Sir George Douglas.

Selection is the soul or art. Find out the thing which for you is physically or morally the most beautiful thing in the world, and worthily reproduce it, and you will produce a masterpiece. But M. Zola has lent the great weight of his authority to the belief that what is rare is not "real." "Go to the nearest draper's shop," he says, "observe the first counter-jumper wheedle a foolish dame into the purchase of shoddy goods, and reproduce that." There is material good enough for the exercise of your art. This may be true enough. In the hands of the great artist the common theme itself becomes great. But then the greatness of the artist's power supplies the element of rarity. And surely the artist whose greatness is not yet approved would at least do well to choose his material with extreme care, and to study it with loving closeness. And this being conceded, let him be as "realistic" as he likes. Indeed, in what I conceive to be the only true sense of "realism"—that of *essential truth*—he cannot possibly be too realistic. And no work of art which in this sense lacks realism can ever be aught else than a futility, a structure in the air without foundations.

The brothers De Goncourt, then, may achieve a realistic success with the Memoirs of a Maid of all Work. But these memoirs are realistic because presumably they contain essential truth, not because they deal with the squalid, miserable and vicious side of life. My ideal of a realistic short story is Tourgueneff's *Le Brigadier*, a little tale which may possibly have suggested to Dr Conan Doyle the idea of his *Story of Waterloo*. In this marvellous little illustration of the truth that in our ashes live their wonted fires, we have the height of pathos and of tragedy without the smallest demand being made on our credulity. Nothing is recounted which we cannot easily believe to have happened. Another admirable example of this best kind of realism is the late Dr Brown's tale of *Rab and his Friends*. And these two stories illustrate the honest and sane side of realism—that which dispenses with the insipid "poetic license" of the old-fashioned fiction, wages war against convention, and disdaining approximations labours to add fact to fact and touch to touch in giving a local habitation and a well-defined individuality to its creations. In bringing about this reform, realism has rendered good service to fiction. In deluding us into a belief that what is ugly is more real than what is beautiful, it has wrought grievous harm. For I suppose that the existence of the Lakes of Killarney is no more open to dispute than that of Mr Whiteley's establishment, and that the heroism of Chinese Gordon, the philanthrophy or Lord Shaftesbury, the devotion or Father Damian, Grace Darling, or Alice Ayres, is to the full as capable of demonstration as M. Zola's obscenity, Carlyle's irritable nerves, or the extravagant interest displayed by Thackeray in the small details of vulgar house-keeping.

V.—George Gissing.

One could wish to begin with, that the words *realism* and *realist* might never again be used, save in their proper sense by writers on scholastic philosophy. In relation to the work of novelists they never had a satisfactory meaning, and are now become mere slang. Not long ago I read in a London newspaper, concerning some report of a miserable state of things among a certain class of work-folk, that "this realistic description is absolutely truthful," where by *realistic* the writer simply meant painful or revolting, with never a thought of tautology. When a word has been so grievously mauled, it should be allowed to drop from the ranks.

Combative it was, of course, from the first. Realism, Naturalism, and so on, signified an attitude of revolt against insincerity in the art of fiction. Go to, let us picture things as they are. Let us have done with the conventional, that is to say, with mere tricks for pleasing the ignorant and the prejudiced. Let the novelist take himself as seriously as the man of science; be his work to depict with rigid faithfulness the course of life, to expose the secrets of the mind, to show humanity in its eternal combat with fate. No matter how hideous or heart-rending the results; the artist has no responsibility save to his artistic conscience. The only question is, has he wrought truly, in matter and form? The leaders of this revolt emphasized their position by a choice of vulgar, base, or disgusting subjects; whence the popular understanding of the term *realist*. Others devoted themselves to a laborious picturing of the dullest phases of life; inoffensive, but depressing, they invested *realism* with another quite accidental significance. Yet further to complicate and darken the discussion, it is commonly supposed that novelists of this school propound a theory of life, by preference that known as "pessimism." There is but one way out of this imbroglio: to discard altogether the debated terms and to inquire with regard to any work of fiction, first, whether it is sincere, secondly, whether it is craftsmanlike.

Sincerity I regard as of chief importance. I am speaking of an art, and, therefore, take for granted that the worker has art at his command; but art, in the sense of craftsman's skill, without sincerity of vision will not suffice. This is applicable to both branches of fiction, to romance and to the novel; but with romance we are not here concerned. It seems to me that no novel can possess the slightest value which has not been conceived, fashioned, elaborated, with a view to depicting some portion of human life as candidly and vividly as is in the author's power. Other qualities may abound in the work; some others must needs be present. Tragic power, pathos, humour, sportiveness, tenderness: the novelist may have them one or all; constructive ability and the craft of words he cannot dispense with. But these gifts will not avail him as a novelist, if he lack the spirit of truthfulness,—which, be it added, is quite a different thing from saying that no novel can be of worth if it contain errors or observation, or fall short of the entire presentment of facts.

What do we mean by "reality"? Science concerns itself with facts demonstrable to every formal understanding; the world of science we call "real," having no choice but to accept it as such. In terms of art, reality has another signification. What the artist sees is to him only a part of the actual; its complement is an emotional effect. Thus it comes about that every novelist beholds a world of his own, and the supreme endeavour of his art must be to body forth that world as it exists for him. The novelist works, and must work, subjectively. A demand for objectivity in fiction is worse than meaningless, for apart from the personality of the workman no literary art can exist. The cry arose, of course, in protest against the imperfect method of certain novelists, who came forward in their own pages, and spoke as showmen; but what can be more absurd than to talk about the "objectivity" of such an author as Flaubert, who triumphs by his extraordinary power of presenting life as he, and no other man, beheld it? There is no science of fiction. However energetic and precise the novelist's preparation for his book, all is but dead material until breathed upon by "the shaping spirit of imagination," which is the soul of the individual artist. Process belongs to the workshop; the critic of the completed work has only to decide as to its truth—that is to say, to judge the spirit in which it was conceived, and the technical merit of its execution.

Realism, then, signifies nothing more than artistic sincerity in the portrayal of contemporary life; it merely contrasts with the habit of mind which assumes that a novel is written "to please people," that disagreeable facts must always be kept out of sight, that human nature must be systematically flattered, that the book must have a "plot," that the story should end on a cheerful note, and all the rest of it. Naturally that question arises: What limits does the independent novelist impose upon himself? Does he feel free to select *any* theme, from the sweetest to the most nauseating? Is it enough to declare that he has looked upon this or that aspect of life, has mirrored it in his imagination, and shows it forth candidly, vividly? For my own part, I believe that he must recognize limits in every direction; that he will constantly reject material as unsuitable to the purposes of art; and that many features of life are so completely beyond his province that he cannot dream of representing them. At the same time I joyfully compare the novelist's freedom in England of to-day with his bondage of only ten or twelve years ago. No doubt the new wine of liberty tempts to excess. Moreover, novels nowadays are not always written for the novel's sake, and fiction cries aloud as the mouthpiece of social reform. The great thing is, that public opinion no longer constrains a novelist to be false to himself. The world lies open before him, and it is purely a matter for his private decision whether he will write as the old law dictates or to show life its image as he beholds it.

VI.—W. H. Mallock.

If by realism is meant the artistic reproduction of life literally as it is or of even a single scene exactly as it occurred, realism is impossible, and even unthinkable. If we take, for instance, any single human being, sculpture might reproduce his form with complete exactitude; but it would be a reproduction that was exact for a single moment only. A painter again would represent such a human being not only under a momentary aspect, but would represent one side or view only of a solid body. Even in a photograph everything depends on the point from which it is taken, and the happy disposition of a moment's light and shadow; and only one aspect is given or a scene, a house or a figure, each of which has a thousand aspects. Art, in fact, is a process of representing, or attempting to represent a whole, by a very small number of selected parts; and whether the representation is true to life, or in other words, whether it expresses a reality, and is in any deep sense realistic, does not depend only on the accuracy of each part, but on the general impression which the parts, when put together, produce. If M. Zola had witnessed and described the Crucifixion, he would probably have devoted more care to describing a heap or filth at the foot of the Cross, than the aspect and behaviour or the Sufferer; but he would not for that reason be more realistic than the Evangelists, who omit such details altogether. The fact is that in every incident of life and history, there are any number of realities, only one or a few of which can be represented by one artist, or one work of art; and all artists are equally realistic if they represent with equal fidelity the aspects which their temperaments, or their faiths, or their philosophies, lead them severally to regard as the most important and see with the clearest vision. Let us take, for instance, some serious domestic crisis in humble or vulgar life: the persons concerned will infallibly use expressions or gestures, or betray some turn of thought, which to persons more highly bred will seem odd or ridiculous; and two novelists might describe such a scene, one of whom brought out the reality of its serious aspect, the other the reality of its absurd aspect. The former would probably, so far as was possible, eliminate all peculiarities or vulgarisms of speech, accent, and demeanour; the latter would dwell on them, and call attention to them; and thus two accounts might be written of the same scene, taking place in the same room, each of which was equally realistic, yet neither of which had more than a few details in common. Realism, in novel writing, is vulgarly used to mean a full and unshrinking description of the operation of the sexual appetites, especially in their lower manifestations; but whether such description is, in any true sense, realistic or not, depends altogether on proportion. Does the novelist leave with the reader an impression that these appetites play a larger part in human life than they do, or a less part than they do, or the exact part that they do? A kind of realism, however exact in detail, which leaves on the mind of the reader any impression that the depraved impulses of human nature are more extended in their presence and operation than they are, may be easily more unreal than an art—and this is saying a great deal—which refuses to take account of such impulses altogether.

The above considerations appear to me to touch the root of the matter, though it is impossible in a short space to explain them fully.

VII.—Richard Pryce.

A curious association of ideas (whereby humanity is paid indirectly a sufficiently poor compliment!) seems so to have warped the word Realism, that its just significance is lost. I read in a review of a recent book that parts of it were "realistic to a degree, but true to life." The ingenuous *but* spoke volumes. With such dogged and humorless persistence have we used "realism" to indicate things that are sordid or unsavoury (the things themselves, moreover, apart from the expression of them) that it stands maligned, distorted and unclassed—very outcast in the world of words. But white lives are to be found as well as black, and, oftener than either, lives that are black and white in patches, or grey by the blending of tones. Cannot a presentment of purity, of impulsive goodness and evil, of average morality be as realistic as an "exploiting" of depravity and vice? Can the one-sided book be realistic at all? Pilate asked, What is truth? To the writer of fiction truth is realism, and realism, truth.

VIII.—Adeline Sergeant.

In a certain sense, and to a certain degree, I hold with the Realists. That is to say, I believe (though I do not always practise all that I believe) in minute accuracy and scrupulous fidelity to life. I think these qualities essential to good fiction, without regard to the pleasantness or unpleasantness of the subject treated. Indeed, I feel something akin to contempt, I fear, for the feeble folk who look for a mere fairy tale when they take up a novel, who demand a "happy ending" and "nice" characters before they find enjoyment in fiction. They forget how unsatisfactory Life's "endings" usually are, and how seldom we meet with perfection even in our dearest friends. Above everything, I would have the novelist true to life, and therefore a Realist.

But if a novel is to be a transcript from life, and valuable for its truthfulness as well as its artistic form, we must guard against its being levelled to the comprehension of children. It is almost a pity that very young people read novels at all. For if the novel is to do its proper work, which is to expound the true meaning of life, it must deal with the dark as well as the bright side or the world. Its writer must not shrink from the presentation or the most terrible problems, the most heart-rending situations, the deepest desolation or spirit known in the history of man. A great deal of life is full of sin, misery, and unrest: it is worse than useless to gloss over its wretchedness by calling darkness, light, and sickness, health. Let us have *Esther Waters* and *Lourdes* by all means; teach us to know the extremes of human agony as of human blessedness, to realise the depths of vice as well as the heights of sanctity. They are all a part of human experience: we cannot afford to set aside the shadows in any picture of the great tragic-comedy that we call Life.

But there is the other side. We cannot dispense with the shadow, but we need not live in it. The fault of your Realist is that he cares too much for the study of abnormal growths, of "strange sins," of disease and death. Now this is work for the physician, not for the artist. The doctor should study disease that he may cure it, and he devotes himself to that side of the world's history; but the artist should see life "whole." There is a blue sky overhead as well as a dunghill at our feet. Why become a specialist on dunghills because you wish to produce a picture of life?

And, as all specialists magnify their office, it follows that the Realist's work has a tendency towards magnifying the importance of the ills which he describes. He is apt to forget (what it should surely be one object of the true artist to point out) the tremendous compensations for human misery which meet us on every side. It has, indeed, been argued that there is no such thing as an especially miserable lot—that all human lives are, on the whole, pretty much at the same level as regards happiness and misery. Disease of body is balanced by a mirthful spirit, poverty by a contented mind or the love of friends; all unhappiness is, at worst, intermittent and terminable. Every constitution adapts itself in time to its environment. What is torture to one person, is almost a pleasure to another—it is all a question of temperament. We ought to hesitate as much to call a man wretched in this life, as the ancients did to call him happy. We cannot judge—values are relative—we can but point what lies before us, remembering that the more faithfully and minutely we reproduce human life, the more likely we are to get the "true inwardness"—the moral and meaning—of the story. Life is immoral only when we draw the half of it instead or the whole, where, if we find ugliness, we find also beauty, and joy, and noble aims, and high achievements. In these also consist the true Realism of Life, and of the Fiction which claims to represent Life.

IX.–Frederick Wedmore.

It has taken seventeen years to sell four editions of the first of my collections of short stories, yet, of my three little volumes of imaginative pieces, those contained in *Pastorals of France* are, I believe, the least markedly unpopular. The state of my pocket makes me painfully aware that the well-informed public which buys its stories where it buys its railway rugs and paper knives, has scarcely heard of *English Episodes*, or of *Renunciations*. I should take it, therefore, as a personal kindness if someone would allay my curiosity and put me in possession of the reason why I am invited to say anything about Realism in Fiction. But meanwhile, to the point.

The importance of Realism in Narrative Fiction, as well as in the Drama, has got chiefly to be experienced as "a felt want," since the world has become less naïve. The demand for it has scarcely been made by the dweller in remote ages or in a remote place. To unsophisticated youth, and in the youth of the world, the unreality of a thing, or its mere strangeness, constituted its charm. From this, in the condition of omniscience at which we have at present arrived, there has been a strong reaction, and the extreme of that reaction—its unjustified excess—is shown in contemporary fiction, as in play-writing and in pictorial art, by these two things—the enthusiastic pursuit of the entirely hideous and the undue adoration of the merely true.

Realism, in many people's minds, has come to be confused with the steady presentation of ugliness and the self-satisfied exhibition of vice. There are folk who consider that it is much more penetrating to pourtray, with however lamentable a crudeness, some creature who has not only broken the commandments, but in whom the instincts of humanity are absent, than to model, with however firm and exquisite a delicacy, some white figure who may still move to reverence as she walks the world unsmirched. Readers for whom Balzac is inevitably closed, by reason of the depth of his thoughtfulness, could not in any case have paid heed to his declaration that it requires far greater art to give interest to a worthy character than to an unworthy.

Other people, whose better instincts, or whose wider and saner social education, may cause them to revolt against the doctrine that the vicious must necessarily be the real, are yet not always delivered from the superstition that mere accuracy has value. Now, personally, I love to register an observation; I love accuracy and try, in my small way, to practise it; but not, I hope, without knowing that in literary art, accuracy is only inestimable when it conduces to the effect that was sought—when it furthers sensibly the scheme of the artist. When it does not do so, it has but little worth. Invaluable in the dictionary or the handbook, the work of literary art can very well, upon occasion, do without it. The realism that it most of all behoves you to conserve or to acquire, is the inner and deeper realism that comes in part of a vision individual and potent. I take it, that a profound sympathy with the selected theme, a watchful tact in the acceptance and rejection of details, the exercise, in a word, of a sane and commanding artistry, placed ever at the service of Nature, but never overwhelmed by her mere affluence or material, makes more for a realism lasting in its effectiveness, than the obtrusive accumulation of five hundred facts, by the industry which suffices to docket details, but does not know how to employ them.

Half of the art of the finer realists, consists, it seems to me, in knowing what to avoid, how not to make mistakes about things, how never to "put your foot in it." As much fact must be got into the picture as the picture can quite safely carry: as much, and very carefully no more. A character of yours works in a factory; I do not see in that any reason for describing every transformation of the fabric, for devoting many pages to an account of where the raw material is brought from, and many more to the eventual bankruptcy of the merchant who, in fullness of time, possessed himself of the manufactured article. But I ask for a few telling touches that shall convey to me the interior, and how, during your factory hand's long day, the hours speed upon his dial. I would invite you to do your work of preliminary study for me, and not to expect that I—your reader—shall do it all in your company. It would bore me to death. The time waxes short; men's reasonable occupations are many; and in the future the realism that is likely to be prized, is not so much the realism of prolixity as the realism of frugal and austere choice.

Of the larger aspects of Realism, or its supposed opposition to Idealism—an opposition far more imaginary than true—a volume might be written, were there any advantage in writing it. Surely the finer Realism is but a development of the older method, of the older conception, a development dictated by the needs of our growth, which needs, whatever be the fashion of the moment, can never permit the exclusion of the ideal—in other words, of the poetic. In the most distinguished of contemporary work, English, American, or French, in that which is written least of all, presumably, with deference to the immediate fancy of the large public, in that in which you find the fewest concessions either to antiquated prejudice or novel whim, it is not, as I conceive it, two principles or two methods that come into contact; nor is it one that has dominance. The art may be so subtle and elusive, the fabric of such individual design, the "story" perhaps so slight an element in the matter created, that we may not receive the thing with the immediate readiness with which we greet the obvious and the hackneyed. But, at least, when we do receive it, it becomes apparent to us that it is neither uninterruptedly "realistic" nor exclusively "ideal"; but that fact and beauty have gone hand in hand; and the thing is acceptable, and perhaps medicinable even, in virtue of their union.

X.—W. H. Wilkins.

Realism has suffered more from its friends than its foes. For assuming that realism is truth, and further, that the truth has many aspects, then it must be admitted that many writers of fiction who dub themselves "realists" have fallen very short of their end, in that they confine themselves to one aspect of the truth only, and that the least pleasing. In the quest for truth it is not enough to be always nosing after nastiness, because life is not altogether nasty; it is not enough to be always raking together and analysing the wreckage of humanity because humanity is not all wreckage. To do these things is the function of the man with the muck-rake; it is not the work of the artist in fiction. He should rather in his search for truth take a broad and liberal view of the human comedy, and recognize the good as well as the bad, the sweet as well as the bitter. Life is not all leaden-hued. In the windows of a squalid slum may sometimes be seen, in spite of grime and fog and smuts, bright-hued flowers, tended by loving hands, little bits of colour in the all-pervading gloom.

So, too, in the crowd of dull, unlovely lives some pure unselfish souls may be found, happy and diffusing their happiness around them. The writer who ignores these salient features is not a true realist, whatever else he may be.

In the fiction of another development of the so-called realistic school, "sex-maniacs," to wit, may be noted a similar incapacity to see more than one side of the truth. "The passion called love," say these in effect, "is physical, moral or immoral, as the case may be, but physical at the core." This is a half-truth, and, like all half-truths, it hides a dangerous fallacy. *Nulla falsa doctrina est, quae non permisceat aliquid veritatis.* This half-truth is the bane of the average French novel which dwells wholly on the physical aspect of love and life. On the other hand, certain of our veteran toilers in the consolidated tale-and-novel-industry ignore that aspect altogether, and deal only with bloodless and impossible emotions. The truth is with neither. As Paul Bourget seeks almost passionately to express, if we have bodies we have also souls. The true realist will remember this, for only by remembering it can he hope to see life whole.

But the excesses or the fleshy and the pessimistic schools are not of the essence of realism. They may rather be regarded as an exaggerated protest against the unreal conventionalities of the ordinary three-volume novel of a few years ago, which, for instance, treated of life as ending with marriage instead of beginning with it. The revolt against these unrealities has at least made it clear that all literature cannot be dragged down to the level of the Young Person's innocence—or ignorance—or to Mrs Grundy's notions of propriety.

Of realism in its fullest and highest sense we cannot have too much. St. Jerome says somewhere, "If an offence come out of the truth, better is it that the offence come than that the truth be concealed." These words strike the keynote of true realism. Let the writer of fiction give us the truth by all means and at all hazards, only let it be the whole truth. Let him give us the beauty of life as well as the ugliness, the purity as well as the impurity, the spiritual as well as the material. And above all, in endeavouring to depict life as it is, let him not lose sight of life as it ought to be.

❧ 75 ❧

On Literary Construction

VERNON LEE

A late nineteenth and early twentieth century writer in the Paterean tradition, Vernon Lee (Violet Paget [1856-1935]) wrote books on Italy and Italian art, novels and criticism. In this essay, she compares the construction of a successful novel to a "gigantic symphony" as opposed to the "little sonata" of the essay. She criticizes the typical nineteenth-century British three-volume novel for its awkward alteration of scene and narrative links and argues that the French and Russian novels more seamlessly render "the force of accumulated action". In a final division between "synthetic" and "analytic" novelists, she applauds the former, exemplified by Thackeray and Tolstoy, for their ability to live inside the characters and to shift point of view while remaining believable and realistic. This essay is an early example of a host of critical writings on novelistic technique. Specifically, it points toward Percy Lubbock's distinction between pictorial and dramatic and the recognition that form and subject matter must closely coincide.

The craft of the writer consists, I am convinced, in manipulating the contents of his reader's mind, that is to say, taken from the technical side as distinguished from the psychologic, in construction. Construction is not only a matter of single words or sentences, but of whole large passages and divisions; and the material which the writer manipulates is not only the single impressions, single ideas and emotions, stored up in the reader's mind and deposited there by no act of his own, but those very moods and trains of thought into which the writer, by his skilful selection of words and sentences, has grouped those single impressions, those very moods and trains of thought which were determined by the writer himself.

We have all read Mr Stevenson's *Catriona*. Early in that book there is a passage by which I can illustrate my meaning. It is David Balfour's walk to Pilrig:

> My way led over Mouter's Hill, and through an end of a clachan on the braeside among fields. There was a whirr of looms in it went from house to house; bees hummed in the garden; the neighbours that I saw at the doorsteps talked in strange

Source: Vernon Lee, "On Literary Construction", *Contemporary Review*, 68, 1895, pp. 404-19.

tongue; and I found out later that this was Picardy, a village where the French weavers wrought for the Linen Company. Here I got a fresh direction for Pilrig, my destination; and a little beyond, on the wayside, came by a gibbet and two men hanged in chains. They were dipped in tar, as the manner is; the wind span them, the chains clattered, and the birds hung about the uncanny jumping jacks and cried.

This half-page sounds as if it were an integral part of the story, one of the things which happened to the gallant but judicious David Balfour. But in my opinion it is not such a portion or the story, not an episode told for its own sake, but a qualifier of something else; in fact, nothing but an adjective, on a large scale.

Let us see. The facts of the case are these: David Balfour, having at last, after the terrible adventures recorded in *Kidnapped*, been saved from his enemies and come into his lawful property, with a comfortable life before him and no reason for disquietude, determines to come forward as a witness in favour of certain Highlanders, whom it is the highest interest of the Government to put to death, altogether irrespective of whether or not they happen to be guilty in the matter about which they are accused. In order to offer his testimony in what he imagines to be the most efficacious manner, David Balfour determines to seek an interview with the Lord Advocate of Scotland; and he is now on his way to his cousin of Pilrig to obtain a letter from him for the terrible head of the law. Now if David Balfour actually has to be sent to Pilrig for the letter of introduction to the Lord Advocate, then his walk to Pilrig is an intrinsic portion of the story, and what happened to him on his walk cannot be considered save as an intrinsic portion also. This would be true enough if we were considering what actually could or must happen to a real David Balfour in a real reality, not what Stevenson wants us to think did happen to an imaginary David Balfour. If a real David Balfour was destined, through the concatenation of circumstances, to walk from Edinburgh to Pilrig by that particular road on that particular day; why, he was destined also—and could not escape his destiny—to come to the gibbet where, on that particular day, along that particular road, those two malefactors were hanging in chains.

But even supposing that Stevenson had been found, for some reason, to make David Balfour take that particular day the particular walk which must have brought him past that gibbet; Stevenson would still have been perfectly free to omit all mention of his seeing that gibbet, as he evidently omitted mentioning a thousand other things which David Balfour must have seen and done in the course of his adventures, because the sight of that gibbet in no way affected the course of the events which Stevenson had decided to relate, any more than the quality of the porridge which David had eaten that morning. And as it happens, moreover, the very fact of David Balfour having walked that day along that road, and of the gibbet having been there, is, as we know, nothing but a make-believe on Stevenson's part, and so there can have been no destiny at all about it. Therefore, I say that this episode, which leads to no other episode, is not an integral part of the story, but a qualifier, an adjective. It acts, not upon what happens to the hero, but on what is felt by the reader. Again, let us look into the matter. This beginning of the story is, from the nature of the facts, rather empty of tragic events; yet tragic events are what Stevenson wishes us to live through. There is something humdrum in those first proceedings of David Balfour's, which are to lead to such hairbreadth escapes. There is something not heroic enough in a young man, however heroic his intentions, going to ask for a letter of introduction to a Lord Advocate. But what can be done? If adventures are invented to fill up these first chapters, these adventures will either actually lead to something which will complicate a plot already quite as complicated as Stevenson requires, or—which is even worse—they will come to nothing, and leave the reader disappointed, incredulous, unwilling to attend further after having wasted expectations and sympathies. Here comes in the admirable invention of the gibbet. The gibbet is, so to speak, the shadow of coming events cast over the smooth earlier chapters of the book. With its grotesque and ghastly vision, it puts the reader in the state of mind desired: it means tragedy. "I was pleased," goes on David Balfour, "to be so far in the still countryside; but the shackles of the gibbet clattered in my head . . . There might David Balfour hang, and other lads pass on their errands, and think light of him." Here the reader is not only forcibly reminded that the seemingly trumpery errand of this boy will lead to terrible dangers; but he is made to feel, by being told that David felt (which perhaps at that moment David, accustomed to the eighteenth-century habit of hanging petty thieves along the roadside might not) the ghastliness of that encounter.

And then note how this qualifier, this adjectival episode, is itself qualified. It is embedded in impressions of peacefulness: the hillside, the whirr of looms and hum of bees, and talk of neighbours on doorsteps; nay, Stevenson has added a note which increases the sense of peacefulness by adding an element of unconcern, of foreignness, such as we all find adds so much to the peaceful effect of travel, in the fact that the village was inhabited by strangers—Frenchmen—to whom David Balfour and the Lord Advocate and the Appin murder would never mean anything. Had the gibbet been on the Edinburgh Grassmarket, and surrounded by people commenting on Highland disturbances, we should have expected some actual adventure for David Balfour; but the gibbet there, in the fields, by this peaceful foreign settlement, merely puts our mind in the right frame to be moved by the adventures which will come slowly in their due time.

This is a masterpiece of constructive craft: the desired effect is obtained without becoming involved in other effects not desired, without any debts being made with the reader; even as in the case of the properly chosen single adjective, which defines the meaning of the noun in just the desired way, without suggesting any further definition in the wrong way.

Construction—that is to say, co-ordination. It means finding out what is important and unimportant, what you can afford and cannot afford to do. It means thinking out the results of every movement you set up in the reader's mind, how that movement will work into, help, or mar the other movements which you have set up there already, or which you will require to set up there in the future. For, remember, such a movement does not die out at once. It continues and unites well or ill with its successors, as it has united well or ill with its predecessors. You must remember that in every kind of literary composition, from the smallest essay to the largest novel, you are perpetually, as in a piece of music, introducing new *themes*, and working all the themes into one another. A theme may be a description, a line of argument, a whole personage; but it always represents, on the part of the reader, a particular kind of intellectual acting and being, a particular kind of mood. Now, these moods, being concatenated in their progression, must be constantly altered by the other moods they meet; they can never be quite the same the second time they appear as the first, nor the third as the second: they must have been varied, and they ought to have been strengthened or made more subtle by the company they have kept, by the things they have elbowed, and been—however unconsciously—compared and contrasted with; they ought to have become more satisfactory to the writer as a result of their stay in the reader's mind.

A few very simple rules might be made, so simple as to sound utterly childish; yet how many writers observe them?

Do not, if you want Tom to seem a villain, put a bigger villain, Dick, by his side; but if, for instance, like Tolstoi, you want Anatole to be the trumpery wicked Don Juan, put a grand, brilliant, intrepid Don Juan—Dologhow—to reduce him to vulgar proportions. Do not, again, break off in the midst of some event, unless you wish that event to become important in the reader's mind and to react on future events; if, for some reason, you have brought a mysterious stranger forward, but do not wish anything to come of his mysteriousness, be sure you strip off his mystery as prosaically as you can, before leaving him. And, of course, *vice versa*.

I have compared literary themes to musical ones. The novel may be considered as a gigantic symphony, opera, or oratorio, with a whole orchestra. The essay is a little sonata, trio, sometimes a mere little song. But even in a song, how many melodic themes, harmonic arrangements, accents, and so forth! I could wish young writers, if they have any ear, to unravel the parts of a fugue, the themes of a Beethoven sonata. By analogy, they would learn a great many things.

Leaving such learning by musical analogy alone, I have sometimes recommended to young writers that they should draw diagrams, or rather *maps*, of their essays or stories. This is, I think, a very useful practice, not only for diminishing faults of construction in the individual story or essay, but, what is more important, for showing the young writer what amount of progress he is making, and to what extent he is becoming a craftsman. Every one will probably find his own kind of map or diagram. The one I have made use of to explain the meaning to some of my friends is as follows: Make a stroke with your pen which represents the first train of thought or mood, or the first group of facts you deal with. Then make another pen-stroke to represent the second, which shall be proportionately long or short according to the number of words or pages occupied, and which, connected with the first pen-stroke, as one articulation of a reed is with another, will deflect to the right or the left according as it contains more or less new matter; so that, if it grow insensibly from stroke number one, it will have to be almost straight, and if it contain something utterly disconnected, will be at right angles. Go on adding pen-strokes for every new train of thought, or mood, or group of facts, and writing the name along each, and being careful to indicate not merely the angle of divergence, but the respective length in lines. And then look at the whole map. If the reader's mind is to run easily along the whole story or essay, and to perceive all through the necessary connection between the parts, the pattern you will have traced will approximate most likely to a perfect circle or ellipse, the conclusion re-uniting with the beginning as in a perfect logical exposition; and the various pen-strokes, taking you gradually round this circle or ellipse, will correspond in length very exactly to the comparative importance or complexity of the matter to dispose of. But in proportion as the things have been made a mess of, the pattern will tend to the shapeless; the lines, after infinite tortuosities, deflections to the right and to the left, immense bends, sharp angles and bags of all sorts, will probably end in a pen-stroke at the other end of the paper, as far off as possible from the beginning. All this will mean that you have lacked general conception of the subject, that the connection between what you began and what you ended with is arbitrary or accidental, instead of being logical and organic. It will mean that your mind has been rambling, and that you have been making the reader's mind ramble hopelessly, in all sorts of places you never intended; that you have wasted his time and strength and attention, like a person pretending to know his way in an intricate maze of streets, but not really knowing which turning to take. Every one of those sharp angles has meant a lack of connection, every stroke returning back upon itself a useless digression, every loop an unnecessary reiteration; end the entire shapelessness of your diagram has represented the atrocious fact that the reader, while knowing what you have been talking about, has not known why you have been talking about it—and is, but for a number of random pieces of information which he must himself re-arrange, no wiser than when you began.

What will this lead to? What will it make the reader expect? What will it actually bring the reader's mind to? This is the meaning of the diagrams. For, remember, in literature all depends on what you can set the reader to do; if you confuse his ideas or waste his energy, you can no longer do anything.

I mentioned just now that in a case of bad construction the single items might be valuable, but that the reader was obliged to rearrange the book; and, if any one is to do that, it had better not be the reader, surely, but rather a more competent writer. When the badly arranged items are themselves good, one sometimes feels a mad desire to hand them over thus to some one else. It is like good food badly cooked. I think I have scarcely ever been so tormented with the desire to get a story re-written by some competent person, or even to re-write it myself, as in the case of one or the little volumes of the Pseudonym Series, a story called "A Mystery or the Campagna." I should like every young writer to read it, as a perfect model of splendid material, imaginative and emotional, of notions and descriptions worthy of Merimée (who would have worked them into a companion piece to the wonderful "Venus d'Ille"), presented in such a way as to give the minimum of interest with the maximum of fatigue. It is a thing to make one cry merely to think of; such a splendid invention, such deep contagious feeling for the uncanny solemnity, the deathly fascination of the country about Rome, worked up in a way which leaves no clear impression at all, or, if any, an impression of trivial student restaurant life.

One of the chief defects of this unlucky little book of genius is that a story of about a hundred pages is narrated by four or five different persons, none of whom has any particular individuality, or any particular reason to be telling the story at all. The result is much as if you were to be made to hear a song in fragments, fragments helter-skelter, the middle first and beginning last, played on different instruments. A similar fault of construction, you will remember, makes the beginning of one of our greatest masterpieces of passion and romance, *Wuthering Heights*, exceedingly difficult to read. As if the step-relations and adopted relations in the story were not sufficiently puzzling, Emily Brontë gave the narrative to several different people, at several different periods, people alternating what they had been told with what they actually witnessed. This kind of construction was a fault, if not of Emily Brontë's own time, at least of the time in which many of the books which had impressed her most had been written, notably Hoffman's, from whose *Majorat* she borrowed much for *Wuthering Heights*. It is historically an old fault for the same reason which makes it a fault with beginners, namely, that it is undoubtedly easier to narrate in the first person, or as an eye-witness, and that it is easier to co-ordinate three or four sides of an event by boxing them mechanically as so many stories one in the other, than to arrange the various groups of persons and acts as in real life, and to change the point or view of the reader from one to the other. These mechanical divisions also seem to give the writer courage: it is like the series or ropes which take away the fear of swimming: one thinks one might always catch hold of one of them, but, meanwhile, one usually goes under water all the same. I have no doubt that most of the stories which we have all written between the ages or fifteen and twenty were either in the autobiographical or the epistolary room, that they had introduction set in introduction like those of Scott, that they shifted narrator as in *Wuthering Heights*, and altogether reproduced, in their immaturity, the forms of an immature period of novel-writing, just as Darwinians tell us that the feet and legs of babies reproduce the feet and legs of monkeys. For, difficult as it is to realise, the apparently simplest form of construction is by far the most difficult; and the straightforward narrative of men and women's feelings and passions, or anything save their merest outward acts; the narrative which makes the thing pass naturally before the reader's mind, is by far the most difficult, as it is the most perfect. You will remember that *Julie* and *Clarissa* are written in letters, *Werther* and *Adolphe* as confessions with post-scripts; nay, that even Homer and the *Arabian Nights* cannot get along save on a system of narrative within narrative; so long does it take to get to the straight-forward narrative of Thackeray, let alone that of Tolstoi. For a narrative may be in the third person, and may leave out all mention of eye-witness narration, and yet be far from what I call straightforward. Take, for instance, the form of novel adopted by George Eliot in *Adam Bede*, *Middlemarch*, *Deronda*—in all save her masterpiece, which has the directness of an autobiography—*The Mill on the Floss*. This form I should characterise as that of *the novel built up in scenes*, and it is well worth your notice because it is more or less the typical form of the English three-volume novel. It represents a compromise with that difficult thing, straightforward narrative; and the autobiographical, the epistolary, the narration-within-narration dodges have merely been replaced by another dodge for making things easier for the writer and less efficacious for the reader, the dodge of arranging the matter as much as possible as in a play, with narrative or analytic connecting links. By this means a portion of the story is given with considerable efficacy; the dialogue and gesture, so to speak, are made as striking as possible; in fact, we get all the apparent lifelikeness of a play. I say the *apparent* lifelikeness, because a play is in reality excessively unlifelike, owing to the necessity of things, which could not have happened together, being united in time and place; to quantities of things being said which never could have been said nor even thought; to scenes being protracted, rendered explicit and decisive far beyond possibility, merely because of other scenes (if we may call them scenes), the hundred other fragments of speech and fragments or action which really made the particular thing happen, having to be left out. This is a necessity on the stage because the scene cannot be changed sufficiently often, and because you cannot let people remain for an instant without talking either to some one else or to themselves. But this necessity when applied to a novel, actually mars the action, and, what is worse, alters the conception of the action, for the form in which any story is told inevitably reacts on the matter.

Take *Adam Bede*. The hero is supposed to be exceedingly reserved, more than reserved, one of those strenuous natures which cannot express their feelings even to themselves, and run away and hide in a hole whenever they do know themselves to be feeling. But, owing to the division of the book into scenes, and connecting links between the scenes, one has the impression of Adam Bede perpetually *en scène*, with appropriate background of carpenter's shop or wood, and a chorus of village rustics; Adam Bede always saying something or doing something, talking to his dog, shouldering his tools, eating his breakfast, in such a way that the dullest spectators may recognise what be is feeling and thinking. Now, to make an inexplicit personage always explain himself is only equalled by making an un-analytical person perpetually analyse himself; and, by the system of scenes, by having to represent the personage walking immersed in thoughts, hurrying along full or conflicting feelings, this is the very impression which we get, on the contrary, about Arthur and Hetty, whose misfortunes were certainly not due to overmuch introspection.

Now you will mark that this division into scenes and connecting links occurs very much less in modern French novels: in them, indeed, when a scene is given, it is because a scene actually took place, not because a scene was a convenient way of showing what was going on; and I think you will all remember that in Tolstoi's great novels one scarcely has the sense or there being any scenes at all, not more so than in real life. Pierre's fate is not sealed in a given number of interviews with Hélène; nor is the rupture between Anna and Wronsky—although its catastrophe is brought about, as it must be, by a special incident—the result of anything save imperceptible disagreements every now and then, varied with an outbreak of jealousy. Similarly, in Tolstoi you never know how many times Levine went to the house of Kitty's parents, nor whether Pierre had twenty or two thousand interviews with Natasha; you only know that it all happens as it inevitably must, and happens, as most things in this world do, by the force of accumulated action.

There are some questions of construction in novels connected with this main question of the really narrative or partially dramatic form of construction, of the directness or complication of arrangement. One of these is the question of what I would call the *passive* description, by which I men the setting up, as it were, of an elaborate landscape, or other background, before the characters are brought on the stage. The expression I have just used, "brought on the stage," shows you that I connect this particular mode of proceeding with the novel in scenes. And it is easy to understand that, once the writer allows himself to think of any event happening as it would on the stage, he will also wish to prepare a suitable background, and, moreover, most often a chorus and set of supernumeraries; a background which, in the reality, the principal characters would perhaps not be conscious of, and a chorus which, also in the reality, would very probably not contribute in the least to the action. Another drawback, by the way, of the construction in scenes and connecting links is, that persons have to be invented to elicit the manifestation of the principal personage's qualities: you have to invent episodes to show the good heart of the heroine, the valour of the hero, the pedantry of the guardian, &c., and meanwhile the real action stops; or, what is much worse, the real action is most unnaturally complicated by such side business, which is merely intended to give the reader information that he either need not have at all, or ought to get in some more direct way. Note that there is all the difference in the word between an episode like that of the gallows on the road to Pilrig, which is intended to qualify the whole story by inducing a particular frame of mind in the reader, and an episode like that of Dorothea (in *Middlemarch*) sharing her jewels with her sister on the very afternoon of Mr Casaubon's first appearance, and which is merely intended to give the reader information that might have been quite simply conveyed by saying, whenever it was necessary, "Now Dorothea happened to be a very ascetic person, with a childishly deliberate aversion to the vanities." This second plan would have connected Dorothea's asceticism with whatever feelings and acts really sprang from it; while the first plan merely gives you a feeling of too many things happening in one day, and of Mr Casaubon appearing, not simply as a mere new visitor, but as the destined husband of Dorothea. For, remember, that the reader tends to attribute to the personages of a book whatever feelings you set up in him, so that, if you make the reader feel that Casaubon is to be the bridegroom, you also, in a degree, make Dorothea feel that Casaubon is to be the bridegroom. And that, even for Dorothea, is rather precipitate.

Another question of construction is the one I should call the question of *retrospects*. The retrospect is a frequent device for dashing into the action at once, and putting off the evil day of explaining why people are doing and feeling in the particular way in which we find them, on the rising of the curtain. This, again, is a dramatic device, being indeed nothing but the narrative to or by the confidants which inevitably takes place in the third or fourth scene of the first act of a French tragedy, with the author in his own costume taking the place of the nurse, bosom friend, captain of the guard, &c. The use of this retrospective, of this sort of folding back of the narrative, and the use of a number of smaller artifices of foreshortening the narrative, seems to me not disagreeable at all in the case of the short story. The short story is necessarily much more artificial than the big novel, owing to its shortness, owing to the initial unnaturalness of having isolated one single action or episode from the hundred others influencing it, and to the unnaturalness of having, so to speak, reduced everybody to be an orphan, or a childless widow or widower, for the sake of greater brevity. And the short story, being most often thus artificially pruned and isolated, being in a measure the artificially selected expression of a given situation, something more like a poem or a little play, sometimes actually gains by the discreet display of well-carried-out artifices. While, so far as I can see, the big novel never does.

There is yet another constructive question about the novel—the most important question of all—whose existence the lay mind probably does not even suspect, but which, I am sure, exercises more than any other the mind of any one who has attempted to write a novel; even as the layman, contemplating a picture, is apt never to guess how much thought has been given to determining the place where the spectator is supposed to see from, whether from above, below, from the right or the left, and in what perspective, consequently, the various painted figures are to appear. This supreme constructive question in the novel is exactly analogous to that question in painting; and in describing the choice by the painter of the point of view, I have described also that most subtle choice of the literary craftsman: choice of the point of view whence the personages and action of a novel are to be seen. For you can see a person, or an act, in one of several ways, and connected with several other persons or acts. You can see the person from nobody's point of view, or from the point of view of one of the other persons, or from the point of view of the analytical, judicious author. Thus, Casaubon may be seen from Dorothea's point of view, from his own point of view, from Ladislaw's point of view, or from the point of view of George Eliot; or he may be merely made to talk and act without any explanation of why he is so talking and acting, and that is what I call nobody's point of view. Much of Wilkie Collins and Miss Braddon is virtually written from nobody's point of view; and so are the whole of the old Norse sagas, the greater part of Homer and the *Decameron*, and the whole of *Cinderella* and *Jack the Giant Killer*. We moderns, who are weary of psychology—for poor psychology is indeed a weariness—often find the lack of point of view as refreshing as plain water compared with wine, or tea, or syrup. But once you get a psychological interest, once you want to know, not merely what the people did or said, but what they thought or felt, the point of view becomes inevitable, for acts and words come to exist only with reference to thoughts and feelings, and the question comes, Whose thoughts or feelings?

This is a case of construction, of craft. But it is a case where construction is most often determined by intuition, and where craft comes to be merged in feeling. For, after having separated the teachable part of writing from the unteachable, we have come at last to one of the thousand places—for there are similar places in every question, whether of choice of single words or of construction of whole books—

where the teachable and the unteachable unite, where craft itself becomes but the expression of genius. So, instead of trying to settle what points of view are best, and how they can best be alternated or united, I will now state a few thoughts of mine about that which settles all questions of points of view, and alone can settle them satisfactorily—the different kinds of genius of the novelist.

I believe that the characters in a novel which seem to us particularly vital are those that to all appearance have never been previously analysed or rationally understood by the author, but are, on the contrary, those which, connected always by a sort of similar emotional atmosphere, have come to him as realities—realities emotionally borne in upon his innermost sense.

Mental science may perhaps some day, by the operation of stored-up impressions, of obscure hereditary potentialities, of all the mysteries of the subconsciousness, explain the extraordinary phenomenon of a creature being apparently invaded from within by the personality of another creature, of another creature to all intents and purposes imaginary. The mystery is evidently connected, if not identical, with the mysterious conception—not reasoned out, but merely felt, by a great actor of another man's movements, tones of voice, states of feeling. In this case, as in all other matters of artistic activity, we have all of us, if we are susceptible in that particular branch of art (otherwise we should not be thus susceptible) a rudiment of the faculty whose exceptional development constitutes the artist. And thus, from our own very trifling experience, we can perhaps, certainly not explain what happens to the great novelist in the act of creation of his great characters, but guess, without any explanation, at what does happen to him. For, in the same way that we all of us, however rudimentally, possess a scrap in ourselves of the faculty which makes the actor; so also we possess in ourselves, I think, a scrap of what makes the novelist; if we did not, neither the actor nor the novelist would find any response in us. Let me pursue this. We all possess, to a certain small degree, the very mysterious faculty of imitating, without any act of analysis, the gestures, racial expression, and tone of voice or other people; nay, more, or other people in situations in which we have never seen them. We feel that they move, look, sound like that; we feel that, under given conditions, they would necessarily move, look, and sound like that. Why they should do so, or why we should feel that they do so, we have no notion whatever. Apparently because for that moment and to that extent we *are* those people: they have impressed us somehow, so forcibly, at some time or other, they or those like them, that a piece of them, a pattern of them, a word (one might think) or this particular vital spell, the spell which sums up their mode of being, has remained sticking in us, and is there become operative. I have to talk in allegories, in formulæ which savour of cabalistic mysticism; but I am not trying to explain, but merely to recall your own experiences; and I am sure you will recognise that these very mysterious things do happen constantly to all of us.

Now, in the same way that we all feel, every now and then, that the gestures and expression and tones or voice which we assume are those of other people and of other people in other circumstances; So likewise do we all of us occasionally feel that certain ways of facing life, certain reactions to life's various contingencies—

certain acts, answers, feelings, passions—are the acts, answers, feelings, passions, the reactions to life's contingencies of persons not ourselves. We say, under the circumstances *I* should do or say so and so, but Tom, or Dick, or Harry would do or say such another thing. The matter would be quite simple if we had seen Tom, Dick, or Harry in exactly similar circumstances; we should be merely repeating what had already happened, and our forecast would be no real forecast, but a recollection. But the point is, that we have *not* seen Tom, Dick, or Harry doing or saying in the past what we thus attribute to him in the future. The matter would also be very simple if we attained to this certainty about Tom, Dick, or Harry's sayings and doings by a process of conscious reasoning. But we have not gone through any conscious reasoning; indeed, if some incredulous person challenges us to account by analysis for our conviction, we are most often unable to answer; we are occasionally even absolutely worsted in argument. We have to admit that we do not know why we think so, nay, that there is every reason to think the contrary; and yet there, down in our heart of hearts, remains a very strong consciousness, a consciousness like that of our own existence, that Tom, Dick, or Harry would, or rather will, or rather—for it comes to that—*does* say or do that particular thing. If subsequently Tom, Dick, or Harry is so perverse as not to say or do it., that, oddly enough, does not in the least obliterate the impression of our having experienced that he did say or do it, an impression intimate, warm, unanalytical, like our impressions of having done or said certain things ourselves. The discrepancy between what we felt sure must happen and what actually did happen is, I think, due to the fact that there are two persons existing under the same name, but both existing equally—Tom, Dick, or Harry as felt by himself, and Tom, Dick, or Harry as felt by us; and although the conduct of these two persons may not have happened to coincide, the conduct of each has been perfectly organic, inevitable with reference to his nature. I suppose it is because we add to our experience, fragmentary as it needs must be, of other folk, the vitality, the unity of life, which is in ourselves. I suppose that, every now and then, whenever this particular thing I am speaking of happens, we have been tremendously impressed by something in another person—emotionally impressed, not intellectually, mind; and that the emotion, whether of delight or annoyance, which the person has caused in us, in some way grafts a portion of that person into our own life, into the emotions which constitute our life; and that thus our experience of the person, and our own increasing experience of ourselves, are united, and the person who is not ourselves comes to live, somehow, for our consciousness, with the same reality, the same intimate warmth, that we do.

I hazard this explanation, at best an altogether superficial one, not because I want it accepted as a necessary premise to an argument of mine, but because it may bring home what I require to make very clear—namely, the absolutely sympathetic, unanalytic, subjective creation of characters by some novelists, as distinguished from the rational, analytic, objective creation of characters by other novelists; because I require to distinguish between the personage who has been borne in upon the novelist's intimate sense, and the personage who has been built up out of fragments of fact by the novelist's intelligent calculation. Vasari, talking of the Farnesina Palace, said that it was not "built, but really born"—*non murato ma veramente nato*. Well, some personages in novels are built up, and very well built up; and some—some personages, but how few!—are really born.

Such personages as are thus not built up, but born, seem always to have been born (and my theory of their coming into existence is founded on this) of some strong feeling on the part of their author. Sometimes it is a violent repulsion—the strongest kind of repulsion, the organic repulsion of incompatible temperaments, which makes it impossible, for all his virtues, to love our particular Dr Fell; the reason why, we cannot tell. Our whole nature tingles with the discomfort which the creature causes in us. Such characters—I take them at random—are Tolstoi's Monsieur Karénine and Henry James's Olive Chancellor. But the greater number, as we might expect, of these really born creatures of unreality are born of love—of the deep, unreasoning, permeating satisfaction, the unceasing ramifying delight in strength and audacity; the unceasing, ramifying comfort in kindliness; the unceasing, ramifying pity towards weakness—born of the emotion which distinguishes the presence of all such as are, by the necessity of our individual nature and theirs, inevitably, deeply, undyingly beloved. These personages may not be lovable, or even tolerable, to the individual reader—he may thoroughly detest them. But he cannot be indifferent to them; for, born of real feeling, of the strongest of real feelings, the love of suitable temperaments, they are real, and awaken only real feeling. Such personages—we all know them!—such personages are, for instance, Colonel Newcome, Ethel Newcome; Tolstoi's Natacha, Levine, Anna, Pierre; Stendhal's immortal Duchess; and those two imperfect creatures, pardoned because so greatly beloved, Tom Jones and Manon Lescaut. Their power—the power of these creatures born of emotion, of affinity, or repulsion—is marvellous and transcendent. It is such that even a lapse into impossibility—though that rarely comes, of course—is overlooked. The life in the creatures is such that when we are told of their doing perfectly incredible things—things we cannot believe that, being what they were, they could have done—they yet remain alive, oven as real people remain alive for our feelings when we are assured that they have done things which utterly upset our conception of them. Look, for instance, at Mr James's Olive Chancellor. It is inconceivable that she should have ever done the very thing on which the whole book rests—taken up with such a being as Verena; yet she lives. Why? Because the author has realised in her the kind of temperament—the mode of feeling and being most organically detestable to him in all womankind. Look again at Meredith's adorable Diana. She could not have sold the secret, being what she was. Well, does she fall to the ground? Not a bit. She remains and triumphs, because she triumphed over the heart of her author. There is the other class of personage—among whom are most of the personages of every novel, most of the companions of those not built up, but born; and among whom, I think, are all the characters of some of those whom the world accounts as the greatest philosophers of the human heart—all the characters, save Maggie and Tom, of George Eliot; all, I suspect, of the characters of Balzac.

Such are the two great categories into which all novelists may, I think, be divided, the synthetic and the analytic, those who feel and those who reason. According as he belongs to one category or the other, the novelist will make that difficult choice about points of view. The synthetic novelist, the one who does not study his personages, but *lives* them, is able to shift the point of view with incredible frequency and rapidity, like Tolstoi, who in his two great novels really *is* each of the principal persons turn about; so much so, that at first one might almost think there was no point of view at all. The analytic novelist, on the contrary, the novelist who does not live his personages, but studies them, will be able to see his personages only from his own point of view, telling one what they are (or what he imagines they are), not what they feel inside themselves, and, at most, putting himself at the point of view of one personage or two, all the rest being given from the novelist's point of view; as in the case of George Eliot, Balzac, Flaubert, and Zola, whose characters are not so much living and suffering and changing creatures, as illustrations of theories of life in general, or of the life of certain classes and temperaments.

It is often said that there are many more wrong ways of doing a thing than right ones. I do not think this applies to the novel, or perhaps to any work of art. There are a great number of possible sorts of excellent novels, all very different from one another, and appealing to different classes of minds. There is the purely human novel of Thackeray, and particularly of Tolstoi—human and absolutely living; and the analytic and autobiographical novel of George Eliot, born, as regards its construction, of the memoir. There is the analytic, sociological novel of Balzac, studying the modes of life of whole classes of people. There is the novel of Zola, apparently aiming at the same thing as that of Balzac, but in reality, and for all its realistic programme, using the human crowd, the great social and commercial mechanisms invented by mankind—the shop, the mine, the bourgeois house, the Stock Exchange—as so much matter for passionate lyrism, just as Victor Hugo had used the sea and the cathedral. There is the decorative novel—the fantastic idyl of rural life or of distant lands—of Hardy and Loti; and many more sorts. There is an immense variety in good work; it appeals to so many sides of the many-sided human creature, since it always, inasmuch as it is good, appeals successfully. In bad work there is no such variety. In fact, the more one looks at it, the more one is struck at its family resemblance, and the small number of headings under which it can be catalogued. In examining it, one finds, however superficially veiled, everlastingly the same old, old faults—inefficacious use of words, scattered, illogical composition, lack of adaptation of form or thought; in other words, bad construction, waste, wear and tear of the reader's attention, incapacity of manipulating his mind, the craft of writing absent or insufficient. But that is not all. In this exceedingly monotonous thing, poor work (as monotonous as good work is rich and many-sided), we find another fatal element of sameness: lack of the particular emotional sensitiveness which, as visual sensitiveness makes the painter, makes the writer.

For writing—I return to my original theory, one-sided, perhaps, but certainly also true in great part—is the art which gives us the emotional essence of the world and of life; which gives us the moods awakened by all that is and can happen, material and spiritual, human and natural—distilled to the highest and most exquisite potency in the peculiar organism called the writer. As the painter says: "Look, here is all that is most interesting and delightful and vital, all that concerns you most in the visible aspect of things, whence I have extracted it for your benefit;" so the writer on his side says: "Read; here is all that is most interesting and delightful and vital in the moods and thoughts awakened by all things; here is the quintessence of vision and emotion; I have extracted it from the world and can transfer it to your mind." Hence the teachable portion of the art of writing is totally useless without that which can neither be taught nor learned—the possession of something valuable, something vital, essential, to say.

We all of us possess, as I have remarked before, a tiny sample of the quality whose abundance constitutes the special artist; we have some of the quality of the philosopher, the painter, the musician, as we have some of the quality of the hero; otherwise, philosophy, painting, music, and heroism would never appeal to us. Similarly and by the same proof, we have all in us a little of the sensitiveness of the writer. There is no one so dull or so inarticulate as never in his or her life—say, under the stress of some terrible calamity—to have said or written some word which was memorable, never to be forgotten by him who read or heard it: in such moments we have all had the power of saying, because apparently we have had something to say; in that tremendous momentary heightening of all our perceptions we have attained to the writer's faculty of feeling and expressing the essence of things. But such moments are rare; and the small fragments of literary or artistic faculty which we all are born with, or those are born with to whom literature and art are not mere dust and ashes, can be increased and made more efficient only to a limited degree. What we really have in our power is either to waste them in cumbering the world with work which will give no one any pleasure, or to put them to the utmost profit in giving us the highest degree of delight from the work of those who are specially endowed. Let us learn what good writing is in order to become the best possible readers.

❦ 76 ❧

Preface to *The Nigger of the Narcissus*

JOSEPH CONRAD

Joseph Conrad (1857–1924), a Pole and later naturalised British subject, wrote a number of his novels and short stories from the perspective of his occupation as a British merchant ship's master. His best known works, in addition to *The Nigger of the Narcissus*, are *Lord Jim* (1900), *Nostromo* (1904) and his novella, *Heart of Darkness* (1902). In the following preface he offers a counter theory to that of French naturalist Zola in his insistence on the transcendental as opposed to the scientific goal of the novelist. For Conrad, the novelist is an excavator of human emotions and motivations whose stated goal is "by the power of the written word to make you hear, to make you feel—it is, before all, to make you *see*. That—and no more, and it is everything." This statement is often interpreted as evidence of Conrad's impressionism. In delivering the "rescued fragment" or, as the narrator of *Heart of Darkness* notes, the halo surrounding the kernel, Conrad follows Walter Pater's artistic theory in the latter's Conclusion to *Studies in the History of the Renaissance* (1873) and anticipates James Joyce's notion of epiphanic moments in the modern novel.

A work that aspires, however humbly, to the condition of art should carry its justification in every line. And art itself may be defined as a single-minded attempt to render the highest kind of justice to the visible universe, by bringing to light the truth, manifold and one, underlying its every aspect. It is an attempt to find in its forms, in its colours, in its light, in its shadows, in the aspects of matter and in the facts of life what of each is fundamental, what is enduring and essential—their one illuminating and convincing quality—the very truth of their existence. The artist, then, like the thinker or the scientist, seeks the truth and makes his appeal. Impressed by the aspect of the world the thinker plunges into ideas, the scientist into facts—whence, presently, emerging they make their appeal to those qualities of our being that fit us best for the hazardous enterprise of living. They speak

Source: Joseph Conrad, "Preface" to *The Nigger of the Narcissus*, 1897, rptd New York: Doubleday, 1927, pp. xi–xvi.

authoritatively to our common-sense, to our intelligence, to our desire of peace or to our desire of unrest; not seldom to our prejudices, sometimes to our fears, often to our egoism—but always to our credulity. And their words are heard with reverence, for their concern is with weighty matters: with the cultivation of our minds and the proper care of our bodies, with the attainment of our ambitions, with the perfection of the means and the glorification of our precious aims.

It is otherwise with the artist.

Confronted by the same enigmatical spectacle the artist descends within himself, and in that lonely region of stress and strife, if he be deserving and fortunate, he finds the terms of his appeal. His appeal is made to our less obvious capacities: to that part of our nature which, because of the warlike conditions of existence, is necessarily kept out of sight within the more resisting and hard qualities—like the vulnerable body within a steel armour. His appeal is less loud, more profound, less distinct, more stirring—and sooner forgotten. Yet its effect endures forever. The changing wisdom of successive generations discards ideas, questions facts, demolishes theories. But the artist appeals to that part of our being which is not dependent on wisdom: to that in us which is a gift and not an acquisition—and, therefore, more permanently enduring. He speaks to our capacity for delight and wonder, to the sense of mystery surrounding our lives; to our sense of pity, and beauty, and pain; to the latent feeling of fellowship with all creation—and to the subtle but invincible conviction of solidarity that knits together the loneliness of innumerable hearts, to the solidarity in dreams, in joy, in sorrow, in aspirations, in illusions, in hope, in fear, which binds men to each other, which binds together all humanity—the dead to the living and the living to the unborn.

It is only such train of thought, or rather of feeling, that can in a measure explain the aim of the attempt, made in the tale which follows, to present an unrestful episode in the obscure lives of a few individuals out of all the disregarded multitude of the bewildered, the simple and the voiceless. For, if any part of truth dwells in the belief confessed above, it becomes evident that there is not a place of splendour or a dark corner of the earth that does not deserve, if only a passing glance of wonder and pity. The motive then, may be held to justify the matter of the work; but this preface, which is simply an avowal of endeavour, cannot end here—for the avowal is not yet complete.

Fiction—if it at all aspires to be art—appeals to temperament. And in truth it must be, like painting, like music, like all art, the appeal of one temperament to all the other innumerable temperaments whose subtle and resistless power endows passing events with their true meaning, and creates the moral, the emotional atmosphere of the place and time. Such an appeal to be effective must be an impression conveyed through the senses; and, in fact, it cannot be made in any other way, because temperament, whether individual or collective, is not amenable to persuasion. All art, therefore, appeals primarily to the senses, and the artistic aim when expressing itself in written words must also make its appeal through the senses, if its high desire is to reach the secret spring of responsive emotions. It must strenuously aspire to the plasticity of sculpture, to the colour of painting, and to the magic suggestiveness of music—which is the art of arts. And it is only through complete, unswerving devotion to the perfect blending of form and substance; it is only through an unremitting never-discouraged care for the shape and ring of sentences that an approach can be made to plasticity, to colour, and that the light of music suggestiveness may be brought to play for an evanescent instant over the commonplace surface of words: of the old, old words, worn thin, defaced by ages of careless usage.

The sincere endeavour to accomplish that creative task, to go as far on that road as his strength will carry him, to go undeterred by faltering, weariness or reproach, is the only valid justification for the worker in prose. And if his conscience is clear, his answer to those who in the fulness of a wisdom which looks for immediate profit, demand specifically to be edified, consoled, amused; who demand to be promptly improved, or encouraged, or frightened, or shocked, or charmed, must run thus:

My task which I am trying to achieve is, by the power of the written word to make you hear, to make you feel—it is, before all, to make you see. That—and no more, and it is everything. If I succeed, you shall find there according to your deserts: encouragement, consolation, fear, charm—all you demand—and, perhaps, also that glimpse of truth for which you have forgotten to ask.

To snatch in a moment of courage, from the remorseless rush of time, a passing phase of life, is only the beginning of the task. The task approached in tenderness and faith is to hold up unquestioningly, without choice and without fear, the rescued fragment before all eyes in the light of a sincere mood. It is to show its vibration, its colour, its form; and through its movement, its form, and its colour, reveal the substance of its truth—disclose its inspiring secret: the stress and passion within the core of each convincing moment. In a single-minded attempt of that kind, if one be deserving and fortunate, one may perchance attain to such clearness of sincerity that at last the presented vision of regret or pity, of terror or mirth, shall awaken in the hearts of the beholders that feeling of unavoidable solidarity; of the solidarity in mysterious origin, in toil, in joy, in hope, in uncertain fate, which binds men to each other and all mankind to the visible world.

It is evident that he who, rightly or wrongly, holds by the convictions expressed above cannot be faithful to any one of the temporary formulas of his craft. The enduring part of them—the truth which each only imperfectly veils—should abide with him as the most precious of his possessions, but they all: Realism, Romanticism, Naturalism, even the unofficial sentimentalism (which like the poor, is exceedingly difficult to get rid of,) all these gods must, after a short period of fellowship, abandon him—even on the very threshold of the temple—to the stammerings of his conscience and to the outspoken consciousness of the difficulties of his work. In that uneasy solitude the supreme cry of Art for Art itself, loses the exciting ring of its apparent immorality. It sounds far off. It has ceased to be a cry, and is heard only as a whisper, often incomprehensible, but at times and faintly encouraging.

Sometimes, stretched at ease in the shade of a road-side tree, we watch the motions of a labourer in a distant field, and after a time, begin to wonder languidly as to what the fellow may be at. We watch the movements of his body, the waving of his arms, we see him bend down, stand up, hesitate, begin again. It may add to the charm of an idle hour to be told the purpose of his exertions. If we know he is trying to lift a stone, to dig a ditch, to uproot a stump, we look with a more real interest at his efforts; we are disposed to condone the jar of his agitation upon the restfulness of the landscape; and even, if in a brotherly frame of mind, we may bring ourselves to forgive his failure. We understood his object, and, after all, the fellow has tried, and perhaps he had not the strength—and perhaps he had not the knowledge. We forgive, go on our way—and forget.

And so it is with the workman of art. Art is long and life is short, and success is very far off. And thus, doubtful of strength to travel so far, we talk a little about the aim—the aim of art, which, like life itself, is inspiring, difficult—obscured by mists. It is not in the clear logic of a triumphant conclusion; it is not in the unveiling of one of those heartless secrets which are called the Laws of Nature. It is not less great, but only more difficult.

To arrest, for the space of a breath, the hands busy about the work of the earth, and compel men entranced by the sight of distant goals to glance for a moment at the surrounding vision of form and colour, of sunshine and shadows; to make them pause for a look, for a sigh, for a smile—such is the aim, difficult and evanescent, and reserved only for a very few to achieve. But sometimes, by the deserving and the fortunate, even that task is accomplished. And when it is accomplished—behold!—all the truth of life is there: a moment of vision, a sigh, a smile—and the return to an eternal rest.

1897.
J.C.

❧ 77 ❧

An Age of Fiction

FREDERICK KARL

In a survey of the progress of the English novel throughout the nineteenth century, Karl recurs to *Don Quixote*, as the prototype of the novel for its fusion of realism and romance. Cervantes' ability to balance reality and illusion foreshadows the later novelist's implicit agreement with the reader "who must suspend both his belief and disbelief and allow himself to be transported into a world he knows logically is untrue." After Cervantes, Karl argues, the principal eighteenth century English novelists—Defoe, Richardson, Fielding and Smollett—set the pattern for the nineteenth-century novel. Of these four, Richardson had the most lasting influence through his combination of character, morality and sentiment, though Austen, especially, was to draw her sense of satire from Fielding. Unlike Dawson and Dawson (see eighteenth-century section), Karl views Austen's realism and Scott's romanticism as two opposing strains that merge into an oxymoronic romantic realism in Dickens's novels. For Karl, the Victorian novel witnesses the ultimate development of the novel in its realistic reflection of the social and political issues of the century. It also deepens the psychological portraiture, reduces the romanticized hero to size and presents realistic dialogue. He views the modern novel from Hardy through Joyce as "a modification and reassessment of what already existed . . ."

One
An Age of Fiction

The determined opposition to the Victorian novel within last few decades has so diminished that we may now foresee an exaggerated swing of the critical pendulum. Critics and general readers who once embraced the contemporary novelist at the artistic expense of his Victorian counterpart have come to qualify both their praise and their disdain, although the discriminating reader never deserted Dickens, Thackeray, George Eliot, and Meredith for the equally rewarding

Source: Frederick Karl, from *An Age of Fiction: The Nineteenth Century British Novel*, New York: Farrar, Straus and Giroux, 1964, pp. 3-26.

Conrad, Lawrence, and Joyce. The more temperate and flexible readers of the English novel have always recognized that every major writer offers particular truths and that to argue that the novel with time and changing conditions "improves" is to destroy with pseudo-scientific reasoning what should be supported with literary taste.

This is not of course to claim that "advances" do not occur: the work of any major novelist can, in one way, be measured by his difference from his predecessors and contemporaries. The quality of each writer, whether Jane Austen or James Joyce, is determined by what the writer is intrinsically and by what he adds to the novel, by the way the novel is refined to say something unique. Thus, certain novels of Dickens and Hardy were as unique in their day as was *Ulysses* in the 1920's and 30's. Nevertheless, preoccupied almost solely with what the novelist adds to the genre, several critics have tended to ignore the broader implications of the work of the nineteenth-century novelists; while, conversely, apologists for the Victorian novelist have often refused to grant deficiencies in their hero. Both groups by exaggerating their views have undermined their positions, one through obsession with form and symbol, the other through the need to counteract the first overstatement with another.

As a social document, a moral structure, and a work of art, the novel from Defoe, Fielding, and Richardson through Jane Austen and Hardy generates the kind of realism that both creates the world it reflects and mirrors the world it creates. The novel is in the peculiar position of defining reality as no other art form does, and yet paradoxically it has, somehow, to avoid a direct representation of reality. The moral focus of the novel does not justify a course of action, but brings it under scrutiny and demonstrates the extent of human variety. Music, poetry, art do not address the same problem as the novel, for no matter how realistic they become, they still contain elements of artificiality. When we listen arbitrarily to sounds, we do not hear music; when we speak, we do not talk in poetry; when we observe phenomena, we do not see in the shape of paintings. When we approach these art forms, we encounter them as elements that recreate or distort reality; they are never the thing itself. When we read a novel, however, whether it be *Don Quixote* or *Ulysses*, we face real situations involving real people and real language. Distortions and originality there may be, but nevertheless a novel occurs at a certain time, in a certain place, with a certain cast of characters. These elements of the real, the substantial, and the solid are ever-present. Yet while the novelist must never lose sight of them, he still must disguise them. If they prevail, his work becomes realistic in the wrong sense; it is journalistic, ephemeral, superficial, not artistic.

In encountering the crucial issue of what is real and what is illusory, *Don Quixote* is in essence the first novel. Through the Don, Cervantes asks which is more real, the world of practicality and daily events, or the conceptual world, the world of fantasy and illusions, the world of imagination and art. Cervantes carries us back to the medieval mind which saw everything as symbol and emblem. The Don indeed sees real things, but chooses to ignore them in favour of his conception of them. Since, to him, the earthly object derives from the ideal heavenly or imaginative object, man's mind must vault phenomena to get at the real thing, to move behind the physical to the spiritual. Consequently, the Don's so-called madness is the madness of every artist who tells the reader or observer that *his* insights of metaphors are the stuff of reality rather than what the reader senses his own reality to be.

As an artist, the Don recreates the world in his own image, making his adventures into poetic metaphors that seem untruthful, even mad, upon analysis. The Don illustrates that he is concerned with more than social justice, although to seek justice is surely part of his quest. His true vocation, however, is to create a way of seeing, just as every novelist must transform reality into something both more and less than the original object. In his quest for this different kind of reality, the Don convinces nearly everyone, including the reader, that his vision is preferable to what he encounters, and that individual interpretations can never be dissociated from the real.

Like a poet, a revolutionary, a "sane madman," the Don forces a re-evaluation of one's assumptions, for his image-making mind is constantly reforming events. Even if we claim that his vision is mad, we cannot embrace what he denies. No matter how mad he is, his motives are altruistic, just, good; while those around him, neither all good nor bad, have the voice of the real, semi-corrupt world. Under his tutelage, we remember, Sancho progresses from a pleasant but greedy hanger-on to a just and shrewd governor.

Yet such is Cervantes' realistic insight into the ambiguous world he created that he knows that the Don and his metaphors must not prevail. No matter how superior his imagination is to reality, reality must triumph. The norm for Cervantes is a God-driven universe in which man must make a final choice between illusion and reality, as the Don himself does. And when man makes his choice, he sorrowfully rejects poetry and imagination, and then dies. Since Cervantes' is not a romantic view of things, man is not immortal; he must be reduced. Such is the tragic nature of the world, such is Unamuno's tragic sense of life. Man may heroically assume that he is more than he is, but inevitably he must return to body and substance and forgo his dreams.

What Cervantes says about the Don becomes a paradigm for the novel itself. No matter what metaphors the writer establishes—whether those of Earwicker's imaginative dreams in *Finnegans Wake* or Robinson Crusoe's more tepid premonitions on his island—the ultimate effect heightens reality without rejecting it. In *Don Quixote*, the scene in the Cave of Montesinos (Chapter 23, Part II) is so significant because there the Don has to maintain his role as artist (novelist) at the same time he is aware of the illusory nature of his experience below ground. As he later tells Sancho, he will protect Sancho's illusions if Sancho will protect his. So the novelist makes a pact with the reader, who must suspend both his belief and disbelief and allow himself to be transported into a world he knows logically is untrue.

To effect this condition, every eighteenth-century novelist, no matter how conservative, attempted to mask the real nature of his material, or, conversely, to reveal the real nature of his material. From Defoe's reliance on "true history" and Richardson's on the epistolary method to Fielding's emphasis on the episodic narrative and Sterne's on the break-up of plot, the novelist, like the Don, imposed a particular kind of vision upon daily events. Jane Austen herself, with her essentially classical approach to fiction, employed irony to take the edge off a directly moralistic treatment of man's imperfections.

The eighteenth-century English novel, to which Jane Austen, Dickens, and Thackeray were much indebted—a debt that extended also to Meredith (through Dickens) and to George Eliot (through Jane Austen)—provided the principal form and substance of what we now know as the novel. Our use of the term "novel, as Ian Watt has remarked, did not arise until near the end of the eighteenth century, although the content itself was formed earlier in the century by Defoe, Richardson, Fielding, and Smollett. The dominant form of the novel was realism, defined not only by the kind of life it represented (individualized people, everyday affairs, material concerns) but by the way it presented it (denotative prose, use of clock and calendar time, solidity of setting, details of dress). In Defoe, early in the century, we see an emphasis upon particularity and individuality of situation, detail, language, a reliance upon real time. In Richardson, we see even more clearly the stress upon a single person in a trying situation, the analysis of which becomes the plot of the novel. In part contrary to Richardson's practice, we find in *Tom Jones* a prose comic epic that assumes the importance of plot over character and of normal life over heroic action. But while Fielding appears to have influenced novels as diverse as *Pickwick Papers* and *Vanity Fair*, it is really Richardson who became the chief literary influence on the nineteenth-century novel.

Although Defoe had particularized man in his physical setting and had also used language realistically, Richardson—that bourgeois author of conduct-books—evolved the novel of character, morals, and sentiment. The conflict of social behavior in every nineteenth-century author from Jane Austen through George Meredith is suggested in Pamela's reward for virtuous behavior in the face of temptation. Furthermore, the strong moralism implicit in Pamela's defense, a mixture of exemplum and embonpoint, was especially to appeal to nineteenth-century writers restricted by a middle-class reading public. Although Pamela lacks Elizabeth Bennet's penetrating wit, her independence and self-sufficiency under trial identify her as possessing the mettle of a Jane Austen heroine. Jane Austen, who began writing seriously less than four decades after Richardson's death, also found in Sir Charles Grandison, the virtuous hero of Richardson's last novel, a model for several of her male characters—Knightley, Edmund Bertram, Captain Wentworth. In Darcy himself, once his pride has been defeated, we see a less athletic Mr B. (*Pamela*), a less egoistic and sadistic Lovelace (*Clarissa*).

But if Richardson's mise en scène seems restricted, then it is in Fielding that we find a greater range of situation and a more flexible morality. Jane Austen found in Fielding's novels the irony so congenial to her own nature, although his unconventionality did not suit her temperament. Close to Richardson on moral issues and on norms of behavior, Jane Austen and her successors were to make Fielding's sense of mockery and parody into a dangerous social weapon. The fact that Richardson's epistolary style does not reappear in the major nineteenth-century novels indicates that while his ideas and attitudes had been absorbed into the mainstream of fiction his methods were uncongenial. Fielding's use of dialogue to reveal character was more suitable, reaching its most effective usage in Dickens' novels, wherein conversational idiom is character. In Jane Austen, who, in many ways, provides that elusive creature, the transitional figure, the main characters also reveal themselves in their talk. Like Henry James later, Jane Austen early recognized that emotional significance can replace dramatic violence, and incisiveness of character and situation the discursiveness of the romantic novelist. Through the dramatization of short scenes, she intermixed Fielding's reliance on plot with Richardson's realistic analysis of character. This became, with varying revisions, the dominant mode of nineteenth-century realism. The main influences on the later novel came predominantly from the first half of the eighteenth century; Defoe was dead in 1731, Fielding in 1754, Richardson in 1761, and Smollett ten years later. In the latter half of the century, the novel faltered and sprayed its energies in a series of minor efforts: the novel of sensibility, the Gothic romance, the novel of sentiment (an extension of Richardson and Sterne), all of which Jane Austen satirized directly in *Sense and Sensibility* and *Northanger Abbey* and indirectly in her other works. At this time, from about 1760 through 1795, the novel was a relatively unstable commodity. Since it did not have the standing of either poetry or drama, the novelist himself was considered slightly disreputable, an opportunist of a sort. It is not surprising that few novelists took their work seriously or deemed themselves professionals. In her close study of the popular novel in England (1770-1800), Dr. J. M. S. Tompkins asserts that during the years "that follow the death of Smollett [1771], last of the four great novelists of the mid-eighteenth century, the two chief facts about the novel are its popularity as a form of entertainment and its inferiority as a form of art." Later she comments that "the business of the novel was to teach those who by nature and upbringing were unqualified for serious study."

The novel, in brief, had become more a means to something else than a unified narrative with developed characters and an "artistic" intent. The composition of the reading public was itself undergoing several shifts, and this fact had a great deal to do with the changing tastes in fiction. In the second half of the eighteenth century, the reading public became a modern one, that is, one no longer united in common tastes or assumptions, or rooted in a common tradition, as the public once fixed in Augustan principles of order and objectivity or an earlier one based on the recognition of religious revelation. The relative success of *Pamela* in the 1740's already signalled the change in tastes, with its popular theme of the successful servant girl and its reliance upon sentiment rather than classical impersonality. After his *Shamela* failed to stem the popularity of *Pamela*, Fielding tried to retain the classical virtues by stressing the epic theme, but his style (plot over character) was not to be influential until the following century. The new reading public was not sophisticated, but, in part, a semi-literate one—particularly servants—who demanded what Pamela provided. On the other hand, the growing merchant class demanded its kind of fiction, one based on practical virtue, not metaphysical truths, and the several circulating libraries near the end of the century catered to these tastes.

Both groups found their desires satisfied in the so-called novel of sensibility, which, like Methodism and Romantic poetry, elicited compassion and suffering. As Walter Allen remarked, this attitude, one in which the reader is easily moved by the pathetic, leads to morbidity, which becomes an end in itself; and reality "is sought only as a stimulus to the exercise of sensibility." Sensibility in itself is not of course to be decried, especially when, as in Fielding, Smollett, and Sterne, it is underlaid by strong doses of humor: Jane Austen was concerned not with sensibility alone but with the wrong kind which led to immoderate and ludicrous decisions—thus her fun at Marianne Dashwood's expense in *Sense and Sensibility*. Novelists like Henry Brooke (*The Fool of Quality*), Henry Mackenzie (*The Man of Feeling*), and Oliver Goldsmith (*The Vicar of Wakefield*) were to cultivate sensibility for itself, often to the exclusion of reason.

This preoccupation with single modes of behavior had its counterpart in the Gothic novel and its emphasis upon a terror-filled past. Walpole's *Castle of Otranto* in 1764, with its synthetic emotions, its unintentionally funny morbidity, its stress upon omens and outlandish horrors, set the pace for novelists like Clara Reeve, Mrs Radcliffe, and "Monk" Lewis. Their excesses are parodied in Jane Austen's *Northanger Abbey*, and the Gothic novel as such seemed to disappear in the early nineteenth century, except perhaps for Maturin's *Melmoth the Wanderer* in 1820.(1) In Mary Shelley's Frankenstein (1818) and Emily Brontë's *Wuthering Heights* (1847), the mode was considerably qualified. With its stress upon the ghostliness of a supernatural past, the Gothic novel was absorbed into Romantic poetry and the Romantic novel, becoming re-evident in Scott's evocation of a historical past and in Dickens's obsessive emphases upon prisons and criminals.

By the time Jane Austen began to write in the mid-1790's, she had been nurtured on the Gothic romance and the novel of sensibility, although amidst their extravagance the novels of Fanny Burney and William Godwin (*Caleb Williams*, 1794) explored new areas. Fanny Burney in particular was trying to write a novel without excesses; in the Preface to *Evelina* (1778), she stated her intentions, which while obvious now did help clear the way for several major novelists who followed. (One need only compare her statement with George Eliot's in *Adam Bede* [Chapter XVII, 'In Which the Story Pauses a Little']):

> Let me, therefore, prepare for disappointment those who, in the perusal of these sheets, entertain the gentle expectation of being transported to the fantastic regions of Romance, where Fiction is coloured by all the gay tints of luxurious imagination, where Reason is an outcast, and where the sublimity of the Marvellous, rejects all aid from sober Probability. The heroine of these memoirs, young, artless, and inexperienced, is
> No faultless Monster, that the world ne'er saw, but the offspring of Nature, and of Nature in her simplest attire.

We find here Richardson's ideas reappearing, and it comes as no surprise that Fanny Burney cast her novel in epistolary form backed by a conscious moralizing attitude. Her subject, like that of *Pamela*, is the triumph of a virtuous young woman in the face of temptation, however superficial Evelina's temptation may seem compared with Pamela's (and Clarissa's) .Although Fanny Burney retained elements of sentimentality from the novel of sensibility, especially in the emotion-filled letters of the Reverend Mr Villars to his ward, nevertheless she was able to objectify her subject and create some memorable minor characters.

The kind of sensibility demonstrated in Fanny Burney's novels was to carryover into the nineteenth century, and her type of heroine—sweet, amiable, sensible, somewhat naive, yet vain enough to know her worth—was to reappear throughout the following century as often as Jane Austen's independent and knowledgeable heroines. By the turn of the nineteenth century, despite the excesses indicated above, the outlines of the genre were becoming firmer: Jane Austen was to indicate one direction and Scott the other. The latter's romances absorbed the Gothic elements and excesses of sensibility; Jane Austen carried on the classical tradition while redirecting the novel of sentiment into the mainstream of Victorian realism. Her classical awareness of form, however, was less important in the Romantic Age than her use of reason and wit in writing about romantic topics. Jane Austen's views prevailed in the nineteenth century in a permanent way denied Scott's, although his immediate influence, unlike hers, was immense. Her reasonableness and comic awareness, rather than his historical imaginative, became the norm, and the kind of moralizing implicit in her plots fitted the views of the rapidly growing middle class audience of later years.

One of the curiosities of literature is that at the very time Rousseauistic sentimental humanism was so strongly evident in the English Romantic poets, Jane Austen was working the opposing stream of realism. Only with Dickens's major fiction did the two streams become absorbed into each other to form the prevailing tone of romantic realism that then predominated in the nineteenth-century English novel until Hardy.

While the novels of the eighteenth and nineteenth centuries do have several important similarities, the emphasis on a common tradition should not destroy the real differences between them. One tends to group novelists for the sake of labeling them and moving them around, although their divergences arc obviously greater than their similarities. One of the chief differences lies in the responsibilities each century places upon its writers. The nineteenth-century novelist not only faced a more severely changing world, but—alone with the prophets and poets—found himself in a greater position of importance.

The serious novelist was becoming increasingly aware of his "role" in society, and the novel itself was becoming socially conscious in a way rarely attained previously. Taking on the qualities of a sermon and an entertainment, the novel reflected the main issues of the day: rapid industrial and commercial growth, passage of democratic legislation and the establishment of democratic institutions, migration to the cities, Benthamite legislation, Evangelical piety and philanthropy, the Oxford Movement, the "new science" the social consequences of evolution, the conflict between faith and doubt. A list of issues always sounds dry, yet such was the economic and social barbarism of the age—in a professedly Christian society—that many responses were shrieks of outrage and abuse.

Although most nineteenth-century novelists were not, categorically, social critics, nevertheless to read the novel from Jane Austen to Thomas Hardy is to gain the flavor and substance of nineteenth-century social, political, and cultural life in a way no other literary mode can provide. Curiously enough, most of these issues—whether modified or not—remain significant in the twentieth century, although the contemporary novelist can no longer deal with specific issues in the same fashion as his predecessors. To find out what people really thought about their pressing problems, the reader must turn from the metaphysical concerns of the present-day writer to the particularities of the Victorian author. In full bloom, the Victorian novel carried the genre through to its development: the modern novel becomes a modification and reassessment of what already existed, even when one allows for the broader range of subject matter and the greater technical facility of the contemporary novelist. If we find elements of Fielding and Smollett in Dickens, then we discover Dickens in Conrad and Lawrence. If Richardson reappears in Jane Austen, then the latter recurs in George Eliot, whose pastoral settings, along with Hardy's, are evident, once again, in Lawrence. And at the end of the major tradition is Joyce, taking bits and pieces from continental as well as English novelists, not the least of whom is Sterne and Dickens. The crucial time for the English novel was clearly the nineteenth century, when it might have either flowered or degenerated into a minor and stunted form.

A large and voracious audience was now a ready market for the novelist who could meet its moral and cultural demands. W. P. Trent estimates that by the end of the eighteenth century there were perhaps 100,000 habitual readers upon whom the book-sellers and circulating libraries could count. In the nineteenth century itself, literacy outdistanced population growth by more than five to one. The Christmas annuals, the hundreds of sentimental novels, the "yellow backs" sold on railway stalls, the shilling number of a novel and then the shilling magazine, the rapid growth of circulating libraries, the prevalence of the three-decker novel—all of these resulted from catering to an audience that desired in fiction an "entertaining morality." There was also, even by mid-century, a basic optimism; if society were not progressing in a linear fashion, at least there was still the possibility of perfection, as the vast Crystal Palace of 1851 indicated. Faith was a positive attitude and not simply a defense against the unknowable, although Tennyson's *In Memoriam* heralded the new note of doubt. The novel responded, and at its worst, as in some of Bulwer-Lytton and Scott, it catered directly to the waiting audience. Even in the major novelists the spirit of compromise was evident, and Dickens, Thackeray, and Meredith, to name only three, worked artistically within what the century allowed: a Christian morality and a Christian view of sex.

At its best the novel demonstrated categorically the triumph of good over evil; and after mid-century only Hardy fully sensed the bleakness that would prevail once faith became an empty phrase and despair a commonplace of everyday life. George Eliot and Meredith still retained a belief, if not in progress and perfectibility, then in the ability of the individual to resurrect himself through self-knowledge. Thackeray maintained a basically sentimental view of life beneath his surface worldliness, and

Dickens qualified his tragic view with happy endings. Only Hardy remained true to a world in which the ceremony of innocence is mocked and smashed. From the self-possessed and confident Jane Austen at the beginning of the century, we pass to Hardy, who recognized that life itself is destructive whether man is basically good or evil. Perhaps nowhere more than in the development of the "hero" does the nineteenth-century novelist reveal his basic assumptions. In the previous century, Defoe had placed his main characters in a recognizable social setting, although he had paid only lip service to human psychology; much more interested in people's houses than in people, he created characters in his own image: rugged individualists with a Puritan (not puritanical) morality. Fielding gave his protagonists a different morality, but while emphasizing plot over character he was not so concerned with under-lying motives as with surface wit and clarity. Unlike Robinson Crusoe, Tom Jones—the "new hero"—can enjoy his appetites as long as he remains basically decent, and can repent without severe suffering. Richardson, moving the emphasis from plot to character, made the heroine's success—indeed her survival—dependent upon her virtue. In contrast, Smollett stressed the undomesticated hero, the picaresque character whose bumptiousness or rascality masks a basically warm and realistic individual. In his hands, the narrative became full of "on the road" episodes, the kind of novel appropriate to rural settings unaffected by industrialization. Sterne himself wrote the first novel without a hero, the first novel with-out a plot. Like Thomas Amory's *Life and Opinions of John Buncle* (1756, 1766), Henry Brooke's *The Fool of Quality* (1766), and Henry Mackenzie's *The Man of Feeling* (1771), Sterne's *The Life and Opinions of Tristram Shandy* (1760-67) reduced all life to whimsy and all people to lovable, frail creatures. The hero is laughed out of existence. When he is five, a window almost destroys his manhood.

By the time Jane Austen began to write near the turn of the century, English traditions had weakened and the eighteenth-century gentleman—the redeemed Tom Jones, Squire Allworthy, Matthew Bramble, Walter Shandy, Mr B., Lovelace—no longer held his undisputed position. The new moneyed classes and increased literacy created a new kind of gentleman: the genteel man of attainments. The stress is now upon what a person is, not solely upon what he has been born into. The gentleman of attainments, further, becomes the sole person capable of holding back the encroaching vulgarity of the industrialized and commercialized middle class, which has no uniform standard of conduct. It is on this frontier of change that Jane Austen places her batteries of wit and irony. Birth, income, and family tradition, while still important, nevertheless become of secondary significance: the man must still prove himself, for his reputation is not sufficient to make him palatable to a Jane Austen heroine. Like Evelina with Lord Orville, Elizabeth Bennet is not prepared to accept a proud (somewhat vulgar) Darcy, no less a Mr B., whom she would mock for his pretensions to supremacy. Jane Austen's heroines themselves desire the kind of equality denied to the eighteenth-century woman, and they demand romantic love as well. Marriage must be prudent, dignified, and romantic. In brief, these clear-eyed girls stand as virtuous individuals with assertive rights. The male can be no undisputed conqueror; he must be civilized and domesticated, brought to heel *before* he offers his name and fortune. The picaresque hero now attends church on Sunday, sips tea in the afternoon, and spends long evenings at home looking through the latest books. Jane Austen celebrates the rites of happy monogamy, and her standard was to prevail for nearly half a century, with the possible exception of *Wuthering Heights*. Furthermore, her break with the episodic eighteenth-century novel heralded a similar break throughout the century, although Dickens in *Pickwick* followed the form he knew best from his early reading; Thackeray also worked in a semi-episodic form in several of his novels, supplying recurring themes, however, to offset episodic stringiness.

In his sometimes valuable book, *The Hero in Eclipse in Victorian Fiction* (1956), Mario Praz develops the point that the Victorian stress on realism made the typical novelist similar to the seventeenth-century Dutch genre painters, who "domesticated" painting by reducing its size and heroism and making it suitable for middle class consumption. The novelist becomes a *Biedermeier*, or solid citizen, interested in goodness, pathos, morality, someone anxious to strike down aberrations and to mute dissonance. Since the novelist is socially democratic, the traditional hero—with his supremacy based on superior birth and position—is incongruous.

The typical Victorian "hero," accordingly, reflects his times. Less grand than his predecessors, he gains virtue from his common sense and compassion. He must be aware of a norm of behavior, as Jane Austen shows us, and if he departs he must be punished before being again accepted. If he departs too far, then he is incorrigible, and he must go into permanent exile or die. If, however, the hero honors social norms—that is, if he lacks ego and vanity—he can gain all, even though his birth and income may be low.

The comic play of the Victorian novel becomes evident as a device for questioning existing standards and for creating social equality. In his essay on Comedy, Meredith remarked that the Comic Spirit would create equality between the sexes; but it does far more. It reveals, and in many cases, purges all anomalies of behaviour—whether for good or ill. By exposing the egoistic, the vainglorious, and the snobbish, the Comic Spirit in a burst of ridicule discloses frailties and unmans the offender. As a side effect, unfortunately, it also discourages originality and imagination. In its pursuit of the personally gauche and the socially unacceptable, it tries to reduce all people to the level of social consistency. It leaves little room for the rebel or revolutionary. What Meredith calls the Comic Spirit, Jane Austen incorporated as irony, and the practice extends, in one form or another, through Dickens, Thackeray, and George Eliot, only to fade out and become meaningless in Hardy, who turned the Comic Spirit which mocks foolishness into the Universal Will that condemns all.

As we shall see, social comedy provided both the great strengths and apparent weaknesses of the novel in nineteenth-century England, indeed of the English novel (with few exceptions) virtually from its beginnings through Joyce Cary and Henry Green. It is a somewhat melancholy thought that until the work of Hardy and Conrad, almost the sole mode of tragedy in the English novel was Gothic. A good deal of the blandness—as well as the positive sense of life as lived—that we find in the novel is the result of its comic conventions. Tradition, history, customs, a past—all those elements that work only in time—are ever-present, and they are the substances that make comedy possible.

Unlike the American novel, the English novel principally takes place in time, not space. Obviously, the temporal novel is most often representative of an old and established culture. It is often a love story, for love is possible when time is plentiful. As soon as time becomes precious, however, love turns to lust. Further, temporal fiction is usually far more realistic than spatial fiction, which is frequently based on the assumption that moving on will bring something better. When the novelist works in a given locale and is aware of the weight of time, he can bring to bear a kind of comic social criticism that all must accept to survive. As soon as characters are given great mobility—as they are in many American novels—there are few common assumptions, and there is accordingly little room for comedy, or for tragedy either. Comedy, like tragedy, then, works on the sharing of suppositions which derive from common traditions. And both depend on time as a factor, for, as the past unfolds, these common assumptions gain the semblance of universal truths.

The major novel of space, on the other hand, is neither comic nor tragic. It conveys an altogether different mode of experience. It may indicate violence, the chase, lust, lurid adventures, chance affairs. It rarely contains solid marriages, mature love, normalizing behavior. It depends on rebellion, dissatisfaction, a sense of drift. The novel of time, conversely, makes possible the cohesion of people within commonly accepted institutions, and when we define comedy and tragedy we almost always do so within the realm of time considerations. As the English novel developed and hero-ism (tragedy) as a credible idea declined, comedy became entrenched as a major mode: a comedy played out in time.

Going further, one may well speculate that the lack of extremism in the English novel—the lack of violence which so clearly differentiates it from American, Russian, and (some) French fiction—results from its stress upon comedy. The converse may be equally true: that the stress upon comedy precludes extremism. If, as we have already seen, comedy works to bring deviates back to social norms, then extremism itself can be contained, or else discredited as a viable way of existence. The extremist, when he does exist, usually drifts away or dies of a broken heart; even Emily Brontë—hardly a comic novelist—follows this tradition with Heathcliff. Working in time as he does, the comic novelist allows little flexibility in his major characters. Only in his minor figures, where being "outside" does not seem to matter significantly, can he countenance controlled deviation and extremism. Thus we have the insipidity of so many male protagonists and their sweet ladies in the nineteenth-century novel, while the peripheral, minor figures generate excitement, interest, and humor.

The bourgeois novelist, like many Elizabethan dramatists, developed a double plot with a double standard. While the nineteenth-century audience required certain norms in its "heroes" and "heroines," it tolerantly relaxed these standards (rarely, however, in sexual matters) when the lower classes were concerned. For comic purposes, Dickens often exploited this double standard: gaining raucous fun from the economically deprived, but requiring respectability from his central characters.

That he could deploy two such attitudes with both dignity and compassion is a mark of his genius. Similarly, George Eliot gained dramatic tensions from her upper-class characters while she exploited the humor of her peasants.

The comic writer obviously cannot tolerate traditional heroism; the hero depends for sustenance upon his ego, and ego is fair target for the darts of the Comic Spirit. Ego and its twin, Vanity, are the basis for the false gentleman, who loses his status when stringent standards of conduct are applied. Thus, Joe Gargery is more of a gentleman than Bentley Drummle, and Adam Bede more than Arthur Donnithorne. Money having become the great equalizer in a commercialized society, standards of excellence came to be based on intrinsic qualities, although a prudent heroine opted for both the true gentleman and a fortune. As Jane Austen demonstrated, prudence and romance are not necessarily alien to each other.

With the reduction of the romantic hero to smaller size, there followed a stress upon the details of everyday life. As the genre painters placed man in his setting, so too the nineteenth-century novelist identified his characters through an explicit and detailed background. Jane Austen's provincials—as later George Eliot's—are recognizable people whose lives fit their surroundings: a novel like *Mansfield Park* conveys the flavor of boredom on a respectable country estate, and *Pride and Prejudice* shows that marriage is the sole ritual of maturity when society provides little else for a girl to do. As closely as Jane Austen's characters are identified with their provincial background, so too Dickens's and Thackeray's characters act like city people. The spirit of place is very much a part of Victorian fiction, understandably so once the novel has lost its episodic nature and the action becomes rooted to a particular spot.

Language itself changed to suit the realistic presentation of characters and situations, the movement reaching its culmination in the unselfconscious dialect of George Eliot's and Thomas Hardy's provincials. As the hero becomes a commonplace character, his language loses the rhetorical flourishes and affectations common in the eighteenth century. Declamation turned to slang (Sam Weller), and speechifying to realistic dialogue (Adam Bede). Communication was established with a large public unaware of "pretty speech," one attuned to the colloquial language of a relatively urbanized existence.

Characters came to reveal themselves by their talk. Lacking a suitable psychological method and yet aware of the "inner man," the nineteenth-century novelist relied on conversation to disclose the unconscious. This is one reason perhaps why the Victorian novel is full of personalities and the Victorian character seems a person rather than an artificial or fictitious creation. Dickens's characters, for example, are close to the reader because their language reveals submerged details of their personality; they are, as it were, speaking directly to the reader. Although not all nineteenth-century novelists were as aware of their audience as was Dickens, most created intimacy of character and situation through the same personal device of realistic conversation. How different the twentieth-century novelist with his objectivity and impersonality, with his removal of his characters from daily life through symbol and suggestion!

The nineteenth-century novelist was interested in conveying the very feel of life in its details, and when taboos disallowed overt statement, he could suggest aberrations. Dickens, after all, created "Dostoyevskian" characters like Steerforth, Dolge Orlick, and Bradley Headstone; sometimes the Thames seemed to signify to him not commerce but death. Even sexual taboos became fixed only in the 1860's, probably the result of the increase in a middle-class reading public and Victoria's own moral stringency. The 1840's and 1850's were not tightly bound by such strictures, although popular authors like Dickens and Thackeray were careful not to offend public taste directly. The Victorian novelist knew that his books were intended for family reading, and therefore he translated sex and passion into sentiment, the sexual act itself into fainting and weeping and shuddering. The careful reader, however, recognizes that beneath the currents of sentiment there lies a great deal of disguised passion and beneath the layers of respectability there rests, particularly in Dickens, a demonic vision of an aberrant world. Even Meredith, whom we generally (mis)interpret as an eternal optimist, presented through his romantic heroes savagely brought to heel a cruel world in which unthinking idealism can lead to personal tragedy. We forget that suggestion is often as effective as detailed analysis.

Comedy, then, gave the novelist a weapon, and he used it to expose the worst of the very middle class which imposed strictures upon him and then read his work. He reviled vulgarity and coarseness, mocked vanity, and ridiculed the affectations of the nouveaux riches. In a way, comedy provided a type of revenge on those who would restrict him to soap opera. The major nineteenth-century novelist was a figure of common sense, redirecting the vulgar and the eccentric into acceptable behavior and burlesquing them if they remained obtuse and selfish. By the time of George Eliot and Thomas Hardy, however, laughter is insufficient in a world in which the innocent as well as the guilty can be destroyed not through their own foibles but through life itself. With Hardy, as with Butler in *The Way of All Flesh*, the Victorian novel had run its course; the beliefs the world had about itself were being modified, and the novel, although fixed in some of its basic forms, was sufficiently flexible to meet change. Hardy's bleak outlook becomes the norm: the novelist no longer suggested darkness in a world of light, but now occasional light in a world of darkness, and frequently the light revealed the path to self-destruction.

Clearly, the Victorian writer was sensitive to the major political, social and intellectual movements of his day, more so than either the eighteenth- or twentieth-century novelist. It is commonplace now to speak of the novel's response to the manners and morals of the age; but it is not unusual that the novel should be rooted in contemporary values, for its very length requires the solidity of a particular society. Often, the nineteenth-century novelist became a political spokesman, although the novels in which political and social ideas dominate *directly* are weak and unconvincing, as George Gissing's sincere but monotonous books demonstrate.

Dickens himself responded to labor unrest (the aftereffects of Chartism) and following the injunctions of Carlyle wrote a "social novel" in *Hard Times*, which exposes the frustrations and evils of the economic system. Of course, virtually all of Dickens's major fiction is concerned with contemporary English life, with only formal religion excluded as a serious topic. Meredith, in *Beauchamp's Career*, dealt directly with the political situation by creating an idealistic young man who wished to change England, and who found instead that good will and idealism are insufficient values to counter entrenched interests. George Eliot was of course immersed in the social (Middlemarch), religious (Adam Bede), and political (Felix Holt) developments of the century. Jane Austen and Thackeray were alike in not responding directly to definite movements, but their works reflect two of the major strains of the day, the growth of democracy and the development of industrial and commercial enterprises. Hardy, writing in the latter third of the century, was strongly affected by Darwin's publications; in *The Mayor of Casterbridge* and *Jude the Obscure*, as well as in several earlier novels, he reflected a Darwinian world in which man gains heroic stature through his struggle against inexplicable forces that will ultimately destroy him. For still later novelists, Darwin was the English Nietzsche.

An army of minor novelists further mirrored various aspects of the economic and political situation and prepared the way for ameliorating legislation that made for shorter hours, better working conditions, and more equitable pay (Disraeli, in his "Young England" novels; Charles Reade, in *Hard Cash*, *It Is Never Too Late to Mend*; Mrs Gaskell, in *Mary Barton*, *North and South*; Harriet Martineau, in nine volumes of *Illustrations of Political Economy*). Under the pressure of several prophets (like Carlyle and Ruskin) and political events themselves (Chartism, Poor Laws, Corn Laws, Reform Bills)—as well as from a sense of moral outrage—the novel became "serious," and the gap between fiction with a message and the novel of sheer entertainment began to widen, until by the end of the century the novel appealed in different ways to two separate reading publics.

Several novels also dealt directly with the Oxford Movement and the significance of Anglo-Catholicism, *Robert Elsmere* by Mrs Humphry Ward being perhaps the most popular and successful. Moreover, by mid-century many Victorian novelists began to deal less with the whole range of society than with significant aspects of it, often restricting their efforts to one segment. With Charles Kingsley, among others, we start to get specialized fiction, a story, for example, about a tailor (*Alton Locke*, 1850) who attempts to raise himself socially and economically. Nevertheless, despite their fierce opposition to abuses in the economic system, both the major and minor writers believed in England herself and assumed that hard work and perseverance—their heritage from the seventeenth century—were sufficient for success. With the exceptions of Gissing and Hardy, most accepted the Horatio Alger-like views of Samuel Smiles (*Self-Help*, 1859; *Character*, 1871; *Thrift*, 1875), who equated diligence with virtue. Dickens, for instance, rejuvenates Pip when the latter realizes, first, that he must work for a living and, second, that snobbery and parasitism are inter-related sins.

In a pre-existential, democratic age, it was perhaps inevitable that virtue should be defined as a man's ability to develop himself to his full potential regardless of his bad beginnings. The need to transcend oneself becomes, then, the religion of a period in which commercial values were generally accepted despite sporadic defiance. Earlier, in Defoe and his successors, the values of a commercial society were the normal, expected ones. In the next century, these values, although attacked fiercely and brilliantly in the vast body of anti-Victorian literature, were still acceptable once outrages were removed. Only in the twentieth century were the values and all their ramifications viewed as villainous. One need only compare the all-consuming silver mine in Conrad's *Nostromo* with the commercial outfit that "saves" Pip after his great expectations have been smashed. Conrad is concerned with showing how commerce can corrupt; while Dickens presents a similar condition as a means of salvation. Even his savage Coketown might have been redeemed if Bounderby and Gradgrind could be transformed. The Victorian novelist believed that a change of heart would improve conditions that were themselves basically sound, even though malpractice created disturbing circumstances. Not until the end of the century did the novelist find conditions themselves self-corrupting and turn inward, to the soul of the individual, to try to redeem him in a world that was beyond visible hope.

The secularization of the novel that began with Defoe was never more apparent than among the Victorians, depending as the form does on a public interested not in metaphysics but in daily events: money, wills, bills to meet, credits, debits, marriage contracts, real estate arrangements, wages, working conditions. Despite the presence of strong religious standards under Victoria, the major novelists were secular in their works, reflecting an age that paid only lip service to the religious prophets. Thackeray, George Eliot, and Hardy were free thinkers; Meredith was a Wordsworthian nature-lover who replaced an orthodox God with the vague trinity of blood, brain, and spirit; Dickens was more concerned with a Christian morality than with the details of orthodoxy, and his characters are graded according to their gentle hearts rather than to their religious declarations. Throughout the century, the clergyman appears as a Chadband (*Bleak House*) or (particularly often) as a High Churchman like Mr Collins of *Pride and Prejudice*, hardly as a devoted man of God. Trollope's secular clergymen are representative of a period in which competitive commercial values left little room for the spirit to flower. Nineteenth-century novelists, Ian Watt points out, "would continue Defoe's serious concern with man's worldly doings without placing them in a religious framework." The dignity of labor became itself the justification of the individual's secularity.

The economic and social nature of the Victorian novel was set, then, in the work of Defoe and Richardson a hundred years earlier. The economic individualism of Robinson Crusoe was readily translated into the ennobling nature of work. Furthermore, work was a means of closing the gap between social classes. A diligent merchant could rise to all but the top of the aristocracy by making a fortune, buying an estate and a town house, bringing his sons up as gentlemen, and marrying his daughters to titled but impecunious men about town. In its various aspects and developments, this world became the stuff of the nineteenth-century novelists. It became the source of much humor and much spite, although its essential nature went unquestioned if the people involved were decent and demonstrated benevolence and compassion. Lest, however, social and political content seem to dominate at the expense of art, we should remember that the Victorian novelist was concerned with art, although not so consciously as were Flaubert, James, Conrad, and Joyce.

While it is true that the novelist often remained an unhappy slave to his reading public, he did recognize that the novel was capable of doing many things. Dickens, while obeying the dictates of a public he tried to cultivate, peppered his letters with references to his craft, and in his later novels was fully conscious of the need for artistic form. *Great Expectations*, whose original ending he changed only at the insistence of Bulwer-Lytton, is itself one of his most carefully wrought works, balanced, unified, and almost completely lacking the episodic stringiness of his earlier fiction. George Eliot, through the advice of George Henry Lewes as well as through her own experience, recognized the limitations of strict realism, and in *Middle-march* tried to fuse art with social reality. The same may be said of nearly all the major novelists, including even Hardy, despite his open disavowal of the novelist's craft.

The Victorian novelist brought to his work a concern with form that for the first time gave weight and depth to longer fiction. Those who do not blindly restrict the criteria of the novel will see that it has changed only in several emphases, not in essentials, from the previous century. David Copperfield, Pip, Pendennis, and Richard Feverel have become Ernest Pontifex, Paul Morel, Leonard Bast, Lord Jim, and Stephen Dedalus; Dorothy Casaubon has changed into Mrs Dalloway and Mrs Ramsay; Becky Sharp has been transformed into one of Aldous Huxley's vampire women, or perhaps into Lady Chatterley herself; Heathcliff is now Lawrence's Gerald Crich. Only Joyce's Leopold Bloom finds no exact counterpart in the nineteenth century, but Bloom is all men who have failed; and the nineteenth-century novelist, culminating in Hardy, knew a great deal about failure in an age of far-reaching success.

Note

1. The Gothic novel did not of course spring ready-made from Walpole, nor did it always manifest uniform qualities. Prior to and contemporaneous with *The Castle of Otranto* was a considerable body of literature which we can identify as Gothic in tone: the supernatural elements of the ballad, the eerie quality of the epic, the extravagance and violence of Elizabethan drama (now being revived), the wildness of pagan Europe caught in Ossian (1760-63) and slightly later in Percy's *Reliques* (1765), the exoticism of Oriental and Near Eastern tales, the excesses of the chivalric romance, the death-orientation of Graveyard Poetry (Young's *Night Thoughts*, 1742; Blair's *The Grave*, 1743; Gray's *Elegy*, 1751), the Rousseauistic admiration for frenzied and disordered nature (manifest in the planned irregularity of English gardens). All these forces and interests operated as emotional counters to the realism of the main tradition of the novel in Fielding, Richardson, and Smollett, although the latter in *Ferdinand Count Fathom* (1753) provided a link between realism and Gothic; and Richardson himself in Clarissa suggested the darknesses and terrors peculiar to the later form. Clarissa dreams of being stabbed (raped) by Lovelace in a churchyard and then tumbled into a deep grave and trampled beneath his feet.

As Gothic developed, it gained in excesses and horrors, so that Mrs Radcliffe (in *A Sicilian Romance*, 1790; *The Romance of the Forest*, 1792; *The Mysteries of Udolpho*, 1794; *The Italian*, 1797) is no more like Matthew Lewis (*The Monk*, 1795; The Bravo of Venice, 1804) or Charles Maturin than Jane Austen seems like Thomas Hardy. Mrs Radcliffe's genteel scenes of eeriness contrast sharply with Lewis's and Maturin's masochistic-sadistic images of torture and brutality in which pain and pleasure blend imperceptibly into each other in one long blood-bath. Calculated to thrill and excite, popular fiction of the early nineteenth century continued the macabre tradition. (See E. S. Turner's *Boys Will Be Boys*).

In the later nineteenth century, Gothic reappeared directly not only in Dickens' unfinished *The Mystery of Edwin Drood* (1870), but in the work of the man who influenced that and earlier Dickens novels, Wilkie Collins. In *Basil* (1852), *The Woman in White* (1860), *Armadale* (1866), and *The Moonstone* (1868), Collins demonstrated that he was heir to the atmospheric devices of Mrs Radcliffe, the sensationalism of the Newgate novels of Bulwer-Lytton and Ainsworth, and the melodramatic tensions of Poe. Like the afore-mentioned Gothic writers—and here unlike Dickens—Collins stressed story-telling at the expense of characterization, comment, humor, even cogent psychology. The thread of mystery is all. As he wrote in the Preface to The Woman in White:

> I have always held the old-fashioned opinion that the primary object of a work of fiction should be to tell a story; and I have never believed that the novelist who properly performed this first condition of his art was in danger, on that account, of neglecting the delineation of character—for this plain reason, that the effect produced by any narrative of events is essentially dependent, not on the events themselves, but on the human interest which is directly connected with them.

From Collins' work to the modern detective story is not distant, although a writer like Graham Greene—and Dostoyevsky and Conrad before him—further transformed the Gothic- and-mystery elements into narratives bearing a philosophical, even a doctrinal, weight. (Author).

The American Novel in the Nineteenth Century

V: Writers on the American Novel

MRS. E. LYNN LINTON	MR. JAMES PAYN	CAPTAIN HAWLEY SMART	MR. F. W. ROBINSON
REV. S. BARING-GOULD	MR. EDMUND YATES	MRS. J. H. RIDDELL	DR. GEORGE MACDONALD
MISS HELEN MATHERS	MR. R. L. FARJEON	MR. WILLIAM BLACK	MR. H. RIDER HAGGARD

MR. W. E. NORRIS	MR. ROBERT BUCHANAN	MR. D. CHRISTIE MURRAY	MRS. T. A. TROLLOPE
MR. J. H. SHORTHOUSE	MISS AMELIA B. EDWARDS	MR. WALTER BESANT	MR. WILKIE COLLINS
MR. R. LOUIS STEVENSON	MR. THOMAS HARDY	MR. W. CLARK RUSSELL	MISS THACKERAY

of the D...

NOTICE

Persons attempting to find a motive in this narrative will be prosecuted; persons attempting to find a moral in it will be banished; persons attempting to find a plot in it will be shot.
>By Order of the Author
>Per G.G., Chief of Ordnance

>[Mark Twain, "Notice" to *The Adventures of Huckleberry Finn*, 1884, rptd New York: P. F. Collier and Son, 1896.]

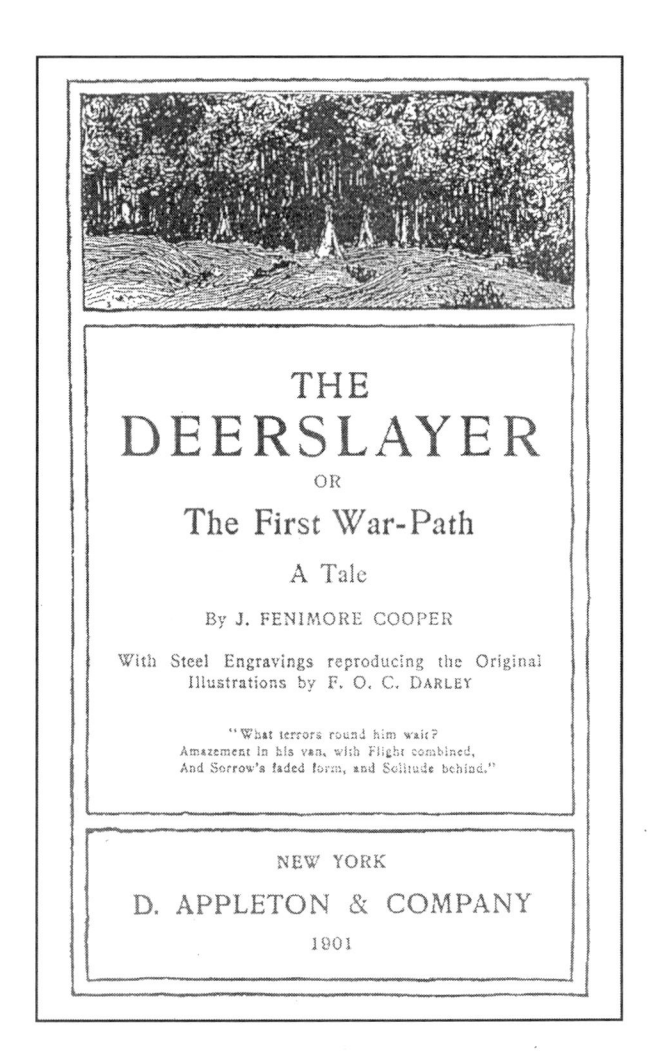

THE DEERSLAYER
OR
The First War-Path
A Tale

By J. FENIMORE COOPER

With Steel Engravings reproducing the Original Illustrations by F. O. C. DARLEY

"What terrors round him wait?
Amazement in his van, with Flight combined,
And Sorrow's faded form, and Solitude behind."

NEW YORK
D. APPLETON & COMPANY
1901

78

Preface to the Leather-Stocking Tales

JAMES FENIMORE COOPER

James Fenimore Cooper (1789-1851) is one of the first recognized American novelists. Primarily a writer of romances, he is best known for his *Leather-Stocking Tales*, a series of five books chronicling the adventures of Natty Bumppo, a sort of noble savage, situated midway between the American Indians and the 'white' civilized society. Though today many of the passages in these novels appear, at best, patronizing and, at worst, racist, Cooper's goal was to entertain the reader while providing a moral standard of conduct, a '*beau idéal*,' as he notes in his Preface. In the Preface he discusses his attempts to mix ideal and real characteristics so as not to make his hero a "monster of goodness". He also addresses the criticism that he has idealized the American Indian, noting that the critic has never witnessed the Indian in his natural surroundings but only in treaty negotiations where his character does not reflect its usual goodness. Cooper's romances have often been likened to the historical romances of Sir Walter Scott. Mark Twain in the following excerpt was to ridicule Cooper's romantic subjection of truth to poetic presentation.

This series of Stories, which has obtained the name of *The Leather-Stocking Tales*, has been written in a very desultory and inartificial manner. The order in which the several books appeared was essentially different from that in which they would have been presented to the world had the regular course of their incidents been consulted. In *The Pioneers*, the first of the series written, the Leather-Stocking is represented as already old, and driven from his early haunts in the forest by the sound of the axe and the smoke of the settler. *The Last of the Mohicans*, the next book in the order of publication, carried the readers back to a much earlier period in the history of our hero, representing him as middle-aged, and in the fullest vigor

Source: James Fenimore Cooper, "Preface to the Leather-Stocking Tales", *The Deerslayer*, 1841, rptd New York: D. Appleton & Company, 1901, pp. iii-vii.

of manhood. In *The Prairie*, his career terminates, and he is laid in his grave. There, it was originally the intention to leave him, in the expectation that, as in the case of the human mass, he would soon be forgotten. But a latent regard for this character induced the author to resuscitate him in *The Pathfinder*, a book that was not long after succeeded by *The Deerslayer*, thus completing the series as it now exists.

While the five books that have been written were originally published in the order just mentioned, that of the incidents, insomuch as they are connected with the career of their principal character, is, as has been stated, very different, Taking the life of the Leather-Stocking as a guide, *The Deerslayer* should have been the opening book, for in that work he is seen just emerging into manhood; to be succeeded by *The Last of the Mohicans*, *The Pathfinder*, *The Pioneers*, and *The Prairie*. This arrangement embraces the order of events, though far from being that in which the books at first appeared. *The Pioneers* was published in 1822; *The Deerslayer* in 1841; making the interval between them nineteen years. Whether these progressive years have had a tendency to lessen the value of the last-named book, by lessening the native fire of its author, or of adding somewhat in the way of improved taste and a more matured judgment, is for others to decide.

If anything from the pen of the writer of these romances is at all to outlive himself, it is, unquestionably, the series of *The Leather-Stocking Tales*. To say this, is not to predict a very lasting, reputation for the series itself, but simply to express. the belief it will outlast any, or all, of the works from the same hand.

It is undeniable that the desultory manner in which *The Leather-Stocking Tales* were written, has, in a measure, impaired their harmony, and otherwise lessened their interest. This is proved by the fate of the two books last published, though probably the two most worthy of an enlightened and cultivated reader's notice. If the facts could be ascertained, it is probable the result would show that of all those (in America, in particular) who have read the three first books of the series, not one in ten has a knowledge of the existence even of the two last. Several causes have tended to produce this result. The long interval of time between the appearance of *The Prairie* and that of *The Pathfinder*, was itself a reason why the later books of the series should be overlooked. There was no longer novelty to attract attention, and the interest was materially impaired by the manner in which, events were necessarily anticipated, in laying the last of the series first before the world. With the generation that is now coming on the stage this fault will be partially removed by the edition contained in the present work, in which the several tales will be arranged solely in reference to their connection with each other.

The author has often been asked if he had any original in his mind for the character of Leather-Stocking. In a physical sense, different individuals known to the writer in early life certainly presented themselves as models, through his recollections; but in a moral sense this man of the forest is purely a creation. The idea of delineating a character that possessed little of civilization but its highest principles as they are exhibited in the uneducated, and all of savage life that is not incompatible with these great rules of conduct, is perhaps natural to the situation in which Natty was placed. He is too proud of his origin to sink into the condition of the wild Indian, and too much a man of the woods not to imbibe as much as was at all desirable, from his friends and companions. In a moral point of view it was the intention to illustrate the effect of seed scattered by the wayside. To use his own language, his 'gifts,' were 'white gifts,' and he was not disposed to bring on them discredit. On the other hand, removed from nearly all the temptations of civilized life, placed in the best associations of that which is deemed savage, and favorably disposed by nature to improve such advantages, it appeared to the writer that his hero was a fit subject to represent the better qualities of both conditions, without pushing either to extremes.

There was no violent stretch of the imagination, perhaps, in supposing one of civilized associations in childhood, retaining many of his earliest lessons amid the scenes of the forest. Had these early impressions, however, not been sustained by continued, though casual connection with men of his own color, if not of his own caste, all our information goes to show he would soon have lost every trace of his origin. It is believed that sufficient attention was paid to the particular circumstances in which this individual was placed, to justify the picture of his qualities that has been drawn. The Delawares only attracted the attention of the missionaries, and were a tribe unusually influenced by their precepts and example. In many instances they became Christians and cases occurred in which their subsequent lives gave proof of the efficacy of the great moral changes that had taken place within them.

A leading character in a work of fiction has a fair right to the aid which can be obtained from a poetical view of the subject. It is in this view, rather than in one more strictly circumstantial, that Leather-Stocking has been drawn. The imagination has no great task in portraying to itself a being removed from the every-day inducements to err, which abound in civilized life, while he retains the best and simplest of his early impressions; who sees God in the forest; hears Him in the winds; bows to Him in the firmament that o'ercanopies all; submits to his sway in a humble belief of his justice and mercy; in a word, a being who finds the impress of the Deity in all the works of nature, without any of the blots produced by the expedients, and passion, and mistakes of man. This is the most that has been attempted in the character of Leather-Stocking. Had this been done without any of the drawbacks of humanity, the picture would have been, in all probability, more pleasing than just. In order to preserve the *vrai-semblable*, therefore, traits derived from the prejudices, tastes, and even the weaknesses of his youth, have been mixed up with these higher qualities and longings, in a way, it is hoped, to represent a reasonable picture of human nature, without offering to the spectator a 'monster of goodness.'

It has been objected to these books that they give a more favorable picture of the redman than he deserves. The writer apprehends that much of this objection arises from the habits of those who have made it. One of his critics, on the appearance of the first work in which Indian character was portrayed, objected that its 'characters were Indians of the school of Heckewelder, rather than of the school of nature.' These words quite probably contain the substance of the true answer to the objection. Heckewelder was an ardent, benevolent missionary, bent on the good of the redman, and seeing in him one who had the soul, reason, and characteristics of a fellow-being. The critic is understood to have been a very distinguished agent of the government, one very familiar with Indians, as they are seen at the councils to treat for the sale of their lands, where little or none of their domestic qualities come in play, and where indeed, their evil passions are known to have the fullest scope. As just would it be to draw conclusions of the general state of American society from the scenes of the capital, as to suppose that the negotiating of one of these treaties is a fair picture of Indian life.

It is the privilege of all writers of fiction, more particularly when their works aspire to the elevation of romances, to present the *beau idéal* of their characters to the reader. This it is which constitutes poetry, and to suppose that the redman is to be represented only in the squalid misery or in the degraded moral state that certainly more or less belongs to his condition, is, we apprehend, taking a very narrow view of an author's privileges. Such criticism would have deprived the world of even Homer.

Preface to
The House of the Seven Gables

NATHANIEL HAWTHORNE

American author Nathaniel Hawthorne (1804-1864), descendent of a New England Puritan family, is known both for his tales and short stories as well as four major novels beginning with *The Scarlet Letter* (1850). In the following Preface he adopts the old distinction between novel and romance but redefines romance, distancing it from its Gothic predecessors of the late eighteenth century. Though he eschews any attempt at realistic representation of actual characters, he warns against emphasizing the marvellous or supernatural save as "a slight, delicate, and evanescent flavour". Like Sir Walter Scott, he attempts to embody the past rather than to historicize it. Though he is not averse to the prevalent nineteenth-century insistence on a story's moral, he refuses to subordinate his novel to one specific end. The romance of the characters and incidents in *The House of the Seven Gables*, like those of its predecessor *The Scarlet Letter*, consists in Hawthorne's focus on symbolic as opposed to realistic portrayal, and connotative in lieu of denotative description.

When a writer calls his work a Romance, it need hardly be observed that he wishes to claim a certain latitude, both as to its fashion and material, which he would not have felt himself entitled to assume had he professed to be writing a Novel. The latter form of composition is presumed to aim at a very minute fidelity, not merely to the possible, but to the probable and ordinary course of man's experience. The former—while, as a work of art, it must rigidly subject itself to laws, and while it sins unpardonably so far as it may swerve aside from the truth of the human heart—has fairly a right to present that truth under circumstances, to a great extent, of the writer's own choosing or creation. If he thinks fit, also, he may so manage his atmospherical medium as to bring out or mellow the lights and deepen

Source: Nathaniel Hawthorne, "Preface", *The House of the Seven Gables*, 1851, rptd Chicago: Houghton, Mifflin and Co., 1883, pp.13-16.

and enrich the shadows of the picture. He will be wise, no doubt, to make a very moderate use of the privileges here stated, and, especially, to mingle the Marvellous rather as a slight, delicate, and evanescent flavor, than as any portion of the actual substance of the dish offered to the public. He can hardly be said, however, to commit a literary crime even if he disregard this caution.

In the present work, the author has proposed to himself—but with what success, fortunately, it is not for him to judge—to keep undeviatingly within his immunities. The point of view in which this tale comes under the Romantic definition lies in the attempt to connect a bygone time with the very present that is flitting away from us. It is a legend prolonging itself, from an epoch now gray in the distance, down into our own broad daylight, and bringing along with it some of its legendary mist, which the reader, according to his pleasure, may either disregard, or allow it to float almost imperceptibly about the characters and events for the sake of a picturesque effect. The narrative, it may be, is woven of so humble a texture as to require this advantage, and, at the same time, to render it the more difficult of attainment.

Many writers lay very great stress upon some definite moral purpose, at which they profess to aim their works. Not to be deficient in this particular, the author has provided himself with a moral,—the truth, namely, that the wrong-doing of one generation lives into the successive ones, and, divesting itself of every temporary advantage, becomes a pure and uncontrollable mischief; and he would feel it a singular gratification if this romance might effectually convince mankind—or, indeed, any one man—of the folly of tumbling down an avalanche of ill-gotten gold, or real estate, on the heads of an unfortunate posterity, there-by to maim and crush them, until the accumulated mass shall be scattered abroad in its original atoms. In good faith, however, he is not sufficiently imaginative to flatter himself with the slightest hope of this kind. When romances do really teach anything, or produce any effective operation, it is usually through a far more subtle process than the ostensible one. The author has considered it hardly worth his while, therefore, relentlessly to impale the story with its moral as with an iron rod,—or, rather, as by sticking a pin through a butterfly,—thus at once depriving it of life, and causing it to stiffen in an ungainly and unnatural attitude. A high truth, indeed, fairly, finely, and skilfully wrought out, brightening at every step, and crowning the final development of a work of fiction, may add an artistic glory, but is never any truer, and seldom any more evident, at the last page than at the first.

The reader may perhaps choose to assign an actual locality to the imaginary events of this narrative. If permitted by the historical connection,—which, though slight, was essential to his plan,—the author would very willingly have avoided anything of this nature. Not to speak of other objections, it exposes the romance to an inflexible and exceedingly dangerous species of criticism, by bringing his fancy-pictures almost into positive contact with the realities of the moment. It has been no part of his object, however, to describe local manners, nor in any way to meddle with the characteristics of a community for whom he cherishes a proper respect and a natural regard. He trusts not to be considered as unpardonably offending by laying out a street that infringes upon nobody's private rights, and appropriating a lot of land which had no visible owner, and building a house of materials long in use for constructing castles in the air. The personages of the tale—though they give themselves out to be of ancient stability and considerable prominence—are really of the author's own making, or, at all events, of his own mixing; their virtues can shed no lustre, nor their defects redound, in the remotest degree, to the discredit of the venerable town of which they profess to be inhabitants. He would be glad, therefore, if—especially in the quarter to which he alluded—the book may be read strictly as a Romance, having a great deal more to do with the clouds overhead than with any portion of the actual soil of the Country of Essex.

LENOX, *January 27, 1851.*

UNCLE TOM'S CABIN;

OR,

LIFE AMONG THE LOWLY.

BY

HARRIET BEECHER STOWE.

ILLUSTRATED EDITION.

COMPLETE IN ONE VOLUME.

DESIGNS BY BILLINGS; ENGRAVED BY BAKER, SMITH, AND ANDREW.

BOSTON:
JOHN P. JEWETT AND COMPANY.
CLEVELAND, OHIO:
JEWETT, PROCTOR, AND WORTHINGTON.
1853.

❦ 80 ❧

Preface to *Uncle Tom's Cabin*

HARRIET BEECHER STOWE

One of the most famous social problem novels of the nineteenth century, Harriet Beecher Stowe's (1811-1896) *Uncle Tom's Cabin* was first serialized in the *National Era* in 1851-52. Though often discounted as an overly sentimentalized version of American slavery (see Baldwin's "Everybody's Protest Novel"), it was believed to have helped instigate the American Civil War. In the following preface, Stowe offers a heavily Christianized message of her goal as a novelist. She proposes to elicit "sympathy and feeling for the African race, as they exist among us" and to expose the unjust system of slavery. Though redolent with paternalistic overtones, Stowe's preface illustrates a common goal of a large number of social problem novels of the nineteenth century: to teach the ruling classes how to acquire a new sympathy for the downtrodden.

The scenes of this story, as its title indicates, lie among a race, hitherto ignored by the associations of polite and refined society; an exotic race, whose ancestors, born beneath a tropic sun, brought with them, and perpetuated to their descendants, a character so essentially unlike the hard and dominant Anglo-Saxon race as for many years to have won from it only misunderstanding and contempt.

But another and better day is dawning; every influence of literature, of poetry, and of art, in our times, is becoming more and more in unison with the great master chord of Christianity,—"Good will to man."

The poet, the painter, and the artist now seek out and embellish the common and gentler humanities of life, and, under the allurements of fiction, breathe a humanizing and subduing influence, favorable to the development of the great principles of Christian brotherhood.

The hand of benevolence is every where stretched out, searching into abuses, righting wrongs, alleviating distresses, and bringing to the knowledge and sympathies of the world the lowly, the oppressed, and the forgotten.

Source: Harriet Beecher Stowe, "Preface", *Uncle Tom's Cabin; or, Life Among the Lowly*, Boston: John P. Jewett and Company, 1853, pp. 5-8.

In this general movement, unhappy Africa at last is remembered; Africa, who began the race of civilization and human progress in the dim, gray dawn of early time, but who, for centuries, has lain bound and bleeding at the foot of civilized and Christianized humanity, imploring compassion in vain.

But the heart of the dominant race who have been her conquerors, her hard masters, has at length been turned towards her in mercy; and it has been seen how far nobler it is in nations to protect the feeble than to oppress them. Thanks be to God, the world has at last outlived the slave trade!

The object of these sketches is to awaken sympathy and feeling for the African race, as they exist among us; to show their wrongs and sorrows, under a system so necessarily cruel and unjust as to defeat and do away the good effects of all that can be attempted for them, by their best friends, under it.

In doing this, the author can sincerely disclaim any invidious feeling towards those individuals who, often without any fault of their own, are involved in the trials and embarrassments of the legal relations of slavery.

Experience has shown her that some of the noblest of minds and hearts are often involved; and no one knows better than they do, that what may be gathered of the evils of slavery from sketches like these is not the half that could be told of the unspeakable whole.

In the Northern States, these representations may, perhaps, be thought caricatures; in the Southern States are witnesses who know their fidelity. What personal knowledge the author has had of the truth of incidents such as here are related will appear in its time.

It is a comfort to hope, as so many of the world's sorrows and wrongs have, from age to age, been lived down, so a time shall come when sketches similar to these shall be valuable only as memorials of what has long ceased to be.

When an enlightened and Christianized community shall have, on the shores of Africa, laws, language, and literature drawn from among us, may then the scenes of the house of bondage be to them like the remembrance of Egypt to the Israelite—a motive of thankfulness to Him who hath redeemed them!

For, while politicians contend, and men are swerved this way and that by conflicting tides of interest and passion, the great cause of human liberty is in the hands of One, of whom it is said,—

> *He shall not fail nor be discouraged*
> *Till He have set judgement in the earth.*

> *He shall deliver the needy when he crieth,*
> *The poop, and him that hath no helper.*

> *He shall redeem their soul from deceit and violence,*
> *And precious shall their blood be in his sight.*

81

Henry James

WILLIAM DEAN HOWELLS

Heralding Henry James as the innovator of a new form of fiction, "an analytic study rather than a story" [28], Howells perceives in the early writings of James a masterful emphasis on character at the expense of plot. Howells credits James's narrators with the impartiality necessary to present characters without the authorial intrusion so characteristic of the preceding age. With the publication of *Daisy Miller* (1879), Howells states that James has founded the "international novel". This genre, he notes, evolves from the realistic fiction of George Eliot and the French realism of Daudet more than from Zola. Howells' attitude towards this new form of fiction is ambivalent. Though he laments the subordination of the romance to the novel, he applauds the Jamesian tendency to say rather than to tell, to expose characters' psyches rather than focus on events and catastrophes. As editor of *Atlantic Monthly*, Howells was responsible for publishing some of James's early fiction.

The events of Mr James's life—as we agree to understand events—may be told in a very few words. His race is Irish on his father's side and Scotch on his mother's, to which mingled strains the generalizer may attribute, if he likes, that union of vivid expression and dispassionate analysis which has characterized his work from the first. There are none of those early struggles with poverty, which render the lives of so many distinguished Americans monotonous reading, to record in his case: the cabin hearth-fire did not light him to the youthful pursuit of literature; he had from the start all those advantages which, when they go too far, become limitations.

He was born in New York city in the year 1843, and his first lessons in life and letters were the best which the metropolis—so small in the perspective diminishing to that date—could afford. In his twelfth year his family went abroad, and after some stay in England made a long sojourn in France and Switzerland. They returned to America in 1860, placing themselves at Newport, and for a year or two Mr James was at the Harvard Law School, where, perhaps, he did not study a great deal of

Source: William Dean Howells, "Henry James", *The Century Illustrated Monthly Magazine*, 25: 3, November 1882, pp. 24-9.

The CENTURY

ILLUSTRATED MONTHLY

MAGAZINE.

November 1882, to April 1883

The CENTURY Co., NEW-YORK.

F. WARNE & Co., LONDON.

Vol. XXV. *New Series Vol. III.*

law. His father removed from Newport to Cambridge in 1866, and there Mr James remained until he went abroad, three years later, for the residence in England and Italy which, with infrequent visits home, has continued ever since.

It was during these three years of his Cambridge life that I became acquainted with his work. He had already printed a tale—'The Story of a Year'—in the 'Atlantic Monthly,' when I was asked to be Mr Field's assistant in the management, and it was my fortune to read Mr James's second contribution in manuscript. 'Would you take it?' asked my chief. 'Yes, and all the stories you can get from the writer.' One is much securer of one's judgement at twenty-nine then, say, at forty-five; but if this was a mistake of mine I am not yet old enough to regret it. The story was called 'Poor Richard,' and it dealt with the conscience of a man very much in love with a woman who adored his rival. He told this rival a lie, which sent him away to his death on the field,—in that day nearly every fictitious personage has something to do with the war,—but Poor Richard's lie did not win him his love. It still seems to me that the situation was strongly and finely felt. One's pity went, as it should, with the liar; but the whole story had a pathos which lingers in my mind equally with a sense of the new literary qualities which gave me such delight in it. I admired, as we must in all that Mr James has written, the finished workmanship in which there is no loss of vigor; the luminous and uncommon use of words, the originality of phrase, the whole clear and beautiful style, which I confess I weakly liked the better for the occasional Gallicisms remaining from an inveterate habit of French. Those who know the writings of Mr Henry James will recognize the inherited felicity of diction which is so striking in the writings of Mr Henry James, Jr. The son's diction is not so racy as the father's; it lacks its daring, but it is as fortunate and graphic; and I cannot give it greater praise than this, though it has, when he will, a splendour and state which is wholly its own.

Mr James is now so universally recognized that I shall seem to be making an unwarrantable claim when I express my belief that the popularity of his stories was once largely confined to Mr Field's assistant. They had characteristics which forbade any editor to refuse them; and there are no anecdotes of thrice-rejected manuscripts finally printed to tell of him; his work was at once successful with all the magazines. But with the readers of 'The Atlantic,' of 'Harper's,' of 'Lippincott's,' of The Galaxy,' of 'The Century,' it was another affair. The flavour was so strange, that, with rare exceptions, they had to 'learn to like' it. Probably few writers have in the same degree compelled the liking of their readers. He was reluctantly accepted, partly through a mistake as to his attitude—through the confusion of his point of view with his private opinion—in the reader's mind. This confusion caused the tears of rage which bedewed our continent in behalf of the 'average American girl' supposed to be satirized in Daisy Miller, and prevented the perception of the fact that, so far as the average American girl was studied at all in Daisy Miller, her indestructible innocence, her invulnerable new-worldliness, had never been so delicately appreciated. It was so plain that Mr James disliked her vulgar conditions, that the very people to whom he revealed her essential sweetness and light were furious that he should have seemed not to see what existed through him. In other words, they would never have liked him better if he had been a worse artist—if he had been a little more confidential.

But that artistic impartiality which puzzled so many in the treatment of Daisy Miller is one of the qualities most valuable in the eyes of those who care how things are done, and I am not sure that it is not Mr James's most characteristic quality. As 'frost performs the effect of fire,' this impartiality comes at last to the same result as sympathy. We may be quite sure that Mr James does not like the peculiar phase of our civilization typified in Henrietta Stackpole; but he treats her with such exquisite justice that he lets *us* like her. It is an extreme case, but I confidently allege it in proof.

His impartiality is part of the reserve with which he works in most respects, and which at first glance makes us say that he is wanting in humor. But I feel pretty certain that Mr James has not been able to disinherit himself to this degree. We Americans are terribly in earnest about making ourselves, individually and collectively; but I fancy that our prevailing mood in the face of all problems is that of an abiding faith which can afford to be funny. He has himself indicated that we have, as a nation, as a people, our joke, and every one of us is in the joke more or less. We may, some of us, dislike it extremely, disapprove it wholly, and even abhor it, but we are in the joke all the same, and no one of us is safe from becoming the great American humorist at any given moment. The danger is not apparent in Mr James's case, and I confess that I read him with a relief in the comparative immunity that he affords from the national facetiousness. Many of his people are humorously *seen*, like Daisy Miller's mother, but these do not give a dominant color; the business in hand is commonly serious, and the droll people are subordinated. They abound, nevertheless, and many of them are perfectly new finds, like Mr Tristam in 'The American,' the bill-paying father in the 'Pension Beaurepas,' the anxiously Europeanizing mother in the same story, the amusing little Madame de Belgarde, Henrietta Stackpole, and even Newman himself. But though Mr James portrays the humorour in character, he is decidedly not on humorous terms with his reader; he ignores rather than recognizes the fact that they are both in the joke.

If we take him at all we must take him on his own ground, for clearly he will not come to ours. We must make concessions to him, not in this respect only, but in several others, chief among which is the motive for reading fiction. By example, at least, he teaches that it is the pursuit and not the end which should give us pleasure; for he often prefers to leave us to our own conjectures in regard to the fate of the people on whom he has interested us. There is no question, of course, but he could tell the story of Isabel in 'The Portrait of a Lady' to the end, yet he does not tell it. We must agree, then, to take what seems a fragment instead of a whole, and to find, when we can, a name for this kind in fiction. Evidently it is the character, not the fate, of his people which occupies him; when he has fully developed their character he leaves them to what destiny the reader pleases.

The analytic tendency seems to have increased with him as his work has gone on. Some of the earlier tales were very dramatic: 'A Passionate pilgrim,' which I should rank above all his other short stories and for certain rich poetical qualities, above everything else that he has done, is eminently dramatic. But I do not find much that

I should call dramatic in 'The Portrait of a Lady,' while I do find in it an amount of analysis which I should call superabundance if it were not all such good literature. The novelist's main business is to possess his reader with a due conception of his characters and the situations in which they find themselves. If he does more or less than this he equally fails. I have sometimes thought that Mr James's danger was to do more, but when I have been ready to declare this excess an error of his method I have hesitated. Could anything be superfluous that had given me so much pleasure as I read? Certainly from only one point of view, and this a rather narrow, technical one. It seems to me that an enlightened criticism will recognize in Mr James's fiction a metaphysical genius working to aesthetic results, and will not be disposed to dent it any method it chooses to employ. No other novelist, except George Eliot, has dealt so largely in analysis of motive, has so fully explained and commented upon the springs of action in the persons of the drama, both before and after the facts. These novelists are more alike than any others in their processes, but with George Eliot an ethical purpose is dominant, and with Mr James an artistic purpose. I do not know just how it should be stated of two such noble and generous types of character as Dorothea and Isabel Archer, but I think that we sympathize with the former in grand aims that chiefly concern others, and with the latter in beautiful dreams that primarily concern herself. Both are unselfish and devoted women, sublimely true to a mistaken ideal in their marriages; but, though they come to this common martyrdom, the original difference in them remains. Isabel has her weaknesses, as Dorothea had, but these seem to me, on the whole, the most nobly imagined and the most nobly intentioned women in modern fiction; and I think Isabel is the more subtly divined of the two. If we speak of mere characterization, we must not fail to acknowledge the perfection of Gilbert Osmond. It was a profound stroke to make him an American by birth. No European could realize so fully in his own life the ideal of a Eurpoean *dilettante* in all the meaning of that cheapened word; as no European could so deeply and tenderly feel the sweetness and loveliness of the English past as the sick American, Searle, in 'The Passionate Pilgrim.'

What is called the international novel is popularly dated from the publication of 'Daisy Miller,' though 'Roderick Hudson' and 'The American' had gone before; but it really began in the beautiful story which I have just named. Mr James, who invented this species in fiction, first contrasted in the 'Passionate Pilgrim' the New World moods, ideals, and prejudices, and he did it there with a richness of poetic effect which he has since never equalled. I own that I regret the loss of the poetry, but you cannot ask a man to keep on being a poet for you; it is hardly for him to choose; yet I compare rather discontentedly in my own mind such impassioned creations as Searle and the painter in 'The Madonnna of the Future' with 'Daisy Miller,' of whose slight, thin personality I also feel the indefinable charm, and of the tragedy of whose innocence I recognize the delicate pathos. Looking back to those early stories, where Mr James stood at the dividing ways of the novel and the romance, I am sometimes sorry that he declared even superficially for the former. His best efforts seem to me those of romance; his best types have an ideal development, like Isabel and Claire Belgarde and Bessy Alden and poor Daisy and even Newman. But, doubtless, he has chosen wisely; perhaps the romance is an outworn form, and would not lend itself to the reproduction of even the ideality of modern life. I myself waver somewhat in my preference—it is a preference—when I think of such people as Lord Warbuton and the Touchetts, whom I take to be all decidedly of this world. The first of these especially interested me as a probable type of the English nobleman, who amiably accepts the existing situation with all its possibilities of political and social change, and insists not at all upon the surviving feudalities, but means to be a manly and simple gentleman in any event. An American is not able to pronounce as to the verity of the type; I only know that it seems probable and that is charming. It makes one wish that it were in Mr James's way to paint in some story the present phase of change in England. A titled personage is still mainly an inconceivable being to us; he is like a goblin or a fairy in a storybook. How does he comport himself in the face of all the changes and modifications that have taken place and that still impend? We can hardly imagine a lord taking his nobility seriously; it is some hint of the conditional frame of Lord Warburton's mind that makes him imaginable and delightful to us.

It is not my purpose here to review any of Mr James's books; I like better to speak of his people than of the conduct of his novels, and I wish to recognize the fineness with which he has touched-in the pretty primness of Osmond's daughter and the mild devotedness of Mr Rosier. A masterly hand is as often manifest in the treatment of such subordinate figures as in that of the principal persons, and Mr James does them unerringly. This is felt in the more important character of Valentin Belgarde, a fascinating character in spite of its detects—perhaps on account of them—and a sort of French Lord Warburton, but wittier, and not so good. 'These are my ideas,' says his sister-in-law, at the end of a number of inanities. 'Ah, you call them ideas!' he returns, which is delicious and makes you love him. He, too, has his moments of misgiving, apparently in regard to his nobility, and his acceptance of Newman on the basis of something like 'manhood suffrage' is very charming. It is of course difficult for a remote plebeian to verify the pictures of the of legitimist society in 'The American,' but there is the probable suggestion in them of conditions and principles, and want of principles, of which we get glimpses in our travels abroad: at any rate, they reveal another and not impossible world, and it is fine to have Newman discover that the opinions and criticism of our world are so absolutely valueless in that sphere that his knowledge of the infamous crime of the mother and brother of his betrothed will have no effect whatever upon them in their own circle if he explodes it there. This seems like aristocracy indeed, and one admires, almost respects, its survival in our day. But I always regretted that Newman's discovery seemed the precursor of his magnanimous resolution not to avenge himself; it weakened the effect of this, with which it had really nothing to do. Upon the whole, however, Newman is an adequate and satisfying representative of Americanism, with his generous matrimonial ambition, his vast good-nature, and his thorough good sense and right feeling. We must be very hard to please if we are not pleased with him. He is not the 'cultivated American' who redeems us from time to time in the eyes of Europe; but he is unquestionably more national, and it is observable that his unaffected fellow-countrymen and women fare very well at Mr James's hands always; it is the Europeanizing sort like the critical little Bostonian in the 'Bundle of Letters.' The ladies shocked at Daisy Miller, the mother in the 'Pension Beaurepas' who goes about trying to be of the 'native' world everywhere, Madame Merle and Gilbert Osmond, Miss Light and her mother, who have reason to complain, if anyone has. Doubtless Mr James does not mean to satirize such Americans, but it is interesting to note how I they strike such a keen observer. We are certainly not allowed to like them, and the other sort find somehow a place in our affections along with his good Europeans. It is little odd, by the way, that in all the printed talk about Mr James—and there has been no end of it—his power of engaging your preference for certain of his people has been so little commented on. Perhaps it is because he makes no obvious appeal for them; but one likes such men as Lord Warburton, Newman, Valentin, the artistic brother in 'The Europeans' and Ralph Touchett, and such women as Isabel, Claire Belgarde, Mrs. Tristram, and certain others, with a thoroughness that is one of the best testimonies to their vitality. This comes about through their own qualities, and is not affected by insinuation or by downright *petting*, such as we find in Dickens nearly always and in Thackeray too often.

The art of fiction has, in fact, become a finer art in our day than it was with Dickens and Thackeray. We could not suffer the confidential attitude of the latter now, nor the mannerism of the former, any more than we could endure the prolixity of Richardson or the coarseness of Fielding. These great men are of the past—they and their methods and interests; even Trollope and Reade are not of the present. The new school derives from Hawthorne and George Eliot rather than any others; but it studies human nature much more in its wonted aspects, and finds its ethical and dramatic examples in the operation of lighter but not really less vital motives. The moving accident is certainly not its trade; and it prefers to avoid all manner of dire catastrophes. It is largely influenced by French fiction in form; but it is the realism of Daudet rather than the realism of Zola that prevails with it, and it has a soul of its own which is above the business of recording the rather brutish pursuit of a woman by a man, which seems to be the chief end of the French novelist. This school, which is so largely of the future as well as the present, find its chief exemplar in Mr James; it is he who is shaping and directing American fiction, at least. It is the ambition of the younger contributors to write like him; he has his following more distinctly recognizable than that of any other English-writing novelist. Whether he will so far control this following as to decide the nature of the novel with us remains to be seen. Will the reader be content to accept a novel which is an analytic study rather than a story, which is apt to leave him arbiter of the destiny of the author's creations? Will he find his account in the unflagging interest of their development? Mr James's growing popularity seems to suggest that this may be the case; but the work of Mr James's imitators will have much to do with the final result.

In the meantime it is not surprising that he has his imitators. Whatever exceptions we take to his methods or his results, we cannot deny him a very great literary genius. To me there is a perpetual delight in his way of saying things, and I cannot wonder that younger men try to catch the trick of it. The disappointing thing for them is that it is not a trick, but an inherent virtue. His style is, upon the whole, better than that of any other novelist I know; it is always easy, without being trivial, and it is often stately, without being stiff; it gives a charm to everything he writes; and he has written so much and in such various directions, that we should be judging him very incompletely if we considered him only as a novelist. His book of European sketches must rank him with the most enlightened and agreeable travelers; and it might be fitly supplemented from his uncollected papers with a volume of American sketches. In his essays on modern French writers he indicates his critical range and grasp; but he scarcely does more, as his criticisms in 'The Atlantic' and 'The Nation' and elsewhere could abundantly testify.

There are indeed those who insist that criticism is his true vocation, and are impatient of his devotion to fiction: but I suspect that these admirers are mistaken. A novelist he is not, after the old fashion, or after any fashion but his own; yet since he has finally made his public in his own way of story-telling—or call it character-painting if you prefer,—it must be conceded that he has chosen best for himself and his readers in choosing the form of fiction for what he has to say. It is, after all, what a writer has to say rather than what he has to tell that we care for nowadays. In one manner or other the stories were all told long ago; and now we want merely to know what the novelist thinks about persons and situations. Mr James gratifies this philosophic desire. If he sometimes forbears to tell us what he thinks of the last state of his people, it is perhaps because that does not interest him, and a large-minded criticism might well insist that it was childish to demand that it must interest him.

I am not sure that my criticism is sufficiently large-minded for this. I own that I like a finished story; but then also I like those which Mr James seems not to finish. This is probably the position of most of his readers, who cannot very logically account for either preference. We can only make sure that we have here an annalist, or analyst, as we choose, who fascinates us from his first page to his last, whose narrative or whose comment may enter into any minuteness of detail without fatiguing us, and can only truly grieve us when it ceases.

82

The Art of Fiction

HENRY JAMES

In a famous essay often thought to inaugurate the criticism of the modem novel, Henry James (1843-1916), author of a considerable number of reviews and essays in British and American journals as well as a host of novels from *The American* (1877) to *The Portrait of a Lady* (1881) and *The Ambassadors* (1903) responds to a lecture by Walter Besant at the Royal Institution in London. James argues for two simple goals of a good novel: (1) that it represent life as a painting represents reality and (2) that it be interesting. His often quoted definition of a novel derives from this essay:

> A novel is in its broadest definition a personal, a direct impression of life: that, to begin with, constitutes its value, which is greater or less according to the intensity of the impression. (507)

James disparages any attempt to prescribe rules for writers of novels, noting that each writer's lived experience is different from another's and thus variously influences the shape of the novel. He refuses to adhere to the old opposition between novel and romance as well as that between novels of incident and those of character, asking, "What is character but the determination of incident? What is incident but the illustration of character?" (512). The essay represents a break from earlier nineteenth-century emphases on the subject matter and morality of the novel. Instead James, like Virginia Woolf several decades later, urges the prospective novelist to "catch the colour of life itself," without regard for a particular message or social opinion.

I should not have affixed so comprehensive a title to these few remarks, necessarily wanting in any completeness, upon a subject the full consideration of which would carry us far, did I not seem to discover a pretext for my temerity in the interesting pamphlet lately published under this name by Mr Walter Besant. Mr Besant's lecture at the Royal Institution—the original form of his pamphlet—appears to indicate that many persons are interested in the art of fiction and are not

Source: Henry James, "The Art of Fiction", *Longman's Magazine*, Fall 1884, pp. 502-21.

indifferent to such remarks as those who practise it may attempt to make about it. I am therefore anxious not to lose the benefit of this favourable association, and to edge in a few words under cover of the attention which Mr Besant is sure to have excited. There is something very encouraging in his having put into form certain of his ideas on the mystery of story-telling.

It is a proof of life and curiosity—curiosity on the part of the brotherhood of novelists, as well as on the part of their readers. Only a abort time ago it might have been supposed that the English novel was not what the French call *discutable*. It had no air of having a theory, a conviction, a consciousness of itself behind it—of being the expression of an artistic faith, the result of choice and comparison. I do not say it was necessarily the worse for that; it would take much more courage than I possess to intimate that the form of the novel, as Dickens and Thackeray (for instance) saw it, had any taint of incompleteness. It was, however, *naïf* (if I may help myself out with another French word); and, evidently, if it is destined to suffer in any way for having lost its *naïveté*, it has now an idea of making sure of the corresponding advantages. During the period I have alluded to there was a comfortable, good-humoured feeling abroad that a novel is a novel, as a pudding is a pudding, and that this was the end of it. But within a year or two, for some reason or other, there have been signs of returning animation—the era of discussion would appear to have been to a certain extent opened. Art lives upon discussion, upon experiment, upon curiosity, upon variety of attempt, upon the exchange of views and the comparison of standpoints; and there is a presumption that that those times when no one has anything particular to say about it, and has no reason to give for practice or preference, though they may be times of genius, are not times of development, are times, possibly even, a little, of dullness. The successful application of any art is a delightful spectacle, but the theory, too, is interesting; and though there is a great deal of the latter without the former, I suspect there has never been a genuine success that has not had a latent core of conviction. Discussion, suggestion, formulation, these things are fertilizing when they are frank and sincere. Mr Besant has set an excellent example in saying what he thinks, for his part, about the way in which fiction should be written, as well as about the way in which it should be published; for his view of the "art," carried on into an appendix, covers that too. Other labourers in the same field will doubtless take up the argument, they will give it the light of their experience, and the effect will surely be to make our interest in the novel a little more what it had for some time threatened to fail to be—a serious, active, inquiring interest, under protection of which this delightful study may, in moments of confidence, venture to say a little more what it thinks of itself.

It must take itself seriously for the public to take it so. The old superstition about fiction being "wicked" has doubtless died out in England; but the spirit of it lingers in a certain oblique regard directed toward any story which does not more or less admit that it is only a joke. Even the most jocular novel feels in some degree the weight of the proscription that was formerly directed against literary levity; the jocularity does not always succeed in passing for gravity. It is still expected, though perhaps people are ashamed to say it, that a production which is after all only a "make believe" (for what else is a "story?") shall be in some degree apologetic—shall renounce the pretension of attempting really to compete with life. This, of course, any sensible wide-awake story declines to do, for it quickly perceives that the tolerance granted to it on such a condition is only an attempt to stifle it, disguised in the form of generosity. The old Evangelical hostility to the novel, which was as explicit as it was narrow, and which regarded it as little less favourable to our immortal part than a stage-play, was in reality far less insulting. The only reason for the existence of a novel is that it *does* compete with life. When it ceases to compete as the canvas of the painter competes, it will have arrived at a very strange pass. It is not expected of the picture that it will make itself humble in order to be forgiven; and the analogy between the art of the painter and the art of the novelist is, so far as I am able to see, complete. Their inspiration is the same, their process (allowing for the different quality of the vehicle) is the same, their success is the same. They may learn from each other, they may explain and sustain each other. Their cause is the same, and the honour of one is the honour of another. Peculiarities of manner, or execution, that correspond on either side, exist in each of them and contribute to their development. The Mahometans think a picture an unholy thing, but it is a long time since any Christian did, and it is therefore the more odd that in the Christian mind the traces (dissimulated though they may be) of a suspicion of the sister art should linger to this day. The only effectual way to lay it to rest is to emphasize the analogy to which I just alluded—to insist on the fact that as the picture is reality, so the novel is history. That is the only general description (which does it justice) that we may give of the novel. But history also is allowed to compete with life, as I say; it is not, any more than painting, expected to apologize. The subject-matter of fiction is stored up likewise in documents and records, and if it will not give itself away, as they say in California, it must speak with assurance, with the tone of the historian. Certain accomplished novelists have a habit of giving themselves away which must often bring tears to the eyes of people who take their fiction seriously. I was lately struck, in reading over many pages of Anthony Trollope, with his want of discretion in this particular. In a digression, a parenthesis or an aside, he concedes to the reader that he and this trusting friend are only "making believe." He admits that the events he narrates have not really happened, and that he can give his narrative any turn the reader may like best. Such a betrayal of a sacred office seems to me, I confess, a terrible crime; it is what I mean by the attitude of apology, and it shocks me every whit as much in Trollope as it would have shocked me in Gibbon or Macaulay. It implies that the novelist is less occupied in looking for the truth than the historian, and in doing so it deprives him at a stroke of all his standing-room. To represent and illustrate the past, the actions of men, is the task of either writer, and the only difference that I can see is, in proportion as he succeeds, to the honour of the novelist, consisting as it does in his having more difficulty in collecting his evidence, which is so far from being purely literary. It seems to me to give him a great character, the fact that he has at once so much in common with the philosopher and the painter; this double analogy is a magnificent heritage.

It is of all this evidently that Mr Besant is full when he insists upon the fact that fiction is one of the fine arts, deserving in its turn of all the honours and emoluments that have hitherto been reserved for the successful profession of music, poetry, painting, architecture. It is impossible to insist too much on so important a truth, and the place that Mr Besant demands for the work of the novelist may be represented, a trifle less abstractly, by saying that he demands not only that it shall be reputed artistic, but that it shall be reputed very artistic indeed. It is excellent that he should have struck this note, for his doing so indicates that there was need of it, that his proposition may be to many people a novelty. One rubs one's eyes at the thought; but the rest of Mr Besant's essay confirms the revelation. I suspect, in truth, that it would be possible to confirm it still further, and that one would not be far wrong in saying that in addition to the people to whom it has never occurred that a novel ought to be artistic, there are a great many others who, if this principle were urged upon them, would be filled with an indefinable mistrust. They would find it difficult to explain their repugnance, but it would operate strongly to put them on their guard. "Art," in our Protestant communities, where so many things have got so strangely twisted about, is supposed, in certain circles, to have some vaguely injurious effect upon those who make it an important consideration, who let it weigh in the balance. It is assumed to be opposed in some mysterious manner to morality, to amusement, to instruction. When it is embodied in the work of the painter (the sculptor is another affair!) you know what it is; it stands there before you, in the honesty of pink and green and a gilt frame; you can see the worst of it at a glance, and you can be on your guard. But when it is introduced into literature it becomes more insidious—there is danger of its hurting you before you know it. Literature should be either instructive or amusing, and there is in many minds an impression that these artistic preoccupations, the search for form, contribute to neither end, interfere indeed with both. They are too frivolous to be edifying, and too serious to be diverting; and they are, moreover, priggish and paradoxical and superfluous. That, I think, represents the manner in which the latent thought of many people who read novels as an exercise in skipping would explain itself if it were to become articulate. They would argue, of course, that a novel ought to be "good," but they would interpret this term in a fashion of their own, which, indeed, would vary considerably from one critic to another. One would say that being good means representing virtuous, and aspiring characters, placed in prominent positions; another would say that it depends for a "happy ending" on a distribution at the last of prizes, pensions, husbands, wives, babies, millions, appended paragraphs and cheerful remarks. Another still would say that it means being full of incident and movement, so that we shall wish to jump ahead, to see who was the mysterious stranger, and if the stolen will was ever found, and shall not be distracted from this pleasure by any tiresome analysis or "description." But they would all agree that the "artistic" idea would spoil some of their fun. One would hold it accountable for all the description, another would see it revealed in the absence of sympathy. Its hostility to a happy ending would be evident, and it might even, in some cases, render any ending at all impossible. The "ending" of a novel is, for many persons, like that of a good dinner, a course of dessert and ices, and the artist in fiction is regarded as a sort of meddlesome doctor who forbids agreeable aftertastes. It is therefore true that this conception of Mr Besant's, of the novel as a superior form, encounters not only a negative but a positive indifference. It matters little that, as a work of art, it should really be as little or as much concerned to supply happy endings, sympathetic characters, and an objective tone, as if it were a work of mechanics; the association of ideas, however incongruous, might easily be too much for it if an eloquent voice were not sometimes raised to call attention to the fact that it is at once as free and as serious a branch of literature as any other.

Certainly, this might sometimes be doubted in presence of the enormous number of works of fiction that appeal to the credulity of our generation, for it might easily seem that there could be no great substance in a commodity so quickly and easily produced. It must be admitted that good novels are somewhat compromised by bad ones, and that the field, at large, suffers discredit from overcrowding. I think, however, that this injury is only superficial, and that the superabundance of written fiction proves nothing against the principle itself. It has been vulgarised, like all other kinds of literature, like everything else, to-day, and it has proved more than some kinds accessible to vulgarisation. But there is as much difference as there ever was between a good novel and a bad one: the bad is swept, with all the daubed canvases and spoiled marble, into some unvisited limbo or infinite rubbish-yard, beneath the back-windows of the world, and the good subsists and emits its light and stimulates our desire for perfection. As I shall take the liberty of making but a single criticism of Mr Besant, whose tone is so full of the love of his art, I may as well have done with it, at once. He seems to me to mistake in attempting to say so definitely beforehand what sort of an affair the good novel will be. To indicate the danger of such an error as that has been the purpose of these few pages; to suggest that certain traditions on the subject, applied *a priori*, have already had much to answer for, and that the good health of an art which undertakes so immediately to reproduce life must demand that it be perfectly free. It lives upon exercise, and the very meaning of exercise is freedom. The only obligation to which in advance we may hold a novel without incurring the accusation of being arbitrary, is that it be interesting. That general responsibility rests upon it, but it is the only one I can think of. The ways in which it is at liberty to accomplish this result (of interesting us) strike me as innumerable and such as can only suffer from being marked out, or fenced in, by prescription. They are as various as the temperament of man, and they are successful in proportion as they reveal a particular mind, different from others. A novel is in its broadest definition a personal impression of life; that, to begin with, constitutes its value, which is greater or less according to the intensity of the impression. But there will be no intensity at all, and therefore no value, unless there is freedom to feel and say. The tracing of a line to be followed, of a tone to be taken, of a form to be filled out, is a limitation of that freedom and a suppression of the very thing that we are most curious about. The form, it seems to me, is to be appreciated after the fact; then the author's choice has been made, his standard has been indicated; then we can follow lines and directions and compare tones. Then, in a word, we can enjoy one of the most charming of pleasures, we can estimate quality, we can apply the test of execution. The execution belongs to the author alone; it is what is most personal to him, and we measure him by that. The advantage, the luxury, as well as the torment and responsibility of the novelist, is that there is no limit to what he may attempt as an executant—no limit to his possible experiments, efforts, discoveries, successes. Here it is especially that he works, step by step, like his brother of the brush, of whom we may always say that he has painted his picture in a manner best known to himself. His manner is his secret, not necessarily a deliberate one. He cannot disclose it, as a general thing, if he would; he would be at a loss to teach it to others. I say this with a due recollection or having insisted on the community of method of the artist who paints a picture and the artist who writes a novel. The painter is able to teach the rudiments of his practice, and it is possible, from the study of good work (granted the aptitude), both to learn how to paint and to learn how to write. Yet it remains true, without injury to the *rapprochement*, that the literary artist would be obliged to say to his pupil much more than the other, "Ah, well, you must do it as you can!" It is a question of degree, a matter of delicacy. If there are exact sciences there are also exact arts, and the grammar of painting is so much more definite that it makes the difference.

I ought to add, however, that if Mr Besant says at the beginning of his essay that the "laws of fiction may be laid down and taught with as much precision and exactness as the laws of harmony, perspective, and proportion," he mitigates what might appear to be an over-statement by applying his remark to "general" laws, and by expressing most for these rules in a manner with which it would certainly be unaccommodating to disagree. That the novelist must write from his experience, that his "characters must be real and such as might be met with in actual life;" that "a young lady brought up in a quiet country village should avoid descriptions of garrison life," and "a writer whose friends and personal experiences belong to the lower middle-class should carefully avoid introducing his characters into Society;" that one should enter one's notes in a common-place book; that one's figures should be clear in outline; that making them clear by some trick of speech or of carriage is a bad method, and "describing them at length" is a worse one; that English Fiction should have a "conscious moral purpose;" that "it is almost impossible to estimate too highly the value of careful workmanship—that is, or style;" that "the most important point of all is the story," that "the story is everything"—these are principles with most of which it is surely impossible not to sympathise. That remark about the lower middle-class Writer and his knowing his place is perhaps rather chilling; but for the rest, I should find it difficult to dissent from anyone of these recommendations. At the same time I should find it difficult positively to assent to them, with the exception, perhaps, of the injunction as to entering one's notes in a common-place book. They scarcely seem to me to have the quality that Mr Besant attributes to the rules of the novelist—the "precision and exactness" of "the laws of harmony, perspective, and proportion." They are suggestive, they are even inspiring, but they are not exact, though they are doubtless as much so as the case admits of; which is a proof of that liberty of interpretation for which I just contended. For the value of these different injunctions—so beautiful and so vague—is wholly in the meaning one attaches to them. The characters, the situation, which strike one as real will be those that touch and interest one most, but the measure of reality is very difficult to fix. The reality of Don Quixote or of Mr Micawber is a very delicate shade; it is a reality so coloured by the author's vision that, vivid as it may be, one would hesitate to propose it as a model; one would expose one's self to some very embarrassing questions on the part of a pupil. It goes without saying that you will not write a good novel unless you possess the sense of reality; but it will be difficult to give you a recipe for calling that sense into being. Humanity is immense and reality has a myriad forms; the most one can affirm is that some of the flowers of fiction have the odour of it, and others have not; as for telling you in advance how your nosegay should be composed, that is another affair. It is equally excellent and inconclusive to say that one must write from experience; to our supposititious aspirant such a declaration might savour of mockery. What kind of experience is intended, and where does it begin and end? Experience is never limited and it is never complete; it is an immense sensibility, a kind of huge spider-web, of the finest silken threads, suspended in the chamber of consciousness and catching every air-borne particle in its tissue. It is the very atmosphere of the mind; and when the mind is imaginative—much more when it happens to be that of a man of genius—it takes to itself the faintest hints of life, it converts the very pulses of the air into revelations. The young lady living in a village has only to be a damsel upon whom nothing is lost to make it quite unfair (as it seems to me) to declare to her that she shall have nothing to say about the military. Greater miracles have been seen than that, imagination assisting, she should speak the truth about some of these gentlemen. I remember an English novelist, a woman of genius, telling me that she was much commended for the impression she had managed to give in one of her tales of the nature and way of life of the French Protestant youth. She had been asked where she learned so much about this recondite being, she had been congratulated on her peculiar opportunities. These opportunities consisted in her having once, in Paris, as she ascended a staircase, passed an open door where, in the household of a *pasteur*, some of the young Protestants were seated at table round a finished meal. The glimpse made a picture; it lasted only a moment, but that moment was experience. She had got her impression, and she evolved her type. She knew what youth was, and what Protestantism; she also had the advantage of having seen what it was to be French; so that she converted these ideas into a concrete image and produced a reality. Above all, however, she was blessed with the faculty which when you give it an inch takes an ell, and which for the artist is a much greater source of strength than any accident of residence or of place in the social scale. The power to guess the unseen from the seen, to trace the implication of things, to judge the whole piece by the pattern, the condition of feeling life, in general, so completely that you are well on your way to knowing any particular corner of it—this cluster of gifts may almost be said to constitute experience, and they occur in country and in town, and in the most differing stages of education. If experience consists of impressions, it may be said that impressions are experience, just as (have we not seen it?) they are the very air we breathe. Therefore, if I should certainly say to a novice, "Write from experience, and experience only," I should feel that this was a rather tantalising monition if I were not careful immediately to add, "Try to be one of the people on whom nothing is lost!"

I am far from intending by this to minimise the importance of exactness—of truth of detail. One can speak best from one's own taste, and I may therefore venture to say that the air of reality (solidity of specification) seems to me to be the supreme virtue of a novel—the merit in which all its other merits (including that conscious moral purpose of which Mr Besant speaks) helplessly and submissively depend. If it be not there, they are all as nothing, and if these be there, they owe their effect to the success with which the author has produced the illusion of life. The cultivation of this success, the study of this exquisite process, form, to my taste, the beginning and the end of the art of the novelist. They are his inspiration, his despair, his reward, his torment, his delight. It is here, in very truth, that he competes with life; it is here that he competes with his brother the painter, in his attempt to render the look of things, the look that conveys their meaning, to catch the colour, the relief, the expression, the surface, the substance of the human spectacle. It is in regard to this that Mr Besant is well inspired when he bids him take notes. He cannot possibly take too many, he cannot possibly take enough. All life solicits him, and to "render" the simplest surface, to produce the most momentary illusion, is a very complicated business. His case would be easier, and the rule would be more exact, if Mr Besant had been able to tell him what notes to take. But this I fear he can never learn in any hand-book; it is the business or his life. He has to take a great many in order to select a few, he has to work them up as he can, and even, the guides and philosophers who might have most to say to him must leave him alone when it comes to the application of precepts, as we leave the painter in communion with his palette. That his characters "must be clear in outline," as Mr Besant says—he feels that down to his boots; but how he shall make them so is a secret between his good angel and himself. It would be absurdly simple if he could be taught that a great deal of "description" would make them so, or that, on the contrary, the absence of description and the cultivation of dialogue, or the absence of dialogue and the multiplication of "incident," would rescue him from his difficulties. Nothing, for instance, is more possible than that he be of a turn of mind for which this odd, literal opposition of description and dialogue, incident and description, has little meaning and light. People often talk of these things as if they had a kind of internecine distinctness, instead of melting into each other at every breath and being intimately associated parts of one general effort of expression. I cannot, imagine composition existing in a series of blocks, nor conceive, in any novel worth discussing at all, of a passage of description that is not in its intention narrative, a passage of dialogue that is not in its intention descriptive, a touch of truth of any sort that does not partake of the nature or incident, and an incident that derives its interest from any other source than the general and only source of the success of a work of art—that of being illustrative. A novel is a living thing, all one and continuous, like every other organism, and in proportion as it lives will it be found, I think, that in each of the parts there is something of each of the other parts. The critic who over the close texture of a finished work will pretend to trace a geography of items will mark some frontiers as artificial, I fear, as any that have been known to history. There is an old-fashioned distinction between the novel of character and the novel of incident, which must have cost many a smile to the intending romancer who was keen about his work. It appears to me as little to the point as the equally celebrated distinction between the novel and the romance—to answer as little to any reality. There are bad novels and good novels, as there are bad pictures and good pictures; but that is the only distinction in which I see any meaning, and I can as little imagine speaking of a novel of character as I can imagine speaking of a picture of character. When one says picture, one says of character, when one says novel, one says of incident, and the terms may be transposed. What is character but the determination of incident? What is incident but the illustration of character? What is a picture or a novel that is not of character? What else do we seek in it and find in it? It is an incident for a woman to stand up with her hand resting on a table and look out at you in a certain way; or if it be not an incident, I think it will be hard to say what it is. At the same time it is an expression of character. If you say you don't see it (character in that—*allons donc*!) this is exactly what the artist who has reasons of his own for thinking he *does* see it undertakes to show you. When a young man makes up his mind that he has not faith enough, after all, to enter the Church, as he intended, that is an incident, though you may not hurry to the end of the chapter to see whether perhaps he doesn't change once more. I do not say that these are extraordinary or startling incidents. I do not pretend to estimate the degree of interest proceeding from them, for this will depend upon the skill of the painter. It sounds almost puerile to say that some incidents are intrinsically much more important than others, and I need not take this precaution after having professed my sympathy for the major ones in remarking that the only classification of the novel that I can understand is into the interesting and the uninteresting.

The novel and the romance, the novel of incident and that of character—these separations appear to me to have been made by critics and readers for their own convenience, and to help them out of some of their difficulties, but to have little reality or interest for the producer, from whose point of view it is, of course, that we are attempting to consider the art of fiction. The case is the same with another shadowy category, which Mr Besant apparently is disposed to set up—that of the "modern English novel;" unless, indeed, it be that in this matter he has fallen into an accidental confusion of standpoints. It is not quite clear whether he intends the remarks in which he alludes to it to be didactic or historical. It is as difficult to suppose a person intending to write a modern English, as to suppose him writing an ancient English, novel; that is a label which begs the question. One writes the novel, one paints the picture, of one's language and of one's time, and calling it modern English will not, alas! make the difficult task any easier. No more, unfortunately, will calling this or that work of one's fellow artist a romance—unless it be, of course, simply for the pleasantness of the thing, as, for instance, when Hawthorne gave this heading to his story of Blithedale. The French, who have brought the theory of fiction to remarkable completeness, have but one word for the novel, and have not attempted smaller things in it, that I can see, for that. I can think of no obligation to which the "romancer" would not be held equally with the novelist; the standard of execution is equally high for each. Of course it is of execution that we are talking—that being the only point of a novel that is open to contention. This is perhaps too often lost sight of, only to produce interminable confusions and cross-purposes. We must grant the artist his subject, his idea, what the French call his *donnée*; our criticism is applied only to what he makes of it. Naturally I do not mean that we are bound to like it or find it interesting: in case we do not our course is perfectly simple—to let it alone. We may believe that of a certain idea even the most sincere novelist can make nothing at all, and the event may perfectly justify our belief; but the failure will have been a failure to execute, and it is in the execution that the fatal weakness is recorded. If we pretend to respect the artist at all we must allow him his freedom of choice, in the face, in particular cases, of innumerable presumptions that the choice will not fructify. Art derives a considerable part of its beneficial exercise from flying in the face of presumptions, and some of the most interesting experiments of which it is capable are hidden in the bosom of common things. Gustave Flaubert has written a story about the devotion of a servant girl to a parrot, and the production, highly finished as it is, cannot on the whole be called a success. We are perfectly free to find it flat, but I think it might have been interesting; and I, for my part, am extremely glad he should have written it; it is a contribution to our knowledge of what can be done—or what cannot. Ivan Turgénieff has written a tale about a deaf and dumb serf and a lap-dog, and the thing is touching, loving, a little masterpiece. He struck the note of life where Gustave Flaubert missed it—he flew in the face of a presumption and achieved a victory.

Nothing, of course, will ever take the place of the good old fashion of "liking" a work of art or not liking it; the more improved criticism will not abolish that primitive, that ultimate, test. I mention this to guard myself from the accusation of intimating that the idea, the subject, of a novel or a picture, does not matter. It, matters, to my sense, in the highest degree, and if I might put up a prayer it would be that artists should select none but the richest. Some, as I have already hastened to admit, are much more substantial than others, and it would be a happily arranged world in which persons intending to treat them should be exempt from confusions and mistakes. This fortunate condition will arrive only, I fear, on the same day that critics become purged from error. Meanwhile, I repeat, we do not judge the artist with fairness unless we say to him,

> Oh, I grant you your starting-point, because if I did not I should seem to prescribe to you, and heaven forbid I should take that responsibility. If I pretend to tell you what you must not take, you will call upon me to tell you then what you must take; in which case I shall be nicely caught! Moreover, it isn't till I have accepted your data that I can begin to measure you. I have the standard; I judge you by what you propose, and you must look out for me there. Of course I may not care for your idea at all; I may think it silly, or stale, or unclean; in which case I wash my hands of you altogether. I may content myself with believing that you will not have succeeded in being interesting, but I shall of course not attempt to demonstrate

it, and you will be as indifferent to me as I am to you. I needn't remind you that there are all sorts of tastes: who can know it better? Some people, for excellent reasons, don't like to read about carpenters; others, for reasons even better, don't like to read about courtesans. Many object to Americans. Others (I believe they are mainly editors and publishers) won't look at Italians. Some readers don't like quiet subjects; others don't like bustling ones. Some enjoy a complete illusion; others revel in a complete deception. They choose their novels accordingly, and if they don't care about your idea they won't, *a fortiori*, care about your treatment.

So that it comes back very quickly, as I have said, to the liking; in spite of M. Zola, who reasons less powerfully than he represents, and who will not reconcile himself to this absoluteness of taste, thinking that there are certain things that people ought to like, and that they can be made to like. I am quite at a loss to imagine anything (at any rate in this matter of fiction) that people ought to like or to dislike. Selection will be sure to take care of itself, for it has a constant motive behind it. That motive is simply experience. As people feel life, so they will feel the art that is most closely related to it. This closeness of relation is what we should never forget in talking of the effort of the novel. Many people speak of it as a factitious, artificial form, a product of ingenuity, the business of which is to alter and arrange the things that surround us, to translate them into conventional, traditional moulds. This, however, is a view of the matter which carries us but a very short way, condemns the art to an eternal repetition of a few familiar *clichés*, cuts short its development, and leads us straight up to a dead wall. Catching the very note and trick, the strange irregular rhythm of life, that is the attempt whose strenuous force keeps Fiction upon her feet. In proportion as in what she offers us we see life *without* rearrangement do we feel that we are touching the truth; in proportion as we see it *with* rearrangement do we feel that we are being put off with a substitute, a compromise and convention. It is not uncommon to hear an extraordinary assurance of remark in regard to this matter of rearranging, which is often spoken of as if it were the last word of art. Mr Besant seems to me in danger of falling into this great error with his rather unguarded talk about "selection." Art is essentially selection, but it is a selection whose main care is to be typical, to be inclusive. For many people art means rose-coloured windows, and selection means picking a bouquet for Mrs. Grundy. They will tell you glibly that artistic considerations have nothing to do with the disagreeable, with the ugly; they will rattle off shallow commonplaces about the province of art and the limits of art, till you are moved to some wonder in return as to the province and the limits of ignorance. It appears to me that no one can ever have made a seriously artistic attempt without becoming conscious of an immense increase—a kind of revelation—of freedom. One perceives, in that case—by the light of a heavenly ray—that the province of art is all life, all feeling, all observation, all vision. As Mr Besant so justly intimates, it is all experience. That is a sufficient answer to those who maintain that it must not touch the painful, who stick into its divine unconscious bosom little prohibitory inscriptions on the end of sticks, such as we see in public gardens—"It is forbidden to walk on the grass; it is forbidden to touch the flowers; it is not allowed to introduce dogs, or to remain after dark; it is requested to keep to the right." The young aspirant in the line of fiction, whom we continue to imagine, will do nothing without taste, for in that case his freedom would be of little use to him; but the first advantage of his taste will be to reveal to him the absurdity of the little sticks and tickets. If he have taste, I must add, of course he will have ingenuity, and my disrespectful reference to that quality just now was not meant to imply that it is useless in fiction. But it is only a secondary aid; the first is a vivid sense of reality.

Mr Besant has some remarks on the question of "the story," which I shall not attempt to criticise, though they seem to me to contain a singular ambiguity, because I do not think I understand them. I cannot see what is meant by talking as if there were a part of a novel which is the story and part of it which for mystical reasons is not—unless indeed the distinction be made in a sense in which it is difficult to suppose that anyone should attempt to convey anything. "The story," if it represents anything, represents the subject, the idea, the data of the novel; and there is surely no "school"—Mr Besant speaks of a school—which urges that a novel should be all treatment and no subject. There must assuredly be something to treat; every school is intimately conscious of that. This sense of the story being the idea, the starting-point, of the novel is the only one that I see in which it can be spoken of as something different from its organic whole; and since, in proportion as the work is successful, the idea permeates and penetrates it, informs and animates it, so that every word and every punctuation-point contribute directly to the expression, in that proportion do we lose our sense of the story being a blade which may be drawn more or less out of its sheath. The story and the novel, the idea and the form, are the needle and thread, and I never heard of a guild of tailors who recommended the use of the thread without the needle or the needle without the thread. Mr Besant is not the only critic who may be observed to have spoken as if there were certain things in life which constitute stories and certain others which do not. I find the same odd implication in an entertaining article in the *Pall Mall Gazette*, devoted, as it happens, to Mr Besant's lecture. "The story is the thing!" says this graceful writer, as if with a tone of opposition to another idea. I should think it was, as every painter who, as the time for "sending in" his picture looms in the distance, finds himself still in quest, of a subject—as every belated artist, not fixed about his *donnée*, will heartily agree. There are some subjects which speak to us and others which do not, but he would be a clever man who should undertake to give a rule by which the story and the no-story should be known apart. It is impossible (to me at least) to imagine any such rule which shall not be altogether arbitrary. The writer in the *Pall Mall* opposes the delightful (as I suppose) novel of *Margot la Balafrée* to certain tales in which "Bostonian nymphs" appear to have "rejected English dukes for psychological reasons." I am not acquainted with the romance just designated, and can scarcely forgive the *Pall Mall* critic for not mentioning the name of the author, but the title appears to refer to a lady who may have received a scar in some heroic adventure. I am inconsolable at not being acquainted with this episode, but am utterly at a loss to see why it is a story when the rejection (or acceptance) of a duke is not, and why a reason, psychological or other, is not a subject when a cicatrix is. They are all particles of the multitudinous life with which the novel deals, and surely no dogma which pretends to make it lawful to touch the one and unlawful to touch the other will stand for a moment on its feet. It is the special picture that must stand or fall, according as it seems to possess truth or to lack it. Mr Besant does not, to my sense, light up the subject by intimating that a story must, under penalty of not being a story, consist of "adventures." Why of adventures more than of green spectacles? He mentions a category of impossible things, and among them he places "fiction without adventure." Why without adventure, more than without matrimony, or celibacy, or parturition, or cholera, or hydropathy, or Jansenism? This seems to me to bring the novel back to the hapless little rôle of being an artificial, ingenious thing—bring it down from its large, free character of an immense and exquisite correspondence with life. And what is adventure, when it comes to that, and by what sign is the listening pupil to recognise it? "It is an adventure—an immense one—for me to write this little article; and for a Bostonian nymph to reject an English duke is an adventure only less stirring, I should say, than for an English duke to be rejected by a Bostonian nymph. I see dramas within dramas in that, and innumerable points of view. A psychological reason is, to my imagination, all object adorably pictorial; to catch the tint of its complexion—I feel as if that idea might inspire one to Titianesque efforts. There are few things more exciting to me, in short, than a psychological reason, and yet, I protest, the novel seems to me the most magnificent form of art. I have just been reading, at the same time, the delightful story of *Treasure Island*, by Mr Robert Louis Stevenson, and the last tale from M. Edmond de Goncourt, which is entitled *Chérie*. One of these works treats of murders, mysteries, islands of dreadful renown, hairbreadth escapes, miraculous coincidences and buried doubloons. The other treats of a little French girl who lived in fine house in Paris and died of wounded sensibility because no one would marry her. I call *Treasure Island* delightful, because it appears to me to have succeeded wonderfully in what it attempts; and I venture to bestow no epithet upon *Chérie*, which strikes me as having failed in what it attempts—that is, in tracing the development of the moral consciousness of a child. But one of these productions strikes me as exactly as much of a novel as the other, and as having a "story" quite as much. The moral consciousness of a child is as much a part of life as the islands of the Spanish Main, and the one sort of geography seems to me to have those "surprises" of which Mr Besant speaks quite as much as the other. For myself (since it comes back in the last resort, as I say, to the preference of the individual), the picture of the child's experience has the advantage that I can at successive steps (an immense luxury, near to the "sensual pleasure" of which Mr Besant's critic in the *Pall Mall* speaks) say Yes or No, as it may be, to what the artist puts before me. I have been a child, but I have never been on a quest for a buried treasure, and it is a simple accident that with M. de Goncourt I should have for the most part to say No. With George Eliot, when she painted that country, I always said Yes.

The most interesting part of Mr Besant's lecture is unfortunately the briefest passage—his very cursory allusion to the "conscious moral purpose" of the novel. Here again it is not very clear whether he is recording a fact or laying down a principle; it is a great pity that in the latter case he should not have developed his idea. This branch of the subject is of immense importance, and Mr Besant's few words point to considerations of the widest reach, not to be lightly disposed of. He will have treated the art of fiction but superficially who is not prepared to go every inch of the way that these considerations will carry him. It is for this reason that at the beginning of these remarks I was careful to notify the reader that my reflections on so large a theme have no pretension to be exhaustive. Like Mr Besant, I have left the question of the morality of the novel till the last, and at the last I find I have used up my space. It is a question surrounded with difficulties, as witness the very first that meets us, in the form of a definite question, on the threshold. Vagueness, in such a discussion, is fatal, and what is the meaning of your morality and your conscious moral purpose? Will you not define your terms and explain how (a novel being a picture) a picture can be either moral or immoral? You wish to paint a moral picture or carve a moral statue; will you not tell us how you would set about it? We are discussing the Art of Fiction; questions of art are questions (in the widest sense) of execution; questions of morality are quite another affair, and will you not let us see how it is that you find it so easy to mix them up? These things are so clear to Mr Besant that he has deduced from them a law which he sees embodied in English Fiction and which is "a truly admirable thing, and a great cause for congratulation." It is a great cause for congratulation, indeed, when such thorny problems become as smooth as silk. I may add that, in so far as Mr Besant perceives that in point of fact English Fiction has addressed itself preponderantly to these delicate questions, he will appear to many people to have made a vain discovery. They will have been positively struck, on the contrary, with the moral timidity of the usual English novelist; with his (or with her) aversion to face the difficulties with which, on every side, the treatment of reality bristles. He is apt to be extremely shy (whereas the picture that Mr Besant draws is a picture of boldness), and the sign of his work, for the most part, is a cautious silence on certain subjects. In the English novel (by which I mean the American as well), more than in any other, there is a traditional difference between that which people know and that which they agree to admit that they know, that which they see and that which they speak of, that which they feel to be a part of life and that which they allow to enter into literature. There is the great difference, in short, between what they talk of in conversation and what they talk of in print. The essence of moral energy is to survey the whole field, and I should directly reverse Mr Besant's remark, and say not that the English novel has a purpose, but that it has a diffidence. To what degree a purpose in a work of art is a source of corruption I shall not attempt to inquire; the one that seems to me least dangerous is the purpose of making a perfect work. As for our novel, I may say, lastly, on this score, that, as we find it in England to-day, it strikes me as addressed in a large degree to "young people," and that this in itself constitutes a presumption that it will be rather shy. There are certain things which it is generally agreed not to discuss, not even to mention, before young people. That is very well, but the absence of discussion is not a symptom of the moral passion. The purpose of the English novel—"a truly admirable thing, and a great cause for congratulation"—strikes me, therefore, as rather negative.

There is one point at which the moral sense and the artistic sense lie very near together; that is, in the light of the very obvious truth that the deepest quality or a work of art will always be the quality of the mind of the producer. In proportion as that mind is rich and noble will the novel, the picture, the statue, partake of the substance of beauty and truth. To be constituted of such elements is, to my vision, to have purpose enough. No good novel will ever proceed from a superficial mind; that seems to me an axiom which, for the artist in fiction, will cover all needful moral ground; if the youthful aspirant take it to heart it will illuminate for him many of the mysteries of "purpose." There are many other useful things that might be said to him, but I have come to the end of my article, and can only touch them as I pass. The critic in the *Pall Mall Gazette*, whom I have already quoted, draws attention to the danger, in speaking of the art of fiction, of generalizing. The danger that he has in mind is rather, I imagine, that of particularizing, for there are some comprehensive remarks which, in addition to those embodied in Mr Besant's suggestive lecture, might, without fear of misleading him, be addressed to the ingenuous student. I should remind him first of the magnificence of the form that is open to him, which offers to sight so few restrictions and such innumerable opportunities. The other arts, in comparison, appear confined and hampered; the various conditions under which they are exercised are so rigid and definite. But the only condition that I can think of attaching to the composition of the novel is, as I have already said, that it be interesting. This freedom is a splendid privilege, and the first lesson of the young novelist is to learn to be worthy of it. "Enjoy it as it deserves," I should say to him;

> take possession of it, explore it to its utmost extent, reveal it, rejoice in it. All life belongs to you, and don't listen either to those who would shut you up into corners of it and tell you that it is only here and there that art inhabits, or to those who would persuade you that this heavenly messenger wings her way outside of life altogether, breathing a superfine air and turning away her head from the truth of things. There is no impression of life, no manner of seeing it and feeling it, to which the plan of the novelist may not offer a place; you have only to remember that talents so dissimilar as those of Alexandre Dumas and Jane Austen, Charles Dickens and Gustave Flaubert, have worked in this field with equal glory. Don't think too much about optimism and pessimism; try and catch the colour of life itself. In France to-day we see a prodigious effort (that of Emile Zola, to whose solid and serious work no explorer of the capacity of the novel can allude without respect), we see an extraordinary effort vitiated by a spirit of pessimism on a narrow basis. M. Zola is magnificent, but he strikes an English reader as ignorant; he has an air of working in the dark; if he had as much light as energy his results would be of the highest value. As for the aberrations of a shallow optimism, the ground (of English fiction especially) is strewn with their brittle particles as with broken glass. If you must indulge in conclusions let them have the taste of a wide knowledge. Remember that your first duty is to be as complete as possible—to make as perfect a work. Be generous and delicate, and then, in the vulgar phrase, go in!

The Future of the Novel

HENRY JAMES

Like several other writer/critics of the 1880s and '90s, especially Thomas Hardy and Vernon Lee, James examines the relationship between the novelist and the reading public, excoriating the levelling of taste that allows for a proliferation of mediocre novels. He blames the increased readership, composed largely of schoolchildren and women, for hindering novelists from experimenting with more varied subject matter and more sophisticated treatment. The "irreflective and uncritical" reader has allowed the novelist to produce vapid works that do not last. Reviewers are equally at fault for their lack of a critical spirit. In a statement ironically prophetic for fiction a century later, James states, "the future of fiction is intimately bound up with the future of the society that produces and consumes it." He urges the prospective reader to develop a greater appreciation for ideas and a more astute capacity for reflection. In Arnoldian fashion, he presses the critic to encourage a free play of ideas for the novelist to enlarge and enliven. Finally he asks the novelist to provide the "anodyne" to revitalize the dormant intellectual climate. Though he has distanced himself from his Victorian predecessors who demanded that a novel convey a moral, James still believes, like Hardy, in the novel's capacity mentally to elevate the reader.

Beginnings, as we all know, are usually small things, but continuations are not always strikingly great ones, and the place occupied in the world by the prolonged prose fable has become, in our time, among the incidents of literature, the most surprising example to be named of swift and extravagant growth, a development beyond the measure of every early appearance. It is a form that has had a fortune so little to have been foretold at its cradle. The germ of the comprehensive epic was more recognizable in the first barbaric chant than that of the novel as we know it to-day in the first anecdote retailed to amuse. It arrived, in truth, the novel, late at self-consciousness; but it has done its utmost ever since to make up for lost opportunities. The flood at present swells and swells, threatening

Source: Henry James, "The Future of the Novel", 1899, rptd *The Future of the Novel; Essays on the Art of Fiction*, ed. by Leon Edel, New York: Vintage Books, 1956.

the whole field of letters, as would often seem, with submersion. It plays, in what may be called the passive consciousness of many persons, a part that directly marches with the rapid increase of the multitude able to possess itself in one way and another of the book. The book, in the Anglo-Saxon world, is almost everywhere, and it is in the form of the voluminous prose fable that we see it penetrate easiest and farthest. Penetration appears really to be directly aided by mere mass and bulk. There is an immense public, if public be the name, inarticulate, but abysmally absorbent, for which, at its hours of ease, the printed volume has no other association. This public—the public that subscribes, borrows, lends, that picks up in one way and another, sometimes even by purchase—grows and grows each year, and nothing is thus more apparent than that of all the recruits it brings to the book the most numerous by far are those that it brings to the "story".

This number has gained, in our time, an augmentation from three sources in particular, the first of which, indeed, is perhaps but a comprehensive name for the two others. The diffusion of the rudiments, the multiplication of common schools, has had more and more the effect of making readers of women and of the very young. Nothing is so striking in a survey of this field, and nothing to be so much borne in mind, as that the larger part of the great multitude that sustains the teller and the publisher of tales is constituted by boys and girls; by girls in especial, if we apply the term to the later stages of the life of the innumerable women who, under modern arrangements, increasingly fail to marry—fail, apparently, even, largely, to desire to. It is not too much to say of many of these that they live in a great measure by the immediate aid of the novel—confining the question, for the moment, to the fact of consumption alone. The literature, as it may be called for convenience, of children is all industry that occupies by itself a very considerable quarter of the scene. Great fortunes, if not great reputations, are made, we learn, by writing for schoolboys, and the period during which they consume the compound artfully prepared for them appears—as they begin earlier and continue later—to add to itself at both ends. This helps to account for the fact that public libraries, especially those that are private and money-making enterprises, put into circulation more volumes of "stories" than of all other things together of which volumes can be made. The published statistics are extraordinary, and of a sort to engender many kinds of uneasiness. The sort of taste that used to be called "good" has nothing to do with the matter: we are so demonstrably in presence of millions for whom taste is but an obscure, confused, immediate instinct. In the flare of railway bookstalls, in the shop-fronts of most booksellers, especially the provincial, in the advertisements of the weekly newspapers, and in fifty places besides, this testimony to the general preference triumphs, yielding a good-natured corner at most to a bunch of treatises on athletics or sport, or a patch of theology old and new.

The case is so marked, however, that illustrations easily overflow, and there is no need of forcing doors that stand wide open. What remains is the interesting oddity or mystery—the anomaly that fairly dignifies the whole circumstance with its strangeness: the wonder in short, that men, women, and children *should* have so much attention to spare for improvisations mainly so arbitrary and frequently so loose. That, at the first blush, fairly leaves us gaping. This great fortune then, since fortune it seems, has been reserved for mere unsupported and unguaranteed history, the *inexpensive* thing, written in the air, the record of what, in any particular case, has not been, the account that remains responsible, at best, to "documents" with which we are practically unable to collate it. This is the side of the whole business of fiction on which it can always be challenged, and to that degree that if the general venture had not become in such a manner the admiration of the world it might but too easily have become the derision. It has in truth, I think, never philosophically met the challenge, never found a formula to inscribe on its shield, never defended its position by any better argument than the frank, straight blow: "Why am I not so unprofitable as to be preposterous? Because I can do *that*. There!" And it throws up from time to time some purely practical masterpiece. There is nevertheless an admirable minority of intelligent persons who care not even for the masterpieces, nor see any pressing point in them, for whom the very form itself has, equally at its best and at its worst, been ever a vanity and a mockery. This class, it should be added, is beginning to be visibly augmented by a different circle altogether, the group of the formerly subject, but now estranged, the deceived and bored, those for whom the whole movement too decidedly fails to live up to its possibilities. There are people who have loved the novel, but who actually find themselves drowned in its verbiage, and for whom, even in some of its approved manifestations, it has become a terror they exert every ingenuity, every hypocrisy, to evade. The indifferent and the alienated testify, at any rate, almost as much as the omnivorous, to the reign of the great ambiguity, the enjoyment of which rests, evidently, on a primary need of the mind. The novelist can only fall back on that—on his recognition that man's constant demand for what he has to offer is simply man's general appetite for a picture. The novel is of all pictures the most comprehensive and the most elastic. It will stretch anywhere—it will take in absolutely anything. All it needs is a subject and a painter. But for its subject, magnificently, it has the whole human consciousness. And if we are pushed a step farther backward, and asked why the representation should be required when the object represented is itself mostly so accessible, the answer to that appears to be that man combines with his eternal desire for more experience an infinite cunning as to getting his experience as cheaply as possible. He will steal it whenever he can. He likes to live the life of others, yet is well aware of the points at which it may too intolerably resemble his own. The vivid fable, more than anything else, gives him this satisfaction on easy terms, gives him knowledge abundant yet vicarious. It enables him to select, to take and to leave; so that to feel he can afford to neglect it he must have a rare faculty, or great opportunities, for the extension of experience—by thought, by emotion, by energy—at first hand.

Yet it is doubtless not this cause alone that contributes to the contemporary deluge; other circumstances operate, and one of them is probably, in truth, if looked into, something of an abatement of the great fortune we have been called upon to admire. The high prosperity of fiction has marched, very directly, with another "sign of the times", the demoralization, the vulgarization of literature in general, the increasing familiarity of all such methods of communication, the making itself supremely felt, as it were, of the presence of the ladies and children—by whom I mean, in other words, the reader irreflective and uncritical. If the novel, in fine, has found itself socially speaking, at such a rate, the book *par excellence*, so on the other hand the book has in the same degree found itself a thing of small ceremony. So many ways of producing it easily have been discovered that it is by no means the occasional prodigy, for good or for evil, that it was taken for in simpler days, and has therefore suffered a proportionate discredit. Almost any variety is thrown off and taken up, handled, admired, ignored by too many people, and this, precisely, is the point at which the question of its future becomes one with that of the future of the total swarm. How are the generations to face, at all, the monstrous multiplications? Any speculation on the further development of a particular variety is subject to the reserve that the generations may at no distant day be obliged formally to decree, and to execute, great clearings of the deck, great periodical effacements and destructions. It fills, in fact, at moments the expectant ear, as we watch the progress of the ship of civilization—the huge splash that must mark the response to many an imperative, unanimous "Overboard!" What at least is already very plain is that practically the great majority of volumes printed within a year cease to exist as the hour passes, and give up by that circumstance all claim to a career, to being accounted or provided for. In speaking of the future of the novel we must of course, therefore, be taken as limiting the inquiry to those types that have, for criticism, a present and a past. And it is only superficially that confusion seems here to reign. The fact that in England and in the United States every specimen that sees the light may look for a "review" testifies merely to the point which, in these countries, literary criticism has sunk. The review is in nine cases out of ten an effort of intelligence as undeveloped as the ineptitude over which it fumbles, and the critical spirit, which knows where it is concerned and where not, is not touched, is still less compromised, by the incident. There are too many reasons why newspapers must live.

So, as regards the tangible type, the end is that in its undefended, its positively exposed state, we continue to accept it, conscious even of a peculiar beauty in an appeal made from a footing so precarious. It throws itself wholly on our generosity, and very often indeed gives us, by the reception it meets, a useful measure of the quality, of the delicacy, of many minds. There is to my sense no work of literary, or of any other, art, that any human being is under the smallest positive obligation to "like". There is no woman—no matter of what loveliness—in the presence of whom it is anything but a man's unchallenged-ably *own* affair that he is "in love" or out of it. It is not a question of manners; vast is the margin left to individual freedom; and the trap set by the artist occupies no different ground—Robert Louis Stevenson had admirably expressed the analogy—from the offer of her charms by the lady. There only remain infatuations that we envy and emulate. When we do respond to the appeal, when we *are* caught in the trap, we are held and played upon; so that how in the world can there *not* still be a future, however late in the day, for a contrivance possessed of this precious secret? The more we consider it the more we feel that the prose picture can never be at the end of its tether until it loses the sense of what it can do. It can do simply everything, and that is its strength and its life. Its plasticity, its elasticity are infinite; there is no colour, no extension it may not take from the nature of its subject or the temper of its craftsman. It has the extraordinary advantage—a piece of luck scarcely credible—that, while capable of giving an impression of the highest perfection and the rarest finish, it moves in a luxurious independence of rules and restrictions. Think as we may there is nothing we can mention as a consideration outside itself with which it must square, nothing we can name as one of its peculiar obligations or interdictions. It must, of course, hold our attention and reward it, it must not appeal on false pretences; but these necessities, with which, obviously, disgust and displeasure interfere, are not peculiar to it—all works of art have them in common. For the rest it has so clear a field that if it perishes this will surely be by its fault—by its superficiality, in other words, or its timidity. One almost, for the very love of it, likes to think of its appearing threatened with some such fate, in order to figure the dramatic stroke of its revival under the touch of a life-giving master. The temperament of the artist can do so much for it that our desire for some exemplary felicity fairly demands even the vision of that supreme proof. If we were to linger on this vision long enough, we should doubtless, in fact, be brought to wondering—and still for very loyalty to the form itself—whether our own prospective conditions may not before too long appear to many critics to call for some such happy *coup* on the part of a great artist yet to come.

There would at least be this excuse for such a reverie: that speculation is vain unless we confine it, and that for ourselves the most convenient branch of the question is the state of the industry that makes its appeal to readers of English. From any attempt to measure the career still open to the novel in France I may be excused, in so narrow a compass, for shrinking. The French, as a result of having ridden their horse much harder than we, are at a different stage of the journey, and we have doubtless many of their stretches and baiting-places yet to traverse. But if the range grows shorter from the moment we drop to inductions drawn only from English and American material, I am not sure that the answer comes sooner. I should have at all events—a formidably large order—to plunge into the particulars of the question of the present. If the day *is* approaching when the respite of execution for almost any book is but a matter of mercy, does the English novel of commerce tend to strike us as a production more and more equipped by its high qualities for braving the danger? It would be impossible, I think, to make one's attempt at an answer to that riddle really interesting without bringing into the field many illustrations drawn from individuals—without pointing the moral with names both conspicuous and obscure. Such a freedom would carry us, here, quite too far, and would moreover only encumber the path. There is nothing to prevent our taking for granted all sorts of happy symptoms and splendid promises—so long, of course, I mean, as we keep before us the general truth that the future of fiction is intimately bound up with the future of the society that produces and consumes it. In a society with a great and diffused literary sense the talent at play ran only be a less negligible thing than in a society with a literary sense barely discernible. In a world in which criticism is acute and mature such talent will find itself trained, in order successfully to assert itself, to many more kinds of precautionary expertness than in a society in which the art I have named holds all inferior place or makes a sorry figure. A community addicted to reflection and fond of ideas will try experiments with the "story" that will be left untried in a community mainly devoted to travelling and shooting, to pushing trade and playing football. There are many judges, doubtless, who hold that experiments—queer and uncanny things at best— are not necessary to it, that its face has been, once for all, turned in one way, and that it has only to go straight before it. If that is what it is actually doing in England and America the main thing to say about its future would appear to be that this future will in very truth more and more define itself as negligible. For all the while the immense variety of life will stretch away to right and to left, and all the while there may be, on such lines, perpetuation of its great mistake of failing of intelligence. That mistake will be, ever, for the admirable art, the only one really inexcusable, because of being a mistake about, as we may say, its own soul. The form of novel that is stupid on the general question of its freedom is the single form that may, a priori, be unhesitatingly pronounced wrong.

The most interesting thing to-day, therefore, among ourselves is the degree in which we may count on seeing a sense of that freedom cultivated and bearing fruit. What else is this, indeed, but one of the most attaching elements in the great drama of our wide English-speaking life! As the novel is at any moment the most immediate and, as it were, admirably *treacherous* picture of actual manners—indirectly as well as directly, and by what it does not touch as well as by what it does—so its present situation, where we are most concerned with it, is exactly a reflection of our social changes and chances, of the signs and portents that lay most traps for most observers, and make up in general what is most "amusing" in the spectacle we offer. Nothing, I may say, for instance, strikes me more as meeting this description than the predicament finally arrived at, for the fictive energy, in consequence of our long and most respectable tradition of making it defer supremely, in the treatment, say, of a delicate case, to the inexperience of the young. The particular knot the coming novelist, who shall prefer not simply to beg the question, will have here to untie may represent assuredly the essence of his outlook. By what it shall decide to do in respect to the "young" the great prose fable will, from any serious point of view, practically see itself stand or fall. What is clear is that it has, among us, veritably never chosen—it has, mainly, always obeyed an unreasoning instinct of avoidance in which there has often been much that was felicitous. While society was frank, was free about the incidents and accidents of the human constitution, the novel took the same robust ease as society. The young then were so very young that they were not table-high. But they began to grow and from the moment their little chins rested on the mahogany, Richardson and Fielding began to go under it. There came into being a mistrust of any but the most guarded treatment of the great relation between men and women, the constant world-renewal, which was the conspicuous sign that whatever the prose picture of life was prepared to take upon itself, it was not prepared to take upon itself not to be superficial. Its position became very much: "There are other things, don't you know? For heaven's sake let *that* one pass!" And to this wonderful propriety of letting it pass the business has been for these so many years—with the consequences we see to-day—largely devoted. These consequences are of many sorts, not a few altogether charming. One of them has been that there is an immense omission in our fiction—which, though many critics will always judge that it has vitiated the whole, others will continue to speak of as signifying but a trifle. One can only talk for one's self, and of the English and American novelists of whom I am fond, I am so superlatively fond that I positively prefer to take them as they are. I cannot so much as imagine Dickens and Scott *without* the "love-making" left, as the phrase is, out. They were, to my perception, absolutely right—from the moment their attention to it could only be perfunctory—practically not to deal with it. In all their work it is, in spite of the number of pleasant sketches of affection gratified or crossed, the element that matters least. Why not therefore assume, it may accordingly be asked, that discriminations which have served their purpose so well in the past will continue not less successfully to meet the case? What will you have better than Scott and Dickens?

Nothing certainly *can* be, it may at least as promptly be replied, and I can imagine no more comfortable prospect than jogging along perpetually with a renewal of such blessings. The difficulty lies in the fact that two of the great conditions have changed. The novel is older, and so are the young. It would seem that everything the young can possibly do for us in the matter has been successfully done. They have kept out one thing after the other, yet there is still a certain completeness we lack, and the curious thing is that it appears to be they themselves who are making the grave discovery, "you have kindly taken," they seem to say to the fiction-mongers,

> our education off the hands of our parents and pastors, and that, doubtless, has been very convenient for *them*, and left them free to amuse themselves. But what, all the while, pray, if it is a question of education, have you done with your own? These are directions in which you seem dreadfully untrained, and in which *can* it be as vain as it appears to apply to you for information?

The point is whether, from the moment it is a question of averting discredit, the novel can afford to take things quite so easily as it has, for a good while now, settled down into the way of doing. There are too many sources of interest neglected—whole categories of manners, whole corpuscular classes and provinces, museums of character and condition, unvisited; while it is on the other hand mistakenly taken for granted that safety lies in all the loose and thin material that keeps reappearing in forms at once ready-made and sadly worse for wear. The simple themselves may finally turn against our simplifications; so that we need not, after all, be more royalist than the king or more childish than the children. It is certain that there is no real health for any art—I am not speaking, of course, of any mere industry—that does not move a step in advance of its farthest follower. It would be curious—really a great comedy—if the renewal were to spring just from the satiety of the very readers for whom the sacrifices have hitherto been supposed to be made. It bears on this that as nothing is more salient in English life to-day, to fresh eyes, than the revolution taking place in the position and outlook of women—and taking place much more deeply in the quiet than even the noise on the surface demonstrates—so we may very well yet see the female elbow itself, kept in increasing activity by the play of the pen, smash with final resonance the window all this time most superstitiously closed. The particular draught that has been most deprecated will in that case take care of the question of freshness. It is the opinion of some observers that when women do obtain a free hand they will not repay their long debt to the precautionary attitude of men by unlimited consideration for the natural delicacy of the latter.

To admit, then, that the great anodyne can ever totally fail to work, is to imply, in short, that this will only be by some grave fault in some high quarter. Man rejoices in an incomparable faculty for presently mutilating and disfiguring any plaything that has helped create for him the illusion of leisure; nevertheless, so long as life retains its power of projecting itself upon his imagination, he will find the novel work off the impression better than anything he knows. Anything better for the purpose has assuredly yet to be discovered. He will give it up only when life itself too thoroughly disagrees with him. Even then, indeed, may fiction not find a second wind, or a fiftieth, in the very portrayal of that collapse? Till the world is an unpeopled void there will be an image in the mirror. What need more immediately concern us, therefore, is the care of seeing that the image shall continue various and vivid. There is much, frankly, to be said for those who, in spite of all brave pleas, feel it to be considerably menaced, for very little reflection will help to show us how the prospect strikes them. They see the whole business too divorced on the one side from observation and perception, and on the other from the art and taste. They get too little of the first-hand impression, the effort to penetrate—that effort for which the French have the admirable expression to *fouiller*—and still less, if possible, of any science of composition, any architecture, distribution, proportion. It is not a trifle, though indeed it is the concomitant of an edged force, that "mystery" should, to so many of the sharper eyes, have disappeared from the craft, and a facile flatness be, in place of it, in acclaimed possession. But these are, at the worst, even for such of the disconcerted, signs that the novelist, not that the novel, has dropped. So long as there is a subject to be treated, so long will it depend wholly on the treatment to rekindle the fire. Only the ministrant must really approach the altar; for if the novel is the treatment, it is the treatment that is essentially what I have called the anodyne.

From *Criticism and Fiction*

WILLIAM DEAN HOWELLS

William Dean Howells (1837-1920) was one of the principal proponents of realism among American novelists of the late 1800s. Editor of the *Atlantic Monthly* from 1866-71 and associate editor of *Harper's Magazine* from 1886-91, he contributed regular essays on the nature of the novel to the latter. These were later compiled and printed in the collection, *Criticism and Fiction*. Though he also wrote romances, he is best known for the social realism of his novels, *The Rise of Silas Lapham* (1885) and *A Hazard of New Fortunes* (1890). In Chapter 15 from *Criticism and Fiction*, he discusses the differences between English and American novels, criticizing the English for reverting after the brilliant realism of Jane Austen to sensational romanticism. In Chapter 18 he laments the immorality of mediocre novels and their adverse effect on behaviour. According to Howells, the most significant criterion for a good novel is its truth to human life. In Chapter 28, he calls for the new realistic novel to assist society in becoming more human by depicting characters and events truthfully. His call for a democratic literature as opposed to "the aristocratic spirit . . . [which] is now seeking to shelter itself in aesthetics" will arouse harsh reactions from modernists of the 1920s.

Chapter XV

Which brings us again, after this long way about, to the divine Jane and her novels, and that troublesome question about them. She was great and they were beautiful, because she and they were honest, and dealt with nature nearly a hundred years ago as realism deals with it to-day. Realism is nothing more and nothing less than the truthful treatment of material, and Jane Austen was the first and the last of the English novelists to treat material with entire truthfulness. Because she sis this, she remains the most artistic of the English novelists, and alone

---

Source: William Dean Howells, from *Criticism and Fiction*, New York: Harper and Brothers, 1892, Chs. 15, 18, 28, pp. 73-7, 92-104, 183-8.

worthy to be matched with the great Scandinavian and Slavic and Latin artists. It is not a question of intellect, or not wholly that. The English have mind enough; but they have not taste enough; or, rather, their taste has been perverted by their false criticism, which is based upon personal preference, and not upon principle; which instructs a man to think that what he likes is good, instead of teaching him first to distinguish what is good before he likes it. The art of fiction, as Jane Austen knew it, declined from her through Scott, and Bulwer, and Dickens, and Charlotte Brontë, and Thackeray, and even George Eliot, because the mania of romanticism had seized upon all Europe, and these great writers could not escape the taint of their time; but it has shown few signs of recovery in England, because English criticism, in the presence of the Continental masterpieces, has continued provincial and special and personal, and has expressed a love and a hate which had to do with the quality of the artist rather than the character of his work. It was inevitable that in their time the English romanticists should treat, as Señor Valdés says, "the barbarous customs of the Middle Ages, softening and disfiguring them, as Walter Scott and his kind did;" that they should "devote themselves to falsifying nature, refining and subtilizing sentiment, and modifying psychology, after their own fancy," like Bulwer and Dickens, as well as like Rousseau and Madame de Staël, not to mention Balzac, the worst of all that sort at his worst. This was the natural course of the disease; but it really seems as if it were their criticism that was to blame for the rest: not, indeed, for the performance of this writer or that, for criticism can never affect the actual doing of a thing; but for the esteem in which this writer or that is held through the perpetuation of false ideals. The only observer of English middle-class life since Jane Austen worthy to be named with her was not George Eliot, who was first ethical and then artistic, who transcended her in everything but the form and method most essential to art, and there fell hopelessly below her. It was Anthony Trollope who was most like her in simple honesty and instinctive truth, as unphilosophized as the light of common day; but he was so warped from a wholesome ideal as to wish at times to be like the caricaturist Thackeray, and to stand about in his scene, talking it over with his hands in his pockets, interrupting the action, and spoiling the illusion in which alone the truth of art resides. Mainly, his instinct was too much for his ideal, and with a low view of life in its civic relations and a thoroughly bourgeois soul, he yet produced works whose beauty is surpassed only by the effect of a more poetic writer in the novels of Thomas Hardy. Yet if a vote of English criticism even at this late day. when all continental Europe has the light of æsthetic truth, could be taken, the majority against these artists would be overwhelmingly in favor of a writer who had so little artistic sensibility, that he never hesitated on any occasion, great or small, to make a foray among his characters, and catch them up to show them to the reader and tell him how beautiful or ugly they were; and cry out over their amazing properties.

Doubtless the ideal of those poor islanders will be finally changed. If the truth could become a fad it would be accepted by all their "smart people," but truth is something rather too large for that; and we must await the gradual advance of civilization among them. Then they will see that their criticism has misled them; and that it is to this false guide they owe, not precisely the decline of fiction among them, but its continued debasement as an art.

Chapter XVIII

In General Grant's confession of novel-reading there is a sort of inference that he had wasted his time, or else the guilty conscience of the novelist in me imagines such an inference. But however this may be, there is certainly no question concerning the intention of a correspondent who once wrote to me after reading some rather bragging claims I had made for fiction as a mental and moral means. "I have very grave doubts," he said,

> as to the whole list of magnificent things that you think novels have done for the race, and can witness in myself many evil things which they have done for me. Whatever in my mental make-up is wild and visionary, whatever is untrue, whatever is injurious, I can trace to the perusal of some work of fiction. Worse than that, they beget such high-strung and supersensitive ideas of life that plain industry and plodding perseverance are despised, and matter-of-fact poverty, or every-day, commonplace distress, meets with no sympathy, if indeed noticed at all, by one who has wept over the impossibly accumulated sufferings of some gaudy hero or heroine.

I am not sure that I had the controversy with this correspondent that he seemed to suppose; but novels are now so fully accepted by every one pretending to cultivate taste—and they really form the whole intellectual life of such immense numbers of people, without question of their influence, good or bad, upon the mind—that it is refreshing to have them frankly denounced, and to be invited to revise one's ideas and feelings in regard to them. A little honesty, or a great deal of honesty, in this quest will do the novel, as we hope yet to have it, and as we have already begun to have it, no harm; and for my own part, I will confess that I believe fiction in the past to have been largely injurious, as I believe the stage play to be still almost wholly injurious, through its falsehood, its folly, its wantonness, and its aimlessness. It may be safely assumed that most of the novel-reading which people fancy an intellectual pastime is the emptiest dissipation, hardly more related to thought or the wholesome exercise of the mental faculties than opium eating; in either case the brain is drugged, and left weaker and crazier for the debauch. If this may be called the negative result of the fiction habit, the positive injury that most novels work is by no means so easily to be measured in the case of young men whose character they help so much to form or deform, and the women of all ages whom they keep so much in ignorance of the world they misrepresent. Grown men have little harm from them, but in the other cases, which are the vast majority, they hurt because they are not true—not because they are malevolent, but because they are idle lies about human nature and the social fabric, which it behooves us to know and to understand, that we may deal justly with ourselves and with one another. One need not go so far as our correspondent, and trace to the fiction habit "whatever is wild and visionary, whatever is untrue, whatever is injurious," in one's life; bad as the fiction habit is it is probably not responsible for the whole sum of evil in its victims, and I believe that if the reader will use care in choosing from this fungus-growth with which the fields of literature teem every day, he may nourish himself as with the true mushroom, at no risk from the poisonous species.

The tests are very plain and simple, and they are perfectly infallible. If a novel flatters the passions and exalts them above the principles, it is poisonous; it may not kill, but it will certainly injure; and this test will alone exclude an entire class of fiction, of which eminent examples will occur to all. Then the whole spawn of so-called unmoral romances, which imagine a world where the sins of sense are unvisited by the penalties following, swift or slow, but inexorably sure, in the real world, are deadly poison: these do kill. The novels that merely tickle our prejudices and lull our judgement, or that coddle our sensibilities or pamper our gross appetite for the marvellous are not so fatal, but they are innutritious, and clog the soul with unwholesome vapors of all kinds. No doubt they too help to weaken the moral fibre, and make their readers indifferent to "plodding perseverance and plain industry," and to "matter-of-fact poverty and commonplace distress.'

Without taking them too seriously, it still must be owned that the "gaudy hero and heroine" are to blame for a great deal of harm in the world. That heroine long taught by example, if not precept, that Love, or the passion or fancy she mistook for it, was the chief interest of a life, which is really concerned with a great many other things; that it was worthy of every sacrifice, and was altogether a finer thing than prudence, obedience, reason; that love alone was glorious and beautiful, and these were mean and ugly in comparison with it. Most lately she has begun to idolize and illustrate Duty, and she is hardly less mischievous in this new role, opposing duty, as she did love, to prudence, obedience, and reason. The stock hero, whom, if we met him, we could not fail to see was a most deplorable person, has undoubtedly imposed himself upon the victims of the fiction habit as admirable. With him, too, love was and is the great affair, whether in its old romantic phase of chivalrous achievement or manifold suffering for love's sake, or its more recent development of the "virile," the bullying, and the brutal, or its still more recent agonies of self-sacrifice, as idle and useless as the moral experiences of the insane asylums. With his vain posturings and his ridiculous splendor he is really a painted barbarian, the prey of his passions and his delusions, full of obsolete ideals, and the motives and ethics of a savage, which the guilty author of his being does his best—or his worst—in spite of his own light and knowledge, to foist upon the reader as something generous and noble. I am not merely bringing this charge against that sort of fiction which is beneath literature and outside of it, "the shoreless lakes of ditch-water," whose miasms fill the air below the empyrean where the great ones sit; but I am accusing the work of some of the most famous, who have, in this instance or in that, sinned against the truth, which can alone exalt and purify men. I do not say that they have constantly done so, or even commonly done so; but that they have done so at all marks them as of the past, to be read with the due historical allowance for their epoch and their conditions. For I believe that, while inferior writers will and must continue to imitate them in their foibles and their errors, no one here-after will be able to achieve greatness who is false to humanity, either in its facts or its duties. The light of civilization has already broken even upon the novel, and no conscientious man can now set about painting an image of life without perpetual question of the verity of his work, and without feeling bound to distinguish so clearly that no reader of his may be misled, between what is right and what is wrong, what is noble and what is base, what is health and what is perdition, in the actions and the characters he portrays.

The fiction that aims merely to entertain—the fiction that is to serious fiction as the opera-bouffe, the ballet, and the pantomime are to the true drama—need not feel the burden of this obligation so deeply; but even such fiction will not be gay or trivial to any reader's hurt, and criticism will hold it to account if it passes from painting to teaching folly.

More and more not only the criticism which prints its opinions, but the infinitely vaster and powerfuler criticism which thinks and feels them merely, will make this demand. I confess that I do not care to judge any work of the imagination without first of all applying this test to it. We must ask ourselves before we ask anything else. Is it true?—true to the motives, the impulses, the principles that shape the life of actual men and women? This truth, which necessarily includes the highest morality and the highest artistry—this truth given, the book cannot be wicked and cannot be weak; and without it all graces of style and feats of invention and cunning of construction are so many superfluities of naughtiness. It is well for the truth to have all these, and shine in them, but for falsehood they are merely meretricious, the bedizenment of the wanton; they atone for nothing, they count for nothing, But in fact they come naturally of truth, and grace it without solicitation; they are added unto it. In the whole range of fiction we know of no true picture of life—that is, of human nature—which is not also a masterpiece of literature, full of divine and natural beauty. It may have no touch or tint of this special civilization or of that; it had better have this local color well ascertained; but the truth is deeper and finer than aspects, and if the book is true to what men and women know of one another's souls it will be true enough, and it will be great and beautiful. It is the conception of literature as something apart from life, superfinely aloof, which makes it really unimportant to the great mass of, mankind, without a message or a meaning for them; and it is the notion that a novel may be false in its portrayal of causes and effects that makes literary art contemptible even to those whom it amuses, that forbids them to regard the novelist as a serious or right-minded person. If they do not in some moment of indignation cry out against all novels, as my correspondent does, they remain besotted in the fume of the delusions purveyed to them, with no higher feeling for the author than such maudlin affection as the habitué of an opium-joint perhaps knows for the attendant who fills his pipe with the drug.

Or, as in the case of another correspondent who writes that in his youth he "read a great many novels, but always regarded it as an amusement, like horse-racing and card-playing," for which he had no time when he entered upon the serious business of life, it renders them merely contemptuous. His view of the matter may be commended to the brotherhood and sisterhood of novelists as full of wholesome if bitter suggestion; and we urge them not to dismiss it with high literary scorn as that of some Bœotian dull to the beauty of art. Refuse it as we may, it is still the feeling of the vast majority of people for whom life is earnest, and who find only a distorted and misleading likeness of it in our books. We may fold ourselves in our scholars' gowns, and close the doors of our studies, and affect to despise this rude voice; but we cannot shut it out. It comes to us from wherever men are at work, from wherever they are truly living, and accuses us of unfaithfulness of triviality, of mere stage-play; and none of us can escape conviction except he prove himself worthy of his time—a time in which the great masters have brought literature back to life, and filled its ebbing veins with the red tides of reality. We cannot all equal them; we need not copy them; but we can all go to the sources of their inspiration and their power; and to draw from these no one need go far—no one need really go out of himself.

Fifty years ago, Carlyle, in whom the truth was always alive, but in whom it was then unperverted by suffering, by celebrity, and by despair, wrote in his study of Diderot:

> Were it not reasonable to prophesy that this exceeding great multitude of novel-writers and such like must, in a new generation, gradually do one of two things: either retire into the nurseries, and work for children, minors, and semi-fatuous persons of both sexes, or else, what were far better, sweep their novel-fabric into the dust-cart, and betake themselves with such faculty as they have to understand and record what is true, of which surely there is, and will forever be a whole infinitude unknown to us of infinite importance to us? Poetry, it will more and more come to be understood, is nothing but higher knowledge; and the only genuine Romance (for grown persons), Reality.

If, after half a century, fiction still mainly works for "children, minors, and semi-fatuous persons of both sexes," it is nevertheless one of the hopefulest signs of the world's progress that it has begun to work for "grown persons," and if not exactly in the way that Carlyle might have solely intended in urging its writers to compile memoirs instead of building the "novel-fabric," still it has, in the highest and widest sense, already made Reality its Romance. I cannot judge it, I do not even care for it, except as it has done this; and I can hardly conceive of a literary self-respect in these days compatible with the old trade of make-believe, with the production of the kind of fiction which is too much honored by classification with card-playing and horse-racing. But let fiction cease to lie about life; let it portray men and women as they are, actuated by the motives and the passions in the measure we all know; let it leave off painting dolls and working them by springs and wires; let it show the different interests in their true proportions; let it forbear to preach pride and revenge, folly and insanity, egotism and prejudice, but frankly own these for what they are, in whatever figures and occasions they appear; let it not put on fine literary airs; let it speak the dialect, the language, that most Americans know—the language of unaffected people everywhere—and there can be no doubt of an unlimited future, not only of delightfulness but of usefulness, for it.

Chaspter XXVIII

But if the humanitarian impulse has mostly disappeared from Christmas fiction, I think it has never so generally characterized all fiction. One may refuse to recognize this impulse; one may deny that it is in any greater degree shaping life than ever before, but no one who has the current of literature under his eye can fail to note it there. People are thinking and feeling generously, if not living justly, in our time; it is a day of anxiety to be saved from the curse that is on selfishness, of eager question how others shall be helped, of bold denial that the conditions in which we would fain have rested are sacred or immutable. Especially in America, where the race has gained a height never reached before, the eminence enables more men than ever before to see how even here vast masses of men are sunk in misery that must grow every day more hopeless, or embroiled in a struggle for mere life that must end in enslaving and imbruting them.

Art, indeed, is beginning to find out that if it does not make friends with Need it must perish. It perceives that to take itself from the many and leave them no joy in their work, and to give itself to the few whom it can bring no joy in their idleness, is an error that kills. This has long been the burden of Ruskin's message: and if we can believe brilliantly William Morris, the common people have heard him gladly, and have felt the truth of what he says, "They see the prophet in him rather than the fantastic rhetorician, as more superfine audiences do;" and the men and women who do the hard work of the world have learned from him and from Morris that they have a right to pleasure in their toil, and that when justice is done them they will have it. In all ages poetry has affirmed something of this sort, but it remained for ours to perceive it and express it somehow in every form of literature. But this is only one phase of the devotion of the best literature of our time to the service of humanity.

No book written with a low or cynical motive could succeed now, no matter how brilliantly written; and the work done in the past to the glorification of mere passion and power, to the deification of self, appears monstrous and hideous. The romantic spirit worshipped genius, worshipped heroism, but at its best, in such a man as Victor Hugo, this spirit recognized the supreme claim of the lowest humanity. Its error was to idealize the victims of society, to paint them impossibly virtuous and beautiful; but truth, which has succeeded to the highest mission of romance, paints these victims as they are, and bids the world consider them not because they are beautiful and virtuous, but because they are ugly and vicious, cruel, filthy, and only not altogether loathsome because the divine can never wholly die out of the human. The truth does not find these victims among the poor alone, among the hungry, the houseless, the ragged; but it also finds them among the rich, cursed with the aimlessness, the satiety, the despair of wealth, wasting their lives in a fool's paradise of shows and semblances, with nothing real but the misery that comes of insincerity and selfishness.

It is needless for me to say, either to the many whom my opinions on this point incense or to the few who accept them, that I do not think the fiction of our own time even always equal to this work, or perhaps more than seldom so. But as I have before expressed, to the still-reverberating discontent of two continents, fiction is now a finer art than it has ever been hitherto, and more nearly meets the requirements of the infallible standard. I have hopes of real usefulness in it, because it is at last building on the only sure foundation; but I am by no means certain that it will be the ultimate literary form, or will remain as important as we believe it is destined to become. On the contrary, it is quite imaginable that when the great mass of readers, now sunk in the foolish joys of mere fable, shall be lifted to an interest in the meaning of things through the faithful portrayal of life in fiction, then fiction the most faithful may be superseded by a still more faithful form of contemporaneous history. I willingly leave the precise character of this form to the more robust imagination of readers whose minds have been nurtured upon romantic novels, and who really have an imagination worth speaking of, and confine myself, as usual, to the hither side of the regions of conjecture.

The art which in the mean time disdains the office of teacher is one of the last refuges of the aristocratic spirit which is disappearing from politics and society, and is now seeking to shelter itself in æsthetics. The pride of caste is becoming the pride of taste; but as before, it is averse to the mass of men; it consents to know them only in some conventionalized and artificial guise. It seeks to withdraw itself, to stand aloof; to be distinguished, and not to be identified. Democracy in literature is the reverse of all this. It wishes to know and to tell the truth, confident that consolation and delight are there; it does not care to paint the marvellous and impossible for the vulgar many, or to sentimentalize and falsify the actual for the vulgar few. Men are more like than unlike one another: let us make them know one another better, that they may be all humbled and strengthened with a sense of their fraternity. Neither arts, nor letters, nor sciences, except as they somehow, clearly or obscurely, tend to make the race better and kinder, are to be regarded as serious interests; they are all lower than the rudest crafts that feed and house and clothe, for except they do this office they are idle; and they cannot do this except from and through the truth.

85

Fenimore Cooper's Literary Offences

MARK TWAIN

Samuel Langhorne Clemens (1835-1910), writing under the pseudonym of Mark Twain, is one of the most prominent American writers of the nineteenth century. He recounts a fictionalized version of his childhood in Missouri in his two best known novels, *Tom Sawyer* (1876) and *The Adventures of Huckleberry Finn* (1884). A humorist and frontier realist, Twain was also a lecturer, essayist and critic. In the following piece, he humorously takes Cooper's *Leather-Stocking Tales* to task for their historical inaccuracy and novelistic flaws. He criticizes Cooper's inventive capacities, his inaccurate eye, his faulty ear, his lack of logic, and notes that the main hero–Pathfinder–lacks all credibility as a character. As a realist, Twain had little respect for the romance tradition with its exaggerated idealism that Cooper represented.

The Pathfinder and *The Deerslayer* stand at the head of Cooper's novels as artistic creations. There are others of his works which contain parts as perfect as are to be found in these, and scenes even more thrilling. Not one can be compared with either of them as a finished whole.

The defects in both of these tales are comparatively slight. They were pure works of art.—*Prof. Lounsbury.*

The five tales reveal an extraordinary fulness of invention.

. . . One of the very greatest characters in fiction, Natty Bumppo. . . .

The craft of the woodsman, the tricks of the trapper, all the delicate art of the forest, were familiar to Cooper from his youth up.—*Prof. Brander Matthews.*

Cooper is the greatest artist in the domain of romantic fiction yet produced by America.—*Wilkie Collins.*

It seems to me that it was far from right for the Professor of English Literature in Yale, the Professor of English Literature in Columbia, and Wilkie Collins to

Source: Mark Twain, "Fenimore Cooper's Literary Offences", *How to Tell a Story and Other Essays*, New York: Harper & Brothers Publishers, 1897, pp. 93-116.

deliver opinions on Cooper's literature without having read some of it. It would have been much more decorous to keep silent and let persons talk who have read Cooper.

Cooper's art has some defects. In one place in *Deerslayer*, and in the restricted space of two-thirds of a page, Cooper has scored 114 offences against literary art out of a possible 115. It breaks the record.

There are nineteen rules governing literary art in the domain of romantic fiction—some say twenty-two. In *Deerslayer* Cooper violated eighteen of them. These eighteen require:

1. That a tale shall accomplish something and arrive somewhere. But the *Deerslayer* tale accomplishes nothing and arrives in the air.

2. They require that the episodes of a tale shall be necessary parts of the tale, and shall help to develop it. But as the *Deerslayer* tale is not a tale, and accomplishes nothing and arrives nowhere, the episodes have no rightful place in the work, since there was nothing for them to develop.

3. They require that the personages in a tale shall be alive, except in the case of corpses, and that always the reader shall be able to tell the corpses from the others. But this detail has often been overlooked in the *Deerslayer* tale.

4. They require that the personages in a tale, both dead and alive, shall exhibit a sufficient excuse for being there. But this detail also has been overlooked in the *Deerslayer* tale.

5. They require that when the personages of a tale deal in conversation, the talk shall sound like human talk, and be talk such as human beings would be likely to talk in the given circumstances, and have a discoverable meaning, also a discoverable purpose, and a show of relevancy, and remain in the neighborhood of the subject in hand, and be interesting to the reader, and help out the tale, and stop when the people cannot think of anything more to say. But this requirement has been ignored from the beginning of the *Deerslayer* tale to the end of it.

6. They require that when the author describes the character of a personage in his tale, the conduct and conversation of that personage shall justify said description. But this law gets little or no attention in the *Deerslayer* tale, as Natty Bumppo's case will amply prove.

7. They require that when a personage talks like an illustrated, gilt-edged, tree-calf, hand-tooled, seven-dollar Friendship's Offering in the beginning of a paragraph, he shall not talk like a negro minstrel in the end of it. But this rule is flung down and danced upon in the *Deerslayer* tale.

8. They require that crass stupidities shall not be played upon the reader as "the craft of the woodsman, the delicate art of the forest," by either the author or the people in the tale. But this rule is persistently violated in the *Deerslayer* tale.

9. They require that the personages of a tale shall confine themselves to possibilities and let miracles alone; or, if they venture a miracle, the author must so plausibly set it forth as to make it look possible and reasonable. But these rules are not respected in the *Deerslayer* tale.

10. They require that the author shall make the reader feel a deep interest in the

person-ages of his tale and in their fate; and that he shall make the reader love the good people in the tale and hate the bad ones. But the reader of the *Deerslayer* tale dislikes the good people in it, is indifferent to the others, and wishes they would all get drowned together.

11. They require that the characters in a tale shall be so clearly defined that the reader can tell beforehand what each will do in a given emergency. But in the *Deerslayer* tale this rule is vacated.

In addition to these large rules there are some little ones. These require that the author shall

12. *Say* what he is proposing to say, not merely come near it.
13. Use the right word, not its second cousin.
14. Eschew surplusage.
15. Not omit necessary details.
16. Avoid slovenliness of form.
17. Use good grammar.
18. Employ a simple and straightforward style.

Even these seven are coldly and persistently violated in the *Deerslayer* tale.

Cooper's gift in the way of invention was not a rich endowment; but such as it was he liked to work it, he was pleased with the effects, and indeed he did some quite sweet things with it. In his little box of stage properties he kept six or eight cunning devices, tricks, artifices for his savages and woodsmen to deceive and circumvent each other with, and he was never so happy as when he was working these innocent things and seeing them go. A favorite one was to make a moccasined person tread in the tracks of the moccasined enemy, and thus hide his own trail. Cooper wore out barrels and barrels of moccasins in working that trick. Another stage-property that he pulled out of his box pretty frequently was his broken twig. He prized his broken twig above all the rest of his effects, and worked it the hardest. It is a restful chapter in any book of his when somebody doesn't step on a dry twig and alarm all the reds and whites for two hundred yards around. Every time a Cooper person is in peril, and absolute silence is worth four dollars a minute, he is sure to step on a dry twig. There may be a hundred handier things to step on, but that wouldn't satisfy Cooper. Cooper requires him to turn out and find a dry twig; and if he can't do it, go and borrow one. In fact, the Leather Stocking Series ought to have been called the Broken Twig Series.

I am sorry there is not room to put in a few dozen instances of the delicate art of the forest, as practised by Natty Bumppo and some of the other Cooperian experts. Perhaps we may venture two or three samples. Cooper was a sailor—a naval officer; yet he gravely tells us how a vessel, driving towards a lee shore in a gale, is steered for a particular spot by her skipper because he knows of an *undertow* there which will hold her back against the gale and save her. For just pure woodcraft, or sailorcraft, or whatever it is, isn't that neat? For several years Cooper was daily in the society of artillery, and he ought to have noticed that when a cannon-ball strikes the ground it either buries itself or skips a hundred feet or so; skips again a hundred feet or so—and so on, till it finally gets tired and rolls. Now in one place he loses some "females"—as he always calls women—in the edge of a wood near a plain at night in a fog, on purpose to give Bumppo a chance to show off the delicate art of the forest before the reader. These mislaid people are hunting for a fort. They hear a cannon-blast, and a cannon-ball presently comes rolling into the wood and stops at their feet. To the females this suggests nothing. The case is very different with the admirable Bumppo. I wish I may never know peace again if he doesn't strike out promptly and *follow the track* of that cannon-ball across the plain through the dense fog and find the fort. Isn't it a daisy? If Cooper had any real knowledge of Nature's ways of doing things, he had a most delicate art in concealing the fact. For instance: one of his acute Indian experts, Chingachgook (pronounced Chicago, I think), has lost the trail of a person he is tracking through the forest. Apparently that trail is hopelessly lost. Neither you nor I could ever have guessed out the way to find it. It was very different with Chicago. Chicago was not stumped for long. He turned a running stream out of its course, and there, in the slush in its old bed, were that person's moccasin-tracks. The current did not wash them away, as it would have done in all other like cases—no, even the eternal laws of Nature have to vacate when Cooper wants to put up a delicate job of woodcraft on the reader.

We must be a little wary when Brander Matthews tells us that Cooper's books "reveal an extraordinary fulness [sic] of invention." As a rule, I am quite willing to accept Brander Matthews's literary judgments and applaud his lucid and graceful phrasing of them; but that particular statement needs to be taken with a few tons of salt. Bless your heart, Cooper hadn't any more invention than a horse; and I don't mean a high-class horse, either; I mean a clothes-horse. It would be very difficult to find a really clever "situation" in Cooper's books, and still more difficult to find one of any kind which he has failed to render absurd by his handling of it. Look at the episodes of "the caves"; and at the celebrated scuffle between Maqua and those others on the table-land a few days later; and at Hurry Harry's queer water-transit from the castle to the ark; and at Deerslayer's half-hour with his first corpse; and at the quarrel between Hurry Harry and Deerslayer later; and at—but choose for yourself; you can't go amiss.

If Cooper had been an observer his inventive faculty would have worked better; not more interestingly, but more rationally, more plausibly. Cooper's proudest creations in the way of "situations" suffer noticeably from the absence of the observer's protecting gift. Cooper's eye was splendidly inaccurate. Cooper seldom saw anything correctly. He saw nearly all things as through a glass eye, darkly. Of course a man who cannot see the commonest little every-day matters accurately is working at a disadvantage when he is constructing a "situation." In the Deerslayer tale Cooper has a stream which is fifty feet wide where it flows out of a lake; it presently narrows to twenty as it meanders along for no given reason, and yet when a stream acts like that it ought to be required to explain itself. Fourteen pages later the width of the brook's outlet from the lake has suddenly shrunk thirty feet, and become "the narrowest part of the stream." This shrinkage is not accounted for. The stream has bends in it, a sure indication that it has alluvial banks and cuts them; yet these bends are only thirty and fifty feet long. If Cooper had been a nice and punctilious observer he would have noticed that the bends were oftener nine hundred feet long than short of it.

Cooper made the exit of that stream fifty feet wide, in the first place, for no particular reason; in the second place, he narrowed it to less than twenty to accommodate some Indians. He bends a "sapling" to the form of an arch over this narrow passage, and conceals six Indians in its foliage. They are "laying" for a settler's scow or ark which is coming up the stream on its way to the lake; it is being hauled against the stiff current by a rope whose stationary end is anchored in the lake; its rate of progress cannot be more than a mile an hour. Cooper describes the ark, but pretty obscurely. In the matter of dimensions "it was little more than a modern canal boat." Let us guess, then, that it was about one hundred and forty feet long. It was of "greater breadth than common." Let us guess, then, that it was about sixteen feet wide. This leviathan had been prowling down bends which were but a third as long as itself, and scraping between banks where it had only two feet of space to spare on each side. We cannot too much admire this miracle. A low-roofed log dwelling occupies "two-thirds of the ark's length"—a dwelling ninety feet long and sixteen feet wide, let us say—a kind of vestibule train. The dwelling has two rooms—each forty-five feet long and sixteen feet wide, let us guess. One of them is the bedroom of the Hutter girls, Judith and Hetty; the other is the parlor in the daytime, at night it is papa's bedchamber. The ark is arriving at the stream's exit now, whose width has been reduced to less than twenty feet to accommodate the Indians—say to eighteen. There is a foot to spare on each side of the boat. Did the Indians notice that there was going to be a tight squeeze there? Did they notice that they could make money by climbing down out of that arched sapling and just stepping aboard when the ark scraped by? No; other Indians would have noticed these things, but Cooper's Indians never notice anything. Cooper thinks they are marvellous creatures for noticing, but he was almost always in error about his Indians. There was seldom a sane one among them.

The ark is one hundred and forty feet long; the dwelling is ninety feet long. The idea of the Indians is to drop softly and secretly from the arched sapling to the dwelling as the ark creeps along under it at the rate of a mile an hour, and butcher the family. It will take the ark a minute and a half to pass under. It will take the ninety foot dwelling a minute to pass under. Now, then, what did the six Indians do? It would take you thirty years to guess, and even then you would have to give it up, I believe. Therefore, I will tell you what the Indians did. Their chief, a person of quite extraordinary intellect for a Cooper Indian, warily watched the canal-boat as it squeezed along under him, and when he had got his calculations fined down to exactly the right shade, as he judged, he let go and dropped. And *missed the house!* That is actually what he did. He missed the house, and landed in the stern of the scow. It was not much of a fall, yet it knocked him silly. He lay there unconscious. If the house had been ninety-seven feet long he would have made the trip. The fault was Cooper's, not his. The error lay in the construction of the house. Cooper was no architect.

There still remained in the roost five Indians. The boat has passed under and is now out of their reach. Let me explain what the five did—you would not be able to reason it out for yourself. No. 1 jumped for the boat, but fell in the water astern of it. Then No. 2 jumped for the boat, but fell in the water still farther astern of it. Then No. 3 jumped for the boat, and fell a good way astern of it. Then No. 4 jumped for the boat, and fell in the water *away* astern. Then even No. 5 made a jump for the boat—for he was a Cooper Indian. In the matter of intellect, the difference between a Cooper Indian and the Indian that stands in front of the cigar-shop is not spacious. The scow episode is really a sublime burst of invention; but it does not thrill, because the inaccuracy of the details throws a sort of air of fictitiousness and general improbability over it. This comes of Cooper's inadequacy as an observer.

The reader will find some examples of Cooper's high talent for inaccurate observation in the account of the shooting-match in The Pathfinder.

> A common wrought nail was driven lightly into the target, its head having been first touched with paint.

The color of the paint is not stated—an important omission, but Cooper deals freely in important omissions. No, after all, it was not an important omission; for this nail-head is *a hundred yards* from the marksmen, and could not be seen by them at that distance, no matter what its color might be. How far can the best eyes see a common house-fly? A hundred yards? It is quite impossible. Very well; eyes that cannot see a house-fly that is a hundred yards away cannot see an ordinary nail-head at that distance, for the size of the two objects is the same. It takes a keen eye to see a fly or a nail-head at fifty yards—one hundred and fifty feet. Can the reader do it?

The nail was lightly driven, its head painted, and game called. Then the Cooper miracles began. The bullet of the first marksman chipped an edge of the nail-head; the next man's bullet drove the nail a little way into the target—and removed all the paint. Haven't the miracles gone far enough now? Not to suit Cooper; for the purpose of this whole scheme is to show off his prodigy, Deerslayer-Hawkeye-Long-Rifle-Leather-Stocking-Path-finder-Bumppo before the ladies.

> "Be all ready to clench it, boys!" cried out Pathfinder, stepping into his friend's tracks the instant they were vacant. "Never mind a new nail; I can see that, though the paint is gone, and what I can see I can hit at a hundred yards, though it were only a mosquito's eye. Be ready to clench!"
>
> The rifle cracked, the bullet sped its way, and the head of the nail was buried in the wood, covered by the piece of flattened lead.

There, you see, is a man who could hunt flies with a rifle, and command a ducal salary in a Wild West show to-day if we had him back with us.

The recorded feat is certainly surprising just as it stands; but it is not surprising enough for Cooper. Cooper adds a touch. He has made Pathfinder do this miracle with another man's rifle; and not only that, but Pathfinder did not have even the advantage of loading it himself. He had everything against him, and yet he made that impossible shot; and not only made it, but did it with absolute confidence, saying, "Be ready to clench." Now a person like that would have undertaken that same feat with a brickbat, and with Cooper to help he would have achieved it, too. Pathfinder showed off handsomely that day before the ladies. His very first feat was a thing which no Wild West show can touch. He was standing with the group of marksmen, observing—a hundred yards from the target, mind; one Jasper raised his rifle and drove the centre of the bull's-eye. Then the Quartermaster fired. The target exhibited no result this time. There was a laugh. "It's a dead miss," said Major Lundie. Pathfinder waited an impressive moment or two; then said, in that calm, indifferent, know-it-all way of his, "No, Major, he has covered Jasper's bullet, as will be seen if anyone will take the trouble to examine the target."

Wasn't it remarkable! How *could* he see that little pellet fly through the air and enter that distant bullet-hole? Yet that is what he did; for nothing is impossible to a Cooper person. Did any of those people have any deep seated doubts about this thing? No; for that would imply sanity, and these were all Cooper people.

> The respect for Pathfinder's skill and for his *quickness and accuracy of sight"* [the italics are mine] "was so profound and general, that the instant he made this declaration the spectators began to distrust their own opinions, and a dozen rushed to the target in order to ascertain the fact. There, sure enough, it was found that the Quartermaster's bullet had gone through the hole made by Jasper's, and that, too, so accurately as to require a minute examination to be certain of the circumstance, which, however, was soon clearly established by discovering one bullet over the other in the stump against which the target was placed.

They made a "minute" examination; but never mind, how could they know that there were two bullets in that hole without digging the latest one out? for neither probe nor eye-sight could prove the presence of any more than one bullet. Did they dig? No; as we shall see. It is the Pathfinder's turn now; he steps out before the ladies, takes aim, and fires.

But, alas! here is a disappointment; an incredible, an unimaginable disappointment—for the target's aspect is unchanged; there is nothing there but that same old bullet-hole!

"If one dared to hint at such a thing." cried Major Duncan, "I should say that the Pathfinder has also missed the target!"

As nobody had missed it yet, the "also" was not necessary; but never mind about that, for the Pathfinder is going to speak.

"No, no, Major," said he, confidently, "that would be a risky declaration. I didn't load the piece, and can't say what was in it; but if it was lead, you will find the bullet driving down those of the Quartermaster and Jasper, else is not my name Pathfinder."

A shout from the target announced the truth of this assertion.

Is the miracle sufficient as it stands? Not for Cooper. The Pathfinder speaks again, as he "now slowly, advances towards the stage occupied by the females":

> "That's not all, boys, that's not all; if you find the target touched at all, I'll own to a miss. The Quartermaster, cut the wood, but you'll find no wood cut by that last messenger."

The miracle is at last complete. He knew—doubtless *saw*—at the distance of a hundred yards—that his bullet had passed into the hole *without fraying the edges*. there were now three bullets in that one hole—three bullets embedded processionally in the body of the stump back of the target. Everybody knew this—somehow or other—and yet nobody had dug any of them out to make sure. Cooper is not a close observer, but he is interesting. He is certainly always that, no matter what happens. And he is more interesting when he is not noticing what he is about than when he is. This is a considerable merit.

The conversations in the Cooper books have a curious sound in our modern ears. To believe that such talk really ever came out of people's mouths would be to believe that there was a time when time was of no value to a person who thought he had something to say; when it was the custom to spread a two-minute remark out to ten; when a man's mouth was a rolling-mill, and busied itself all day long in turning four-foot pigs of thought into thirty-foot bars of conversational railroad iron by attenuation; when subjects were seldom faithfully stuck to, but the talk wandered all around and arrived nowhere; when conversations consisted mainly of irrelevances, with here and there a relevancy, a relevancy with an embarrassed look, as not being able to explain how it got there.

Cooper was certainly not a master in the construction of dialogue. Inaccurate observation defeated him here as it defeated him in so many other enterprises of his. He even failed to notice that the man who talks corrupt English six days in the week must and will talk it on the seventh, and can't help himself. In the *Deerslayer* story he lets Deerslayer talk the showiest kind of book talk sometimes, and at other times the basest of base dialects. For instance, when some one asks him if he has a sweetheart, and if so, where she abides, this is his majestic answer:

> "She's in the forest—hanging from the boughs of the trees, in a soft rain—in the dew on the open grass—the clouds that float about in the blue heavens—the birds that sing in the woods—the sweet springs where I slake my thirst—and in all the other glorious gifts that come from God's Providence!"

And he preceded that, a little before, with this:

> " It consarns me as all things that touches a fri'nd consarns a fri'nd."

And this is another of his remarks:

> "If I was Injin born, now, I might tell of this, or carry in the scalp and boast of the expl'ite afore the whole tribe; or if my inimy had only been a bear"—and so on.

We cannot imagine such a thing as a veteran Scotch Commander-in-Chief comporting himself in the field like a windy melodramatic actor, but Cooper could. On one occasion Alice and Cora were being chased by the French through a fog in the neighborhood of their father's fort:

> "*Point de quartier aux coquins!*" cried an eager pursuer, who seemed to direct the operations of the enemy.
> "Stand firm and be ready, my gallant 60ths!" suddenly exclaimed a voice above them; "wait to see the enemy; fire low, and sweep the glacis."

"Father! father!" exclaimed a piercing cry from out the mist; "it is I! Alice! thy own Elsie! spare, O! save your daughters!"

"Hold!" shouted the former speaker, in the awful tones of parental agony, the sound reaching even to the woods, and rolling back in solemn echo. "'Tis she! God has restored me my children! Throw open the sally-port; to the field, 60ths, to the field; pull not a trigger, lest ye kill my lambs! Drive off these dogs of France with your steel."

Cooper's word-sense was singularly dull. When a person has a poor ear for music he will flat and sharp right along without knowing it. He keeps near the tune, but it is *not* the tune. When a person has a poor ear for words, the result is a literary flatting and sharping: you perceive what he is intending to say, but you also perceive that he doesn't *say* it. This is Cooper. He was not a word-musician. His ear was satisfied with the *approximate* word. I will furnish some circumstantial evidence in support of this charge. My instances are gathered from half a dozen pages of the tale called *Deerslayer*. He uses "verbal," for "oral"; "precision," for "facility"; "phenomena," for "marvels"; "necessary," for "predetermined"; "unsophisticated," for "primitive"; "preparation," for "expectancy"; "rebuked," for "subdued"; "dependant on," for "resulting from"; "fact," for "condition"; "fact," for "conjecture"; "precaution," for "caution"; "explain," for "determine"; "mortified," for "disappointed"; "meretricious," for "factitious"; "materially," for "considerably"; "decreasing," for "deepening"; "increasing," for "disappearing"; "embedded," for "enclosed"; "treacherous," for "hostile"; "stood," for "stooped"; "softened," for "replaced"; "rejoined," for "remarked"; "situation" for "condition"; "different," for "differing"; "insensible," for "unsentient"; "brevity," for "celerity"; "distrusted," for "suspicious"; "mental imbecility," for "imbecility"; "eyes," for "sight"; "counteracting," for "opposing"; "funeral obsequies," for "obsequies."

There have been daring people in the world who claimed that Cooper could write English, but they are all dead now—all dead but Lounsbury. I don't remember that Lounsbury makes the claim in so many words, still he makes it, for he says that *Deerslayer* is a "pure work of art." Pure, in that connection, means faultless—faultless in all details—and language is a detail. If Mr Lounsbury had only compared Cooper's English with the English which he writes himself—but it is plain that he didn't; and so it is likely that he imagines until this day that Cooper's is as clean and compact as his own. Now I feel sure, deep down in my heart, that Cooper wrote about the poorest English that exists in our language, and that the English of *Deerslayer* is the very worst that even Cooper ever wrote.

I may be mistaken, but it does seem to me that *Deerslayer* is not a work of art in any sense; it does seem to me that it is destitute of every detail that goes to the making of a work of art; in truth, it seems to me that *Deerslayer* is just simply a literary *delirium tremens*.

A work of art? It has no invention; it has no order, system, sequence, or result; it has no lifelikeness, no thrill, no stir, no seeming of reality; its characters are confusedly drawn, and by their acts and words they prove that they are not the sort of people the author claims that they are; its humor is pathetic; its pathos is funny;

its conversations are—oh! Indescribable; its love-scenes odious; its English a crime against the language.

Counting these out, what is left is Art. I think we must all admit that.

⸘86⸛

Preface to *The Portrait of a Lady*

HENRY JAMES

James's *The Portrait of a Lady* was serialized first in *Macmillan's Magazine* (October 1880–November 1881) and in *Atlantic Monthly* (November 1880–December 1881). It was published in book form in London in 1881 and in New York in 1882. James added the Preface for the collective New York Edition in 1908. In the Preface he discusses his method of presentation, the placement of "the centre of the subject in the young woman's own consciousness" (xxiii), a method that was to give rise to such later full-fledged stream of consciousness views as those of Joyce, Woolf and Faulkner. Using an architectural metaphor throughout to explain the process of composition, James stresses the need for a central consciousness to provide a window into the "house of fiction".

The Portrait of a Lady was, like *Roderick Hudson*, begun in Florence, during three months spent there in the spring of 1879. Like *Roderick* and like *The American*, it had been designed for publication in The *Atlantic Monthly*, where it began to appear in 1880. It differed from its two predecessors, however, in finding a course also open to it, from month to month, in *Macmillan's Magazine*; which was to be for me one of the last occasions of simultaneous "serialisation" in the two countries that the changing conditions of literary intercourse between England and the United States had up to then left unaltered. It is a long novel, and I was long in writing it; I remember being again much occupied with it, the following year, during a stay of several weeks made in Venice. I had rooms on Riva Schiavoni, at the top of a house near the passage leading off to San Zaccaria; the waterside life, the wondrous lagoon spread before me, and the ceaseless human chatter of Venice came in at my windows, to which I seem to myself to have been constantly driven, in the fruitless fidget of composition, as if to see whether, out in the blue channel, the ship of some right suggestion, of some better phrase, of the next happy twist of my subject, the next true touch for my canvas, mightn't come into sight. But I recall vividly enough that the response most elicited, in general, to these restless appeals was the rather grim

Source: Henry James, "Preface", *The Portrait of a Lady*, 1906, rptd *The Novels and Tales of Henry James*, New York, 1908.

admonition that romantic and historic sites, such as the land of Italy abounds in, offer the artist a questionable aid to concentration when they themselves are not to be the subject of it. They are too rich in their own life and too charged with their own meanings merely to help him out with a lame phrase; they draw him away from his small question to their own greater ones; so that, after a little, he feels, while thus yearning toward them in his difficulty, as if he were asking an army of glorious veterans to help him to arrest a peddler who has given him the wrong change.

There are pages of the book which, in the reading over, have seemed to make me see again the bristling curve of the wide Riva, the large colour-spots of the balconied houses and the repeated undulation of the little hunch-backed bridges, marked by the rise and drop again, with the wave, of foreshortened clicking pedestrians. The Venetian footfall and the Venetian cry—all talk there, wherever uttered, having the pitch of a call across the water—come in once more at the window, renewing one's old impression of the delighted senses and the divided, frustrated mind. How can places that speak *in general* so to the imagination not give it, at the moment, the particular thing it wants? I recollect again and again, in beautiful places, dropping into that wonderment. The real truth is, I think, that they express, under this appeal, only too much—more than, in the given case, one has use for; so that one finds one's self working less congruously, after all, so far as the surrounding picture is concerned, than in presence of the moderate and the neutral, to which we may lend something of the light of our vision. Such a place as Venice is too proud for such charities; Venice doesn't borrow, she but all magnificently gives. We profit by that enormously, but to do so we must either be quite off duty or be on it in her service alone. Such, and so rueful, are these reminiscences; though on the whole, no doubt, one's book, and one's "literary effort" at large, were to be the better for them. Strangely fertilising, in the long run, does a wasted effort of attention often prove. It all depends on *how* the attention has been cheated, has been squandered. There are high-handed insolent frauds, and there are insidious sneaking ones. And there is, I fear, even on the most designing artist's part, always witless enough good faith, always anxious enough desire, to fail to guard him against their deceits.

Trying to recover here, for recognition, the germ of my idea, I see that it must have consisted not at all in any conceit or a "plot," nefarious name, in any flash, upon the fancy, of a set of relations, or in anyone of those situations that, by a logic of their own, immediately fall, for the fabulist, into movement, into a march or a rush, a patter of quick steps; but altogether in the sense of a single character, the character and aspect of a particular engaging young woman, to which all the usual elements of a "subject," certainly of a setting, were to need to be super-added. Quite as interesting as the young woman herself, at her best, do I find, I must again repeat, this projection of memory upon the whole matter of the growth, in one's imagination, or some such apology for a motive. These are the fascinations of the fabulist's art, these lurking forces of expansion, these necessities of upspringing in the seed, these beautiful determinations, on the part of the idea entertained, to grow as tall as possible, to push into the light and the air and thickly flower there; and, quite as much, these fine possibilities of recovering, from some good standpoint on the ground gained, the intimate history of the business—or retracing and reconstructing its steps and stages. I have always boldly remembered a remark that I heard fall years ago from the lips of Ivan Turgenieff in regard to his own experience of the usual origin of the fictive picture. It began for him almost always with the vision of some person or persons, who hovered before him, soliciting him, as the active or passive figure, interesting him and appealing to him just as they were and by what they were. He saw them, in that fashion, as *disponibles*, saw them subject to the chances, the complications of existence, and saw them vividly, but then had to find for them the right relations, those that would most bring them out; to imagine, to invent and select and piece together the situations most useful and favourable to the sense of the creatures themselves, the complications they would be most likely to produce and to feel.

"To arrive at these things is to arrive at my 'story'", he said,

> and that's the way I look for it. The result is that I'm often accused of not having "story" enough. I seem to myself to have as much as I need—to show my people, to exhibit their relations with each other; for that is all my measure. If I watch them long enough I see them come together, I see them *placed*, I see them engaged in this or that act and in this or that difficulty. How they look and move and speak and behave, always in the setting I have found for them, is my account of them—of which I dare say, alas, *que cela manque souvent d'architecture*. But I would rather, I think, have too little architecture than too much—when there's danger of its interfering with my measure of the truth. The French of course like more of it than I give—having by their own genius such a hand for it; and indeed one must give all one can. As for the origin of one's wind-blown germs themselves, who shall say, as you ask, where *they* come from? We have to go too far back, too far behind, to say. Isn't it all we can say that they come from every quarter of heaven, that they are *there* at almost any turn of the road? They accumulate, and we are always picking them over, selecting among them. They are the breath of life—by which I mean that life, in its own way, breathes them upon us. They are so, in a manner prescribed and imposed—floated into our minds by the current of life. That reduces to imbecility the vain critic's quarrel, so often, with one's subject, when he hasn't the wit to accept it. Will he point out then which other it should properly have been?—his office being, essentially *to* point out. *Il en serait bien embarrassé*. Ah, when he points out what I've done or failed to do with it, that's another matter: there he's on his ground. I give him up my "architecture,"

my distinguished friend concluded, "as much as he will."

So this beautiful genius, and I recall with comfort the gratitude I drew from his reference to the intensity of suggestion that may reside in the stray figure, the unattached character, the image *en disponibilité*. It gave me higher warrant than I seemed then to have met for just that blest habit of one's own imagination, the trick of investing some conceived or encountered individual, some brace or group of individuals, with the germinal property and authority. I was myself so much more antecedently conscious of my figures than of their setting—a too preliminary, a preferential interest in which struck me as in general such a putting of the cart before the horse. I might envy, though I couldn't emulate, the imaginative writer so constituted as to see his fable first and to make out its agents afterwards: I could think so little of any fable that didn't need its agents positively to launch it; I could think so little of any situation that didn't depend for its interest on the nature of the persons situated, and thereby on their way of taking it. There are methods of so-called presentation, I believe—among novelists who have appeared to flourish—that offer the situation as indifferent to that support; but I have not lost the sense of the value for me, at the time, of the admirable Russian's testimony to my not needing, all superstitiously, to try and perform any such gymnastic. Other echoes from the same source linger with me, I confess, as unfadingly—if it be not all indeed one much-embracing echo. It was impossible after that not to read, for one's uses, high lucidity into the tormented and disfigured and bemuddled question of the objective value, and even quite into that of the critical appreciation, of "subject" in the novel.

One had had from an early time, for that matter, the instinct of the right estimate of such values and of its reducing to the inane the dull dispute over the "immoral" subject and the moral, recognising so promptly the one measure of the worth of a given subject, the question about it that, rightly answered, disposes of all others—is it valid, in a word, is it genuine, is it sincere, the result of some direct impression or perception of life?—I had found small edification, mostly, in a critical pretension that had neglected from the first all delimitation of ground and all definition of terms. The air of my earlier time shows, to memory, as darkened, all round, with that vanity—unless the difference to-day be just in one's own final impatience, the lapse of one's attention. There is, I think, no more nutritive or suggestive truth in this connexion than that of the perfect dependence of the "moral" sense of a work of art on the amount of felt life concerned in producing it. The question comes back thus, obviously, to the kind and the degree of the artist's prime sensibility, which is the soil out of which his subject springs. The quality and capacity of that soil, its ability to "grow" with due freshness and straightness any vision of life, represents, strongly or weakly, the projected morality. That element is but another name for the more or less close connexion of the subject with some mark made on the intelligence, with some sincere experience. By which, at the same time, of course, one is far from contending that this enveloping air of the artist's humanity—which gives the last touch to the worth of the work—is not a widely and wondrously varying element; being on one occasion a rich and magnificent medium and on another a comparatively poor and ungenerous one. Here we get exactly the high price of the novel as a literary form—its power not only, while preserving that form with closeness, to range through all the differences of the individual relation to its general subject-matter, all the varieties of outlook on life, of disposition to reflect and project, created by conditions that are never the same from man to man (or, so far as that goes, from man to woman), but positively to appear more true to its character in proportion as it strains, or tends to burst, with a latent extravagance, its mould.

The house of fiction has in short not one window, but a million— number of possible windows not to be reckoned, rather; every one of which has been pierced, or is still pierceable, in its vast front, by the need of the individual vision and by the pressure of the individual will. These apertures, of dissimilar shape and size, hang so, all together, over the human scene that we might have expected of them a greater sameness of report than we find. They are but windows at the best, mere holes in a dead wall, disconnected, perched aloft; they are not hinged doors opening straight upon life. But they have this mark of their own that at each of them stands a figure with a pair of eyes, or at least with a field-glass, which forms, again and again, for observation, a unique instrument, insuring to the person making use of it an impression distinct from every other. He and his neighbours are watching the same show, but one seeing more where the other sees less, one seeing black where the other sees white, one seeing big where the other sees small, one seeing coarse where the other sees fine. And so on, and so on; there is fortunately no saying on what, for the particular pair of eyes, the window may *not* open; "fortunately" by reason, precisely, of this incalculability of range. The spreading field, the human scene, is the "choice of subject"; the pierced aperture, either broad or balconied or slit-like and low-browed, is the "literary form"; but they are, singly or together, as nothing without the posted presence of the watcher—without, in other words, the consciousness or the artist. Tell me what the artist is, and I will tell you of what he has *been* conscious. Thereby I shall express to you at once his boundless freedom and his "moral" reference.

All this is a long way round, however, for my word about my dim first move toward *The Portrait*, which was exactly my grasp of a single character—an acquisition I had made, moreover, after a fashion not here to be re-traced. Enough that I was, as seemed to me, in complete possession of it, that I had been so for a long time, that this had made it familiar and yet had not blurred its charm, and that, all urgently, all tormentingly, I saw it in motion and, so to speak, in transit. This amounts to saying that I saw it as bent upon its fate—some fate or other; *which*, among the possibilities, being precisely the question. Thus I had my vivid individual—vivid, so strangely, in spite of being still at large, not confined by the conditions, not engaged in the tangle, to which we look for much of the impress that constitutes an identity. If the apparition was still all to be placed how came it to be vivid?—since we puzzle such quantities out, mostly, just by the business of placing them. One could answer such a question beautifully, doubtless, if one could do so subtle, if not so monstrous, a thing as to write the history of the growth of one's imagination. One would describe then what, at a given time, had extraordinarily happened to it, and one would so, for instance, be in a position to tell, with an approach to clearness, how, under favour or occasion, it had been able to take over (take over straight from life) such and such a constituted, animated figure or form. The figure has to that extent, as you see, been placed—placed in the imagination that detains it, preserves, protects, enjoys it, conscious of its presence in the dusky, crowded, heterogeneous back-shop of the mind very much as a wary dealer in precious odds and ends, competent to make an "advance" on rare objects confided to him, is conscious of the rare little "piece" left in deposit by the reduced, mysterious lady of title or the speculative amateur, and which is already there to disclose its merit afresh as soon as a key shall have clicked in a cupboard-door.

That may be, I recognise, a somewhat superfine analogy for the particular "value." I here speak of the image of the young feminine nature that I had had for so considerable a time all curiously at my disposal; but it appears to fond memory quite to fit the fact—with the recall, in addition, of my pious desire but to place my treasure right. I quite remind myself thus of the dealer resigned not to "realise," resigned to keeping the precious object locked up indefinitely rather than commit it, at no matter what price, to vulgar hands, For there *are* dealers in these forms and figures and treasures capable of that refineme nt. The point is, however, that this single small cornerstone, the conception of a certain young woman affronting her destiny, had begun with being all my outfit for the large building of *The Portrait of a Lady*. It came to be a square and spacious house—or has at least seemed so to me in this going over it again; but, such as it is, it had to be put up round my young woman while she stood there in perfect isolation. That is to me, artistically speaking, the circumstance of interest; for I have lost myself once more, I confess, in the curiosity of analysing the structure. By what process of logical accretion was this slight "personality," the mere slim shade of an intelligent but presumptuous girl, to find itself endowed with the high attributes of a Subject?—and indeed by what thinness, at the best, would such a subject not be vitiated? Millions of presumptuous girls, intelligent or not intelligent, daily affront their destiny, and what is it open to their destiny to *be*, at the most, that we should make an ado about it? The novel is of its very nature an "ado," an ado about something, and the larger the form it takes the greater of course the ado. Therefore, consciously, that was what one was in for—for positively organising an ado about Isabel Archer.

One looked it well in the face, I seem to remember, this extravagance; and with the effect precisely of recognising the charm of the problem. Challenge any such problem with any intelligence, and you immediately see how full it is of substance; the wonder being, all the while, as we look at the world, how absolutely, how inordinately, the Isabel Archers, and even much smaller female fry, insist on mattering. George Eliot has admirably noted it—"In these frail vessels is borne onward through the ages the treasure of human affection." In *Romeo and Juliet* Juliet has to be important, just as, in *Adam Bede* and *The Mill on the Floss* and *Middlemarch* and *Daniel Deronda*, Hetty Sorrel and Maggie Tulliver and Rosamond Vincy and Gwendolen Harleth have to be; with that much of firm ground, that much of bracing air, at the disposal all the while of their feet and their lungs. They are typical, none the less, of a class difficult, in the individual case, to make a centre of interest; so difficult in fact that many an expert painter, as for instance Dickens and Walter Scott, as for instance even, in the main, so subtle a hand as that of R. L. Stevenson, has preferred to leave the task unattempted. There are in fact writers as to whom we make out that their refuge from this is to assume it to be not worth their attempting; by which pusillanimity in truth their honour is scantly saved. It is never an attestation of a value, or even of our imperfect sense of one, it is never a tribute to any truth at all, that we shall represent that value badly. It never makes up, artistically, for an artist's dim feeling about a thing that he shall "do" the thing as ill as possible. There are better ways than that, the best of all of which is to begin with less stupidity.

It may be answered meanwhile, in regard to Shakespeare's and to George Eliot's testimony, that their concession to the "importance" of their Juliets and Cleopatras and Portias (even with Portia as the very type and model of the young person intelligent and presumptuous) and to that of their Hettys and Maggies and Rosamonds and Gwendolens, suffers the abatement that these slimnesses are, when figuring as the main props of the theme, never suffered to be sole ministers of its appeal, but have their inadequacy eked out with comic relief and underplots, as the playwrights say, when not with murders and battles and the great mutations of the world. If they are shown as "mattering" as much as they could possibly pretend to, the proof of it is in a hundred other persons, made of much stouter stuff, and each involved moreover in a hundred relations which matter to *them* concomitantly with that one. Cleopatra matters, beyond bounds, to Antony, but his colleagues, his antagonists, the state or Rome and the impending battle also prodigiously matter; Portia matters to Antonio, and to Shylock, and to the Prince of Morocco, to the fifty aspiring princes, but for these gentry there are other lively concerns; for Antonio, notably, there are Shylock and Bassanio and his lost ventures and the extremity of his predicament. This extremity indeed, by the same token, matters to Portia—though its doing so becomes of interest all by the fact that Portia matters to *us*. That she does so, at any rate, and that almost everything comes round to it again, supports my contention as to this fine example of the value recognised in the mere young thing. (I say "mere" young thing because I guess that even Shakespeare, preoccupied mainly though he may have been with the passions of princes, would scarce have pretended to found the best of his appeal for her on her high social position.) It is an example exactly of the deep difficulty braved—the difficulty of making George Eliot's "frail vessel," if not the all-in-all for our attention, at least the clearest of the call.

Now to see deep difficulty braved is at any time, for the really addicted artist, to feel almost even as a pang the beautiful incentive, and to feel it verily in such sort as to wish the danger intensified. The difficulty most worth tackling can only be for him, in these conditions, the greatest the case permits of. So I remember feeling here (in presence, always, that is, of the particular uncertainty of my ground), that there would be one way better than another—oh, ever so much better than any other!—of making it fight out its battle. The frail vessel, that charged with George Eliot's "treasure," and thereby of such importance to those who curiously approach it, has likewise possibilities of importance to itself, possibilities which permit of treatment and in fact peculiarly require it from the moment they are considered at all. There is always the escape from any close account of the weak agent of such spells by using as a bridge for evasion, for retreat and flight, the view of her relation to those surrounding her. Make it predominantly a view of their relation and the trick is played: you give the general sense of her effect, and you give it, so far as the raising on it of a superstructure goes, with the maximum of ease. Well, I recall perfectly how little, in my now quite established connexion, the maximum of ease appealed to me, and how I seemed to get rid of it by an honest transposition of the weights in the two scales. "Place the centre of the subject in the young woman's own consciousness," I said to myself,

> and you could get as interesting and as beautiful a difficulty as you could wish. Stick to that—for the centre; put the heaviest weight into that scale, which will be so largely the scale of her relation to herself. Make her only interested enough, at the same time, in the things that are not herself, and this relation needn't fear to be too limited. Place meanwhile in the other scale the lighter weight (which is usually the one that tips the balance of interest): press least hard, in short, on the consciousness of your heroine's satellites, especially the male; make it an interest contributive only to the greater one. See, at all events, what can be done in this way. What better field could there be for a due ingenuity? The girl hovers, inextinguishable, as a charming creature, and the job will be to translate her into the highest terms of that formula, and as nearly as possible moreover into all of them. To depend upon her and her little concerns wholly to see you through will necessitate, remember, your really "doing" her.

So far I reasoned, and it took nothing less than that technical rigour, I now easily see, to inspire me with the right confidence for erecting on such a plot of ground the neat and careful and proportioned pile of bricks that arches over it and that was thus to form, constructionally speaking, a literary monument. Such is the aspect that to-day *The Portrait* wears for me: a structure reared with an "architectural" competence, as Turgenieff would have said, that makes it, to the author's own sense, the most proportioned of his productions after *The Ambassadors*—which was to follow it so many years later and which has, no doubt, a superior roundness. On one thing I was determined; that, though I should clearly have to pile brick upon brick for the creation of an interest, I would leave no pretext for saying that anything is out of line, scale or perspective. I would build large—in fine embossed vaults and painted arches, as who should say, and yet never let it appear that the chequered pavement, the ground under the reader's feet, fails to stretch at every point to the base of the walls. That precautionary spirit, on re-perusal of the book, is the old note that most touches me: it testifies so, for my own ear, to the anxiety of my provision for the reader's amusement. I felt, in view of the possible limitations of my subject, that no such provision could be excessive, and the development of the latter was simply the general form of that earnest quest. And I find indeed that this is the only account I can give myself of the evolution of the fable: it is all under the head thus named that I conceive the needful accretion as having taken place, the right complications as having started. It was naturally of the essence that the young woman should be herself complex; that was rudimentary—or was at any rate the light in which Isabel Archer had originally dawned. It went, however, but a certain way, and other lights, contending, conflicting lights, and of as many different colours, if possible, as the rockets, the Roman candles and Catherine-wheels of a "pyrotechnic display," would be employable to attest that she was. I had, no doubt, a groping instinct for the right complications, since I am quite unable to track the footsteps of those that constitute, as the case stands, the general situation exhibited. They are there, for what they are worth, and as numerous as might be; but my memory, I confess, is a blank as to how and whence they came.

I seem to myself to have waked up one morning in possession of them—of Ralph Touchett and his parents, of Madame Merle, of Gilbert Osmond and his daughter and his sister, of Lord Warburton, Caspar Goodwood and Miss Stackpole, the definite array of contributions to Isabel Archer's history. I recognised them, I knew them, they were the numbered pieces of my puzzle, the concrete terms of my "plot." It was as if they had simply, by an impulse of their own, floated into my ken, and all in response to my primary question: "Well, what will she do?" Their answer seemed to be that if I would trust them they would show me; on which, with an urgent appeal to them to make it at least as interesting as they could, I trusted them. They were like the group of attendants and entertainers who come down by train when people in the country give a party; they represented the contract for carrying the party on. That was an excellent relation with them—a possible one even with so broken a reed (from her slightness of cohesion) as Henrietta Stackpole. It is a familiar truth to the novelist, at the strenuous hour, that, as certain elements in any work are of the essence, so others are only of the form; that as this or that character, this or that disposition of the material, belongs to the subject directly, so to speak, so this or that other belongs to it but indirectly—belongs intimately to the treatment.

This is a truth, however, of which he rarely gets the benefit—since it could be assured to him, really, but by criticism based upon perception, criticism which is too little of this world. He must not think of benefits, moreover, I freely recognise, for that way dishonour lies: he has, that is, but one to think of—the benefit, whatever it may be, involved in his having cast a spell upon the simpler, the very simplest, forms of attention. This is all he is entitled to; he is entitled to nothing, he is bound to admit, that can come to him, from the reader, as a result on the latter's part of any act of reflection or discrimination. He may *enjoy* this finer tribute—that is another affair, but on condition only of taking it as a gratuity "thrown in," a mere miraculous windfall, the fruit of a tree he may not pretend to have shaken. Against reflection, against discrimination, in his interest, all earth and air conspire; wherefore it is that, as I say, he must in many a case have schooled himself, from the first, to work but for a "living wage." The living wage is the reader's grant of the least possible quantity of attention required for consciousness of a "spell." The occasional charming "tip" is an act of his intelligence over and beyond this, a golden apple, for the writer's lap, straight from the wind-stirred tree. The artist may of course, in wanton moods, dream of some Paradise (for Art) where the direct appeal to the intelligence might be legalised; for to such extravagances as these his yearning mind can scarce hope ever completely to close itself. The most he can do is to remember they *are* extravagances.

All of which is perhaps but a gracefully devious way of saying that Henrietta Stackpole was a good example, in *The Portrait*, of the truth to which I just adverted—as good an example as I could name were it not that Maria Gostrey, in *The Ambassadors*, then in the bosom of time, may be mentioned as a better. Each of these persons is but wheels to the coach; neither belongs to the body of that vehicle, or is for a moment accommodated with a seat inside. There the subject alone is ensconced, in the form of its "hero and heroine," and of the privileged high officials, say, who ride with the king and queen. There are reasons why one would have like this to be felt, in one's work, that one has one's self contributively felt. We have seen, however, how idle is that pretension, which I should be sorry to make too much of. Maria Gostrey and Miss Stackpole then are cases, each, of the light *ficelle*, not of the true agent; they may run beside the coach "for all they are worth," they may cling to it till they are out of breath (as poor Miss Stackpole all so visibly does), but neither ceases for a moment to tread the dusty road. Put it even that they are like the fishwives who helped to bring back to Paris from Versailles, on that most ominous day of the first half of the French Revolution, the carriage of the royal family. The only thing is that I may well be asked, I acknowledge, why then, in the present fiction, I have suffered Henrietta (of whom we have indubitably too much) so officiously, so strangely, so almost inexplicably, to pervade. I will presently say what I can for that anomaly and in the most conciliatory fashion.

A point I wish still more to make is that if my relation of confidence with the actors m my drama who *were*, unlike Miss Stackpole, true agents, was an excellent one to have arrived at, there still remained my relation with the reader, which was another affair altogether and as to which I felt no one to be trusted but myself. That solicitude was to be accordingly expressed in the artful patience with which, as I have said, I piled brick upon brick. The bricks for the whole counting-over—putting for bricks little touches and inventions and enhancements by the way—affect me in truth as wellnigh innumerable and as ever so scrupulously fitted together and packed in. It is an effect of detail of the minutest; though, if one were in this connection to say all, one would express the hope that the general the ampler air of the modest monument still survives. I do at least seem to catch the key to a part of this abundance of small anxious, ingenious illustration as I recollect putting my finger, in my young woman's interest on the most obvious of her predicates.

> What will she "do"? Why, the first thing she'll do will be to come to Europe; which in fact will form, and all inevitably, no small part of her principal adventure. Coming to Europe is even for the "frail vessels," in this wonderful age, a mild adventure; but what is truer than that on one side—the side of their independence of flood and field, of the moving accident, of battle and murder and sudden death— her adventures are to be mild? Without her sense of them, her sense *for* them, as one may say, they but are next to nothing at all; but isn't the beauty and the difficulty just in showing their mystic conversion by that sense, conversion into the stuff of drama or, even more delightful word still, of "Story"?

It was all as clear, my contention as a silver bell. Two very good instances, I think of this effect of conversion, two cases of the rare chemistry, are the pages in which Isabel, coming into the drawing-room at Gardencourt, coming in from a wet walk or whatever, that rainy afternoon, finds Madame Merle in possession of the place, Madam Merle seated, all absorbed but all serene, at the piano, and deeply recognises, in the striking of such an hour, in the presence there, among the gathering shades, of this personage, of whom a moment before she had never so much as heard, a turning-point in her life. It is dreadful to have too much, for any artistic demonstration, to dot one's i's and insist on one's intentions, and I am not eager to do it now; but the question here was that of producing the maximum of interest with the minimum of strain.

The interest was to be raised to its pitch and yet the elements to be kept in their key; so that, should the whole thing duly impress, I might show what an "exciting" inward life may do for the person leading it even while it remains perfectly normal. And I cannot think of a more consistent application of that ideal unless it be in the long statement, just beyond the middle of the book, of my young woman's extraordinary meditative vigil on the occasion that was to become for her such a landmark. Reduced to its essence, it is but the vigil of searching criticism; but it throws the action further forward than twenty "incidents" might have done. It was designed to have all the vivacity of incident and all the economy of picture. She sits up, by her dying fire, far into the night, under the spell of recognitions on which she finds the last sharpness suddenly wait. It is a representation simply of her motionless *seeing*, and an attempt withal to make the mere still lucidity of her act as "interesting" as the surprise of a caravan or the identification of a pirate. It represents, for that matter, one of the identifications dear to the novelist, and even indispensable to him; but it all goes on without her being approached by another person and without her leaving her chair. It is obviously the best thing in the book, but it is only a supreme illustration of the general plan. As to Henrietta, my apology for whom I just left incomplete, she exemplifies, I fear, in her superabundance, not an element of my plan, but only an excess of my zeal. So early was to begin my tendency to *overtreat*, rather than undertreat (when there was choice or danger) my subject. (Many members of my craft, I gather, are far from agreeing with me, but I have always held overtreating the minor disservice.) "Treating" that of *The Portrait* amounted to never forgetting, by any lapse, that the thing was under a special obligation to be amusing. There was the danger of the noted "thinness"—which was to be averted, tooth and nail, by cultivation of the lively. That is at least how I see it to-day. Henrietta must have been at that time a part of my wonderful notion of the lively. And then there was another matter. I had, within the few preceding years, come to live in London, and the "international" light lay, in those days, to my sense, thick and rich upon the scene. It was the light in which so much of the picture hung. But that is another matter. There is really too much to say.

VI. Critics on the American Novel

·≫·87·≪·

The Didactic and the Sentimental

LILLIE DEMING LOSHE

In an informative history of early American precursors of the great nineteenth-century novelists, Loshe acknowledges the debt of many American writers to the English tradition and particularly to the novels of Richardson. Like their British counterparts, American novelists generally defined the goals of the novel as moralistic and didactic. After the American Revolution, however, the Puritan distrust of the novel was weakened by a new colonial spirit, and a number of female novelists published largely sentimental works in the last decade of the eighteenth century. The first American novel is generally agreed to be Sarah Wentworth Morton's *The Power of Sympathy* in 1789. This was followed by Susanna Haswell Rowson's *Charlotte Temple*, published in London in 1790 and in the United States in 1794. The other successful novel of the period was Hannah Webster Foster's *The Coquette* (1797). Loshe discusses the importance of the *Massachusetts Magazine*, a journal that serialized a number of quasi-novels mainly by women. Concurrent with the didactic and sentimental traditions in the novel was the less frequent romantic tradition in which novelists aimed principally for adventure and amusement. The last genres to achieve a large readership were the educational tales represented by Reverend Enos Hitchcock, the Quixote-influenced satire practiced by Hugh Henry Brackenridge, and the adventurous travel novel by, among others, Royall Tyler. Loshe concludes that these early American novelists ultimately failed to distinguish themselves from their British mentors in spite of assertions of independence.

When the Revolution made a conscious separation between American and English literature, America had already developed a considerable literary activity. Among the fruits of this incipient literary culture were a mass of religious writing, much verse, some history, a few attempts at drama, and a large amount of political and controversial writing. The *genre* most noticeably absent from this list is

Source: Lillie Deming Loshe, "The Didactic and the Sentimental", *The Early American Novel*, New York: Columbia University Press, 1907, Chapter 1, pp. 1-28.

the novel. Colonial America had produced no novelist, although in England the great novels of the century had long been written. In view of the active interest shown in poetry and the drama, such apparent neglect of a prevailing literary fashion cannot be attributed to lack of literary ambition and effort. Its causes are rather to be sought in two important aspects of early American culture,—the surviving Puritan spirit, and the colonial spirit.

The Puritan attitude toward the lighter forms of literature is too well known to need discussion here. Its survival is evident in the words of Timothy Dwight, whose taste for poetry, and music, and other unpuritanical joys could not reconcile him to the sudden development of fiction which took place in his day. "Between the Bible and novels there is a gulf fixed," he says,[1]

> which few novel readers are willing to pass. The consciousness of virtue, the dignified pleasure of having performed one's duty, the serene remembrance of a useful life, the hope of an interest in the Redeemer, and the promise of a glorious inheritance in the favor of God are never found in novels.

The novelists of the earlier period in America show, in their prefaces, a nervous consciousness of the possibility of such censure, and endeavor to forestall it by showing that they are not as other novelists—that their works are calculated, not to mislead, but to direct, the young mind. The Reverend Enos Hitchcock, one of our earliest writers of fiction, and, like Timothy Dwight, a Revolutionary chaplain, makes his heroine utter the warning[2]—"Nothing can have a worse effect on the mind of our sex than the free use of those writings which are the offspring of modern novelists." The same dread of the pernicious effects of novel reading appears in Mrs Foster, Mrs Rowson, and the other literary ladies who were our first novelists.

Puritanism, of course, did not control the opinions of the whole country. More general was the colonial spirit, under whose influence Americans looked to England as their mother country, gave their sons an English education, whenever possible, and sought in English manners a model for their own. Readers filled with such a spirit naturally satisfied their taste for fiction with the stories of English life which constant traffic and intercourse made accessible.

This spirit of filial acceptance could not survive the Revolution. When the confusion of war had had time to subside, thoughtful people, gazing with a pardonable complacency on what they had already accomplished, decided that thereafter manners and letters, as well as laws, should be home-made. "We have already," said the Reverend Enos Hitchcock, "suffered by too great an avidity for British customs and manners, it is now time to become independent in our maxims, principles of education, dress, and manners, as we are in our laws and government."[3] Ardent patriots at once applied themselves to the task of supplying a literature which should reflect American manners. Thus the new spirit of national self-consciousness united with the unbending of the Puritan spirit to make the last decade of the eighteenth century one of novel writing, as well as of novel reading. Royall Tyler, in the preface to his *Algerine Captive*,[4] published in 1797, illustrates both the changed attitude toward the reading of fiction and the demand for a novel of native manners.

One of the first observations the author of the following sheets made upon his return to his native country, after an absence of seven years, was the extreme avidity with which books of mere amusement were purchased and perused by his countrymen. When he left New England, books of biography, travels, and modern romances were confined to our seaports; or if known in the country were read only in the families of clergymen, physicians, and lawyers; while certain funeral discourses, the last words and dying speeches of Bryan Shaheen and Levi Ames, and some dreary somebody's day of Doom, formed the most diverting parts of the farmer's library.

When he returned, however, he found that libraries and book-sellers had filled the land with

modern travels and novels almost as incredible....No sooner was a taste for amusing literature diffused, than all orders of country life with one accord forsook the sober sermons and practical pieties of their fathers for the gay stories and splendid impieties of the traveller and the novelist. The worthy farmer no longer fatigued himself with Bunyan's Pilgrims up the hill of difficulty . . . but quaffed wine with Brydone in the hermitage of Vesuvius, or sported with Bruce in the fairy land of Abyssinia.

The dairymaid and the hired man, he says, no longer wept over the ballad of the cruel step-mother, but amused themselves into an agreeable terror with the haunted houses and hobgoblins of Mrs Radcliffe.

Two things, however, the author finds to be deplored.

The first is that while so many books are vended they are not of our own manufacture[5] . . . The second misfortune is that, novels being the picture of the time, the New England reader is insensibly taught to admire the levity, and often the vices, of the mother country . . . .If the English novel does not inculcate vice, it at least impresses on the young mind an erroneous idea of the world in which she is to live. It paints the manners, customs, and habits of a strange country; excites a fondness for false splendors; and renders the habits of her own country disgusting. "There are two things wanted," said a friend to the author, "that we write our own books of amusement and that they exhibit our own manners."

Tyler's own tale was to "display a portrait of New England manners hitherto unattempted."

To English novelists, however, the aspiring authors looked for models. *Humphrey Clinker*, the last book of any of the great novelists of the century, had been published in 1771. Between its publication and that of the first American novel in 1789 only one novel of real merit had appeared—Fanny Burney's *Evelina* in 1781. The production of novels in this period, however, had been astonishing in quantity. The hopelessness of any attempt to characterize this mass of fiction, or to classify it according to influences, is pleasantly illustrated by the fact that Mr Raleigh[6] describes Robert Bage as coming nearest of all imitators to Richardson, while Mr, Saintsbury[7] finds in him an imitator of Fielding and Smollett with the addition of a deliberately immoral purpose, and Mr Cross[8] says that Bage had "posed in literature as a second Sterne." Certain types and characteristic themes can, nevertheless, be distinguished among the countless "memoirs," "histories," "adventures," "domestic stories," "sacred novels," and "tales of real life," written by "ladies of quality," "ladies of distinction," "sons of Neptune," and assumers of other elegant aliases.

The various adventures are usually strings of incidents, so far beyond the scope of one man's possible experience that they are assigned to some object easily capable of passing from one hand to another, such as a guinea, a shilling, a gold-headed cane, or a lap-dog. The purpose of these is satirical, and this intention is shared by the various Quixotes, the female Quixote, the spiritual Quixote, the benevolent Quixote, the infernal Quixote, and the like.

The various histories, domestic stories, and tales of real life, of every degree of romance and realism, of every condition of life from the cottage to the castle, have elements inherited from their great predecessors. The influence of Richardson persists rather in subject than in manner. He has contributed the fascination exerted by tales of seduction, as Fielding has given the nobly devoted wife, who becomes one of the stock figures of the domestic tale. But, while Fielding merely left the character of his Booth somewhat colorless in order that the virtues of his Amelia might shine more brightly, later writers, craving more vivid contrasts, painted the unfortunate marital background a sooty black. The influence of Sterne, which seems generally to be filtered through Mackenzie, is present in forms varying from a melting sensibility, "a dropping of warm tears," if one may borrow that phrase, to a scarcely perceptible humidity of atmosphere. Of these three influences that of Fielding is the least felt, in part, perhaps, because it is the least easy to detect, but more decidedly because the first requisite for a novelist at this time seems to have been the entire absence of any sense of humor.

The favorite ingredients of these tales are a lovely and gifted heroine, a devoted wife and mother with a brutal and vicious husband, or a vain and negligent mother, whose kind and pious spouse expires early in the first volume leaving his daughter without a protector, a heartless relative or guardian, preferably an aunt, a confidante who is usually, as one of them describes herself, "a sprightly toad," a virtuous hero, a designing villain, and one or two faithful retainers. Many of these tales can be reduced to the trials of a helpless maiden, consequent upon ill-treatment by an unfeeling relative. The alluring simplicity of this formula, and its infinite possibilities of variation, commended it to the many aspiring novelists of the day. It supplied, in particular, a theme to the women novelists whose band had grown in numbers and prosperity[9] since Smollett had said of novel-writing:

> That branch of business is now engrossed by female authors who publish merely for the propagation of virtue, with so much ease, and spirit, and delicacy, and knowledge of the human heart, and all in the serene tranquillity of high life, that the reader is not only enchanted by their genius but reformed by their morality.[10]

Although these conventional themes and personages were most abundant in the novels of the century's last three decades, other elements were then entering fiction. The growing spirit of romanticism is seen not only in the more romantic situations of these tales, exemplified in Mrs Bennett's melodrama *De Valcourt*, but in the popularity of other forms, the oriental tale and apologue, the educational romance inspired by Rousseau, and the educational tales for the edification of the young, influenced by Madame de Genlis, of which the classic example is *Sandford and Merton*.

Toward the end of the period the pseudo-historical novel and the tale of terror flourished side by side. French and German fiction, in part through Holcroft's translations, reached English readers, and the "heroine in the Kotzebue taste," so displeasing to Miss Edgeworth, was introduced to the Ellens, Emmelines, and Elizas of the "female novelists."

It is to these female novelists, rather than to the great writers who preceded them or to the more dignified schools of Gothic, historical, and revolutionary fiction which filled the last decade of the century, that we owe our first novelists. The women who wrote fiction in England had, for the most part, little power of construction and less of character-drawing; their stories were encumbered by "episodes" without organic relation to the plot; and their style was often both essentially weak and disfigured by Della Cruscan ornamentation. Their experience of life was apparently small, their invention limited to new combinations of well-worn situations and personages. It was scarcely to be expected that their sisters and heirs, the first American novelists, should produce works of enduring literary merit.

Didacticism and sentimentality were the chief characteristics of the British novel in the period immediately preceding the vogue of the Gothic. Naturally the same moods and purposes appear in the first American novels,[11] most of which, like their British models, were the work of women. The writings of these women fall into two groups: the first of which includes the more directly didactic tales, whose authors proclaim their moral purpose, while the second consists of stories more romantic in spirit, describing sentimental vicissitudes for their own sake, rather than for the moral lessons they suggest. Slightly different influences appear in the few men who wrote novels before Charles Brockden Brown. But their work is so usually didactic in purpose, and so frequently sentimental in tone, that it may conveniently be considered in connection with that of the more numerous women novelists who represent sentimental didacticism in its most typical form.

The first to attempt the moral regeneration of the youth of America, through the persuasive art of fiction, was the New England poetess, Mrs Sarah Wentworth Morton.[12] She had observed that "didactic essays are not always capable of engaging the attention of young ladies. We fly from the laboured precepts of the essayist to the sprightly narrative of the novelist." Mrs Morton was doubtless supported in the undertaking by the consciousness of an established literary reputation.[13] Her poems earned for her the title of "the American Sappho." To her novel, *The Power of Sympathy*, she prefixed a solemn dedication to the young ladies of Columbia, which the printer, perceiving the greatness of the occasion, adorned with eleven different kinds and sizes of type. Her preface proclaims the purpose of the work "to expose the dangerous Consequences of Seduction and to set forth the advantages of female Education."

The story itself is more easily described by showing what it is intended to be than by trying to explain what it is. The personages of the tragedy obviously belong to types monotonously familiar in the fiction of the time. The lovely injured heroine is present in the person of Harriet Fawcet; Myra Harrington is the playful but warm-hearted confidante, Mrs Francis, with whom Harriet lives as companion, the unfeeling relative, and Worthy is the sensible friend of the volatile hero. This hero, Harrington, originally intended for a gay young Lovelace, says of himself, at the outset of the narrative, that the moralist and the amoroso, sentiment and sensibility, are so interwoven in his constitution that "nature and grace are at continual fisticuffs." One glance of Harriet's eye, however, ends forever both the fisticuffs and his designs upon her peace of mind. Thereafter he exhibits, in happy combination, the thrilling sensibility of a Marianne Dashwood, with the erudite morality of a Mary Bennett. Animated by the spirit of the latter, he says of a dance to which he is to accompany Harriet: "These elegant relaxations prevent the degeneracy of human nature, exhilarate the spirits, and wind up this machine of ours for another revolution of business." Harriet and Harrington are at once betrothed, and the author is at liberty to turn to the real object of the work, sentimental and moral discussions of education, literature, and manners, with emphasis on the consequences of seduction, and anecdotes to point the moral. These discussions are carried on under the auspices of Mrs Holmes, a "serious sentimentalist," devoted to rural retirement, who sits in one of the "temple" summer-houses dear to the "elegant female" of the eighteenth century, quoting Sterne and moralizing. Her part, that of the middle-aged patroness and adviser, is consistently carried out. After Mrs Morton has preached her sermon, she enforces its precepts by the fate of her lovers. When Harrington insists on marrying Harriet, in spite of paternal opposition, his conscience-stricken father confesses that Harriet is his sister. Harriet dies of a broken heart, in a lingering, graceful manner. A few days later Harrington is found slain by his own hand. On his table, beside his last will and testament, lies *The Sorrows of Werther*.[14]

The story is without construction or attempt at characterization. Its sentiment, a tepid infusion of Sterne, may be judged from Worthy's tribute to Myra's sampler:

> "It is the work of Myra," said I to myself. "Did not her fingers trace these beautiful expanding flowers? Did she not give to this carnation its animated glow, and to this opening rose its languishing grace? Removed, as I am," continued I, in a certain interior language that every son of nature possesses—"Removed as I am, from the amiable object of my tenderest affection, I have nothing to do but admire this offspring of industry and art. It shall yield more fragrance to my soul than all the boquets in the universe."

Of the many passages of attempted poetical style, the most elaborate are a Dante-inspired vision of the lower world shown to the guilty father, and the history of Fidelia, a pink-ribboned New England Ophelia, whose morbid interest in the brook is justified by the fact that her lover once drowned himself in it. Poems are also inserted in the text, a practice common in that period and particularly acceptable to Mrs Morton who had been a poet before she became a novel writer. One extract from Harrington's epitaph, composed by himself, may illustrate the gift of the American Sappho.

> *When on their urn celestial care descends,*
> *Two lovers come, whom fair success attends,*
> *O'er the pale marble shall they join their heads,*
> *And drink the falling tears each other sheds,*

Then sadly say, with mutual pity mov'd,
O! may we never love as these have loved.

Mrs Susanna Haswell Rowson, whose most successful novel, *Charlotte Temple*, was published in 1790, had a more eventful career than Mrs Morton. She was born in England, in 1762, but was brought to America four years later when her father, a naval officer on the American station, married an American lady, was retired, and settled at Nantasket. The hardships of the voyage were later described in *Rebecca*. The quiet life of the Haswell family was interrupted by the Revolutionary War. Mr Haswell would not serve against the king, and consequently was regarded as a suspicious person, whose situation would make it easy for him to aid the king's ships. After some harrowing adventures, which appear in *Rebecca* the Haswells were ordered to remove to Hingham, and the next year to Abington. Later they were allowed to go to Halifax, and thence to England.

In London Susanna's trials really began. To help in the struggle for maintenance, she became a governess. In 1786 she married, to please her family, her father's friend, William Rowson, who combined the activities of a hardware merchant with those of a trumpeter in the Royal Horse Guards. Mrs Rowson's opinion of matrimony was never enthusiastically favorable. Nason, her biographer, sensibly observes that the warning prefixed to her *Sarah, or the Exemplary Wife*, "do not marry a fool," was probably the result of experience.[15]

In 1793, Mr Rowson's business having completely failed, the stage was tried as a last resort. The Rowson family, consisting of Mr and Mrs Rowson and a young sister of the former, appeared in the provinces for a season, apparently with no remarkable success, and were glad to obtain an engagement at the Chestnut Street Theater in Philadelphia. This brought Mrs Rowson back to America where the rest of her life was spent. From 1793 to 1797 the Rowsons remained on the stage. During these years Mrs Rowson, who had already published several novels, became a playwright as well as an actress.[16]

In Boston, in 1797, Mrs Rowson began what was destined to be a long and illustrious pedagogical career, with a school containing one pupil. By the end of the year she had a hundred scholars and a waiting list; "yet," her biographer exclaims with pardonable pride, "she suffered not the ink to dry upon her graceful pen." For the rest of her life she enjoyed a long-delayed prosperity. Her literary reputation made her the center of a group of learned ladies. In 1802 she became the editor of a new periodical, the *Boston Weekly Magazine*. Three years later this was superseded by the *Monthly Anthology*, to which she was a frequent contributor. To the *New England Galaxy*, started in 1815, she made contributions of a religious character. The most important of her works in prose were a series of papers modelled on the *Spectator*, and a serial novel, *Sincerity*, published, in 1813, as *Sarah, or the Exemplary Wife*. In 1804 her miscellaneous poems were published. She wrote much occasional verse, many recitations for the use of her scholars,[17] and some educational works in prose.[18] She died in 1824.

Mrs Rowson's career as a novelist began in the year of her marriage. Her first novel *Victoria* appeared in 1786, followed the next year by *Mary, or the Test of*

Honour, and in 1788 by *The Inquisitor, or the Invisible Rambler*. In 1790 *Charlotte Temple* was published. *Mentoria, or the Young Ladies Friend* (1791) embodied some of Mrs Rowson's own experiences as a governess. Soon after appeared *Rebecca, or the Fille de Chambre*.

The earliest of Mrs Rowson's works accessible in an American edition is *The Inquisitor or the Invisible Rambler*, professedly in the manner of Sterne. Mrs Rowson, however, possessed little sentiment and no humor. The *Inquisitor*, her would-be sentimentalist, whose beneficent undertakings are furthered by a magic ring, suggests the able and efficient agent of a charity organization society. Indeed so admirable is his economy of effort, that if he rescues a betrayed and forsaken maiden, she is sure to be the long lost daughter of the penniless old soldier whom he had saved from insult the week before.

Charlotte Temple, a Tale of Truth (London, 1790, New York, 1794), established Mrs Rowson's reputation, and still maintains it, although among a somewhat different class of readers. It is the story of a young girl, Charlotte Temple, or Stanley, who is lured away from a boarding school by a young officer and a wicked French governess, taken to New York, and abandoned to die in misery. Nothing that can heighten the sensational effect is spared,—two of the very blackest villains obtainable are employed to bring about the catastrophe. The question at once suggests itself—why should this story have survived, to linger out a dishonored old age in yellow paper covers, when all its equally harrowing contemporaries have long been forgotten? The answer lies in Mrs Rowson's undeniable command of the sensational, and in the comparative simplicity and directness of the story itself.[19] There are many such tales, treated merely as episodes in Mrs Rowson's other novels, which, if worked out separately with the same brevity and workmanlike construction, might have won the same reputation.

Lucy Temple, or the Three Orphans is the story of Charlotte's daughter. As Lucy Blakeney, she has been brought up in ignorance of her mother's history. She is about to marry a young man named Franklin when it is discovered, as in *The Power of Sympathy*, that he is the son of her mother's betrayer. The more practical bent of Mrs Rowson appears in Lucy's decision to found a school instead of dying of a broken heart. The general tone of the novel is educational, in contrast to the pure sensationalism of *Charlotte*.

The Trials of the Human Heart (1795) is best described in the definition of a novel[20] given by the translator of Alexis, "a concatenation of events which taken separately will be worthy of belief." In its four volumes horrors worthy of the tragedy of blood are seen domesticated in London. Mrs Rowson's sensationalism differs from that of most of her contemporaries—from that of Mrs Bennett for example—in its complete lack of romance. Her theme here, as in *Rebecca* and in *Sarah*, is the bitter struggle of a poor and friendless woman to maintain herself in a world in which her beauty and accomplishments are only added dangers. Meriel, the heroine, after years of vicissitudes, individually conceived with some crude force, but collectively incredible because of their number, emerges from the ordeal, apparently with not a curl displaced, to marry her first love.

In the choice of her horrors, and in the presentation of them, Mrs Rowson is essentially a realist,[21] whose trick of giving vividness by touches of homely detail was probably learned from Richardson, who got it from Defoe. The description of the room furnished for Meriel by her benefactor, with its tent-bedstead and its box containing a piece of grey lutestring, and two pieces of dark chintz enough for a gown, and a piece of fine linen, resembles one of Pamela's conscientious catalogues. This crude realism of situation, without any corresponding truth of character, has given Mrs Rowson a high place among successful exploiters of domestic melodrama, and it separates her didactic sensationalism from the more politely imaginative world of her "female" contemporaries.

Similar in its moral aim to *The Power of Sympathy* and *Charlotte Temple*, Mrs Hannah Webster Foster's[22] *The Coquette* (1797) has neither the extreme sentimentality of Mrs Morton nor the sensationalism of Mrs Rowson. Like *Charlotte* it is founded on fact, on the unfortunate story of a connection of the Foster family.[23] It is superior to its predecessors in interest and especially in character-drawing; the personages are individuals not types, speaking well in character, in letters as vivacious as the epistolary conventions of the time would allow. Some development can be traced in the character of the heroine, while the catastrophe is kept well in mind from the first. The virtuous hero is not represented as absolutely impeccable—although neither the heroine nor the author quite grasps the fact that he is an estimable prig—and the villain is allowed his softer side.

Of all the tales of these women novelists, *The Coquette* remains the most readable, and preserves a faded appeal to the sympathies of a public which has lost its taste for tragedy in letters. Early in the nineteenth century *The Coquette's* popularity rivalled that of *Charlotte*. Many editions were bought and wept over,[24] and a reprint was made as late as 1874.

Another example of the elegantly edifying type of fiction is Caroline Matilda Warren's novel, *The Gamesters; or, Ruins of Innocence* (1805). Presented to the public, the author says, "not as the labored production of erudition, but as the efforts of a mind rather of a contemplative turn, whose principal amusement is derived from such pursuits," it is, as the title indicates, directed against the evil of gambling. In addition to this main theme it points many other morals, and consequently has a more complicated action than *The Power of Sympathy* or *The Coquette*. Mrs Warren makes some parade of her acquaintance with "polite authors," among whom it is a pleasure to find Shakespeare, and she seems to have had a fondness for the study of physiognomy inspired by Lavater. In a suicide scene there is the novelty of substituting Addison's *Cato* for the usual *Werther* opened at an appropriate passage. Another innovation is the introduction of Tom Tarpaulin, "an honest son of Neptune," and his sweetheart Peggy. Otherwise there is little that is new in this attempt to "blend instruction with amusement, and at once to regale the imagination, and reform the heart."

More didactic, even pedagogic in intention, are two novels by Helena Wells, whose books were published in London. On the title page of *The Stepmother*,[25] the author is described as "of Charlestown, South Carolina," both *The Stepmother*

(1799) and *Constantia Neville, or the West Indian* (1800) went into second editions soon after their publication. Their aim, as stated in the preface to *The Stepmother*, "by pointing out the superior advantages of a religious education, is to counteract the pernicious tendency of modern philosophy," and to check the prevailing taste for "the marvellous and the terrible."

In a somewhat later work by Rebecca Rush, *Kelroy* (1812), the didactic novel, while retaining its moralizing tone, shows the influence of the novel of social manners. *Kelroy* owes, perhaps, to its later date, its comparative freedom from the naive absurdities of many of its predecessors. Its style also, while still studied, has lost the excessive "elegance" of diction characteristic of Mrs Morton's time.

One can hardly leave the subject of sentimental didacticism without referring to the *Massachusetts Magazine*, which was its shrine. Here the gifted ladies of Mrs Morton's circle were sure of a welcome. The editor sometimes spoke sharply, in his acknowledgments to patrons and correspondents, of contributions from manly hands; but all ladies were received with a sugared politeness. Mrs Morton, under her poetical name of Philenia, was referred to as "the Daughter of Genius—the Queen of elegance in thought and word and deed." Another lady, known as "Sabina," had contributed the history of a woman carried off by pirates to the harem of a Turkish noble, where her instructions led to the liberation of all the slaves. In recompense she received this editorial tribute:

> Sabina, authoress of *Louisa*, an interesting novel, is sincerely thanked for a momentary renunciation of domestick labours. Her sex, her country, and mankind at large have reason to acknowledge their obligation to the virtuous fair, who divide their time between family economy and the dissemination of universal instruction.

Long serial stories, except for occasional translations, are rare in periodicals before 1800, although many tales run through two or three issues. The space given to fiction, which in the *Massachusetts Magazine* is large, is occupied by various forerunners of the short story, the character, the anecdote, the apologue, and the condensed novel. The Oriental tale was the most favored of all types, and no issue of the *Massachusetts Magazine* was complete without one; very few, however, were of American origin. In original work this magazine made a specialty of "historiettes," tragic, sentimental, or amusing. Pastorals and bits of prose poetry were favorite efforts of the fair contributors, perhaps a touching scene from a projected novel. One of the most moving of these pastoral productions is *Fidele, or the Faithful Shepherd*, which appeared in 1791, signed by "Caloc." The Shepherd Fidele loves Zephyra; Almira, a town beauty, sees Fidele and falls into a decline for love of him. Her parents send for the shepherd, but he is already pledged to Zephyra. "His sensibility was too exquisite. The news of Almira's gradual decline preyed heavily on a slender constitution. Zephyra caught the weakening contagion, and three celestial spirits languished into life together." The mistress of this branch of poetic prose was "Lavinia." Other contributors were Laurinda, Alouette, Menander, Evander, and Lindor.

So much of this magazine work is left unsigned, so little scruple is felt at borrowing from foreign sources, or from one American magazine to another, that a formidable tangle of possible authorships awaits any venturesome person who may undertake to investigate the early American short story, or its forerunners. Although the *Massachusetts Magazine* virtuously declared that "all pieces which have been published in any other vehicle than the *Massachusetts Magazine* we deem *antique* composition," others did not share its fastidiousness; indeed the *New York Magazine* seems to have used its New England contemporary as a regular source of supply, and even paid it the compliment of reprinting one story twice under different titles.

While the didactic sentimentality of Mrs Morton, Mrs Foster, and other Massachusetts ladies is the most striking feature of early American novel writing, other types, both of didacticism and of sentimentality, are to be found among the novelist of the day. The educational, the religious, and the satirical varieties of didacticism all are present. Consideration of these, however, may be postponed to that of the other variety of novel popular among the women writers of the last decade of the eighteenth century and the first of the nineteenth—the tale similar in quality of sentiment to those already discussed, but romantic where they are didactic, and aiming to amuse rather than to instruct.

This more romantic and less deliberately edifying type of female fiction[26] is well represented by *The Hapless Orphan, or Innocent Victim of Revenge*, "By an American lady" (1793). The orphan is a lovely and defenceless creature, afflicted with a hard-hearted relative,—a situation popular in the fiction of the time. This relative, an aunt, although "for her own child all the feelings of a parental bosom vegetated in luxuriance," is so unkind to the niece that the unfortunate Caroline is forced to seek another home. Hence arise all her difficulties, for at Princeton, whither she has fled, she falls in love with the miniature of a charming youth already betrothed to another, the jealous Eliza. At the tender moment when the youth, on his knee, is presenting to Caroline a locket adorned with a figure of Hope, and two doves drinking from a fountain, elegantly done in hair-work, which, he assures her, is his own "performance," the lovers are discovered by Eliza. After the suicide of the too attractive youth the frantic Eliza vows vengeance. Thenceforth Caroline is hounded by every conceivable persecution,—pursuit by masked villains, by men in women's garments, slander, purloining of letters, attempted abduction, and more elaborate machinations affecting even the happiness of her friends, and successfully poisoning against her the mind of her betrothed who is at a distance fighting Indians.

The unreality of the tale is heightened by the absurd juxtaposition of blood-curdling plots, harrowing escapes, and prim discourses full of the self-centered, calculating common-sense which makes Caroline a true child of her century. "I had long established it a maxim of prudence and a dictate of reason," she says, "to make as easy as possible the various incidents which occur in this journey of life." Even when most occupied in foiling villains, she finds leisure for discourses on the necessity of education, and gentle Pamela-like moralizings, "Death, my dear Maria, is a serious event." The course of the narrative is impeded by her pauses to retail the private history of everyone she meets,—the young lady whose mind has been poisoned by too much novel-reading, the young man who is led by *The Sorrows of Werther* to shoot his disdainful fair one and then himself, the irate father who slays the brutal husband of his daughter and then falls into fits. Caroline, herself, is not without sensibility,– "frequently," she tells us, "doth the great drop burst from my eye." She invariably retains her composure, however, even when her betrothed is killed in battle. Indeed, she soon begins to cast an eye of favor on an another suitor, Mr Helen, but remarks, with her usual propriety, "great as my present partialities are, I should be disgusted with an immediate declaration of his attachment." Her arrangement to give funereal honors to the memory of her betrothed may serve as a sample of the "elegance" of the author's imagination:

> As a memento of my uniform attachment, I will cause a monument to be raised, on the base of which shall be represented, upon one side an urn which shall be supposed to contain the ashes of my friend, over which two cupids shall hold a cypress wreath; under the urn shall be displayed the fatal trophies of war, while the figure of a female shall be seated under the friendly shade of a weeping willow, in a melancholy attitude, pointing to a number of angels that will be seen above. The urn shall be inscribed to friendship, bravery, and virtue. Upon the opposite side of the base an urn shall represent the sacred remains of my dear Lucretia, while a figure, whose eyes shall emit an insatiable revenge, shall hold in her hand a dart, which she is aiming at the bosom of a female who stands weeping over the ashes of her friend. At one end shall be engraved in capitals. "SUPPRESS EVERY MOTIVE OF REVENGE."

After this tribute to the departed she accepts Mr Helen.

At length the malevolent Eliza triumphs. Caroline is carried off by villains in Eliza's pay, and the devoted Helen, flying in pursuit, only arrives in time to save her body from a company of medical students. Nothing happens to Eliza.

Although the principle of poetic justice is violated in *The Hapless Orphan*, it usually governs the dénouements of tales of this class; the rejected lovers of the heroine console themselves with young ladies who have sighed in vain for the hero, and long-lost uncles reappear from strange lands, in time to endow all the principals with "handsome" fortunes, and the faithful attendants with "genteel" annuities. On the title page a "Lady of Quality" and the like have been replaced by "A Lady of Worcester County," "A Young Lady of the State of New York," or "A Lady of Philadelphia." In the tale itself nothing but the geographical situation is changed; the atmosphere is unreal, the lady is unfortunate, the hero is of a wax-work perfection, the villain is of a mechanical iniquity, just as in the numberless similar British romances.

The trials of this engaging type of heroine did not meet with universal compassion. In her *Female Quixotism exhibited in the Romantic opinions and Extravagant Adventures of Dorcasina Sheldon* (1808), Mrs Tabitha Tenney ridiculed the effect of such romantic tales on the mind of a country girl, much as Mrs Lennox, fifty years before, had satirized in her *Female Quixote*, the influence of the heroic romances of the Clélie and Cléopâtre type. Mrs Tenney's[27] heroine, who changes her homely appellation of Dorcas to Dorcasina, has been led to see a disguised hero in every horseboy, and a romance in every chance acquaintance. The story of her many disappointments and absurd mishaps, as a result of the credulity which makes her an ever ready dupe, is told with some humor; but the humor too often has the roughness and cruelty which in many of Smollett's practical jokes turns the reader's sympathies to the victim rather than to the perpetrator. Indeed, the chief distinction between Mrs Lennox's satire and that of Mrs Tenney is that one lived before, and the other after, Smollett.

Leaving this second type of feminine achievement, and turning to other varieties of didacticism, one finds first, in point of time, the educational tale represented by *The Memoirs of the Bloomsgrove Family* by the Reverend Enos Hitchcock, D.D.[28] (1790). This learned author, after serving through the Revolutionary War as a chaplain, had acquired fame as a preacher. His purpose in novel writing was not only didactic but patriotic; to furnish a system of education suited to American conditions was his design. This is accomplished in a series of letters describing the training of the youthful Osander and Rozella Bloomsgrove under the supervision of their humane and enlightened parents. Incidentally, the views on education of Rousseau, Locke, Lord Kaimes, Mrs Chapone, and Mme. de Genlis are weighed and sifted. The educational effect of dressing dolls is solemnly discussed—for the author was convinced that "females should inure themselves to the exercise of thinking."[29] His acquaintance with eighteenth century fads appears in the little didactic Oriental tales which occasionally point his morals, and in the enthusiasm for landscape gardening shown in his descriptions of the Bloomsgrove domain, with its lawn, and summer-house, and paths running in a "vermicular direction." Of his style an example is furnished by his paraphrase of the speech of the Mother of the Gracchi, which he expands to a more elegant form. "These, my good friends," Cornelia says, "are my ornaments and all that I have of a toilet."

In 1293 Hitchcock published a work of a like improving tendency, *The Farmer's Friend, or the History of Mr Charles Worthy*, designed to show the progressive steps by which an individual can rise by his own struggles.

Similarly edifying in purpose is *The Art of Courting*, which shows characteristics both of the educational and of the religious tale, but differs from both in its avowed intention to "impress the minds of young people with a lively sense of the love and favor of heaven in granting to the human race the institution of marriage, which is so admirably calculated to promote their improvement, pleasure, and happiness." "The delightful business of courting" is the theme of the work, and is illustrated, the author says, by "several instances of courtship not unworthy of the imitation of the American youth."[30]

Seven typical courtships are followed out in detail by means of the letters of the lovers and an explanatory narrative by the author. These include a didactic courtship, a religious courtship, the courtship of an old maid and an old bachelor, of a widower and a widow, of an old man and a young girl, the courtship of Braggadocius and Numskuldia, inserted not for example but for warning, and finally, as a crowning triumph, the conversion, through love, of Damon, who had been a charming youth but a "finished deist."

The narrative is enlivened by the insertion of verses, the composition of various lovers. Of them all the following tribute from Oliva to Emilius is perhaps the most touching:

469

The beauties of the blooming spring,
Fresh to my mind Emilius bring,
The flowers which give a fragrant smell,
Do emulate his virtues well.

The inspiration, if so it may be called, to this undertaking probably came from Defoe's popular work on *Religious Courtship*, but there is a great difference not only in form, the substitution of letters for dialogues, but in feeling and style, both of which have the sentimentality and fondness for ornament of contemporary fiction, rather than the precision and matter of fact qualities of Defoe. Any connection there may be between *The Art of Courting* and the *Religious Courtship* is one of suggestion rather than of close imitation.

In addition to the educational and the religious, the satirical form of didacticism, which gave rise to the large family of eighteenth century Quixotes, is represented in America by Hugh Henry Brackenridge's[31] *Modern Chivalry*: containing the *Adventures of Captain John Farrago and Teague O'Regan his Servant*. This story, which displays more ability than any other American tales before those of Charles Brockden Brown, describes the travels of a thoughtful man whose ideas of life have been derived entirely from books. He is accompanied by an ignorant Irish servant, half-fool, half-knave, who by constantly getting into difficulties affords a text for satirical moralizings by his master.

In the earlier portions the satirical note is more sustained, and the adventures follow a fixed plan. At each stage of their journey the Captain and his servant fall in with some foolish assemblage, now of scientists seeking recruits for their society, now of citizens about to elect a representative, and the like. Each foolish group finds something to admire in the foolish and vain Teague O'Regan, and offers him membership or office. To prevent his acceptance the Captain is obliged to invent ridiculous objections, and then follows a chapter of reflections by the author, suggested by the previous adventure. This order, however, is gradually abandoned toward the end of the first part of the story, and is not resumed in the second. After a visit to Philadelphia, where Teague is a social success and an idol of young ladies, he has an interview with the President, and is led to expect political preferment. At last he obtains the office of exciseman. In that capacity he becomes involved in the Whiskey Rebellion, is tarred and feathered by indignant citizens, captured by a scientific society, caged as a strange animal, and finally sent to France where, in the character of an Esquimau, he figures in the train of Anacharsis Cloots.

The second part of the story, added later, is devoted to the description of a new settlement founded by the Captain and his friends, the governmental problems which arise being mere pretexts for long chapters setting forth Brackenridge's political beliefs. The relief given by comic adventure and satiric reflection to the educational intention of the first part is often lacking here, and there is no real plot.

At his best Brackenridge shows great satiric rower, and a vigor and clearness of style unusual in that day of somewhat tawdry elegance in fiction. Although he took the form of his narrative from Cervantes, he is nearer rather in spirit. Indeed it was his original intention to put his story into Butlers jolting couplets, and a beginning was actually made, but he finally abandoned the idea and adopted the prose form for his narrative. Another popular *genre* in the British fiction of the day, allied with the romantic rather than the didactic novel, was the tale of adventurous travel, whose rise is due partly to the influence of Smollett, partly to that of the books of travel and description which were being produced in considerable quantity. This type is early represented in America by two novels, both of which appeared in 1797, and both of which deal in part with the Algerine pirates, then a serious menace to commerce, as well as a picturesque peril appealing to many purveyors of light literature. Although, in so far as they possess the elements of action and enterprise, these two tales have a relationship with the adventure novels to be discussed in a later chapter, they have elements, one of the sentimental, the other of the didactic type, sufficient to give them a place here. Similar as are their subjects, the two authors employ quite opposite methods of treatment; one follows the traditional romance of high-born captives and gory-minded captors, while the other attempts an iconoclastic realism.

Fortune's Football, or, the Adventures of Mercutio possesses all the hairbreadth escapes, the rapid succession of improbable situations, familiar in the modern novel of this type, but differs from it in the share in the conduct of affairs assigned to the hero. As the title implies, Mercutio is the sport of fortune, not its master. Things happen to him; he does not make them happen to other people. Even the passion of love, which nerves the modern hero to many interesting impossibilities, has no such stimulating effect on Mercutio. As each object of his affections is snatched from him by death, he sheds a few tears, and replaces her by another even more desirable. Of him, far more truly than of Sir Charles Grandison, may it be said, "all the world is *his* Emily." Of perils by land and sea he has an endless series, once, indeed, owing his preservation to the humble agency of a friendly hen-coop. On another occasion his ship remains stuck between two rocks in mid-sea for five days, to the great annoyance of the passengers. In Venice he elopes with the Doge's daughter and an ebony box crammed full of ducats, while his final exploit is the conversion of the Sophi of Persia to monogamy and English cavalry tactics. The progress of the story is constantly interrupted by Mercutio's reunions with various long-lost friends, including an earl and a retired highwayman. The main narrative is abandoned while each friend recounts the tale of his adventures during his separation from the hero, thus causing a dislocation of the course of events. Mercutio's captivity among the pirates, although short, is as harrowing as his other experiences; he is chained to an oar and forced to row night and day. Among his fellow prisoners he finds equals and friends whose plight, like his own, is viewed as a romantic hardship.

In *The Algerine Captive*, on the other hand, Royall Tyler[32] has a more didactic purpose. After devoting the first part of his book to a satirical account of New England customs, he gives a serious picture of the terrors of a slave-ship. Finally, when he brings his hero to Algiers, he ridicules the romantic ideas of Algerian slavery generally derived from books, and gravely applies himself to a somewhat tedious account of actual conditions.

> I am loath [he says] to destroy the innocent gratifications which the readers of novels or plays derive from the works of a Behn and a Colman; but the sober character of the historian compels me to assure my readers that, whatever may have happened in the sixteenth century, I never saw during my captivity a man of any rank, family, or fortune among the menial slaves.

Tyler's style was clear and correct, without ornamentation or artificiality, very well fitted for story telling. Unfortunately, however, a flood of information submerged whatever story he may have meant to tell.

Not one of these early novels, with the possible exception of *Modern Chivalry*, whether intended for edification or for amusement, can claim any enduring literary merit, or any real originality. All belong to types common in contemporary British fiction, and many of them seem to be put forward in a tentative and apologetic spirit. This very amateurishness gives many of them a naïvely amusing quality, and seems to have been a source of innocent pride to some of the compatriots of their authors. At a time when American fiction was for a few years, at least, represented by a professional man of letters, Charles Brockden Brown, we find a plea for the amateur prefixed by Mrs Wood's Baltimore publisher to her *Ferdinand and Elmira* (1804). The "advertisement" to the work announces that

> the writer of this instructive and amusing work has heretofore published the effusions of her Pen in New England; and there, where the flights of fancy (as if chilled by the frigid blasts of the north) are not received with that friendly welcome which they receive in the south and middle states, commanded that applause which Genius and fancy never fail of producing on those liberal and candid minds who will take the trouble to discriminate between the ordinary day-labor of the common English novelist, who works for a living, similar to a mechanic, and has no other end in view than to bring forth a fashionable piece of Goods, that will suit the taste of the moment and remunerate himself, and the Lady of refined sentiments and correct taste, who writes for the amusement of herself, her friends, and the public.

The zeal for novel reading which underlay this zeal for novel-writing appears in the number of small towns or cities in which the earliest American novels were published. Before 1800 novels of native authorship had been printed in Newburyport, Northampton, Leominster, Hallowell, Dedham, Walpole, and Portsmouth. In other towns the most popular British novels were reprinted, and many, of course, were imported directly. While the American tales were usually kept at a medium price, the British varied greatly in cost, so that no thirst for fiction need have remained ungratified. The extravagant could obtain *The Beggar Girl and her Benefactors* for three dollars; the frugal might console themselves with *The Man of Real Sensibility* for thirty-seven and a half cents. Although this eager consumption of British fiction was deprecated by the patriotic American novelist, it must have suggested alluring possibilities of success.

Any attempt to sum up the importance of these early exercises in the didactic and the sentimental must give results chiefly negative. What their direct moral influence was, cannot be ascertained. It is certain, however, that they did not supplant British fiction in the affections of the reading public. Nor did they give any adequate expression to American life and ideals. Again they cannot he said to have great importance as evidence of an incipient literary culture. That culture was already showing itself in the cultivation of other literary forms. And although the authors of didactic fiction were often connected with self-conscious literary groups, they did not approach the novel from the point of view of art. The function of the novel, in their estimation, was almost entirely utilitarian. It is a significant fact that nearly all the directly didactic novels are by known writers—writers of literary or educational importance in their day—while, on the other hand, the stories designed chiefly for amusement, but related to their didactic contemporaries by similarity of sentiment and manner, are almost invariably by unknown authors. Apparently a novelist without a definite lesson to impart did not venture to appear in person before the public. The attitude of even the most edifying story tellers is apologetic. Such an attitude toward novel writing was not likely to bring about a search for new material in actual human experience or a more artistic handling of the well worn themes already in use.

These early novelists, in spite of their common aims, represent no concerted movement: they do not even form a group possessing any real unity. They discovered no new or characteristic type of novel, but sought their models in the very British fiction whose influence they were trying to destroy. Unfortunately, they followed the methods of British fiction in its most uninspired and uninspiring period. From these British models they derived the didacticism which is the guiding spirit of the novels brought together in this chapter. But many of these novels show also the influence of other aspects of contemporary thought. Consequently, although it is convenient to consider them in one large group characterized by this didactic and sentimental spirit, it would be possible, with equal consistency, to divide them into a number of small groups, several of which would consist of one novel each.

Yet inconsiderable as was their accomplishment from the point of view of literary merit they have a certain interest as documents in the history of taste. For their authors, and presumably their readers, were of the cultivated class, of the class which would consciously seek what it supposed to be the best. More than this, it should be remembered that to introduce novel writing to America at all was an achievement of real importance. Although the Gothic novel, the historical romance, and other newer forms of fiction followed in a very few years, the honor of leading the way in the new field belongs to the already old fashioned novel of the didactic Richardsonian tradition.

Notes

1. *Travels in New England and New York*, London, 1823, Vol. I, p. 477.
2. *Memoirs of the Bloomsgrove Family*, Boston, 1790, Vol. II, p. 82.
3. *Memoirs of the Bloomsgrove Family*, Vol. I, p. 16.
4. *The Algerine Captive, or the Life and Adventures of Dr Updike Underhill, a Prisoner among the Algerines*, Walpole, Vt., 1797.

The Nineteenth Century Novel

5. See also the *Massachusetts Magazine*, 1791, Vol. III, p. 662. "On modern novels and their effects."

6. Walter Raleigh, *The English Novel*, New York, 1906, p.211.

7. "An imitator of Fielding and Smolett in general plan, of the latter especially in the dangerous scheme of narrative by letter,—Bage added to their methods the purpose of advocating a looser scheme of morals and a more anarchical system of government." *A History of Nineteenth Century Literature*. London and New York, 1899, p.42.

8. W. L. Cross, *The Development of the English Novel*, New York and London, 1904, p.88.

9. The first edition of *Vancenza, or the Dangers of Credulity*, by Mrs M. Robinson, is said to have been "Sold off in London before 12 o'clock of the day on which it first issued from the press." *New York Magazine*, Vol. I, p. 303.

10. Smollett, *Miscellaneous Works*, Vol. VI, *Humphrey Clinker*, p. 136.

11. A few novels of these earliest years of American fiction belong to new and different types and will be discussed in Chapter III.

12. A woman of American birth, Mrs Charlotte Lennox, had been a popular novelist in England nearly forty years before the publication of *The Power of Sympathy*. But she left America while still a child and can hardly be claimed as an ornament of American literature. Her satirical novel, *The Female Quixote*, was much read, and was honored with a dedication from the hand of Dr Johnson. She was the author of several novels, of *Shakespeare Illustrated or Novels and Histories on which his plays are founded*, and of a variety of other literary efforts. (See *Dict. of Nat. Biog.*)

13. Mrs Morton, who was born in 1759, married Percy Morton, later Attorney-General of Massachusetts. She was early a contributor to the *Massachusetts Magazine* and became one of the chief adornments of a literary circle. Her verse is of an elegant and Della Cruscan insipidity.

14. The influence of the *Sorrows of Werther* on the mind of impulsive youth appears in many of our nearly novels, for example, in *The Hapless Orphan* and *The Letters of Ferdinand and Elizabeth*, and one tale, *The Slave of Passion, or the Fruits of Werther*, Philadelphia, 1802, is deliberately directed against this insidious evil.

15. Elias Nason, *A Memoir of Mrs Susanna Rowson with Elegant and Illustrative Extracts front her Writings in Prose and Poetry*, Albany, N.Y., 1870.

16. One of her productions: a comedy, called *Americans in England, or Lessons for Daughters*, was presented at a benefit in 1797. Others were *The Female Patriot*, *The Volunteers*, and an opera, *Slaves in Algiers*.

17. *A Present for Young Ladies containing Poems, Dialogues, Addresses . . . as Recited by the Pupils of Mrs Rowson's Academy at the annual exhibition*. Boston, 1811.

18. *Bible Dialogues between a Father and his Family*, Boston, 1822. *Exercises in History*, etc., Boston, 1822.

19. A more dignified reprint of the first edition has recently been issued, edited, with an introduction and a bibliography, by Francis W. Halsey, New York, 1905.

20. *Alexis, or the Cottage in the Woods*, a novel from the French. Boston, 1796. (*Alexis: ou la Maisonnette dans les Bois . . . .Par l'Auteur de Lolotte et Fanfan*, Liège, 1790.)

21. In *Reuben and Rachel* (1798) Mrs Rowson shows the more romantic influence of the increasing school of historical fiction. The tale, which seems to have been educational in intention, begins in the time of Columbus. Subsequently it describes the marriage of his granddaughter to a son of Lady Jane Grey, and of their son to an Indian princess, and of their son to a member of the Penn family.

22. Hannah Foster, 1759-1840, was the wife of a Massachusetts minister, the Rev. John Foster. She was the author of *The Boarding School* (1796) and *Lessons of a Preceptress* (1798).

23. The story is told at length in Mrs C. H. Dall's *Romance of the Association*, 1875.

24. The thirtieth appeared in Boston in 1833. Wegelin, *Early American Fiction*, 1902, p. 14.

25. *The Stepmother* was favorably reviewed in the *Gentleman's Magazine* for July, 1800.

26. Among the tales of this type may be mentioned: *Cynthia, with the tragical account of the unfortunate loves of Almerin and Desdemona*, Northampton, Mass., 1798; *The Fortunate Discovery, Or the History of Henry Villars*, New York, 1798; *Moreland Vale, or the Fair Fugitive*, New York, 1801; *Monima, or the Beggar Girl*, Philadelphia, 1803; *Margaretta*, Philadelphia, 1807. In a review in the *Massachusetts Magazine*, 1792, Vol. IV, p. 367, *The Hapless Orphan* is severely criticised, apparently for its lack of edifying tendency, and because the foibles of the aunt are "rather

sneered at by stoical apathy than consoled in the language of sensibility."

27. Tabitha Tenney was born in Exeter, N. H., in 1762. In 1788 she married Samuel Tenney who in 1800 became a member of Congress. She died in Exeter in 1837.

28. The Rev. Enos Hitchcock was born in Springfield, Mass., in 1744, and died in Providence, R. I., in 1803. He was graduated from Harvard in 1767, and became a chaplain in the Revolutionary army in 1780. He published, beside his novels, a *Treatise on Education*, Boston, 1790, and *Catechetical Instructions and Forms of Devotion for Children and Youth*, 1788.

29. A different view was taken by the writer who, in 1792, contributed to the *American Museum*, Vol. XI, lines addressed to a lady who had desired the establishment of a university for women. Of the blighting effect of science he says:

> At her approach the roses fade,
> Each charm forsakes the astonished maid;
> And o'er her cheek of sickly pale,
> Thought slowly draws its loathsome veil.

30. Of this work the *Massachusetts Magazine* remarks, 1796 (Vol. VIII, p. 68), "Here is nothing of the delicate demeanor and gentle affection, none of the tender sensibilities or winning attention, and little of the modest innocence or chaste reservedness which bespeak a refined attachment."

31. Hugh Henry Brackenridge was born in 1748, in Scotland, but came to America when five years old. His boyhood was spent on a farm in York County, Pa., where he managed to obtain an education. By teaching school he earned the money necessary for study at Princeton, and was graduated in 1771 with James Madison and Philip Freneau. He continued at the college as a tutor, studied divinity, and later taught in an academy in Maryland where he composed a dramatic poem, *Bunker's Hill*, recited by his pupils, and published in 1776. He became editor of the *United States Magazine* in 1776. After serving as chaplain in the war, he studied law at Annapolis. In 1781 he moved to Pittsburg, and later became a member of the Legislature. He was much interested in the Whiskey Rebellion and in 1795 published *Incidents of the Insurrection in the Western Part of Pennsylvania in 1794*. In 1799 he was made judge of the Supreme Court of Pennsylvania. He died in 1816.

32. Royall Tyler was born in Boston in 1756, was of the class of 1776 at Harvard, and studied law with John Adams. He served for some time in the army. His comedy, *The Contrast*, was acted in 1786. The next year he produced *May Day, or New York in an Uproar*. To the *Farmer's Weekly Museum*, and other papers, he contributed numerous productions "from the shop of Messrs. Colon and Spondee," and to the *Port Folio*, in 1801, a series of *An Author's Evenings*. In the same year some of his *Farmer's Museum* papers were collected and published. He composed much occasional verse, and contributed to various periodicals, including the *New England Galaxy*. In 1800 he was made Chief Justice of the Supreme Court of Vermont, and held the office for several years. He died in 1812.

·֍·88·֍·

The Beginnings of Fiction

CARL VAN DOREN

Carl Van Doren (1885-1950), editor of *The Nation* (1919-22) and *Century* (1922-25), was a literary critic, biographer and historian, primarily of American literature and history. His best known works include *Contemporary American Novelists, 1900-1920* (1922), *Benjamin Franklin* (1938) and *The American Novel* (1921), from which the first chapter (printed below) is taken. Van Doren argues that the American novel was heavily influenced by Richardson's *Pamela* and, to a lesser extent, by Fielding, Smollett and Sterne. Van Doren proceeds to discuss a host of now little known novels and novelists from Sarah Wentworth Morton's *The Power of Sympathy* (1789) to Charles Brockden Brown to James Fennimore Cooper. Van Doren attributes the paucity of good American novels before the mid nineteenth century to the belief that "fiction belonged to the Old World, fact to the new" (16) and that the American novelist had first to discover typically American subjects about which to write. The American novel, heavily weighted toward romance, drew upon patriotic materials from the Revolution, the Indian wars and the frontier. It was Cooper's attempt to deal with the latter two themes that pushed him to prominence in the 1820s and 30s. Van Doren devotes the second chapter of the book to Cooper's works.

1. Arguments and Experiments

Prose fiction, by the outbreak of the American Revolution one of the most popular forms of literature in Europe, had as yet a small and insecure reputation in the British colonies which subsequently became the United States. Not only were there still no native novels, but the great English masters of the art had little vogue. Richardson's *Pamela*, indeed, a book read everywhere as much for its piety as for its power to entertain, had been printed in 1744 at Philadelphia by that shrewd judge of public taste and private profits, Benjamin Franklin, and there

Source: Carl Van Doren, "The Beginnings of Fiction", *The American Novel*, New York: Macmillan, 1921, pp. 1-23.

were editions the same year at New York and Boston. But Richardson's later novels, like Fielding's *Joseph Andrews* and *Tom Jones*, did not appear for more than forty years, when all of them were brought out in abridged editions in 1786. Even *Robinson Crusoe* had to wait nearly fifty years for an American printer, while *Rasselas* and *The Vicar of Wakefield* only tardily crossed the Atlantic. English editions, of course, had a moderate circulation, but it could not have been great or a keener rivalry would have been awakened in such towns as Boston and Philadelphia in spite of the coldness of utilitarians and Puritans. Probably the Southern and Middle colonies read more novels than New England. William Byrd of Virginia, owner of one of the largest private libraries in America, possessed novels by Defoe, Fielding, Smollett, Le Sage, and Cervantes (who as satirist and moralist was widely admired), as well as more trivial performances. There was at least one copy of *Joseph Andrews* in Philadelphia in 1744, for Dr. Alexander Hamilton of Maryland, then on a leisurely vacation, read it there and thought it the best work of the kind he had ever seen. And New England was by no means innocent of novels. Jonathan Edwards himself, conspicuous among the saints, read *Sir Charles Grandison*, and with such interest that he resolved to correct his own hitherto neglected style upon the example of Richardson; while Stephen Burroughs, as conspicuous among the sinners, later charged many of his offenses to his early reading of such books as *Guy, Earl of Warwick*, which he read about the time of the Revolution.

In part this apathy to fiction was due to the common colonial tendency to lag behind in matters of, taste and culture. Pope in poetry and Addison in prose long sufficed for models among the Americans, and theological and political discussion proceeded with little reference to prevailing modes in imaginative literature. But even more important than mere apathy was the positive antipathy which showed itself when, soon after the Revolution, novel reading began to increase with great rapidity, and native novelists appeared in respectable numbers. The moralists were aroused and exclaimed against the change—their cries appearing in the magazines of the day side by side with moral tales. Nearly every grade of sophistication applied itself to the problem. The dullest critics contended that novels were lies; the pious, that they served no virtuous purpose; the strenuous, that they softened sturdy minds; the utilitarian, that they crowded out more useful books; the realistic, that they painted adventure too romantic and love too vehement; the patriot, that, dealing with European manners, they tended to confuse and dissatisfy republican youth. In the face of such censure American novelists came forward late and apologetically, armed for the most part with the plea that they told the truth, pointed to heaven, or devoutly believed in the new republic. Before 1800 the sweeping abuse of the older school had been forced to share the field of criticism with occasional efforts to distinguish good novels from bad. The relative merits of Fielding and Smollett were discussed almost as frequently as, fifty years later, were those of Dickens and Thackeray, and in much the same confusion of ethical and æsthetic considerations. Fielding was of course preferred by the enlightened, Smollett by the robustious, Sterne by the "sensible," and Richardson, most popular of all it will be seen, by the domestic and sentimental. Indeed, to the influence of Richardson, with something from Sterne, must be credited the first regular American novel, *The Power of Sympathy*, a poor and stilted narrative in epistolary form which was published by Sarah Wentworth Morton at Boston in 1789.

Political allegory, however, had already begun to prepare the way for invented narratives. The eighteenth century would have been less than itself had it brought forth in America only sentimental romances. Franklin is but one of many evidences that humor and satire were not silent. Francis Hopkinson, also of Philadelphia, produced an allegory which lies nearly as close to fiction as to history. In *A Pretty Story* (1774) he set forth, after the fashion earlier established by Dr. Arbuthnot, the history of a certain nobleman (the king) who had an old farm (England) and a new farm (the colonies) in the management of which his wife (Parliament) and his steward (the ministry) constantly interfered to the annoyance of his sons (the colonists) and to the great derangement of his own affairs. The story breaks off abruptly with Jack (Boston) shut up in his farm and turning for help to his brothers. The satire was without much bitterness or indignation, and perhaps for that reason all the more effective through its shrewd and amusing narrative. Jeremy Belknap, the learned historian of New Hampshire, likewise tried his hand at allegory in *The Foresters* (1792, enlarged 1796). His foresters are the colonists, whose career he follows in a mild comic history, consistently allegorized, from the days of settlement, through the colonial wars, the Revolution, the Confederation, the Constitution, the establishment of the Republic, and the polemic episode of Citizen Genêt.

Neither Hopkinson nor Belknap is to be compared, for comic force and satirical point and power of observation, to the Pennsylvanian Hugh Henry Brackenridge (1748–1816), who between 1792 and 1805 published the various parts of his satirical novel *Modern Chivalry*. It is indicative of the changing taste of his time that he began his book in 1787 in the meter of *Hudibras*, recently employed with such success in Trumbull's *McFingal*, but later changed to prose. By his own confession, he followed the style of Hume, Swift, and Fielding—like Swift in *A Tale of a Tub* alternating Chapters of narrative with ironical essays on all manner of subjects. Captain Farrago, the hero, is a new Don Quixote, who whimsically takes it into his head to leave his farm in western Pennsylania "and ride about the world a little, with his man Teague at his heels, to see how things were going on here and there, and to observe human nature." A description of manners in the early days of the Republic the book is unapproached by any other. Races, elections, rural conjurors, village "philosophers" or pseudo-scientists, inns, duels and challenges, treaties with Indians, the Society of the Cincinnati, hedge parsons, brothels, colleges, Congress, Quakers, lawyers, theatres, law courts, Presidential levees, dancing masters, excise officers, tar and feathers, insurrections—all these are displayed in the first part of the book with obvious verisimilitude and unflagging spirit. Much of the action of this part is furnished by the doings of Teague, a grotesque and witless Sancho Panza, whose impudent ambition survives the most ludicrous and painful misadventures. Brackenridge regards him as typical of the political upstarts of the period, and his triumphs as an accusation properly to be brought against the public which followed such sorry leaders. In Part II Captain Farrago, after a brief hiatus spent on his farm, resumes his travels, which at first do not take him beyond the limits of the nearest village, with its newspaper, academy, lunatic asylum, and fair, but which eventually bring him to a settlement in the black country of which he becomes governor. The remainder of the book, ostensibly a chronicle of the new settlement, is practically a burlesque of the history of civilization in America. The settlers war with the Indians and make it a constitution. They legislate like madmen, under the guidance of a visionary from Washington who holds that beasts should have the vote as well as men, and actually persuades his fellows to commission a monkey clerk and admit a hound to the bar. Brackenridge aimed his satire primarily at doctrinaires and demagogues, but he whipped as well almost all the current follies and affectations, revising his book from time to time to keep pace with new absurdities. For half a century *Modern Chivalry* was widely popular, and nowhere more so than along the very frontier which it satirized and which read it as more or less a true history. It was among the earliest books printed west of the Alleghanies.

Satire had to be helped by sentiment, however, before fiction could win the largest audience. Indeed, until Scott had definitely established a new mode of fiction for the world, the potent influence in American fiction was Richardson. The amiable ladies who produced most of the early sentimental novels commonly held, like Mrs. Rowson, that their knowledge of life had been "simply gleaned from pure nature," because they dealt with facts which had come under their own observation; but like other amateurs they saw in nature what art had assured them would be there. Nature and Richardson they found the same. Whatever bias they gave this Richardsonian universe was due to a pervading consciousness that their narratives would be followed chiefly by women. The result was a highly domestic world, limited in outlook, where the talk was of careless husbands, of grief for dead children, of the peril of many childbirths, of the sentiment and the religion without which it used to be thought women could not endure their sex's destiny. Over all hangs the unceasing menace of the seducer, who appears in such multitudes that modern readers might think that age one of the most illicit on record if they did not understand that Richardson's Lovelace is merely being repeated in different colors and proportions. It is true, however, that the two most important novels of this sort, as well as *The Power of Sympathy*, were based on actual happenings. Sarah Webster Foster's *The Coquette* (1797) recorded the tragic and widely known career of Elizabeth Whitman of Hartford, who, having coquetted with the Reverend Joseph Buckminster, was seduced by a mysterious rake generally identified with Jonathan Edwards's son Pierrepont, and died in misery at the Old Bell Tavern in Danvers, Massachusetts, 1788. *The Coquette* saw thirty editions in forty years, and was known in almost every household of the Connecticut Valley. It has not survived as has Susannah Haswell Rowson's *Charlotte* (1794), one of the most popular novels ever published in the United States. Mrs. Rowson, an American only by immigration, had probably written the novel in England (where it seems to have been published in 1790), but *Charlotte Temple*, to call it by its later title, was thoroughly naturalized and has had its largest circulation here. It has persuaded an increasingly naïve underworld of fiction readers—housemaids and shopgirls—to buy more than a hundred editions and has built up a legend about a not too authentic tomb in Trinity Churchyard, New York, which at least since about 1845 has borne the name "Charlotte Temple" in concession to the legend but which probably contains the ashes of a certain Charlotte Stanley whom a British officer named Montrésor seduced from her home in England and deserted her in New York, much as in the novel. This simple story Mrs. Rowson embroidered with every device known to the romancer—sentimentalism, bathos, easy tears, high-flying language, melodrama, moralizings without stint or number; and yet something universal in the theme has kept it, in its way, still alive without the concurrence of critics or historians of literature.

The tradition that Abigail Stanley, mother of Elizabeth Whitman, was a cousin of Charlotte, serves to illustrate the process by which *Charlotte Temple* and *The Coquette* won a hearing from a community which winced at fiction: like sagas they stole upon their readers in the company of facts. A similar companionship appears in Royall Tyler's *The Algerine Captive* (1797). The hero, Updike Underhill, after an account of his youth and education in the backwoods of New England, and of his experiences as a schoolmaster there, goes on to Boston, begins the practice of medicine, proceeds to Philadelphia where he meets Franklin, and to Virginia, where he is shocked at encountering a figure quite unknown to New England, a sporting parson: later he goes to sea, visits London, tells of Tom Paine, observes the horrors of a slave ship, and is captured by the Algerines, among whom he spends the six years recounted in the second volume. The value of the book lies largely in its reports of facts, which it gives clearly and freshly. That Tyler thought of the traveler and the novelist as about equally his models appears from his preface, upon which the fame of *The Algerine Captive* principally depends. In 1787, it should be remembered, he had produced our earliest comedy, *The Contrast*, opposing to foreign affectations the rustic worth of the first "stage Yankee." Now ten years later he renewed his demand for nativism, while pointing out that the status of fiction had greatly changed in the interim. Formerly, he says,

> books of Biography, Travels, Novels, and modern Romances, were confined to our sea ports; or, if known in the country, were read only in the families of Clergymen, Physicians, and Lawyers; while certain funeral discourses, the last words and dying speeches of Bryan Shakeen, and Levi Ames, and some dreary somebody's Day of Doom, formed the most diverting part of the farmer's library.

But

> no sooner was a taste for amusing literature diffused than all orders of country life, with one accord, forsook the sober sermons and Practical Pieties of the fathers, for the gay stories and splendid impieties of the Traveller and the Novelist. The worthy farmer no longer fatigued himself with Bunyan's Pilgrim up the "hill of difficulty" or through the "slough of despond"; but quaffed wine with Brydone in the hermitage of Vesuvius, sported with Bruce on the fairy land of Abyssinia: while Dolly, the diary [sic] maid, and Jonathan, the hired man, threw aside the ballad of the cruel stepmother, over which they had so often wept in concert, and now amused themselves into so agreeable a terrour, with the haunted houses and hobgoblins of Mrs. Ratcliffe [sic], that they were both afraid to sleep alone.

Such addiction to romance, Tyler argued, was too exciting for plain Americans; their novels like their clothes ought to be homespun.

It was in the very year of Royall Tyler's preface that the first American to make authorship his sole profession decided upon fiction as the form he should undertake. Charles Brockden Brown (1770-1810) of Philadelphia as a schoolboy aspired to be an epic poet, and contemplated epics on Columbus, Pizarro, and Cortez, possibly desiring to rival Timothy Dwight, whose *Conquest of Canaan* appeared in 1785, or Joel Barlow, whose *Vision of Columbus* followed two years later. But after reading William Godwin's *Caleb Williams* (1794) Brown acquired a new ambition. He would patriotically try for reality as some others were trying; and of course he would lay stress on the moral tendency of his performances, as all had done. In addition he hoped "to enchain the attention and ravish the souls of those who study and reflect." At the same time, he was too good a democrat to write for geniuses alone, and he believed that while they were being stirred by the ideas of a novel the plain people could be captured by its plot.

Brown's important books were written in a few vivid months, spent mostly in New York. His specific indebtedness to Godwin appears chiefly in a fondness for the central situation of *Caleb Williams*: an innocent and somewhat hapless youth in the grasp of a patron turned enemy. The parallel is exact in *Arthur Mervyn* (1799-1800), which brings a young man of that name to Philadelphia, makes him blunder into the secret of a murder, and subjects him to elaborate persecutions from the murderer. A surviving fragment of the lost *Sky-Walk* (written in 1797) shows that Brown there varied the Godwin situation by making the patron a woman. In *Ormond* (1799) by still another variation a woman is the victim, Constantia Dudley, pursued by the enthusiast and revolutionary Ormond until in self-defense she is obliged to kill him. Constantia won the passionate regard of a greater among Godwin's disciples, Shelley, to whom she was the type of virtuous humanity oppressed by evil custom. But Brown's victims do not have to undergo the cumulative agony of Godwin's, for the reason that Brown worked too violently to be able to organize a scheme of circumstances all converging upon any single victim. And more than his vehement methods of work handicapped him in his rivalry with Godwin: to be a master of the art of calm and deliberate narrative he must have had Godwin's cold and consistent philosophy of life. As a matter of fact, while the leaven of revolutionary rationalism stirs in his work, it does not, as with Godwin's, pervade the mass.

The Godwinian elements in Brown now seem less impressive than certain effects which he was able to produce by the use of native material. In 1793 he had fled with his family to the country to escape the epidemic of yellow fever which then visited Philadelphia; five years later he had gone through a similar invasion of the plague at New York. His letters show how deeply he was moved by the only personal contact he ever had with such affairs of danger and terror as he chose to write about. Composing *Ormond* almost before the pestilence had receded, Brown transferred his impressions from the New York of 1798 to the Philadelphia of 1793, as he did in *Arthur Mervyn*, perhaps for some gain in perspective; but in both he wrote with an eye on the fact as nowhere else in his books. With unsparing, not to say sickening, veracity, he reproduced the physical horrors of the plague—its loathsome symptoms and its fearful stenches; he was even more veracious in his account of the mental and spiritual horrors which accompanied it: the superstitious dread and foolhardy courage which sprang in different people from the current ignorance with regard to infection; the pusillanimous flight of many who were deeply needed; the brutal callousness of certain wretches who stayed to nurse the sick and then neglected them; the general moral collapse. Less successful than these experiments was that in Edgar Huntly (1799), wherein he turned to the material which beyond any other was to be celebrated in American fiction for half a century: frontier adventure. Brown claimed for this book the merit

> of calling forth the passions and engaging the sympathy of the reader by means hitherto unemployed by preceding authors. Puerile superstition and exploded manners, Gothic castles and chimeras, are the materials usually employed for this end. The incidents of Indian hostility, and the perils of the Western wilderness, are far more suitable; and for a native of America to overlook these would admit of no apology.

As far as his knowledge and his prepossessions allowed him, Brown succeeded in his experiment. But he knew little of the frontier, either its scenery or its customs, and no more of the Indians than he could have picked up from books or casual meetings in the towns.

What he did was to substitute new devices for calling forth much the same passions and sympathies as had been addressed by the older Gothic romances. His wild regions and his wild adventurers are all seen through an intensely romantic temperament with only occasional intervals for realism. As in his handling of the yellow fever, Brown shows power to set forth grisly details of blood and suffering, and he treats his Indians without the glamour with which they were already invested by certain sentimentalists. But so far as reality of impression is concerned, the visible Indians are none of them so memorable as the old woman called Queen Mab, who never appears in person and who exists chiefly as a symbol of a race vanquished and yet still clinging to its old domains with a tenacity that is poetic. Vivid, too, is the impression of the feverish, nocturnal wanderings, without much aim or sequence, to which Huntly devotes his time. Here again Brown's shambling narrative methods dull the edge of his story: like most of the romancers of his age, he moved forward through a cloud.

As a rationalist he tried to solve the mystery of the cloud about *Edgar Huntly* by explaining that both Clithero, the suspected villain who is really innocent, and Huntly are addicted to sleep-walking, a subject which was just then, as contemporary journals show, under discussion and much debated. Also illustrative of Brown's attempt to fuse mystery with science, and in itself more effective than this sleep-walking, is the ventriloquism which plays a prominent part in his best—that is, his most compact, most psychological, and most powerful—novel, *Wieland* (1798). Its plot was primarily founded upon the deed of an actual religious fanatic of Tomhannock, New York, who in a mad vision had heard himself commanded to destroy all his idols, and had murdered his wife and children with ferocious brutality. With this theme Brown involved the story of Carwin, the "biloquist," to make the "voices seem less incredible than in the original. It may be assumed that ventriloquism did not seem a pinchbeck solution in 1798, when it was a trick little known or practised; and Brown, too much an artist to make his ventriloquist a mere instigator to murder, makes him out a hero-villain whose tragedy it is that he has to sin, not as the old morality had it, because of mere wickedness, but because of the driving power of the spirit of evil which no man can resist and from which only the weak are immune. Yet though Carwin by his irresponsible acts of ventriloquism in and out of season actually sets going in Theodore Wieland's mind the train of thought which terminates in the crimes, he does no more than to arouse from unsuspected depths a frenzy already sleeping in Wieland's nature. These were cases of speculative pathology which Brown had met in his Godwinian twilights, beings who had for him the reality he knew best, that of dream and passion; from them comes the fever in the climate which gives the book its shuddering power. To a notable extent Wieland fulfills the rules Brown had laid down in his announcement of *Sky-Walk*. Ventriloquism, religious murder, and a case of spontaneous combustion make up the "contexture of facts capable of suspending the faculties of every soul in curiosity." These were for the unlearned. The apparent scene of action is laid upon the banks of the Schuylkill; this was patriotic realism. But for those of his readers who might have "soaring passions and intellectual energy," as Brown had, the absorbing thing was the clash of mighty forces, the din of good and evil, which resound throughout the story, and which in spite of awkward narrative, strained probabilities, and a premature solution lift it above the ephemeral—the earliest American romance of distinction.

2. The Three Matters of American Romance

Except for the work of Irving, who deliberately chose short stories to avoid any rivalry with Scott, the first twenty years of the nineteenth century produced no memorable fiction, whatever in the United States. Even the example of Scott, who was immensely popular, at first failed to arouse imitators. Indeed, the brilliance of his achievement served to discourage his warmest admirers. Such learning, such experience, such humor, such abundance as the "Author of Waverley" displayed—who dared match his powers against them? Moreover, the elements which gave Scott his vogue, and which for a time seemed the essential elements of fiction, were not easily transportable to another soil. The attitude of Americans in the matter was well set forth by John Bristed in his book on *The Resources of the United States* in 1818:

> Of native *novels* we have no great stock, and none good; our democratic institutions placing all the people on a dead level of political equality; and the pretty equal diffusion of property throughout the country affords but little room for varieties, and contrasts of character; nor is there much scope for fiction, as the

country is quite new and all that has happened from the first settlement to the present hour, respecting it, is known to every one. There is, to be sure, some traditionary romance about the Indians; but a novel describing these miserable barbarians, their squaws, and papooses, would not be very interesting to the present race of American readers.

To Bristed, as to most contemporaries, it seemed impossible for the novel to flourish in a country which had no aristocracy, no distinct classes of society, no wide range of poverty and wealth, no legendary and semi-legendary lore like that of the English-Scottish border. A genuine task challenged the American imagination before any considerable body of fiction could be achieved. Whatever man of genius might appear, there was still the problem of reaching a public taught that fiction belonged to the Old World, fact to the New; taught to look for the pleasures of the imagination on the soil where they had long existed and to which even the most self-conscious and politically independent American had been accustomed to look back with admiration, with some vague nostalgia to the spirit. Yet at the very moment when Bristed wrote, national passions were awake which within a half-dozen years had not only elicited a great romancer but had shown a popular imagination unexpectedly prepared for him. Out of such emotions come, in the proper ages, ballads and epic lays. In the United States, though prose fiction was the form at hand, the narratives were all romantic, and the literary process but repeated the processes of romantic ages. As in medieval France there were three "matters" of romance,

> De France, et de Bretagne, et de Rome la grant,

so in the United States there were also three: the Revolution, the Settlement, and the Frontier.

The revolutionary generation had been an age of myth-making. Washington, for instance, to his very face was apotheosised by his followers with a passion of language which notoriously embarrassed him. Almost before his bones were cold appeared Parson Weems's astounding tract, miscalled a biography, to catch the popular fancy at once and to establish the absurd legend of Washington's superhuman virtues. "Private Life," Weems avowed, "is real life"; and though, lacking first-hand knowledge, he was obliged to invent, he seemed intimate and credible to an audience somewhat overwhelmed by the heavy splendour of the more official orations and odes and sermons called forth by Washington's death. Thereafter the legend grew unchecked, until the pious Catherine Maria Sedgwick, in 1835, apologising for the introduction of the hero in her novel *The Linwoods*, could write "

> in extenuation of what may seem presumption, that whenever the writer has mentioned Washington, she has felt a sentiment resembling the awe of the pious Israelite when he approached the ark of the Lord."

The legends of Arthur and Charlemagne grew no more rapidly in the most legend-breeding age—indeed, did not grow so rapidly as this. And around Washington, as around Arthur his knights and around Charlemagne his peers, were speedily grouped such minor heroes as Francis Marion, whose life was also written by Weems,

Israel Putnam, whom David Humphreys celebrated, Patrick Henry, whose biographer was no less a person than William Wirt, Attorney-General of the United States, Ethan Allen, who wrote his own record, and others whose fame or infamy (as in the case of Benedict Arnold) depended less specifically upon books. As all these heroes were constantly whitened by their biographers, so was the cause for which they fought; until the second generation after the Revolution had hardly a chance to suspect—at least so far as popular literature was concerned—that the Revolution had been anything but a melodrama victoriously waged by stainless Continental heroes against atrocious villains in British scarlet, followed by a victory without ugly revenges and crowned by a reconstruction culminating in the divinely-inspired Constitution. George Bancroft himself, a scholar of large attainments, could write as late as 1860 such words as these concerning the Declaration of Independence:

> This immortal state paper, which for its composer was the aurora of enduring fame, was "the genuine effusion of the soul of the country at that time," the revelation of its mind, when in its youth, its enthusiasm, its sublime confronting of danger, it rose to the highest creative powers of which man is capable. The bill of rights which it promulgates, is of rights that are older than human institutions, and spring from the eternal justice that is anterior to the state. Two political theories divided the world; one founded the commonwealth on the reason of state, the policy of expediency; the other on the immutable principles of morals: the new republic, as it took its place among the powers of the world, proclaimed its faith in the truth and reality and unchangeableness of freedom, virtue, and right. The heart of Jefferson in writing the declaration, and of congress in adopting it, beat for all humanity; the assertion of right was made for the entire world of mankind and all coming generations, without any exception whatever; for the proposition which admits of exceptions can never be self-evident. As it was put forth in the name of the ascendant people of that time, it was sure to make the circuit of the world, passing everywhere through the despotic countries of Europe; and the astonished nations as they read that all men are created equal, started out of their lethargy, like those who have been exiles from childhood, when they suddenly hear the dimly remembered accents of their mother tongue.

This, the most patriotic American must now admit, is the language of romance.

The deeds and personages of the Revolution, steadily growing in the popular imagination under the stimulus of an exultant and hopeful independence, were naturally first expressed and most highly regarded of the new national themes. But side by side with them, in part aroused and drawn along by the Revolution, went the matter of the Settlement, consisting of the tales told in every state about its colonial days. Here again Parson Weems took a hand and wrote folk-books about William Penn and Benjamin Franklin. Weems, himself a Virginian, in his choice of these Pennsylvania worthies as subjects for his art illustrates the national feeling which gradually superseded the old colonial memories and prejudices. The new states no sooner pooled their national resources than they began unconsciously to pool their resources of tradition, of legend, of local poetry. Their wealth was as unequal in this respect as in any other, and widely different in quality. Certain themes from the first assumed a prominence that attracted to them the national imagination as it was attracted to no others. The landing of the Pilgrims, the witchcraft mania at Salem, Connecticut and its Charter Oak, the Dutch on the Hudson, Penn's liberality and tolerance, the settlement at Jamestown, Pocahontas and her career, Bacon's Rebellion, John Locke's schemes for the Carolinas, the debtors in Georgia, and, somewhat later, the siege of Louisburg and Braddock's defeat: each of these early became the center of an increasing legend. Particularly important was a theme which in some form or other belonged to every colony—the warfare with the Indians for undisturbed possession of the soil from which they have been driven. So long as the natives had been dangerous to the invaders there had existed that bitterness of race-hatred which goes along with race-menace, and which kept out of the records of the old Indian wars, from Maine to Florida, any real magnanimity or sympathy for the disposed owners of the land. They were as paynims to Christian Knights, as the sons and daughters of Amalek to the invaders of Canaan. King Philip's War in New England having begotten better books than any other, it lived in the popular memory more vividly than did the equally bitter and important but unrecorded Tuscarora and Yemassee wars in the Carolinas, for instance. The Deerfield raid, in large measure because of the Rev. John Williams's narrative of his captivity, became classic while similar episodes elsewhere were forgotten. Toward the end of the eighteenth century, however, when the Indian was no longer in any way a menace, he had begun to be sentimentalised by admirers of the natural man, with whom he was commonly identified by Europeans and not infrequently by the descendants of the very Americans who had hated him so bitterly a century before.

The Indian was a link connecting the matter of the Settlement with the matter of the Frontier, the only one which had a contemporary aspect. It was the frontier not as remembered for the beginnings but as reported from the more distant territories where it still lay in the early years of the new century. Even before the revolution not a few imaginations had turned inland. The settlement of Kentucky had excited the seaboard, and Daniel Boone, though not the greatest of the pioneers, before 1800 was already beginning to be the most famous of all of them, a true folk-hero. Literature unquestionably did him this service, in the person of the eccentric schoolmaster John Filson, who wrote for Boone his *Adventures* in 1784. Later the Louisiana Purchase drew still more eyes to the West, while the government expedition conducted by Lewis and Clark, rather less through its reports than through busy rumor, had an influence upon the popular imagination perhaps larger than that ever produced by any other American exploring venture. As contrasted with the tradition of the Settlement or of the Revolution, the reports concerning the contemporary frontier came as news, but there was still about them the haze of distance—distance in miles if not in years. The Great Lakes, the prairies, the plains and mountains beyond, the fever lands of the lower Mississippi, and especially the broad rivers and blue-grass of Kentucky, all of these constituted a sort of hinterland for the national imagination which writers were not slow to take advantage of. Nor did the frontier lie entirely inland. The sea also was a frontier. From every port of the New England coast, and to a less degree from the Atlantic coast generally, ships went out to every corner of the world, particularly to the mysterious Pacific, with its strange calms and rich pastures for fishermen, and to the exotic countries beyond, but also to the crowded Mediterranean, the banks of Newfoundland, the neighborly West Indies. The new nation was setting out in every direction to become acquainted with its own immense domain and to establish communications between it and all the rest of the world, real or imaginative.

Such potentialities, of course, still ran a long way before the facts at the time Bristed made his unhopeful prophecy. What he said of existing American fiction suited its recent examples accurately enough. John Davis, a visiting Englishman, had taken a fancy to the Pocahontas legend and had dealt with it in three versions in his *Travels* (1803), *Captain Smith and Princess Pocahontas* (1805), and *The First Settlers of Virginia* (1806). Preposterous as they all are, they are interesting as the first treatment of one of the most persistent of American legends. A rollicking anti-romance, *Female Quixotism* (1808?) by Tabitha Tenney, which made very good fun of the novels of the day by showing into how many follies its heroine could blunder by taking the manners of such novels for her guide, was far less popular than the absurdly sentimental performance, probably by Isaac Mitchell, *The Asylum* (1811), which achieved at least a score of editions and exhibits the worst qualities of Mrs. Radcliffe to an extent which now makes it incredibly amusing. The nadir of the old-fashioned, sensational, sentimental romance was reached, however, in Samuel Woodworth's *The Champions of Freedom* (1816), written to order to celebrate the second war with England. Pompous language (Ossian mixed with Sterne and Cicero), a ghost that walks like a man, shrieking patriotism, and ineffable sentimentality are all it has to commend it. No wonder that from such monstrosities the public turned with delight to a story-teller by comparison so natural, so rational, so critical, so sensible as Fenimore Cooper.

"Come Back to the Raft Ag'in, Huck Honey!"

LESLIE FIEDLER

Perhaps best known for his literary landmark, *Love and Death in the American Novel* (1960), Leslie Fiedler captures here in an early essay what he terms a peculiarly American obsession—the homoerotic love between white and "coloured" men in American fiction. This innocently portrayed theme tends to surface most often in books either written for or nevertheless securing a children's audience. This obsession of the white man for a companion of a different race arises from the nostalgic vision of boyhood in American culture, a vision that many of the principal nineteenth-century American male authors depict. Especially Cooper, Melville and Twain, Fiedler argues, present their protagonists in lonely isolation, either in water or in the forest. Amidst this isolation, they forge unlikely bonds with people of a different race—Natty Bumpo with Chingachgook, Ishmael with Queequeg, and Huck Finn with Jim. Fiedler suggests that this persistent theme is connected with American guilt, a legacy of Puritanism, that must seek to absolve itself in a relation between the outcast and the victim.

It is perhaps to be expected that the Negro and the homosexual should become stock literary themes, compulsive, almost mythic in their insistence, in a period when the reassertion of responsibility and of the inward meaning of failure has become again a primary concern of our literature. Their locus is, of course, discrepancy—in a culture which has no resources (no tradition of courtesy, no honoured mode of cynicism) for dealing with a contradiction between principle and practice. It used once to be fashionable to think of puritanism as a force in our life encouraging hypocrisy; quite the contrary, its rigid emphasis upon the singleness of belief and action, its turning of the most prosaic areas of common life into arenas where one's state of grace is symbolically tested, confuse the outer and

Source: Leslie Fiedler, "Come Back to the Raft Ag'in, Huck Honey!", *Partisan Review* 15.6, June 1948, pp. 664–71.

the inner and make among us, perhaps more strikingly than ever elsewhere, hypocrisy *visible*, visibly detestable, a cardinal sin. It is not without significance that the shrug of the shoulders (the acceptance of circumstance as a sufficient excuse, the vulgar sign of self-pardon before the inevitable lapse) seems in America an unfamiliar, an alien gesture.

And yet before the underground existence of crude homosexual love (the ultimate American epithets of contempt notoriously exploit the mechanics of such affairs), before the blatant ghettos in which the cast-off Negro conspicuously creates the gaudiness and stench that offend him, the white American must over and over make a choice between coming to uneasy terms with an institutionalized discrepancy, or formulating radically new ideologies. There are, to be sure, stop-gap devices, evasions of that final choice; not the least interesting is the special night club: the fag café, the black-and-tan joint, in which fairy or Negro exhibit their fairyness, their Negro-ness as if they were mere divertissements, gags thought up for the laughs and having no reality once the lights go out and the chairs are piled on the tables for the cleaning-women. In the earlier minstrel show, a negro performer was required to put on with grease paint and burnt cork the formalized mask of blackness.

The situations of the Negro and the homosexual in our society pose precisely opposite problems, or at least problems suggesting precisely opposite solutions: Our laws on homosexuality and the context of prejudice and feeling they objectify must apparently be changed to accord with a stubborn social fact, whereas it is the social fact, our overt behavior toward the Negro, that must be modified to accord with our laws and the, at least official, morality they objectify.

It is not, of course, quite so simple. There is another sense in which the fact of homosexual passion contradicts a national myth of masculine love, just as our real relationship with the Negro contradicts a myth of that relationship, and those two myths with their betrayals are, as we shall see, one.

The existence of overt homosexuality threatens to compromise an essential aspect of American sentimental life: the camaraderie of the locker-room and ball park, the good fellowship of the poker game and fishing trip, a kind of passionless passion, at once gross and delicate, homoerotic in the boy's sense, possessing an innocence above suspicion. To doubt for a moment this innocence, which can survive only as *assumed*, would destroy our stubborn belief in a relationship simple, utterly satisfying, yet immune to lust; physical as the hand-shake is physical, this side of copulation. The nineteenth-century myth of the Immaculate Young Girl has failed to survive in any *felt* way into our time; rather in the dirty jokes shared among men in the smoking-car, the barracks, or the dormitory there is a common male revenge against women for having flagrantly betrayed that myth, and under the revenge, there is the rather smug assumption of the chastity of the group as a masculine society. From what other source could that unexpected air of good clean fun which overhangs such sessions arise? It is this self-congratulatory buddy-buddiness, its astonishing naiveté, that breeds at once endless opportunities for inversion and the terrible reluctance to admit its existence, to surrender the last believed-in stronghold of love without passion.

It is, after all, what we know from a hundred other sources that is here verified: the regressiveness, in a technical sense, of American life, its implacable nostalgia for the infantile, at once wrongheaded and somehow admirable. The mythic America is boyhood—and who would dare be startled to realize that two (and the two most popular, the two most absorbed, I think) of the handful of great books in our native heritage are customarily to be found, illustrated, on the shelves of the Children's Library. I am referring of course to *Moby Dick* and *Huckleberry Finn*, splendidly counterpoised in their oceanic complexity and fluminal simplicity, but alike children's books, or more precisely, boys' books.

Among the most distinguished novelists of the American past, only Henry James escapes completely classification as a writer of juvenile classics; even Hawthorne, who did write sometimes for children, must in his most adult novels endure, though not as Mark Twain and Melville submit to, the child's perusal; a child's version of *The Scarlet Letter* would seem a rather far-fetched joke if it were not a part of our common experience. On a lower level of excellence, there are the Leatherstocking Tales of Cooper and Dana's *Two Years Before the Mast*, books read still, though almost unaccountably in Cooper's case, by boys. What do all these novels have in common?

As boys' books we would expect them shyly, guilelessly as it were, to proffer a chaste male love as the ultimate emotional experience—and this is spectacularly the case. In Dana, it is the narrator's melancholy love for the *kanaka*, Hope; in Cooper, the lifelong affection of Natty Bumpo and Chingachgook; in Melville, Ishmael's love for Queequeg; in Twain, Huck's feeling for Nigger Jim. At the focus of emotion, where we are accustomed to find in the world's great novels some heterosexual passion, be it Platonic love or adultery, seduction, rape or long-drawn-out flirtation, we come instead upon the fugitive slave and the no-account boy lying side by side on a raft borne by the endless river towards an impossible escape, or the pariah sailor waking in the tatooed arms of the brown harpooner on the verge of their impossible quest. "Aloha, aikane, aloha nui," Hope cries to the lover who prefers him above his fellow-whites; and Ishmael, in utter frankness, tells us: "Thus, then, in our heart's honeymoon, lay I and Queequeg—a cosy, loving pair." Physical it all is, certainly, yet of an ultimate innocence; there is between the lovers no sword but a child-like ignorance, as if the possibility of a fall to the carnal had not yet been discovered. Even in the *Vita Nuova* of Dante there is no vision of love less offensively, more unremittingly chaste; that it is not adult seems sometimes beside the point.

The tenderness of Huck's repeated loss and refinding of Jim, Ishmael's sensations as he wakes under the pressure of Queequeg's arm, the role of almost Edenic helpmate played for Bumpo by the Indian—these shape us from childhood: we have no sense of first discovering them, of having been once without them.

Of the infantile, the homoerotic aspects of these stories we are, though vaguely, aware, but it is only with an effort that we can make to a consciousness of how, among us who at the level of adulthood find a difference in color sufficient provocation for distrust and hatred, they celebrate, all of them, the mutual love of *a white man and a colored*.

So buried at a level of acceptance which does not touch reason, so desperately repressed from overt recognition, so contrary to what is usually thought of as our ultimate level of taboo—the sense of that love can survive only in the obliquity of a symbol, persistent, archtypical, in short, as a myth: the boy's homoerotic crush, the love of the black fused at this level into a single thing.

I hope I have been using here a hopelessly abused word with some precision; by myth I mean a coherent pattern of beliefs and feelings, so widely shared at a level beneath consciousness that there exists no abstract vocabulary for representing it, and (this is perhaps another aspect of the same thing) so "sacred" that unexamined, irrational restraints inhibit any explicit analysis. Such a complex achieves a formula or pattern story, which serves both to embody it, and, at first at least, to conceal its full implications. Later the secret may be revealed, the myth (I use a single word for the formula and what is formulized) "analyzed" or "allegorically interpreted" according to the language of the day.

I find the situation we have been explicating genuinely mythic; certainly it has the concealed character of the true myth, eluding the wary pounce of Rowells or of Mrs. Twain who excised from *Huckleberry Finn* the cussin' as unfit for children, but left, unperceived, a conventionally abhorrent doctrine of ideal love. Even the writers in whom we find it, attained it, in a sense, dreaming. The felt difference between *Huckleberry Finn* and Twain's other books must lie surely in the release from conscious restraint inherent in the author's assumption of the character of Huck; the passage in and out of darkness and river mist, the constant confusion of identities (Huck's ten or twelve names—the questions of who is the real uncle, who the true Tom), the sudden intrusions into alien violences without past or future, give the whole work for all its carefully observed detail, the texture of a dream. For *Moby Dick*, such a point need scarcely be made. Even Cooper, despite his insufferable gentlemanliness, his civilized tedium, cannot conceal from the kids who continue to read him the secret behind the overconscious, stilted prose: the childish impossible dream. D. R. Lawrence saw in him clearly the kid's Utopia: the absolute wilderness in which the stuffiness of home yields to the wigwam and "My Wife" to Chingachgook.

I do not recall ever having seen in the commentaries of the social anthropologist or psychologist an awareness of the role of this profound child's dream of love in our relation to the Negro. (I say Negro, though the beloved in the books we have mentioned is variously Indian and Hawaiian, because the Negro has become more and more exclusively for us *the* colored man, the colored man par excellence.) Trapped in what has by now become a shackling cliché: the concept of the white man's sexual envy of the Negro male, they do not sufficiently note the complementary factor of physical attraction, the mythic love of white male and black. I am deliberately ignoring here an underlying Indo-European myth of great antiquity, the Manichaean notion of an absolute Black and White, hostile yet needing each other for completion, as I ignore more recent ideologies that have nourished the view that concerns us: the Shakespearian myth of good homosexual love opposed to an evil heterosexual attachment, the Rousseauistic concept of the

Noble Savage; I have tried to stay within the limits of a single unified myth, reenforced by disparate materials.

Ishmael and Queequeg, arm in arm, about to ship out, Huck and Jim swimming beside the raft in the peaceful flux of the Mississippi,—it is the motion of water which completes the syndrome, the American dream of isolation afloat. The Negro as homoerotic lover blends with the myth of running off to sea, of running the great river down to the sea. The immensity of water defines a loneliness that demands love, its strangeness symbolizes the disavowal of the conventional that makes possible all versions of love.

In *Two Years Before the Mast*, in *Moby Dick*, in *Huckleberry Finn* the water is there, is the very texture of the novel; the Leather-stocking Tales propose another symbol for the same meaning: the virgin forest. Notice the adjective—the virgin forest and the forever inviolable sea. It is well to remember, too, what surely must be more than a coincidence, that Cooper who could dream this myth invented the novel of the sea, wrote for the first time in history the sea-story proper. The rude pederasty of the forecastle and the Captain's cabin, celebrated in a thousand jokes, is the profanation of a dream. In a recent book of Gore Vidal's an incipient homosexual, not yet aware of the implications of his feelings, indulges in the apt reverie of running off to sea with his dearest friend. The buggery of sailors is taken for granted among us, yet it is thought of usually as an inversion forced on men by their isolation from women, though the opposite case may well be true, the isolation sought more or less consciously as an occasion for male encounters. There is a context in which the legend of the sea as escape and solace, the fixated sexuality of boys, the dark beloved are one.

In Melville and Twain at the center of our tradition, in the lesser writers at the periphery, the myth is at once formalized and perpetuated; Nigger Jim and Queequeg make concrete for us what was without them a vague pressure upon the threshold of our consciousness; the proper existence of the myth is in the realized character, who waits, as it were, only to be asked his secret. Think of Oedipus biding in silence from Sophocles to Freud.

Unwittingly we are possessed in childhood by the characters and their undiscriminated meaning, and it is difficult for us to dissociate them without a sense of disbelief. What! these household figures clues to our subtlest passions! The foreigner finds it easier to perceive the remoter significance; D. H. Lawrence saw in our classics a linked mythos of escape and immaculate male love; Lorca in *The Poet in New York* grasped instinctively the kinship of Harlem and Walt Whitman, the fairy as bard. Yet in every generation of our own writers the myth appears; in the Gothic reverie of Capote's *Other Voices, Other Rooms*, both elements of the syndrome are presented, though disjunctively: the boy moving between the love of a Negro maid-servant and his inverted cousin.

In the myth, one notes finally, it is always in the role of outcast, ragged woodsman, or despised sailor (Call me Ishmael!), or unregenerate boy (Huck before the prospect of being "sivilized" cries, "I been here before!") that we turn to the love of a colored man. But how, we must surely ask, does the vision of the white American as pariah correspond with our long-held public status: the world's beloved, the success? It is perhaps only the artist's portrayal of *himself*, the notoriously alienated writer in America, at home with such images, child of the town drunk, the survivor. But no, Ishmael is all of us, our unconfessed universal fear objectified in the writer's status as in the sailor's: that compelling anxiety, which every foreigner notes, that we may not be loved, that we are loved for our possessions and not ourselves, that we are really—*alone!* It is that underlying terror which explains our almost furtive incredulity in the face of adulation or favor, what is called (once more the happy adjective) our "boyish modesty."

Our dark-skinned beloved will take us, we assure ourselves, when we have been cut off, or have cut ourselves off from all others, without rancor or the insult of forgiveness; he will fold us in his arms saying "Honey" or "Aikane!", he will comfort us, as if our offense against him were long ago remitted, were never truly *real*. And yet we cannot really forget our guilt ever; the stories that embody the myth dramatize almost compulsively the role of the colored man as victim: Dana's Hope is shown dying of the white man's syphilis; Queequeg is portrayed as racked by fever, a pointless episode except in the light of this necessity; Cooper's Indian smolders to a hopeless old age conscious of the imminent disappearance of his race; Jim is shown loaded down with chains, weakened by the hundred torments of Tom's notion of bullyness. The immense gulf of guilt must be underlined, just as is the disparity of color (Queequeg is not merely brown but monstrously tatooed, Chingachgook is horrid with paint, Jim is shown as the Sick A-rab dyed blue), so that the final reconciliation will seem more unbelievable, more tender. The myth makes no attempt to whitewash our outrage as a fact; it portrays it as meaning-less in the face of love.

There would be something insufferable, I think, in that final vision of remission if it were not for the apparent presence of a motivating anxiety, the sense always of a last chance; behind the white American's nightmare that someday, no longer tourist, inheritor, or liberator, he will be rejected, refused—he dreams of his acceptance at the breast he has most utterly offended. It is a dream so sentimental, so outrageous, so desperate that it redeems our concept of boyhood from nostalgia to tragedy.

In each generation we *play* out the impossible mythos, and we live to see our children play it, the white boy and the black we can discover wrestling affectionately on any American street, along which they will walk in adulthood, eyes averted from each other, unwilling to touch. The dream recedes; the immaculate passion and the astonishing reconciliation become a memory, and less, a regret, at last the unrecognized motifs of a child's book. "It's too good to be true, Honey," Jim says to Huck. "It's too good to be true."

Everybody's Protest Novel

JAMES BALDWIN

James Baldwin (1924–87), author of *Go Tell It on the Mountain* (1953), *Notes of a Native Son* (1955), and the play, *Blues for Mister Charley* (1964), is one of the principal African American writers after Richard Wright. In the following essay he decries the African American protest novel for its refusal to escape black and white stereotypes in its attempt to homogenize people. He views Richard Wright's *Native Son* as an inheritor of the theological terror of damnation incited by Stowe's *Uncle Tom's Cabin*. The latter work is, he argues, a bad novel because of its excessive sentimentality. Such sentimentality tends to avoid the brutality that attended slavery. According to Baldwin, the protest novel of the twentieth century, like Stowe's novel, denies a black man or woman humanity in its acceptance of a white standard to which all must submit.

In *Uncle Tom's Cabin* that cornerstone of American social protest fiction, St. Clare, the kindly master, remarks to his coldly disapproving Yankee cousin, Miss Ophelia, that, so far as he is able to tell, the blacks have been turned over to the devil for the benefit of the whites in this world—however, he adds thoughtfully, it may turn out in the next. Miss Ophelia's reaction is, at least, vehemently right-minded: "This is perfectly horrible!" she exclaims. "You ought to be ashamed of yourselves!"

Miss Ophelia, as we may suppose, was speaking for the author her exclamation is the moral, neatly framed, and incontestable like those improving mottoes sometimes found hanging on the walls of furnished rooms. And, like these mottoes, before which one invariably flinches, recognizing an insupportable, almost an indecent glibness, she and St. Clare are terribly in earnest. Neither of them questions the medieval morality from which their dialogue springs: black, white, the devil, the next world—posing its alternatives between heaven and the flames—were realities for them as, of course, they were for their creator. They spurned and were terrified of the darkness, striving mightily for the light; and considered from this aspect, Miss

Source: James Baldwin, "Everybody's Protest Novel", *Partisan Review*, 16.6, June 1949, pp. 578–85.

Ophelia's exclamation, like Mrs Stowe's novel, achieves a bright, almost a lurid significance, like the light from a fire which consumes a witch. This is the more striking as one considers the novels of Negro oppression written in our own, more enlightened day, all of which say only: "This is perfectly horrible! You ought to be ashamed of yourselves!" (Let us ignore, for the moment, those novels of oppression written by Negroes, which add only a raging, near-paranoiac postscript to this statement and actually reinforce, as I hope to make clear later, the principles which activate the oppression they decry.)

Uncle Tom's Cabin is a very bad novel, having, in its self-righteous, virtuous sentimentality, much in common with *Little Women*. Sentimentality, the ostentatious parading of excessive and spurious emotion, is the mark of dishonesty, the inability to feel; the wet eyes of the sentimentalist betray his aversion to experience, his fear of life, his arid heart; and it is always, therefore, the signal of secret and violent inhumanity, the mask of cruelty. *Uncle Tom's Cabin*—like its multitudinous hardboiled descendants—is a catalogue of violence. This is explained by the nature of Mrs Stowe's subject matter, her laudable determination to flinch from nothing in presenting the complete picture; an explanation which falters only if we pause to ask whether or not her picture is indeed complete; and what constriction or failure of perception forced her to do so depend on the description of brutality—unmotivated, senseless—and to leave unanswered and unnoticed the only important question: what it was, after all, that moved her people to such deeds.

But this, let us say, was beyond Mrs Stowe's powers; she was not so much a novelist as an impassioned pamphleteer; her book was not intended to do anything more than prove that slavery was wrong; was in fact, perfectly horrible. This makes material for a pamphlet but is hardly enough for a novel; and the only question left to ask is why we are bound still within the same constriction. How is it that we are so loath to make a further journey than that made by Mrs Stowe, to discover and reveal something a little closer to the truth?

But that battered word, truth, having made its appearance here, confronts one immediately with a series of riddles and has, moreover, since so many gospels are preached, the unfortunate tendency to make one belligerent. Let us say, then, that truth, as used here, is meant to imply a devotion to the human being, his freedom and fulfillment; freedom which cannot be legislated, fulfillment which cannot be charted. This is the prime concern, the frame of reference; it is not to be confused with a devotion to Humanity which is too easily equated with a devotion to a Cause; and Causes, as we know, are notoriously bloodthirsty. We have, as it seems to me, in this most mechanical and interlocking of civilizations, attempted to lop this creature down in the status of a time-saving invention. He is not, after all, merely a member of a Society or a Group or a deplorable conundrum to be explained by Science. He is—and how old-fashioned the words sound!—something more than that, something resolutely indefinable, unpredictable. In overlooking, denying, evading his complexity—which is nothing more than the disquieting complexity of ourselves—we are diminished and we perish; only within this web of ambiguity, paradox, this hunger, danger, darkness, can we find at once ourselves and the power that will free us from ourselves. It is this power of revelation which is the business of the novelist, this journey toward a more vast reality which must take precedence over all other claims. What is today parroted as his Responsibility—which seems to mean that he must make formal declaration that he is involved in, and affected by, the lives of other people and to say something improving about this somewhat self-evident fact— is, when he believes it, his corruption and our loss; moreover, it is rooted in, interlocked with and intensifies this same mechanization. Both *Gentleman's Agreement* and *The Postman Always Rings Twice* exemplify this terror of the human being, the determination to cut him down to size. And in *Uncle Tom's Cabin* we may find foreshadowing of both: the formula created by the necessity to find a lie more palatable than the truth has been handed down and memorized and persists yet with a terrible power.

It is interesting to consider one more aspect of Mrs Stowe's novel, the method she used to solve the problem of writing about a black man at all. Apart from her lively procession of field-hands, house-niggers, Chloe, Topsy, etc,—who are the stock, lovable figure presenting no problem—she has only three other Negroes in the book. These are the important ones and two of them may be dismissed immediately, since we have only the author's word that they are Negro and they are, in all other respects, as white as she can make them. The two are George and Eliza, a married couple with a wholly adorable child—whose quaintness, incidentally, and whose charm, rather puts one in mind of a darky boot-black doing a buck and wing to the clatter of condescending coins. Eliza is a beautiful, pious hybrid, light enough to pass—the heroine of *Quality* might, indeed, be her reincarnation—differing from the genteel mistress who has overseered her education only in the respect that she is a servant. George is darker, but makes up for it by being a mechanical genius, and is, moreover, sufficiently un-Negroid to pass through town, a fugitive from his master, disguised as a Spanish gentleman, attracting no attention whatever beyond admiration. They are a race apart from Topsy. It transpires by the end of the novel, through one of those energetic, last-minute convolutions of the plot, that Eliza has some connection with French gentility. The figure from whom the novel takes its name, Uncle Tom, who is a figure of controversy yet, is jet-black, wooly-haired, illiterate; and he is phenomenally forbearing. He has to be; he is black; only through this forbearance can he survive or triumph. (Cf. Faulkner's preface to *The Sound and the Fury*: These others were not Compsons. They were black:—They endured.) His triumph is metaphysical, unearthly; since he is black, born without the light, it is only through humility, the incessant mortification of the flesh, that he can enter into communion with God or man. The virtuous rage of Mrs Stowe is motivated by nothing so temporal as a concern for the relationship of men to one another— or, even, as she would have claimed, by a concern for their relationship to God— but merely by a panic of being hurled into the flames, of being caught in traffic with the devil. She embraced this merciless doctrine with all her heart, bargaining shamelessly before the throne of grace: God and salvation becoming her personal property, purchased with the coin of her virtue. Here, black equates with evil and white with grace; if, being mindful of the necessity of good works, she could not cast out the blacks—a wretched, huddled mass, apparently, claiming like an obsession, her inner eye—she could not embrace them either without purifying them of sin. She must cover their intimidating nakedness, robe them in white, the garments of salvation; only thus could she herself be delivered from ever-present sin, only thus could she bury, as St. Paul demanded, "the carnal man, the man of the flesh." Tom, therefore, her only black man, has been robbed of his humanity and divested of his sex. It is the price for that darkness with which he has been branded.

Uncle Tom's Cabin, then, is activated by what might be called theological terror, the terror of damnation; and the spirit that breathes in this book, hot, self-righteous, fearful, is not different from that spirit of medieval times which sought to exorcize evil by burning witches; and is not different from that terror which activates a lynch mob. One need not, indeed, search for examples so historic or so gaudy; this is a warfare waged daily in the heart, a warfare so vast, so relentless and so powerful that the interracial handshake or the interracial marriage can be as crucifying as the public hanging or the secret rape. This panic motivates our cruelty, this fear of the dark makes it impossible that our lives shall be other than superficial; this interlocked with and feeding our glittering, mechanical, inescapable civilization which has put to death our freedom.

This, notwithstanding that the avowed aim of the American protest novel is to bring greater freedom to the oppressed. They are forgiven, on the strength of these good intentions, whatever violence they do to language, whatever excessive demands they make of credibility. It is, indeed, considered the sign of a frivolity so intense as to approach decadence to suggest that these books are both badly written and wildly improbable. One is told to put first things first, the good of society coming before niceties of style or characterization. Even if this were incontestable—for what exactly is the "good" of society?—it argues an insuperable confusion, since literature and sociology are not one and the same; it is impossible to discuss them as if they were. Our passion for categorization, life neatly fitted into pegs, has led to an unforseen, paradoxical distress; confusion, a break-down of meaning. Those categories which were meant to define and control the world for us have boomeranged us into chaos; in which limbo we whirl, clutching the straws of our definitions. The "protest" novel, so far from being disturbing, is an accepted and comforting aspect of the American scene, ramifying that framework we believe to be so necessary. Whatever unsettling questions are raised are evanescent, titillating; remote, for this has nothing to do with us, it is safely ensconced in the social arena, where, indeed, it has nothing to do with anyone, so that finally we receive a very definite thrill of virtue from the fact that we are reading such a book at all. This report from the pit reassures us of its reality and its darkness and of our own salvation, and "As long as such books are being published," an American liberal once said to me, "everything will be all right."

But unless one's ideal of society is a race of neatly analysed, hard-working ciphers, one can hardly claim for the protest novel the lofty purpose it claims for itself or share the present optimism concerning them. They emerge for what they are: a mirror of our confusion, dishonesty, panic, trapped and immobilized in the sunlit prison of the American dream. They are fantasies, connecting nowhere with reality, sentimental; in exactly the same sense that such movies as *The Best Years of Our Lives* or the works of Mr James M. Cain are fantasies. Beneath the dazzling pyrotechnics of these current operas one may still discern, as the controlling force, the intense theological preoccupations of Mrs Stowe, the sick vacuities of *The Rover Boys*. Finally, the aim of the protest novel becomes something very closely resembling the zeal of those alabaster missionaries to Africa to cover the nakedness of the natives, to hurry them into the pallid arms of Jesus and thence into slavery. The aim has now become to reduce all Americans to the compulsive, bloodless dimensions of a guy named Joe.

It is the peculiar triumph of society—and its loss—that it is able to convince those people to whom it has given inferior status of the reality of this decree; it has the force and the weapons to translate its dictum into fact, so that the allegedly inferior are actually made so, insofar as the societal realities are concerned. This is a more hidden phenomenon now than it was in the days of serfdom, but it is no less implacable. Now, as then, we find ourselves bound, first without, then within, by the nature of our categorization. And escape is not effected through a bitter railing against this trap; it is as though this very striving were the only motion needed to spring the trap upon us. We take our shape, it is true, within and against that cage of reality bequeathed us at our birth; and yet it is precisely through our independence on this reality that we are most endlessly betrayed. Society is held together by our need; we bind it together with legend, myth, coercion, fearing that without it we will be hurled into that void, within which, like the earth before the Word was spoken, the foundations of society are hidden. From this void—ourselves—it is the function of society to protect us; but it is only this void, our unknown selves, demanding, forever, a new act of creation, which can save us—"from the evil that is in the world." With the same motion, at the same time, it is this toward which we endlessly struggle and from which, endlessly, we struggle to escape.

It must be remembered that the oppressed and the oppressor are bound together within the same society; they accept the same criteria, they share the same beliefs, they both alike depend on the same reality. Within this cage it is romantic, more, meaningless, to speak a "new" society as the desire of the oppressed, for that shivering dependence on the props of reality which he shares with the *Herrenvolk* makes a truly "new" society impossible to conceive. What is meant by a new society is one in which inequalities will disappear, in which vengeance will be exacted; either there will be no oppressed at all or the oppressed and the oppressor will change places. But, finally, as it seems to me, what the rejected desire is, is an elevation of status, acceptance within the present community. Thus, the African, exile, pagan, hurried off the auction block and into the fields, fell on his knees before that God in Whom he must now believe; who had made him, but not in His image. This tableau, this impossibility, is the heritage of the Negro in America: *Wash me*, cried the slave to his Maker, *and I shall be whiter, whiter than snow!* For black is the color of evil; only the robes of the saved are white. It is this cry, implacable on the air and in the skull, that he must live with. Beneath the widely published catalogue of brutality—bringing to mind, somehow, an image, a memory of church-bells burdening the air—is this reality which in the same nightmare notion, he both flees and rushes to embrace. In America, now, this country devoted to the death of the paradox—which may, therefore, be put to death by one—his lot is as ambiguous as a tableau by Kafka. To flee or not, to move or not, it is all the same, his doom is written on his forehead, it is carried in his heart, In *Native Son*, Bigger Thomas stands on a Chicago street corner watching air-planes flown by white men racing against the sun and "Goddamn" he says, the bitterness bubbling up like blood, remembering a million indignities, the terrible, rat-infested house, the humiliation of home-relief, the intense, aimless, ugly bickering, hating it; hatred smoulders through these pages like sulphur fire. All of Bigger's life is controlled, defined by his hatred and his fear. And later, his fear drives him to murder and his hatred to rape; he dies, having come, through this violence, we are told, for the first time, to a kind of life, having for the first time redeemed his manhood. Below the surface of this novel there lies, as it seems to me, a continuation, a complement of that monstrous legend it was written to destroy. Bigger is Uncle Tom's descendant, flesh of his flesh, so exactly opposite a portrait that, when the books are placed together, it seems that the contemporary Negro novelist and the dead New England woman are locked together in a deadly, timeless battle; the one uttering merciless exhortations, the other shouting curses. And, indeed, within this web of lust and fury, black and white can only thrust and counter-thrust, long for each other's slow, exquisite death; death by torture, acid, knives and burning; the thrust, the counter-thrust, the longing making the heavier that cloud which blinds and suffocates them both, so that they go down into the pit together. Thus has the cage betrayed us all, this moment, our life, turned to nothing through or terrible attempts to insure it. For Bigger's tragedy is not that he is cold or black or hungry, not even that he is American, black; but that he has accepted a theology that denies him life, that he admits the possibility of his being sub-human and feels constrained, therefore, to battle for his humanity according to those brutal criteria bequeathed him at his birth. But our humanity is our burden, our life, we need not battle for it; we need only do what is infinitely more difficult, that is, accept it. The failure of the protest novel lies in its rejection of life, the human being, the denial of his beauty, dread, power, in its insistence that it is his categorization alone which is real and which cannot be transcended.

⸙ 91 ⸙

Paleface and Redskin

PHILIP RAHV

In the first essay in the book, Rahv outlines two opposing tendencies, represented by Whitman and James, in American literature. The "redskin" (Whitman, Twain, Dreiser, Anderson, Steinbeck, Hemingway) immerses himself in experience at the expense of intellect or reflection; the "paleface" (James, Hawthorne, Melville) inherits the Puritan legacy of introspection and discipline. The former represents the "low-brow," the latter the "high-brow." Rahv notes that the "paleface" writer dominated the literature of the nineteenth century but that the "redskin" has held ascendancy in the twentieth. In spite of his unfortunate choice of terms, Rahv, like D. H. Lawrence and other non-American critics, perceives a fatal split between these two types of writers. He blames this schism both on the Puritan inheritance and on the practical drive toward the frontier.

Viewed historically, American writers appear to group themselves around two polar types. Paleface and redskin I should like to call the two, and despite occasional efforts at reconciliation no love is lost between them.

Consider the immense contrast between the drawing-room fictions of Henry James and the open air poems of Walt Whitman. Compare Melville's decades of loneliness, his tragic failure, with Mark Twain's boisterous career and dubious success. At one pole there is the literature of the lowlife world of the frontier and of the big cities; at the other the thin, solemn, semi-clerical culture of Boston and Concord. The fact is that the creative mind in America is fragmented and one-sided. For the process of polarization has produced a dichotomy between experience and consciousness—a dissociation between energy and sensibility, between conduct and theories of conduct, between life conceived as an opportunity and life conceived as a discipline.

The differences between the two types define themselves in every sphere. Thus while the redskin glories in his Americanism, to the paleface it is a source of endless ambiguities. Sociologically they can be distinguished as patrician vs. plebeian, and

Source: Philip Rahv, "Paleface and Redskin", *Image and Idea: Twenty Essays on Literary Themes*, 1949; rev. ed. London, Weidenfeld and Nicolson, 1957, pp. 1-6.

in their aesthetic ideals one is drawn to allegory and the distillations of symbolism, whereas the other inclines to a gross, riotous naturalism. The paleface is a "highbrow," though his mentality—as in the case of Hawthorne and James—is often of the kind that excludes and repels general ideas; he is at the same time both something more and something less than an intellectual in the European sense. And the redskin deserves the epithet "low-brow," not because he is badly educated—which he might or might not be-but because his reactions are primarily emotional, spontaneous, and lacking in personal culture. The paleface continually hankers after religious norms, tending toward a refined estrangement from reality. The redskin, on the other hand, accepts his environment, at times to the degree of fusion with it, even when rebelling against one or another of its manifestations. At his highest level the paleface moves in an exquisite moral atmosphere; at his lowest he is genteel, snobbish, and pedantic. In giving expression to the vitality and to the aspirations of the people, the redskin is at his best; but at his worst he is a vulgar anti-intellectual, combining aggression with conformity and reverting to the crudest forms of frontier psychology.

James and Whitman, who as contemporaries felt little more than contempt for each other, are the purest examples of this dissociation.[1] In reviewing *Drum Taps* in 1865 the young James told off the grand plebeian innovator, advising him to stop declaiming and go sit in the corner of a rhyme and meter school, while the innovator, snorting at the novelist of scruples and moral delicacy, said "Feathers!" Now this mutual repulsion between the two major figures in American literature would be less important if it were mainly personal or aesthetic in reference. But the point is that it has a profoundly national and social-historical character.

James and Whitman form a kind of fatal antipodes. To this, in part, can be traced the curious fact about them that, though each has become the object of a special cult, neither is quite secure in his reputation. For most of the critics and historians who make much of Whitman disparage James or ignore him altogether, and vice versa. Evidently the high valuation of the one is so incongruous with the high valuation of the other that criticism is chronically forced to choose between them—which makes for a breach in the literary tradition without parallel in any European country. The aristocrat Tolstoy and the tramp Gorky found that they held certain values and ideas in common, whereas James and Whitman, who between them dominate American writing of the nineteenth century, cannot abide with one another. And theirs is no unique or isolated instance.

The national literature suffers from the ills of a split personality. The typical American writer has so far shown himself incapable of escaping the blight of one-sidedness: of achieving that mature control which permits the balance of impulse with sensitiveness, of natural power with philosophical depth. For the dissociation of mind from experience has resulted in truncated works of art, works that tend to be either naive and ungraded, often flat reproductions of life, or else products of cultivation that remain abstract because they fall short on evidence drawn from the sensuous and material world. Hence it is only through intensively exploiting their very limitations, through submitting themselves to a process of creative yet cruel self-exaggeration, that a few artists have succeeded in warding off the failure that threatened them. And the later novels of Henry James are a case in point.

The palefaces dominated literature throughout the nineteenth century, but in the twentieth they were overthrown by the redskins. Once the continent had been mastered, with the plebeian bourgeoisie coming into complete possession of the national wealth, and Puritanism had worn itself out, degenerating into mere respectability, it became objectively possible and socially permissible to satisfy that desire for experience and personal emancipation which heretofore had been systematically frustrated. The era of economic accumulation had ended and the era of consummation had arrived. To enjoy life now became one of the functions of progress—a function for which the palefaces were temperamentally disqualified. This gave Mencken his opportunity to emerge as the ideologue of enjoyment. Novelists like Dreiser, Anderson, and Lewis—and, in fact, most of the writers of the period of "experiment and liberation"—rose against conventions that society itself was beginning to abandon. They helped to "liquidate" the lag between the enormous riches of the nation and its morality of abstention. The neo-humanists were among the last of the breed of palefaces, and they perished in the quixotic attempt to re-establish the old values. Eliot forsook his native land, while the few palefaces who managed to survive at home took to the academic or else to the "higher" and relatively unpopular forms of writing. But the novelists, who control the main highway of literature, were, and still are, nearly all redskins to the wigwam born.

At present the redskins are in command of the situation, and the literary life in America has seldom been so deficient in intellectual power. The political interests introduced in the nineteen-thirties have not only strengthened their hold but have also brought out their worst tendencies; for the effect of the popular political creeds of our time has been to increase their habitual hostility to ideas, sanctioning the relaxation of standards and justifying the urge to come to terms with semi-literate audiences.

The redskin writer in America is a purely indigenous phenomenon, the true-blue offspring of the western hemisphere, the juvenile in principle and for the good of the soul. He is a self-made writer in the same way that Henry Ford was a self-made millionaire. On the one hand he is a crass materialist, a greedy consumer of experience, and on the other a sentimentalist, a half-baked mystic listening to inward voices and watching for signs and portents. Think of Dreiser, Lewis, Anderson, Wolfe, Sandburg. Caldwell, Steinbeck, Farrell, Saroyan: all writers of genuine and some even of admirable accomplishments, whose faults, however, are not so much literary as faults of raw life itself. Unable to relate himself in any significant manner to the cultural heritage, the redskin writer is always on his own; and since his personality resists growth and change, he must continually repeat himself. His work is ridden by compulsions that depress the literary tradition, because they are compulsions of a kind that put a strain on literature, that literature more often than not can neither assimilate nor sublimate. He is the passive instead of the active agent of the *Zeitgeist*, he lives off it rather than through it, so that when his particular gifts happen to coincide with the mood of the times he seems modern and contemporary, but once the mood has passed he is in danger of being quickly discarded. Lacking the qualities of surprise and renewal, already Dreiser and Anderson, for example, have a "period" air about them that makes a re-reading of their work something of a critical chore; and one suspects that Hemingway, that perennial boy-man, is more accurately understood as a descendant of Natty Bumppo, the hero of Fenimore Cooper's Leather-stocking tales, than as the portentously disillusioned character his legend makes him out to be.

As for the paleface, in compensation for backward cultural conditions and a lost religious ethic, he has developed a supreme talent for refinement, just as the Jew, in compensation for adverse social conditions and a lost national independence, has developed a supreme talent for cleverness. (In this connection it is pertinent to recall T. S. Eliot's remark about Boston society, which he described as "quite refined, but refined beyond the point of civilization.") Now this peculiar excess of refinement is to be deplored in an imaginative writer, for it weakens his capacity to cope with experience and induces in him a fetishistic attitude toward tradition; nor is this species of refinement to be equated with the refinement of artists like Proust or Mann, as in them it is not an element contradicting an open and bold confrontation of reality. Yet the paleface, being above all a conscious individual, was frequently able to transcend or to deviate sharply from the norms of his group, and he is to be credited with most of the rigors and charms of the classic American books. While it is true, as John Jay Chapman put it, that his culture is "secondary and tertiary" and that between him and the sky "float the Constitution of the United States and the traditions and forms of English literature"—nevertheless, there exists the poetry of Emily Dickinson, there is *The Scarlet Letter*, there is *Moby Dick*, and there are not a few incomparable narratives by Henry James.

At this point there is no necessity to enter into a discussion of the historical and social causes that account for the disunity of the American creative mind. In various contexts a number of critics have disclosed and evaluated the forces that have worked on this mind and shaped it to their uses. The sole question that seems relevant is whether history will make whole again what it has rent asunder. Will James and Whitman ever be reconciled, will they finally discover and act upon each other? Only history can give a definite reply to this question. In the meantime, however, there are available the resources of effort and understanding, resources which even those who believe in the strict determination of the cultural object need not spurn.

Note

1. According to Edith Wharton, James changed his mind about Whitman late in life. But this can be regarded as a private fact of the Jamesian sensibility, for in public he said not a word in favor of Whitman.

The Novel of Manners in America

ARTHUR MIZNER

American critic and biographer of F. Scott Fitzgerald (*The Far Side of Paradise* 1951) and Ford Maddox Ford (*The Saddest Story: A Biography of Ford Maddox Ford* 1971), Arthur Mizner (1907-1988) reflects on the split between aesthetic and social consciousness in the American novel after World War I. Citing the opposition between internal and external experience in Conrad and Wells respectively, Mizner discusses the failure of most American novelists to incorporate the impersonal world within the personal world of the writer. He views Faulkner, Fitzgerald and Hemingway as the only post war writers who were able to bridge the gap between inner and outer experience or between aesthetic and social concerns. Dos Passos errs on the side of what Trilling would term "social realism," while Fitzgerald demonstrates Trilling's ideal of "moral realism." (See Trilling's "Manners, Morals, and the Novel", 1950).

Mr Blackmur has recently suggested in the pages of *The Kenyon Review* (Winter, 1949) that we are probably in for a little "new criticism" of the novel; he does not anticipate this event with any great enthusiasm, for he is obviously worried that the visible hardening into a kind of dogma of the New Criticism's concern for verbal and structural analysis will lead it astray. "The Henry James novel, the Joyce novel, the Kafka novel, the Mann novel and the Gide novel together," he says, "will kill us yet if we do not realize soon that these novelists do not depend on what we think of as their 'novels' except in the first instance." In these feelings I follow Mr Blackmur without qualification. Yet how we are to deal with the novel remains a problem for us. It is our drunken, disreputable cousin, never mentioned when the subject can be avoided but forever turning up on the front porch at the most embarrassing times. It is not a theoretical or remote problem at all, but an immediate and practical one. I have no doubt, having read a good many and written a few, that remarks about novels such as we write now are something the editors of the quarterlies would do away with altogether if they could; and if you look into the books, the situation

Source: Arthur Mizner, "The Novel of Manners in America", *The Kenyon Review* 12.1, Winter 1950, pp. 1-19.

is at least as bad: so far as criticism of the novel is concerned, we are—with *The Craft of Fiction* and *Aspects of the Novel* and the rest—still living in the age of Sir Arthur Quiller-Couch and A. C. Bradley—which, in fact, we are not. Yet novels must be dealt with, not because of any passion we may have for an orderly aesthetic of the novel, but because we have to talk about them, in print, in the classroom, and among our intelligent, unprofessional friends; and it is awkward to be at a stand to know what kind of talk is relevant and what kind is not.

It is important, too, that the novel is the last of the verbal forms to retain wide popularity, important, I mean, to those whose business it is to talk about the novel. It is about all we any longer share with the common reader, and whatever the reasons for his interest may be, they are very probably not the kind which concerned Henry James so much of the time in his prefaces and still concern those for whom the mechanical techniques of the novel are its main interest. No doubt what Mr Blackmur himself has called for James the Art of the Novel is also important; it is certainly still the best kind of talk about the novel we have, the one that convinces you most continuously that as far as it goes it is to the point. We cannot do without it, whatever else we may need to say about the novel; for if it is not enough for us to say that the novel, as largely practised in English, is a perfect paradise of the loose end or for the novelist to go forth to encounter the reality of experience with no better means of communion with it than silence, exile and cunning, neither is it enough not to say and do these things. Whatever there is to be said, for example, for Hardy as a novelist, what James said against him is also to be said. We feel ourselves as critics forced to choose, then, between a kind of talk which seems to us relevant but inadequate—and seriously misleading if it is not treated so—and a kind of talk which would get at what the art of the novel does not; and the second of these choices is known to us only either as something we haven't got or as a discouraging confusion of traditional talk about Gentle Jane's charm and Hardy's philosophy and Dos Passos' socialist realism, most of which is either downright false or clearly beside the point.

But this need to choose between a conception of the novel which we feel inadequate and a conception which does not exist, and the further need to bring the two into accord, appears to be only a secondary manifestation of a choice and a struggle for reconciliation which the novelists themselves have faced. The problem goes a long way back beyond the New Criticism and has nothing really to do with it, except as the New Criticism is itself a manifestation of one of the conflicting attitudes. I think this fact comes out with remarkable clarity in the history of the American novel between the two world wars, and most of the conditions which have contributed to the problem as it confronts the novelists are especially clear in the America of that time. It was a time when the novel, as distinguished from the synthetic product more or less deliberately manufactured to some advertising research organization's specification, probably achieved its maximum popularity. It was a time, that is, when the genuine article was subject to great commercial pressure but had not yet to meet the competition of a synthetic substitute. These are probably the conditions of a healthy literary form in any society, and we ought perhaps not to complain about their effect. They did, certainly, great damage. Because of them, many bad novels were published and publicized and many good ones discouraged and neglected. But because of them, too, the serious novelist could write pretty directly for a large audience, while the poet, as Yeats bitterly remarked, could say anything he wanted to because nobody read him.

At the beginning of the period between the two wars, the novel participated vigorously in the life of society. It was very much a party to the new and shocking ideas about war and politics and The American Way of Life. The novelists were, that is to say, trying to represent experience as we ordinarily know it and to imply the immediate judgments and attitudes which that experience seemed to call for. However inadequate the evaluation of experience and however wooden the prose which expresses it in Hergesheimer, for example, his novels were an attempt to represent what was, for the time, a critical part of experience for large numbers of people. Had they not had this characteristic, it would be quite impossible to explain how novels which were at once so tediously earnest and so bad achieved such success. There could hardly be better evidence of how the novels of the early 'twenties succeeded for their time in representing familiar experience than the way they were criticized. Those who disliked them did not say they were not life; they only said they were a much less widespread kind of life than their authors thought. Even Max Perkins, one of the most sympathetic members of the older generation, thought that, though there may have been a few soldiers like Dos Passos' three, they were not representative; and Heywood Broun was sure *This Side of Paradise* was a case of not kissing but telling just the same.

I suspect that when we find a proper way of talking about the novel it will be because we have learned to discriminate between the novels which provide this kind of experience for readers in a valuable way and the novels which do not. Those which do not may be simply bad novels like Hergesheimer's, and then they have little interest except to social historians. But they may also be, in other ways, good novels, like Joyce's later work. But Joyce's work will, I think, seem nonetheless deficient in an important respect for all its special greatness. This kind of deficiency, in a much less significant way, exists in poetry; it is marked in *Paradise Lost*, for example. But it is probably a far more important element in the novel than in poetry.

In any event, the pressures of the 'twenties and 'thirties were such that the novels which provided this kind of experience had a harder and harder time surviving. For one thing they were under pressure on the literary side. Mr Bennett's view of Mrs Brown was discovered to be hopelessly old-fashioned and Joyce and Gertrude Stein and The Revolution of the Word began to be taken very seriously among all literary people who kept abreast of things. "My husband is finishing his first novel, you see," says Violet McKisco in *Tender Is The Night*. "It's on the idea of Ulysses. Only instead of taking twenty-four hours my husband takes a hundred years. He takes a decayed old French aristocrat and puts him in contrast with the mechanical age. . . ." The novel was also under pressure, as time went on, on the social side. The successful serious novels of the 'twenties were almost all in the general sense radical.

This is equally true of the home-grown novelists like Dreiser, Lewis, and Anderson and of the more "advanced" exile writers like Hemingway. With rare exceptions, where these radicals were not swayed toward the Revolution of the Word, they were affected by Marxist ideas, which in other quarters were nearly as stylish. This drift carried a whole series of novelists into a kind of writing where the life they saw and imagined became a means of illustrating prior, doctrinaire social theories; for only a few writers were Marxist ideas instruments of discovery American experience seems to bear out Trotsky's argument that a proletarian literature is impossible.

Both of these pressures encouraged, then, novels very different from the kind Dreiser and Lewis and Dos Passos and Fitzgerald were writing. On the whole they wrote Mr Bennett's kind of novel; and, ill-defined though it is in her pamphlet, it was Mrs Woolfs kind of novel Mrs Woolf preferred, as it was nearly raw preachment of the line that *The New Masses* and the John Reed Clubs wanted. These forces, together with a generous share of the characteristic scorn of any period for its immediate predecessors, served effectively to conceal the fact that the main intellectual and formal influence on the novel after the first war was still the tradition which came down through the 'nineties and the Georgian period. "No one," remarked Edmund Wilson much later, "seems to have noticed that *Axel's Castle* and *To the Finland Station* are complementary books." It is quite true. And, making due allowance for the difference in the two men's ages, there is a clear similarity between the values of *Axel's Castle* and of the Thomas Parke D'Invilliers who set Amory Blaine to reading so energetically in Swinburne and Wilde and—the list is worth taking, name by name—"Shaw, Chesterton, Barrie, Pinero, Yeats, Synge, Ernest Dowson, Arthur Symons, Keats, Sudermann, Robert Hugh Benson, The Savoy Operas." (*This Side of Paradise*.) Here—brought up to date—are the previous periods' two apparently discrepant lines of interest, the aesthetic assertion of the value of the individual consciousness and the socio-political assertion of the value of the community. Whether they are really complementary is the question. The people who were in college when the first war broke out were still reading Swinburne almost as a contemporary; even in the 'thirties, in one of the finest and most angry of the "Camera Eye" passages, Dos Passos was quoting from *Song in Time of Order* to support a revolutionary attitude. Like Swinburne himself, the writers who came of age in the period of the first World War committed themselves to both the aesthetic attitude and the social conscience without—at least at first—any sense of conflict. They were a generation that read Dowson and Wilde, Shaw and Wells indiscriminately. It is not easy now to understand how Wells could have seemed so important to them until you see how he appeared, for a moment, to have solved the problem inherent for them in the tradition. As the technical innovations forced more and more into the open the discordance of the two strains in the tradition, writers were more and more forced to face the question of whether the passionate, sensitive inner life constitutes reality and so, represented in one form or another, is the business of the novel, or whether the world of the social and political theorists' conceiving is reality and its representation the novel's business. Should the novel, that is, move toward the condition of the lyric with Joyce and Virginia Woolf, or should it move toward the condition of the case history with Dreiser and Farrell?

So many young novelists were telling each other that the H. G. Wells of *Tono Bungay* and *The New Machiavelli* ("that queer confused novel," Wells called it twenty-five years later) was a great novelist because he seemed to have solved this problem. You can certainly see even today how Wells's political talk, for all its thinness, sounded exciting and carried for the period an air of "metaphysical pathos." But what seemed to have struck the writers was the way Wells managed to make the political novel personal, to make a survey of contemporary history a part of the life of his hero so that, like the really fine account of Remington's childhood and the accounts of his affairs with Margaret and Isabel, the endless essay-writing of the political sections of *The New Machiavelli* appeared human and personally significant. "The glorious intoxicated efforts of H. G. Wells," Amory Blaine in *This Side of Paradise* called Wells's novels, "to fit the key of romantic symmetry into the elusive lock of truth." So he had seemed then.

Wells's solution was a kind of picaresque novel of ideas. Compton Mackenzie, whose *Sinister Street* (1913) was, as Frances Newman said, also "the apple of one's eye," wrote a similar kind of novel and had a similar appeal; *Youth's Encounter* is even referred to in *Manhattan Transfer*. Here, for a moment anyway, appeared to be a solution to the problem of representing the intricate inner life of the individual and also doing a kind of social history of the times. Therefore *This Side of Paradise* (1920) turned out, in Edmund Wilson's words, to be "an exquisite burlesque of Compton Mackenzie with a pastiche of H. G. Wells thrown in at the end." A number of other novels like *The Briary Bush* (1921) followed suit and even Dos Passos' *Three Soldiers* (1921) showed the influence, though it made a significant change in the form. It is ironic that Wells of all people should have had this effect, "for though he certainly had a gift for the kind of romance Fitzgerald is talking about, he was himself belligerently opposed to any novelist's spending much time on that kind of thing. He believed the novel was primarily an instrument for setting forth social arguments and ideas and firmly distinguished himself from James and Conrad on exactly this point.

> I remember a dispute we had one day as we lay on Sandgate beach and looked out to sea. How, [Conrad] demanded, would I describe how that boat out there sat or rode or danced or quivered on the water? I said that in nineteen cases out of twenty I would just let the boat be there in the commonest phrase possible...if I wanted to make it important then the phrase to use would depend on the angle at which the boat became significant. But it was all against Conrad's oversensitive receptivity that a boat could ever be just a boat. He wanted to see it with a definite vividness of his own. But I wanted to see it and to see it only in relation to something else—a story, a thesis. (*Experiment in Autobiography*.)

There is, of course, a wonderful confusion in all this. Wells is probably right that Conrad sometimes indulged the fine shades of his awareness of detail at the expense of the whole and even, occasionally, took more interest in the evocative rhetoric of his thesis than in its point; "essentially sentimental and melodramatic," Wells called his work, anticipating almost exactly Dos Passos' later judgment of Fitzgerald's. But if there is something in this judgment, Wells is himself either disingenuous or remarkably innocent about a boat's being just a boat—whatever that is. He seems to have some notion that there is an easily available objective boat which Conrad wants to clutter up with all sorts of decorative qualities, whereas Wells is content to present the simple boat itself, which Conrad knows as well as he does if he will only be sensible. Yet Wells has a point; he wants to see things primarily "in relation to...a story." If it is a mistake to suppose that the shared world of familiar ways of seeing things is made up of boats which are "just boats," and that its realization does not involve a gift and a great deal of care and attention, it is also true that this is a world which it is perilous to omit from a fiction. In the end Wells failed because he became so interested in his thesis that his natural gift for realizing this world was more and more neglected in his books and they thinned out into endless and dreary lecturing. But if he could have done with more of Conrad's regard for receptivity, Conrad could certainly have done with more of Wells's interest in presenting the world as the everyday awareness receives it and Wells's consequent concern for what that world is about ("My dear Wells," he would say, apparently genuinely puzzled, "what is this Love and Mr Lewisham about?")

As Wells's interest in the particulars of the world he dealt with declined with his growing interest in social generalizations about it, the solution to the problem of the novel which he had seemed to offer lost influence. Almost simultaneously he and Mackenzie faded out, both as writers and as influences, so that by 1925, when the two generations met in the persons of Fitzgerald and Mackenzie, Fitzgerald was saying: "You get no sense from him that he feels his work has gone to pieces. . . . The war wrecked him as it did Wells and many of that generation."

Meanwhile, under the influences I have mentioned, the novel of inner experience was rapidly developing an elaborate and self-conscious form which made more and more delicate and lyrical accounts of that experience possible largely by excluding more and more of the world of ordinary, everyday apprehension; and the naturalistic novel was excluding more and more of the inner experience of its characters and narrator in order to be what was called the collective novel. With the most gifted and responsible novelists the dilemma created by this split remained, apparently inescapable. There is a dramatic display of its consequences in a letter Dos Passos wrote Fitzgerald in 1936 when Fitzgerald published "The Crack-Up." "There are always those," Fitzgerald remarked in another connection, "to whom all self-revelation is contemptible. . . ." It is the interest of Dos Passos' protest that he had more serious grounds than these for complaining about "The Crack-Up."

There has always been in Dos Passos, as there was not in Wells, a novelist of inner experience; this novelist wrote the earliest things, turned up only slightly disguised as John Andrews in *Three Soldiers*, and made an appearance looking like Joyce and E. E. Cummings in the "Camera Eye" passages of *U. S. A.*; the degree to which Dos Passos is capable in these passages of isolating his awareness in the small world of sensory responses is remarkable and disturbing:

> the raindrops fell one by one out of the horsechestnut tree over the arbor onto the table in the abandoned beergarden and the puddly gravel and my clipped skull

where my fingers move gently forward and backward over the fuzzy knobs and hollows...shyly tingling fingers feel out the limits of the hard immortal skull under the flesh a deathshead and skeleton sits wearing glasses in the arbor under the lucid occasional raindrops inside the new khaki uniform inside my twentyone-yearold body that's been swimming in the Marne in red and whitestriped trunks in Chalons in the spring.

Most of the time, however, Dos Passos is a social novelist, and the social novelist is completely unacquainted with this thin-skinned and tingling-fingered death's-head in glasses. It is almost as if Dos Passos had solved the personal problem of living in an everyday world which can neither be satisfactorily imagined nor decently ignored by making that world his main business. Yet what makes even this main business better in Dos Passos than it is in other social novelists is the way his narrative—despite an almost deliberate impoverishment—does something more than present the interplay of typical social attitudes. Malcolm Cowley, in one of the best things that has ever been written about Dos Passos, observed that "we are likely to remember [*The Big Money*] as a furious and sombre poem, written in a mood of revulsion even more powerful than that which T. S. Eliot expressed in "The Waste Land."' The comparison is perhaps not very apt, but the point about Dos Passos is true. The effect of *U.S.A.* is the effect of a world in which no man wins, whether he "succeeds" as do Charlie Anderson and Richard Savage and Margo Dowling, or fails as do Mary French and Ben Compton and Evelin Hutchins; their defeat in either case is a defeat beyond political redress.

Yet on the whole Dos Passos' characters are the two-dimensional sort we expect in the Jonsonian tragedy of humors, and his events are thin and diagrammatic rather than full of the felt contingency of experience. *U.S.A.* has the characteristic brilliant architecture of the Jonsonian tragedy on a very large scale, but what it organizes is a set of notes—often brilliant notes—for people and events, rather than the fully realized things. It is devastating, for example, to compare the scene where Daughter and Dick Savage decide not to have their baby with Hemingway's "Hills like White Elephants." This is the significant part of Dos Passos' scene:

> Dick was hoping she'd go, everything she did drove him crazy. There were tears in her eyes when she came up to him. "Give me a kiss, Dick...don't worry about me...I'll work things out somehow."
> "I'm sure it's not too late for an operation," said Dick. "I'll find out an address tomorrow and drop you a line to the Continental...Anne Elizabeth...it's splendid of you to be so splendid about this."
> She shook her head, whispered goodby and hurried out of the room.
> "Well, that's that," said Dick aloud to himself. He felt terribly sorry about Anne Elizabeth.

What must be the deliberate and calculated thinness of this dialogue, the deliberate reduction of it to a set of outlined clichés, is clear enough if you put it beside an equal amount of Hemingway's dialogue, alive as it is in every phrase with the immediate movement of feeling in the characters and, ultimately, with Hemingway's feeling about the whole situation.

"It's really an awfully simple operation, Jig," the man said. "It's not really an operation at all."

The girl looked at the ground the table legs rested on.

"I know you wouldn't mind it, Jig. It's really not anything. It's just to let the air in."

The girl did not say anything.

"I'll go with you and I'll stay with you all the time. They just let the air in and then it's an perfectly natural."

"Then what will we do afterward?"

"We'll be fine afterward. Just like we were before. . . . "

"And you think then we'll be all right and be happy."

"I know we will. You don't have to be afraid. I've known lots of people that have done it."

"So have I," said the girl. " And afterward they were all so happy."

The same thing happens if you put a passage of Dos Passos' narrative beside a passage of Fitzgerald's. This is Dos Passos' account of Dick's arrival at Harvard.

> He sent his trunk and suitcase out by the transfer company from South Station and went out on the subway. He had on a new grey suit and a new grey felt hat and was afraid of losing the certified check he had in his pocket for deposit in the Cambridge bank...Kendall Square . . . Central Square...Harvard Square. The train didn't go any further; he had to get out, something about the sign on the turnstile *Out to the College Yard* sent a chill down his Spine.

"He was afraid of losing the certified check. . . . " "Something about the sign . . . sent a chill down his spine." These are the merest notations of sentiments. Like Dos Passos' dialogue, they are deliberately deprived of all Dos Passos' sense of immediate experience, which has been drained off into the "Camera Eye" passages. This, in contrast, is one of Fitzgerald's schoolboys on his first week-end away from a school where he has been desperately and humiliatingly unpopular.

> . . . he went for luncheon to the Manhattan Hotel, near the station, where he ordered a club sandwich, French fried potatoes and a chocolate parfait. Out of the corner of his eye he watched the nonchalant, debonair, blasé New Yorkers at neighboring tables.... School had fallen from him like a burden; it was no more than an unheeded clamor, faint and far away. He even delayed opening the letter from the morning's mail which he found in his pocket, because it was addressed to him at school. He wanted another chocolate parfait, but being reluctant to bother the busy waiter any more, he opened the letter and spread it before him instead. [This letter is from Basil's mother, suggesting a trip to Europe which will take him away from the school for the rest of the year.] Basil got up from his chair with a dim idea of walking over to the Waldorf and having himself locked up safely until his mother came. Then, impelled to some gesture, he raised his voice and in one of his first basso notes called boomingly and without reticence for the waiter. . . . It required the din of Forty-second Street to sober his maudlin joy. With his hand on his purse to guard against the omnipresent pickpocket, he moved cautiously toward Broadway.

Fitzgerald is here dealing with a far simpler being than Dos Passos' Dick Savage, yet where Dos Passos is thin, Fitzgerald is richly concrete; moreover, every detail Fitzgerald introduces is there because it is a characteristic part of the awareness of young manhood and forces our minds to summon up and share Basil's feelings. We not only know in this way what Basil felt and assent to it; we also measure, with the guidance of Fitzgerald's irony the distance between ourselves and boyhood, the exact distance we have come from club sandwiches and chocolate parfaits, from boyhood's habit of *finding* our morning's mail in our pocket, from the fear of the busy waiter and the omnipresent pickpocket, from all the simple, intense suffering and joy of young manhood. With Dos Passos we merely note the individual character's feelings and slide into a simple attitude toward him, but with Fitzgerald, as with Hemingway, we feel in imagination what he feels and grow gradually into an attitude toward all he is. This attitude is neither simple nor static, because it has not been built up by details which I have almost no purpose except to repeat the generalized idea of the paragraph as a whole. Our attitude toward what Hemingway and Fitzgerald tell us is complex and dramatic because each of the details which have contributed to creating it has had a considerable independent life of its own, and what they write provides us in Coleridge's phrase "such delight from the *whole*, as is compatible with a distinct gratification from each component *part*." In Dos Passos the component parts are, with a kind of deliberation, given only the kind of interest that reflect from the whole.

Yet If Dos Passos characters are two-dimensional and if their experience is never more than outlined for us, still the effect of the world of his narrative as a whole unstylish as some of its more superficial implications may be at the moment, is impressive. If you ignore the intrusive or undigested material like the "Camera Eye" passages and the biographies then the pattern of successes and failures with their common defeat, the controlled accumulation and variety of recognizable if slightly realized people and experiences have a value which I think it is impossible to achieve without Dos Passos' large-scale design. Because the basic evaluation of experience which develops, at least through the latter half of *U. S. A.*, is consistent and is in one way or another a part of the presentation of every person and event, it takes on a kind of weight and meaning for us which the feeling in, for instance, A *Farewell to Arms*, with its comparatively small scope and intense and very particular realization, never quite does.

But the Dos Passos who wrote the narrative of *U. S. A.* is, nonetheless, only part of Dos Passos, the public man and his public feelings, and as Auden once remarked,

> Private faces in public places
> Are wiser and nicer
> Than public faces in private places.

The Fitzgerald whom Dos Passos was taking to task about "The Crack-Up," on the other hand, was a novelist who made a lifework of being his personal self and of trying to understand what that was. His self was profoundly affected by the world he lived in and in his way he understood that, but it was not affected in a way that can be represented by the techniques of the social novelist.

> Dos [he wrote Edmund Wilson in 1933] was here, & we had a nice evening—we never quite understand each other & perhaps that's the best basis for an enduring

friendship. . . . He told me to my amazement that you had explained the fundamentals of Leninism, even Marxism the night before, & Dos tells me that it was only recently made plain thru the same agency to the *New Republic*. I little thought when I left politics to you & your gang in 1920 you would devote your time to cutting up Wilson's shroud into blinders! Back to Mallarmé!

No doubt Wilson, who, if he has never been able to reconcile them, has never ignored either Mallarmé or Lenin, was similarly attacked by Dos Passos when he appeared to be sliding back to Mallarmé.

As a novelist Fitzgerald works always with action and action characteristic of his society and familiar to us all; that is why even his finest stories have something for the dullest readers and could be sold to popular magazines. Yet his lifelong desire to understand himself involved him in trying to grasp the conduct of the people around him by getting at that part of their inner moral experience which coincided, in kind, with his own. As a result all the action in his novels is, like his account of Basil, a tracing—in events, gestures, turns of thought—of the movement of awareness in his characters or in himself as narrator. In his best work even the smallest detail of action is governed by this kind of understanding ("She was alseep—he stood for a moment beside her bed [,]sorry for her, because she was asleep, and because she had set her slippers beside her bed"), and this kind of interest in the movement of awareness as it demonstrates itself in action is what Mr Lionel Trilling, in a fine recent article, has called an interest in "manners." "My manners," says Dick Diver in *Tender Is The Night*, "are a trick of the heart"; and so are all the minutely observed manners, good or bad, kind- or hard-hearted, in Fitzgerald's novels. It was in this respect that he found that "the very rich are different from you and me." "Almost for that remark alone," Mr Trilling quite rightly says, "he has been received in Balzac's bosom in the heaven of novelists."

Fitzgerald's "Crack-Up" is an account of a major moral crisis in his life. To the task of understanding it he brought all his considerable resources and because he was in so many ways a representative man, such an understanding has a good deal more than a merely biographical interest. But Dos Passos felt that Fitzgerald was fiddling while Rome burned, as in a way he was. Fitzgerald's account of his Crisis—completely honest and fully imagined as it is—omits entirely all that Dos Passos thought most real. Social forces, those more or less personified abstractions, which have, at whatever remove, had their part in reducing him to the state he describes hardly figure in his awareness of it. Not that Fitzgerald has not a sense of history, just as Dos Passos has a sense of the personal life; a kind of history, in fact, fascinated Fitzgerald. But his history is never abstract forces; he knows these "forces" only as they exist in the personal moral experience of himself and the people he understands. Such history as he could realize is fully experienced history.

> By 1927—he could for instance write—a wide-spread neurosis began to be evident, faintly signalled, like a nervous beating of the feet, by the popularity of cross-word puzzles. I remember a fellow ex-patriate opening a letter from a mutual friend of ours, urging him to come home and be revitalized by the hardy, bracing qualities of the native soil. It was a strong letter and it affected us both deeply, until we noticed that it was headed from a nerve sanitarium in Pennsylvania.

This is Fitzgerald's way of knowing the everyday world which surrounds him and his characters, and in his novels it can be very impressive. It shows an incurable preference for experiencing things, with however superior a sensitiveness, in essentially the same way the ordinary imagination of his time does; he had a happy incapacity for subduing his imagination to any system of abstract categories. This incapacity held him always in contact with the familiar world of our everyday awareness, and so unenslaved by either an aesthetic or a social theory. It also left him, unfortunately, without any general theory, a thing which—so long as it does not corrupt the imagination—a writer can surely never have too much of. As a result Fitzgerald never quite reaches the point where you feel he has constructed a fable adequate to the whole occasion of which it is a particular instance; the personal aspect of individual experience bulks too large. "Life," he confessed to having thought when he was young, "was something you dominated if you were any good." Life taught him better than that, but it is the pathos of his personal life that he never admitted to himself the extent to which it dominated *him*.

Dos Passos, on the other hand, knows the everyday world of ordinary apprehension—in which the essential Dos Passos appears to be so self-consciously not at home—as the movement of whole groups and classes and the clash of group prejudices. He is so preoccupied with representing these movements by newspaper headlines, historical figures, and, above all, by type characters that he reduces the movement of awareness in his characters to the simplified pattern we ascribe to the imaginary average man. You do not know his people except as you know the journalist's average businessman, Vassar girl, or labor leader; nor can you believe that the drama of their lives represents Dos Passos' full awareness of experience; the stifling personal and sensory awareness of the "Camera Eye," so completely isolated from any larger context, is the Dos Passos who is omitted from the narrative: it is his Mallarmé, as the narrative is his Lenin. The unbridged gap between these two has always been in Dos Passos. It is quite as clear, for instance, in *Three Soldiers*, between Fuselli, who lives entirely in terms of the clichés of a laissez-faire society, and John Andrews, who lives in a world of imagination which can absorb the arts and nature but is aware of the ordinary social world only as an unpleasant and frequently intolerably humiliating intrusion.

Thus when Dos Passos, speaking as the man who wrote the narrative part of *U.S.A.*, protests in his letter to Fitzgerald against "The Crack-Up's" neglect of his kind of history, his complaint sounds like a bad editorial. The very fact that this is a personal letter underlines the superficial rhetorical quality of these attitudes toward the world of common experience, their lack of any deep roots in his intimate personal experience.

> Why Scott—you poor miserable bastard—he wrote—it was—damned handsome of you to write me. . . . I've been wanting to see you, naturally, to argue about your *Esquire* articles—Christ, man, how do you find time in the middle of the general conflagration to worry about all that stuff? . . . most of the time the course of world events seems so frightful that I feel absolutely paralysed. . . . We're living in one of the damnedest tragic moments in history. . . . Forgive the locker room peptalk.

Locker room pep talk indeed; certainly this sounds uncomfortably strained, like so much of our talk about ideas which we know ought to move us but don't, and don't because a moment in history is not tragic. Only a person is tragic. It is true that forces which are more or less public or at least not merely personal must produce the situation in which the person suffers or his story becomes sentimental and insignificant, as Dos Passos obviously feels Fitzgerald's had become. Yet the situation, the moment in history, is not itself tragic; it only provides the occasion on which the aware individual suffers the experience of unavoidable moral choices. No matter what the occasion, there is no tragedy where the forces of circumstances are not transmuted into personal experience. There is only indignation, rhetoric—locker room or otherwise. "We can do only within the heart," says the subadar in Faulkner's "Ad Astra," "while we see beyond the heart." Dos Passos' letter is an attempt to say as if from the heart something that exists for him almost entirely as something seen beyond the heart. This is his characteristic fault, as Fitzgerald's is that he never saw beyond the heart in a conscious and controlled way at all.

The problem for the novelist is today what it was in Wells's and Conrad's time, the problem of absorbing into the felt, personal awareness out of which good writing comes the huge, impersonal world presented with such deadening inhumanity by journalists and historians. Yet the efforts of most of the talented writers of our time have gone into developing the resources of the novel either for the intense, personal apprehension of experience or for the collective social apprehension of it. A considerable number of them have taken the first course, and their concentration on the development of formal techniques for expressing nuances of feeling has drawn these writers further and further away from the kind of awareness of which they have too little to begin with. For all the critical hullabaloo in the 'thirties over such geniuses as Clara Weatherwax, very few really talented writers besides Dos Passos have taken the second course, perhaps only Steinbeck and Farrell. The really disturbing thing about the social novel is that, in a cruder, more journalistic form, it seems to be capturing the serious novelist's audience. The Richard Wrights and the Lillian Smiths have powerful social problems to pose and simple solutions to suggest. The thing they have not got at all is the thing that gives Dos Passos' narrative its distinction, a refinement of moral feeling which, if it is not fully realized, is still there in the movement of the novel's action. The result is books in which brutality and lust of the most violent kind are authorized for virtuous consumption by a pitifully vague but entirely respectable humanitarian attitude. It is easy to think of any number of novelists of some talent who have written more or less impoverished novels with skill and elegance, from Cabell and Frances Newman to Eudora Welty and Eleanor Clark. It is equally easy to follow the line of the social novel which scorns mere receptivity and form, from Dreiser and Upton Sinclair through the authorities on the American peasant in the 'twenties and the proletarian novelists of the 'thirties to the less dialectical but more sensational problem novelists of the 'forties. The novelists it is difficult to find in any numbers are those who can write what Mr Trilling calls the novel of manners.

No doubt the perfect novel of manners will never be written. There are rigidities in the Jamesian "given" in both of the worlds the novelist must unite which probably can never be wholly reduced. But a reasonable solution of these difficulties is nonetheless the task the 20th Century novelist has to face, and along with him the critic. The possibility for such a solution is always present in writers like Fitzgerald and Faulkner and Hemingway. Still none of these writers has as yet produced a novel in which the eccentrically conceived and obsessive personal moral problem has not to some extent seriously distorted or even excluded a satisfactory account of the conditions which were its occasion, and to this extent Dos Passos was right to protest against Fitzgerald's attitude in "The Crack-Up." Yet if the novel of manners is to come from any place, it will probably come from Fitzgerald's kind of novel rather than from Dos Passos'; for Fitzgerald's kind of novel starts with manners, even though it may not include enough of them or the most significant. But Dos Passos' kind of novel hardly ever gets around to manners at all.

Naturalism: No Teacup Tragedies

MALCOLM COWLEY

American critic Malcolm Cowley details the history and influence of naturalism from Émile Zola's Darwinian definition in the late 1800s (see Zola entry) through its application by American novelist Frank Norris (see Norris entries) to the new, more optimistic naturalism of Algren, Ellison and Bellow. Though he disagrees with the pessimism of the naturalistic method, Cowley offers a useful interpretation of its impact on American fiction of the first half of the twentieth century. Arguing against naturalism as an extension of realism, he explores the romantic element of naturalism in its tendency to magnify events, people and forces. After Norris, American naturalism resurfaced as a response to the depression years of the 1930s in Steinbeck's *The Grapes of Wrath* and Dos Passos and Farrell's trilogies. Among all the representatives of naturalism Cowley decries a deficiency of language in the novelists' attempts to present an objective reality. Such objectivity, he claims, ultimately fails, as no good novelist can be dispassionate about his or her subject. After a long discussion of the problems of socialist realism among Communist writers, Cowley presents evidence of a new brand of naturalism among American writers. They are, he states, more optimistic about the efficacy of the individual struggle against oppressive social and economic conditions. Even though the protagonists are ultimately defeated by these conditions, they retain an individuality their naturalistic predecessors lacked.

1.

Several times in these chapters I have objected to the disparaging fashion in which some critics use words derived from "naturalism" and to their habit of applying the bad words to any novel with a social and general subject. One reason for

Source: Malcolm Cowley, "Naturalism: No Teacup Tragedies", *The Literary Situation*, New York: The Viking Press, 1954, pp. 74-95.

objecting to the habit is that it conceals a purpose which ought to be clearly stated: the critics mean to advocate a rather narrow and specialized conception of what good novels should or shouldn't do. Any novel that does more than present a crisis in the lives of a few individuals they regard as "naturalistic," and not worth talking about. But there is another objection too: the critics are spoiling words that can be very useful when properly applied. "Naturalism" and "naturalistic" belong to a definite literary tradition, one that was originated by several French authors, but was taken over and named by Émile Zola in 1869. During the next two decades it spread over Europe, which in those easier days included Spain and Russia. It was introduced to this country in the early 1890s and still plays a fairly important part in American writing. It isn't my tradition, for I disagree with its doctrines and even more with the slipshod manner in which they are usually applied. Nevertheless, it has produced some admirable novels, not all of them by European authors, and it has contributed to our picture of the modern world.

Naturalism appeared in this country almost surreptitiously, with the private printing in 1893 of Stephen Crane's *Maggie: A Girl of the Streets*. Maggie's story was that of a tenement girl mistreated by her drunken mother, seduced by a tough, forced into prostitution, deserted and driven to suicide; like other naturalistic heroines, she was a pawn on a chessboard and the victim of forces beyond her control. In dedicating a copy of the book to a Baptist minister, Crane said, "It tries to show that environment is a tremendous thing in this world and often shapes lives regardlessly. If I could prove that theory, I would make room in heaven for all sorts of souls (notably an occasional street girl) who are not confidently expected to be there by many excellent people," he was helping to set the naturalistic pattern, both in his emphasis on environment and in his defiance of many excellent people.

Except for a brief period and indirectly, Crane was not a disciple of Zola's. he was to write a second naturalistic novel *George's Mother*, but most of his short career was devoted to a less objective type of writing that was closer to his personal vision. Frank Norris—who was a year older than Crane, but less precocious—would be the first American novelist to become a formal convert to naturalism and, with a few infidelities, to cherish its doctrines to the end. He didn't learn them in France, where he spent two of his most impressionable years. Norris was a very young art student in Paris, not a writer, and the books he read were chiefly concerned with medieval history and romance. It was after he returned to this country and entered the university of California in 1890 that he discovered Zola. For the next four years, so his classmates reported, he was usually to be seen with one of Zola's yellow-backed novels in his hand.

What did he learn from the novels? In Zola's working notes, which Norris of course had never seen, but which one might say that he divined from the published fiction, the founder of naturalism had indicated some of his aims as a writer. He was trying to create a new type of fiction ruled by scientific laws, based on scientific methods; if successful, he would recapture for himself, and for literature, some of the prestige that had begun to surround the great scientists. "sturdy men as simple elements and note the reactions," he said. Notebook in hand, he studied them as if they were specimens in a biological laboratory. Many of the specimens were thieves, drunkards, or prostitutes and Matthew Josephson's life of Zola tells how the great novelist and respectable family man—wearing a velvet-collared overcoat, a bowler hat, and pince-nez glasses—could be seen taking notes in houses of assignation. "What matters most to me," he said, "is to be purely naturalistic, purely physiological. Instead of having principles (royalism, Catholicism) I shall have laws (heredity, atavism)." And again, "Balzac says that he wishes to paint men, women, and things. I count men and women as the same, while admitting their natural differences, and *subject men and women to things.*" In that last phrase, which Zola underlined, he expressed the central naturalistic doctrine, derived from the whole Darwinian movement: that men and women are part of nature, subject to natural laws, and indeed the helpless victims of natural force.

The characteristics of naturalism in the proper sense of the word—not in the critics loose sense—are derived from the practice of Zola and other novelists who accepted the doctrine. Naturalism is pessimistic about the fate of individuals; it holds that there is no reward on earth or in heaven for moral actions, or punishment for vice. Naturalism is rebellious, or at least defiant. With each new work it says again to respectable society, "Here is life with the veils stripped away; here are better men than you, broken and obliterated through no fault of their own; here is an end to your complacency." At the same time naturalism claims to be objective; it claims that an author can deliberately choose a subject, observe it, take notes, and present the results like a laboratory report. It approaches situations and characters from the outside; if the novelist projects himself into a character he is in danger of losing his objectivity. Naturalism is inclusive rather than selective, being an attempt to present the totality of a big subject; it is literature in breadth rather than depth. In practice it is careless about the sound or style of the words it uses, being based on the eyes (and the nose) rather than the ears. Things play an important part in it—not the novelist's impression of things, but the actual hard, angular, soiled, and smelly objects. In practice as in theory it leads to a magnification of forces, crowds, conditions, and a minification of persons.

Frank Norris, in his American adaptation of naturalism, carried this last tendency to an extreme that Zola never reached. "Men were nothings, mere animalculae, mere ephemerides that fluttered and fell and were forgotten between dawn and dusk," he said in the next-to-last chapter of *The Octopus*. "Men were naught, life was naught; FORCE only existed—FORCE that brought men into the world, FORCE that made the wheat grow, FORCE that garnered it from the soil to give place to the succeeding crops." But Norris was also impressed by two other characteristics of naturalism. In an editorial on Zola, written at the beginning of his own literary career, he said:

> Terrible things must happen to the characters of the naturalistic tale. They must be twisted from the ordinary, wrenched from the quiet, uneventful round of everyday life and flung into the throes of a vast and terrible drama that works itself out in unleashed passions, in blood and in sudden death. The world of M. Zola is a world of big things; the enormous, the formidable, the terrible is what counts; no

teacup tragedies here.... Everything is extraordinary, imaginative, grotesque even, with a vague note of terror quivering throughout like the vibration of an enormous and low-pitched diapason.... Naturalism is a form of romanticism, not an inner circle of realism.

Bigness and romance: these were two qualities that Norris tried to embody in all his novels. He thought he had found a perfect expression for them in 1899, when he laid the plans for his "Epic of the Wheat." It was to consist of three novels, the first dealing with California as producer of wheat, the second with Chicago as distributor, and third with Europe (or India, in a later plan) as consumer. All three books, he said in a letter to William Dean Howells, would

> keep to the idea of this huge Niagara of wheat rolling from West to East. I think a big epic trilogy could be made out of such a subject, that at the same time would be modern and distinctly American. The idea is so big that it frightens me at times, but I have about made up my mind to have a try at it.

He had his try at it; he wrote the first volume bravely, *The Octopus*, and the second doggedly, *The Pit*; then he died before he could start the third. Although his trilogy—which would have been the second in the history of serious American writing, after Cooper's *The Littlepage Manuscripts*—was never finished, his dream of bigness lived in the minds of many novelists who followed him. Dreiser, Upton Sinclair, David Graham Phillips, Sinclair Lewis, and many others tried to find epical, modern, distinctly American subjects—no teacup tragedies here—and most of them planned trilogies or whole interrelated series of novels that would be realistic in treatment but would be based on an essentially romantic emotion.

It seems to us now that the 1930s were the great age of naturalistic fiction. They were also the depression years and a time of social bad conscience, so that most of the novels dealt with the under-nourished third of the nation. If they ended with a hopeless strike or a parade of the unemployed, or with the hero risking his life by urging hungry men to unite, like Tom Joad in *The Grapes of Wrath*, they were known as proletarian or revolutionary novels. Most of these are remembered dimly for their political innocence and wooden writing, but among them were two powerful works that will continue to be read for a long time: one was of course *The Grapes of Wrath*, and the other was James T. Farrell's *Studs Lonigan* trilogy. Erskine Caldwell was a naturalist and a good one in his particular fashion; probably he is still good, although most of the critics have stopped reading the books in which he keeps applying the same formula to slightly different groups of degraded characters. Not all the naturalists wrote about starving people. John Marquand, with a more conservative cast of mind, became the most accurate observer of almost upper-class families in the Eastern sea-board states, and John O'Hara the most accurate observer of cafe society. Finally there is John Dos Passos, whose trilogy *U. S. A.* is the most impressive and possibly the best of American works in the naturalistic tradition. In any case, he deals with the biggest subject of all—not an industry, like Sinclair in *The Jungle*; not a profession, like Lewis in *Arrowsmith*, or a background, like Farrell in *Studs Lonigan*; but thirty years of the whole country, with many of its industries, many professions, a diversity of backgrounds, and hundreds of characters, all driven to failure, even the richest of them, by forces beyond their control.

Although the naturalistic tradition is at present loosely defined and widely condemned, it is by no means abandoned. Among the postwar writers those who are naturalistic in the proper sense of the word form a third group that might be set beside the combat novelists (note that some of these, including Norman Mailer, are naturalistic too) and the new fictionists. It is not a group in the social sense, for its members are scattered over the country and seem to be hardly conscious of one another's existence; yet their work retains a family likeness, as if they had all inherited the same sharp eyes and indifferent sense of hearing. In general they seem to be less certain of what they believe than were the naturalists of the 1930s. They are also less ambitious in their search for material, and not one of them has displayed anything like Dos Passos' curiosity about everything that happens in American life. Retaining the objective point of view and the naturalistic interest in conditions that "often shape lives regardlessly," they prefer to write about a special community or background, usually their own. Some of their postwar subjects have been a small city with its interwoven lives (*Sironia, Texas*), a Midwestern county over the years (*Raintree County*), boys going wrong in the Chicago slums (*Knock on Any Door*), the motion-picture business (*What Makes Sammy Run*), a military school (*End as a Man*), and the younger generation on the Pacific Coast (*Corpus of Joe Bailey*).

The plot or theme of such novels, as distinguished from the subject, is usually simple. In some the protagonist—we can't often call him a hero—is warped by his environment, tempted into crime, and shot down by the police (or taken to the electric chair); the mood is always passive. In others the protagonist succeeds in business because of faults that keep him from being truly human. In still others a community is morally ruined by industrialism or commercialism. Almost all the characters in all the stories are victims of forces beyond their control, but there are some naturalistic novels—like *Corpus of Joe Bailey*—in which the protagonist resists the forces and achieves a sort of emotional maturity. Since the novelist is interested in the social background that leads to success, and more often to failure, and since he deals at length with many other characters who cross the path of the hero-victim-villain, he ends by writing a very long book. If a manuscript comes to a publisher's office in a single neat folder, it is likely to be new-fictional. If it arrives in a suitcase or a wooden packing box, it is either historical or naturalistic.

In their effort to achieve bigness and totality, the new naturalists, like their predecessors, are likely to be careless about the structure and texture of their novels. Some of the episodes will occupy a disproportionately large space in the disproportionately long manuscript—unless an editorial reader blue-pencils them—while others will be foreshortened. Frank Norris—not Crane, who cared about words—was the grandfather of these novelists, and he often expressed his contempt for careful writing. "What pleased me most in your review of *McTeague*," he said in a letter to Isaac Marcosson, "was "disdaining all pretensions to style." It is precisely what I try most to avoid. I detest "fine writing," "rhetoric," "elegant English"—

tommyrot. Who cares for fine style! Tell your yarn and let your style go to the devil. We don't want literature, we want life." Yet Norris's novels are full of fine writing in the bad sense and usually end with a deep-purple passage. "Annixter dies," he says on the last page of The Octopus, "but in a far distant corner of the world a thousand lives are saved. The larger view always and through all shams, all wickednesses, discovers the Truth that will, in the end, prevail, and all things, surely, inevitably, resistlessly work together for good." That is not only illogical, as a deduction from the story he has told; it is shameless and self-hypnotizing in its use of language.

With a few exceptions the present-day naturalists have followed Norris, both in his contempt for elegant English and in his failure to see that he often wrote with bogus elegance. That is one reason why—to make a confession of faith—I couldn't ever accept their tradition as my own. I have always felt by instinct that language was the central problem, of any writer, in any creative medium. If he lacks the sense of words he may be an admirable scholar, a moral philosopher, a student of human behavior, or a contriver of big dramatic scenes, but he isn't properly a writer. Yeats said that style in literature is what corresponds to the moral element in men of action. I think he meant that style is the result of an infinite number of choices, all determined by standards of what is linguistically right and wrong. "Books live almost entirely because of their style," he said—and he was echoing a long line of creative artists who felt that until the right words have been found for an action it does not exist in words, in literature.

There are other objections to naturalism, and one of them is based on the human implications of the doctrine. When the naturalists say that men are subject to natural laws they usually mean that human destinies are determined by the principles of mechanics, or chemistry, or genetics, or physiology, or a rather mechanical type of economics. Each novelist seems to have his favorite science: for Zola it was the laws, or imagined laws, of heredity that bound together his enormous series of novels. For Jack London the explanation of human behavior lay in biology— "I mean," says his auto-biographical hero, Martin Eden, "the real interpretative biology, from the ground up, from the laboratory and the test tube and the vitalized inorganic right on up to the widest esthetic and social generalizations." No activity was strictly human for London, not even administering a charity or producing a work of art; they were all applications of biology. For Dreiser the key science was chemistry, and he explained the failure of his brother Paul by the "lack of a little iron or sodium or carbon dioxide in his chemical compost." For Dos Passos the laws were economic and governed the concentration of "power superpower." Every year, so he believed, a smaller number of always larger corporations was exercising a closer control over the lives of more and more Americans. His central purpose in U. S. A. was to explain how people were ruined by "the big money."

All these novelists and many others were trying to explain the personal by the impersonal and the complicated in terms of the simple: society in terms of selfishness, man in terms of his animal inheritance, and the organic in terms of the inorganic. Something was always omitted at each stage in this process of reduction. To say, as many naturalistic writers have done, that man is a beast of prey, or "a mechanism, undevised and uncreated," or a collection of chemical compounds, or a simple economic unit, is a faulty way of describing man, since it omits his special characteristics. It is a metaphor, not a scientific statement, and a metaphor that subtracts from literature the whole notion of responsible purposes, the whole possibility of tragic action.

Finally I would object that naturalism involves a false conception of the writer himself. It holds that a novelist or a dramatist should be a dispassionate observer, like a scientist in his laboratory; that he should choose an important subject, methodically gather material, arrange it into a dramatic pattern, and then submit his report. But good novels are seldom written in that fashion; they are written because the novelist has been chosen by his subject and because the material, forced upon him by everything in his past, urgently demands to be expressed. The fact is that most naturalistic writers have violated, in practice, their own ideal of objectivity. There is an autobiographical element in the best of the naturalistic novels, from *Sister Carrie* to *U. S. A.* and beyond; it helps to explain their emotional power. The element is present even in novels that seem far from the authors' lives, as we learn from reading their memoirs. Thus Upton Sinclair said of his best book, *The Jungle*:

> I wrote with tears and anguish, pouring into the pages all that pain which life had meant to me. Externally, the story had to do with a family of stockyard workers, but internally it was the story of my own family. Did I wish to know how the poor suffered in Chicago? I had only to recall the previous winter in a cabin, when we had only cotton blankets, and had put rags on top of us, shivering in our separate beds. . . . Our little boy was down with pneumonia that winter, and nearly died, and the grief of that went into the book.

After the success of his novel about the meat-packing industry in Chicago, Sinclair wrote novels about other cities (Denver, Boston) and other industries (oil, coal, whisky, automobiles). He demonstrated his capacity for research, for telling stories, and for painting broad pictures. but the subjects were outside his personal experience and he didn't write about them with the warmth of feeling that distinguished *The Jungle*. Other naturalistic novelists, almost all of them, have had the same failures in sympathy. They are at their best not when they are scientific or objective in accordance with their own doctrines, but when they are least naturalistic, most subjective and lyrical.

2.

Lately a change has been evident in the leading ideas of many naturalistic writers. Their novels still follow the pattern established by Crane, Norris, and Dreiser—that is, their heroes are still victims, betrayed by circumstances into criminal follies that lead to disasters—but now the follies are likely to be excused in a new fashion. They used to be the result of either the heroes' bad heredity (*McTeague*) or more often of their bad environment (*An American Tragedy*, *Native Son*). In recent years heredity has played a rather small part in naturalistic novels and social environment isn't so often presented as the only reason why the heroes or heroines were victimized. Instead of being ruined by poverty or wealth or racial prejudice, they are in many cases deformed by some traumatic experience in childhood. The heroine is seeking for a lost father image (see William Styron's brilliant first novel, *Lie Down in Darkness*), or else she was raped by an older man (as in John O'Hara's *Butterfield 8*), with the result that she became a frigid nymphomaniac. The hero was rejected by his mother—sometimes we are told that she weaned him too soon—or else he hates his father as a sexual rival and an image of authority (see *Prince Bart*, by Jay Richard Kennedy). All the heroes are Oedipus; the heroines are either Electra or Messalina.

This Freudian myth in its various forms is of course not confined to naturalistic novels. It appears still oftener in what I have called the new fiction—as note all the stories about sensitive young men with possessive mothers—and even furnishes plots for musical comedies and motion pictures (with subplots for soap operas). Besides showing that the public is familiar with notions derived or distorted from Freudian psychology, this wide use of the myth is also connected with a general literary movement that seems to be dominant everywhere in Western literature: a movement from sociology to psychology, from political to personal problems, in a word, from the public to the private.

East of the Elbe—and, with variations, among the minority of Communist writers in France and Italy—there is a movement in the opposite direction, that is, from novels about individual lives to novels about masses of men, written with a public purpose. In France and Italy the purpose is to prove that the workers are mistreated and hence to prepare them for a Communist seizure of power; the novels are revolutionary. In Russia they are patriotic, conformist, and their purpose is to advance various programs of the Soviet state. Every Communist who appears in the novels is supposed to be heroic; the non-Communists can become heroic by accepting Communist leadership; the anti-Communists are always villains. All the characters represent political tendencies or attitudes toward the state, and so little is said about their private lives that they almost cease to be persons.

There are substantial rewards and punishments for Russian writers. Those who follow instructions earn a great deal of money—often more than they can spend—and occupy a more privileged social position than their colleagues in the West. Those who disobey the watchful critics aren't published at all, no matter how popular their past works may have been. Fantastic as the situation seems to us, it bears a resemblance to some American practices. Radio and television writers in this country are under almost as close surveillance by patriotic pressure groups. Some of the mass-circulation magazines—though by no means all of them—present subjects for treatment by fiction writers they can trust. "Why don't you do a two-fisted serial about oil prospecting in the Gulf of Mexico?" the editor says persuasively. "It's very much in the news." During World War II the imposed subject was often the result of a government directive: for example, the Air Force asked for help from the mass-circulation magazines when it had difficulty persuading men to be tail gunners on bombing planes, and the magazines obliged by ordering stories with tail gunners as heroes. Even in peacetime some of our weeklies outdo the Russians by presenting a novelist with both a subject and a ready-made plot, asking him only to provide descriptions and dialogue.

Here the parallel ends. If the American novelist refuses the subject or the plot, if he prefers to deal with more personal themes, he has other avenues of publication. Many writers earn comfortable incomes without once appearing in the mass-circulation magazines, and they are admired for preserving a sort of artistic chastity. For a real parallel with Russia we should have to imagine that the *Saturday Evening Post* and *Collier's*, with a very few others, were the only magazines to print fiction, that they were interlocked with the only publishing houses, that they were staffed by government and party functionaries, and that novelists who wouldn't follow their directives not only couldn't be published but would become politically suspect. We might also have to imagine that a novel approved and published in 1945 would have to be withdrawn from circulation in 1948, although it was still extremely popular, because the directives had changed. Exactly that happened in the case of Fadeyev's *The Young Guard*, whose author had to make a public confession of error and then had to revise his picture of the war before the novel could be reissued by the State Publishing House.

It would be a mistake, however, to judge Soviet literature in theory by its practice of the last few years. The theory, known as "socialist realism," has always taken for granted that literature exerts a direct effect on social life, and therefore has always been willing to admit that a wise society, a workers' society, would control its novelists for their own good. On the other hand, the theory did not contemplate that the control would be so rigid, so comprehensive, and so anti-esthetic as it has been in Russia since 1948. There were special reasons for that period of repression, and the cold war was only one of them. There was the Russian habit, which is also an American habit, of carrying everything to extremes; there was Stalin's attitude toward art—that of a tired businessman; and there was the single-minded Communist efficiency of Andrei A. Zhdanov, who had taken charge of cultural affairs. In 1953, after both men were dead, signs appeared that artists in all fields, including fiction, might be granted a somewhat greater degree of freedom. Even the bureaucrats themselves were beginning to admit that "a creative problem cannot be solved by bureaucratic means," as Aram Khachaturian, one of the composers scolded by Zhdanov, was finally allowed to say in the magazine *Soviet Music*.[1]

As a theory, socialist realism should be judged by its achievements in years like those from 1932 to 1936 and from 1943 to 1947, when novels were being written and published with somewhat less interference from the Soviet bureaucrats. It might also be judged by novels of the school that were produced in France, England, and America during the 1930s and are now being produced by Communist writers in France and Italy. On this basis, that of its best periods and productions, socialist realism proves to be a theory of fiction which, like naturalism, has produced many valuable and impressive works. As a matter of fact it developed out of naturalism, at least on the technical side, and has retained many characteristics of the earlier school. Some of these are the close study of social environments, the interest in the behavior of crowds, the approach to characters from the outside—as if they were specimens for dissection—and, most of all, the emphasis on subject matter at the expense of form. In Russia "formalism" and "subjectivism" are serious charges against a writer, almost the equivalent of political crimes. The Russian doctrine resembles naturalism in holding that novelist can deliberately choose a subject for treatment, almost without respect to his past experience, but it goes a step farther by holding that the subject can also be chosen for the novelist by the workers' party or by the state.

In 1948 Russian writers were collectively scolded because they hadn't produced a sufficient number of articles about the new irrigation projects. In 1953 some of those projects were deferred, and the Central Committee of the Communist Party adopted a new program calling for a greatly increased production of foodstuffs and consumer goods. In December of that same year the writers were scolded again, this time because the new program, after three months, still hadn't been reflected in more and better novels about the collective farms. Although writers were being given a little more freedom, consumer goods and foodstuffs were the pressing need and hence an imposed subject for novels. Said the *Literary Gazette*, in a leading article translated for the *New York Times*:

> No substantial improvement in the activities of the secretariat of the Union of Soviet Writers is evident, even since the September plenary session of the Central Committee.... A great and difficult task lies before our writers: to produce books that help the people in their great creative activities. To depict accurately and profoundly the life of the people in all its aspects and in every sphere of activity, to express the all-pervasive grandeur of the Soviet man and to express the fundamental and typical processes of our epoch—such is the task of Soviet literature. But contemporary Soviet life will not be truly portrayed unless it is shown that the struggle for the prosperity of collective and state farms has become a matter of supreme importance for the people in general.

The Literary Gazette was explaining that writers' aims, even in a period of comparative freedom, must still be those of the state, and that a socially imposed subject must be executed without delay. Earlier in this chapter I tried to explain the faults of naturalism. Socialist realism has almost all of them, and it also has a serious fault of its own, growing out of its political conformity: novelists are expected to "depict accurately and profoundly the life of the the people in all its aspects," but their picture must agree with that of the Central Committee, which is the final judge of literary truth. Old-fashioned naturalists look for and sometimes discover truths of their own. With this exception, however, socialist realism has most of the virtues of naturalism. It presents us with big, dramatic subjects, it treats them in a bold fashion, and it gives the reader a feeling that the novelist isn't running away from life but is embracing it in all its ugliness and infinite fertility. The doctrine also has one virtue in which naturalism is conspicuously lacking: it offers a system of moral values and allows its characters to choose between good and evil. Sometimes they choose to do good at the cost of their lives, and then the socialist realist is able to write in something that approaches the tragic spirit. When Malraux was a socialist realist he wrote *Man's Fate*, which is a tragic novel. *The Silent Don*, by Mikhail

Sholokhov, is a collective tragedy, that of the Cossack people, and it is the novel of our time that comes closest to being another *War and Peace*. I might add that both Malraux and Sholokhov were writing from experience, or from an imaginative projection of experience, and that neither of them produced his book to order.

It has sometimes been suggested that the ideal might lie somewhere between the present Western and the present Russian practice. One could start with either, I have heard it said, and arrive at better novels by a mixture of qualities selected from West and East. Thus, one could start with the Soviet novel, subtract the bureaucratic control, add a greater psychological depth and more attention to form, and the result would be possible masterpieces. Again, one could start with the American novel, give it broader subjects, more interest in contemporary problems, more social responsibility—without surrendering any of its virtues—and the result would be almost the same. The one weakness of this most attractive program is that novels aren't compounded by a judicious mixture of ingredients. Sift together one cup of psychological depth with two cups of subject matter, knead into form, bake in a medium oven, and the result is nothing.

The Western ideal of novels based on personal experience is essentially right and the present Russian ideal of socially useful novels produced to order is wrong. The Western ideal is right because novels should be true at all levels and because such truth can't be achieved without a long accumulation of feelings and observations. The Russian ideal is wrong because social aims and political programs—especially new ones—are likely to be accepted only on the top level of the mind. It is always conceivable that some novelists might write very well about the new irrigation projects or about the new program for collective farms, but that would be chiefly by accidents of personality. That is, the novelists might be obsessed, as many persons are, by the image of running water; or they might have risen from the peasantry and might be excited by the vision of new lives for families like their own. But where one novelist would write well about the projects and programs, a dozen others would be unable to make the personal connection, and their books would be dutiful, shallow, and nonexistent as literature.

The newer American criticism has provided us with methods for understanding the weakness of novels written to order (including those whose authors agreed with the order and thought they were performing their simple duty). If we examine the language and structure of such books; if we analyze their rhythms, their images, their use of symbols, their choice of significant details, we find that all of these are out of keeping with the novelists' conscious purposes. The optimism is revealed to be forced, the convictions to be hollow, the characters to be not of a piece. Subconsciously the novelists have rebelled against the subject imposed on them and have refused to assimilate the information gathered in a pile of notebooks; it is merely information, not experience. "Man," said Marcel Proust, "is the creature who cannot get outside himself, who knows others only in himself, and when he says the contrary he lies." That is an extreme statement of the limitation under which we operate as writers and human beings, but the limitation can be transcended, as Proust showed in *Remembrance of Things Past*. Man does know others, if only in and through himself, and each life is the mirror of many others: By looking intently at our own experience, each of us can find social institutions and values, the diminished reflection of the world in which we live, so that even the purest type of personal or subjective novel has implications for its age and country. When Proust started to explain what a dinner party meant to himself, he ended by explaining a considerable area of French society.

The weakness of many American novelists today is that the books they write are based on a narrow segment of their experience and that the experience itself has been too narrow. Life on a college faculty or in a narrow circle of sophisticated people doesn't often give the novelist a sense of living in history, nor does it often lead to any broad knowledge of men and manners. I should hesitate to advise a change of life for anyone who has already made a place for himself, though I do think that apprentice novelists should pause and reflect before they decide to combine writing with teaching. For somewhat older novelists there is the possibility of making a more intensive use of what they are. "Look in your hearts and write," I heard one of them say to his students with an apologetic smile. If the novelists looked deeply enough into their own hearts and minds, they would find a broader image of American life than most of them have been presenting. I think of one example, that of William Faulkner, who lived in a Mississippi town and wrote essentially for himself, sometimes without thinking, so he said, that strangers might read what he wrote; yet when strangers did read it they found that his books contained a picture of the Deep South and an interpretation of Southern history—even a system of values and a myth of the sort that critics had been admiring in Hawthorne and Melville.

3.

Two men are spending the night in a police station on Division Street, in the Polish quarter of Chicago. They aren't sure why they have been arrested, but they work for Zero Schwiefka, who runs a gambling house, and they guess that he tried to get out of paying his weekly tribute to Police Sergeant Kvorka. One of the men is Francis Macjinek, alias Frankie Machine, who is a wizard with cards but can't do anything with people, including himself. Frankie has two great sorrows: that his wife Sophie is a psychotic invalid and that he can't stop taking morphine—"can't get the monkey off my back." His one devoted henchman is the other prisoner, Sparrow Saltskin, whose trade is steering clients into the gambling house, when he isn't stealing dogs or committing other forms of petty larceny. Sparrow is "a little offbalanced," as he likes to say, "but oney on one side. So don't try offsteerin' me, you might be tryin' my good-balanced side."

In the morning a roach falls into the slop bucket in their cell. It reminds Frankie of his own fate and he starts to rescue it, but then he changes his mind. "You ain't get tin' out till I get out," he says. Zero Schwiefka bails out his two employees. Climbing the stairs to freedom, Frankie turns back to take the roach out of the bucket, but finds that it has drowned. The roach is the familiar animal symbol that is introduced at the beginning of so many naturalistic novels; one remembers the land turtle in *The Grapes of Wrath*, crawling obstinately to no destination, just as the Joad family would crawl westward on the highway; and one remembers the cornered rat that Bigger Thomas killed in the first chapter of *Native Son*, as Bigger himself would be killed at the end of the story. This time, however, the symbol is a mixture of the grotesque and the absurd, with a hint that the author feels a wry affection for his characters and even for the roach.

I have been retelling the first episode of Nelson Algren's novel, *The Man with the Golden Arm*. The rest of the story will follow the naturalistic pattern, but with a mixture of new qualities foreshadowed by the symbol. Frankie is another hero as victim; he was an orphan and never had a chance; he had been expelled from parochial school when the coppers raided a crap game and took him off to jail; he had never been taught a trade except dealing cards; Sophie had forced him to marry her by pretending to be pregnant; in the Army he had been severely wounded and had been given morphine to deaden the pain, until he learned to steal the drug when the doctors stopped prescribing it. Back in Chicago he had smashed a second-hand car when Sophie and he were drunk, and Sophie, in her sub-conscious desire to retain his affection, had convinced herself that she was hopelessly crippled. Now the pattern of victimization will be traced to the end. Frankie will be badgered into killing a dope peddler; he will be hunted by the police, while Sophie is taken to the county asylum; he will be hidden for a time by a strip teaser who loves him (she is another victim); then at last he will be cornered in a cheap hotel and driven to commit suicide; all his life will be written in the passive mood. Most of the minor characters are also driven and deformed by conditions beyond their power to change, as in every naturalistic novel since Zola, but there is some0 thing different in the author's approach to the story. Instead of repeating that vast forces are grinding these people down, he takes the forces for granted. What he emphasizes is the other side of the picture, the rebellions and lies and laughter by means of which they retain, even the most repulsive of them, some remnants of human pride.

The most repulsive of all the characters is Piggy-O, the blind dope peddler who hates more fortunate people and hasn't bathed since he lost his sight, because he enjoys the idea that he is inflicting his smell on mankind. Like the others, he drinks in the Tug & Maul bar, but Anton the Owner makes him stand at the end of the bar, next to the men's toilet, so that the smell of disinfectant will deaden the smell of Piggy. Anton asks him why he hasn't pride enough to bathe, and Piggy-O answers, "I got *my* kind of pride, 'n you got yours—I'm proud of being how *I* am too." That pride in being themselves makes the characters something more than the specimens they would be in purely naturalistic novels. Instead of being a clinical study in degradation, the book comes close to being a poem about degradation, written in sometimes lyrical prose. Instead of leaving us with a feeling of defeat, it celebrates the unconquered personality and humor in the lowest of men: hustlers, junkies, stoolies, dips, stewbums, "the Republic's crummiest lushes...even the most maimed wreck of them all," the author says, "held, like a pennant in that drifting light, some frayed remnant of laughter from un-frayed years."

The Invisible Man, by Ralph Ellison, is another novel that starts with social conditions and ends as a defense of the separate personality. Its unnamed hero, who tells his own story, has been expelled from a Southern Negro college for no fault of his own. Still eager to succeed, he finds work in a white-paint factory on Long Island and is injured through the malice of another Negro. In the factory hospital he is given electric-shock treatments because the doctors want a subject for experiment. The scene shifts to Harlem, where he is recruited by the Communists and, on revealing a talent for public speaking, is made their district leader. Soon the Communists abandon and betray him; they have changed their policy and decided to foment a race riot by supporting a group of Negro fanatics. In the midst of the riot he is pursued by the fanatics and narrowly escapes being lynched. Once again the hero has been a victim whose story can be told in the passive mood, but *The Invisible Man* is far from being a naturalistic novel. The technique is closer to that of the expressionists: every scene is exaggerated, even caricatured, in order to convey what the novelist thinks is the essential truth about it. Almost every act has a symbolic value, and many of the scenes are too fatly symbolic—like the picture of black men working in a sub-basement to make a black liquid that, when carried upstairs into the sunlight, will turn paint dazzlingly white.

At the end of the novel even the plot ceases to be naturalistic and becomes a sort of parable. The hero falls through a manhole into a coal cellar and thus escapes from the black mob that is trying to lynch him. After finding an unused basement room, he lives there alone and meditates on his past life. He decides that everybody has regarded him simply as a material, a natural resource to be used. Nobody has ever seen him as a person; he has been the invisible man. For all the resentment he feels against the white race, he realizes that his dilemma is not merely that of a Negro; it is the dilemma of all men in a mechanized civilization. "Who knows," he says to the presumably white reader at the end of the novel, "but that, on the lower frequencies, I speak for you?"

Still another novel—*The Adventures of Augie March*, by Saul Bellow—leads by a more roundabout path to a somewhat similar conclusion. This time the background is Chicago in the depression years. The hero is a Jewish boy who, at the beginning of the story, is living with his meek, half-blind mother and his two brothers. The youngest, Georgie, is feeble-minded, and the father is a shiftless failure who has deserted the family. At present the Marches are miserably poor, but this isn't the sort of novel that will pursue them to the point where their lives are crushed out by conditions and forces. Simon, the oldest brother, has an inner force that is capable of surmounting conditions. He is determined to get rich, he makes a brilliant marriage, and at the end of the book he is an overbearing, pot-bellied, unhappy man of affairs. Augie March is less certain of what he wants to do. He is bright, engaging, uncommitted, so that dozens of persons want to pick a career for him, enlist him in their schemes, adopt him as a son, or take him for a lover—and Augie always consents in the beginning, but there is something stubborn in him that makes him follow his own path even though he isn't certain where it goes. Always he remains uncommitted; always he breaks away and is ready to start a new adventure.

Some of the adventures are criminal: Augie is the friend of gangsters, he helps to rob a leather-goods store, and later, while attending lectures at the university, he supports himself by stealing books. Other adventures are grotesque, as when he becomes chauffeur and delivery boy for a boarding kennel that calls itself a dogs' club, or when he is employed as secretary and ghost writer by a demented millionaire. In one chapter he is a union organizer pursued by goons; in the next he is driving to Mexico with a rich woman bent on hunting iguanas with an eagle. The adventures, interesting as they are in themselves, are chiefly occasions for introducing new characters. Each of these has a separate life, and many have something more than that, a sort of demonic power. Among others there is Anna Coblin, who appears at the beginning of the book. "As she had great size and terrific energy of constitution," Augie says of her, "she produced all kinds of excesses. Even physical ones: moles, blebs, hairs, bumps on her forehead, huge concentrations on her neck; she had spiraling reddish hair springing with no negligible beauty and definiteness from her scalp." Most of Bellow's Chicago characters are like that: excessive, but with definite features of no negligible beauty.

Augie, who tells their stories, has a feeling for the integrity of each separate person; he is ready to love and admire them all, so long as each embodies a different pattern or principle of life. His own development from one episode to another is simply toward a greater awareness of his own nature. "I have always tried to become what I am," he tells a wise old rascal named Mintouchian, whom he also loves and admires. At the end of the book Augie is living in Paris and acting as Mintouchian's agent in black-market deals. He adores his wife, but she is getting ready to deceive him with a French aristocrat, and he has had to relinquish his dream of starting a foster home in which to educate many children. But he is happy enough simply observing people in their endless variety. "Why," he says at last, "I am a sort of Columbus of those near-at-hand and believe you can come to them in this immediate *terra incognita* that spreads out in every gaze."

All three of these novels have "big" subjects of the types that are usually treated in naturalistic fiction. All three are concerned with social forces, but they don't leave us with the impression that the forces were everything or that the characters were "nothings, mere animalculae," as Norris called them at the end of *The Octopus*. A few other novelists have been writing in much the same spirit; I might mention Herbert Gold (*Birth of a Hero* and *The Prospect before Us*) and Harvey Swados (*Out Went the Candle*). I suspect that these novels and others belong to a new category of postwar fiction, smaller but no less important for the future than the categories described in earlier chapters. Is there a name for this new tendency or group or school? Perhaps the name is suggested in Swados' first novel, which I read in manuscript. At one point the hero, on a visit to Pompeii, is accosted by a little boy selling filthy souvenirs. He buys them all and throws them away. "There are times," he explains, "when you have to do things you know are useless. . . . It isn't just conscience-salving. It's a way of proving to yourself that you're still a person. And that's something you have to prove over and over."

Since all the novelists end by affirming the value of separate persons in conflict with social forces, I have thought of calling them personalists. The name, of course, has been used in other connections, but it has the present advantage of applying to the different styles in which the novels are written as well as to the doctrine they all imply. Each of the novelists seems to believe that the author himself should be a personality instead of a recording instrument, and therefore he keeps trying to find a personal approach and a personal manner of writing. The effort is sometimes carried too far and in fact all the novels have faults that are easy to discern: Algren, for example, keeps falling into a burlesque of himself, Ellison sacrifices his sense of reality to his passion for symbols, and Bellow, though he writes with more authority than the others, still has trouble holding his long book together and making it more than a series of adventures. These faults, however, are the price each of them pays for taking risks that other novelists have been a little too willing to avoid.

Yet other postwar novelists have written some admirable books, whatever the category in which we place them—new fiction, combat novels, or old-fashioned naturalism. There is a weakness in the topographical or taxonomic method I have been following in these chapters—I mean the method that consists in surveying American writing as if from a distance and naming its recent types and tendencies. The method reveals the sorts of qualities, usually faults or foibles, that are common to a group, but not the more important qualities that make a novel survive as a separate work of art. Take for example *The Member of the Wedding*, by Carson McCullers. From the taxonomic standpoint it belongs to the genus New Fiction, species Southern, variety Coming to Knowledge of Pre-adolescent Girl (or *rite de passage*), and thus can be filed away with half a dozen books by other writers. What the survey does not reveal is that it is written with an intensity of feeling and a rightness of language that the others fail to achieve; it has the power over the reader of a correctly spoken incantation.

Or take a not widely read novel by Harriette Arnow, *Hunter's Horn*. This time the genus is Naturalism (with symbolic overtones), the species Hillbilly, the variety Obsessive Pursuit of a Wild Animal. Once again the survey does not reveal the special quality of the novel, which is partly the poetry of earth, partly the sense of a community, and partly a sort of in-feeling for the characters, especially the women, that hadn't appeared in any other novel about the Kentucky hill people since Elizabeth Madox Roberts's *The Time of Man*.

The postwar period has not produced any novels that the future is likely to call great—only the future is entitled to speak of greatness—but it has produced many works, famous or neglected, that are unique in their species and varieties and deserve to be read for many years. Perhaps the central fault of the period is that novelists as a class have been cautious in their choice of subjects and methods and timid about expressing their convictions. As justification for timidity they can plead the climate of the age, which has not been friendly to experiments in living or thinking. Yet the age has effected some fundamental changes in the American character, and these have not been mirrored in the novels, most of which are traditional in their form, as in their sense of life. Many of the novelists are serious, skillful, and perceptive, but one feels that most of them are without a definite direction—not stumbling, or not enough, but walking briskly, heads erect, eyes forward, within imaginary fences. A very few, including those I called personalists, have been more reckless than the rest, and perhaps they are finding directions that others can follow. The immediate future of American writing depends largely on the writers themselves. At the same time it depends on what the naturalists would describe as conditions and forces—that is, on the state of the world and whether it remains at peace, on the continuing vigor and freedom of American culture, and on the daily lives of men and women who write for the public. Since their books have to be printed before they are read, the future of literature also depends on the health of the publishing industry.

Note

1. By the summer of 1954, Khachaturian had been reproved for his bourgeois deviation; the bureaucratic control of literature was being tightened again.

The Cult of Experience in American Writing

PHILIP RAHV

In the second essay in the book, Rahv explores the American author's quest (especially that of James) for experience as a rebellion against the Puritan "morality of abstention." While European writers automatically accept experience as a given from which they struggle with values, the American author begins with a naïve sense of life as something to be sought. Such a pursuit, Rahv argues, allows neither for the intellect nor ideas, both of which are suspect in the American author's preference for concrete reality. In the modern period, Hemingway epitomizes this spontaneous drive toward experience while Faulkner, though less straightforward, also values immediate experience over order or judgment. In comparing American literature to European, Rahv attributes the former's one-sidedness to the historical successes of the American Revolution and Civil War. James (and occasionally Melville) is one of the first American novelists to deepen his themes, to juxtapose American experience to European and thus to acknowledge an historical consciousness. Rahv concludes the essay with the recognition that international forces have finally superceded national ones in influencing American writing.

Every attentive reader of Henry James remembers that highly dramatic scene in *The Ambassadors*—a scene singled out by its author as giving away the "whole case" of his novel—in which Lambert Strether, the elderly New England gentleman who had come to Paris on a mission of business and duty, proclaims his conversion to the doctrine of experience. Caught in the spell of Paris, the discovery of whose grace and form is marked for him by a kind of meaning and intensity that can be likened only to the raptures of a mystic vision, Strether feels moved to renounce publicly the morality of abstention he had brought with him from Woollett, Mass.

Source: Philip Rahv, "The Cult of Experience in American Writing", *Image and Idea: Twenty Essays on Literary Themes*. 1949; rev. ed. London: Weidenfeld and Nicolson, 1957, Pp. 7-25.

And that mellow Sunday afternoon, as he mingles with the charming guests assembled in the garden of the sculptor Gloriani, the spell of the world capital of civilization is so strong upon the sensitive old man that he trembles with happiness and zeal. It is then that he communicates to little Bilham his newly acquired piety toward life and the fruits thereof. The worst mistake one can make, he admonishes his youthful interlocutor, is not to live all one can.—

> Do what you like so long as you don't make my mistake . . . Live! . . . It doesn't so much matter what you do in particular, so long as you have your life. If you haven't had that, what *have* you had? . . . This place and these impressions...have had their abundant message for me, have just dropped *that* into my mind. I see it now...and more than you'd believe or I can express. . . . The right time is now yours. The right time is any *time* that one is still so lucky as to have . . . Live, Live!

To an imaginative European unfamiliar with the prohibitive American past and the long-standing national habit of playing hide and seek with experience, Strether's pronouncements in favour of sheer life may well seem so commonplace as scarcely to be worth the loving concentration of a major novelist. While the idea that one should "live" one's life came to James as a revelation, to the contemporary European writers this idea had long been a thoroughly assimilated and natural assumption. Experience served them as the concrete medium for the testing and creation of values, whereas in James's work it stands for something distilled or selected from the total process of living; it stands for romance, reality, civilization—a self-propelling, autonomous "presence" which in the imagination of Hyacinth Robinson, the hero of *The Princess Casamassima*, takes on a form at once "vast, vague, and dazzling—an irradiation of light from objects undefined, mixed with the atmosphere of Paris and Venice."

The significance of this positive approach to experience and identification of it with life's "treasures, felicities, splendors and successes" is that it represents a momentous break with the then dominant American morality of abstention. The roots of this morality are to be traced on the one hand to the religion of the puritans and, on the other, to the inescapable need of a frontier society to master its world in sober practice before appropriating it as an object of enjoyment. Such is the historical content of that native "innocence" which in James's fiction is continually being ensnared in the web of European "experience." And James's tendency is to resolve this drama of entanglement by finally accepting what Europe offers on condition that it cleanse itself of its taint of evil through an alliance with New World virtue.

James's attitude toward experience is sometimes overlooked by readers excessively impressed (or depressed) by his oblique methods and effects of remoteness and ambiguity. Actually, from the standpoint of the history of the national letters, the lesson he taught in *The Ambassadors*, as in many of his other works, must be understood as no less than a revolutionary appeal. It is a veritable declaration of the rights of man—not, to be sure, of the rights of the public, of the social man, but of the rights of the private man, of the rights of personality, whose openness to experience provides the sole effective guaranty of its development. Already in one of his earliest stories we find the observation that "in this country the people have rights but the person has none." And in so far as any artist can be said to have had a mission, his manifestly was to brace the American individual in his moral struggle to gain for his personal and subjective life that measure of freedom which, as a citizen of a prosperous and democratic community, he had long been enjoying in the sphere of material and political relations.

Strether's appeal, in curiously elaborated, varied, as well as ambivalent forms, pervades all of James's work; and for purposes of critical symbolization it might well be regarded as the compositional key to the whole modern movement in American writing. No literature, it might be said, takes on the qualities of a truly national body of expression unless it is possessed by a basic theme and unifying principle of its own. Thus the German creative mind has in the main been actuated by philosophical interests, the French by the highest ambitions of the intelligence unrestrained by system or dogma, the Russian by the passionately candid questioning and shaping of values. And since Whitman and James the American creative mind, seizing at last upon what had long been denied to it, has found the terms and objects of its activity in the urge toward and immersion in experience. It is this search for experience, conducted on diverse and often conflicting levels of consciousness, which has been the dominant, quintessential theme of the characteristic American literary productions—from *Leaves of Grass* to *Winesburg, Ohio* and beyond; and the more typically American the writer—a figure like Thomas Wolfe is a patent example—the more deeply does it engulf him.

It is through this preoccupation, it seems to me, that one can account, perhaps more adequately than through any other factor, for some of the peculiarities of American writing since the close of its classic period. A basis is thus provided for explaining the unique indifference of this literature to certain cultural aims implicit in the aesthetic rendering of experience—to ideas generally, to theories of value, to the wit of the speculative and problematical, and to that new-fashioned sense of irony which at once expresses and modulates the conflicts in modern belief. In his own way even a writer as intensely aware as James shares this indifference. He is the analyst of fine consciences, and fine minds too, but scarcely of minds capable of grasping and acting upon those ineluctable problems that enter so prominently and with such significant results into the literary art developed in Europe during the past hundred years. And the question is not whether James belonged among the "great thinkers"—very few novelists do—but whether he is "obsessed" by those universal problems, whether, in other words, his work is vitally associated with that prolonged crisis of the human spirit to which the concept of modernity is ultimately reducible. What James asks for, primarily, is the expansion of life beyond its primitive needs and elementary standards of moral and material utility; and of culture he conceives as the reward of this expansion and as its unfailing means of discrimination. Hence he searches for the whereabouts of "Life" and for the exact conditions of its enrichment. This is what makes for a fundamental difference between the inner movement of the American and that of the European novel, the novel of Tolstoy and Dostoevsky, Flaubert and Proust, Joyce, Mann, Lawrence, and

Kafka, whose problem is invariably posed in terms of life's intrinsic worth and destiny.

The intellectual is the only character missing in the American novel. He may appear in it in his professional capacity—as artist, teacher, or scientist—but very rarely as a person who dunks with his entire being, that is to say, as a person who transforms ideas into actual dramatic motives instead of merely using them as ideological conventions or as theories so externally applied that they can be dispensed with at will. Everything is contained in the American novel except ideas. But what are ideas? At best judgments of reality and at worst substitutes for it. The American novelist's conversion to reality, however, has been so belated that he cannot but be baffled by judgments and vexed by substitutes. Thus his work exhibits a singular pattern consisting, on the one hand, of a disinclination to thought and, on the other, of an intense predilection for the real: and the real appears in it as a vast phenomenology swept by waves of sensation and feeling. In this welter there is little room for the intellect, which in the unconscious belief of many imaginative Americans is naturally impervious, if not wholly inimical, to reality.

Consider the literary qualities of Ernest Hemingway, for example. There is nothing Hemingway dislikes more than experience of a make-believe, vague, or frigid nature, but in order to safeguard himself against the counterfeit he consistently avoids drawing upon the more abstract resources of the mind, he snubs the thinking man and mostly confines himself to the depiction of life on its physical levels. Of course, his rare mastery of the sensuous element largely compensates for whatever losses he may sustain in other spheres. Yet the fact remains that a good part of his writing leaves us with a sense of situations unresolved and with a picture of human beings tested by values much too simplified to do them justice. Cleanth Brooks and Robert Penn Warren have recently remarked on the interrelation between qualities of Hemingway's style and his bedazzlement by sheer experience. The following observation in particular tends to bear out the point of view expressed in this essay:

> The short simple rhythms, the succession of coordinate clauses, the general lack of subordination—all suggest a dislocated and un-unified world. The figures which live in this world live a sort of hand-to-mouth existence perceptually, and conceptually, they hardly live at all. Subordination implies some exercise of discrimination—the sifting of reality through the intellect. But Hemingway has a romantic anti-intellectualism which is to be associated with the premium which he places upon experience as such.[1]

But Hemingway is only a specific instance. Other writers, less gifted and not so self-sufficiently and incisively one-sided, have come to grief through this same creative psychology. Under its conditioning some of them have produced work so limited to the recording of the unmistakably and recurrently real that it can truly be said of them that their art ends exactly where it should properly begin.

"How can one make the best of one's life?" André Malraux asks in one of his novels. "By converting as wide a range of experience as possible into conscious thought." It is precisely this reply which is alien to the typical American artist, who all too often is so absorbed in experience that he is satisfied to let it "write its own ticket"—to carry him, that is, to its own chance or casual destination.

In the first part of *Faust* Goethe removes his hero, a Gothic dreamer, from the cell of scholastic devotion in order to embroil him in the passions and high-flavored joys of "real life." But in the second part of the play this hero attains a broader stage of consciousness, reconciling the perilous freedom of his newly released personality with the enduring interests of the race, with high art, politics, and the constructive labor of curbing the chaotic forces in man and nature alike. This progress of Faust is foreshadowed in an early scene, when Mephisto promises to reveal to him "the little and then the great world."—*Wir sehen die kleine, dann die grosse Welt.*—The little world is the world of the individual bemused by his personal experience, and his sufferings, guilt-feelings, and isolation are to be understood as the penalty he pays for throwing off the traditional bonds that once linked him to God and his fellow-men. Beyond the little world, however, lies the broader world of man the inhabitant of his own history, who in truth is always losing his soul in order to gain it. Now the American drama of experience constitutes a kind of half-*Faust*, a play with the first part intact and the second part missing. And the Mephisto of this shortened version is the familiar demon of the Puritan morality-play, not at all the Goethian philosopher-sceptic driven by the nihilistic spirit of the modern epoch. Nor is the plot of this half-*Faust* consistent within itself. For its protagonist, playing Gretchen as often as he plays Faust, is evidently unclear in his own mind as to the role he is cast in—that of the seducer or the seduced?

It may be that this confusion of roles is the inner source of the famous Jamesian ambiguity and ever-recurring theme of betrayal. James's heroines—his Isabel Archers and Milly Theales and Maggie Ververs—are they not somehow always being victimized by the "great world" even as they succeed in mastering it? Gretchen-like in their innocence, they none the less enact the Faustian role in their uninterrupted pursuit of experience and in the use of the truly Mephistophelean gold of their millionaire-fathers to buy up the brains and beauty and nobility of the civilization that enchants them. And the later heroes of American fiction—Hemingway's young man, for instance, who invariably appears in each of his novels, a young man posing his virility against the background of continents and nations so old that, like Tiresias, they have seen all and suffered all—in his own way he, too, responds to experience in the schizoid fashion of the Gretchen-Faust character. For what is his virility if not at once the measure of his innocence and the measure of his aggression? And what shall we make of Steinbeck's fable of Lennie, that mindless giant who literally kills and gets killed from sheer desire for those soft and lovely things of which fate has singularly deprived him? He combines an unspeakable innocence with an unspeakable aggression. Perhaps it is not too far-fetched to say that in this grotesque creature Steinbeck has unconsciously created a symbolic parody of a figure such as Thomas Wolfe, who likewise crushed in his huge caresses the delicate objects of the art of life.

The disunity of American literature, its polar division into above and below or paleface and redskin writing, I have noted elsewhere. Whitman and James, who form a kind of fatal antipodes, have served as the standard examples of this dissociation. There is one sense, however, in which the contrast between these two archetypal Americans may be said to have been overdrawn. There is, after all, a common ground on which they finally, though perhaps briefly, meet—an essential Americanism subsuming them both that is best defined by their mutual affirmation of experience. True, what one affirmed the other was apt to negate; still it is not in their attitudes toward experience as such that the difference between them becomes crucial but rather in their contradictory conceptions of what constitutes experience. One sought its ideal manifestations in America, the other in Europe. Whitman, plunging with characteristic impetuosity into the turbulent, formless life of the frontier and the big cities, accepted experience in its total ungraded state, whereas James, insisting on a precise scrutiny of its origins and conditions, was endlessly discriminatory, thus carrying forward his ascetic inheritance into the very act of reaching out for the charms and felicities of the great European world. But the important thing to keep in mind here is that this plebeian and patrician are historically associated, each in his own incomparable way, in the radical enterprise of subverting the puritan code of stark utility in the conduct of life and in releasing the long compressed springs of experience in the national letters. In this sense, Whitman and James are the true initiators of the American line of modernity.

If a positive approach to experience is the touchstone of the modern, a negative approach is the touchstone of the classic in American writing. The literature of early America is a sacred rather than a profane literature. Immaculately spiritual at the top and local and anecdotal at the bottom, it is essentially, as the genteel literary historian Barrett Wendell accurately noted, a "record of the national inexperience" marked by "instinctive disregard of actual fact." For this reason it largely left untouched the two chief experiential media—the novel and the drama. Brockden Brown, Cooper, Hawthorne, and Melville were "romancers" and poets rather than novelists. They were incapable of apprehending the vitally new principle of realism by virtue of which the art of fiction in Europe was in their time rapidly evolving toward a hitherto inconceivable condition of objectivity and familiarity with existence. Not until James did a fiction-writer appear in America who was able to sympathize with and hence to take advantage of the methods of George Eliot, Balzac, and Turgenev. Since the principle of realism presupposes a thoroughly secularized relationship between the ego and experience, Hawthorne and Melville could not possibly have apprehended it. Though not religious men themselves, they were nevertheless held in bondage by ancestral conscience and dogma, they were still living in the afterglow of a religious faith that drove the ego, on its external side, to aggrandize itself by accumulating practical sanctions while scourging and inhibiting its intimate side. In Hawthorne the absent or suppressed experience reappears in the shape of spectral beings whose function is to warn, repel, and fascinate. And the unutterable confusion that reigns in some of Melville's narratives (*Pierre, Mardi*) is primarily due to his inability either to come to terms with experience or else wholly and finally to reject it. Despite the featureless innocence and moral enthusiastic air of the old American books, there is in some of them a peculiar virulence, a feeling of discord that does not easily fit in with the general tone of the classic age. In such worthies as Irving, Cooper, Bryant, Longfellow, Whittier, and Lowell there is scarcely anything more than meets the eye, but in Poe, Hawthorne, and Melville there is an incandescent symbolism, a meaning within meaning, the vitality of which is perhaps only now being rightly appreciated. D. H. Lawrence was close to the truth when he spoke of what serpents they were, of the "inner diabolism of their underconsciousness." Hawthorne, "that blue-eyed darling," as well as Poe and Melville, insisted on a subversive vision of human nature at the same time as cultivated Americans were everywhere relishing the orations of Emerson who, as James put it, was helping them "to take a picturesque view of one's internal possibilities and to find in the landscape of the soul all sorts of fine sunrise and moonlight effects." Each of these three creative men displays a healthy resistance to the sentimentality and vague idealism of his contemporaries; and along with this resistance they display morbid qualities that, aside from any specific biographical factors, might perhaps be accounted for by the contradiction between the poverty of the experience provided by the society they lived in and the high development of their moral, intellectual, and affective natures—though in Poe's case there is no need to put any stress on his moral character. And the curious thing is that whatever faults their work shows are reversed in later American literature, the weaknesses of which are not to be traced to poverty of experience but to an inability to encompass it on a significant level.

The dilemma that confronted these early writers chiefly manifests itself in their frequent failure to integrate the inner and outer elements of their world so that they might stand witness for each other by way of the organic linkage of object and symbol, act and meaning. for that is the linkage of art without which its structure cannot stand. Lawrence thought that *Moby Dick* is profound *beyond* human feeling—which in a sense says as much against the book as for it. Its further defects are dispersion, a divided mind: its real and transcendental elements do not fully interpenetrate, the creative tension between them is more fortuitous than organic. In *The Scarlet Letter* as in a few of his shorter fictions, and to a lesser degree in *The Blithedale Romance*, Hawthorne was able to achieve an imaginative order that otherwise eluded him. A good deal of his writing, despite his gift for precise observation, consists of phantasy unsupported by the conviction of reality.

Many changes had to take place in America before its spiritual and material levels could fuse in a work of art in a more or less satisfactory manner. Whitman was already in the position to vivify his democratic ethos by an appeal to the physical features of the country, such as the grandeur and variety of its geography, and to the infinite detail of common lives and occupations. And James too, though sometimes forced to resort to makeshift situations, was on the whole successful in setting up a lively and significant exchange between the moral and empiric elements of his subject-matter. Though he was, in a sense, implicitly bound all his life by the morality of Hawthorne, James none the less perceived what the guilt-tossed psyche of the author of *The Marble Faun* prevented him from seeing—that it is not the man trusting himself to experience but the one fleeing from it who suffers the "beast in the jungle" to rend him.

The Transcendentalist movement is peculiar in that it expresses the native tradition of inexperience in its particulars and the revolutionary urge to experience in its generalities. (Perhaps that is what Van Wyck Brooks meant when, long before prostrating himself at his shrine, he wrote that Emerson was habitually abstract where he should be concrete, and vice versa.) On a purely theoretical plane, in ways curiously inverted and idealistic, the cult of experience is patently prefigured in Emerson's doctrine of the uniqueness and infinitude, as well as in Thoreau's equally steep estimate, of the private man. American culture was then unprepared for anything more drastic than an affirmation of experience in theory alone, and even the theory was modulated in a semiclerical fashion so as not to set it in too open an opposition to the dogmatic faith that, despite the decay of its theology, still prevailed in the ethical sphere. "The love which is preached nowadays," wrote Thoreau, "is an ocean of new milk for a man to swim in. I hear no surf nor surge, but the winds coo over it." No wonder, then, that Transcendentalism declared itself most clearly and dramatically in the form of the essay—a form in which one can preach without practicing.

Personal liberation from social taboos and conventions was the war cry of the group of writers that came to the fore in the second decade of the century. They employed a variety of means to formulate and press home this program. Dreiser's tough-minded though somewhat arid naturalism, Anderson's softer and spottier method articulating the protest of shut-in people, Lewis's satires of Main Street, Cabell's florid celebrations of pleasure, Edna Millay's emotional expansiveness, Mencken's worldly wisdom and assaults on the provincial pieties, the early Van Wyck Brook's high-minded though bitter evocations of the inhibited past, his ideal of creative self-fulfillment—all these were weapons brought to bear by the party of rebellion in the struggle to gain free access to experience. And the secret of energy in that struggle seems to have been the longing for what was then called "sexual freedom"; for at the time Americans seeking emancipation were engaged in a truly elemental discovery of sex whose literary expression on some levels, as Randolph Bourne remarked, easily turned into "caricatures of desire." The novel, the poem, the play—all contributed to the development of a complete symptomatology of sexual frustration and release. In his Memoirs, written toward the end of his life, Sherwood Anderson recalled the writers of that period as "a little band of soldiers who were going to free life . . . from certain bonds." Not that they wanted to overplay sex, but they did want "to bring it back into real relation to the life we lived and saw others living. We wanted the flesh back in our literature, wanted directly in our literature the fact of men and women in bed together, babies being born. We wanted the terrible importance of the flesh in human relations also revealed again." In retrospect much of this writing seems but a naive inversion of the dear old American innocence, a turning inside out of inbred fear and reticence, but the qualities one likes in it are its positiveness of statement, its zeal and pathos of the limited view.

The concept of experience was then still an undifferentiated whole. But as the desire for personal liberation, even if only from the less compulsive social pressures, was partly gratified and the tone of the literary revival changed from eagerness to disdain, the sense of totality gradually wore itself out. Since the nineteen-twenties a process of atomization of experience has forced each of its spokesmen into a separate groove from which he can step out only at the risk of utterly disorienting himself. Thus, to cite some random examples, poetic technique became the special experience of Ezra Pound, language that of Gertrude Stein, the concrete object was appropriated by W. C. Williams, super-American phenomena by Sandburg and related nationalists, Kenneth Burke experienced ideas (which is by no means the same as thinking them), Archibald MacLeish experienced public attitudes, F. Scott Fitzgerald the glamor and sadness of the very rich, Hemingway death and virile sports, and so on and so forth. Finally Thomas Wolfe plunged into a chaotic recapitulation of the cult of experience as a whole, traversing it in all directions and ending nowhere.

Though the crisis of the nineteen-thirties arrested somewhat the progress of the experiential mode, it nevertheless managed to put its stamp on the entire social-revolutionary literature of the decade. A comparison of European and American left-wing writing of the same period will at once show that whereas Europeans like Malraux and Silone enter deeply into the meaning of political ideas and beliefs, Americans touch only superficially on such matters, as actually their interest is fixed almost exclusively on the class war as an experience which, to them at least, is new and exciting. They succeed in representing incidents of oppression and revolt, as well as sentimental conversions, but conversions of the heart and mind they merely sketch in on the surface or imply in a gratuitous fashion. (What does a radical novel like *The Grapes of Wrath* contain, from an ideological point of view, that agitational journalism cannot communicate with equal heat and facility? Surely its vogue cannot be explained by its radicalism. Its real attraction for the millions who read it lies elsewhere—perhaps in its vivid recreation of "a slice of life" so horridly unfamiliar that it can be made to yield an exotic interest.) The sympathy of these ostensibly political writers with the revolutionary cause is often genuine, yet their understanding of its inner movement, intricate problems, and doctrinal and strategic motives is so deficient as to call into question their competence to deal with political material. In the complete works of the so-called "proletarian school" you will not find a single viable portrait of a Marxist intellectual or of any character in the revolutionary drama who, conscious of his historical role, is not a mere automaton of spontaneous class force or impulse.

What really happened in the nineteen-thirties is that due to certain events the public aspects of experience appeared more meaningful than its private aspects, and literature responded accordingly. But the subject of political art is *history*, which stands in the same relation to experience as fiction to biography; and just as surely as failure to generalize the biographical element thwarts the aspirant to fiction, so the ambition of the literary Left to create a political art was thwarted by its failure to lift experience to the level of history. (For the benefit of those people who habitually pause to insist on what they call "strictly literary values," I might add that by "history" in this connection I do not mean "history books" or anything resembling what is known as the "historical novel" or drama, A political art would succeed in lifting experience to the level of history if its perception of life—any life—were organized around a perspective relating the artist's sense of the *society* of the dead to his sense of the *society* of the living and the as yet unborn.)

Experience, in the sense of "felt life" rather than as life's total practice, is the main but by no means the total substance of literature. The part experience plays in the aesthetic sphere might well be compared to the part that the materialist conception of history assigns to economy. Experience, in the sense of this analogy, is the substructure of literature above which there rises a superstructure of values, ideas, and judgments—in a word, of the multiple forms of consciousness. But this base and summit are not stationary: they continually act and react upon each other.

It is precisely this superstructural level which is seldom reached by the typical American writer of the modern era. Most of the well-known reputations will bear out my point. Whether you approach a poet like Ezra Pound or novelists like Steinbeck and Faulkner, what is at once noticeable is the uneven, and at time quite distorted, development of the various elements that constitute literary talent. What is so exasperating about Pound's poetry, for example, is its peculiar combination of a finished technique (his special share in the distribution of experience) with amateurish and irresponsible ideas. It could be maintained that for sheer creative power Faulkner is hardly excelled by any living novelist, yet the diversity and wonderful intensity of the experience represented in his narratives cannot entirely make up for their lack of order, of a self-illuminating structure, and obscurity of value and meaning. One might naturally counter this criticism by stating that though Faulkner rarely or never sets forth values directly, they none the less exist in his work by implication. Yes, but implications incoherently expressed are no better than mystifications, and nowadays it is values that we can least afford to take on faith. Moreover, in a more striking manner perhaps than any of his contemporaries, Faulkner illustrates the tendency of the experiential mode, if pursued to its utmost extreme, to turn into its opposite through unconscious self-parody. In Faulkner the excess, the systematic inflation of the horrible is such a parody of experience. In Thomas Wolfe the same effect is produced by his swollen rhetoric and compulsion to repeat himself—and repetition is an obvious form of parody. This repetition-compulsion has plagued a good many American writers. Its first and most conspicous victim, of course, was Whitman, who occasionally slipped into unintentional parodies of himself.

Yet there is a positive side to the primacy of experience in late American literature. For this primacy has conferred certain benefits upon it, of which none is more bracing than its relative immunity from abstraction and other-worldliness. The stream of life, unimpeded by the rocks and sands of ideology, flows through it freely. If inept in coping with the general, it particularizes not at all badly; and the assumptions of sanctity that so many European artists seem to require as a kind of guaranty of their professional standing are not readily conceded in the lighter and clearer American atmosphere. "Whatever may have been the case in years gone by," Whitman wrote in 1888, "the true use for the imaginative faculty of modern times is to give ultimate vivification to facts, to science, and to common lives, endowing them with glows and glories and final illustriousness which belong to every real thing, and to real things only." As this statement was intended as a prophecy, it is worth noting that while the radiant endowments that Whitman speaks of—the "glows and glories and final illustriousness"—have not been granted, the desired and predicted vivification of facts, science, and common lives has in a measure been realized, though in the process Whitman's democratic faith has as often been belied as confirmed.

It is not the mere recoil from the inhibitions of puritan and neopuritan times that instigated the American search for experience. Behind it is the extreme individualism of a country without a long past to brood on, whose bourgeois spirit had not worn itself out and been debased in a severe struggle against an old culture so tenacious as to retain the power on occasion to fascinate and render impotent even its predestined enemies. Moreover, in contrast to the derangements that have continually shaken Europe, life in the United States has been relatively fortunate and prosperous. It is possible to speak of American history as "successful" history. Within the limits of the capitalist order—and until the present period the objective basis for a different social order simply did not exist here—the American people have been able to find definitive solutions for the great historical problems that faced them. Thus both the Revolutionary and the Civil War were complete actions that virtually abolished the antagonisms which had initially caused the breakdown of national equilibrium. In Europe similar actions have usually led to festering compromises that in the end reproduced the same conflicts in other forms.

It is plain that until very recently there has really been no urgent need in America for high intellectual productivity. Indeed, the American intelligentsia developed very slowly as a semi-independent grouping; and what is equally important, for more than a century now and especially since 1865, it has been kept at a distance from the machinery of social and political power. What this means is that insofar as it has been deprived of certain opportunities, it has also been sheltered and pampered. There was no occasion or necessity for the intervention of the intellectuals—it was not mentality that society needed most in order to keep its affairs in order. On the whole the intellectuals were left free to cultivate private interests, and, once the moral and aesthetic ban on certain types of exertion had been removed, uninterrruptedly to solicit individual experience. It is this lack of a sense of extremity and many-sided involvement which explains the peculiar shallowness of a good deal of American literary expression. If some conditions of insecurity have been known to retard and disarm the mind, so have some conditions of security. The question is not whether Americans have suffered less than Europeans, but of the quality of whatever suffering and happiness have fallen to their lot.

The consequence of all this has been that American literature has tended to make too much of private life, to impose on it, to scour it for meanings that it cannot always legitimately yield. Henry James was the first to make a cause, if not a fetish, of personal relations; and the justice of his case, despite his vaunted divergence from the pioneer type, is that of a pioneer too, for while Americans generally were still engaged in "gathering in the preparations and necessities" he resolved to seek out "the amenities and consummations." Furthermore, by exploiting in a fashion altogether his own the contingencies of private life that fell within his scope, he was able to dramatize the relation of the new world to the old, thus driving the wedge of historical consciousness into the very heart of the theme of experience. Later not a few attempts were made to combine experience with consciousness, to achieve the balance of thought and being characteristic of the great traditions of European art. But except for certain narratives of James and Melville, I know of very little American fiction which can unqualifiedly be said to have attained this end.

Since the decline of the regime of gentility many admirable works have been produced, but in the main it is the quantity of felt life comprised in them that satisfies, not their quality of belief or interpretive range. In poetry there is evidence of more distinct gains, perhaps because the medium has reached that late stage in its evolution when its chance of survival depends on its capacity to absorb ideas. The modern poetic styles—metaphysical and symbolist—depend on a conjunction of feeling and idea. But, generally speaking, bare experience is still the *Leit-motif* of the American writer, though the literary depression of recent years tends to show that this theme is virtually exhausted. At bottom it was the theme of the individual transplanted from an old culture taking inventory of himself and of his new surroundings. This inventory, this initial recognition and experiencing of oneself and one's surroundings, is all but complete now, and those who resist in going on with it are doing so out of mere routine and inertia.

The creative power of the cult of experience is almost spent, but what lies beyond it is still unclear. One thing, however, is certain: whereas in the past, throughout the nineteenth and well into the twentieth century, the nature of American literary life was largely determined by national forces, now it is international forces that have begun to exert a dominant influence. And in the long run it is in the terms of this historic change that the future course of American writing will define itself.

Note

1. Cf. "The Killers," by Cleanth Brooks and Robert Penn Warren, in *American Prefaces*, Spring 1942.

95

The Broken Circuit

RICHARD CHASE

In one of the major critical studies of American literature in the 1950s, Richard Chase attempts to define the peculiar character of the American novel, most often a hybrid of novel and romance in its greatest authors—Hawthorne, Twain, Melville, Hemingway and Faulkner. According to Chase, following Tocqueville, the American novel reflects the unresolved contradictions in American society. Instead of seeking to resolve these contradictions as the typical nineteenth-century English novel does, American authors depict a Manichaean quality inherited from early Puritan society. Thus the recurrent the nineteenth and early twentieth centuries. Chase further contrasts the American with the English novel, noting that the former tends toward narrowness and depth, the latter toward panorama. He credits Hawthorne with deepening and psychologizing romance and ultimately legitimizing the novel-romance genre. He concludes this chapter with a discussion of James's attempts to unite realism and romance by emphasizing a "circuit of life among extremes or opposites" (27). The authors of the novel-romances have often broken that circuit in emphasizing the romantic over the real.

A Culture of Contradictions

The imagination that has produced much of the best and most characteristic American fiction has been shaped by the culture. In a sense this may be true of all literatures of whatever time and place. Nevertheless there are some literatures which take their form and tone from polarities, opposites, and irreconcilables, but are content to rest in and sustain them, or to resolve them into unities, if at all, only by special and limited means. The American novel tends to rest in contradictions and among extreme ranges of experience. When it attempts to resolve contradictions, it does so in oblique, morally equivocal ways. As a general rule it does so either in

Source: Richard Chase, "The Broken Circuit", *The American Novel and Its Tradition*, New York: Anchor Books, 1957, pp. 1-28.

melodramatic actions or in pastoral idylls, although intermixed with both one may find the stirring instabilities of "American humor." These qualities constitute the uniqueness of that branch of the novelistic tradition which has flourished in this country. They help to account for the strong element of "romance" in the American "novel."

By contrast the English novel has followed a middle way. It is notable for its great practical sanity, its powerful engrossing composition of wide ranges of experience into a moral centrality and equability of judgment. Oddity, distortion of personality, dislocations of normal life, recklessness of behavior, malignancy of motive—these the English novel has included. Yet the profound poetry of disorder we find in the American novel is missing, with rare exceptions, from the English. Radical maladjustments and contradictions are reported but are seldom of the essence of form in the English novel, and although it is no stranger to suffering and defeat or to triumphant joy either, it gives the impression of absorbing all extremes, all maladjustments and contradictions into a normative view of life. In doing so, it shows itself to derive from the two great influences that stand behind it—classic tragedy and Christianity. The English novel has not, of course, always been strictly speaking tragic or Christian. Often it has been comic, but often, too, in that superior form of comedy which approaches tragedy. Usually it has been realistic or, in the philosophical sense of the word, "naturalistic." Yet even its peculiar kind of gross poetic naturalism has preserved something of the two great traditions that formed English literature. The English novel, that is, follows the tendency of tragic art and Christian art, which characteristically move through contradictions to forms of harmony, reconciliation, catharsis, and transfiguration.

Judging by our greatest novels, the American imagination, even when it wishes to assuage and reconcile the contradictions of life, has not been stirred by the possibility of catharsis or incarnation, by the tragic or Christian possibility. It has been stirred, rather, by the aesthetic possibilities of radical forms of alienation, contradiction, and disorder.

The essential difference between the American novel and the English will be strongly pointed up to any reader of F. R. Leavis's *The Great Tradition*. Mr Leavis's "great tradition of the novel is really Anglo-American, and it includes not only Jane Austen, George Eliot, Conrad, and Henry James but, apparently, in one of its branches Hawthorne and Melville. My assumption in this book is that the American novel is obviously a development from the English tradition. At least it was, down to 1880 or 1890. For at that time our novelists began to turn to French and Russian models and the English influence has decreased steadily ever since. The more extreme imagination of the French and Russian novelists has clearly been more in accord with the purposes of modern American writers than has the English imagination. True, an American reader of Mr Leavis's book will have little trouble in giving a very general assent to his very general proposition about the Anglo-American tradition. Nevertheless, he will also be forced constantly to protest that there is another tradition of which Mr Leavis does not seem to be aware, a tradition which includes most of the best American novels.

Ultimately, it does not matter much whether one insists that there are really *two* traditions, the English and the American (leaving aside the question of what writers each might be said to comprise) or whether one insists merely that there is a radical divergence within one tradition. All I hold out for is a provisional recognition of the divergence as a necessary step towards understanding and appreciation of both the English and the American novel. The divergence is brought home to an American reader of Leavis's book when, for example, he comes across the brief note allotted to the Brontës. Here is Leavis's comment on Emily Brontë:

> I have said nothing about *Wuthering Heights* because that astonishing work seems to me a kind of sport . . . she broke completely, and in the most astonishing way, both with the Scott tradition that imposed on the novelist a romantic resolution of his themes, and with the tradition coming down from the eighteenth century that demanded a plane-mirror reflection of the surface of "real" life. Out of her a minor tradition comes, to which belongs, most notably, *The House with the Green Shutters*.

Of course Mr Leavis is right; in relation to the great tradition of the English novel, *Wuthering Heights* is indeed a sport. But suppose it were discovered that *Wuthering Heights* was written by an American of New England Calvinist or Southern Presbyterian background. The novel would be astonishing and unique no matter who wrote it or where. But if it were an American novel it would not be a sport; it has too close an affinity with too many American novels, and among them some of the best, like many of the fictions discussed in this book *Wuthering Heights* proceeds from an imagination that is essentially melodramatic, that operates among radical contradictions and renders reality indirectly or poetically, thus breaking, as Mr Leavis observes, with the traditions that require a surface rendering of real life and a resolution of themes, "romantic" or otherwise.

Those readers who make a dogma out of Leavis's views are thus proprietors of an Anglo-American tradition in which many of the most interesting and original and several of the greatest American novels are sports. *Wieland* is a sport, and so are *The Scarlet Letter* and *The Blithedale Romance*, *Moby-Dick*, *Pierre*, and *The Confidence Man*, *Huckleberry Finn*, *The Red Badge of Courage*, *McTeague*, *As I Lay Dying*, *The Sun Also Rises*—all are eccentric, in their differing ways, to a tradition of which, let us say, Middlemarch is a standard representative. Not one of them has any close kinship with the massive, temperate, moralistic rendering of life and thought we associate with Mr Leavis's "great tradition."

The English novel, one might say, has been a kind of imperial enterprise, an appropriation of reality with the high purpose of bringing order to disorder. By contrast, as Lawrence observed in his *Studies in Classic American Literature*, the American novel has usually seemed content to explore, rather than to appropriate and civilize, the remarkable and in some ways unexampled territories of life in the New World and to reflect its anomalies and dilemmas. It has not wanted to build an imperium but merely to discover a new place and a new state of mind. Explorers see more deeply, darkly, privately and disinterestedly than imperialists, who must perforce be circumspect and prudential. The American novel is more profound and clairvoyant than the English novel, but by the same token it is narrower and more arbitrary, and it tends to carve out of experience brilliant, highly wrought fragments rather than massive unities.

For whatever reason—perhaps the nagging scrupulosity of the Puritan mind has something to do with it—the American novel has sometimes approached a perfection or art unknown to the English tradition, in which we discover no such highly skilled practitioners as Hawthorne, Stephen Crane, Henry James, or Hemingway. These writers, often overestimated as moralists, seem content to oppose the disorder and rawness of their culture with a scrupulous art-consciousness, with aesthetic forms—which do, of course, often broaden out into moral significance.

In a well known passage Allen Tate refers to the "complexity of feeling" that everyone senses in the American novel and that, as Mr Tate says, "from Hawthorne down to our own time has baffled our best understanding." The complexity of the American novel has been much exaggerated. With the exception of one or two of James's novels no American fiction has anything like the complexity of character and event of *Our Mutual Friend*, for example. In *The Scarlet Letter* or *Moby-Dick* the characters and events have actually a kind of abstracted simplicity about them. In these books character may be deep but it is narrow and predictable. Events take place with a formalized clarity. And certainly it cannot be argued that society and the social life of man are shown to be complex in these fictions.

But of course Tate says "complexity of feeling," and he is right about that. The states of feeling, and the language in which they are caught, are sometimes very intricate in American novels. Yet these musing tides of feeling and language that make such a rich poetry in our fiction often seem to be at variance with the simplified actions and conceptions of life our novels present, the origins of this apparent anomaly must be sought in the contradictions of our culture.

Marius Bewley takes up Tate's remark in an essay called "Fenimore Cooper and the Economic Age" and traces this "complexity of feeling" to a "tension" which he finds not only in Cooper but in Hawthorne and James. It is, he thinks, a political tension in its origins, although as embodied in the works of these authors, it assumes many forms. This tension, he says,

> was the result of a struggle to close the split in American experience, to discover a unity that—for the artist especially—almost sensibly *was not there*. What was the nature of the division that supported this conflict? It took on many forms concurrently; it was an opposition between tradition and progress or between the past and the future; between Europe and America, liberalism and reaction, aggressive acquisitive economics and benevolent wealth. These same divisions existed in Europe also, but there they were more ballasted by a denser social medium, a richer sense of the past, a more inhibited sense of material possibilities.

Mr Bewley's apt discussion of the matter needs to be amended in one fundamental way. The kind of art that stems from a mind primarily moved by the impulse toward aesthetic and cultural unities and thus "struggles to close the split in American experience" as an artist might wish to close it—this kind of art is practised often, though not always, by Henry James, but less often by Hawthorne and Cooper, and much less often by Faulkner, Melville, and Mark Twain. That fact is that many of the best American novels achieve their very being, their energy and their form, from the perception and acceptance not of unities but of radical disunities.

Like many readers of American literature, Bewley makes the mistake of assuming both that our writers have wanted to reconcile disunities by their art and their intelligence and that this is what they *should* have wanted to do. Behind this assumption is a faulty historical view, as well as a certain overplus of moralism, which neglects to observe that there have been notable bodies of literature, as well as of painting and sculpture, that have proposed and accepted an imaginative world of radical, even irreconcilable contradictions, and that with some important exceptions, the American novel (by which I mean its most original and characteristic examples) had been one of these bodies of literature.

Surely Cooper (as will be noted later) is not at his best in a novel like *Satanstoe*, which is a "culture-making" novel and in which his mind is moved by an image of aesthetic and political harmony. On the contrary he is at his best in a book like *The Prairie*, where the search for unity is not at the center of the stage and he can accept without anxiety or thought the vivid contradictions of Natty Bumppo and his way of life—those contradictions which, as Balzac saw, made him so original a conception. In this book Cooper is not inspired by an impulse to resolve cultural contradictions half so much as by the sheer romantic exhilaration of escape from culture itself, into a world where nature is dire, terrible, and beautiful, where human virtues are personal, alien, and renunciatory, and where contradictions are to be resolved only by death, the ceaseless brooding presence of which endows with an unspeakable beauty every irreconcilable of experience and all the irrationalities of life.

Mr Bewley is not alone in assuming it to be the destiny of American literature o reconcile disunities rather than to pursue the possibility it has actually pursued— that is, to discover a putative unity *in* disunity or to rest at last among irreconcilables. In *Democracy in America* Tocqueville tried to account for a number of related contradictions in American life. He noted a disparity between ideals and practice, a lack of connection between thought and experience, a tendency of the American mind to oscillate rather wildly between ideas that "are all either extremely minute and clear or extremely minute and clear or extremely general and vague."

Tocqueville sought a genetic explanation for these disparities. He pointed out that in aristocratic societies there was a shared body of inherited habits, attitudes and institutions that stood in a meditating position between the individual and the state. This, he observed, was not true in a democracy, where "each citizen is habitually engaged in the contemplation of a very puny object: namely, himself. If he ever looks higher, he perceives only the immense form of society at large or the still more imposing aspect of mankind.... What lies between is a void." Tocqueville believed that this either/or habit of mind also owed much to the sharp distinctions made by Calvinism and its habit of opposing the individual to his God, with a minimum of mythic or ecclesiastical mediation. He found certain advantages in this "democratic" quality of mind, but he warned Americans that it might produce great confusion in philosophy, morals, and politics and a basic instability in literary and cultural values, and that consequently Americans should try to discover democratic equivalents for those traditional habits of mind which in aristocracies had moderated and reconciled extremes in thought and experience.

Tocqueville knew that the dualistic kind of thought of which he spoke was specifically American only in the peculiar quality of its origin and expression. He saw that with the probable exception of England, Europe would characteristically concern itself during the nineteenth century with grand intellectual oppositions, usually more or less of a Hegelian order. But even though the tendency of thought Tocqueville predicated belonged to Western culture generally, one is nevertheless struck by how often American writers conceive of human dilemmas according to his scheme, and how many make aesthetic capital out of what seemed to him a moral and intellectual shortcoming.

In his studies of the classic American writers, D.H. Lawrence presented his version of the contrariety, or, as he said, "duplicity" of the American literary mind by saying that he found in writers like Cooper, Melville, and Hawthorne "a tight mental allegiance to a morality which all their passion goes to destroy," a formulation which describes perfectly the inner contradiction of such products of the American imagination as the story of Natty Bumppo. In general Lawrence was thinking of an inherent conflict between "genteel" spirituality and a pragmatic experientialism which in its lower depths was sheer Dionysian or "Indian" energy and violence. Acute enough to see that the best American artistic achievements had depended in one way or another on this dualism, he seemed ready nevertheless to advocate, on moral grounds, a reconciliation of opposites, such as he thought he discerned in the poems of Whitman.

In short, like all the observers of American literature we are citing in these pages, Lawrence was trying to find out what was wrong with it. He is a sympathetic and resourceful reader—one of the best, surely, ever to turn his attention to the American novel. But he thinks that the American novel is sick, and he wants to cure it. Perhaps there is something wrong with it, perhaps it is sick—but a too exclusive preoccupation with the wrongness of the American novel has in some ways disqualified him for seeing what, right or wrong, it *is*.

Finally, there is the division of American culture into "highbrow" and "lowbrow" made by Van Wyck Brooks in 1915 in his *America's Coming-of-Age*. Brook's essay is a great piece of writing; it is eloquent, incisive, and witty. But we have lived through enough history now to see its fundamental error—namely, the idea that it is the duty of our writers to heal the split and reconcile the contradictions in our culture by pursuing a middlebrow course. All the evidence shows that whatever American literature has pursued the middle way it has tended by a kind of native fatality not to reconcile but merely to deny or ignore the polarities of our culture. Our middlebrow literature—for example, the novels of Howells—has generally been dull and mediocre. In the face of Brooks's desire to unite the highbrow and the lowbrow on a middle ground, there remains the fact that our best novelists have been, not middlebrows, but either highbrows like James, lowbrows like Mark Twain, Frank Norris, Dreiser, and Sherwood Anderson, or combination highbrow-lowbrows like

Melville, Faulkner, and Hemingway. Here again American fiction contrasts strongly with English. The English novel at its best is staunchly middlebrow. The cultural conditions within which English literature has evolved have allowed it to become a great middlebrow literature—the only one, it may be, in history.

Let us in all candor admit the limited, the merely instrumental value of the terms used in the last paragraph. They work very well, and are in fact indispensable, in making large cultural formulations. But in applying them to individual authors the terms must be constantly re-examined. We might ask, for example, whether from one point of view both Hawthorne and James performed the unlikely feat of becoming great middlebrow writers. Both of them, at any rate, achieve a kind of contemplative centrality of vision within the confines of which their minds work with great delicacy and equanimity. In so far as they do this, one certainly cannot chide them for shying away from some of the more extreme contradictions, the more drastic forms of alienation, the more violent, earthly, or sordid ranges of experience which engage the minds of Melville and Faulkner, and in fact most of our best writers. Yet to achieve a "contemplative centrality of vision" certainly requires an action of the mind; whereas the word "middlebrow," although suggesting centrality of vision, inevitably suggests, judging by our American literature, a view gained by no other means than passivity and the refusal of experience.

To conclude this brief account of the contradictions which have vivified and excited the American imagination, these contradictions see traceable to certain historical facts. First, there is the solitary position man has been placed in in this country, a position very early enforced by the doctrines of Puritanism and later by frontier conditions and, as Tocqueville skilfully pointed out, by the very institutions of democracy as these evolved in the eighteenth and nineteenth centuries.

Second, the Manichaean quality of New England Puritanism, which, as Yvor Winters and others have shown, had so strong an effect on writers like Hawthorne and Melville and entered deeply into the national consciousness. From the historical point of view, this Puritanism was a back-sliding in religion as momentous in shaping the imagination as the cultural reversion Cooper studied on the frontier. For, at least as apprehended by the literary imagination, New England Puritanism—with its grand metaphors of election and damnation, its opposition of the kingdom of light and the kingdom of darkness, its eternal and autonomous contraries of good and evil—seems to have recaptured the Manichaean sensibility. The American imagination, like the New England Puritan mind itself, seems less interested in redemption than in the melodrama of the eternal struggle of good and evil, less interested in incarnation and reconciliation than in alienation and disorder. If we may suppose ourselves correct in tracing to this origin the prevalence in American literature of the symbols of light and dark, we may doubtless suppose also that this sensibility has been enhanced by the racial composition of our people and by the Civil War that was fought, if more in legend than in fact, over the Negro.

More obviously, a third source of contradiction lies in the dual allegiance of the American, who in his intellectual culture belongs both to the Old World and the New. These are speculative ideas which I can only hope to make concrete and relevant in the succeeding pages. I would hope to avoid, at the same time, the rather arid procedure that would result from trying to find a "contradiction" behind every character and episode.

Novel vs. Romance

Nothing will be gained by trying to define "novel" and "romance" too closely. One of their chief advantages is that as literary forms go, they are relatively loose and flexible. But especially in discussing American literature, these terms have to be defined closely enough to distinguish between them, even though the distinction itself may sometimes be meaningless as applied to a given book and even though, following usage, one ordinarily uses the word "novel" to describe a book like Cooper's *The Prairie* which might more accurately be called a "romance" or a "romance-novel."

Doubtless the main difference between the novel and the romance is in the way in which they view reality. The novel renders reality closely and in comprehensive detail. It takes a group of people and sets them going about the business of life. We come to see these people in their real complexity of temperament and motive. They are in explicable relation to nature, to each other, to their social class, to their own past. Character is more important than action and plot, and probably the tragic or comic actions of the narrative will have the primary purpose of enhancing our knowledge of and feeling for an important character, a group of characters, or a way of life. The events that occur will usually be plausible, given the circumstances, and if the novelist includes a violent or sensational occurrence in his plot, he will introduce it only into such scenes as have been (in the words of Percy Lubbock) "already prepared to vouch for it." Historically, as it has often been said, the novel has served the interests an aspirations of an insurgent middle class.

By contrast the romance, following distantly the medieval example, feels free to render reality in less volume and detail. It tends to prefer action to character, and action will be freer in a romance than in a novel, encountering, as it were, less resistance from reality. (This is not always true as we see in what might be called the static romances of Hawthorne, in which the author uses the allegorical and moral, rather than the dramatic, possibilities of the form.) The romance can flourish without providing much intricacy of relation. The characters, probably rather two-dimensional types, will not be complexly related to each other or to society or to the past. Human beings will on the whole be shown in ideal relation—that is, they will share emotions only after thee have become abstract or symbolic. To be sure, characters may become profoundly involved in some way, as in Hawthorne or Melville, but it will be a deep and narrow, an obsessive, involvement. In American romances it will not matter much what class people come from, and where the novelist would arose our interest in a character by exploring his origin, the romancer will probably do so by enveloping it in mystery. Character itself becomes, then, somewhat abstract and ideal, so much so in some romances that it seems to be merely a function of plot. The plot we may expect to be highly coloured. Astonishing events may occur, and these are likely to have a symbolic or ideological, rather than a realistic, plausibility. Being less committed to the immediate rendition of reality than the novel, the romance will more freely veer toward mythic, allegorical, and symbolistic forms.

The Historical View

Although some of the best works of American fiction have to be called, for purposes of criticism, romances rather than novels, we would be pursuing a chimera if we tried, except provisionally, to isolate a literary form known as the American prose romance, as distinguished from the European or the American novel. In actuality the romances of our literature, like European prose romances, are literary hybrids, unique only in their peculiar but widely differing amalgamation of novelistic and romance elements. The greatest American fiction had tended towards the romance more often than the greatest European fiction. Still, our fiction is historically a branch of the European tradition of the novel. And it is the better part of valor in the critic to understand our American romances as adaptations of traditional novelistic procedures to new cultural conditions and new aesthetic aspirations. It will not damage our appreciation of the originality and value of *Moby-Dick* or *The Blithedale Romance* to say that they both seem to begin as novels but then veer off into the province of romance, in the one case making a supreme triumph, in the other, a somewhat dubious but interesting medley of genres and intentions.

Inevitably we look to the writings of James Fenimore Cooper, for it was he who first exemplified and formulated the situation of the novelist in the New World. His first book, *Precaution*, was a novel of manners, somewhat in the style of Jane Austen. Considering this a failure, he wrote *The Spy*, a story of the Revolution, in which, following Scott, he put his characters in a borderland (in this case between the American and British armies) where the institutions and manners of society did not obtain, he sketched out in Harvey Birch the semilegendary hero who would find his full development in Natty Bumppo. As for characterization and realism of presentation, he contented himself with what he called in *Notions of the Americans* "the general picture" and "the delineation of principles" this being, as he said, all that could be expected of the American writer, given the "poverty of materials" and the uniformity of behaviour and public opinion. He introduced an element of melodrama, believing that this might be suitable to scenes set in the American forest, even though we had no mysterious castles, dungeons, or monasteries. He introduced also a certain "elevation" of style and a freedom in arranging events and attributing moral qualities to his characters. It is thus apparent that if American conditions had forced Cooper to be content with "the general picture" and "the delineation of principles" this was, if a step away from the novel form proper, a step *toward* the successful mythic qualities of the Leather-Stocking tales. Here was proof of Tocqueville's idea that although the abstractness and generality of the democratic imagination would make unavailable some of the traditional sources of fiction, this abstractness would in itself be a new source of mythic ideality.

In Cooper's books we see what was to be the main drift of American fiction. Responding to various pressures, it would depart markedly from the novelistic tradition. When it did so, it would with variations that may be observed in such writers as Hawthorne, Melville, Mark Twain, Faulkner, and Hemingway—become either melodrama or pastoral idyl, often both.

Although Cooper gave an indubitably American tone to romance he did so without ceasing to be, in many ways, a disciple of Scott. Another disciple of Scott, and to a lesser extent of Godwin, was Cooper's near contemporary, the South Carolina journalist and romancer William Gilmore Simms. This author is no less convinced than Cooper that romance is the form of fiction called for by American conditions. Historical romance was his particular *forte*, and his *Views and Reviews* (1845) contains an interesting investigation of the materials available to the American romancer. In his prefatory letter to *The Yemassee*, his most popular tale of Indian warfare (first published in 1835), Simms defines the romance as the modern version of epic:

> You will note that I call *The Yemassee* a romance, and not a novel. You will permit me to insist on the distinction . . . What are the standards of the modern Romance? What is the modern Romance itself? The reply is immediate. The modern Romance is the substitute which the people of the present day offer for the ancient epic. The form is changed; the matter is very much the same; at all events, it differs much more seriously from the English novel than it does from the epic and the drama, because the difference is one of material, even more than of fabrication. The reader who, reading *Ivanhoe*, keeps Richardson and Fielding beside him, will be at fault in every step of his progress. The domestic novel of those writers, confined to the felicitous narration of common and daily occurring events, and the grouping and delineation of characters in the ordinary conditions of society, is altogether a different sort of composition; and if, in a strange doggedness or simplicity of spirit, such a reader happens to pin his faith to such writers alone, circumscribing the boundless horizon of art to the domestic circle, the Romances of Maturin, Scott, Bulwer, and others of the present day, will be little better than rhapsodical and intolerable nonsense.
>
> When I say that our Romance is the substitute of modern times for the epic or the drama, I do not mean to say that they are exactly the same things, and yet, examined thoroughly . . . the differences between them are very slight. These differences depend upon the material employed, rather than upon the particular mode in which it is used. The Romance is of loftier origin than the Novel. It approximates the poem. It may be described as an amalgam of the two. It is only with those who are apt to insist upon poetry as verse, and to confound rhyme with poetry, that the resemblance is unapparent. The standards of the Romance . . . are very much those of the epic. It interests individuals with an absorbing interest—it hurries them rapidly through crowding and exacting events in a narrow space of time—it requires the same unities of plan, or purpose, and harmony of parts, and it seeks for its adventures among the wild and wonderful. It does not confine itself to what is known, or even what is probable. It grasps at the possible; and, placing a human agent in hitherto untried situations, it exercises its ingenuity in extricating him from them, while describing his feelings and his fortunes in the process.

Loosely written as it is, this statement, with its echoes of Aristotle's Poetics, remains something of a classic in the history of American criticism, its general purport being one which so many of our prose fictionists have accepted. American fiction had been notable for its poetic quality, which is not the poetry of verse not yet the domestic or naturalistic poetry of the novel but the poetry of romance. In allying romance to epic Simms was reflecting his own preoccupation with panoramic settings, battles, and heroic deeds; doubtless he had also in mind, vociferous nationalist that he was, the power of epic to mirror the soul of a people. There are many American fictions besides *The Yemassee* which reminds us of epics, large and small: Cooper's *Prairie*, *Moby-Dick*, *The Adventures of Huckleberry Finn*, Faulkner's *As I Lay Dying*, for example. Yet on the whole, American fiction had approximated the poetry of idyl and of melodrama more often than of epic.

Not all of Simms's own romances have the epic quality. *Confession: or the Blind Heart* (1841), *Beauchampe* (1842), and *Charlemont* (1856) are "tales of passion" and have to do with seduction, murder, revenge, and domestic cruelty. They are dark studies in psychology that reflect Godwin and the Gothic tradition at the same time that in their pictures of town life, lawyers, court trials, and local customs they forecast later Southern writers, such as Faulkner and Robert Penn Warren. Simms's tales of passion, however, are fatally marred by the carelessness and crudity with which they are thrown together, and it was in the work of Hawthorne that for the first time the psychological possibilities of romance were realized.

As we see from the prefaces to his longer fictions, particularly *The Marble Faun*, Hawthorne was no less convinced than Cooper and Simms that romance, rather than the novel, was the predestined form of American narrative. In distinguishing between forms, his Preface to *The House of the Seven Gables* makes some of the same points Simms had made:

> When a writer calls his work a romance it need hardly be observed that he wishes to claim a certain latitude, both as to its fashion and material, which he would not have felt himself entitled to assume, had he not professed to be writing a novel. The latter form of composition is presumed to aim at a very minute fidelity, not merely to the possible, but to the probable and ordinary course of man's experience. The former—while, as a work of art, it must rigidly subject itself to laws, and while it sins unpardonably so far as it may swerve aside from the truth of the human heart—has fairly a right to present that truth under circumstances, to a great extent, of the writer's own choosing or creation. If he thinks fit, also, he may so manage his atmospherical medium as to bring out or mellow the lights, and deepen and enrich the shadows, of the picture. He will be wise, no doubt, to make a very moderate use of the privileges here stated, and especially, to mingle the marvellous rather as a slight, delicate, and evanescent flavour, than as any portion of the actual substance of the dish offered to the public. He can hardly be said, however, to commit a literary crime, even if he disregard this caution.

As Hawthorne sees the problem confronting the American author, it consists in the necessity of finding (in the words of the Introduction to *The Scarlet Letter*) "a neutral territory, somewhere between the real world and fairy-land, where the Actual and the Imaginary may meet, and each imbue itself with the nature of the other." Romance is, as we see, a kind of "border" fiction, whether the field of action is in the neutral territory between civilization and the wilderness, as in the adventure tales of Cooper and Simms, or whether, as in Hawthorne and later romancers, the field of action is conceived not so much as a place as a state of mind—the borderland of the human mind where the actual and the imaginary intermingle. Romance does not plant itself, like the novel, solidly in the midst of the actual. Nor when it is memorable, does it escape into the purely imaginary.

In saying that no matter what its extravagances romance must not "swerve aside from the truth of the human heart," Hawthorne was in effect announcing the definitive adaptation of romance to America. To keep fiction in touch with the human heart is to give it a universal human significance. But this cannot be done memorably in prose fiction, even in the relatively loose form of the romance, without giving it a local significance. The truth of the heart as pictured in romance may be more generic or archetypal than in the novel; it may be rendered less concretely; but it must still be made to belong to a time and a place. Surely Hawthorne's romances do. In his writings romance was made for the first time to respond to the particular demands of an American imagination and to mirror, in certain limited ways, the American mind. In order to accomplish this Hawthorne had to bring into play his considerable talent for psychology. Cooper was not a psychologist of any subtlety and outside of the striking conception of the stoic inner life of Natty Bumppo, he gave to romance no psychological quality that might not find its close analogue in Scott. Although no one would mistake a fiction of Simms for one of Scott, Simms's originality was circumscribed by his apparent belief, as stated in the quotation above, that American romance would differ from earlier forms only because it had different material. His claim to originality was severely limited by the crudity and indecision of his literary form and his psychological insights.

In the writings of Brockden Brown, Cooper, and Simms we have the first difficult steps in the adaptation of English romance to American conditions and needs. Following these pioneers we have had, ever since, two streams of romance in pour literary history. The first is the stream that makes the main subject of this book and includes Hawthorne, Melville, James, Mark Twain, Frank Norris, Faulkner, Hemingway, and others who have found that romance offers certain qualities of thought and imagination which the American fiction writer needs but which are outside the province of the novel proper. These are writers who each in his own way have followed Hawthorne both in thinking the imagination of romance necessary and in knowing that it must not "swerve aside from the truth of the human heart."

The other stream of romance, justly contemned by Mark Twain and James, is one which also descends from Scott, and includes John Esten Cooke's *Surry of Eagle's Nest* (1886), Lew Wallace's *Ben Hur* (1880), Charles Major's *When Knighthood Was In Flower* (1899), and later books like *Gone with the Wind* and the historical tales of Kenneth Roberts. Although these works may have their points, according to the taste of the reader, they are, historically considered, the tag-end of a European tradition that begins in the Middle Ages and has come down into our own literature without responding to the forms of imagination which the actualities of American life have inspired. Romances of this sort are sometimes defended because "they tell a good story"—as opposed to the fictions of, say, Faulkner and Melville, which allegedly don't. people who make this complaint have a real point; yet they put themselves in the position of defending books which have a fatal inner falsity.

The fact is that the word "romance" begins to take on its inevitable meaning, for the historically minded American reader, in the writing of Hawthorne. Ever since his use of the word to describe his own fiction, it has appropriately signified the peculiar narrow profundity and rich interplay of lights and darks which one associates with the best American writing. It has also signified, to be sure, that common trait shared by the American romances which are discussed in this book and all other romances whatsoever—namely, the penchant for the marvellous, the sensational, the legendary, and in general the heightened effect. But the critical question is always: To what purpose have these amiable tricks of romance been used? To falsify reality and the human heart or to bring us round to a new, significant and perhaps startling relation to them?

James on the Novel vs. the Romance

In the two preceding sections of this chapter, I have tried to formulate preliminary definitions of "romance" and the "novel" and then look at the matter in a historical perspective. In order to amplify the discussion, in both the abstract and the concrete, it will be of value at this point to return, with the aid of Henry James's prefaces, to the question of definition. In doing so, I shall risk repeating one or two observations which have already been made.

The first four prefaces James wrote for the New York edition of his works set forth, or at least allude to, the main items of his credo as a novelist, and although they are perhaps well known, there may be some advantage in looking them over again before noticing what James had to say directly about the relation of the romance to the novel. The four prefaces are those to *Roderick Hudson*, *The American*, *The Portrait of a Lady*, and *The Princess Casamassima*.

We might take as a motto this sentence, from the Preface to *The Princess*: "Experience, as I see it, is our apprehension and our measure of what happens to us as social creatures." Although James himself does not overtly contrast his procedure with that of romance until he comes to the Preface to *The American*, we shall be justified in ourselves making the contrast, since James is obviously seeking to show, among other things, how the imperfections of romance may be avoided. And thus we reflect that, in a romance, "experience" has less to do with human beings as "social creatures" than as individuals. Heroes, villains, victims, legendary types, confronting other individuals or confronting mysterious or otherwise dire forces—this is what we meet in romances.

When James tells us that the art of the novel is the "art of representation," the practice of which spreads "round us in a widening, not in a narrow circle," we reflect on the relative paucity of "representation" in the older American romances and their tendency towards a concentrated and narrow profundity. Again we hear that "development" is "of the very essence of the novelist's process," and we recall how in romances characters appear really to be given quantities rather than emerging and changing organisms responding to their circumstances as these themselves develop one out of another. For if characters change in a romance, let's say as Captain Ahab in *Moby-Dick* or the Reverend Dimmesdale in *The Scarlet Letter* change, we are not shown a "development"; we are left rather with an element of mystery, as with Ahab, or a simplified and conventionalised alteration of character, as with Dimmesdale. Similarly, the episodes of romance tend to follow each other without ostensible causation; here too there is likely to be an element either of mystery or convention. To "treat" a subject, James says, is to "exhibit . . . relations"; and the novelist "is in the perpetual predicament that the continuity of things is the whole matter, for him, of comedy and tragedy." But in a romance much may be made of unrelatedness, of alienation and discontinuity, for the romancer operates in a universe that is less coherent than that of the novelist.

As for the setting, James says that it is not enough merely to report what it seems to be the author to be, in however minute detail. The great thing is to get into the novel not only the setting but somebody's *sense* of the setting. We recall that in *The Scarlet Letter* the setting, although sketchy, is pictorially very beautiful and symbolically *à propos*. But none of the characters has a sense of the setting; that is all in the author's mind and hence the setting is never dramatized but remains instead a handsomely tapestried backdrop. In *Moby-Dick* the setting is less inert; it becomes, in fact, a kind of "enveloping action." Still, only in some of the scenes do we have Ishmael's sense of the setting; during most of the book Ishmael himself is all but banished as a dramatic presence.

The whole question of the "point of command" or "point of view" or "center of intelligence" is too complicated to go onto here. Suffice it to say that the allotment of intelligence, the question of what character shall be specially conscious of the meaning of what happens to and around him so that we see events and people more or less through his eyes, thus gaining a sense of dramatic coherence—these questions are less and less pertinent as fiction approaches pure romance. Natty Bumppo need be conscious only of what the Indians are going to do next. Hawthorne's Chillingworth and Melville's Ahab are clairvoyantly conscious, but with a profoundly obsessive distortion of the truth. They are not placed in context in order to give concrete dramatic form to a large part of what the author sees, as is the "point of command" in a James novel; all we learn from them is how *they* see. And as I shall suggest in speaking of *The Blithedale Romance*, the dyed-in-the-wool romancer like Hawthorne merely proves that you mustn't have a central observer in your story, because if you do you simply point up the faults of romance and admit your incapacity to follow out a fully developed novelistic procedure. In the romance too much depends on mystery and bewilderment to risk a generally receptive intelligence in the midst of things. Too often the effect you are after depends on a universe that is felt to be irrational, contradictory, and melodramatic—whereas the effect of a central intelligence is to produce a sense of verisimilitude and dramatic coherence.

One or two further items from the prefaces may point up the contrast. A character, especially "the fictive hero," as James says, "successfully appeals to us only as an eminent instance, as eminent as we like, of our own conscious kind." He must not be "a morbidly special case"—but in romance he may well be. Again, says James, when economy demands the suppression of parts of the possible story they must not be merely "eliminated"; they must be foreshortened, summarized, compressed but nevertheless brought to bear on the whole. But in the looser universe of the romance, we may think "elimination" will be less criminal and unexplained hiatuses and discontinuities may positively contribute to the effect. To take an obvious case, in *Moby-Dick* we are content to think the sudden elimination of Bulkington an interesting oddity rather than a novelistic blunder and we gladly draw on the poetic capital Melville makes of it.

As for the moral significance of the novel, James sees a "prefect dependence of the 'moral' sense of a work of art on the amount of felt life concerned in producing it." We must ask, he says, "is it valid, in a word, is it genuine, is it sincere, the result of some direct impression or perception of life." These questions bear less on the romance, on of the assumptions of which is that it need not contain a full amount of felt life, that life may be felt indirectly, though legend, symbol, or allegory. Not does the romance need the sincerity of the novel; indeed, as Lawrence points out, American romances, especially, tend to make their effect by a deep "duplicity" or ironic indirection.

To come finally to James's specific comments on the question we are considering. In the prefaces he follows his own advice as that had been expressed twenty-odd years earlier in "The Art of Fiction"—he sees no reason, that is, why the practicing writer should distinguish between novel and romance. There are good novels and bad ones, novels that have life and those that haven't—and this, for the novelist, is the only one relevant question. The implication is that the novelist will be also the romancer if the "life" he is rendering extends in to the realm of the "romantic." But if we are not, except as critics and readers, to distinguish between novel and romance, we still have to distinguish, within the novel that may be also a romance, the "romantic" from the "real." And this James essays in his Preface to *The American*.

In rereading this early novel James found a large element of romance in the free and easy way in which he had made his semilegendary hero Christopher Newman behave on his European travels, particularly, James thought, the picture of the Bellegard family was "romantic." James had made them reject Newman as a vulgar manufacturer when actually common sense tells us that "they would positively have jumped at him," and James comments that "the experience here represented is the disconnected and uncontrolled experience—uncontrolled by our general sense of 'the way things happen'—which romance alone more or less successfully palms off on us." At the same time James finds an unexpected pleasure in rereading *The American*, which somewhat compensates for the lapses of verisimilitude. And his description of this pleasure makes a fair definition of the pleasure of romance—"the free play of so much unchallenged instinct . . . the happiest season of surrender to the invoked muse and the projected fable."[1]

"The disconnected and uncontrolled experience," then, is of the essence of romance, and any adequate definition must proceed form this postulate. First, however, one may clear out of the way certain conventional but inadequate descriptions of romance. It is not "a matter indispensably of boats, or of caravans, or of tigers, or of "historical characters," or of ghosts, or of forgers, or of detectives, or of beautiful wicked women, or of pistols and knives"—although one might perhaps be a little readier than James to think that these things might be of service. Yet one follows him assentingly when he decides that the common element in sensational tales is "the facing of danger" and then goes on to say that for most of us the danger represented by caravans and forgers is certainly benign or impotent compared with the "common and covert" dangers we face in our everyday existence, which may "involve the sharpest hazards to life and honor and the highest instant decisions and intrepidities of action."

The "romantic" cannot be defined, either, as "the far and the strange," since, as such, these things are merely unknown, whereas the "romantic" is something we know, although we know it indirectly. Nor is a novel romantic because its hero or heroine is. "it would be impossible to have a more romantic temper than Flaubert's Madame Bovary, yet nothing less resembles a romance than the record of her adventures." Nor can we say the presence or absence of "costume" is a crucial difference, for "where . . . does costume begin or end."

James then arrives at the following formulation:

> The only *general* attribute of projected romance that I can see, the only one that fits all its cases, is the fact of the kind of experience with which it deals—experience liberated, so to speak; experienced disengaged, disembroiled, disencumbered, exempt from the conditions that we usually know to attach to it and, if we wish so to put the matter, drag upon it, and operating in a medium which relieves it, in a particular interest, of the inconvenience of a *related*, a measurable state, a state subject to all our vulgar communities.

And James goes on in words that are particularly illustrative of his own art:

> The greatest intensity may so be arrived at evidently—when the sacrifice of community, of the "related" sides of situations, has not been too rash. It must to this end not flagrantly betray itself; we must even be kept if possible, for our illusion, from suspecting any sacrifice at all.

In a fully developed art of the novel there is, as James says, a "latent extravagance." In novelists of "largest responding imagination before the human scene," we do not find only the romantic or only reality but a "current . . . extraordinarily rich and mixed." The great novelist responds to the "need of performing his whole possible revolution, by the law of some rich passion in him for extremes."

To have a rich passion for extremes is to grasp both the real and the romantic. By the "real," James explains, he means "the things we cannot possibly *not* know, sooner or later, in one way or another." By the "romantic" he means "the things that, with all the facilities in the world, all the wealth and all the courage and all the wit and all the adventure, we never *can* directly know; the things that can reach us only through the beautiful circuit and subterfuge of our thought and our desire."

We hear much in these prefaces of the novelist's rich and mixed "current," of the possible "revolution" of his mind among extremes, of the "circuit" of thought and desire. James speaks too, of the "conversion" that goes on in the mind of the novelist's characters between what happens to them and their *sense* of what happens to them, and of "the link of connection" between a character's "doing" and his "feeling." In other words James thinks that the novel does not find its essential being until it discovers what we may call the circuit of life among extremes or opposites, the circuit of life that passes through the real and the ideal, through the directly known and the mysterious or the indirectly known, through doing and feeling. Much of the best American fiction does not meet James's specifications. It has not made the circuit James requires of the "largest responding imagination." And the closer it has stuck to the assumptions of romance the more capital it has made, when any capital has been made, exactly by leaving the Jamesian circuits broken. That very great capital can be made in this way James does not acknowledge or know, and hence his own hostility, and that of may of his followers, to the more extreme forms of American fiction—these we associate, for example, with Brockden Brown, Poe, Melville, and Faulkner.

Nevertheless James's theory of the novel, his idea of the circuit of life which allows him to incorporate in his novels so many of the attributes of romance, is the most compete and admirable theory, as at their best Jamses's are the most complete and admirable novels yet produced by an American. And it is against James's theory and often, though certainly not always, his practice that we have to test the achievements of his compatriots. But the danger is that in doing so we should lapse into an easy disapproval of that "rich passion . . . for extremes" which James praised on his own grounds but which may be seen operating to advantage on other grounds too.

Note

1. Cf. Melville's plea to his reality-minded readers for latitude in the depiction of character and incident. The ideal reader, he says, will "want nature . . . ; but nature unfettered, exhilarated, in effect transformed . . . .It is with fiction as with religion; it should present another world, and yet one to which we feel the tie." (*The Confidence Man*, Chapter 33.)

96

The Question of Form

MARIUS BEWLEY

Following Trilling's essay, "Manners, Morals, and the Novel" (1950), Bewley argues that American authors lacked the formal European sense of community and tradition requisite to the novel of manners. Instead, nineteenth-century American authors, Cooper, Hawthorne, Melville and James, replaced this void with symbolic renditions of tensions inherent in American society. Consequently, their work is more abstract, growing out of a sense of deprivation. Beginning with Cooper, all these authors strive in vain to heal a tension that runs throughout American literature. While this tension assumes various forms from the opposition between tradition and progress, European and American, liberalism and conservatism, it is most prominent in the conflict between the isolated individual and society. For Cooper, the conflict is more concrete: the individual is literally caught between the wilderness and civilization. By the time of Hawthorne and Melville and even later that of Fitzgerald, these two poles are internalized within the individual. As Bewley notes, "The American novel has had to find a new experience and discover how to put that experience into art." The form of the novel, then, has arisen as a response to the nature of the individual American experience.

I
The Question of Form

Form is an elusive, even a frightening, word. A word that stands for so much sometimes ends up by meaning little, and therefore at the outset I wish to define the limits within which I shall use it in this book. Sir Herbert Read has written that we should realize that "form is the natural effect of the poet's integrity", and that we should be concerned not so much with "'the life of form,' . . . but rather the form of life".[1] I doubt if an investigation of aesthetic form that tried to push beyond these sensible boundaries would lead us very far towards understanding the peculiar

Source: Marius Bewley, "The Question of Form", *The Eccentric Design: Form in the Classic American Novel*, 1957; rptd New York: Columbia University Press, 1963 pp. 13-21.

constitution and problems of the American novel.

"The form of life" results from emotions and ideas coming together in various combinations in the moulds provided by the conventions and manners of a given society. As the novelist's subject is man in society, his subject must also be the texture of manners and conventions by which social man defines his own identity. In saying this I do little more than paraphrase the arguments of two illuminating essays by Mr Lionel Trilling, "Manners, Morals, and the Novel", and "Art and Fortune". It is at this point, as Mr Trilling makes clear, that a distinction between the American and the European novel becomes evident. In the earlier of the two essays he writes:

> Now the novel as I have described it has never really established itself in America. Not that we have not had very great novels but that the novel in America diverges from its classic intention, which, as I have said, is the investigation of the problem of reality beginning in the social field. The fact is that American writers of genius have not turned their minds to society. The reality they sought was only tangential to society.[2]

And enlarging on this in the second essay, "Art and Fortune", Mr Trilling says that "In this country the real basis of the novel has never existed—that is, the tension between a middle class and an aristocracy which brings manners into observable relief as the living representation of ideals and the living comment on ideas." The American novel has sheered towards abstraction. Even its great characters, Natty Bumppo and Captain Ahab, "tend to be mythic because of the rare finesse and abstractness of the ideas they represent; and their very freedom from class gives them a large and glowing generality".[3]

These remarks suggest that the matrix of form for the American novel is not manners or society. "Many of us forget", Mr Trilling continues, "how in the novel ideas may be as important as character and as essential to the given dramatic situation." There was that in the American ethos which gave an emotional primacy to ideas, which made them the proper subject-matter of the novelist's art, while at the same time the novelist was deprived of that richness of nuance and tone which a traditional society alone can provide. The American novelist was necessarily at a disadvantage when he attempted to create character. The traditional codes and manners by which the European novelist creates his men and women were not at his disposal; but before the middle of the nineteenth century he had discovered his great alternative in symbolism. It is a gross simplification to say that symbol in art stands in relation to idea as character in fiction stands in relation to the values represented by traditional social patterns, but the statement has its measure of truth. If the American novelist, deprived of an adequate social density, has never been able to approach nearer to Emma Bovary than poor Sister Carrie, it is also true to say that no English or French novelist has ever come so near to the White Whale. *Moby-Dick* and *Madam Bovary* may be taken as examples of contrasting modes of fiction, each representative (in so far as a masterpiece can ever be representative) of its particular world, and of different ways of searching out truth in art. Therefore, when I say that I am chiefly concerned in the following pages with ideas rather than with manners it is not with any intention of minimizing the overwhelming importance of the latter for the European tradition, nor of maintaining that the absence of a rich texture of manners in American life may not have resulted, on many levels, in artistic impoverishment. But the most casual reading of Fenimore Cooper, Hawthorne, or Melville—the most significant American novelists before Henry James—is sufficient to indicate that they did not draw on social observation to achieve their profoundest effects, nor search traditional social forms for their values. If the case of Cooper will call for certain qualifications later, it will be found nevertheless that his deepest meaning is at variance with anything he was able to read in patterns of American social behaviour. The popularity of such writers as Scott and Dickens in the United States was responsible for a large number of American imitators, but where the American novelist was successful enough to create genuine art it will usually be found that it is a deep and emotional concern with abstractions which is the controlling factor in the motives and organization of his work.

This should not surprise us, given the conditions under which the American writer had to create. Jane Austen, to take the ideal example, was able to move progressively into her values in the course of any given novel, to reveal them in the very circumstances of her story, in the inflections of her characters' speeches, or the way they wore their inherited manners. Her values *pre-existed* in the materials and conditions of her art, even if it took her genius to reveal them. Her art is essentially an art of ironic illumination, of revealing in a new light what had been there all along. Her judgements and insights have the sureness and strength that come from the corroboration of traditional sanctions. But the American novelist had only his *ideas* with which to begin: ideas which, for the most part, were grounded in the great American democratic abstractions. And he found that these abstractions were disembodied, that there was no social context in which they might acquire a rich human relevance. For the traditional novelist, the universal and the particular come together in the world of manners; but for the American artist there was no social surface responsive to his touch. The scene was crude, even beyond successful satire, as Dickens was to discover. There was really only one subject available to the nineteenth-century American novelist—his own unhappy plight. And the essence of that plight was his isolation. The American novelist before James, in his most successful work, turns his back on manners and society as such. In doing so he confronts his own emotional and spiritual needs which his art becomes the means of comprehending and analysing. Under such circumstances these novelists ran the risk of becoming exponents of the romantic agony; it is to the credit of certain elements in the American intellectual climate, as well as to their personal stature as artists, that they became metaphysical novelists instead. Obviously such a description must apply to the artists treated here in widely different ways and in different degrees, but when they were writing most intensely they were intent on discovering and defining a reality that the traditions and orthodoxy of the Old World had presented pre-packaged to the European novelists to do with what they would. If the American novelists were deprived of great riches, it is also true that the starkness of their situation invited extraordinary creative originality. It was a situation in which the artist had to be great or abdicate his role entirely. And it is true that America produced several of the greatest novels written in English in the nineteenth century (in *Moby Dick* quite probably the greatest), but no minor novels that we can take very seriously.

I hope I have not suggested that what the great American novelists of the period in question have in common is mainly a matter of deprivation, though it is, of course, in the shadow of deprivation that the truly great ones have made their beginning. Our concern in the following pages is with common problems growing out of that common deprivation; problems which the novelists with whom we shall be dealing could not have shirked without a loss of intellectual integrity or stature. If we agree with Sir Herbert Read that form is the natural effect of the poet's integrity, then it is also the stance in which, as a creative artist, he meets and resolves those problems that form the medium in which he lives his intellectual and emotional life.

The American novelists whose works we shall consider in the following pages are Cooper, Hawthorne, Melville, and Henry James. Under the wide diversity of types their art represents, we are aware of a concealed fellowship among them. I have already suggested, somewhat obliquely, the nature or the grounds of the resemblance, but I should like to be more explicit. The likeness does not exist in the texture of their writings, or their enthusiasms or aversions, though these elements may, on occasion, play their parts. It is not even, strictly speaking, rooted in their technical equipment as artists, although it colours that equipment and enriches it. Mr Allen Tate has a passage that is suggestive in his essay, "Techniques in Fiction":

> There are "good" popular novelists who have done much to make us physically at home in our own country; they have given us our scenes, our people, and above all our history; and these were necessary to the preliminary knowledge of ourselves, which we have been a little late in getting and which must be got and assimilated if we are going to be a mature people. Possibly the American novel had to accomplish the task that in Europe had been done by primitive chronicle, memoire, ballad, strolling player. The American novel has had to find a new experience, and only in our time has it been able to pause for the difficult task of getting itself written. That is an old story with us, yet beneath it lies a complexity of feeling that from Hawthorne down to our time has baffled our best understanding.[4]

The American novel has had to find a new experience and discover how to put that experience into art. And the process by which it has been done was one of progressive self-discovery for the nation. Mr Tate is speaking of "popular" novelists, and perhaps he is thinking more of the surfaces of American life than of the more inaccessible problems and conflicts. But the preliminary knowledge of ourselves out of which mature art grows is no more a sense of one's own people and history than of one's own tensions and inner struggles. Indeed, these are one's history and one's sense of racial self. And yet the deepest tensions that have contributed to establishing the American identity are extremely elusive. They are ultimately grounded in the sense of deprivation I spoke of before, the sense of being without certain kinds of reality that men ought to have: the sense that there is a world of abstract ideas and ideals, and a world of bitter fact, but no society or tradition or orthodoxy in which the two worlds can interact and qualify each other. If we are justified in searching "popular" American fiction in the nineteenth century for a mirror image of ourselves, shall we be less justified in searching the works of the great American novelists for some clue to what those characteristic spiritual problems—intensified by the deprivations of American society—may have been, and possibly are? Referring to this deeper and more complex question, Mr Tate names Hawthorne as a significant starting point. But I think the problem may be presented on a more elementary and unambiguous level if we move a step farther back in time to Hawthorne's greatest predecessor in American fiction, James Fenimore Cooper.

Behind much of Cooper's writing there is a fundamental conflict or tension that grows out of his sense of American society and history. In successive novels he tried to solve this tension, but without complete success. This tension was inherited later by such novelists as Hawthorne, Melville, and James, who saw it in different lights and colours, and they too tried to resolve it—each in his own way. It is, then, at this point of crucial strain in American experience that the writers to be treated here resemble each other. Each great, or even successful, work of art is an attempt to surmount a crisis in experience. The crisis is both private and impersonal; both cruelly one's own, and participating in the wide cycle of history. This tension which passed down from Cooper through Hawthorne and Melville to James is, at bottom, a matter of American history; and yet each writer felt it intimately as his own. It is because each suffered it privately in his unique way that we sometimes lose sight of how they also suffered it in common. The tension I am speaking of has grown more complex with time, and it is therefore worthwhile to trace it back, if we can, to its earliest distinguished expression in our literature.

In its most basic definition this tension was the result of a struggle to close the split in American experience, to discover a unity that, for the artist especially, almost sensibly *was not there*. The nature of the division that supported this conflict was partly determined by those deprivations in American society I have discussed above: deprivations of which the practising American novelist was deeply aware, for they confronted him with a society in which the abstract idea and the concrete fact could find little common ground for creative interaction. From a more positive point of view the division took on many different forms concurrently: it was an opposition between tradition and progress, between democratic faith and disillusion, between the past and the present and future; between Europe and America, liberalism and conservatism, aggressive acquisitive economics and benevolent wealth. These same divisions existed in Europe also, but there they were ballasted by a denser social medium, a richer sense of the past, a more inhibited sense of material possibilities. At bottom the tension is political in character. But it is in Cooper that we are able to trace its political grounding most clearly and to see how the tension in its political sense is at one with the tension in its social, economic, and international senses. At this point I should like to offer some explanation of the apportionment of space allotted to the novelists treated in the following chapters. I am not concerned with presenting here a series of critical evaluations of each novelist in his turn, but in discovering what elements, if any, common among them all, may be isolated as characterizing a tradition in the novel that is distinctly American. I have looked for these common elements, not in American manners, conventions, or language, but in the very structure of thought and in the nature of the emotional drive out of which each novelist created. I have done this because, as I said above, the absence of a traditional social medium in America compelled the original American artist to confront starkly his own emotional and spiritual needs which his art then became the means of comprehending and analysing. It is in this hidden and comparatively inaccessible area that we must look for the roots of any generalization about form in the American novel. In the following pages it will be found that I treat the work of Fenimore Cooper at somewhat greater length than that of Melville, or Henry James, but no comparative evaluation is implied thereby. Although I believe with Joseph Conrad that Cooper "is a rare artist"[5] and that he can sometimes reach "the heights of inspired vision",[6] my purpose in treating him at greater length in the present context than the other writers is practical: he touches the argument at more points than they.

In writing of Hawthorne my principal concern will be the tension between isolation and social sympathy which is, perhaps, the dominant theme of his work. Melville touches my argument principally in the conflict between democratic faith and despair; James, in the everlasting dialectic between Europe and America. These respective tensions are all reflections, at different levels, of the basic split or tension in American experience. But Cooper reflects this basic tension not in one, but in various ways. His work shows us, for example, the creative tension between aristocracy and democracy, but operating in a very different mode from that "tension between a middle class and an aristocracy" which Mr Lionel Trilling, in an earlier quotation, mentioned as "the real basis of the novel". We also find the tension between acquisitive economics and benevolent wealth—one of the most persistent of the American historical tensions—becoming a structural idea out of which he shapes the form of at least one of his novels. Most fundamental of all, he celebrates the tension between the American wilderness (which emotionally corresponds to the solitude of Hawthorne) and the new American industrial civilization. He endeavours to resolve these tensions artistically in specific novels in ways that make them ideal platforms on which to demonstrate how abstractions rather than manners became the material out of which the American novelist constructed the form of his art. Intellectually he was far more deeply and sensitively aware of the political grounding of these tensions he was dealing with in his novels than any of his successors, and by virtue of that awareness we are able to see more clearly the relation between certain abiding factors in American history and the disturbing problems which became the substance of his fictions, and of other writers' fictions later on. Chronologically he stands at the beginning. "He wrote", as Conrad said, "before the great American language was born,"[7] and in that clear and simple light one is able to trace the outlines of the problems dealt with here, more unambiguously and more simply in their relations, than in Melville's metaphysical shadows or James's nuanced atmosphere. In his modest way he stands at or near the beginning of the symbolist tradition in American fiction—that tradition by which the American artist was able to overcome, in a handful of great books, the impoverishment of his social milieu. This is a role with which Cooper has rarely, if ever, been credited,[8] but Natty Bumppo is, as I shall endeavour to show, a beautifully realized symbol through which Cooper expresses his highly complex reaction to American civilization. But before proceeding to an analysis of Cooper's novels I should like to sketch in very briefly the background against which these tensions developed. To do so adequately would require a much longer study than is possible here, but even a slight sketch may add weight to our later discussion of the novels. As the tensions I have been speaking of are, in some considerable part, a reflection of tensions that existed in the early intellectual climate of America, it may be possible to avoid a random discursiveness by concentrating on the writings of those political theorists of the national formative period whose political and social doctrines, meeting in polemical hostility, not only established the shape of the Republic, but generated that variegated pattern of tensions that is to be so largely the subject of the present argument.

Notes

1. Sir Herbert Read, *The True Form of Feeling*, New York, 1953, p. 9.
2. Lionel Trilling, *The Liberal Imagination*, New York, 1953, p.206.
3. *Ibid.*, 249.
4. Allen Tate, *On the Limits of Poetry*, New York, 1948, p. 135.
5. Conrad, Letter to Arthur Symonds, 1908.
6. Joseph Conrad, *Notes on Life and Letters*, London, 1949, p. 56.
7. *Ibid.*
8. He has been, by implication at least, excluded from the symbolist phase of literature by Charles Feidelson, *Symbolism and American Literature*, Chicago, 1953.

The Novel and America

LESLIE A. FIEDLER

The following essay introduces Fiedler's major contribution to American literary theory, Love and Death in the American Novel *(1960). In the first section he attempts to define the American novel as distinct from its European counterpart. Lacking a native novelistic tradition, American authors eschewed both Richardsonian sentimentalism and Fieldingesque comedy to espouse a form of Gothic terror. In this "American" genre the isolated protagonist, pitted against civilization, flees toward the frontier. One of the principal novelistic ingredients—love—is pushed aside in favor of a more abstract conflict between innocence and original sin. From Hawthorne and Melville to such authors as Eudora Welty and John Hawkes, Fiedler argues, American writers have pursued "a literature of darkness and the grotesque in a land of light and affirmation." In the second section, Fiedler opposes the rationalism of Jeffersonian democracy to the romantic "Break-through," inspired by Rousseau, noting that the latter predominates in the nineteenth and twentieth century novel.*

Between the novel and America there are peculiar and intimate connections. A new literary form and a new society, their beginnings coincide with the beginnings of the modern era and, indeed, help to define it. We are living not only in the Age of America but also in the Age of the Novel, at a moment when the literature of a country without a first-rate verse epic or a memorable verse tragedy has become the model of half the world. *The Age of the American Novel*, a French critic calls a book on contemporary writing; and everywhere in the West there are authors who quite deliberately turn from their own fictional traditions to pursue ours—or at least something they tale for ours.

We have known for a long time, of course, that our national literary reputation depends largely upon the achievement of our novelists. The classical poetic genres revived by the Renaissance had lost their relevance to contemporary life before America entered the cultural scene; and even the lyric has provided us with occasions

Source: Leslie A. Fiedler, "The Novel and America", *Partisan Review*, 27.1, Winter 1960, pp. 41–61.

for few, and unlimited, triumphs. Whitman, Poe, and Dickinson—beyond these three, there are no major American poets before the twentieth century; and even about their merits we continue to wrangle. It is Melville and Hawthorne and James (together with such latter-day figures as Faulkner and Hemingway) who possess the imagination of a already committed to the novel as the prevailing modern form. Not only in the United States, though pre-eminently there, literature has become for most readers quite simply prose fiction; and our endemic fantasy of writing "the Great American Novel" is only a local instance of a more general obsession. The notions of greatness once associated with the heroic poem have been transferred to the novel; and the shift is a part of that "Americanization of culture" which some European intellectuals continue ritually to deplore.

But is there, as certain continental critics have insisted, an "American novel," a specific sub-variety of the form? If we turn to these critics for a definition, we come on such terms as "neo-realist" "hard-boiled" "naïve" and "anti-traditional"—terms derived from a standard view of America as an "anti-culture," an eternally maintained preserve of primitivism. This view (notoriously exemplified by André Gide) ends by finding in Dashiell Hammett the same values as in William Faulkner, and is more a symptom of European cultural malaise than a useful critical distinction. While America is, in a very real sense, a constantly recreated fact of the European imagination, it is not only, or even pre-eminently, that. It is tempting to insist on the pat rebuttal that, far from being an anti-culture, we are merely a branch of Western culture; and that there is no "American novel," only local variants of standard European kinds of fiction: American sentimental, American gothic, American historical romance, etc. Certainly no single sub-genre of the novel was invented in the United States. Yet the peculiarities of our variants seem more interesting and important than their resemblances to the parent forms.

There is a real sense in which our prose fiction is immediately distinguishable from that of Europe, though this is a fact that is difficult for Americans (oddly defensive and flustered in its presence) to confess. In this sense, our novels seem not primitive, perhaps, but innocent, unfallen in a disturbing way, almost juvenile. The great works of American fiction are notoriously at home in the children's section of the library, their level of sentimentality precisely that of a pre-adolescent. This is part of what we mean when we talk about the incapacity of the American novelist to develop; in a compulsive way he returns to a limited world of experience, usually associated with his childhood, writing the same book over and over again until he lapses into silence or self-parody.

Merely finding a language, learning to talk in a land where there are no conventions of conversation, no special class idioms and no dialogue between classes, no continuing literary language—this exhausts the American writer. He is forever *beginning*, saying for the first time (without real tradition there can never be a second time) what it is like to stand alone before nature, or in a city as appallingly lonely as any virgin forest. He faces, moreover, another problem, which has resulted in a failure of feeling and imagination perceptible at the heart of even our most notable works. Our great novelists, though experts on indignity and assault, on loneliness and terror, tend to avoid treating the passionate encounter of a man and a woman, which we expect at the center of a novel. Indeed, they rather shy away from permitting in their fictions the presence of any full-fledged, mature women, giving us instead monsters of virtue or bitchery, symbols of the rejection or fear of sexuality.

To be sure, the theme of "love" in so simple a sense is by no means necessary to all works of art. In the *Iliad*, for instance, and in much Greek tragedy, it is conspicuously absent; and in the heroic literature of the Middle Ages, it is peripheral where it exists at all. The *"belle aude"* of the *Chanson de Roland* is a supernumerary, and the only female we remember from *Beowulf* is a terror emerging from the darkness at the bottom of the waters. The world of the epic is a world or war, and its reigning sentimental relationship is the loyalty of comrades in arms; but by the eighteenth century the notion of a heroic poem without romance had come to seem intolerable. The last pseudo-epics of the baroque had been obsessed with the subject of love, and the rococo had continued to elaborate that theme. Shakespeare himself appeared to the English Augustans too little concerned with the "reigning passion" to be quite interesting without revision. Why, after all, should Cordelia not survive to marry Edgar, they demanded of themselves—and they rewrote *King Lear* to prove that she should.

The novel, however, was precisely the product of the sentimentalizing taste of the eighteenth century; and a continuing tradition of prose fiction did not begin until the love affair of Lovelace and Clarissa (a demythicized Don Juan and a secularized goddess of Christian love) had been imagined. The subject par excellence of the novel is love or, more precisely—in its beginnings at least—seduction and marriage; and in France, Italy, Germany, and Russia, even in England, spiritually so close to America, love in one form or another has remained the novel's central theme, as necessary and as expected as battle in Homer or revenge in the Renaissance drama. When the Romantic impulse led in Germany to a technical recasting of the novel form, even the wildest experimentalists did not desert this traditional theme; Schiller's *Lucille* is a dialogue on freedom and restraint in passion. But our great Romantic *Unroman*, our typical anti-novel, is the woman-less *Moby-Dick*.

Where is our *Madame Bovary*, our *Anna Karenina*, our *Pride and Prejudice* or *Vanity Fair*? Among our classic novels, at least those before Henry James, who stands so oddly between our own traditions and the European ones we rejected or recast, the best attempt at dealing with love is *The Scarlet Letter*, in which the physical consummation of adultery has occurred and all passion burned away before the novel proper begins. Our *Madame Bovary* is a novel about adultery with the adultery off-stage; and the child who is its product is so elfin and ethereal that it is hard to believe her engendered in the usual way. For the rest, there are *Moby-Dick* and *Huckleberry Finn*, *The Last of the Mohicans*, *The Red Badge of Courage*, the stories of Edgar Allan Poe—books that turn form society to nature or nightmare out of a desperate need to avoid the fats of wooing, marriage, and child-bearing.

The figure of Rip Van Winkle presides over the birth of the American imagination; and it is fitting that our first successful homegrown legend should memorialise, however playfully, the flight of the dreamer from the shrew—into the mountains and out of time, away from the drab duties of home and town toward the good companions and the magic keg of beer. Ever since, the typical male protagonist of our fiction has been a man on the run, harried into the forest and out to sea, down the river or into combat—anywhere to avoid "civilization," which is to say, the confrontation of a man and woman which leads to the fall to sex, marriage, and responsibility. One of the factors that determine these and form in our great books is this strategy of evasion, this retreat to nature and childhood which makes our literature (and life!) so charmingly and infuriatingly "boyish."

The child's world is not only asexual, it is terrible: a world of fear and loneliness, a haunted world; and the American novel is pre-eminently a novel of terror. To "light out for the territory" or seek refuge in the forest seems easy and tempting from the vantage point of a chafing and restrictive home; but civilization once disavowed and Christianity disowned, the bulwark of woman left behind, the wanderer feels himself without protection, more motherless child than free man. To be sure, there is a substitute for wife or mother presumably waiting in the green heart of nature: the natural man, the good companion, pagan and unashamed— Queequeg or Chingachgook or Nigger Jim. But the figure of natural man is ambiguous, a dream and a nightmare at once. The other face of Chingachgook is Injun Joe, the killer in the graveyard and the haunter of caves; Nigger Jim is also the Babo of Melville's "Benito Cereno," the humble servant whose name means "papa" holding the razor to his master's throat; and finally the dark-skinned companion becomes the "Black Man," which is a traditional American name for the Devil himself.

The enemy of society on the run toward "freedom" is also the pariah in flight from his guilt, the guilt of that very flight; and new phantoms arise to haunt him at every step. American literature likes to pretend, of course, that its bugaboos are all finally jokes: the headless horseman a hoax, every manifestation of the supernatural capable of rational explanation on the last page—but we are never quite convinced. *Huckleberry Finn*, that euphoric boys' book, begins with its protagonist holding off at gun point his father driven half mad by the D. T.'s and ends (after a lynching, a disinterment, and a series of violent deaths relieved by such humorous incidents as soaking a dog in kerosene and setting him on fire) with the revelation of that father's sordid death. Nothing is spared; Pap, horrible enough in life, is found murdered brutally, abandoned to float down the river in a decaying house scrawled with obscenities. But it is all "humor" of course, a last desperate attempt to convince us of the innocence of violence, the good clean fun of horror. Our literature as a whole at times seems a chamber of horrors disguised as an amusement park "fun house," where we pay to play at terror and are confronted in the innermost chamber with a series of inter-reflecting mirrors which present us with a thousand versions of our own face.

In our most enduring books, the cheapjack machinery of the gothic novel is called on to represent the hidden blackness of the human soul and human society. No wonder our authors mock themselves as they use such devices; no wonder Mistress Hibbins in *The Scarlet Letter* and Fedallah in *Moby Dick* are treated jocularly, half melodramatically, though each represents in his book the Faustian pact, the bargain with the Devil, which our authors have always felt as the essence of the American experience. However shoddily or ironically treated, horror is essential to our literature. It is not merely a matter of terror filling the vacuum left by the suppression of sex in our novels, of Thanatos standing in for Eros. Through these gothic images are projected certain obsessive concerns for our national life: the ambiguity of our relationship with Indian and Negro, the ambiguity of our encounter with nature, the guilt of the revolutionist who feels himself a patricide—and, not least of all, the uneasiness of the writer who cannot help believing that the very act of composing a book is Satanic revolt. "Hell-fires," Hawthorne called *The Scarlet Letter*, and Melville thought his own *Moby Dick* a "wicked book."

The American writer inhabits a country at once the dream of Europe and a fact of history; he lives on the last horizon of an endlessly retreating vision of innocence on the "frontier," which is to say, the margin where the theory of original goodness and the fact of original sin come face to face. To express this "blackness ten times black" and to live by it in a society in which, since the decline of orthodox Puritanism, optimism has become the chief effective religion, is a complex and difficult task.

It was to the novel that the American writer turned most naturally, as the only *popular* form of sufficient magnitude for his vision. He was, perhaps, not sufficiently sophisticated to realize that such learned forms as epic and tragedy had already outlived their usefulness; but, working out of a cultural background at best sketchy and unsure, he felt insecure before them. His obligations urged him in the direction of tragedy, but traditional verse tragedy was forbidden him; indeed, a chief technical problem for American novelists has been the adaptation of non tragic forms to tragic ends. How could the dark vision of the American—his obsession with violence and his embarrassment before love—be expressed in the sentimental novel of analysis as developed by Samuel Richardson or the historical romance as practiced by Sir Walter Scott? These subgenres of fiction, invented to satisfy the emotional needs of a merchant class in search of dignity or a Tory squirearchy consumed by nostalgia, could only by the most desperate expedients be tailored to fit American necessities. Throughout their writing lives, such writers as Charles Brockden Brown and James Fenimore Cooper devoted (with varying degrees of self-consciousness) all their ingenuity to this task, yet neither Brown nor Cooper finally proved capable of achieving high art; and the literary types invented by both have fallen since into the hands of mere entertainers—that is, novelists able and willing to attempt anything *except* the projection of the dark vision of America we have been describing. The Fielding novel, on the other hand, the pseudo-Shakespearean "comic epic" with its broad canvas, its emphasis upon reversals and recognitions, and its robust masculine sentimentality, turned out, oddly enough, to have no relevance to the American scene; in the United States it has remained an exotic, eternally being discovered by the widest audience and raised to best-sellerdom in its latest imported form, but seldom home-produced for home consumption.

It is the gothic form that has been most fruitful in the hands of our best writers:

the gothic symbolically understood, its machinery and decor translated into metaphors for a terror psychological, social, and metaphysical. Yet even treated as symbols, the machinery and decor of the gothic have continued to seem vulgar and contrived; symbolic gothicism threatens always to dissolve into its components, abstract morality and shoddy theater. A recurrent problem of our fiction has been the need of our novelists to find a mode of projecting their conflicts which would contain all the dusky horror of gothic romance and yet be palatable to discriminating readers, palatable at first of all to themselves.

Such a mode can, of course, not be subsumed among any of those called "realism," and one of the chief confusions in our understanding of our own literature has arisen from our failure to recognize this fact clearly enough. Our fiction is essentially and at its best non-realistic, even anti-realistic; long before *symbolisme* had been invented in France and exported to America, there was a full-fledged native tradition of symbolism. That tradition was born of the profound contradictions of our national life and sustained by the inheritance from Puritanism of a "typical" (even allegorical) way of regarding the sensible world—not as an ultimate reality but as a system of signs to be deciphered. For too long, historians of American fiction have mistakenly tried to impose on the course of a brief literary history a notion of artistic "progress" imported from France or, more precisely perhaps, from certain French literary critics. Such historians have been pleased to speak of "The Rise of Realism" or "The Triumph of Realism," as if the experience of Hawthorne or Poe or Melville were half-misguided fumblings toward the final excellence of William Dean Howells!

But the moment at which Flaubert was dreaming *Madame Bovary* was the moment when Melville was finding *Moby-Dick*, and considered as a "realistic" novel the latter is a scandalous botch. To speak of a counter-tradition to the novel, of the tradition of "the romance" as a force in our literature, is merely to repeat the rationalizations of our writers themselves; it is certainly to fail to be *specific* enough for real understanding. Our fiction is not merely in flight from the physical data of the actual world, in search of a (sexless and dim) Ideal; from Charles Brockden Brown to William Faulkner or Eudora Welty, Paul Bowles or John Hawkes, it is, bewilderingly and embarrassingly, a gothic fiction, nonrealistic and negative, sadist and melodramatic—a literature of darkness and the grotesque in a land of light and affirmation.

Moreover—and the final paradox is necessary to the full complexity of the case—ours is a literature of horror for boys. Truly shocking, frankly obscene authors we do not possess; Edgar Allan Poe is our closest approximation, a child playing at what Baudelaire was to live. A Baudelaire, a Marquis de Sade, a "Monk" Lewis, even a John Cleland is inconceivable in the United States. Our flowers of evil are culled for the small girl's bouquet, our novels of terror (*Moby-Dick*, *The Scarlet Letter*, *Huckleberry Finn*, the tales of Poe) are placed on the approved book lists of Parents' Committees who nervously fuss over the latest comic books. If such censors do not flinch at necrophilia or shudder over the book whose secret motto is "I baptise you not in the name of the Father . . . but of the Devil," or fear the juvenile whose hero at his greatest moment cries out, "All right, I'll *go* to Hell," it is only another irony of life in a land where the writers believe in hell and the official guardians of morality do not. As long as there's no *sex*!

Yet our authors are as responsible as the P.T.A.'s for the confusion about the true nature of their books; though they may have whispered their secret to friends, or confessed it in private letters, in their actual works they assumed what camouflage prudence dictated. They *wanted* to be misunderstood. *Huckleberry Finn* is only the supreme instance of a subterfuge typical of our classic novelists. To this very day, it is heresy in some quarters to insist that this is not finally the jolliest, the *cleanest* of books; Twain's ironical warning to significance hunters, posted just before the title page, is taken quite literally, and the irreverent critic who explicates the book's levels of terror and evasion is regarded as a busybody and scandalmonger. It is at last hard to say which is more remarkable, the eccentricity of American books or our critics' conspiracy of silence in this regard. (Or is it the critics' *unawareness* of the fact?) Why, one is driven to ask, why the distortion and why the ignorance? But the critics, after all, are children of the same culture as the novelists they discuss; and if we answer one question we will have answered both.

Perhaps the whole odd shape of American fiction arises simply (as simplifying Europeans are always ready to assure us) because there is no real sexuality in American life and therefore there cannot very well be any in American art. What we cannot achieve in Our relations with each other it would be vain to ask our writers to portray or even our critics to miss. Certainly many of our novelists have themselves believed, or pretended to believe, this. Through *The Scarlet Letter*, there is a constant mournful undercurrent, a series of asides in which Hawthorne deplores the sexual diminution of American women. Mark Twain in *1601* somewhat similarly contrasts the vigor of Elizabethan English-women with their American descendants; contrasting the sexual utopia of pre-colonial England with a fallen America where the men copulate "but once in seven yeeres"; and his pornographic sketch, written to amuse a clergyman friend (for men only!), ends on the comic-pathetic image of an old man's impotent lust that "would not stand again." Such pseudo-nostalgia cannot be taken too seriously, however; it may, indeed, be the projection of mere personal weakness and fantasy. Certainly, outside their books, Hawthorne and Twain seem to have fled rather than sought the imaginary full-breasted, fully sexed woman from whom American ladies had presumably declined. Both married, late in life, pale hypochondriac spinsters, intellectual invalids—as if to assert publicly that they sought in marriage not sex but culture!

Such considerations leave us trapped in the chicken-egg dilemma. How can one say whether the quality of passion in American life suffers because of a failure of the writer's imagination or vice versa? What is called "love" in literature is a rationalization, a way of coming to terms with the relationship between man and woman that does justice, on the one hand, to certain biological drives and, on the other, to certain generally accepted conventions of tenderness and courtesy; and literature, expressing and defining those conventions, tends to influence "real life" more than such life influences it. For better or for worse and for whatever reasons, the American novel is different from its European prototypes, and one of its essential differences arises from its chary treatment of woman and of sex.

To write, then, about the American novel is to write about the fate of certain European genres in a world of alien experience. It is not only a world where courtship and marriage have suffered a profound change, but also one in the process of losing the traditional distinctions of class; a world without significant history or a substantial past; a world which had left behind the terror of Europe not for the innocence it dreamed of, but for new and special guilts associated with the rape of nature and the exploitation of dark-skinned people; a world doomed to play out the imaginary childhood of Europe. The American novel is only *finally* American; its appearance is an event in the history of the European spirit—as, indeed, is the very invention of America itself.

II

Though it is necessary, in understanding the fate of the American novel, to understand what European prototypes were available when American literature began, as well as which ones nourished and which ones disappeared on our soil, it is even more important to understand the meaning of that moment in the mid-eighteenth century which gave birth to Jeffersonian democracy and Richardsonian sentimentality alike: to the myth of revolution and the myth of seduction. When Charles Brockden Brown, the first professional American author, sent a copy of his *Wieland* to Thomas Jefferson in 1798, he must, beneath his modest disclaimers, have had some sense of his and the President's kinship as revolutionaries. "I am therefore obliged to hope," Brown wrote, "that . . . the train of eloquent and judicious reasoning . . . will be regarded by Thomas Jefferson with as much respect as . . . me." But if Jefferson ever found the time to read Brown's novel, he left no record; we know only that he expressed general approval of "works of the imagination" as being able, more than history, to "possess virtue in the best and vice in the worst forms possible." It is a chillingly rational approach to art and a perhaps sufficient indication of the hopelessness of Brown's attempting in those sensible years to live by his writing.

Yet despite the fact that no professional novelist of real seriousness was to find a supporting public in America for twenty-five or thirty years more, Brown's instincts had not deceived him. He and Jefferson were engaged in a common enterprise; the novel and America did not come into existence at the same time by accident. They are the two great inventions of the bourgeois, Protestant mind at the moment when it stood, on the one hand, between Rationalism and Sentimentalism, and on the other, between the drive for economic power and the need for cultural autonomy. The series of events which includes the rise of modern psychology, and the triumph of the lyric in poetry, adds up to a psychic revolution as well as a social one—perhaps first of all to a psychic revolution. This revolution, viewed as an overturning of ideas and artistic forms, has traditionally been called "Romantic"; but the term is paralyzingly narrow, defining too little too precisely, and leading to further pointless distinctions between Romanticism proper, pre-Romanticism, *Stürm und Drang*, Sentimentalism, *Symbolisme*, etc. It seems preferable to call the whole continuing, complex event simply "the Break-through," thus emphasizing the dramatic entry of a new voice into the dialogue of Western man with his various selves.

The Break-through is characterized not only by the separation of psychology from philosophy, the displacement of the traditional leading genres by the personal lyric and analytic prose (with the consequent subordination of plot to character); it is also marked by the promulgation of a theory of revolution as a good in itself and, most notably perhaps, by a new concept of inwardness. One is almost tempted to say, by the invention of a new kind of self, a new level of mind; for what has been happening since the eighteenth century seems more like the development of a new organ than the mere finding of a new way to describe old experience. The triumph, for instance, of the theory that insanity is not possession by forces outside the psyche but a failure within the psyche itself is a representative aspect of the change-over.

It was Diderot who represented a first real awareness (as Freud represents a final one) that man is *double* to the final depths of his soul, the prey of conflicting psyches both equally himself. The conflict had, of course, always been felt, but had traditionally been described as occurring between man and devil, or flesh and spirit; that the parties to the dispute are both man and spirit was a revolutionary suggestion. In his demi-novel, *Rameau's Nephew*, Diderot projected the conflicting divisions within man's mind as the philosopher and the parasite, the rationalist and the underground man, debating endlessly the cause of the head versus that of the gut. And in his pornographic *Bijoux Indiscrets*, he proposed another version of the same dialogue: the enchanted (and indiscreet) genitals speak the truth which the mouth will not avow, thus comprising an allegorical defense of pornography in the guise of a pornographic work. In the same year in which Richardson's sentimental novel Clarissa was published, John Cleland's long-lived dirty book *The Memoirs of Fanny Hill* was making a stir. Pornography and obscenity are, indeed, hallmarks of the age of the Break-through. Not only pious novels but titillating ones show the emergence of the underground emotions (of what the period itself euphemistically called "the heart") into high culture. Quite as influential as Diderot (or Richardson or Rousseau) in the bouleversement of the eighteenth century is the Marquis de Sade, who stands almost emblematically at the crossroads of depth psychology and revolution.

Not only did de Sade shed new light on the ambivalence of the inner mind, revealing the true darkness and terror implicit in the drive which the neo-classical age (revolting against Christian notions of sin) had been content to celebrate as simple "pleasure" or polite "gallantry"; he may even have caused that symbolic storming of an almost empty prison with which the French Revolution begins. Himself a prisoner in the *Tour de la liberté* of the Bastille, de Sade, through an improvised loud speaker made of a tube and funnel, screamed to bystanders to rescue his fellow inmates who were having their throats cut—and scattered handwritten leaflets complaining about jail conditions to the crowd he attracted.

On July 3, 1798, he was finally transferred elsewhere to insure "the safety of the building," but not before he has started to write *Justine, or the Misfortunes of Virtue*, that perverse offshoot of the Richarsonian novel, and had thus begun to create the first example of revolutionary pornography. Maurice Blanchot, in an essay called *Lautréamont et Sade*, describes his method as follows:

> What is striking is this: the language of de Sade is precisely opposite to the cheating language of hangmen; it is the language of the victim; he invented it in the Bastille . . . .He put on trial, reversing the process of his own judgement, the men who condemned him, God himself, and—in general—every limitation against which his frenzy clashed . . .

In the Marquis de Sade, the Break-through found its most stringent and spectacular spokesman: the condemned man judging his judges, the pervert mocking the normal, the advocate of destruction and death sneering at the defenders of love and life; but his *reductio* follows logically enough from assumptions shared by Jefferson and Rousseau, Richardson and Saint-Just. Whatever has been suspect, outcast, and denied is postulated as the source of good. Before the Break-through, no one, Christian or Humanist, had doubted the inferiority of Passion to reason, of impulse to law; and though it is possible sophistically to justify all eighteenth-century reversals by quoting the verse which says the last shall be first, Christianity is dead from the moment such a justification is made. The Break-through, the triumphant intrusion of the libido into the place of virtue and reason, is profoundly anti-Christian though it is not always willing to appear so. There is a brief age of transition when the Enlightenment and Sentimentalism exist side by side, when it is still possible to pretend that true reason and true feeling, the urgings of passion and the dictates of virtue are identical—and that all are alike manifestations of the orthodox God. But Sentimentalism yields quickly to the full Romantic revolt; in a matter of months, Don Juan, enemy of heaven and the family, has been transformed from villain to hero; and before the process is finished, audiences have learned to weep for Shylock rather than laugh him from the stage. The legendary rebels and outcasts, Prometheus and Cain, Judas and the Wandering Jew, Faust and Lucifer himself are one by one redeemed. The parricide becomes an object of veneration, and tourists (among them that good American abroad, Herman Melville) carry home as an icon Guido's picture of Beatrice Cenci, slayer of her father!

The process is continuous and nearly universal. Even the values of language change: "gothic" passes from a term of contempt to one of description and then of praise, while "baroque" makes more slowly the same transition; meanwhile terms once used honorifically to describe desired traits—"condescension," for example—become indicators of disapproval. The child is glorified over the man, the peasant over the courtier, the dark man over the white, the rude ballad over the polished sonnet, the weeper over the thinker, colony over mother country, the commoner over the king—nature over culture. At first, all this is a game: the ladies of the court in pastoral dress swing high into the air to show their legs with a self-consciousness quite unlike the abandon of children to which they are pretending. But in a little while, Jean-Jacques Rousseau has fainted on the road to Vincennes and awakened to find his waistcoat soaked with tears; and it is suddenly all in earnest. Whatever was down is now up, as the under-mind heaves up out of the darkness: barricades are erected and the novel becomes the reigning form; the Jew walks openly out of the ghetto, and otherwise sensible men hang on their walls pictures of trees and cattle. The conjunctions are comic in their unexpectedness and variety.

It is hard to say what was cause and what effect in the complex upheaval; everything seems the symptom of everything else. Yet deep within the nexus of causes (gods must die for new genres to be born) was that "death of God" that has not yet ceased to trouble our peace. Somewhere near the beginning of the eighteenth century, Christianity (more precisely, perhaps, that desperate compromise of the late Middle Ages and early Renaissance, Christian Humanism) began to wear out. It was not merely, or even primarily, a matter of the destruction of the political and social power of one Church or another, much less of the lapse of economic control by the priests. The divisions within Christendom surely contributed to the final collapse, but they are perhaps better regarded as manifestations than as causes of the insecurity over dogma that was at work deep within. Institutionalized Christianity at any rate began to crumble when its God began to fail, that is to say, when its mythology no longer proved capable of controlling and revivifying the imagination of Europe.

The darker motive forces of the psyche refused any longer to accept the names and ranks by which they had been demeaned for almost two thousand years; once worshiped as "gods," had been made demons by fiat, but now they stirred again in discontent. Especially the Great Mother—cast down by the most patriarchal of all religions (to the Hebrews, she was Lilith, the bride of darkness), ambiguously redeemed as the Blessed Virgin and denied once more by a Hebraizing Protestantism—clamored to be honored once more. The very distinction between God and Devil, on which the psychic balance of Europe had for so long been staked, was threatened. It did not matter that some people (chiefly women) continued to go to church, or even that there were revivals within the framework of surviving sects; fewer and fewer men lived by the legends of the church, and the images of saints represented not living myths but "mythology" in a literary sense, tales to be read for amusement or "analyzed" in the light of the teachings of anthropology or psychology. There remained only the job of carrying the news of God's death to those who had not yet heard the word.

The effect of the growing awareness (an awareness, to be sure, at first shared by only a handful of advanced thinkers) of this cosmic catastrophe was double: a sense of exhilaration and a spasm of terror, to which correspond the two initial and over-lapping stages of the Break-through. There was first of all the conviction of the Age of Reason and its spokesmen, the *philosophes*, grave-diggers of the Christian God, that they—and all of mankind—were at last *free*, free of the superstition and ignorance so long sponsored by the priests for their own selfish ends. Those demons into which the early Christian apologists had translated the gods of antiquity seemed to the *philosophes* idle inventions of the Church itself: bugaboos to scare the pious into unquestioning subservience. Even the Christian God seemed to them such a contrivance, demonic and irrational. In the imagined universe presided over by their own "Author of Creation," there could be no place for mystery or blackness. Once "l'infâme," the scandalous Church, had been crushed, all monsters would be eliminated forever, and man could take up his long, baffled march toward perfection in a sweet, sunlit, orderly world. Just such a vision, however modified by circumstance, moved the Deist intellectuals who founded America, especially that Thomas Jefferson to whom C. B. Brown, himself a follower of the *philosophes*, proffered his gothic novel.

Insofar as America is legendary, a fact of the imagination as well as one of history, it has been shaped by the ideals of the Age of Reason. To be sure, the European mind had dreamed for centuries before the Enlightenment of an absolute West: Atlantis, Ultima Thule, the Western Isles—a place of refuge beyond the seas, to which the hero retreats to await rebirth, a source of new life in the direction of the setting sun which seems to stand for death. Dante, however, on the very brink of an age which was to turn the dream into the actualities of exploration, had prophetically sent to destruction in the West, Ulysses, the archetypal explorer. The direction of his westward journey through the great sea is identified with the sinister left hand; and Ulysses himself comes to stand for man's refusal to accept the simple limits of traditional duty: "not the sweetness of having a son, nor the pious claim of an old father, nor the licit love that should have made Penelope rejoice could quench in me the burning to become familiar with the vice of men and men's valor." It is a fitting enough epigraph to represent that lust for experience which made America. There is, indeed, something blasphemous in the very act by which America was established, a gesture of defiance that began with the symbolic breaching of the pillars of Hercules, long considered the divine signs of limit.

To be sure, the poets of later Catholicism made an effort to recast the dream of America in terms viable for their Counter-Reformation imaginations, to forge a myth that would subserve new political exigencies. It was not accident, they boasted, that the discoverer of America (sponsored by those most Catholic defenders of the Faith) had been called Cristoforo Colombo, "the Christ-bearing dove." Had he not carried orthodoxy into a world of unredeemed pagans, a reservoir of souls providentially kept in darkness until they were needed to replace the lapsed Christians of heretical northern Europe?

It is however, the Enlightenment's vision of America rather than that of the Church that was written into our documents and has become the substance of our deepest sense of ourselves and our destiny. If North America had remained Latin, the story might have been different; but Jefferson himself presided over the purchase of the Louisiana Territory, which settled that question once and for all. History sometimes provides suitable symbolic occasions, and surely one of them is the scene that finds Jefferson and Napoleon, twin heirs of the Age of Reason, preparing the way for Lewis and Clark, that is to say, for the first actors in our own drama of a perpetually retreating West. Napoleon, it must be remembered, was the sponsor of the painter David and Jefferson the planner of Monticello; good neo-classicists both, they place the American myth firmly in the classicizing, neo-Roman tradition of the late eighteenth century. The New World is, of course, in one sense an older one than Europe, a preserve of the primitive, last refuge of antique virtue; indeed the writers and artists of the Empire period could never quite tell the difference between Americans, red or white, and the inhabitants of the Roman Republic. The face of Washington, as rendered in bronze by Houdon, is that of the noblest Roman of them all, or, in Byron's phrase (already a cliché), "the Cincinnatus of the West."

But America is not exclusively the product of Reason—not even in the area of legend. Behind its neo-classical facade, ours is a nation sustained by a sentimental and Romantic dream, the dream of an escape from culture and a renewal of youth. Beside the *philosophes*, with whom he seemed at first to accord so well that they scarcely knew he was their profoundest enemy, stands Rosseau. It is his compelling vision of a society uncompromised by culture, of simple piety and virtue bred by "Nature," i.e., the untended landscape, that has left the deepest impress on the American mind. The heirs of Rousseau are Chateaubriand and Cooper, after whom the world of togas and marble brows and antique heroism is replaced by the sylvan scene, across which the melancholy refugee plods in search of the mysterious Niagara, or where Natty Bumppo, buckskinned savior, leans on his long rifle and listens for the sound of a cracking twig. The bronze face of a bewigged Washington gives way to the image of young Abe splitting logs in a Kentucky clearing.

The dream of the Republic is quite a different thing from that of the Revolution. The vision of blood and fire as ritual purification, the need to cast down what is up, to degrade the immemorial images of authority, to impose equality as the ultimate orthodoxy—these came from the *Encyclopédie*, perhaps, as abstract ideas; but the spirit in which they were lived was that of full-blown Romanticism. The Revolution of 1789 (for which ours was an ideological dress rehearsal) may have set up David as its official interpreter, but it left the world to Delacroix; and though it enthroned Reason as its goddess, it prepared for a more unruly Muse.

In Sentimentalism, the Age of Reason dissolves in a debauch of tearfulness; sensibility, seduction, and suicide haunt its art even before ghosts and graveyards take over-strange images of darkness to usher in an era of freedom from fear. And beneath them lurks the realization that the devils which had persisted from antiquity into Christianity were not dead but only driven inward; that the "tyranny of superstition," far from being the fabrication of a Machiavellian priesthood, was a projection of a profound inner insecurity and guilt, a hidden world of nightmare not abolished by manifestos or restrained by barricades. The final horrors, as modern society has come to realize, are neither gods nor demons, but intimate aspects of our own minds.

A Figure in the Carpet: Irony and the American Novel

HAROLD BEAVER

British critic Harold Beaver diagnoses the principal flaw in the American novel as a failure of detachment that would allow for an ironic voice in novelists from Cooper to the Beat Generation writers. Following Lawrence, Fiedler and Rahv, Beaver blames the lack of social tradition for the American tendency to retreat to the frontier, away from civilization. The absorption in the personal gave rise to the dominant genre in nineteenth-century American literature—the sentimental novel, a type inimical to irony. Apart from Twain's *Huck Finn*, a novel that attains a perfect ironic balance, according to Beaver, only the urban sophisticates James and Wharton possessed an ironic eye. Beaver discusses the disillusionment that beset American authors after World War I and the increased bitterness evident in the social realists of the 1920s and 30s. Like Marius Bewley, he perceives a "dissociated sensibility" between inner experience and outer world among American novelists, one that could be healed by the ironic realism that Russian, French and English writers bring to their work. Only J.D. Salinger's *Catcher in the Rye*, Beaver believes, achieves the supreme irony of *Huck Finn* among twentieth-century novelists.

American literature, after years of colonial status, has now become respectable. It has, we are told, come of age. Just how this happened is not clear, but the event seems to have occurred some time after the First World War and to have received international recognition only after the Second. The crowning of William Faulkner and Ernest Hemingway with Nobel wreaths in 1950 and 1954 brought the initiation ceremonies to a public conclusion.

Since then the literary reviews have increasingly devoted their supplements or special articles to the subject; academic courses on American literary topics at British

Source: Harold Beaver, "A Figure in the Carpet: Irony and the American Novel", *Essays and Studies*, 15, 1962, pp. 101-14.

universities have rapidly multiplied and the appearance of new work from across the Atlantic has been received with the awe earlier reserved only for French or Russian imports. Nevertheless, not everyone is happy. Doubts have arisen, and even the most confident Americans seem to feel them.

Naturally, some reply. American is not a *major* literature. How can it be? American history—the experience of the white race and the mingling of all races on that northern continent—is still too short. America has no past, no myths, no gods, no ancient drama, no ancient rituals.

Still—one ponders the answer—four hundred and fifty years is not so short a span. However new the people, the continent itself is old and its government the oldest republican form of government in the world. Many of its songs derive from Britain, much of the folklore from the Indian or Negro, yet American as its own ballads, its own oral tradition of tall tales, its own epic of conquest, its own myths of workers and warriors. The Civil War is the American Iliad; the expansion westward the American Odyssey; its cowboys and gunmen are the American heroes; and the miners of Nevada, the whale-boatmen and lumbermen, the American Jasons of the Golden Fleece.

The epic is recent. It is squeezed into the narrow confines of the nineteenth century but there lies the essence of its hypnotic power. While the European male was already servant of the top hat, the machine and the counting-house, the American was still free. He served violence and progress. He carried the gun, the hatchet and the prayer-book. He had escaped out into the vastness of the virgin forests, the prairies, the Sierras and the hot, untamed landscape of the Mexican border. The frontier was the earliest and most enduring of native myths. Fenimore Cooper was its first exponent, Francis Parkman its first historian. Out of the lawless tussle of sheriffs, cattlemen and Indians was slowly created that morality of right and wrong, good guy and bad guy, which is still the major attraction of film and television.

Length of history alone, therefore, cannot be a final answer. It is with Pushkin, after all, and, his nineteenth-century successors that Russian literature became significant. Whatever the origins and epics, its span is embraced by one miraculous century.

There comes another reply: American experience has until recently been lopsided. Subduing this vast continent has been a man's work. A cult of virility, of male companionship, of danger, pursuit, flight and death dominated the American imagination. This was no place for the traditional novel of social forces, of a delicate web of male and female relationships. Life on the Mississippi was a long way from Barchester. In fact, it was precisely to escape the world of Barchester, with its patronage of church and state, prelate and nobility, that the immigrant had crossed over to the New World. He was the new Adam in a new-found land. He had fled authority and all responsibility—including adult sexual responsibility—in a search not only for new opportunity but for renewed innocence. This, or something like it, is the recent thesis of Leslie A. Fiedler. Its most original portions were borrowed from D. H. Lawrence; by and large, they are still true.

An outline of an answer emerges. The American frontier denied the past. Out in the virgin wilds all men, of all nationalities, could begin again as equals. Here was the point of return, of rebirth to a true manhood, of a new start. But in life—even in America—there is never a new start. The past is always there to haunt and overshadow the present. The taming of the Frontier was itself a denial of innocence; and as the old civilization caught up, the Frontier—the dream of the wilderness—receded ever westward.

This conflict between dream and reality is the stuff of the American imagination. It was with the closing of the Frontier that final disillusion set in. It was the post-World War I writers who were labelled "The Lost Generation". Americans had always projected their dreams forward; previously there had always been routes of escape. After the rapid scramble for their continent was over, they could only project their dreams into the past, or into themselves, or into an alien world that defied their image. In this borderland between dream and reality, their writers from Hawthorne to Poe, Melville to Faulkner to Hemingway, have traced the ironic bitterness of existence.

But ironic bitterness, ironic techniques or a feeling for the dramatic irony of the fate of mankind is not the same as a grasp of reality. It is also no substitute for it. Making his accounts on the borderlines of dream and actuality, the American prose-writer has often been closer to the working of poetry, allegory or romance. There is a grandeur among their great writers, a depth not often sounded in English fiction; but there is also rhetoric, a fatal fluency, an inability to stand aside, to grasp and measure emotion and experience.

A strand is lacking. Reviewing an anthology of French poetry in *The Times Literary Supplement* a critic wrote:

> There is no true realism without irony, because irony is the power to penetrate the reality of things. It is a detachment, but it is not an indifference, and that is why it is compatible with intense personal feeling. It is knowing the truth about one's emotions and experience. It is one of several forms of transcendence, and it is the one peculiarly native to the French genius.

It is also the form peculiarly foreign to the American genius. One strain, and an essential strain, is almost completely lacking in American artistic output. In a phrase, it is the failure to achieve a tradition of ironic realism equal to that of the great Russians from Gogol to Chekhov, to that of the great French from Stendhal to Flaubert to Proust, to that of the great English from Jane Austen to Dickens to E. M. Forster, which raises the lingering doubt whether American literature is to be considered their equal. English prose fiction too has had its visionaries from Emily Bronte to D. H. Lawrence, but American literature even today—with so much contemporary achievement from Carson McCullers to Saul Bellow—still seems lopsided, too full of adolescent phantasy and self-concern, too full of lust and guilt and hankerings after a vanished Eden.

Who have been the American ironists? In the main they sprang from a small sophisticated urban class. They took pride in an English ancestry, a generation or more of money and a secure social position in circles centring on Boston or New

York, Harvard or Yale. Theirs was a culture which flourished precariously above the teeming immigrant millions in the expansive age which followed the Civil War. They were aristocratic and pessimistic and so detached that their main representative writers, Henry Adams, Henry James and Edith Wharton deserted America entirely for long periods of their lives. Yet, in their aristocratic way, they pointed a path which is not merely that of the paleface versus the redskin (in Philip Rahv's metaphor) but that of informed irony versus lyrical self-commitment which has been too seldom followed since.

For critical intelligence was easily divorced from art; the splintering can already be seen at work in Henry James. Once the background of material culture was removed, the rapid growth of American criticism, the New Criticism, resulted between the wars. It is far easier to take a detailed view of literature than of life. Van Wyck Brooks became the guide and curator of the historical cult: while T. S. Eliot, heir-apparent of this fin-de-siècle culture and himself a refugee to Europe, has continued to walk a tightrope balance between the creative and critical intelligence throughout his life. On the East Coast it is only the Ivy League universities who are now heirs and guardians of this Brahmin tradition. But their influence is, of course, enormous; and no longer confined to parts of New England and the mid-Atlantic States but spreading through hundreds of universities and the whole body politic.

Detachment is an aristocratic virtue. The immigrant workers were, above all, anxious to belong. It was not for them to question the promised land or the philosophical assumptions on which it was founded. To have crossed the Atlantic was itself an irrevocable act of commitment and this act continued to colour both their thought and literature. How much vaunted American realism, from William Dean Howells's "truthful treatment of material" to Sinclair Lewis's *Babbitt* has not consisted, at bottom, of sentiment dressed as a vehicle for wishful thinking or for propaganda—even if, as in many cases, the propaganda was adverse. Lyrical candour took the place of detachment. Too often American writers isolated themselves in the flood of their own emotions. The self-rapt outpourings of a Thomas Wolfe or a Henry Miller or the more recent Howls of the Beat Generation—a lyricism sickened and carried to hysterical excess—has been a constant long drawn-out refrain of American fiction.

In all such cases sentiment is the pervasive trap, and the sentimental mode is the most distinctive mode of American writing. Irony is the corrective of sentiment, especially of that sentimental vision which sees the whole world as emanating from the writer, all objects as part of the stream of his emotions. But while some—notably today the sociologists, William Whyte, Vance Packard, David Riesman, C. Wright Mills and others—are busy questioning *everything* in American society, the novelists as often as not, are only intent on proclaiming the uniqueness of their personal experience. There is a dichotomy here between the vast sweeping question and the intense personal avowal, a lack of equilibrium which is part of the dissociated sensibility within which most modern American writers have had to perform.

The sociological criticism is part of what D. H. Lawrence rudely labelled the "mind-consciousness" of American culture: the personal pre-occupation of a Norman Mailer, the cult of total confession ("One's self I sing, a single separate person"), is all attempt to rediscover the American myth in a unique identity when all else has failed. The first lacks the intense personal feeling of self-knowledge: the second lacks the proper aesthetic distance. One form of inquiry is ultimately arid: the second, hysterical and self-frustrating. Both lack, what Halldor Laxness called, "that Icelandic talent, straight from the sagas, of speaking mockingly of what was nearest the heart".

Of course there have been rebels from this self-consuming democratic ethos. But the rebels were either considered outsiders by others or themselves (like Nathanael West) or made exiles of themselves to Europe, like the Negro writer Richard Wright who ended his days in Paris. For the traditional role of the American rebel has been simply to withdraw, just as Thoreau withdrew from Concord to the loneliness of Walden Pond, Natty Bumppo withdrew from the town of Templeton to the wild forests, Melville from New York and the whaling towns to the Taipi Valley in the South Seas, and Huck Finn determined, at the end of his saga, to escape from Aunt Sally and "light out for the territories". Modern America, after all, was itself born of withdrawal. Away from the oppressive cities, in uncomplicated nature, an American dreams of rediscovering his identity and his lost purpose. It is always from this standard of untainted nature the natural perfection that society has fallen. Such is the legacy of Rousseau to the American psyche!

Such is also the legacy of early Nineteenth Century Romanticism. For it is not only the gothic horror novel, with its cult of perversion, rape, homicide and sadism, which left its mark on the whole school of Southern writers from Poe to Tennessee Williams, but also the tongue of romantic prophecy which descended on every American who sings the Song of Himself—the intoning priestly voice of Walt Whitman barding in Brooklyn, Henry Miller mouthing his black mass of sexual release in Paris apartments, and Jack Kerouac bumming in San Francisco. The Puritans turned their eyes inward to their consciences. The Romantics turned third eyes inward to their emotions. The immigrants turned their eyes inward to search for their new identity. No wonder it took some time before eyes turned outward and actually inspected the new land and society around them. It was mainly the foreigners, Crèvecoeur and Tocqueville from France, Mrs. Trollope and Dickens from England, who were left to make the detailed inventory. When the virgin land, the rough and tumble past, the shadowy Indians and their legends had all but disappeared, only then were writers like Mark Twain or Willa Cather moved to recreate the lost land in a lyrical surge of longing.

A further obstacle was, and remains, that of language. Mark Twain is credited with the formulation of the distinctive American prose style. Which is true to an extent. But this voice—Huck Finn's speaking voice—had not solved a more fundamental literary problem. It is very well for a critic like Richard Chase to call Huckleberry Finn "a joyous exorcism of traditional literary English", but what remains? Even Americans still need the subtle, pliant tool of literary English. How is an American to achieve a realistic prose style without writing an English which is too obviously English?

Once the younger generation had turned their back on the biblical rhetoric of Melville, Hawthorne, Poe and Whitman—or the involuted self-communions of the later Henry James—the problem could no longer be avoided. In practice, however, it was avoided. Most academic writers, especially academic critics, continued to elaborate an inflated verbiage (the special brain-child of the universities) which had lost touch not only with their own speaking voice but with the English of its supposed origin. Southern writers, too, still gloried in the old purple tradition of inflated prose, which left Faulkner breathlessly chasing adjectives, metaphors and adjectival clauses down page after page.

Gertrude Stein, in her muddled way, did see the problem. She returned in all seriousness to a kind of kindergarten or Berlitz School textbook English. She wrote a whole autobiography for her friend, Alice Toklas, in this infinitely boring pastiche before she turned the language in upon itself creating daisy-chain patterns whose purpose was as much to exclude as to include meaning. Hemingway, her chief disciple, certainly learnt a simplicity from her which he could stretch and spring in the tense violence of his action. But too often the style grew trite, repetitious, naïve. In the main, Hemingway was happy to discard narrative altogether. It was easier to concentrate on dialogue, reducing narrative to little more than commentary and a few stage-directions.

Perhaps Gertrude Stein's experiments were seen to lead to a dead end. Perhaps Hemingway's style felt too cramped within the limits of journalism. At any rate younger writers, like Philip Roth, Bernard Malamud, J. D. Salinger, or James Purdy, have all returned to a chunkier prose, handled flatly and impersonally. As a medium it lacks both pliancy and warmth. It attempts a frontal assault on the outer world (like that of film or camera) when that world has yielded more readily to insinuation, to the poise and recoil of irony. For irony, that weapon which alone penetrates reality, is also a weapon from the armory of the optic imagination.

So the problem remains unsolved. At their happiest and most brilliant Faulkner, Wolfe, Salinger, Twain, Dreiser, Hemingway, Joel Chandler Harris, Ring Lardner, Scott Fitzgerald, Erskille Caldwell—all resort to the speaking voice, the native gusto of the streets, the slow yarning drawl of the country. Resigned to the third person, only a few like James Thurber have been able to keep the folksy, intimate tone of the front stoop or saloon bar: the prose of the others almost invariably grows stilted or inflated. Either the brain takes over or the tension slackens: sentiment and rhetoric creep in. Each labours with language as if each were the first to hew his way through the dictionary jungle. All measuring-rods are lacking.

Mark Twain, by imbibing the Southern vernacular and folksy grandiloquence of the tall tales into the texture of his prose, had created a very personal idiom. It was bantering. It was easy. Its button-holing intimacy prompted a host of imitators. It released spurts of colloquial energy, but it was no substitute for a common literary language. For the voice of Mark Twain, the travelling showman, and of Huck Finn, his lost boyhood, concealed a far sadder, more embittered individual. The Style itself was a mask and it was not until his last decade that Samuel Clemens himself was allowed to speak.

His case makes an interesting study. "A vein of irony" (that was William Dean Howells's phrase) runs through his work right from the start. But at first he used it only at the expense of others—the Sandwich islands, Italy, the Holy Land—at any place that he visited as a reporter, at anything that was abroad. He was the buoyant American optimist casting a sardonic eye at the old fogies outside God's Own country, and the folks at home, who read his despatches, loved him. *The Innocents Abroad* established Mark Twain. But if in 1869 (despite the four years' butchery of the Civil War) Europe still seemed a pretty second-hand and second-rate affair compared to the brand-new shining virtues of the American republic, twenty years later the satire was a good deal more double-edged. Though the Connecticut Yankee provides his "new deal" for the downtrodden people of England, though he transforms King Arthur's realm with marvels of gunpowder and mechanics, the author's sardonic eye is now on the American. "This Yankee of mine," wrote Twain, "is a perfect ignoramus; he is boss of a machine shop, he can build a locomotive or a Colt's revolver, he can put up and run a telegraph line, but he's an ignoramus nevertheless."

Meanwhile disillusion had set in. Already in *The Gilded Age* Mark Twain had satirized the political corruption of Washington and the frenzied speculation of New York. By 1882, after his return trip to the Mississippi, the disillusion was complete. In the second half of *Life on the Mississippi* he puts on a brave face, dutifully admiring the material progress up and down the river; but, at heart, he had retreated farther and farther into the past. He never returned to the river. He stayed on at Hartford completing *Huckleberry Finn*.

That book was compounded of deeply-felt nostalgia and ironic bitterness. The golden age had now dropped for ever below the horizon of the past, to a time which was always "before the War", when rafts and boys and steamboats owned the open river. And there he found his hero. Huck was the perfect ironic hero. He was the frontier Candide, the clear-eyed, practical youth, brought up outside the confines of the city, by his drunken "pap", in the wilds of nature. This motherless outcast, this child of nature, had no masters, no book-learning, no Docteur Pangloss. He learnt of life from the source of life itself; from the wide brown waters of the Mississippi and from his companion Jim, whose Negro people had not yet lost communion with the spirits of nature.

The raft floats down the river; and each adventure brings its spiritual lesson; and each lesson stands in ironic contrast to the civilized life as it is lived on the shores of the Mississippi, the little towns with their fraudulent hucksters, murderous brawls and pious slave-owning spinsters. This "christian" civilization, in fact, is rotten. Its surface is all violence and humbug. Huck's moral crisis, the victory over his "yaller dog" conscience in helping a nigger to escape, is not just victory over the morality of St. Petersburg but over all morality which denies the common humanity of man.

In this one book Mark Twain found the true balance. As sometimes happens, it is doubtful whether he fully realized it. When, almost ten years later, in *The Tragedy of Pudd'nhead Wilson*, he returned to a riverside village with its slaves and decayed gentry, the irony had turned scornful, the nostalgia sour. For a while longer he could act the professional jokester, the popular one-man burlesque mixing laughter and satire and pathos. But the bitterness was showing through. In his last books, in *The Man that Corrupted Hadleyburg, King Leopold's Soliloquy, What is Man? Extract from Captain Stormfield's Visit to Heaven, The Mysterious Stranger*, the scorn breaks fiercely to the surface. He attacked the sham respectability of the small town, the morality of missionaries, the exploitation of underdeveloped countries, the smug self-satisfaction of man. The great earth itself was renamed the Wart. Again and again, with the Swiftian fury of the King of Brobdingnag, he attacked "the nasty stinking little human race", "a museum of diseases, a home of impurities", a "race of cowards' constituting the most consummate sham and lie that was ever invented".

In such paroxysms of despair the great humorist burnt himself out. As the Angel said to the boys of Eseldorf in the final, posthumous book:

> No sane man can be happy, for to him life is real, and he sees what a fearful thing it is . . . There is no God, no Universe, no human race, no earthly life, no heaven, no hell. It is all a dream—a grotesque and foolish dream. Nothing exists but you. And you are but a *thought*—a vagrant thought, a useless thought, a homeless thought, wandering forlorn among the empty eternities.

Bleak nihilism could go no farther.

Other Americans—one thinks of Nathanael Wesst, or Scott Fitzgerald's last years in Hollywood—found their way into this same dark night. The overwhelming emotion is disgust, a furious disgust at the inherent unhappy evil in the world. The disgust is brother to despair. Mark Twain's early optimism, his marvellous optimism, were the bracing effects of a tremendous personal commitment, an exuberant belief in the uniqueness of the United States. Once that crumbled, once disillusion set in, there was nothing to take its place. Samuel Clemens had no positive idea to offer. Nor did Nathanael West have a positive idea to offer. Nor did Scott Fitzgerald, in *The Last Tycoon*, have a positive idea to offer. Mark Twain returned to the sheet-anchor of his youth. There, for a time, he found courage and hope.

The Brahmins were poised more firmly. Henry James continually questioned life, holding each scene, each person up for scrutiny like some aesthetic object. Henry Adam created such self-imposed sceptical distances between himself and his environment that he even wrote his autobiography in the third person. But those of the post-war generation who turned their backs on the urban novel also turned their backs on the English—English of the Brahmins and the irony which was their medium. Faulkner hymned his prose epics of the rural South. Steinbeck upheld the rights of the migrant farm-workers in California. Hemingway (like Stephen Crane, Jack London and Ring Lardner before him) gloried in the muscular exploits of hunters, sportsmen, sailors, soldiers, and bullfighters. The clock was turned back full circle to the backwoodsmen, to the Davy Crocketts and Paul Bunyans in modern guise, who have always been welcomed as true American heroes at the expense of urban, civilized man.

But the jazz age was a city culture. Scott Fitzgerald's and everyone else's New York and Chicago and Greenwich Village were all city cultures. If irony was too detached, too aristocratic a weapon, if irony seemed to put too great a distance between the speaker and his fellow American, the wisecrack was slick, urban and democratic. The wisecrack was Damon Runyan; the wisecrack was O. Henry, that large-minded Texan urbanized by the largest city in the Universe. The wisecrack today is essentially the style of *Time* magazine, as well as of Mort Sahl and his fellow jesters of despair.

But the wisecrack, whatever its rôle (hearty, complacent, or swashbuckling with H. L. Mencken against the "booboisie") could not replace a more searching irony. It was J. D. Salinger who made the supreme transition. He reintroduced Huck Finn, a modern Huck Finn, one Holden Caulfield, a prep-schoolboy who had flunked out of three schools, into the maelstrom of the modern city. The immense popularity of the book reflects the immense popularity of the new folk-hero. Millions of Americans could identify with this renewed longing for innocence—the adolescent, with his crazy red cap worn back to front, looking back to the thresholds of his childhood.

As always he had to be all adolescent. Only an adolescent now stood, clear and well-defined, between the borderlines of innocence and experience where American myth has always crystallized. Only an adolescent could still move like a Don Quixote through the garish vulgarity of the modern city, and with his boyish code of chivalry and boyish disillusion create that ironic counterpoint between ideal and actuality. "Phony! Boy, was it phony!" Prep-school, Harvard, business, film, theatre, any and every adult hierarchy or organization are all a "big, big deal", "strictly phony", "strictly for the birds". But Holden Caulfield, like any adolescent, rejects not only the organized ways of the world, he rejects the whole of modern American civilization: "'Well, *I* hate it. Boy. do I hate it,' I said. 'But it isn't just that. It's everything. I hate living in New York and all.'"

Like every American rebel. Holden dreams his dream of escape. But when he dreams, this mid-twentieth century boy can only imagine working at a roadside garage, somewhere out West:

> "They'd let me put gas and oil in their stupid cars, and they'd pay me a salary and all for it, and I'd build me a little cabin somewhere with the dough I made and live there for the rest of my life. I'd build it right near the woods, but not right *in* them, because I'd want it to be sunny as hell all the time."

That is the irony of his fate. There is no Walden Pond left for Holden. There are no more Territories for him to light out to. He is caught, immersed in the civilization of the Lavender Room and the Roquettes and Radio City and garages. He is part of the modern neuroticism—mechanically immersed fighting mechanism. Huck was still happily at the centre of his world: Holden Caulfield, nervous, depressed, lonesome, is modern maladjusted man. Huck was escaping the Miss Watsons and Aunt Sallies of the world: Holden is escaping everybody and himself. No wonder he is heading for a nervous breakdown. He is a lost soul and must end up the hands of that American mechanic of the soul, the "psychoanalyst guy". The irony is self-destructive.

The immediate theme of *The Catcher in the Rye* is that of mixed-up adolescence;

and in that ambiguous territory some of the finest contemporary novelists—Carson McCullers in *The Member of the Wedding*, Truman Capote in *Other Voices, Other Rooms*, James Purdy in *63: Dream Palace*—have felt the moral pulse of American life.

The more obvious ironies have, by and large, been left to foreigners or to first-generation Americans, like the Rumanian Steinberg or the Russian Vladimir Nabokov.

The eyes of the newcomers were still uncluttered. They had not gone soft at heart. What they saw—the sabre-toothed ears, the diabolic sunglasses, the women in leather-fringed cowboy suits—they could hold to open ridicule. The supreme comedy of Nabokov's *Lolita* is that now a European, charming, ruthless, perverted Humbert Humbert, is let loose among the American innocents. The innocents are no longer observed abroad, but at home. And none are quite as innocent as they seemed. *Lolita* is not so much a satire on America, as an ironic *jeu d'esprit*, built on a base of pornography, and filled with a minute personal observation of American life, where everything is seen as supremely odd and supremely ridiculous—women smoking, garage mechanics, suburban lawns, prefabricated hotels. The style, to suit these absurdities, is as ironically groomed as that of another Oscar Wilde, lecturing to an audience of cowboys.

So there is a line of descent. Somewhere from Mark Twain to James Thurber to J. D. Salinger, from Edith Wharton to Sinclair Lewis to Vladimir Nabokov, there is a tradition of American irony. But though the scope and achievement of American letters, the carpet—to use Henry James's metaphor—has long been ample, this figure, this strand of perception, is still a slight one. It needs some scrutiny to find it. Here and there it shows boldly. Over large areas it disappears altogether.

Passages of satire, or invective, or irony, naturally occur in most great American prose writers—it would be odd if this were not so in a literature of the last two centuries—but, by and large, Americans have not viewed themselves, or their world, with a glittering eye. They have not seen life coldly nor seen it whole. Their realism, as Eugene O'Neill said of himself, remained "fog-bound".

✥ 99 ✥

The Sociological Matrix of the Novel of Manners

JAMES W. TUTTLETON

In the first chapter of his book, Tuttleton defends the American novel of manners against charges from Hawthorne through James to Chase that America lacked the requisite social stratification and cultural milieu to produce such novels. Adopting Trilling's definition of "a culture's hum and buzz of implication," Tuttleton argues that America did possess sufficient social differentiation among groups for the novelist to depict conflicts and interactions between individuals and society. In the second section, he addresses the argument that the predominant American fictional mode was the romance. He disagrees with both Cooper's and Hawthorne's laments at the paucity of realistic subject matter, and he faults James for advancing Hawthorne's complaint into the twentieth century. Though Wharton followed James's opinion that American writers lacked the necessary cultural stimulus to write great novels, Tuttleton notes that many of them, Wharton included, proved their own verdicts wrong.

Contemporary actuality may indeed be so strange that the imagination cannot compete with it. "It is now life and not art," Lionel Trilling has remarked, "that requires the willing suspension of disbelief."[1] And it is doubtless true that modern sociologists and psychologists have appropriated fields once reserved to the novelist. But it is by no means decided that the novel is dead—despite the claim of critics like F. W. Bateson and Sir Harold Nicolson that "the future of imaginative prose lies with history and biography."[2] The novel persists because still today—as Henry James observed of the American scene some sixty years ago in "The Future of the Novel"— "there are too many sources of interest neglected—whole categories of manners, whole corpuscular classes and provinces, museums of character and condition; unvisited."[3] The function of the novelist has always been, and is now, to observe and to order the social facts about us and to dramatize them in a new imaginative interpretation

Source: James W. Tuttleton, "The Sociological Matrix of the Novel of Manners", *The Novel of Manners in America*, Chapel Hill: University of North Carolina Press, 1972, pp. 7-27.

of human experience. The charge that the novel is dead, so often heard in the literary criticism of the 1950s, is today a dead issue.

There is one type of novel, though, which is generally held to be deader than usual—especially in this country. And when, in our recent criticism, writers have reflected on the death of the American novel, they have usually meant a certain kind of novel—the American novel of manners. The obituaries pronounced by our critics upon this kind of novel are primarily oversimplifications of a point of view expressed by Lionel Trilling in his provocative essay "Manners, Morals, and the Novel." (I have no wish to rehearse the extensive arguments this essay provoked in the 1950s and 1960s. The interested reader will find a sampling of them listed in my notes.)[4] Trilling's description of "manners" is of such interest that it deserves to be quoted in full:

> What I understand by manners, then, is a culture's hum and buzz of implication. I mean the whole evanescent context in which its explicit statements are made. It is that part of a culture which is made up of half-uttered or unutterable expressions of value. They are hinted at by small actions, sometimes by the arts of dress or decoration, sometimes by tone, gesture, emphasis, or rhythm, sometimes by the words that are used with a special frequency or a special meaning. They are the things that separate them from the people of another culture. They make the part of a culture which is not art, or religion, or morals, or politics, and yet it relates to all these highly formulated departments of culture. It is modified by them; it modifies them; it is generated by them; it generates them. In this part of culture assumption rules, which is often so much stronger than reason.[5]

I find this a brilliant observation about the content of the novels of manners considered in this study. But let me declare at the outset that I do not consider satisfactory some of the critical observations which have been inferred from it—namely, that American society has no hum and buzz; that we have never had in this country a hierarchy of social classes; that we have never had and do not now have a variety of manners and mores—those small actions, arts, gestures, emphases, and rhythms that express value; that, consequently, the novel of manners never really established itself in America; and that our best writers are therefore idea-oriented symbolic romancers. When Richard Chase claims in *The American Novel and Its Tradition* that American "novels" are inferior to our prose romances and that only second- or third-rate writers spend time on novels, he means that our novels of manners and their authors are inferior. Are we compelled to regard only our romances as great books? In view of the extraordinary achievement of *The Portrait of a Lady*, *The American*, *The House of Mirth*, and *The Great Gatsby*, it is remarkable that some of our critics have concluded that "we do not have the novel that touches significantly on society, on manners."[6]

To understand this issue of the relation of the American novel to our society—it has had a long and controversial history—requires of us assent to the proposition that, as James somewhere remarked, "kinds" are the very life of literature, and truth and strength come from the complete recognition of them. We need also to be aware of some aspects of the history of the American romance and of a special kind of American novel which is the subject of this book—the American novel of manners.

I

Dr. Johnson once observed that one of the maxims of civil law is that definitions are hazardous. This maxim holds true in the field of literary criticism. Although no "kind" or genre of literature has been more difficult to define than the novel of manners, formulating an acceptable definition of it is the first order of business. Without a satisfactory definition, misunderstanding rather than enlightenment is the result; and along with misunderstanding usually comes irrelevant arguments about whether America is capable of producing a novel of manners.

To formulate a definition of the American novel of manners, let us regard as polarities the concept of the individual and the concept of the group, of society. Neither of these extremes can of course be the focus of the novel. Yet every novel locates itself somewhere between these extremes. If the novel deals largely with the self, personal experience, or the individual consciousness, the result will be a work which gravitates toward autobiography or "lyric or informal philosophy." If the self is refined out of existence in favor of social documentations, the result is history or chronicle. As Mark Schorer puts it:

> The problem of the novel has always been to distinguish between these two, the self and society, and at the same time to find suitable structures that will present them together . . . .The novel seems to exist at a point where we can recognize the intersection of the stream of social history and the stream of the soul. This intersection gives the form its dialectical field, provides the source of those generic tensions that make it possible at all.[7]

Near the center of this convergence, where the streams of the self and of social history intersect, is the novel of manners. It is probably not amiss to say that the form emphasizes social history more than lyric, confessional, or autobiographical statement.

Perhaps a useful test of the definition of the novel of manners—to borrow a term from Irving Howe's definition of the political novel—is its "inclusiveness," rather than its narrowness, for narrow definitions have provoked some of the controversies which always attend a discussion of this genre. If we are inclusive, we may define the novel of manners as a novel in which the closeness of manners and character is of itself interesting enough to justify an examination of their relationship. By a novel of manners I mean a novel in which the manners, social customs, folkways, conventions, traditions, and mores of a given social group at a given time and place play a dominant role in the lives of fictional characters, exert control over their thought and behavior, and constitute a determinant upon the actions in which they are engaged, and in which these manners and customs are detailed realistically—with, in fact, a premium upon the exactness of their representation.

The representation of manners may be without authorial prejudice, in which case the novelist merely concerns himself, without comment, with his society's hum and buzz of implication. But more often the portrait of manners is put to the service of an ideological argument. The center of the novel of manners, that is, may be an idea or an issue—for example, the idea of social mobility, of class conflict, of professional ambition, of matchmaking, of divorce. But if, in the development of such "ideas," significant attention is paid to a realistic notation of the customs and conventions of the society in which these ideas arise and are acted out, then we are dealing with a novel of manners. That a novel is "about" a subject does not necessarily disqualify it as a novel of manners. Jane Austen's *Pride and Prejudice*, for example, is "about" the problem of finding suitable husbands for a household of girls; and Scott Fitzgerald's *The Great Gatsby* is "about" the failure of the American dream. But enough attention is directed to the traditions of the early nineteenth-century English middle class, in the one, and to jazz-age manners and mores, in the other, to justify our examination of both of them as novels of manners. A useful extension of this definition, therefore, would be to say that the analysis of manners yields, from the point of view of this definition, profitable insights into the meaning of the novel without any distortion of its total significance.

Since the novel of manners inclines more toward social history than toward subjective psychologies or autobiography, it is, in a fundamental sense, sociologically oriented. That is, the novelist of manners is in some sense a "sociologist" who manipulates his data in terms of a narrative rather than a scientific or "logical" framework. This fact need not prejudice our attitude toward the novelist of manners or the genre created by his observation and notation. Many good novels survive the freight of social documentation intrinsic to the form. The influence of Comte's positivism is clearly evident in George Eliot's best studies of manners in midland England, yet we are never bothered by it. With the rise of sociology as a "science," in fact, novelists discovered a new set of tools for dissecting man in society. Many worthwhile novels have in fact major characters who are sociologists, anthropologists, or students of these disciplines—for example, Edith Wharton's Ralph Marvell of *The Custom of the Country*; Sinclair Lewis's Carol Kennicott of *Main Street*, who studied sociology at college; William Dean Howells's protagonist in *The Vacation of the Kelwyns*, a professor of historical sociology at Harvard; and Marquand's Malcolm Bryant, a sociologist in Point of No Return who has come to Clyde, Massachusetts, to analyze its social structure.

If we look to sociology for a systematic analysis of society, we soon find ourselves dealing with five areas of social experience which may be described as follows:

> Firstly, a set of social conventions and taboos regarding relations between the sexes, between parents and children, as well as people's behavior in the company of their fellowmen. Secondly, a set of commonly, or at any rate widely accepted ethical standards. Thirdly, a set of religious and philosophical beliefs, or more often a miscellany of such beliefs, concerning the position and role of man in the universe. Fourthly, a given type of economic organization, with a greater or lesser emphasis on the importance of material possessions. Lastly, the political structure of a given community, embodying certain conceptions of government, of the individual's position in the state, and of international relations.[8]

The first category, "a set of social conventions and taboos," is of course the most important area of human experience for the novel of manners. For manners represent the expression, in positive and negative form, of the assumptions of society at a given time and place. Dramatic violations of commonly held ethical values are also endemic to the novel of manners. (Sometimes morals and manners are so inextricably mixed that we cannot tell whether characters act as they do because they think it is morally right or because it is socially proper. And in the novels of Henry James we cannot always be sure that there is any difference.) From the sociological point of view, in fact, a system of ethics merely represents the crystallization of the folkways of a society. Religious or philosophical beliefs are less important to the novel of manners, but if religious or philosophical assumptions did not subtly affect the behavior of fictional characters, the novel of manners would be other than it is. Economic considerations also play a less significant role in the development of the novel of manners, though wealth is often a particularly useful device for the freedom it provides a novelist in dramatizing certain social values. Whenever religious, philosophical, or economic "ideas" tend to be blown up out of proportion, the novel of manners becomes something else—the propaganda novel advocating religious opinions, philosophical systems, or economic dogmas. This point also applies to political considerations in the novel: if they become obtrusive, not merely a part of the fabric of the fictive social world, the novel becomes something other than a novel of manners—it becomes a radical or political novel.

To put it another way, the novel of manners is primarily concerned with social conventions as they impinge upon character. These other concerns are less central to it, but they help to define the ethos of the society portrayed, they provide a body of assumptions about experience which underlie its social code, and they affect the thought and behavior of fictional characters. To return to the analogy offered by Mark Schorer, as long as the impulse of the novelist does not push him too far toward propaganda or the extreme of chronicle or history, I see him as writing the novel of manners. I assume throughout this study, incidentally, that the novel of manners is a novel and not another thing—not, for example, as Ralph Ellison puts it, disguised sociology.

"Society," as used in this study, ordinarily refers to the structure of "classes," cliques, or groups by which specific American communities are organized. More particularly, "society" may refer to whatever group is presumed by the author to constitute the class defining itself through "polite manners," such as the commercial aristocracy of Edith Wharton's Old New York or the Brahmin patriciate of Marquand's New England. In a novel of manners, the illusion of society may be generated in two ways. First, the sense of society may be created by a vast number of characters who sprawl and swarm across the printed page and who, by very mass and number, give the novel the illusion of social density, of that "substantiality" characteristic of actual society. Novelists like Balzac, Proust, Thackeray, and O'Hara develop the illusion of society by this documentary technique. On the other hand, society may be merely felt as an abstract force; that is, the novel may "deal" with only a few individuals who embody various social attitudes. Howells was this kind of novelist—he liked to focus on three or four characters whose conflicting manners stand for the values of the social classes to which they belong.

What is important to this genre is that there be for analysis groups with recognizable and differentiable manners and conventions. These groups need not be stable, in the sense of enduring for centuries (e.g., the English or French hereditary aristocracy). They need not even be typical of the general culture of a particular country (e.g., James's American colony in Rome). For the novel of manners it is necessary only that there be groups large enough to have developed a set of differing conventions which express their values and permanent enough for the writer's notation of their manners. Frequently the most successful novels of manners treat classes which have existed briefly or during transitional periods when one group is in the process of decay while another is rising to supplant it. Hence it need not be assumed that the novel of manners features only an aristocratic class in conflict with the bourgeoisie; any stratified groups will do. In America, Cable found such groups in New Orleans; Ellen Glasgow in Richmond; J. P. Marquand in New England; Louis Auchincloss in New York; John O'Hara in the mid-Pennsylvania coal district; and Edith Wharton in New York. To deny the reality of these distinctive groups as "social classes" is largely to miss the point of the social analysis contained in the fiction of these writers. Their fiction suggests that, once and for all, the criterion for distinguishing the novel of manners is execution—what James would have called "treatment"—rather than subject matter.

II

The novel of manners in America has not always been a popular genre with our writers. And any discussion of this form must deal with two objections which frequently attend it. One has to do with the alleged superiority of symbolic romances over the realistic novel. In part, this objection, which I shall discuss later on, is an extension of the old theory of a hierarchy of literary genres. The other objection is based on the claim that America lacks the social differences which are the sine qua non of the novel of manners. Can the novel of manners flourish in a democratic country which supposedly lacks adequate social density and a clearly stratified and stable class structure? A surprisingly large number of serious novelists and critics of the past century and a half have contended that American social experience is and has been too meager and limited to nourish a fiction that portrays men involved in the social world and perhaps even establishing through it their personal identities. A concomitant argument is often put this way: The absence of clear and stable class lines prohibits a meaningful portrayal of American manners—everybody has middle-class manners; without a diversity of manners based on class distinctions there can be no contrasts in the values, customs, or traditions of fictional characters; and without such contrasts, there can be no intrinsic interest, conflict, or "solidity of specification" in the portrait of American society. As W. M. Frohock has ironically phrased it:

> At first glance the syllogism seems unattackable: only a firmly (but not too firmly) stratified society can furnish the materials of which novels are made; the society of

the United States is not firmly stratified; therefore the novel in the United States is out of the question. And the corollary is that the best we can hope for is romances.[9]

Both of these objections, in their earliest form, appear as a general criticism of what was once called "the poverty for the artist of native American materials." This issue is no longer as relevant as it was a century ago, but if we know what some of our writers and critics have felt about American society, we may be better able to understand the dilemma they saw themselves as confronting.

James Fenimore Cooper was the first major novelist to indict America on the grounds of its cultural poverty. His observation is my point of departure because he first isolated the issue, and he articulated it so fully that most subsequent references to America's social thinness are mere repetitions, mostly thoughtless, of views Cooper presented in 1828:

> The second obstacle against which American literature has to contend [the first was the pirating and copyright problem], is in the poverty of materials. There is scarcely an ore which contributes to the wealth of the author, that is found, here, in veins as rich as in Europe. There are no annals for the historian; no follies (beyond the most vulgar and commonplace) for the satirist; no manners for the dramatist; no obscure fictions for the writer of romance; no gross and hardy offences against decorum for the moralist; nor any of the rich artificial auxiliaries of poetry. The weakest hand can extract a spark from the flint, but it would baffle the strength of a giant to attempt kindling a flame with a pudding-stone. I very well know there are theorists who assume that the society and institutions of this country are, or ought to be, particularly favourable to novelties and variety. But the experience of one month, in these States, is sufficient to show any observant man the falsity of their position. The effect of a promiscuous assemblage anywhere, is to create a standard of deportment; and great liberty permits every one to aim its attainment. I have never seen a nation so much alike in my life, as the people of the United States, and what is more, they are not only like each other, but they are remarkably like that which common sense tells them they ought to resemble. No doubt, traits of character that are a little peculiar, without, however, being either very poetical, or very rich, are to be found in remote districts; but they are rare, and not always happy exceptions.[10]

This passage, expressing Cooper's characteristic ambivalence toward our "national conformity," is suspect in the very rhetorical extravagance of his description of our social dullness. The fact is that the example of his own fiction belies the assumptions here expressed. *Home As Found* and *The Pioneers*, for example, are rich in the depiction of native manners, national follies, and social offenses. But it cannot be escaped that Cooper *believed* that the character of American society prevented his writing the *roman de moeurs*, even though he wanted to. Under the inspiration of Scott, therefore, he took his characters out of the drawing room and trailed them into the woods. It should not be forgotten, however, that even in the Leatherstocking series, the real issues are sometimes social issues masked in the adventure of the romance genre. In *The Pathfinder*, for example, Cooper's real purpose is to explore the question of whether a man of the hunter class (however much a "nature's gentleman") can find settlement happiness married to a girl whose manners have been polished by real ladies—the wives of the garrison officers.

But Cooper was not alone in pointing out the deficiencies in American society for the novelist. In "Some Reflections on American Manners" in *Democracy in America*, Alexis de Tocqueville, one of the most perceptive foreign critics of American ways, remarked in 1835 that in a new democratic society, the forms of social experience are so transitory that even if a code of good breeding were formulated no one could enforce it. "Every man therefore behaves after his own fashion, and there is always a certain incoherence in the manners of such times, because they are molded upon the feelings and notions of each individual rather than upon an ideal model proposed for general imitation." The absence of an authoritative code might make for more sincerity and openness in the American character, but Tocqueville felt that "the effect of democracy is not exactly to give men any particular manners, but to prevent them from having manners at all."[11] This alleged absence of observable manners, however beneficial to the political citizen, Cooper regarded as fatal to the novelist because it deprived him of the raw material of his social portrait.

III

Some of their contemporaries, however, argued that it was an easier task to draw the portrait of American manners than Cooper and Tocqueville admitted. Social witnesses of the stature of William Cullen Bryant, John Neal, and William Hickling Prescott argued that American society, for all its apparent formlessness, still offered a rich field for fiction. As Bryant observed in his 1825 review of Catharine Maria Sedgwick's *Redwood*, American social novels do not need the European class of idle aristocrats who "have leisure for that intrigue, those plottings and counter plottings, which are necessary to give a sufficient degree of action and eventfulness to the novel of real life."[12] Though lacking a class with "polite manners," he argued, the annals of our people "are abundantly fertile in interesting occurrences, for all the purposes of the novelists." Since "distinctions of rank, and the amusements of elegant idleness, are but the surface of society," the American novelist is uniquely capable of dramatizing character through the representation of different manners. "Whoever will take the pains to pursue this subject into its particulars," Bryant observed, will be surprised at the infinite variety of forms of character, which spring up under the institutions of our country." Bryant went on to suggest the "innumerable and diverse influences upon the manners and temper of our people": the variety of religious creeds, geographical differences (North and South, East and West, seacoast and interior, province and metropolis), diversifications in manners produced by massive immigrations, and the like. "When we consider all these innumerable differences of character, native and foreign," he concluded, "this infinite variety of pursuits and objects, this endless diversity of change of fortunes, and behold them gathered and grouped into one vast assemblage in our own country, we shall feel little pride in the sagacity or the skill of that native author, who asks for a richer or a wider field of observation."[13]

Put in this way, nineteenth-century America does seem to have been an immensely rich source of social materials for the novelist. Bryant makes us wonder seriously whether Cooper's social vision was as perspicuous as we might wish. I do not mean to say that early American novelists did not face formidable obstacles. They surely did. But the problem of the "materials" was less crucial than the artist's felt need for those "romantic associations" which these materials could not provide. By this I mean that some of our early novelists seriously resented the notion that fiction ought to deal with the actualities of American life. A strictly realistic portrait of men's ordinary lives was held inferior because it made "few demands upon the imagination." Writing novels based on everyday actualities was merely imitating, unimaginatively, what men did. And what men did in this country, in the early years of the republic, was mainly a variety of disagreeable things incident to clearing and settling the country.

More and more our writers fixated on the need for "romantic settings" to evoke aesthetic emotions. Isaac Mitchell even went to the extreme of creating a medieval castle for Long Island in his *Alonzo and Melissa* (1804). "Romance" and "novel" cannot be defined too precisely, but the differences between them were so important to early American writers that to understand the relation of the American novel of manners to American fiction, we would do well to consider them.

The basic differences, as they develop in the eighteenth and nineteenth centuries, are loosely as follows. The novel was held to be a "truthful" representation of ordinary reality; it detailed with satisfactory realism the actualities of the social world. The romance, on the other hand, less committed to the realities of ordinary life, sought to leave "the powers of fancy at liberty to expatiate through the boundless realms of invention."[14] In the romance, in other words, invention rather than observation or description was valued. The novel emphasized character as revealed in everyday life—in the religious, business, political, moral, and social relationships of people. The romance, however, was concerned very little with the interaction of men in society; in fact, in the romance social relations were often so thinly represented that the characters seem less complex, less rounded, and therefore less credible as "real people." In the romance, the representation of character often resulted in abstractions or idealizations of social types—gentleman, heroes, villains, soldiers, aristocrats. In the novel, extremes of characterization were avoided in favor of multidimensional or rounded characters, most of them drawn from the middle class.

The novel usually did not have a complicated plot, heroic action, or improbabilities. Plotting in the romance, however, was often elaborately worked out on the basis of coincidence or chance and was, if not incredible, often implausible. In many respects, the romance extended into prose some of the characteristics of the medieval verse romance, from which it derived not only its name but its tendency toward the "poetic," the legendary, and the highly imaginative, wonderful scenes of the distant past or the strange and faraway. Since it is "less committed to the immediate rendition of reality than the novel," as Chase has observed, "the romance will more freely veer toward mythic, allegorical, and symbolic forms."[15]

Clara Reeve's early history of prose fiction, *The Progress of Romance*, defined what in 1785 was understood to be the nature of the novel:

> The Novel is a picture of real life and manners, and of the time in which it is written . . . .The Novel gives a familiar relation of such things, as pass every day before our eyes, such as may happen to our friend, or to ourselves; and the perfection of it, is to represent every scene, in so easy and natural a manner, and to make them appear so probable, as to deceive us into a persuasion (at least while we are reading) that all is real, until we are affected by the joys or distresses, of the persons in the story, as if they were our own.[16]

This definition will not of course do any more. It stands as a generally reliable definition of the novel of manners, though, except for the claim that the novel must deal with the time in which it is written. There is no reason why a novel of manners reflecting all of these qualities may not be laid in the past, say (like *Waverley*) "sixty years since."

To find a definition of the American romance, let us move down into the 1830s, for Scott's treatment of history gave fresh direction to the romance in this country. William Gilmore Simms, a follower of Cooper in the Scott tradition of the historical romance, provided a definitive description of the form in the preface to his *The Yemassee: A Romance of Carolina* (1835):

> The question briefly is—What are the standards of the modern Romance? What is the modern Romance itself? The reply is immediate. The modern Romance is the substitute which the people of the present day offer for the ancient epic. The form is changed: the matter is very much the same; at all events it differs much more seriously from the English novel than it does from the epic and the drama, because the difference is one of material, even more of fabrication. The reader who, reading Ivanhoe, keeps Richardson and Fielding beside him, will be at fault in every step of his progress. The domestic novel of those writers, confined to the felicitous narration of common and daily occurring events, and the grouping and delineation of characters in ordinary conditions of society, is altogether a different sort of composition; and if, in a strange doggedness, or simplicity of spirit, such a reader happens to pin his faith to such writers alone, circumscribing the boundless horizon of art to the domestic circle, the Romances of Maturin, Scott, Bulwer, and others of the present day, will be little better than rhapsodical and intolerable nonsense.
>
> When I say that our Romance is the substitute of modern times for the epic or the drama, I do not mean to say that they are exactly the same things, and yet, examined thoroughly, the differences between them are very slight. These differences depend on the material employed, rather than upon the particular mode in which it is used. The Romance is of loftier origin than the Novel. It approximates the poem. It may be described as an amalgam of the two. It is only with those who are apt to insist upon poetry as verse, and to confound rhyme with poetry that the resemblance is unapparent. The standards of the Romance—take such a story, for example, as the Ivanhoe of Scott, or the Salathiel of Croly,—are very much those of the epic. It invests individuals with an absorbing interest—it hurries them rapidly through crowding and exacting events, in a narrow space of time—it requires the same unities of plan, of purpose, and harmony of parts, and it seeks for its adventures among the wild and wonderful. It does not confine itself to what is known, or even what is probable. It grasps at the possible; and, placing a human agent in hitherto untried situations, it exercises its ingenuity in extricating him from them, while describing his feelings and his fortunes in his progress.[17]

While this definition rationalizes Simms's own practice, it is a reliable statement of what romances after Scott were conceived to be and what they aimed to do. We should note the relationship alleged between the romance and the epic poem; the indifference to actuality in favor of extravagance or improbability; the corresponding distaste for the novel of manners, which is alleged to be limited to the trivialities of the domestic circle; and the bald assertion that the romance is altogether a loftier genre than the novel. These assumptions carry over, in part, into the twentieth century, where symbol-searching critics have exhibited "an attitude of distaste toward the actuality of experience—an attitude of radical devaluation of the actual if not downright hostility to it."[18] Irving Howe has likewise remarked how

> the contemporary eagerness to interpret works of literature as symbolic patterns is often due to a fear or distaste of direct experience—sometimes, of direct literary experience . . . .When hardened into critical dogma, this mode of interpretation supports the assumption that truth or reality is always "behind" what we see and sense—that an essence lurks in the phenomenon, a ghost in the machine, a spirit in the tree.[19]

This prejudice against actuality, against the experience of the ordinary world as we know it in society, led Simms to castigate savagely the novel of manners:

> In works of this class, the imagination can have little play. The exercise of the creative faculty is almost entirely denied. The field of speculation is limited; and the analysis of minute shades of character, is all the privilege which taste and philosophy possess, for lifting the narrative above the province of mere lively dialogue, and sweet and fanciful sentiment. The ordinary events of the household, or of the snug family circle, suggest the only materials; and a large gathering of the set, at ball or dinner, affords incident of which the novelist is required to make the highest use. Writers of much earnestness of mood, originality of thought, or intensity of imagination seldom engage in this class of writing. Scott attempted it in St. Ronan's Well, and failed;—rising only into the rank of Scott, in such portions of the story as, by a very violent transition, brought him once more into the bolder displays of wild and stirring romance. He consoled himself with the reflection that male writers were not good at these things. His conclusion, that such writings were best handled by the other sex, may be, or not, construed into a sarcasm."[20]

It was no sarcasm, of course. Scott's respect for novelists of manners like Edgeworth and Austen was so great that he launched his career as a writer of fiction in imitation of them. But rarely has the outworn hierarchy of literary genres—evident in Simms's praise of the romance as epic—played more havoc with the fundamental impulse of American fiction—a realistic impulse grounded in the commonplace actualities of our daily experience.

IV

The growing popularity of the romance in the nineteenth century explains in part the indifference of our novelists to American society and manners. The scope of this indifference expands as the distinction between the romance and the novel becomes more rigid. American society appears deficient not only to the novelist but also to the romancer, who demands the privilege of disengaging experience from the actualities we know. Hawthorne complained that the American character was too dully matter-of-fact, too pragmatic and commonsensical, to accord much significance to the kind of liberated experience he liked to deal with: "In the old countries, with which fiction has long been conversant, a certain conventional privilege seems to be awarded to the romancer; his work is not put exactly side by side with nature; and he is allowed a license with regard to every-day probability, in view of the improved effects which he is bound to reproduce thereby."[21] These views are expressed in the preface to *The Blithedale Romance*, a book which proved to be an extremely interesting failure. In the beautifully enclosed world of the Brook Farm community, Hawthorne had the materials for a first-rate novel. And certain scenes— for example, the search for Zenobia's body—are portrayed with masterful realism and a substantiality that we are not accustomed to find in Hawthorne. But the book is ruined for some readers by Hawthorne's addiction to the contrived mystifications of the third-rate romance.

Hawthorne's attempt to escape the representation of American society merely testifies to the eminence, if not preeminence, of society, as a factor in the creation of fiction. Even in the attempt to ignore it, Hawthorne acknowledged its fascination as a subject for fiction. Justifying the European setting of *The Marble Faun*, he remarked:

> No author, without a trial, can conceive of the difficulty of writing a romance about a country where there is no shadow, no antiquity, no mystery, no picturesque and gloomy wrong, nor anything but a commonplace prosperity, in broad and simple daylight, as is happily the case with my dear native land. It will be very long, I trust, before romance-writers may find congenial and easily handled themes, either in the annals of our stalwart republic, or in any characteristic and probable events of our individual lives.[22]

This view is questionable as a description of the American scene in the 1840s and 1850s. But Henry James was quick to seize upon its implications in his biography *Hawthorne* (1879). Speaking of the preface to *The Blithedale Romance*, James remarked the thinness of Hawthorne's notebooks:

> The perusal of Hawthorne's American Note-Books operates as a practical commentary upon this somewhat ominous text. It does so at least to my own mind; it would be too much perhaps to say that the effect would be the same for the usual English reader. An American reads between the lines—he completes the suggestions—he constructs a picture. I think I am not guilty of any gross injustice in saying that the picture he constructs from Hawthorne's American diaries, though by no means without charms of its own, is not, on the whole, an interesting one. It is characterised by an extraordinary blankness—a curious paleness of colour and paucity of detail. Hawthorne, as I have said, has a large and healthy appetite for detail, and one is therefore the more struck with the lightness of the diet to which his observation was condemned. For myself, as I turn the pages of his journals, I seem to see the image of the crude and simple society in which he lived. I use these epithets, of course, not invidiously, but descriptively; if one desires to enter as closely as possible into Hawthorne's situation, one must endeavour to reproduce

his circumstances. We are struck with the large number of elements that were absent from them, and the coldness, the thinness, the blankness, to repeat my epithet, present themselves so vividly that our foremost feeling is that of compassion for a romancer looking for subjects in such a field. It takes so many things, as Hawthorne must have felt later in life, when he made the acquaintance of the denser, richer, warmer European spectacle—it takes such an accumulation of history and custom, such a complexity of manners and types, to form a fund of suggestion for a novelist.[23]

Then James continues, enumerating the characteristics of what he calls "high civilization," qualities allegedly typical of European countries which Hawthorne as an American writer lacked for his art; and the implication of the passage is that nothing is left for the American novelist to work with:

The negative side of the spectacle on which Hawthorne looked out, in his contemplative saunterings and reveries, might, indeed, with a little ingenuity be made almost ludicrous; one might enumerate the items of high civilization, as it exists in other countries, which are absent from the texture of American life, until it should become a wonder to know what was left. No State, in the European sense of the word, and indeed barely a specific national name. No sovereign, no court, no personal loyalty, no aristocracy, no church, no clergy, no army, no diplomatic service, no country gentlemen, no palaces, no castles, nor manors nor old country-houses, nor parsonages, nor thatched cottages nor ivied ruins; no cathedrals, nor abbeys, nor little Norman churches; no great Universities nor public schools—no Oxford, nor Eton, nor Harrow; no literature, no novels, no museums, no pictures, no political society, no sporting class—no Epsom nor Ascot! Some such list as that might be drawn up of the absent things in American life—especially in the American life of forty years ago,—the effect of which, upon an English or a French imagination, would probably as a general thing be appalling.[24]

Put in this way it sounds pretty appalling even to an American imagination. And although James ascribes these deficiencies to the America of the 1840s, he seriously believed that his own fiction suffered from the same limitations.

Howells disagreed in his review of James's biographical study of Hawthorne. Howells complained of the attention Hawthorne and James paid to what he called the "dreary and worn-out paraphernalia" of European novels. He argued that Hawthorne's sensibility kept him from exploiting the social world of America, just as later critics have said of James. Howells pointed out that *The Marble Faun*, which drew upon the "complex social machinery" of Europe, was inferior to Hawthorne's New England romances. Such paraphernalia, Howells believed, needed to be eliminated from the novel, for beneath them was the proper subject of the novelist— man and human nature: "After leaving out all those novelistic "properties," as sovereigns, courts, aristocracy, gentry, castles, cottages, cathedrals, abbeys, universities, museums, political class, Epsoms, and Ascots, by the absence of which Mr James suggests our poverty to the English conception, we have the whole of human life remaining, and a social structure presenting the only fresh and novel opportunities left to fiction, opportunities manifold and inexhaustible. No man would have known less what to do with that dreary and worn-out paraphernalia than Hawthorne. . . ."[25]

Howells sent the review to James, but James was not convinced, and in a letter dated 31 January 1880, James replied:

> I sympathize even less with your protest against the idea that it takes an old civilization to set a novelist in motion—a proposition that seems to me so true as to be a truism. It is on manners, customs, usages, habits, forms, upon all these things matured and established, that a novelist lives—they are the very stuff his work is made of; and in saying that in the absence of these "dreary and worn-out paraphernalia" which I enumerate as being wanting in American society, "we have simply the whole of human life left," you beg (to my sense) the question, I should say we had just so much less of it as these same "paraphernalia" represent, and I think they represent an enormous quantity of it. I shall feel refuted only when we have produced (setting the present high company—yourself and me—for obvious reasons apart) a gentleman who strikes me as a novelist—as belonging to the company of Balzac and Thackeray.[26]

This complaint underlies, in part, James's expatriation to Europe, a culture he believed to be more nourishing than America to the novelist interested in the relation between character and society. Many years later, though, James undertook to reexamine American society, and his conclusions suggest an interesting shift in attitude. The purpose of *The American Scene* as a travel work was to investigate "the great adventure of a society reaching out into the apparent void for the amenities, the consummations, after having earnestly gathered in so many of the preparations and necessities."[27] His travels in America led him to believe that it is indeed possible that new societies may be even more interesting than old societies, "especially if they are "backed" by unlimited funds and an inexhaustible will for self-improve-ment."[28] These remarks tend to suggest that between the 1880s, when Hawthorne was writing the major romances, and 1907, when James published *The American Scene*, the United States had begun to assume some of the complexities and amenities of social experience that are the lifeblood of the novel of manners. Howells argued that the social complexity was available in the 1880s, and the witness of our social historians suggests that Howells was right: a limitation of James's sensibility prevented him from making fictional use of what was already there.

But Edith Wharton, the disciple of James who had the richest European experience of any of these novelists, tended to agree with the Master. Arguing that a great novel must have, in Hilton's phrase, a "great argument," but that America was capable only of "the perpetual chronicling of small beer," she denied that American society offered the novelist an adequate field. She viewed Lewis's *Main Street* as an illustration of the conditions of American life which stifle the imagination:

> If it be argued that the greatest novelists, both French and English, have drawn some of their richest effects from the study of narrow lives and parochial problems, the answer is that Balzac's provincial France, Jane Austen's provincial England, if limited in their external contacts compared to a Main Street linked up to the universe by telephone, motor, and wireless, nevertheless made up for what they lacked in surface by the depth of the soil in which they grew. This indeed is still true of the dense old European order, all compounded of differences and *nuances*, all interwoven with intensities and reticences, with passions and privacies, inconceivable to the millions brought up in a safe, shallow, and shadowless world.

It is because we have chosen to be what Emerson called "mixed of middle clay" that we offer, in spite of all that patriotism may protest to the contrary, so meagre a material to the imagination. It is not because we are middle-class but because we are middling that our story is so soon told.[29]

These writers have suggested in varying ways that society in America has been too shallow for the novel of manners to flourish. Even the romance, for Hawthorne, seemed too difficult of execution in this country. The conclusions of these writers, however, do not strike me as totally convincing. The element of special pleading in the tone of their remarks suggests a rationalization of obvious limitations in their talent and sensibilities. Their own novels of manners—Hawthorne excepted—surprisingly transcend conditions that seemed to them insurmountable. We have always had significant novels of manners because, despite these complaints, America has always had those variegated customs, that complexity of manners and types, that hum and buzz of implication, which forms a fund of suggestion for our writers. Still, Cooper, for example, resolutely held to the myth of our cultural homogeneity and late in his career bemoaned the absence of any "standard for opinion, manners, social maxims, or even language."[30] To overcome these felt deficiencies was a formidable task—a task to which, fortunately, Cooper at least was equal.

Notes

1. Lionel Trilling, "The Novel Alive or Dead," *A Gathering of Fugitives*, Boston, 1956, p. 125.
2. Harold Nicolson, "Is the Novel Dead?" *Observer*, 29 August 1954. Cited in John O. McCormick, "The Novel and Society," *Jahrbuch fur Amerikastudien*, I, 1956: 70.
3. Henry James, "The Future of the Novel," in *The Future of the Novel: Essays on the Art of Fiction*, ed. Leon Edel, New York, 1956, p. 40.
4. See particularly Trilling's "Manners, Morals, and the Novel" and "Art and Fortune" in his *The Liberal Imagination*, Garden City, N.Y., 1950; Richard Chase's *The American Novel and Its Tradition*, Garden City, N.Y., 1957; Marius Bewley's *The Eccentric Design*, London, 1959 ; John W. Aldridge's *After the Lost Generation*, New York, 1958 and *In Search of Heresy*, New York, 1956. These works touch on the general argument that the novel of manners never established itself in this country. For representative counterstatements, see David H. Hirsch's "Reality, Manners, and Mr Trilling," *Sewanee Review* 72, 1964: 425; William Barrett's "American Fiction and American Values," *Partisan Review* 18, 1951: 681-90, a reply to Barrett is Aldridge's "Manners and Values," *Partisan Review* 19 [1952]: 347; Delmore Schwartz's "The Duchess' Red Shoes," *Partisan Review* 20, 1953: 58; Hilton Kramer's "Unreal Radicalism," *Partisan Review* 23, 1956: 554; Arthur Mizener's "The Novel of Manners in America," *Kenyon Review* 12, 1950: 19; W. M. Frohock's *Strangers to This Ground: Cultural Diversity in Contemporary American Writing*, Dallas, 1961; and *The Living Novel: A Symposium*, ed. Granville Hicks, New York, 1957—particularly John Brooks's "Some Notes on Writing One Kind of Novel," Ralph Ellison's "Society, Morality, and the Novel," Flannery O'Connor's "The Fiction Writer and His Country," and Hicks's "Introduction." For ancillary discussions of the argument, see Trilling's "William Dean Howells and the Roots of Modern Taste," in *The Opposing Self: Nine Essays in Criticism*, New York, 1955; Allen Tate's "What Is a Traditional Society?" in *Reason in Madness*, New York, 1941 ; David Riesman's *The Lonely Crowd*, Garden City, N.Y., 1953, together with Trilling's "Two Notes on David Riesman" in *A Gathering of Fugitives*; Ludwig Lewisohn's *Expression in America*, New York, 1932, p. 252; Louis Auchincloss's *Reflections of a Jacobite*, New York, 1961; Flannery O'Connor's *Mystery and Manners*, ed. Sally Fitzgerald and Robert Fitzgerald, New York, 1969; Charles C. Walcutt, "*Sister Carrie*: Naturalism or the Novel

of Manners?" *Genre* I, 1968: 76-85.

5. Trilling, "Manners, Morals, and the Novel," pp. 200-201.

6. Chase, *American Novel and Its Tradition*, pp. 157-59; Trilling, "Manners, Morals, and the Novel," p. 207.

7. Mark Schorer, "Foreword: Self and Society," in *Society and Self in the Novel: English Institute Essays, 1955*, New York, 1956, pp. viii-ix.

8. W. Witte, "The Sociological Approach to Literature," *Modern Language Review* 36, 1951: 87-88.

9. W. M. Frohock, *Strangers to This Ground*, p. 28.

10. James Fenimore Cooper, *Notions of the Americans, Picked Up by a Travelling Bachelor*, ed. Robert E. Spiller, 2 vols., New York. 1963, 2: 108-9

11. Alexis de Tocqueville, *Democracy in America*, ed. Phillips Bradley, 2 vols., New York, 1958, 2: 229-30.

12. William Cullen Bryant, review of *Redwood* by Catherine M. Sedgwick, *North American Review* 20, April 1825; reprinted in *William Cullen Bryant: Representative Selections*, ed. Tremaine McDowell, New York, 1935, pp. 182-83.

13. Ibid.

14. Horace Walpole, "The Castle of Otranto," in *Shorter Novels: Eighteenth Century*, ed. Philip Henderson, London, 1930, p. 102

15. Chase, *American Novel and Its Tradition*, p. 13.

16. Clara Reeve, *The Progress of Romance*, Facsimile Text Society, ser. 1, vol. 4, 1785; reprint ed. New York, 1930, p. 111.

17. William Gilmore Simms, *The Yemassee: A Romance of Carolina*, ed. C. Hugh Holman, Boston, 1962, pp. 5-6.

18. Philip Rahv, "Fiction and the Criticism of Fiction," *Kenyon Review* 18, 1956: 285.

19. Irving Howe, "The Passing of a World," in *Twentieth Century Interpretations of "The Sound and the Fury,"* ed. Michael H. Cowan, Englewood Cliffs, N.J., 1968, p. 38.

20. William Gilmore Simms, *Views and Reviews in American Literature, History and Fiction: First Series*, ed. C. Hugh Holman, Cambridge, Mass., 1962, p. 259.

21. Nathaniel Hawthorne, *The Blithedale Romance*, Boston, 1876, p. vi.

22. Nathaniel Hawthorne, *The Marble Faun*, Boston, 1880, pp. vii-viii.

23. Henry James, *Hawthorne*, London, 1879, p. 43.

24. Ibid., pp. 43-44.

25. William Dean Howells, "James's Hawthorne," *Atlantic Monthly* 45, February 1880: 284.

26. Henry James, *The Letters of Henry James*, ed. Percy Lubbock, 2 vols., New York, 1920, 1:72.

27. Henry James, *The American Scene*, London, 1907, p. 12.

28. F. W. Dupee, *Henry James*, Garden City, N.Y., 1956, p. 238.

29. Edith Wharton, "The Great American Novel," *Yale Review*, n.s. 16, 1927: 649.

30. James Fenimore Cooper, *Home As Found*, ed. Lewis Leary, New York, 1961, p. xxviii.